A History and Criticism

of

American Public Address

VOLUME II

A History and Criticism

of

American Public Address

PREPARED UNDER THE AUSPICES OF

The Speech Association of America

VOLUME II

WILLIAM NORWOOD BRIGANCE

Editor

New York

RUSSELL & RUSSELL

Contents

v

Contents

Contents

17

Ralph Waldo Emerson

by HERBERT A. WICHELNS

Ralph Waldo Emerson was born in Boston, May 25, 1803. He was graduated from Harvard University, 1821; taught school; was licensed to preach as a Unitarian, October, 1826; was ordained as assistant pastor of the Second Church, Boston, March, 1829; resigned September, 1832, because of reluctance to administer communion; continued to preach for about fifteen years but was chiefly a lecturer on ethical and literary subjects in the spreading lyceum system; published essays, recast from lectures, which won him regard as the leading American thinker of his time; died in Concord, April 27, 1882.

In February, 1832, Emerson preached a sermon entitled "Find Your Calling." Every man, he said, has his appointed vocation, in which alone he can work with ease of soul and with all his power. Six months later he resigned his pastorate and began again the search for his calling. Almost at once he embarked on the mixed career of preacher in others' pulpits, lecturer in the growing lyceum system, writer of essays reworked from his lectures; and as writer and lecturer he continued until his death. But Emerson's "coming out" of the Unitarian church was only the beginning of his discovery of his true vocation. He needed a decade or more to determine the nature and proper use of his gift of expression and to find his right relation to his audience.

For one of Emerson's temperament and constitution, the right relation to his audience was not easy to find. He had great admiration for the civic leader and great respect for the power of persuasion. His ideal speaker was a man thoroughly at home in the community, on easy terms with its members, leading and commanding them by force of personality, strength of mind, and power of statement. Nor was the ideal speaker far removed in thought from those he led. Yet Emerson himself was reserved and awkward in social contacts, unhappy in enforced intimacy with his fellows, hesitant in speech. His early struggle with tuberculosis had left him with reduced energy and low vitality. The course of his thought had deprived him of common ground with any large section of his fellow citizens. Hence, seeking outlet for his undoubted gift of expression, he was gradually but inevitably driven to deny his own ideal. In resigning his pastorate, he gave up the conception of active civic leadership with which he had started and, retiring from Boston to Concord, took a house at the end of the village street—fit symbol of his new attitude to his community. Presently he was to release himself also from that intellectual accountability to his peers which every writer and speaker—on the higher levels at least—customarily acknowledges. As we review his changing conception of his own function—and his performance—we shall see that Emerson in the end found his true calling and his right relation to his hearers by making himself thoroughly independent of them.

Yet at no time did he doubt that his task in life was to practice eloquence. That calling was never questioned. To have thoughts, to write them, to rework them and read them to others—this was his natural mode of functioning. He might speak of himself as born with a pen, not with a tongue, or declare himself no orator or regret his dependence upon a manuscript, but always he wrote, and always he found an audience to listen. In the lecture on "Inspiration" he spoke of the fullness of thoughts that makes a diary a joy as well as a necessity. And in his apprentice days as a sermon maker he bade his elder brother send him topics or whole outlines, "for much of my time is lost in choosing a subject"[1]—as if the message were less important than to be a messenger.

The family history and the family training combined to foster respect for the true word spoken. There were in the Emerson connection ministers, learned ladies, and businessmen. But the businessmen of the Haskins family, to which his mother belonged, seem to have given little help to the widow and to have shaped not at all the ambitions of her sons. "These boys were born to be educated," said Aunt Mary Moody Emerson, as gifted as she was eccentric. And educated they were, though the mother kept a boardinghouse, though there was but one overcoat for two boys, though the undergraduates taught school in the intervals of their own schooling. The long ministerial tradition of the family, with its accompaniment of an honored place in the community, had its part too in shaping ambition for professional careers in Emerson and his brothers. And the influence of the aunt especially created a respect for the life of the mind and a sense of the reality of intellectual experience. In the Harvard of 1817–1821, the prizes of college life were for literary and oratorical talent; Emerson's success in the competitions, though not outstanding, was yet more a success than his middling academic rank. Above all, the times confirmed the Emersonian valuation of the power of speech, for the society of 1820 lived far more by oral discourse than by the printed word.

---

[1] *Letters of Ralph Waldo Emerson* (R. L. Rusk, ed., New York, 1939), I, 211. This work is hereafter cited as Rusk.

In his journal for April 18, 1824, when he was just entering into his majority, Emerson wrote out his reasons for rejecting the law and choosing the ministry as a career; the passage clearly reveals his first conception of eloquence. His reasoning powers he found weak; his imagination strong, so strong as to cause an "immoderate fondness for writing." And the best preaching, and that most in vogue, he thought, was "the fruit of a sort of moral imagination." He noted in himself, and ascribed to his inheritance, "a passionate love for the strains of eloquence" and confidently wrote of public preaching (though without attaching reasons), "Entire success . . . is the lot of few, but this I am encouraged to expect." The same entry contains the severest faultfinding with his personal address in ordinary intercourse, connects his want of address with unfitness for legal debate, but makes no connection at all between that same defect and the exercise of the pastor's "private influence" on his parishioners! And though the humiliating awkwardness in social intercourse receives most emphasis in his catalogue of delinquencies, it is not the fault that he undertakes to remedy. He "would sacrifice inclination to the interest of mind and soul"; that is, he will eat less for three days "and so see if it be a fact that I can understand more clearly." The unconscious choice is there: if the flow of thought and play of mind can by any means be enriched, those means must be tried. As to social awkwardness—it is a fact of nature, unalterable. The passage has one remarkable insight—moral imagination is noted as the diarist's peculiar strength; but on the whole it betrays the very young man's conception of public address as an exhibition of his powers as a stylist—from behind a desk and with the aid of manuscript—and the introvert's flight from contact or combat on equal terms with his fellows. It was a conception that a more mature Emerson could rebuke in a younger brother but that his own practice could never completely reverse.

During the scant six years of his preaching as a regular member of the Unitarian church—from 1826 until he approached the resignation of his pastorate in 1832—Emerson held the conventional attitudes toward his function as preacher. He was, he thought, the organ of an established institution and of a tradition, a body of doctrine and experience, which it was his duty to vivify, interpret, and apply for his congregation. As is plain from his two sermons on taking the pastorate of the Second Church in March, 1829, Emerson entered upon his work with the convictions a Christian minister of the Unitarian persuasion should have and with zeal for the work of preacher and pastor. Christianity, he told his congregation, is true; its truths he would try to bring home to them; he believed in public prayer, in miracles, and in the Lord's Supper; he spoke feelingly of the death that must come to each of his hearers and of his own office as comforter in the hour of mortality. If he showed an appropriate diffidence as to his task of instructing the congregation from the pulpit, he hailed with enthusiasm the life of a minister in intimate contact with his parishioners.

These were the correct things to say; and Emerson meant them, as many a young preacher before and since. Correct and conventional, too, were the disclaimer of any wish for the praise of eloquence and the proposal to measure his success by the changes his ministry should work in the lives of his people:

> But if I can add any distinctness to your idea of God, any beauty to your notion of virtue; if I can represent the life of Christ in such vivid and true colours as to exalt your love; if I can persuade one young man to check the running tide of sensual pleasure . . . ; if I can prevail with one old man to forgive an injury . . . then, my brethren, it is praise enough.[1]

He was, then, not to be remote from the community, or a Sabbath exhibition before it, but to be an active, vigorous member of it. His chief instrument was to be persuasion, direct, forceful counsel given in the face of all. He would take positions and maintain them and by eloquence would make the world better. In sum, Emerson saw himself as the scholar in the thick of the fight, living in intimate touch with the practical as well as the intellectual life of the community. The letters of his early years reveal this attitude even more plainly than the sermons. Just a year after he began to preach, he said, "The agency of an individual may be immense. The nature of man or the face of society is wonderfully plastic."[2] And a little later: "I aspire always to the production of present effect, for a strong present effect is a permanent impression."[3] Presently he analyzed the failure of his brother Charles in a college contest: "He is a *spectacle* instead of being an *engine;* a fine show at which we look, instead of an agent that moves us," with more to drive home the point that the orator requires above all communicative urgency, "must not wrap himself in himself, but must wholly abandon himself to the sentiment he utters, and to the multitude he addresses."[4] And to the same brother he suggested public opinion as the subject of an oration; in his sketch the climax was the power of the individual to alter the opinions of the many. In a letter to the older minister whom he was to succeed, he expressed his serious ambition to make preaching "as effectual an engine as I can."[5] He watched keenly the platform methods of experienced ministers—Dr. Lowell, Dr. Taylor. He commented on the cracked voice, doubtful taste, and majestic action of the old John

[1] *Young Emerson Speaks* (A. C. McGiffert, ed., Boston, 1938), p. 30. This work is hereafter cited as McGiffert.

[2] Rusk, I, 188.

[3] *Ibid.*, I, 211.

[4] *Ibid.*, I, 238–240.

[5] *Ibid.*, I, 245, 257.

Quincy Adams. He admired the fine Indian eloquence of a Cherokee, Walker-on-the-Mountains, and was glad that Channing heard Dr. Taylor in a stirring sermon to raise money for a sailor's mission; it was what the head of the Unitarians could not do. He still had some of Everett's sermons by him, in manuscript, and noted their simple style. But his admiration was now, among preachers, for Dr. Channing, even though he lacked evangelistic fervor, and, among secular orators, for Webster.[1]

This attitude toward the speaker's function was in no way different from that of thousands of speakers over many generations. Personal force, intellectual resource, platform technique—all were to be combined in the defense of causes dear to both audience and speaker.

There were, it is true, some qualifications of the conventional attitude. Shortly before being licensed to preach in October, 1826, Emerson wrote to his aunt the much-quoted sentences: "Others laugh, weep, sell, or proselyte. I admire."[2] As so often, the passing phrase betrayed the real bent of his mind, though years elapsed before he realized it. The first sermon Emerson ever preached likewise suggested a bias from the standard doctrine and attitude. The leading thought was that all our prayers are answered; let us take heed, therefore, for the things we seek in prayer. Here was the unusual remark upon a usual practice. Here were the centering of attention upon the individual and the deposit of duty squarely upon his own shoulders. Here was the quiet ignoring of Christian dogma and an optimism unrelated to the articles of faith.

The opening sermons at the Second Church, conventional as they were in the main, yet held some novelties. The young pastor promised to use "new forms of address, new modes of illustration, and varied allusions." He meant to advert often, he indicated, "to the printing press and the loom, to the phenomena of steam and of gas, to the magnificence of towns, to free constitutions, and a petulant and vain nation." Nor was the change of style all. The topics, too, must change. Preaching had been too straightened, had walked in a narrow round, had harped on a few and ancient strings, expounding texts and the terms of dogma—grace, justification, atonement. Unfaithful teachers had permitted their people to forget "that Christianity is an infinite and universal law which touches all action, all passion, all rational being; . . . that it . . . teaches us to attain the highest good of intelligent nature."[3] And last among the novelties—the preacher must give to his own mind the highest cultivation, not only in the critical study of the Scriptures but in the contemplation of the life around him.

---

[1] *Ibid.*, I, 303, 304, 321, 328, 344.

[2] *Journals of Ralph Waldo Emerson with Annotations* (E. W. Emerson and W. E. Forbes, eds., Boston and New York, 1909–1914), II, 111. This work is hereafter cited as *Journals*.

[3] McGiffert, pp. 22ff.

The wisdom of hindsight enables us to see what neither Emerson nor his audience could see at the time: the preacher was already preparing his mind for the shift from Christian revelation to the nature of man as the ultimate sanction, yet he was by no means so clear about his basic premise as about the consequences of that premise upon the style of his illustrations and the matter of his allusions.

The sermons number 170 or a little more. They are half-hour discourses, more or less, as their author's own notes on the margins of some indicate, and were read rather slowly to the small congregation, the rate being close to a hundred words a minute. Two dozen only were prepared in the journeyman years from October, 1826, to March, 1829. Ill-health doubtless was one reason why he came to his pastorate with so small a supply; but the custom of exchange of pulpits, frequently availed of, reduced the strain of weekly preparation of new material, and allowed the beginner to fill his barrel slowly. Half a dozen only of the sermons date from the years immediately following his separation from the church. This stock enabled Emerson to preach, altogether, more than nine hundred times. His own record of the sermons read, with place and date, is extant but is known to be incomplete; its total is 885. Fewer than twenty of the sermons were used but once. More than fifty were delivered twice in his own church, generally at a year's interval. Several were read fifteen or sixteen times, and one, "On Showing Piety at Home," twenty-seven times, though not after 1831. The preaching years were not over with the resignation from the Second Church, nor when, in 1838, he gave up the little pulpit of East Lexington, but continued to a date not accurately known. McGiffert has found record of a sermon delivered in 1839; Cabot mentions that Nantucket heard one in 1847.[1]

Emerson tells us that he generally selected a subject Friday night, by jotting down the first five or six ideas that came to him and then taking "the mean" of these as his theme. His journal occasionally noted promising subjects. Writing was the work of Saturday. Some of the manuscripts, as McGiffert tells us, show signs of haste, some of initial difficulty in finding the right expression or more rarely of difficulty in finding the right mode of treatment. Drafts on the journals to fill out the sermons were less than in later years, with more change of wording. Corrections for second readings were few and were generally in the introductions and conclusions.

In the main he avoided both doctrinal subjects and social themes and dealt with the individual, his virtues, his conduct, and his attitudes. After a year at the Second Church, he defended his choice of topics in a retrospective sermon: "I do not think it necessary to say to you, Do not worship

---

[1] *Ibid.*, pp. xviiff., 261ff.; J. E. Cabot, *Memoir of Ralph Waldo Emerson* (Boston, 1893), p. 498. This work is hereafter cited as Cabot.

idols, . . . Do not kill; Do not steal; Do not commit adultery; . . . but I do think it important to say, Love the Lord thy God . . . Love thy neighbor as thyself. Do not bear false witness; Be temperate; Pray; Give."[1] Emerson was trying hard to deal with the individuals actually before him and to give them the counsels they needed. The result was dull. He never paid his flock the compliment of warning against the colorful sins; never gave them the old strong doctrinal preaching that he knew they loved; never gave them the joy of beholding him victor in sharp intellectual combat, for he rarely refuted opposing views—merely put them aside. He had promised to refer often to a petulant and vain nation, but he never treated the congregation to a rousing attack on the degeneracy of the times—nor did the sinners before him receive more than gentle rebukes and mild persuasions. No wonder he received into the church fewer new members than his predecessor.

Emerson was right in his wish not to publish his sermons. They are—to judge from the twenty-five brought together by McGiffert—orderly, lucid, painstakingly sincere, but dry and juiceless. Now and then there is a glow, but a faint one. Whether he defends miracles or explains the importance of self-culture or the unimportance of trifles, the chief impression is of stiffness and effort, of illustration painfully sought, of thought not freely moving, of a personality remote from the hearers. The general tone is often that of a stilted sentence in the sermon he chose oftenest to deliver: "My friends, I should esteem myself most happy and successful if the doctrine I have attempted to recommend might weigh with any of you to set yourselves to this experiment, to make this small venture for your everlasting welfare."[2] Or take this passage from the ninetieth sermon, written late in 1830:

Brethren, I beg each of you to remember, whether, when you have in any instance forsaken your first impressions of a book, or a character, or a question of duty, and adopted new ones from complaisance, you have not by and by been compelled to receive your own again, with the mortification of being overcome by your own weapons.[3]

The sermon is on a theme of which Emerson never tired—trust yourself. But compare the same idea as the Emerson of 1841 turned it in the essay on "Self-reliance":

Great works of art have no more affecting lesson for us than this. They teach us to abide by our spontaneous impression with good-humored inflexibility then most when the whole cry of voices is on the other side. Else to-morrow a stranger

---

[1] McGiffert, p. 71.
[2] *Ibid.*, p. 21.
[3] *Ibid.*, pp. 109, 110.

will say with masterly good sense precisely what we have thought and felt all the time, and we shall be forced to take with shame our own opinion from another.[1]

With different emphasis and a few more words, all told, the second passage makes a far clearer image for reader or hearer. No words are spent begging the brethren to apply their minds; the writer has learned how to make them apply their minds.

Strain—when occasionally it came in the quiet sermon-writing years—was good for the young man's style. It helped him to speak out, tell his thought more simply and directly. In 1831 Emerson met the cruelest test to which a congregation can put their minister. Less than two weeks after his wife's death, he delivered, in the fashion of the times, a sermon on the consolations of the mourner, reaffirming his faith and reassuring his flock. He discharged the impossible task well, in a discourse stronger, more varied in movement, sharper in phrasing, less labored in exposition than his sermons on more general themes. The awkwardness of the young minister before the elders of his congregation disappeared, and the tone was exactly right in its mixture of sincerity and reserve.

There were strain and tension, too, in the sermon on the Lord's Supper, with its announcement, at the end, of his resignation. It fulfills admirably its purpose, to state distinctly his reasons for parting from his congregation. The argument is orderly and careful, the tone frank, dispassionate, friendly. Perhaps because this address is half again as long as the average, the exposition of ideas has lost the cramped, awkward quality often to be seen in the earlier sermons. It is good debating, in a controlled, clear style, without excitement and without undue ramming home of points, though to the audience the summations may have seemed forcible enough. Emerson's son[2] gives credit for the scriptural argument to a manuscript by the preacher's older brother William, who turned from the ministry to the law. The style, however, was often equaled by Emerson in his later addresses on public questions. Much has been made of the lordly sentence near the close: "That is the end of my opposition, that I am not interested in it." Read in its context, however, the sentence loses its overbearing quality, for it is prefaced thus: "The reason of my determination [to resign] is shortly this: It is my desire, in the office of a Unitarian minister, to do nothing that I cannot do with my whole heart." With this speech, Emerson appears to have come to intellectual and emotional maturity and to be speaking, for the first time, with ease and mastery.

The resignation of his charge was a relief to Emerson, set his mind working more freely, strengthened his command both of thought and of

[1] *Complete Works* (E. W. Emerson, ed., Centenary ed., Boston and New York, 1903–1904) II, 46. This edition is hereafter cited as *Works*.

[2] *Ibid.*, XI, 550–551.

expression, made him more willing to declare his own views. If in his ordination sermon he had hinted at a sanction for religion above and beyond the Christian revelation, in the sermon on "The Genuine Man," delivered six weeks after his resignation, but before it had been accepted, he could say:

> The conviction must be produced in our minds that *this truth of character is identical with a religious life;* that they are one and the same at once; that . . . it is the direct revelation of your Maker's Will, not written in books many ages since nor attested by distant miracles but in the flesh and blood, in the faculties and emotions of your constitution.[1]

A year later, on his return from Europe, he faced his old congregation again with a glowing sermon on the historical function of Christianity and on the "revolution of religious opinion taking effect around us."[2] In this, he handles ideas with very little of his old stiffness. There are more energy, more of the commanding drive of the confident persuader, less of the plaintive, timid exhortation of the bulk of the sermons. There is still awkwardness in the forms of direct address, still visible effort to find illustrations that will fit the audience, but the items are more tellingly stated and better marshaled. He has begun to take his own advice, "not to wrap himself in himself, but to abandon himself to the sentiment he utters and the multitude he addresses."

The new confidence and force, the stronger imagination and clearer utterance must find a new channel. Emerson had been made moderately secure by the inheritance of his wife's small fortune, which promised to bring him $1,200 a year, or as much as he had earned on first coming to his pastorate, and therefore he could safely follow his bent. One hundred years later his choice would naturally have fallen upon a writing career, but in 1834 the printing press offered no plethora of vocations, if, indeed, any settled career could be founded on it. He meditated "something more seriously than ever before the adventure of a periodical paper, which shall speak truth without fear or favor to all who desire to hear it, with such persuasion as shall compel them to speak it also."[3] But his choice fell upon lecturing, perhaps because he recognized that a paper entailed fixed responsibilities; as long ago as 1830 he had told his congregation that "the services of the church are periodical, but the development of truth within the mind is not."[4] Perhaps he was as much moved by the fact that the traditional modes of social influence involved public address—in 1834 the

[1] McGiffert, pp. 188–189.
[2] *Ibid.*, pp. 191–202.
[3] Cabot, pp. 216, 218.
[4] McGiffert, pp. 70, 71.

leading citizen still faced his people. The new type of lecturing called for the reading of a written discourse and so meant no change of method. But it offered as free a platform as a man could wish and was an institution visibly growing in public favor. One might lecture before the Mechanics' Institute or the Society for the Diffusion of Useful Knowledge or before the lyceum organized by a community for the express purpose of hearing lectures; or one might, in a city as large as Boston, advertise one's own course and owe responsibility to no man except for the rental of the hall. The lecturer's career promised a minimum of routine duties, imposed no allegiance to the community's code and fund of ideas, offered an audience— or series of audiences—to which there was no responsibility beyond the lecture itself. Yet it offered influence. And influence without full civic responsibility was exactly what Emerson desired. Brother Charles might tell Aunt Mary that Waldo "needs to be dragged closer to people by some practical vocation, however it may irk his tastes."[1] Waldo sensed both his limitations and his strength and refused to be dragged closer to people. He had tried the leadership of a parish and found it wanting. Now, in his house at the end of the village, he set himself apart from the community and narrowed his function to what his eloquence could accomplish without the aid of organizations.

The views that he wished to express, it is true, were those of a critic and reformer of society. He still wished to "press and prevail over the false judgments, the rebel passions, and corrupt habits of men"[2] as he had written years before. And of course the critic was often tempted to realize his aims by joining one or another of the many organized movements of the time. The experiments in communal living at Brook Farm and at Fruitlands attracted him strongly; but in the end he held aloof, preferring "the robe of inaction." Yet his criticisms of existing institutions in the first ten years or so of his lecturing were direct and forthright enough to align him plainly with the liberals and the agitators. In "Man the Reformer" we find a synopsis of his views. Trade is a system of selfishness, perjury, and fraud; professional men have a dapper complaisance and a vicious readiness to compromise; no class is more faithless than the scholars and intellectual men. Wealth is tainted; the inheritor of wealth is a puny, protected person; no man's title to his land is good whilst another man has none. The reformers themselves stoop to management and trickery and clamor, exaggerate the worth of their schemes, and forget the principle they should assert. The conservatives, to whom another lecture was devoted, fared on the whole rather better than one would expect. Emerson balanced

[1] Cabot, p. 174.
[2] *Journals*, I, 367.

their claims against those of the liberals and, though he left no doubt of his own sympathies, allowed a sweeping victory to neither.

In the address to the Divinity School of Harvard, delivered in the summer of 1838, the critical attack is still more sustained and unqualified: Too much has been made of the person of Jesus; historical Christianity has become a fetish; preaching is lifeless, meaningless; it would be criminal to tell the younger generation of ministers that the faith of Christ is preached today. This attack, so forthright and severe, was in part directed against the body of orthodox beliefs of the time, but in larger part it was directed against the ministers themselves as plodding, uninspired, ineffective. They were not slow to take up the challenge and to make public rebuttal. Emerson found himself a storm center and did not relish the experience. He avoided replies, but to his former superior in the Second Church he protested—or proclaimed—his incapacity in methodical writing and his inability to argue or even to recognize "what arguments mean in reference to any expression of a thought." He added, "I shall go on, just as before, seeing whatever I can, and telling what I see."[1] To the "men of strong understanding," the hard and trenchant debaters, the pose of artlessness must have seemed an evasion. To Emerson himself, it did not appear so; polemics were genuinely distasteful to him, not because they aroused enmity but because the stream of thought was dammed by the wrangling process of debate. Why pause to justify a contention when there was so much else to be seen and told? Why linger over the soundness of a position stated when the mind had other thoughts clamoring for expression? It was not long until, in his first volume of essays, he published the much-quoted passage against consistency as the hobgoblin of little minds. Self-reliance in the face of opposition, yes, but not self-reliance that would compel him to defend today the thoughts of yesterday. As in 1824, the flow of his own thoughts, the play of his own mind, came before all else. He might stumble into controversies, but he would not stay to answer his adversaries. The thrust and parry of debate were to him a hindrance and a delay. Zeal to state the truth he had, but not zeal to cudgel it into the skulls of the recalcitrant.

The taste of polemics, however, taught him something. He laid added stress on "preaching the affirmative," and in so doing avoided the scathing tones of criticism. In the lecture of 1842 on "The Transcendentalist" he noted the difficulty of passing beyond criticism to construction, with humor and sympathy, but also with the acknowledgment that a mature man must do more than criticize and reject—must attempt and achieve a positive formulation of his beliefs.

To find and state a positive doctrine in a form that would have meaning for others—this was Emerson's main task as he settled into his lecturing

[1] Cabot, pp. 693, 694.

career. It had been easy to give up the unwelcome duties of the pastorate, easy to renounce the unsatisfying traditions of his church, easy to have his fling at criticism of plainly imperfect institutions. It was not so easy to give clear expression to the thoughts that seemed to him important, to set forth in plain words the "new revelation" that had come to him. In 1833 he had written in his journal of being haunted by "that which I cannot yet declare." In 1836 he had tried to expound his system, and had compressed into the pamphlet "Nature" a great deal of his sense of the correspondence between mind and nature and of his moral intuitionism as the sanction for the final choices in life. In 1838 in the Divinity School address, he exclaimed repeatedly that "the soul" is not preached, but "to preach the soul" had a mawkish sound and carried little meaning. By 1840 he thought of the "infinitude of the private man" as the core of his doctrine. By 1841 the five essays—"History," "Self-reliance," "Compensation," "Spiritual Laws," and "The Over-soul"—that carry his leading ideas were in print (none of them was originally a lecture, though all apparently made some draft on his lecture sheets). Twenty-five years of lecturing and half a dozen volumes advanced but slightly his exposition of his system of thought. But construction of a well-articulated system in the philosophical sense was never his main interest. He found other less formal ways of preaching the affirmative, and these, since they let him tell what he saw, sufficed him.

What did he see? He saw "the harmonies that are in the soul and in matter" and the correspondences between the two. He saw constantly a connection between the mere fact and the thing of beauty and between these and what men call good. Hence he could write, in "Nominalist and Realist," that money is "in its effects and laws, as beautiful as roses" and that property is always moral (this last without a backward glance to earlier and very different sentences). In the same essay, Emerson wrote what might almost constitute his literary creed and the secret of his success as a lecturer. "General ideas are essences. They are our gods: they round and ennoble the most partial and sordid way of living." He was fond of the word *abstractionist;* it represented to him his function as a perceiver of harmonies and connections in diverse things, as a generalizer to whom the particular fact was nothing until he had linked it with other facts and different orders of experience. "The old principles which books exist to express are more beautiful than any book," he said in the lecture on "Courage." At other times he wrote of himself as a painter and of his lectures as picture speeches; but always he had in mind the same process of combining diverse or even opposed facets of experience, giving them new coloring and setting them in a different light. And always his expression tended to round and ennoble the more partial way of living by linking other, less sordid particulars to it and grouping both under a generalizing idea that he did not always express but did make reader or hearer feel.

In sum, Emerson was blissfully at home in the universe and led his followers from room to room, from object to object, as might an unsystematic but enthusiastic guide. It is not unfair to say that he solved the problem of construction as he solved the problem of criticism in 1838—by avoidance, by talking of something else, by confining himself to "telling what he saw." In leaving the pastorate he had released himself from close social responsibility to ordinary, commonplace citizens. In leaving the field of debate and of systematic development of his opinions, he released himself from intellectual responsibility to his peers.

Thus Emerson reached his final attitude toward his subjects and his audience. "I make rockets: must I therefore be a good senator?" he wrote in his journal for November, 1839. "We are by nature observers, and thereby learners. That is our permanent state," he said in the lecture "Love" as early as 1838; and "not talent but sensibility," in the much later lecture on "Success." At times, indeed, perception of the law of things was made all men's highest duty, and action existed only because there was instruction in it. More often he recognized the division of labor in society and used the term *scholar* to describe himself and his function of observing and reporting; but inevitably those who heard him were expected to take the observer's point of view toward life, at least for the period of the lecture. Those who came to the maker of rockets must not expect senatorial counsel, but counsel of a very different sort and on other themes than those debated in senates. For Emerson's prime impulse was ethical. The variety of his subjects conceals a single theme, the conduct of life—not only the active life among men, but the life of the mind and spirit, the life of perception and reflection, of enjoyment and appreciation. All his discourses are counsels on this theme. But they are a rocket-maker's counsels, not set in the framework of a church's code and creed, not shaped to the demands of close-reasoning, systematic thinkers.

His rockets were his insights into the connection of things and his affirmations of the value he discerned in life. The connections were numerous, ingenious, stimulating—the connection of homely incidents with moral principles, of chemical reactions with human concerns, of Napoleon with the middle class (both devoted to success, both without principle), of the farmer with the number of marriages in a community (weddings increase in time of abundance). And, to tantalize the system-makers, there were ample hints of a theory of connection and unity adopted as a philosophical principle.

The value that he affirmed was always that of the individual—his capacities, his achievements, his power of growth. Each man has an aptitude born with him; each is wise; each is made equal to every event. With such aphorisms he set every heart vibrating to the iron string of "Trust thyself." The work of ordinary men was often seen in a flattering light. The farmer has for his servants, not Irish immigrants, but chemistry and geology. The merchant's decisions take a soldier's courage. But the common laborer on the railroads or in the fields was not often in his mind; his Man with a Hoe (the phrase was Emerson's before it was Markham's) was a prosperous farmer. In the national achievement of railroad building and western settlement, Emerson saw the work of enterprising, courageous men. Government subsidies for the roads and government regulation of land occupancy did not lodge in his mind—an institution is the lengthened shadow of a man. His praise of America was not of the form of government, nor yet of the founding fathers to whom Webster and Everett devoted eulogies, but of men of lesser note, sometimes named, sometimes mere types. Nonconformity, of course, had special value to the preacher of self-reliance and the infinitude of the private man.

If there was praise for action and admiration for power, there was protest too against the endless doing of men whose energy narrowed their minds; affirmation of the value of sensitivity and enjoyment; and assessment, with gentle criticism and practical suggestion, of the uses of clubs and books and friendships and domestic life. The dominant tone in the earlier years was enthusiastic, even rapturous; in the later, optimistic and forward looking. "Great men exist that there may be greater men."[1] "Life is a series of surprises"[2] and would not otherwise be worth while. Whatever art or task you select, it is attainable on simple terms: select that in which you are apt; begin at the beginning; proceed in order, step by step. Whether you are on a lonely farm or in a busy city, the rule for self-development is the same:

The secret of culture is to learn that a few great points steadily reappear . . . the escape from all false ties; courage to be what we are, and love of what is simple and beautiful; independence and cheerful relation, these are the essentials—these, and the wish to serve, to add somewhat to the well-being of men.[3]

For the presentation of such counsels on "the private, self-supplied powers of the individual,"[4] system was less needed than style; reasoning power was less needed than the moral imagination that early in life Emerson had discerned as his peculiar gift; the treatise was less suitable by far than the shorter and less formal lecture or essay. Hence Emerson could—and

[1] *Works*, IV, 35.
[2] *Ibid.*, III, 67.
[3] *Ibid.*, VI, 278.
[4] *Ibid.*, III, 260.

did—announce courses of lectures under such titles as "Human Life," "Human Culture," "Philosophy of History," "The Times," "The Conduct of Life," "Life and Literature." Prudence, heroism, trade, art, love, manners, politics, religion—these were the subjects of single lectures. Speaking on such topics for 50 minutes left the orator free indeed to give the "results of his studies" in any form or order the spirit moved him to use.

Let Emerson take superstition as a lecture subject, as he did in 1839. His title will be "Demonology." He will begin with a clear-cut definition, proceed to a poetical disquisition on the witchcraft of sleep and dreams, and will then suggest that animals have a consciousness like our own in dreaming. This will explain how Ovid got the hint for his metamorphoses and lead us on to the truth in dreams, which is that our own characters predetermine the things that befall us. Goethe, Swedenborg, Homer, Euripides, Lucian, Napoleon will be quoted by the way. Spiritism, animal magnetism, mesmerism, and table rapping will be briefly condemned, not without epigrams and an apt Shakespearian line. The belief that luck attends some men will be described as the peculiar form of superstition in the modern mind, with an illuminating reminder of the ancient belief in the guardian genius. The conclusion will be a protest against impatience with superstition—the persistence of belief in the supernatural "indicates the inextinguishableness of wonder in man; betrays his conviction that behind all your explanations is a vast and potent and living Nature, inexhaustible and sublime, which you cannot explain." What a man cannot tell adequately he will tell wildly and fabulously. "Demonology is the shadow of Theology."

The subject is slight, and for that reason perhaps the essay reveals Emerson's method of rocket-making so clearly. He takes a topic that has a current or a universal interest—in this case some mysterious knockings and other like phenomena had had wide recent report. He defines in good professorial style. Then he lets his mind range, following Burke's advice "to diversify the matter infinitely in your own mind." His illustrations are numerous and varied—homely and dignified, literary and historical, near and remote. As a result, the current events become the least part of the whole; the sensible and intelligent attitude toward them is adopted, but they are not made prominent in the landscape. This with Emerson is not merely a device but a habit of thought: what fills the public mind occupies but a corner of his. What the public has not noticed (the superstition of the modern mind) Emerson as a good observer and comparer reports with quiet emphasis. And, indeed, the whole assemblage of points and comments represents what the public has not noticed but what a man of reading and reflection, who keeps a journal, can offer. The wealth of instances and of allusions has a kaleidoscopic effect, but this is counterbalanced by introducing a few general ideas in which the mind can rest—universal law is repeatedly asserted against the belief in luck and omens; demonology itself is fitted into the scheme of things as the shadow of true knowledge; in the end, the subject is placed in the stream of time and the process of nature. The tone is optimistic: men's strange beliefs are not very harmful but curious and interesting and are a forecast of better types of knowledge and belief. The exposition follows what Emerson himself called the *order of wonder*, omitting connectives and skipping some links in the chain of thought. In another mood he condemned this trait of his writing as pebbliness; generations of critics have followed his lead and faithfully underscored his lack of coherence. Unity of subject, of treatment, and of mood exists, however; but the effect of progression is not strongly marked. Climax and peroration are forbidden by the ramifying method, but the final image or detail left with the hearer is carefully chosen.

The method just described needs but a few additions to serve for Emerson's lectures generally. He had a command of incandescent phrase—now direct exhortation, now homely image, now sparkling metaphor, now concrete fact in condensed and forcible statement. His sentences were usually short and crisp; even the longer ones were simple and uninvolved; he was not fond of twisting ideas together into the elaborately woven strands of a Burke. The effect was direct and conversational, even when the ideas were abstract. He could at times control the structure of the whole composition to good effect, as in the discourse on Napoleon, with its forecast of the final condemnation. There was an artful variety in the length and impact of the numerous details—from mere allusion to word picture and sustained narrative, but on the whole he moved with too great speed for a popular audience. We must make allowance for the fact that some of the lectures were compressed in printing and some expanded; yet the impression of overcrowding is too constant to be explained away. The unfamiliarity of the instances—brought from sources the auditor had never read, never heard of—was, of course, part of the rocket-maker's design: his whole plan was to cast new light, to bring the new to bear upon the old and familiar; it was not a good method for producing a clear conviction, but it was admirable for kindling imagination.

The subjects of his lectures changed little over 30 years. He preferred the abstract theme: greatness, resources, civilization, eloquence, wealth, power, fate. But he also spoke on clubs, gifts, farming, domestic life. As he accumulated new matter, a new lecture with a slightly different title might appear: "Heroism," in 1838, was followed by "Courage," in 1859, and "Manners," by "Behavior." In the forties he was interested in men; the results of this interest were a series of lectures on New England, the more famous series on representative men—Plato, Shakespeare, Montaigne,

Swedenborg, Napoleon, Goethe—and, after his travels and lectures there, a group on England. Most often delivered, apparently, were lectures on manners, on domestic life, and on Napoleon. The audiences, it would seem, preferred the more concrete theme. Probably, too, they preferred these three lectures because—to judge from the printed versions—they have less of the kaleidoscopic effect, more evident sequence of ideas, and ampler treatment of each topic.

When Emerson took the platform, generally without a chairman to introduce him, he glided suddenly to the reading desk, put down the inevitable manuscript with nervous rapidity, and opened in a low tone, almost a whisper. Some of his auditors saw a figure tall, thin, aquiline, with an eye piercing and fixed. Others šaw a man

a little above the medium height, with head high, very deep from front to back, and narrow from ear to ear; eyes deep set, with the pupil looking as if from beyond; nose, a prominent triangle; chin prominent, while the mouth occupied a retired position between the two salients. His habit was plain and rather old style and seemed to button him into a little house of his own, saying for him in words of its master: "I am I and you are you!"[1]

A portrait painter noted in 1848, "His appearance is severe, and dry, and hard." Most observed that the eyes, which his son reports as of a clear, rather dark blue, were only occasionally raised from the manuscript and then in such a way that only those at the side of the room met his glance. None felt that he had the usual platform manner of the experienced speaker. We read of "a shapeless delivery" without gestures save nervous twitches and angular movements of the hands and arms—"curious to see and even smile at"—and a slight rocking of the body. Moses C. Tyler, who had a kind of success as a lecturer on both sides of the Atlantic, mentioned in 1870 "the hesitation, the awkwardness, the peculiar prim intonation." Hesitancy in utterance, even from manuscript, was noted by English auditors in 1848 and seems, indeed, to have been habitual, both in conversation and on the platform.

The voice, which James Russell Lowell described to the readers of the *Nation* in 1868 as a rich baritone, in earlier years struck on Margaret Fuller's ear as full and sweet rather than sonorous, yet flexible and haunted by many modulations. But others thought there was little variation. George Gilfillan, who heard him in England, reported a reading "without excitement, without energy, scarcely even with emphasis. . . . There is

[1] *Dansville Advertiser*, Jan. 19, 1865, by the courtesy of Mrs. Rena S. Kramer. For other descriptions of Emerson's appearance, see Rusk, IV, 20; *Works*, VI, 383; G. W. Cooke, *Ralph Waldo Emerson* (Boston, 1882), pp. 115, 116; *Independent*, 22, No. 1118 (May 5, 1870); 1; Alexander Ireland, *In Memoriam: Ralph Waldo Emerson* (London, 1882), pp. 16, 17.

no betrayal of emotion except . . . a slight tremble in his voice." On the whole, however, Emerson's voice was his most effective instrument. If it lacked what an English newspaper called "regular intonation," yet it had range, sweetness, and a commanding quality.[1]

Perhaps because of the manuscript, from which he seldom departed long, Emerson's auditors generally felt that he was not in direct communication with them. A public monologist, ráther than a lecturer, one of his English hearers styled him, and though the earnestness and simplicity of the speaker bespoke sympathy and respect, yet always there was a distance between the speaker and his hearers. Emerson himself reported that some Boston ladies thought he was always on stilts and, for himself, that he saw even the members of his own household as from across a gulf. And as to speaking without a manuscript, "What would I not do or suffer to buy that ability?"[2] There were, of course, successes. Preaching in Concord, N. H., in 1828, Emerson was described as a "man of force and popular address," under whom the congregation constantly increased. (The congregation included Ellen Tucker, to whom Emerson was presently betrothed.) The speech of 1859 on Robert Burns won clamorous applause. And Lowell's account in the *Nation* suggests that under Emerson's hesitant unoratorical style there was the old campaigner's art of engaging sympathy and attention. Yet the lectures seem to have had small audiences in the main, drawn, however, from the upper classes, especially from the intellectual classes, of society. George William Curtis found lecture committees saying, "We can have Mr. Emerson once every three or four years."[3] Emerson, in short, was no Beecher. The sweep and power of the popular orator was not his. Yet for the right audience, he had a quiet strength that left a deep impression, though it provoked no tumult of response.

He had steadiness under fire, too. Remoteness from the audiences meant independence of them. Departures of displeased auditors left Emerson untroubled. Once at Cambridge, in the time of the Fugitive Slave Act, there were hisses and catcalls from Harvard Southerners. Emerson only looked over the turbulent crowd calmly, curiously, as at a new phenomenon. He uttered no sentence he had not written, but the manuscript that night took a little longer in the reading. In 1861 at a turbulent antislavery meet-

[1] For comment on Emerson's voice, see *Nation*, 7 (Nov. 12, 1868): 389; Margaret Fuller, *Life Without and Within* (Boston, 1895), p. 194; George Gilfillan, *Second Gallery of Literary Portraits* (Edinburgh, 1852), p. 133; Cooke, *loc. cit.*; Ireland, *loc. cit.*

[2] On Emerson's attitude to his audience: Gilfillan, *loc. cit.*; *Journals*, V, 324; Rusk, IV, 9; W. C. Brownell, *American Prose Masters* (New York, 1909), p. 112.

[3] Rusk I, 222; E. R. Hoar, in *Tributes to Longfellow and Emerson by the Massachusetts Historical Society* (Boston, 1882), pp. 37–39; G. W. Curtis, *From the Easy Chair* (New York, 1893), p. 23.

ing, he was much interrupted, and his own account is that he retired. Yet the stenographic report in the *Liberator* shows that he made a speech of about ten minutes—he was not the principal speaker—and that he closed his remarks easily and appropriately.[1]

Emerson introduced himself to the lecture-attending public of 1833 by a few discourses that various Boston societies invited him to deliver— probably because he had just returned from some months of European travel—and by courses of eight or ten lectures in Boston; these he himself managed. A Boston lecturer was naturally called out to the New England towns and villages and, after a time, to New York and Philadelphia, to Pittsburgh and Rochester, and thence to the Middle West. In the thirties he was chiefly in New England, in the forties he ranged more widely in the East, in the fifties and sixties there were annual trips to the West—as far west, that is, as Missouri and Iowa. London and numerous English and Scottish towns heard him in 1847–1848. In old age, a pleasure trip brought him to California, where a lecture or two were read.

Though Emerson had faith in the lyceum movement as a large element in popular education, he believed that the laborer deserved his hire and ought to protect his interests. Hence he was watchful against the occasional invitation that did not mention pay. He took pains to prevent too full publication of his addresses in the newspapers—though not always with success. He found it wiser not to sell a lecture to *Graham's Magazine*. He noted that he did better when he appeared under his own management than when a committee of some society organized a series for him and divided the profits with him. In Boston in 1842 the price for a ticket to a series of eight lectures was $2; a ticket to a single lecture, 50 cents. Emerson earned $320 by the eight lectures. The journal for February 9, 1838, gives a detailed computation for the Boston season of ten lectures that had just closed. The prices were those which still prevailed in 1842; 319 season tickets had been sold and 373 single tickets; expenses amounted to $225. He adds, "Deduct error somewhere—$13," and arrives, wrongly, at a gain of $568. It was a highly successful season; Emerson still remembered it when, almost ten years later, he discussed with Alexander Ireland the English venture. For lectures in the country towns of Massachusetts he was paid $5 or $10 and expenses. Fees rose as he moved westward, but Emerson's fee was $75 a night when Murdoch the elocutionist received $100. In London in 1848 a series netted £80 instead of the £200 that his friends had hoped it would bring; and on the whole, the gains of the English venture were not pecuniary.[2]

[1] E. P. Whipple, *Recollections of Eminent Men* (Boston, 1886), pp. 140, 141; *Liberator*, 30 (Feb. 1, 1861): 5.
[2] On lecture prices and profits: Rusk, II, 218, 219; III, 14, 164, 298, 380; IV, 103.

As the Middle West grew, lecture agents appeared, whose services Emerson found a considerable help, both in schedule making and in raising prices. But sometimes a local committee corresponded with the lecturer in the autumn and with his agent in the winter and kept the correspondence. The fee paid was always the lower figure, which he himself had set. After the Civil War, friends managed his Boston appearances—now become fewer—to far greater profit than he had known. But on the whole his gains from lecturing were extremely modest.

The literary messenger and lyceum express, as Emerson styled himself for his wanderings over the country, had, of course, his share of the burdens and accidents of his trade. When too much bored by committees of entertainment, he evaded them by not signing the hotel register. The good committee members, knowing that the last train had arrived, were left to a frantic search of the town for their lecturer, their anxiety not relieved until Emerson had had his nap. But as all lecturers must, he took his engagements seriously. If a special train must be hired in Indiana, he hired it. If the ice-locked Mississippi must be crossed on foot, he crossed it thus— twice at St. Louis in 1853, once at Davenport, Iowa, in 1855. And once he was rowed across on the surface of ice that was not yet safe for pedestrians; the oarsmen levered their oars against the rough surface, and the trip was successfully accomplished. Once, at least, a lecture was delivered against the clock—a train had to be caught—and he could not conceal from the Iowa audience his concern over the time; they saw him skipping leaves of the manuscript and felt cheated.

Apparently lectures were steadily under revision; if Emerson settled in a city to deliver a series, he was either compelled to finish or impelled to refinish the papers he had brought with him. Now and then he found it necessary to send back to Concord for a lecture that he had not expected to use but that was called for. Sometimes he tried out a new lecture on a country audience before bringing it to the larger cities. But in the main, lecture committees were conservative. The lectures they had heard of, perhaps had read, in large part, in the newspapers were the lectures they chose. Hence the Boston lectures were often the newest and made their way westward only by an irregular infiltration in the course of several years. In England especially committees were unresponsive to the speaker's pleas for change, and since the program was a long and heavy one, Emerson found his task doubly burdensome. But the vicissitudes of the lecturing trade are but a small part of the traveler's reports to his family. The greater part by far of the things he thought worth noting concerned the persons met, the sights seen, the observations made. The oft-remarked mixture in Emerson of mysticism and shrewdness, of poet and Yankee was not altogether inborn. The travel enforced by his profession kept his feet on the ground and his eyes open to the daily life of America.[1]

Naturally, the work of a minister, and even more that of an unattached lecturer of some note, included preparing addresses for various ceremonial occasions. These vary from the long speech in which Emerson reviewed the history of Concord after two hundred years to the speech at the Manchester Athenaeum in 1847 and that at the Harvard commemoration of Civil War heroes in 1865. They include various "literary orations" delivered before college gatherings; of these the Phi Beta Kappa address is the best known and the best. The speech on an occasion, with Emerson the orator of the day, perhaps, but compelled to adjust himself to the mood and expectation of the audience, suited him less than the "unappropriated lyceum hour," in which he and his thoughts were the sole object of interest. When he had to consider audience and situation he could; the work was easier and the result was better when the part assigned him gave scope for more than compliments. These he did not turn easily. The short speeches at the Bryant festival and at the Harvard commemoration have a bare adequacy to the occasion, but no felicity either of thought or of expression. The historical discourse at Concord, in 1835, shows Emerson in full sympathy with his subject, in full command of the long narrative, and quite able to subordinate reflection and generalization to the facts. The speech has no coruscations but sustains interest as well as any of Emerson's discourses. The afterdinner occasion at Manchester put Emerson on his mettle, for he was to follow Richard Cobden. He turned the necessary compliments with more grace than was usual for him and went on to a short but inspiring challenge to England and Englishmen to work through the troublous times then confronting them; and he made good use of his own position as a transatlantic guest. In the Phi Beta Kappa address, as in that entitled "Literary Ethics," Emerson had a relatively free hand; the occasion dictated only that a thoughtful and considered discourse should be read: he was able therefore to follow the method of his lectures, with a little more formality of tone and organization.

In another form of ceremonial address—the memorial speech for a dead friend or public figure—Emerson was highly successful. His method was to confine himself to a character sketch. He had an eye for character; he could make anecdote or incident reveal it; he told the truth as he saw it; he kept his attention fixed on the person he described, ignoring almost completely the mood of the mourners. Thus he spoke of Thoreau, of Ezra

---

[1] On the vicissitudes of the lecturing trade: Rusk, III, 137, 138, 143; IV, 4, 278–280, 540; V, 196, 491; VI, 39, 55; Whipple, *op. cit.*, p. 146; H. H. Hoeltje, "Ralph Waldo Emerson in Iowa," *Iowa Journal of History and Politics*, 27 (1927): 237, 245, 263; *Journals*, X, 223.

Ripley, of his aunt Mary Moody Emerson, of Theodore Parker. Thus, too, of Lincoln. The result in each case is a spare and sober record from which a living figure emerges, to win such esteem as the facts allow.

Political speeches, as one might expect, are relatively few in the list of Emerson's works. Those that do appear are concerned, as was inevitable, with the slavery question. As early as 1837 we find mention of a lecture on slavery; apparently it was prepared for his friends in Concord rather than for a larger public. Emancipation in the British West Indies in 1834 was the occasion for a long historical discourse on the treatment of the Negroes. Again the audience was that which Concord could provide. Those who attended the Boston lecture series of 1838 heard a pointed sentence on Lovejoy in the discourse on heroism, and in 1841 the lecture on the times cited "the fury with which the slave-trader defends every inch of his bloody deck and his howling auction platform." But such references as these, while they show Emerson's willingness to speak his mind, show also his unwillingness to enter outright into the agitation. If the principle under discussion can be illustrated by mention of Lovejoy, well and good; but the prime business is to discuss the principle; it is for this that Emerson takes the platform; agitation of the slavery question in the realm of politics he leaves to others; his fellow citizens of Concord shall hear his opinions if they wish, but Concord is almost within the domestic circle. This seems in effect to have been Emerson's attitude until the passage of the Fugitive Slave Act in 1850. After that event, he entered the political arena; with the Emancipation Proclamation, he left it. His political speeches did not supplant his proper work of lecturing but were added to it; they were not numerous, or very often repeated, but for this decade Emerson returned to the earliest view he had had of the function of his eloquence and undertook to press rather than to display his opinions.

The speeches dealt first with the Fugitive Slave Act, then with the assault upon Senator Sumner and affairs in Kansas, finally with John Brown and emancipation. Most are short; they represent Emerson as a supplementary speaker at a mass meeting rather than as the principal agitator. The best, by far, is the speech of 1851 on the Fugitive Slave Act. Vigorous in argument, vigorous in denunciation, the speech moves and kindles. The treatment of Webster is scathing: "No moral perception, no moral sentiment, but in that region, to use the phrase of the phrenologists, a hole in the head." Having been prepared in haste, the speech contains some almost involuntary revelations of Emerson's attitude to public affairs and is franker and more personal in tone than others. There is a note of complaint that government now demands the attention and correction of quiet citizens who have their own work to do; and there is the striking passage on the higher law, with its touching statement of a personal creed:

I had thought, I confess, what must come at last would come at first, a banding of all men against the authority of this statute. I thought it a point on which all sane men were agreed, that the law must respect the public morality. I thought that all men of all conditions had been made sharers of a certain experience, that in certain rare and retired moments they had been made to see how man is man, or what makes the essence of rational beings, namely, that whilst animals have to do with eating the fruits of the ground, men have to do with rectitude, with benefit, with truth, with something which *is*, independent of appearances: and that this tie makes the substantiality of life, this, and not their ploughing, or sailing, their trade or the breeding of families. I thought that every time a man goes back to his own thoughts, these angels receive him, talk with him, and that, in the best hours, he is uplifted in virtue of this essence, into a peace and into a power which the material world cannot give: that these moments counterbalance the years of drudgery, and that this owning of a law, be it called morals, religion, or godhead, or what you will, constituted the explanation of life, the excuse and indemnity for the errors and calamities which sadden it. In long years consumed in trifles, they remember these moments, and are consoled. I thought it was this fair mystery, whose foundations are hidden in eternity, which made the basis of human society, and of law; and that to pretend anything else, as that the acquisition of property was the end of living, was to confound all distinctions, to make the world a greasy hotel, and, instead of noble motives and inspirations, and a heaven of companions and angels around and before us, to leave us in a grimacing menagerie of monkeys and idiots. All arts, customs, societies, books, and laws, are good as they foster and concur with this spiritual element: all men are beloved as they raise us to it; hateful as they deny or resist it. The laws especially draw their obligation only from their concurrence with it.[1]

In the speech on the Emancipation Proclamation, Emerson mentions the orator who, after compliments and pleasantries and conventional argument, "suddenly, lending himself to some happy inspiration, announces with vibrating voice the grand human principles involved." Only once in the course of his political speaking did Emerson attain such inspiration. The political discourses after 1851 are pedestrian affairs, except perhaps for that on the proclamation itself. They register Emerson's indignation; they align him with the movement of protest; they have their effective passages. But the speech of political agitation, molding opinion and intensifying emotion to an immediate practical issue, was not Emerson's forte. For more than fifteen years he had lectured on topics of his own choice, at times assessing institutions and customs, but addressing himself in the main to the concerns of the individual. He had sent up his rockets of insight and affirmation, confident that those whose thoughts he expressed would come to him, as he himself said of Theodore Parker. The political speaker's complete involvement in the situation, his close grasp of its

[1] *Works*, XI, 188–190.

details, his clear sense of the next step to be taken, his outreach for instant assent, and his power to compel it—these Emerson could not muster. The scholar, when he descended into the market place, was a scholar still.

Emerson's activity covered almost forty years, ending, in essentials, shortly after the Civil War. During more than thirty years he brought his lectures to many towns and cities, won more readers than listeners, established his fame. Once he had found his calling, he followed his own maxim, "Do your work," with almost undeviating purpose. "A lecture," he wrote in 1839, "is a new literature, which leaves aside all tradition, time, place, circumstance, and addresses an assembly as mere human beings, no more."[1] The lecturer lays aside, he might have added, the office of civic leader and the office of expositor and defender of a system of thought. He makes no concessions to men's accepted beliefs, or to their established intellectual habits, or to their expectations of direct and commanding communication from the platform. He deals with the timeless problems of the individual, imparts his vision of the first things in life, but always in his own language and with his own logic. No speaker, it would seem, ever found and held an audience, even a small and select one, as Emerson's essentially was, on terms so rigorously independent of it. In a measure, this independence was necessary to his function, which was to alter men's thinking by re-placing the emphasis and changing the direction, to find a new vocabulary of ideas and a different frame of reference. Yet in the main points—the break with theological tradition, the glowing individualism, the strong Americanism, the hopeful and expansive view—he was only a little ahead of his times. In larger measure, then, the independence he so carefully cherished was a need of his own nature—a nature in which faith in his ideas and ambition of social influence were mingled with reluctance to come to grips with the society he sought to influence.[2]

SELECTED BIBLIOGRAPHY

Of Emerson's lectures and addresses, as delivered, we have few exact texts; stenographic reports exist in but one or two instances. Emerson delivered the same lecture, by title, over many years, but he altered much, and he revised drastically for the printer. Some lectures were redistributed into others, not by copying, but by transferring the sheets. Hence reconstitution of the texts appears impossible. The lectures delivered in the last years, and the versions printed, are not entirely of Emerson's own making; he relied much on his friend and assistant, J. E. Cabot. Sermons were omitted from the *Complete Works*, with the single exception of that on the Lord's Supper. McGiffert's selection of twenty-five sermons leaves more than a hundred still unprinted.

[1] *Journals*, V, 234.

[2] For leave to include excerpts from the *Works*, the *Journals*, and *Young Emerson Speaks*, acknowledgment is made to Houghton Mifflin Company; for excerpts from *The Letters of Ralph Waldo Emerson*, to the Columbia University Press and the Ralph Waldo Emerson Memorial Association.

Ralph Waldo Emerson

Primary Sources

The Complete Works of Ralph Waldo Emerson, Edward Waldo Emerson, ed., Centenary ed., 12 vols., Boston and New York, 1903–1904.
Young Emerson Speaks, Arthur Cushman McGiffert, Jr., ed., Boston, 1938.
Ralph Waldo Emerson: Uncollected Writings, New York, 1912.
Journals of Ralph Waldo Emerson with Annotations, Edward Waldo Emerson and Waldo Emerson Forbes, eds., 10 vols., Boston and New York, 1909–1914.
The Letters of Ralph Waldo Emerson, Ralph L. Rusk, ed., 6 vols., New York, 1939.
The Correspondence of Thomas Carlyle and Ralph Waldo Emerson, Boston and New York, 1884.

Secondary Sources

Brooks, Van Wyck: *The Life of Emerson*, New York, 1932.
Cabot, James Elliott: *A Memoir of Ralph Waldo Emerson*, 2 vols., Boston, 1887.
Conway, Moncure D.: *Emerson at Home and Abroad*, Boston, 1882.
Firkins, Oscar W.: *Ralph Waldo Emerson*, Boston, 1915.
Holmes, Oliver Wendell: *Ralph Waldo Emerson*, Boston, 1884.
Ireland, Alexander: *In Memoriam: Ralph Waldo Emerson*, London, 1882.

18

Charles W. Eliot

by Louis M. Eich

Charles William Eliot was born in Boston, March 20, 1834. He was educated in the Boston Latin School and in Harvard College (class of 1853); studied chemistry and investigated educational methods in Europe, 1863–1865; assistant professor of mathematics and chemistry, 1858–1863, Lawrence Scientific School, Harvard; professor of chemistry, Massachusetts Institute of Technology, 1865–1869; president of Harvard University, 1869–1909; president National Education Association, 1902–1903. Died August 22, 1926.

Le Baron Russell Briggs, who, as professor and dean at Harvard, was closely associated with Charles W. Eliot for many years, referred to him as "this greatest of all the men whom I have known"; and, again, "All in all he was the finest speaker I have ever heard."[1] William Allan Neilson, authorized biographer, characterizes Eliot as "a guide not merely in educational matters but in all the great questions that have agitated the public mind, political, industrial, social, and moral. Other great leaders of opinion have come and gone, and some for a time have been more conspicuous; but it is impossible to name a figure who so continuously dominated our intellectual horizon for so long a period."[2] Discounting as he will these evaluations by close friends and ardent admirers, the student of Eliot will assign him a high place among the leaders of thought of America during the last thirty years of the nineteenth century and the first quarter of the twentieth.

Let us note the heritage and training that produced such leadership. Charles William Eliot was a descendant of Andrew Eliot of Devonshire, England, who settled at Beverly, Mass., in 1632. His great-grandfather Samuel Eliot was one of the first book publishers in the United States. His grandfather Samuel Eliot was a prominent merchant of Boston and founder of the Eliot Professorship at Harvard. His father was a leading citizen of Boston, mayor of the city, legislator, and congressman. Charles W. Eliot was educated by tutors and at a private school for boys until the age of ten, when he entered Boston Latin School. This school had a very

[1] L. R. Briggs, "As Seen by a Disciple," *Atlantic Monthly*, November, 1929, p. 595.

[2] W. A. Neilson, *"Charles W. Eliot: The Man and His Beliefs"* (2 vols., New York, Harper & Brothers, 1926), I, 9.

high reputation, but in that day, the curriculum was the traditional classical one, and the boy seems to have found his education rather dull, although he did his duties faithfully and well. The one bright spot seems to have been the programs of "declamation." Oratory of the declamatory type was very popular in the schools and colleges of the time, and Charles was frequently selected to deliver declamations on the "exhibition days." He was chosen to deliver the "Salutatory Address" in Latin at his graduation. He seems to have enjoyed his boyhood speaking experiences and, many years later, delighted in his ability to repeat portions of the orations that he had given half a century before. He possessed a good singing voice and loved to participate in part singing. A quite normal life was led by the boy in matters of recreation, pastimes, and outdoor life. Regular church attendance was the rule of the Eliot family. The finest of life in the home was his. Every resource of generations of English and American culture was available to him.

Like most of the graduates of the Boston Latin School, Eliot went to Harvard, from which he was graduated in 1853. At Harvard, the traditional curriculum continued, with Latin, speech, and mathematics dominating his studies. "Declamations" continued also, consisting largely of the recital of memorized passages. Eliot's "strong melodious voice" is commented upon by one of his classmates.[1] He ranked second in his class at graduation and at commencement declaimed an oration on "The Last Hours of Copernicus,"[2] which, incidentally, was the forty-third oration of a series of forty-four delivered at that commencement.[3] Young Eliot must have had sound nerves to have awaited his turn.

Very early we recognize signs of the educational leader and reformer. Although an excellent student at Harvard, he was dissatisfied with the traditional methods of instruction in American colleges and universities. His experiences as a teacher confirmed his opinions.[4] Two years of study in Europe (1863–1865) gave him the opportunity to observe European educational methods. His views became definite as to what was needed in the American educational program. In 1869, he became president of Harvard and remained in that position for forty years, retiring in 1909. His "Inaugural Address" at once placed him in the front rank among educational reformers and prophets.[5] In this address Eliot pointed forward

---

[1] Henry James, *Charles W. Eliot* (2 vols., Boston, Houghton Mifflin Company, 1930), I, 37.

[2] *Ibid.*, p. 51.

[3] Charles W. Eliot, *A Late Harvest* (Atlantic Monthly Press Publications, 1924), p. 3.

[4] Upon graduation, Eliot became tutor in mathematics at Harvard. From 1858 to 1863 he was assistant professor of mathematics and chemistry in Lawrence Scientific School. After study abroad, he became professor of chemistry in the Massachusetts Institute of Technology.

[5] Delivered Oct. 19, 1869; Neilson, *op. cit.*, I, 1–37.

to the major changes in higher education that were to be accomplished or at least well started during his generation. He advocated the extension of the elective system of studies, greater freedom and responsibility for student conduct, the need of higher salaries to attract talented young men to the teaching profession, and more restrictive entrance requirements. He believed in a thorough study of languages, natural and physical sciences, mathematics, history, and philosophy. "This university," the new president stated, "recognizes no real antagonism between literature and science, and consents to no such narrow alternatives as mathematics *or* classics, science *or* metaphysics. We would have them all, and at their best." It is curious to note his attitude toward coeducation in 1869. He advised that the university "maintain a cautious and expectant policy."

Assuming leadership in educational circles upon his inauguration, Eliot maintained his commanding position throughout his long career as president of Harvard. With decision and firmness, and often against the bitter opposition of the orthodox and conservative, he remodeled Harvard in accordance with his views. At the time of his inauguration Harvard was "an unprogressive provincial college with two or three inefficient professional schools attached to it."[1] Eliot lengthened the school terms, instituted written examinations where only oral examinations had been the rule, and began to point toward the graduate basis in the medical and law schools. His innovations soon became firmly established in American higher education, and Harvard became the model for colleges and universities throughout the United States.

In numerous addresses and published articles, Eliot reiterated his views and kept himself prominent in educational leadership. Let us examine some of this material. In 1884 Eliot spoke at Johns Hopkins University on the subject "What Is a Liberal Education?"[2] His points were: the number of admissible studies needs to be much enlarged; a considerable range of choice should be allowed from an earlier age than now; the existing order of studies in the secondary schools should be changed to permit the study of science earlier; English, French, and German should have full and equal academic standing with Greek, Latin, mathematics, natural and social science. He insists on the withdrawal of the artificial protection given to the classics. They must rely upon merit to retain their places among the studies that belong to a liberal education. He even goes so far as to state: "Greek literature compares with English as Homer with Shakespeare, that is, as infantile with adult civilization."[3] There seems to

[1] Neilson, I, 11.
[2] In *Educational Reform* (The Century Company, 1898); also in Neilson's biography, I, 38–71.
[3] Charles W. Eliot, *Educational Reform* (New York, The Century Company, 1898), p. 98.

be a positive animus in his attitude: "Are not the Greek tragedies means of culture? Yet they are full of incest, murder, and human sacrifice to lustful and revengeful gods."[1]

In 1897 he states *the function of education in a democratic society.*[2] The main elements of instruction and discipline in a democratic society he believes to be the study of nature, the study of the human race through biography and history, and the study of household duties. The supreme attainment of such education is strength and loveliness of character.

In 1905, he boldly attacks the evils of college football, declaring in his opening sentence: "The game of football has become seriously injurious to rational academic life in American schools and colleges, and it is time that the public should understand and take into earnest consideration the objections to this game."[3]

In 1908 we find him again defending the elective system.[4] It is "not a wide open miscellaneous bazaar" but a well-ordered series of consecutive courses in each large subject. Of all the items of his educational program the one perhaps stressed most frequently and emphatically was the extension of the elective choice of studies in connection with the inclusion of more contemporary subjects.

Speaking at the opening of the laboratories of Rockefeller Institute for Medical Research in 1906, Eliot insists: "The educated public needs to obtain a clearer idea than it now has of scientific research, of its objects and results, and of the character and capacity of the men who devote themselves to it."[5] He points to the marvelous achievements in medical research, and pleads that the boundaries of knowledge be ever extended, no matter how severe the battle against ignorance.

We can think, then, of Charles W. Eliot as being continuously before the public as a practical educator presenting definitions of education, matters of curriculum, and details of administration. One can appreciate, also, that he would be regarded as a guide in matters of conduct, ethics, and even aesthetics. In "The New Definition of the Cultivated Man"[6]

[1] Charles W. Eliot, "The New Definition of the Cultivated Man," *Present College Questions* (D. Appleton and Company, 1903).

[2] "The Function of Education in a Democratic Society," in *Educational Reform*, pp. 401–418; also in Neilson's biography, I, 97–114.

[3] "The Evils of College Football," *Woman's Home Companion*, November, 1905; also in Neilson's biography, I, 115–120.

[4] "The Elective System," in *University Administration* (Houghton Mifflin Company, 1908); also in Neilson's biography, I, 132–159.

[5] "The Character of the Scientific Investigator," *The Educational Review*, September, 1906; also in Neilson's biography, I, 121–131.

[6] Address delivered before the National Education Association, Boston, July 6, 1903, published in *Present College Questions* (D. Appleton and Company, 1903); also in Neilson's biography, I, 189–204.

he stresses character as the most important ideal of the modern world. The religious ideal in education,[1] according to Eliot, "is a combination of three ideals which are the supreme result of the best human thinking and feeling through all recorded time. These ideals are truth, beauty or loveliness, and goodness." These ideals are to be taught "incessantly" in the schools. Children from six to eighteen should learn how truth is to be sought. They must learn facts, truth and untruths, as they are manifested in all lines of education. The religious ideal of beauty or loveliness is to be inculcated as it is shown in nature, in the literatures of the world, in the fine arts. The ideal of goodness in the sense of cooperation should be the object of constant teaching.

Again and again Eliot spoke and wrote on such subjects as "The Happy Life,"[2] "The Character of a Gentleman,"[3] "The Durable Satisfactions of Life,"[4] "The Appreciation of Beauty."[5] As was natural, much of his advice is directed to the young men of college age whom he knew so well. The happy life means rational, responsible living. The "gentleman" implies a quiet person, one who is generous in his judgment of others, who sees the superiorities rather than the inferiorities of his associates. The "durable satisfactions of life" for the educated man are health, a wholesome capacity for hard work, and a life of honor. New students at Harvard are cautioned as to their new-found freedom and are advised to choose with the utmost care their studies and their companions.[6] The opening statement of his address on the appreciation of beauty, an address delivered at the opening of a public art gallery, reveals the speaker's idealistic conception of a democracy: "The ultimate object of democracy is to increase the satisfactions and joys of life for the great mass of people."

But Eliot did not confine himself to utterances on education and on life. He entered, with characteristic vigor, into discussion of political and sociological problems of the day. For example, he had quite decided views on the capital-labor controversy. In two extensive lectures, "The Future of Trades Unionism in a Democracy" and "The Future of Capitalism in a

[1] "The Religious Ideal in Education," *The Outlook*, Oct. 21, 1911.

[2] In *The Happy Life* (New York, Thomas Y. Crowell Company, 1895); also in Neilson's biography, II, 413.

[3] Address delivered to new students at Harvard, Oct. 12, 1904; also in Neilson's biography, II, 539–543.

[4] Address delivered to new students at Harvard, Oct. 3, 1903; this and preceding address published in *Training for an Efficient Life* (Houghton Mifflin Company, 1915); also in Neilson's biography, II, 549–553.

[5] Address delivered at the opening of the Albright Art Gallery, Buffalo, N. Y., published in *The Critic* (G. P. Putnam's Sons, 1905).

[6] Address delivered to new students at Harvard, Oct. 3, 1903.

Democracy,"[1] he states his credo in definite style. "It is high time it should be generally understood that trades unionism in important respects works against the very best interests of democracy." He opposes, therefore, uniform wage and limitation of output, leading to higher prices. He opposed "joint agreements" between labor and capital that operate "to determine wages and conditions of work on the one hand and profits on the other, with the least regard to the consumers." In the discussion of any point in dispute the fundamental question should always be: "What terms can the two parties acting together exact for the community at large?" Both the unions and capital have become monopolistic, and it may be necessary for democracy to protect itself against both monopolies by such measures as widespread reduction of consumption of the articles in question or by legislative regulation limiting such monopolies. Vigorously Eliot opposes the secrecy with which the affairs of both unions and employers' associations are carried on. It is a discredit to unions that they do not prevent violence in strikes. The closed shop is far from being a democratic institution. "It is a means of promoting the interests of a certain group or class against the interests of the mass." Where there is mutual confidence between employers and employees the discipline of the shop may be entrusted to an association of employees. Matters of hours, wages, and shop rules are fair subjects for discussion between managers and workmen, but the improvement of the products and a stable and profitable business are also involved. The duty of the union is to promote cooperative good will.

What democracy needs for its capitalists, said Eliot, are such ideals as the following: (1) sympathy with democratic ideals must include responsibility to society for the products; (2) the interests of the whole community must be served; (3) responsibility must be felt for improving the lot of faithful workmen and for disability and old-age provisions; (4) there must be responsibility for the education of the children of employees; (5) democracy would force publicity on corporations. Monopolies are to be avoided in labor as in capital. There is grave danger when unions use such monopolistic means as the boycott, the closed shop, and the union label. Capital should resist such measures in the interests of democracy. One might characterize Eliot, then, as a moderate conservative, with the interests of the general public uppermost in his mind.

Quite consistently, Eliot preaches joy in work. He applies this philosophy to the laborer as well as to the man of culture. "The winning of satis-

[1] These two addresses were delivered at the Larwill Lecture Foundation at Kenyon College in 1909; published, 1910, by Kenyon College; also in Neilson's biography, I, 255-288 and 289-317.

faction and content in daily work is the most fundamental of all objects for an industrial democracy. Unless this satisfaction and content can be habitually won on an immense scale, the hopes and ideals of democracy cannot be realized. Therefore, joy in work should be the all pervading subject of the industrial discussion; for it is at once motive, guide, and goal."[1] A contemporary note is struck in his declaration that there are two tendencies adverse to satisfaction in daily toil: the minute division of types of labor and the monotonous character of machine labor. According to William Allan Neilson,[2] Eliot, although an independent in politics, usually was a Democrat, largely because he found in the Democratic party "more sympathy with ordinary humanity, with the less comfortable and happy classes, and with the dejected or discontented portion of the American population."

Eliot was also a spokesman on the subject "War and Peace."[3] He devoted especial attention to this subject after his retirement from the presidency of Harvard. In 1911 he made a tour of the world on behalf of the Carnegie Endowment for International Peace. National distrusts, he insists, are fostered by ignorance and by unscrupulous newsmongers. His views on American relations with Japan sound quite naïve. Japan has no intention of dominating the Pacific. "All Japanese statesmen and political philosophers recognize the fact that Japan is and always will be unable to dominate the Pacific."[4] "The right state of mind of Americans toward Japan is one of hearty goodwill and cordial admiration."[5] While Europe was at war in 1915, Eliot wrote:

We look forward with hope to a diminution in Europe of the autocratic forms and an increase of the constitutional forms (of government), as well as to better security for both large and small states against sudden invasion. This better security implies a federal council of a few powerful states, the reduction of national armaments, and the creation of a federal force competent to impose peace.[6]

As one would expect, Eliot supported Woodrow Wilson.

The range of Eliot's themes as speaker and writer shows an enormous diversity and catholicity of interests. In "The Intellectual Life of Women"[7] he eulogizes homemaking in its opportunities for intellectual concerns as

---

[1] "Content in Work," *World's Work* (July, 1904), also in Neilson's biography, I, 243.

[2] Neilson's biography, I, 15.

[3] A series of articles published under the title *The Road to Peace* (Houghton Mifflin Company, 1915); also in Neilson's biography, I, 353–382, II, 384–409.

[4] "Present and Future Causes of War," *The Road to Peace* (Houghton Mifflin Company, 1915); also in Neilson's biography, I, 353–372.

[5] *Ibia.*, p. 370.

[6] *Ibid.*, p. 406.

[7] *Ladies' Home Journal*, January, 1908; also in Neilson's biography, II, 568–575.

well as service. "The Religion of the Future"[1] emphasizes the need of change and adaptation in religion if it is to survive. "Public Opinion and Sex Hygiene"[2] is a frank discussion of venereal disease, prostitution, and segregation of vice districts in cities. There were numerous addresses and writings of the biographical and interpretative type on Franklin, Washington, Channing, Emerson, etc. There were detailed studies of governmental problems such as "Civil Service Reform and Popular Government"[3] and "City Government by Fewer Men."[4]

We have thus made a survey of representative writings and addresses of Charles William Eliot. We saw him as a man of many associations, of interests in a large variety of fields of thought and activity, as a spokesman on a wide range of subjects. Primarily he was the professional educator, dealing directly with problems of education or interpreting his topics in the light of their effects upon the intellectual and moral life of the people. Doubtless the greatest number of his listeners were students, teachers, and college administrators. But one can readily appreciate that, as president of a great university, he would be regarded as a guide by many not directly connected with the educational field. Predominantly his messages are hopeful. He was a reformer, dissatisfied with things as they were, but he had steadfast faith in the individual human life, in educational institutions, in democratic ideals, in the possibility of international peace. Sympathetic, he is yet eminently fair-minded: no faction shall have unfair advantage over any other; no stratum in society shall gain increase at the expense of the general public.

Perhaps enough quotations have been cited to illustrate Eliot's rhetorical style. Professor E. K. Rand referred to the "attic style of President Eliot." Professor Rand finds similarity between the literary styles of Eliot and St. Gregory. Significantly he states: "Gregory's literary style is formed on the simplest models. Here is a man educated in the old training, who deliberately threw it away. It often happens, today, that advocates of a new education in which the classics have no part owe their own culture to the system that they would have us abandon."[5] There is no question to whom Professor Rand refers! Significant, too, is Professor Rand's further comparison between Eliot and St. Gregory: "It is fair, I think, to say that these two masters of education, the ancient and ecclesiastic,

---

[1] In *The Durable Satisfactions of Life* (1910).

[2] Published 1913; also in Neilson's biography, II, 649–663.

[3] Address delivered at annual meeting of the National Civil Service Reform League, Philadelphia, 1911, published by the league, 1912.

[4] *World's Work*, October, 1907; also in Neilson's biography, II, 753–774.

[5] E. K. Rand, *Founders of the Middle Ages* (Harvard University Press, 1928). Professor Rand draws comparisons between St. Gregory and Eliot, p. 27.

the modern and anti-ecclesiastic, both manifest a vigorous desire to have done with the follies of the past, and to build on what is sound, and useful, and contemporary."[1]

Although he was schooled in the classics, recommending in his *Harvard Classics*[2] essays of Bacon and Emerson and Milton's *Areopagitica*, there is no suggestion of heaviness in his mode of presentation. "Direct speech at any cost was an article of his faith,"[3] stated Dean Briggs, who, as student, teacher, and dean, observed Eliot from 1871 to 1925. Quoting at random from "The Religion of the Future,"[4] Eliot said: "Religion is not a fixed but a fluent thing. It is, therefore, wholly natural and to be expected that the conceptions of religion prevalent among educated people should change from century to century. Modern studies in comparative religion and in the history of religions demonstrate that such has been the case in times past." This is a very characteristic passage. Perhaps his style is repetitious and obvious to some, particularly as we read his speeches without the vitalizing spirit of his delivery, but this is part of Eliot's scheme of clarity in meaning and conversational method. "Direct speech at any cost."

There is no consistency in length of sentences. There is a mixture of short, long, and moderate-length sentences. One can find no particular philosophy of style on this point. There is a characteristic crispness in his style even when the sentences are rather lengthy. Beginning an address on Channing,[5] Eliot said:

We commemorate today a great preacher. It is the fashion to say that preaching is a thing of the past, other influences having taken its place. But Boston knows better; for she had two great preachers in the nineteenth century, and is sure that an immense and enduring force was theirs, and through them, hers. Channing and Brooks! Men very unlike in body and mind, but preachers of like tendency and influence from their common love of freedom and faith in mankind. This city has learned by rich experience that preaching becomes the most productive of all human works the moment the adequate preacher appears—a noble man with a noble message. Such was Channing.

Note, also, the pronounced rhythm of the passage. In an address on Emerson[6] Eliot begins: "Emerson was not a logician or reasoner, and not a

---

[1] *Ibid.*

[2] The so-called "Five-foot Shelf," naming also works by Benjamin Franklin, Plato, Epictetus, and Marcus Aurelius.

[3] L. R. Briggs, "As Seen by a Disciple," *Atlantic Monthly*, November, 1929, p. 589.

[4] Address delivered at Harvard School of Theology, July 22, 1909.

[5] Address delivered at the unveiling of the Channing statue, Boston, June 1, 1903; also in Neilson's biography, II, 505-511.

[6] Address delivered in Boston, May 24, 1903; also in Neilson's biography, II, 512-538.

rhetorician, in the common sense. He was a poet, who wrote chiefly in prose, but also in verse. His verse was usually rough, but sometimes finished and melodious; it was always extraordinarily concise and expressive." While the choice of words is on the level of the educated man, as would be natural considering Eliot's customary audiences, clarity is never sacrificed for any display of scholarship. The traditional tripartite "to teach, to please, to move" seems to motivate his writing and his speaking.

Dean Briggs states on the matter of Eliot's logic:

> Logical consistency, some of us thought he had not. To draw an illustration from football, not, by the way, his favorite sport, he had developed a magnificently strong offense and let the defense take care of itself. In the eagerness of debate he repeatedly laid himself open to a reductio ad absurdum. . . . His mind was essentially affirmative. Accustomed to command he was often an authority himself, giving his views without sufficient evidence to satisfy one who disagreed with him.[1]

It is true that such all-inclusive statements, without substantiation, as the following, will sometimes appear: "All Japanese statesmen and political philosophers recognize the fact that Japan is and always will be unable to dominate the Pacific." Undoubtedly the authoritative position he occupied would be reflected in this "essentially affirmative" type of mind.

The regularity of his composition would satisfy the rhetoricians, ancient and modern, although the detailed rules as to such matters as emphasis of space may not always be fulfilled. An excellent example of the orderliness of material is found in "Five American Contributions to Civilization."[2] After a brief background introduction, closing with a definite transition sentence, we have "the first and principal contribution," etc. This is handled in definite pattern arrangement, with summaries and with refutation of possible opposing points. Then follows "the second eminent contribution," etc. There are a summary of all five points in conclusion and a final appeal.

Widely heard in our own time, there is abundant testimony of "eye and ear witnesses" as to the actual speaking method of Eliot. As we have noted, he had been interested in public speaking since boyhood. He was an unusually tall man, impressive looking, stately, extremely dignified. "Even as an old man, he retained the muscular bearing of youth, without the slightest suggestion of infirmity."[3]

---

[1] L. R. Briggs, "As Seen by a Disciple," *Atlantic Monthly*, November, 1929, p. 594.

[2] In A. M. Drummond and E. L. Hunt, *Persistent Questions in Public Discussion* (New York, The Century Company, 1924), pp. 3–24.

[3] Quoted from Dr. Eugen Kuehnemann, *Charles W. Eliot* (Boston, Houghton Mifflin Company, 1909), p. 79. Dr. Kuehnemann, from the University of Breslau, was exchange professor of German at Harvard, 1906–1907 and 1908–1909.

His voice was rich and deep and had fine carrying power, readily filling the average auditorium. Many are the comments upon that marvelous low voice. "He began to speak, and one said to oneself, 'This must be the voice of a great man.'"[1] Professor C. T. Copeland once described Eliot's voice as "sounding as if it issued from channels that had been warmed with old port wine."[2] No matter how large the room, the conversational method sufficed. His enunciation was rather sharp; there was the crispness notable in animated conversation. Of facial expression, gesture, or other action, there was very little. A dark birthmark, prominent on one side of his face, may quite possibly account for the lack of facial expression and for the rather rigid manner. This birthmark, however, at least after the first momentary curiosity of the audience had been appeased, did not detract from the general impressiveness of his appearance. He readily rose above the impediment. A certain consciousness of this blemish must have been there, however, since all photographs for which he posed carefully presented the normal profile.

The formality of his manner before an audience was often interpreted as coldness. Restraint, lack of gesture, lack of emotional appeal were very much a part of his style of speaking. Eliot once debated with Wendell Phillips on the subject of admitting women to Harvard. The contrast of Eliot's fact-presenting method with the emotional arguments of Phillips is said to have been most striking. Perhaps his statement in an essay entitled "How I Have Kept My Health and Working Power till Eighty" may be apropos here: "I could always spend a long evening in stirring debate or in public speaking, and go to sleep, on getting home, without delay or need of any calming process."[3] Eliot was often characterized as phlegmatic, cold, lacking in a sense of humor. While his friends deny this[4] and insist that he was really congenial and "sedately jocular," there was unquestionably a certain austerity and brusqueness about him that carried over into his speaking.[5]

On October 11, 1923, the Massachusetts Historical Society celebrated the fiftieth anniversary of Eliot's election to its membership. On that occasion he said (he was then eighty-nine):

[1] Allen Davis, *The Public Speaking Review*, October, 1911.

[2] James, *op. cit.*, II, 102.

[3] Charles W. Eliot, *A Late Harvest: Miscellaneous Papers* (Atlantic Monthly Press Publications, 1924), p. 12.

[4] On his seventieth birthday the tribute sent to him under the auspices of thousands of Harvard alumni contained the sentence: "Your outward reserve has concealed a heart more tender than you have trusted yourself to reveal."

[5] Eliot was in rather marked contrast with his contemporary James B. Angell, who was president of the University of Michigan during almost identical years and who was noted for the warmth of his personality as a speaker.

Charles W. Eliot

In all the early part of my career as a teacher and an educational administrator, I was much engaged in controversy, not to say combat, and that at home as well as outside of Harvard. In all my public appearances during those years, I had a vivid sense that I was addressing an adverse audience. Now today is a very delightful illustration of a change that has come over my experience. For twenty years past, I should think, I have found myself often in the presence of a favoring audience—of one that wished, at any rate, to agree with me, or, if it could not, regretted that it could not.[1]

Retelling the anecdote so often told of Eliot will show the occasional brusqueness for which he was noted. Discussing a successor for Phillips Brooks at a meeting at which Bishop Lawrence was present, Eliot spoke to this effect: "We need a man of education, of culture, but with no claims to brilliance or oratory, such a man as [turning to Lawrence] "—why Bishop Lawrence, you are just the man. You should be Brooks' successor."[2] In contrast, and for further insight, let us quote a letter to Eliot by George Herbert Palmer:

·I cannot let this memorial day go by without expressing to you my gladness for the twenty-five years that are gone. Twenty-four of them I have spent with you, and every one has made me more deeply your debtor. Without you I should not have known myself. . . . No living man has had a larger share than you in shaping my ideals and powers.

At the first I saw how significant you were to be for me and—though disliking— I set myself to study you. My comprehension was slow, and resisted. Few members of the faculty have voted against you more times than I, but sympathy was growing through the years when our radical difference of temper was becoming plain. Smoothly and with no violent change I passed through distrust, tolerance, respect, admiration, liking, in the hearty friendship—I might say the love—which makes it a delight to work with you now, whether in opposition or alliance.[3]

It is significant that in reply to this letter, Eliot refers to himself as "by nature reserved except with intimates, and even with some of them." That characteristic of the man naturally colored his manner of speaking.

Charles W. Eliot, then, occupies a high place among American educators who were effective speakers. How much of his influence was due to his speaking it is, of course, impossible to measure. Undoubtedly his prestige as speaker and writer were greatly enhanced by his position as president of Harvard. Henry James quotes from a letter Eliot wrote to his sister-in-law,

[1] Charles W. Eliot, *A Late Harvest: Miscellaneous Papers* (Atlantic Monthly Press Publications, 1924), p. 12 of Introduction.

[2] "Last Seen," in Archie Butt's *Intimate Letters of Archie Butt, Military Aide to William H. Taft and Theodore Roosevelt* (New York, Doubleday, Doran & Company, Inc., 1930).

[3] May, 19, 1894; letter given in Henry H. Saunderson, *Charles W. Eliot, Puritan Liberal* (New York, Harper & Brothers, 1928), pp. 8ff.

January 26, 1870: "I am getting used to being treated with distinguished consideration. Official station is a curious power. There is lots of human nature in the saying *a tout seigneur tout honneur;* even when the *seigneur* is a mean or inadequate person, the station is still sacred."[1]

Eugen Kuehnemann said of him: "The people have come to expect to hear from President Eliot in every great question of American life, and, when he speaks, America listens."[2] A great moral force during his lifetime he certainly was. His most direct influence, however, will always be as the "great statesman of American pedagogics,"[3] the prophet and the practical builder of new ideals and practices in the American educational program.

SELECTED BIBLIOGRAPHY

Life

Briggs, L. R.: "As Seen by a Disciple," *Atlantic Monthly*, November, 1929.

Chapman, John Jay: *Memories and Milestones,* including essay on "President Eliot," Harvard University Press, 1909.

Eliot, Charles W.: *Harvard Memories*, Harvard University Press, 1923.

James, Henry: *Charles W. Eliot*, 2 vols., Boston, Houghton Mifflin Company, 1930.

Kuehnemann, Eugen: *Charles W. Eliot*, Boston, Houghton Mifflin Company, 1909.

Neilson, William A.: *Charles W. Eliot: The Man and His Beliefs*, 2 vols., New York, Harper & Brothers, 1926.

Proceedings of the Harvard Alumni Association—Ninetieth Birthday of Charles W. Eliot, Harvard University Press, 1924.

Saunderson, Henry H.: *Charles W. Eliot: Puritan Liberal*, New York, Harper & Brothers, 1928.

Addresses and Writings

"Academic Freedom," address, Press of Andrus and Church, Ithaca, N. Y., 1907.

"American Education since the Civil War," address, Rice Institute, Houston, Tex., 1907.

"The Appreciation of Beauty," address delivered at opening of Albright Art Gallery, Buffalo. published in *The Critic*, G. P. Putnam's Sons, 1905.

Certain Defects in American Education, U. S. Bureau of Education, 1918.

"Changes Needed in American Secondary Education," New York, General Education Board, 1916.

"Channing," address delivered at unveiling of the Channing statue, Boston, 1903, published by American Unitarian Association.

"The Character of a Gentleman," address to new students at Harvard, Oct. 12, 1904.

"The Character of the Scientific Investigation," address, *The Educational Review*, September, 1906.

Charles Eliot, Landscape Architect, Boston, Houghton Mifflin Company, 1902.

"City Government by Fewer Men," *World's Work*, October, 1907.

"Conflict between Individualism and Collectivism," three lectures, New York, Charles Scribner's Sons, 1910.

---

[1] James, *op. cit.*, p. 302.

[2] Eugen Kuehnemann, *Charles W. Eliot* (Boston, Houghton Mifflin Company, 1909), pp. 76 and 84.

[3] *Ibid.*

"Contemporary American Conception of Equality," address, University of Missouri Press, 1909.

"Content in Work," *World's Work*, July, 1904.

"The Durable Satisfactions of Life," address, *Training for an Efficient Life*, Boston, Houghton Mifflin Company, 1915.

"Educational Reforms," *Essays and Addresses*, The Century Company, 1898.

"The Elective System," *University Administration*, Boston, Houghton Mifflin Company, 1908.

"Emerson," address delivered in Boston, May 24, 1903, published by American Unitarian Association.

"The Evils of College Football," *Woman's Home Companion*, November, 1905.

"Five American Contributions to Civilization," published by A. M. Drummond and E. L. Hunt, *Persistent Questions in Public Discussion*, New York, The Century Company, 1924.

"Fruits of Medical Research with the Aid of Anaesthesia," Boston, Barta Press, 1909.

"The Function of Education in a Democratic Society," *Educational Reform*, The Century Company, 1898.

"The Fundamental Reform," address on civil service, National Civil Service League, 1910.

"The Future of Capitalism in a Democracy," address published by Kenyon College, 1910.

"The Future of Trades Unionism in a Democracy," address published by Kenyon College, 1910.

"The Happy Life," in *The Happy Life*, New York, The Thomas Y. Crowell Company, 1895.

Harvard Classics, New York, P. F. Collier & Son, Inc., 1909.

"Inaugural Address as President of Harvard University, 1869," Neilson's biography and numerous other sources.

"The Independence of 1776 and the Dependence of 1911," address, Documents of the City of Boston, 1911.

"The Intellectual Life of Women," *Ladies' Home Journal*, January, 1908.

"Japanese Characteristics," New York, American Association for International Conciliation, 1913.

A Late Harvest: Miscellaneous Papers, Atlantic Monthly Press Publications, 1924.

Latin and the A. B. Degree, New York, General Education Board, 1917.

Manual of Qualitative Chemical Analysis, 1869.

"The Meaning of the War," New York, The Macmillan Company, 1915.

More Money for the Public Schools, New York, Doubleday, Page and Company, 1903.

"The New Definition of the Cultivated Man," address before the National Education Association, published in *Present College Questions*, D. Appleton and Company, 1903.

"Public Opinion and Sex Hygiene," 1913.

"The Religion of the Future," *The Durable Satisfactions of Life*, New York, The Thomas Y. Crowell Company, 1910.

"The Religious Ideal in Education," *The Outlook*, Oct. 21, 1911.

"Shortening and Enriching the Grammar School Course," National Education Association, 1892.

Tendency to the Concrete and Practical in Modern Education, Boston, Houghton Mifflin Company, 1908.

University Administration, Boston, Houghton Mifflin Company, 1908.

"War and Peace," *The Road to Peace*, Boston, Houghton Mifflin Company, 1915.

"What Is a Liberal Education," address at Johns Hopkins University, 1884, in Neilson's biography.

Edwin A. Alderman

by CHARLES A. FRITZ

Edwin Anderson Alderman was born in Wilmington, N. C., May 15, 1861. He was graduated from the University of North Carolina, 1882; superintendent of public schools, Goldsboro, N. C., 1884–1887; assistant state superintendent of schools, North Carolina, 1889–1892; professor of English and history at North Carolina State Normal College, 1892–1893; professor of education in the University of North Carolina, 1893–1896; president of the University of North Carolina, 1896–1900; president of Tulane University, 1900–1904; President of University of Virginia, 1904–1931. Alderman was editor in chief of *Library of Southern Literature*, 1907; editor, *Classics Old and New*, a series of school readers, 1906–1907; author of *A Brief History of North Carolina*, 1896; *J. L. M. Curry*, a biography, 1911. He died April 29, 1931.

Born in the first year of the Civil War, Edwin A. Alderman spent his most impressionable years in the darkest period of the South's history. He saw around him the bitterness of sectional feeling, the political corruption of the Reconstruction period, and, above all, the poverty and ignorance of the masses of the people. In the cause of the education of these masses he decided to spend his life. For a number of years he was a teacher and administrator, chiefly in the public-school system of North Carolina, but from the time that he became president of the University of North Carolina in 1896 he was perhaps the outstanding force in the elevation of the educational standards of the South. His prominence as an educator and administrator led him to the presidencies of three Southern universities. It was in the last position, the presidency of the University of Virginia, that he rose to national prominence as an administrator and a speaker.

Alderman's chief interest, both to the historian of educational movements and to the student of oratory, lies in the fact that he was a prominent educator who, because he was also a very skillful speaker, was able to exert a considerable influence toward raising the educational standards of the South, not only for the higher institutions but also for the submerged masses, both white and black. He wrote a few books and a number of articles on educational topics that, although they may have added to his reputation as an educator at the time they were written, deserve no more attention at the present time than hundreds of other books or articles written by educators in the past fifty years. But by reason of his recognition as the greatest educational spokesman in the South during its period of rebuilding he has been given a place in this collection of studies.

Kinds of Speeches

During his lifetime Alderman made a great many speeches,[1] and fortunately, he kept in his files copies—or else newspaper notices—of most of them. Almost all of them were of the kind that we usually term *occasional*.[2] In very few was the aim that of securing direct action but rather that of impressing upon the hearers the significance of the immediate occasion, the meaning of the event commemorated, or the lessons for history in the life of the man being eulogized. He was much in demand, particularly in the South and occasionally in the North, to deliver the main address at such occasions as commencements, inaugurations, dinners, anniversaries, and memorial meetings. It was perhaps as a memorial speaker that he was at his best, his skill in that form of address, together with the fact that he was a friend of Woodrow Wilson, causing him to be chosen in 1924 to deliver the oration before both houses of Congress at the memorial service for Wilson. Chiefly remembered by the students at his universities will be his academic addresses—notably the talks that he gave each year at the Founders' Day exercises and those at the finals at the University of Virginia. In these speeches and in his commencement addresses can be found most of his educational philosophy.

Topics

A few main topics recurred again and again in Alderman's speeches. Naturally, the ones most often mentioned dealt with education—the need

[1] In the library at the University of Virginia is a special Alderman file containing about one thousand cards representing entries in newspapers, magazines, and the University of Virginia daily. Many of these are not yet (April, 1938) available to the reader. The writer had access to from two hundred to three hundred speeches filed in the library—some in typed manuscript; some in *College Topics*, the University of Virginia newspaper; some in the *Alumni News;* some printed in separate covers. For the purpose of this study seventy-one of Alderman's speeches were read, twenty-six studied more carefully.

[2] Of the seventy-one speeches examined for this study fifteen may be classified as commemorative (memorial addresses or eulogies); eight were inaugural addresses, either at his own installation or at those of other university presidents; four were before graduating classes; seven were delivered at dinners, but some of these—the one before the New England Society, for example—were speeches of praise; eleven were given before the student body of the institution of which he was at the time president; five were commencement addresses; one was of acceptance, one of introduction, one of response, and one of welcome; seventeen were delivered on various occasions before such bodies as bankers' associations, religious bodies, and educational associations where he was asked to make the main address.

for it in the South, its advancement in the South, and the necessity for making it more democratic everywhere. In his early speeches, when he was going all over North Carolina trying to arouse sentiment for the betterment of public education in that state, he stressed the importance of education and tried to show the people of that section that the South could be lifted materially and socially only through the agency of a truly popular education and that to secure this there must be a system of good free schools supported by local taxation.[1] This popular education, he held, should be available not only to the children of the white population but—and this at a time when Negroes had no schooling at all—to all children in the South without reference to color.

His idea of the great democratizing force of education extended also to the university. In short, *all* education from the elementary school to the university must, as he said, be "a great unified force molding national character, free to all, obligatory upon all."[2] He held, too, that the universities must at all times adjust themselves to the practical needs of the people. Of this idea, John Finley, speaking on Alderman before the American Academy of Arts and Letters, said: "The old idea that it was the duty of the state to care for the university was in his administration turned about, making it the primary duty of the university to care for the state."[3] And in his Founders' Day speech at the University of Virginia, Alderman said: "No university or college, in the future, will long endure which is not in fairly close touch with the community to whose needs it must minister. I stand on the principle that a university's chief task is, first, to teach its own students faithfully and well, not primarily for their sakes as individuals, but as a means of state and national enrichment."[4] To some it may seem strange that a man with all these ideas of democracy in education should strongly oppose coeducation, but, as he said in a speech at the University of Virginia, January 6, 1921, he felt that the sexes thrown together in college distracted each other and became overstimulated. This we can understand, but believers in learning for its own sake may wonder why it was that in all his addresses to college students, Alderman, while speaking often of the value of an education and the function of a university, should say so little about pure scholarship or the dignity of the

[1] William P. Trent, "President Alderman and the University of Virginia," *American Review of Reviews*, 31 (April, 1905): 449.

[2] This is from Alderman's article "The Nation's Supreme Task," in *World's Work*, 41: 129, but the same idea was expressed in some of his speeches.

[3] *Academy Publications*, No. 77 (1932), pp. 61–69.

[4] "The University and Reconstruction," *University of Virginia Alumni Bulletin*, 12, No. 2 (April, 1919): 184.

life of the scholar.[1] This seeming neglect was due no doubt to the fact that to his mind the purpose of education was not so much to enrich the soul of the learner as to enable him to serve society more efficiently. We may conclude this from the fact that Alderman talked so much about democracy. He upheld many times the democratic ideal[2] but often stressed the idea that democracy can be gained only through the medium of a popular education.[3] Perhaps the best statement of his thought on this topic is in the following passage taken from an address that he made in 1922:

> There is but one great question in this world—how to make men and women better and fitter for life in a democracy and there is but one answer—the right sort of *education*. Education is the supreme essential of democracy while democracy is the supreme opportunity of education. . . . The acid test of all public teaching, especially the higher education—which simply means more education—would seem to be, therefore, the quality and quantity of the service it can render to society in promoting its welfare.[4]

When Alderman spoke of education and democracy, he usually had in mind the people of the South. To other problems of the South he also gave a great deal of attention. One great ambition of his life was to bring about a better understanding of the South and her problems on the part of other sections of the country. In speech after speech he brought in this appeal, usually praising the contributions of the South and pointing out her advances. In one of the most important of these addresses, that delivered before the Civic Forum in New York on March 22, 1908,[5] his theme was the building spirit at work in the South—"the self-reliant effort of the Southern states of this Union to transform their economic and social life, to master the weapons of an industrial civilization, and to breathe easily the spirit of twentieth century Americanism, without sacrificing their deepest political and social instincts." This referred, of course, partly to the growing industrialization of the South, which he mentioned at other times with the hope that the change would not commercialize her soul. When speaking on the subject of the South he often referred to the Southern boy, his heritage, and of how he found himself; often he praised the idealism

---

[1] Reference was made to this in one speech, that given in 1928 at the University of Virginia finals.

[2] In ten of the speeches studied, democracy, either in education or in national life, was the chief topic.

[3] This was the dominant idea in a speech entitled "The Growth of Public Education in America," which Alderman delivered at the Jamestown Exposition, Oct. 12, 1906.

[4] Address delivered at the Virginia Polytechnic Institute Semicentennial, May 29, 1922.

[5] *The Growing South* (New York, The Civic Forum, 1908), p. 3.

of the South, holding that the South was the most idealistic section in America and that the nation sorely needed this idealism.[1] Of the purpose usually in his mind when speaking of the South, the following sentence is probably the best statement:

It is my purpose to speak to you today of the southern section of our country, made distinctive by inheritance, by isolation, by physical influence in economic history, in order that this region, being better understood, may be better served by the force that would aid in the slow process of renationalization.[2]

Not only did he praise the South; he loved particularly the state of Virginia and spoke often of her people, her heroes, and her contributions to the life of the nation. One of his most important speeches[3] was in its entirety a rather fulsome eulogy of the state of Virginia. In his speeches outside the state he usually managed to get in a word of praise for Virginia or to mention the sympathy existing between her and the state in which he was speaking.

While he praised the South, Alderman, however, did not fail to realize that she had serious problems to solve and that the most serious problem was that of the Negro. Of this he spoke in several of his addresses. He held that since the white race was superior to the black, it was the duty of the whites to give to the blacks a chance for education.[4] All his ideas on the subject, stated separately in several speeches, are brought together in the following passage:

For sixty years the South stood ready to die, and did die, for the doctrine of State sovereignty. It now sees that that doctrine and more especially, slavery, as a labor system, stood opposed to the spirit of the modern world. To-day it would die with even more amazing oneness of mind for the doctrine of racial integrity or the separateness of the two races. . . . The best Southern people not only do not hate the negro, but come nearer to having affection for him than any other people on earth. . . . They . . . know . . . that it is a solemn duty of the white man to see that the negro gets his chance in everything save social equality and political

[1] Most clearly expressed in "The Value of Southern Idealism," Alderman's address of welcome to the American Historical Association and the American Economic Association, New Orleans, La., Dec. 29, 1903.
[2] From "The Spirit of the South," Charter Day address at the University of California, Mar. 23, 1906, MS, p. 4.
[3] "Virginia," delivered in response to the toast "Virginia" at the banquet given by the citizens of Petersburg, Va., to the President of the United States and the governor of Pennsylvania on May 19, 1909 (published by the Michie Company, 1909).
[4] "The Race Problem," an address delivered in New York in 1904.

control. . . . In the meantime the white must control our political life, and the negro must build his own society.[1]

Another problem about which he spoke was that of the still existing sectional feeling on the part of both North and South. To him there was one kind of sectionalism that was praiseworthy—that which "symbolizes love of home, and interest and affection from one's neighbors."[2] But the kind of sectionalism in which sections distrusted each other he deplored and pleaded for greater sympathy between the peoples of each. In his speech before the New England Society,[3] he made a plea for the unity of the North and South, for tolerance on the part of each, for an appreciation by each of what the other had done; and looking into the future, foresaw sectionalism growing into nationalism.

Outside the discussion of the Negro problem one finds in Alderman's speeches little recognition of the great economic and social forces at work in the first quarter of the present century. The nearest approach to such recognition was in the following passage from the speech on "Sectionalism and Nationality":

No democracy has ever been tempted like this one. . . . No such field of exploitation has ever opened before any democracy, and never before has the current of the world's genius contributed to perfecting machinery for such vast exploitation. . . . This is not a corrupt nation. . . . Its public men are honest and its merchants are honest.[4]

Speech Structure

In structure Alderman's speeches showed considerable variety, the arrangement of ideas depending on the kind of speech. We can best consider the structure here through an examination of a few of the types of speeches that he delivered.

In the eulogies the method was in some cases selective—a measure of the man's services and influence—and in others biographical or chrono-

[1] "The Value of Southern Idealism: A brief address of welcome to the American Historical Association and the American Economic Association on the Evening of December 29th, 1903, by Edwin Anderson Alderman, President of Tulane University," pp. 9–11.

[2] "The National Spirit," delivered before the Washington Association of New Jersey at Washington Headquarters, Morristown, Feb. 21, 1911, printed in the *Proceedings of the Washington Association of New Jersey*, 1911, p. 11.

[3] "*Sectionalism and Nationality*: A speech by Dr. Edwin A. Alderman, President of the University of Virginia, before the New England Society in the City of New York. December 22, 1906."

[4] *Ibid.*, p. 14.

logical. An example of his use of the selective method was the eulogy of Jefferson,[1] which had the following main heads:

1. Jefferson was the first great philosopher and intelligent radical in American life.

2. Jefferson was the greatest liberal that has appeared in American history.

3. Jefferson was the first great American Democrat.

4. Jefferson was a great poet.

A method largely biographical in order, although with elements of the selective, was used in his eulogy of Woodrow Wilson.[2] In it the speaker reviewed the various phases of Wilson's career from his childhood to his death, stressing under each phase the qualities of the man as brought out by the events or using each event as a point of departure for the discussion of its significance. For example, he narrated the events of Wilson's career at Princeton and during the First World War and sought to justify his course at those times.

Among Alderman's best speeches were the ones that he delivered each year before the graduating class of the university over which he presided. Some of these developed only one main point. In an address to the graduating class of the University of Virginia in June, 1926, he stated his main idea as:

The watchword I would present to you to inform your philosophy of life is *magnanimitas*. . . . Men and women of 1926, take with you into life as a buckler and shield as a common guide, *magnanimitas*—that quality in character which enables one to encounter danger and trouble with tranquility and firmness, to disdain injustice, envy or revenge.[3]

In what is probably the best of these, in point of style at least, he talked to the seniors about what they had gained from the university, about the meaning of success, and sought to impress upon them the idea that he wished for them *public spirit*, the ideal of which is "loyalty to men and the betterment of the social life."[4]

As an example of the structure of his inaugural addresses, the one delivered at his installation as president of Tulane University (March 12, 1901) is typical. He divided it into four main heads:

[1] Delivered at the unveiling of the bust of Jefferson at the Hall of Fame, New York University, May 13, 1924.

[2] "Woodrow Wilson," memorial address delivered before a joint session of both houses of Congress, Dec. 15, 1924 (Washington, D. C., Government Printing Office, 1924).

[3] *Magnanimitas:* Address of President Alderman to the Graduating Classes. Finals of 1926, University of Virginia," *University of Virginia Alumni News*, 14, No. 10, (June–July, 1926): 250–251.

[4] "President Alderman's Farewell Message, 1920," *University of Virginia Alumni Bulletin*, 3d series, 13: 255.

1. The growth of the university and what it has meant.
2. The essentials of a university.
3. The conception of a president.
4. What Tulane will try to do.

Alderman usually, however, especially in his longer speeches, treated a number of points and often did not follow a very coherent order except within the main topics. In the commemorative addresses and in those before special gatherings he made much use of the expository method. This was predominantly the method of the eulogy of Wilson, in which he presented the facts of Wilson's life. He was mainly expository also in his speech before the Virginia Bankers' Association,[1] wherein his purpose was "to discuss what research and scientific ways of thinking might do for this great profession." Again in a commencement address at the Medical College of Virginia[2] he took as his theme: "What is a trained medical man in this year of our Lord, 1929, and in what direction lie his chiefest opportunities for public service?" He then explained in detail the advances made in medicine and the changes needed in the preparation of a medical man.

As the concluding example of this expository method, which is at the same time a typical representation of Alderman's speech structure, nothing will serve better than his address "The Growing South." He said in beginning the body of the speech: "My particular theme is the building spirit now at work in the States of the South."[3] To understand the present South, he continued, it is necessary to have for background five other Souths:

1. The nationalistic and imperial South, to 1830.
2. The self-centered and defensive South, 1830–1860.
3. The militant South, 1861–1865.
4. The submerged South, 1865–1880.
5. The emergent and growing South, 1880–.

Under the latter head the speaker told at length of the great advances the South had made in education, in the solution of the race problem, and in the development of character. It was a speech entirely given to facts; but implicit in the facts was a plea for an understanding of the South and its problems.

In beginning his speeches, Alderman's favorite method was to refer to the occasion and his pleasure at being present. Often he brought the greetings of Virginia or the University of Virginia and stressed the bonds

[1] "Science and Research in the Service of Business," June, 1929, *University of Virginia Extension Series*, 14, No. 6 (December, 1929): 5.

[2] May 28, 1929, MS, p. 2.

[3] *Op. cit.*, p. 4.

of sympathy between them and the section or university where he happened to be speaking. Sometimes he began with a general statement and applied it to his immediate theme. Whatever the method of introduction, he usually brought into it a clear statement of his particular purpose. Since there is space here for only one example, possibly the best one is the introduction to the address on Woodrow Wilson.

In his oration in memory of the first Athenians who fell in the Peloponnesian War, Pericles commended the fitness of the Athenian public funeral, but doubted the wisdom of any speech, declaring that where men's deeds have been great they should be honored in deed only, and that the reputation of many should never depend upon the judgment or want of it of one, and their virtue exalted or not, as he spoke, well or ill. I can, in some faint measure, comprehend what was passing in the mind of the great Athenian as I stand here today, in the Chamber which has often resounded with his own lucid eloquence, to seek to make clear in brief speech the character and achievement of Woodrow Wilson, the twenty-eighth President of the United States.[1]

Persuasive Materials

While most of Alderman's speeches were of the occasional type, he did at times, as in his campaign in North Carolina for better public support of schools and in one or two speeches before his state assembly setting forth the needs of his university, work for a delayed or immediate response. *World's Work*, commenting editorially on one of his speeches before the legislature, said: "When last winter he made a statement of the needs of the university and of the public school system to the Virginia Legislature, he produced an impression which caused men to recall the great oratorical feats in Virginia history. . . . The state increased its education appropriations beyond all precedent."[2]

In all his speaking, however, Alderman by various means gained the good will of his hearers and rendered them better disposed to accept his message. Perhaps his chief persuasive power lay in his graceful and charming manner of speaking, of which more will be said later. One gathers from the testimony about this that he said things in such a way that they seemed more important at the moment of hearing than the mere words indicated. Then, too, he always had a word of appreciation for the immediate section or audience. In his own state he frequently praised Virginia or the South. When speaking outside the state he often repeated the method that he used in a speech in California.[3] There he spent some time in alluding to

---

[1] *Op. cit.*, p. 1.
[2] 12 (July, 1906): 7728.
[3] "The Spirit of the South," delivered at the University of California in 1906.

what the West had accomplished in the nation and to the spirit of the West. The speeches were few in which there was not some tactful praise of the audience before him or of the state in which he was speaking.

Contemporary testimony indicates that in his informal speeches he accomplished much through his natural and spontaneous humor.[1] In these speeches there were many stories, mostly about Southern men or Negroes. One of his colleagues referred to his "keen sense of the ridiculous, . . . [with a] fund of apt illustrations and happy anecdotes."[2] In the more formal speeches, however, there were very few humorous stories, but sometimes a rather humorous reference to a serious subject.

But perhaps the greatest source of persuasion in Alderman's speaking was the man himself. His sincerity was attested by a number of contemporary testimonies; from a study of his speeches and of his career one gains the impression that Alderman believed intensely in the causes for which he spoke. No doubt his hearers also felt this. Many have spoken, too, of his likable personality—a charm of manner that naturally rendered his hearers well disposed toward him. As the *New York Times* said editorially: "It was the charm of his personality that won all hearts and was ble to persuade men almost out of their settled conviction."[3]

Style

In Alderman's spoken style there was great variation as to both quality and methods. The language of some of his speeches was merely commonplace prose. In the very early speeches the rhetoric was so high flown as to be turgid. But at its best, as it was in a few important addresses, the language was simple and incisive, often rising to rhythmic eloquence. Robert Underwood Johnson said of it: "The oratory of no American of our time has exceeded his exalted tone and the literary style of his high-minded utterances on public subjects."[4] The *New York Times*, speaking editorially of the oration on Wilson, mentioned its "high grace of literary form" and compared it in style to the Funeral Oration of Pericles.[5] That at times there were purple patches the reader of Alderman's speeches will discover as soon as he comes to the eulogy of Lee in the address "Virginia." But taken as a whole, the language was conversational; it flowed easily— a fact soon evident even to the reader of the speeches. Few of his words

[1] Editorial, *Nation*, 132 (May 31, 1931): 522.
[2] Professor Albert Lefevre, Tulane University, "Dr. Alderman as an Orator," *University of Virginia Alumni Bulletin*, October, 1904, pp. 240–241.
[3] May 1, 1931, p. 26.
[4] *The New York Times*, May 1, 1931, p. 27.
[5] Dec. 21, 1924, p. 4.

were other than simple and familiar ones; there was nothing that could not be instantly understood by those listening.

In his use of sentences Alderman managed a number of times to gain an effect of contrast and comparison or of contrast and antithesis. In his speech on "Sectionalism and Nationality," for example, he contrasted the men who came to New England with those who came to Virginia. In "Virginia" he said, "There was poverty in Virginia and throughout the South, but it begot strength: there was wounded pride, but it begot in big hearts, a noble humility: there was lack of energy in law and order in society, but it begot self-reliance and constructiveness: and somehow the love of millions, lightened the gloom of the war-smitten land."[1]

Balanced structure in sentences he used, too, but not often. The following will suffice as an example of these:

The Scotch-Irishman in Virginia and the Puritan in Massachusetts were blood kin in spirit and in their moral point of view. The character of each was formed by his religion. The theory of life of each demanded education. Each held to his form of truth and stood ready, and even counted it a glory, for an opportunity to fight for its prevalence, with a fierce intensity of conviction.[2]

In Alderman's speeches there were few figures of speech; it was only in his best known commemorative addresses that any distinctive imagery appeared. A passage from his eulogy of Woodrow Wilson is representative of this imagery at its best. Describing Wilson as he gave his War Address before Congress, Alderman said:

I saw President Wilson for the last time in the fullness of his strength on the evening of April 2, 1917. He was standing at this desk, speaking the momentous words which were to lead this democracy into war, and to teach to all free peoples, then bewildered and depressed, the meaning of the conflict, and to lift up their hearts. All mankind was his audience. The air of this hall was tense with emotion, and the dullest sensed the historic significance of the great scene. There were then etched into my mind, in lines never to be erased, the face and form and manner of Woodrow Wilson—the lithe figure, the bony structure of the forehead, the lean, long visage as a covenanter, somber with fixed purpose. The culture of generations was in his tones, the scholar's artistry in his words, the inheritance of a gentleman's breeding in his manner, and calm courage in his discerning eyes. I was somehow reminded of the unbending lineaments and figure of Andrew Jackson, whom Woodrow Wilson resembled physically; and, in the very soul of him, morally exhibiting the same grim resolution, as of a stranger to the fear that weaklings feel.[3]

[1] *Op. cit.*, p. 9.
[2] From "Sectionalism and Nationality," p. 7.
[3] *Op. cit.*, p. 9.

Edwin A. Alderman

His sentences in length and construction were varied sufficiently to avoid any impression of monotony. In some passages they were predominantly short, in others long, but usually were a combination of both short and long. They were rarely involved; the thought contained in them was always easy to comprehend, the movement of them often rhythmical. The following passage will illustrate this variety of length and structure:

The profession of medicine stands in a class all by itself among human callings. Its ancestry is as old as pain and body decay. Its slow and blundering but majestic progress through the ages, since the Greek intellect gave it scientific form, illustrates so impressively the triumphs of the human mind and the human spirit; its service to mortal man has been so immeasurable that merely to laud it is to touch it with the commonplace. Sir James Paget once declared with admirable insight and restraint, that in this calling were to be found the complete and constant union of the three qualities which have the greatest charm for pure and active minds—novelty, utility and charity. To him, therefore, whom the truth allures by ever new revelations, in some form of Medicine, here is the world of experiment, wonder and reward. To him whose instincts incline him to advance human progress—here is the most inspiring and tremendous arena. To him whose genius runs to patience and exercises of tender charity toward his fellow creatures—here is the field illimitable.[1]

Alderman used few allusions in his speeches and, on the whole, few illustrations. There were some flowery passages, as we have seen, but these were in the eulogies or memorial addresses. On the whole, however, the language was mainly that of direct, expository statement.

Preparation for Speaking

Alderman's future promise as an orator was evident in his student days, for there he seized every speaking opportunity that came his way. At the University of North Carolina he belonged to a debating society, the Dialectic. On April 27, 1881, he represented the Dialectic Society in the interliterary society contest with the oration "Ireland and Her Woes." This oration, which exists in Alderman's handwriting with corrections, was well written for an early composition, but the language was a bit stilted and high-flown, in keeping with the prevailing rhetorical style of the time. On April 2, 1882, he delivered the senior-class prophecy on the occasion of the senior-class tree planting. With an oration entitled "The Influence of Corporate Power" he won the W. P. Magnum Oratory Medal Contest at the University of North Carolina on May 2, 1882. The manuscripts of these last two speeches are also in the files at the library of the University

---

[1] From the commencement address at the Medical College of Virginia, May 28, 1929, MS, p. 2.

of Virginia. That he was a reader of oratorical literature is indicated by the fact that among his personal papers may be found a considerable number of speeches, notably memorial addresses, given by various well-known speakers. Writers on Alderman agree that he had as a background for his speaking a broad knowledge derived from a wide and varied reading. In the words of the editor of *World's Work*, he was "less a technical scholar (although he is an authority on educational history and methods) than a man of a general culture of the modern kind."[1]

In the preparation of each of his speeches he was said to have used infinite care.[2] That he wrote them out in full is shown by the fact that in the Alderman file at the University of Virginia are typed or printed copies of most of them. With a number of the speeches there exists also a second copy typed on small sheets that Alderman evidently held in his hand or placed before him while he was speaking. In a few cases he even made a third copy, as, for example, he did in preparing a speech to be given on April 17, 1929, before the New York alumni of the University of Virginia. Among his papers was found a copy of this speech in his own handwriting on 5- by 8-inch sheets, a typed copy on regular 8- by 11-inch paper, and another typed copy on about 6- by 7-inch sheets to be used during the delivery of the speech. Infrequently, however, only a part of the speech was written out in full, the remainder of the manuscript containing catchwords or phrases. The existing notes, for example, of an address before the Richmond University of Virginia alumni[3] are contained on six and one-half typewritten pages. The beginning is indicated as follows: "No set speech. 'Branch.'" The latter word probably refers to a story about "branching out," which he sometimes told. The substance of the entire speech is included on these sheets, but in phrases and short sentences, something like a paragraph outline.

Delivery

In the preparation of this study the writer talked with a number of men who had heard Alderman speak, some of them former students at the University of Virginia. Unanimously they spoke of his smooth and easy delivery, his excellent speaking voice—and remembered little of what he had said. Of the excellence of his voice there are also some written testimonies. "The wealth, the beauty, the depth of Dr. Alderman's modulation cannot be described, they must be felt" were the words of the Tulane

---

[1] *World's Work*, 12 (July, 1906): 7728.

[2] Dumas Malone, *Edwin A. Alderman* (New York: Doubleday, Doran & Company, Inc., 1940), p. 341. This point was also mentioned in an article on Alderman by John Finley in *The American Scholar*, 1 (January, 1932): 107–110.

[3] Jan. 24, 1929.

University *Olive and Blue*[1] in reporting one of his speeches. And John Finley on the same point said: "I am sure Pericles would not have spoken with a more melodious voice. It was that of a well loved viol."[2] There is little doubt, therefore, that Alderman's pleasing voice, his charm of manner, and his ease and dignity of bearing on the platform accounted in no inconsiderable degree for his popularity and influence as an orator.

Alderman's speech has been described as belonging to the type of vivid conversation,[3] even though he made a practice of writing his speeches and seldom spoke extemporaneously. Contemporary testimony agrees that he usually spoke with manuscript or notes before him but never allowed them to interfere with the naturalness of his conversational style. It is pertinent in this connection to quote what the *New York Times* had to say about the eulogy of Wilson before Congress: "Dr. Alderman read his address from manuscript, but seemingly knew his lines so well that he gave the appearance of speaking without notes. His voice was low and clear. He spoke without any effort at oratorical display. It was obvious as he proceeded, however, that the eloquence of his diction made a profound impression on that silent gathering. . . . "[4]

Contemporary Judgment

It cannot be denied that Alderman occupied a high place in the judgment of his contemporaries, particularly in the South. The immediate effect of his speeches on his hearers is one of those imponderables about which it is vain to generalize. That his listeners liked his speaking we know. They liked the delivery, the flow of the language, the dignified utterances, and the charm of the man's personality. At times he stirred their emotions. He aroused their pride in their state and in their own South. He caused them to feel the enjoyment of oratory as art. But whether his hearers were moved beyond mere enjoyment or a fuller appreciation of the man's topic is as hard to judge as is the immediate effect of any academic orator speaking to an audience of students or educators.

The esteem in which he was held, both as a man and as an orator, may be judged to some extent from a reading of the tributes written at his death and before. The *Nation* said editorially: "Here was a man with extraordinary oratorical gifts who refused to exploit them for private profit or

---

[1] Nov. 17, 1903.

[2] Address, "Edwin Anderson Alderman," *Publications of the American Academy of Arts and Letters*, No. 77 (1932): 61–69.

[3] C. Alphonse Smith, "Edwin A. Alderman," *American Education*, July, 1909. Also Malone, *op. cit.*, p. 368.

[4] *The New York Times*, Dec. 16, 1924, p. 8.

personal political advancement."[1] *World's Work* called him "one of the most accomplished public speakers in the United States."[2] In the opinion of George Gordon Battle, "He was an orator of extraordinary force and charm."[3] The *New York Times*, in an editorial, seemed to sum up the country's judgment in the following words: "His grace of manner, his felicity and pungency of speech, his ready and almost instinctive adaptability to every variety of audience that he was called upon to address, have often been recorded."[4]

It is vain to look into the future and predict Edwin A. Alderman's place in American oratory. He cannot be remembered for his influence upon the history of the nation or upon the promulgation of a great cause, as many orators will be, except as he made the South more conscious of the value of education; too much of what he said pertained only to the moment. Some of his speeches may stand as models of style, but on the whole they were too uneven in language to cause him to be considered a great stylist. The thoughts he uttered were not profound; too many of them were commonplaces. Although he often repeated his ideas, the wonder is that speaking so much he did not do it more frequently; in only three of his speeches were there found passages using identical words and phrases. But he will stand out in the judgment of posterity for his high sincerity, for his ideals, for his complete absorption in the cause of education for the South, and for his faith in his own people. He will be remembered as meeting, in as great a degree as any other man, Cato's definition of an orator, quoted by Quintilian, as that of "a good man skilled in speaking."

SELECTED BIBLIOGRAPHY

Biography

Malone, Dumas: *Edwin A. Alderman: A Biography*, New York, Doubleday, Doran & Company, Inc., 1940.

Articles

Alderman, Edwin A.: "The Functions and Needs of Schools of Education in Universities and Colleges," *Publications of the General Education Board, Occasional papers*, No. 4, 1917.
———: "Obligations and Opportunities of Scholarship," *Proceedings of the National Education Association*, 1900.
———: "The University of Today: Its Work and Needs," *North Carolina University Magazine*, June, 1900.
———: "The Nation's Supreme Task," *World's Work*, 41: 129.
Dabney, R. H.: "Edwin Anderson Alderman," *Outlook*, 77 (Aug. 6, 1904): 806–807.
Finley, John: "Edwin Anderson Alderman," *The American Scholar*, 1 (1932): 107–110.

[1] 132 (May 31, 1931): 522.
[2] 12 (July, 1906): 7728.
[3] *The New York Times*, May 1, 1931, p. 27.
[4] May 1, 1931, p. 26.

———: "Edwin Anderson Alderman," address, printed in *Publications of the American, Academy of Arts and Letters*, No. 77 (1932): 61–69.

Lefevre, Albert: "Dr. Alderman as an Orator," *University of Virginia Alumni Bulletin* October, 1904.

Smith, C. Alphonso: "Edwin A. Alderman," *American Education*, July, 1909.

Trent, William P.: "President Alderman and the University of Virginia," *American Review of Reviews*, 31: 449.

Nation, 132 (May 31, 1931): 522, editorial.

The New York Times, Dec. 21, 1924; May 1, 1931; July 6, 1931; Apr. 30, 1931; Dec. 16 1931, editorials.

Outlook, 106 (Apr. 18, 1914): 828, editorial.

Review of Reviews, 83 (June, 1931): 39–40, editorial.

Richmond News Leader, June 11, 1921, editorial.

World's Work, 12 (July, 1906): 7728, editorial.

Speeches

Listed below are the most important of Alderman's speeches. Except where the source is indicated they exist mainly in manuscript form.

"The Achievement of a Generation," address delivered at the Conference for Education in the South, Lexington, Ky., May 4, 1906.

Address at Founders' Day Exercises, University of Virginia, Apr. 13, 1931.

Address to the graduating class, University of Virginia, June, 1920.

Address at the Guilford battleground on the occasion of the dedication of the monument to the Maryland soldiers, Oct. 15, 1892.

Address at the induction of Harry A. Garfield as president of Williams College, Oct. 7, 1908.

Address at the installation of Nicholas Murray Butler as president of Columbia University, June, 1902, *Columbia University Quarterly*, 1902, pp. 89–92.

Address at the installation of Edward K. Graham as president of the University of North Carolina, Apr. 21, 1915.

Address at the installation of Thomas E. Hodges as president of the University of West Virginia, Nov. 3, 1911.

"Address on the Life of William Hooper," delivered at the Guilford battleground, July 4, 1894, Chapel Hill, University of North Carolina Press, 1894.

Address before the Presbyterian General Assembly, Charlottesville, Va., May 26, 1930.

Address before the University of Virginia Alumni Association at Richmond, Va., Jan. 24, 1929.

Address at the University of Virginia finals, June, 1928.

Address at the Virginia Polytechnic Institute Semi-centennial, May 29, 1922.

"Can Democracy Be Organized?" delivered before the Literary and Historical Association of North Carolina at Raleigh, Nov. 9, 1915, reprinted from the *Proceedings of the Association.*

Commencement address at the Medical College of Virginia, May 28, 1929.

Commencement-day address at John's Hopkins University, Feb. 23, 1903.

"Edward M. Shepard," address delivered at the College of the City of New York, Oct. 29, 1911.

Farewell to the graduating class, University of Virginia, June, 1920.

"The Growing South," address delivered before the Civic Forum, New York City, Mar. 23, 1908, New York, The Civic Forum, 1908.

"The Growth of Public Education in America," delivered at the Jamestown Exposition, Oct. 12, 1906.

"Inaugural Address on Installation as President of Tulane University," Mar. 12, 1901, Boston, George H. Ellis Company, 1904.

Inaugural address as President of Tulane University, Mar. 12, 1901.

"J. L. M. Curry," a memorial address, delivered at Richmond, Va., Apr. 26, 1903, under the auspices of the Conference for Education in the South, Brooklyn, Eagle Press, 1903.

"James Monroe," address at the Monroe Doctrine Centenary, Richmond, Va., Dec. 3, 1923.

"The Making of a National Spirit," delivered at the banquet of the New York Chamber of Commerce, Nov. 21, 1905.

"The National Spirit," delivered at Morristown, N. J., Feb. 21, 1911, printed in the *Proceedings of the Washington Association of New Jersey*, 1911.

"Obligations and Opportunities of Scholarship," address before the N. E. A., in *Proceedings of the National Education Association*, 1900, pp. 266–276.

"Poe and the University," address at a reception given Apr. 29, 1911, by the Pewter Platter Club, of Norfolk, in honor of Governor Woodrow Wilson.

"The Race Problem," New York City," 1904.

"Science and Research in the Service of Business," delivered before the Virginia Bankers' Association, June, 1929, *University of Virginia Extension Series*, 14, No. 6 (December, 1929).

"Sectionalism and Nationality," delivered in New York City, Dec. 22, 1906.

"The Spirit of the South," Charter Day address at the University of North Carolina, Mar. 23, 1906.

"Thomas Jefferson," address at the unveiling of the bust of Jefferson at the Hall of Fame, New York University, May 13, 1924.

"The University in the Service of Democracy," commencement address at the University of North Carolina, June, 1912.

"The University and State in the South," before the National Education Association, 1890.

"The University of Virginia in the Life of the Nation," inaugural address as president of the University of Virginia, Apr. 13, 1905.

"The Value of Southern Idealism," address of welcome to the American Historical Association and the American Economic Association, New Orleans, La., Dec. 29, 1903.

"Virginia," address delivered at Petersburg, Va., May 19, 1909.

"Woodrow Wilson," memorial address delivered before a joint session of both houses of Congress, Dec. 15, 1924, Washington, D. C., Government Printing Office, 1924.

20

Samuel Gompers

by WALTER B. EMERY

Samuel Gompers was born in London, January 27, 1850; came with his parents to New York in 1863, where he became a cigar maker by trade and later a trade-unionist leader. His first public speech for labor was made in 1874, and by 1886 his ability as a spokesman for labor was widely recognized. In the latter year he led in the organization of the American Federation of Labor and was elected as its first president. Excepting for one year, he held that position until his death, December 13, 1924. During these 38 years he spoke not only to labor but in behalf of labor to business, political, and educational groups in both America and Europe.

I. *The Labor Background*

The march of events during the 20 years following the Civil War was not favorable to labor. Capitalists, chiefly concerned with maintaining stable and profitable business, gave little thought to the needs of workers. Excessive hours of labor, continued wage reductions, unhealthful working conditions, and exploitation of women and children engendered a spirit of revolt.[1]

Various organizations had been set up to alleviate these conditions, but all had failed. The National Labor Union had succumbed to politics and workshop nostrums.[2] The Knights of Labor, the largest labor organization of the day, had become enmeshed in radical political enterprises and had provoked widespread criticism.[3] The Federation of Organized Trades and Labor Unions, created in 1881, functioned largely as an agency for legislative reform and benefited organized labor very little.[4]

In the year 1886, with increasing unrest among the wage earners and public indignation over the activities of revolutionaries,[5] the time was

[1] *Report of Industrial Commission* (Washington, D.C., 1901), XIV, 578 and XIX 1902, 789. See also John R. Commons, *et al., History of Labour in United States* (New York, 1918), I, 89–107, and Ida M. Van Etten, *The Conditions of Women Workers*, published by American Federation of Labor, 1891.

[2] Mary Beard, *Short History of the Labor Movement* (New York, 1920), pp. 78–79.

[3] *The New York Times*, Dec. 26, 1886, p. 3; *The New York Sun*, Dec. 16, 1886, p. 2; Henry Clews, "The Labor Crisis," *North American Review*, June, 1886, pp. 598–599.

[4] Samuel Gompers, *Seventy Years of Life and Labor* (New York, 1925), I, 225.

[5] *Ibid.*, II, 177.

ripe for a new type of labor leadership—one that could build and direct an organization consistent with the real psychology of the workingmen and the great middle class of America. This new leadership would have to profit from the mistakes of earlier leaders, most of whom thought in terms of foreign conditions and ideologies and failed to adapt themselves to the true American scene.[1]

The man to seize this opportunity was a Dutch-Jewish immigrant, Samuel Gompers. At the annual meeting of the Federation of Organized Trades and Labor Unions on December 7, 1886, he clearly showed that he understood the psychology of the time. In his speech to the convention he reviewed the work of trade-unionists and pointed out that "they tended to the enlightenment of all, and were conservators of the public peace." He declared they were "against riot, tumult, and anarchy, and society in all its bearings is safe with trade Unions"[2] and urged the delegates to create a closer and stronger federation of unions.

His speech evoked a favorable response. The American Federation of Labor was established at the meeting, and Gompers was elected president. Ten days later the *New York Times*, referring to the new organization, said:

> Already it has assumed formidable proportions, having attained a membership not far from 370,000. At the head of this great democratic—not politically—association is one who said last night that he would not exchange his position with any man in the land. . . . He has an abiding faith in the principles of the association, and believes them to be the only ones by which the great army of skilled labor can remain steadfast.[3]

Thus Gompers emerged as foremost spokesman for American labor. Until his death in 1924, he maintained his position of leadership in the Federation and vigorously defended the cause of "pure and simple" trade-unionism.

II. *The Speaker*

1. *His Training.* By experience and training he was well prepared for his task. Born in 1850 in the London ghetto, he started life in a community inhabited by poor wage earners. The father was a cigar maker by trade. Unable to provide adequately for his wife and five boys, he took Samuel out of public school and put him to work making cigars in the home. The boy found some opportunities for the development of aesthetic tastes.

---

[1] Selig Perlman, *A Theory of the Labor Movement* (New York, 1928). Much of the book supports this thesis.

[2] *The New York Sun*, Dec. 8, 1886, p. 1.

[3] *The New York Times*, Dec. 19, 1886, p. 7.

He attended concerts when the meager family income would allow and occasionally went to the opera. He seemed to have a natural love for dramatic art and as he watched the actors "lived with them the scenes of the play."[1]

Many scenes and experiences of his early life in London impressed him with the insecurity of the working classes. In 1861 there were more than 200,000 men out of work in the manufacturing districts of London.[2] "One of my most vivid early recollections," he wrote in his later years, "is the great trouble that came to the silk weavers when machinery was invented to replace their skill and take their jobs. . . . The narrow street echoed with the tramp of men walking the streets in groups with no work to do. Burned into my mind, was the indescribable effect of the cry of these men, 'God, I've no work to do. Lord strike me dead—my wife, my kids want bread and I've no work to do.'"[3] Through these early experiences he developed a strong sympathy with the wage earners, a feeling that later became the guiding impulse in his life.

Finding it increasingly hard to make a living in London, the Gompers family came to America in the summer of 1863 and settled in the immigrant section on the East Side of New York. Samuel soon secured a job as a cigar maker and joined the Cigar Makers' Local Union 16. Much of his knowledge of labor problems came as a result of his union activities. He attended meetings and observed the union regulations. As he grew older he became more active, and by 1875 he had become a recognized labor leader in New York and had been elected president of a new and stronger Cigar Makers' Local Union, which he had helped establish.

There were many obstacles to overcome in building this new organization. There were financial difficulties, frequent violation of rules, intimidations and bribes by employers, and interference from officers of the law. The economic depression of the seventies brought added difficulties. But in spite of disturbing events, Gompers worked on, preaching the gospel of trade-unionism. "We held mass meetings regularly and kept up educational work by means of talks and circulars. . . . The slogans we raised for the guidance of all were: 'Unions for all working people.' 'Reduce the hours of work.' 'Bring worst paid workers to the level of the highest.'"[4]

Through these experiences in the Cigar Makers' Local Union he acquired a general understanding of labor problems, particularly those of trade-unionism. In 1886 his knowledge and ability were being recognized. Following his election to the presidency of the A.F. of L., the *New York Times*

---

[1] Gompers, *op. cit.*, pp. 1–10.
[2] *London Times*, Feb. 11, 1862, p. 8.
[3] Gompers, *op. cit.*, p. 5.
[4] *Ibid.*, pp. 136–37.

commented that he was considered one of the cleverest leaders in the trade unions of the country.[1]

The dusty workshop became a university for Gompers. Working side by side with such men as Ferdinand Laurrell and Andrew Strasser, labor intellectuals of New York, he acquired knowledge of conflicting social and economic theories. "Every turn and twist of Labor's struggle was followed by the men at the benches. . . . Socialism, anarchism, communism, greenbackism, and cooperation, all passed in review."[2]

His association with Ferdinand Laurrell had a powerful influence on his life. Laurrell, an intelligent, well-read Swede, at one time was a revolutionary but had learned through bitter experience to distrust radical methods. He became a firm believer in a trade-unionism that would conform to the basic pattern of American life. His stimulating talks at the workbench had much to do with shaping Gompers's philosophy and making him ready for his role of national leader.[3]

The man to lead the trade-union movement in 1886 needed not only an understanding of labor problems but ability to articulate his ideas effectively through speech. Since the officers of the A.F. of L. were given no power to issue commands to the unions, they would have to rely upon persuasion to win support for their program, both within and outside the organization.[4]

Gompers was prepared to meet the test. For many years he had trained to develop his speaking ability. As a young man he was known to stammer at times.[5] As late as 1877 he addressed a labor group in New York City, and a reporter wrote that "the last speaker was Mr. Gompers of the Cigarmakers' Union, who made a miserable fist at it."[6] But Gompers wanted to be an effective speaker and worked hard to improve his skill.

He received comparatively little formal instruction. The record shows that he did enroll in a night class in "elocution" at Cooper Union Institute, in New York, but does not tell what success he had with it. Most of his training was received outside the classroom. At the age of fourteen he joined with some of the boys in the neighborhood and organized a club for the study of debate and parliamentary practice.[7]

The free-for-all debates at the workbench gave him opportunity to develop his argumentative ability and was an important part of his training

[1] *The New York Times*, Dec. 12, 1886, p. 1.

[2] Rowland Hill Harvey, *Samuel Gompers* (Stanford University, Calif., Stanford University Press, 1935), pp. 15–16.

[3] Gompers, *op. cit.*, pp. 10–75.

[4] Selig Perlman and Philip Taft, *History of Labor in the United States*, 1896–1932 (New York, 1935), p. 353.

[5] Gompers, *op. cit.*, pp. 112–113.

[6] *The New York Times*, July 27, 1877, p. 8.

[7] Gompers, *op. cit.*, p. 28.

for the extemporaneous speaking he later did as president of the A.F. of L. "In fact, these discussions in the shops," wrote Gompers, "were more like public debating societies or what we call these days 'labor forums.'"

Later he was taking part in the discussions of Die Zehn Philosophen, an organization made up of a small group of wage earners devoted to the principles of trade-unionism.[1]

As he became involved in the work of labor organization in New York, he had increasing opportunities for public speaking. In his campaigns to build up the Cigarmakers' Local Union, he spoke frequently to mass meetings of workers. In the strike of this union against the tenement-house system in 1877, Gompers served as one of the leading spokesman for the strikers, attending many conferences and addressing mass meetings in different parts of the city.

In the famous New York mayoralty campaign of 1886 he was appointed director of the speakers' bureau for Henry George, the labor candidate.[2] By the end of the campaign Gompers's ability as a speaker was being widely recognized, and the same year he was chosen as the leading emissary to agitate for the new federation of trade-unions. His speeches were effective in arousing sentiment for the new national organization, and with the launching of the Federation he was the logical choice for president.

2. *His Appearance.* Gompers had a striking appearance. Though short in stature, about 5 feet 3 inches, he had broad, powerful shoulders and a heavy chest.[3] He had an amazingly large head, supported by a massive neck, and a long-armed torso and heavy abdomen, on short, stubby legs.[4]

His face was expressive and was an effective agent for getting and holding attention. William Allen White, giving his impressions of Gompers in action at the Industrial Conference in 1919, wrote: "His face is mobile. His mouth is large and strong. His jaw is rather brutal and indomitable. He has the big nose of the ruler, but his eyes—there is the mystery—they are sheathed with thin saturnine lids, and when he opens them wide he gives a flaming effect to his face."[5] These impressions have been confirmed by Benjamin Stolberg, who wrote that Gompers had a "congenitally histrionic face"[6] capable of expressing varied moods and emotions.

Reports of observers clearly indicate that he did not move very much while speaking. His body, however, was alive and responsive, and he never

[1] *Ibid.*, pp. 81–88.
[2] *Ibid.*, p. 317.
[3] *New York Evening Sun*, Aug. 30, 1919.
[4] These descriptions are based upon a study of photographs of Samuel Gompers in the economics department of the New York Public Library. The photographs are found in the Samuel Gompers collection of scrap books.
[5] William Allen White, *Washington Herald*, Oct. 20, 1919.
[6] Benjamin Stolberg, "What Manner of Man Was Gompers?" *Atlantic Monthly* (March, 1925), pp. 404–412.

gave the impression of being imbedded in the floor. As to the exact amount of gesticulation he used, the testimony is conflicting, but it is clear that he used some. His gestures were not the fidgety type[1] but were strong and well executed. The extended arm with the pointed finger, the occasional striking with the closed fist the palm of the other hand for emphasis, suggestive gestures with the hands and arms constituted, for the most part, the visible action in his address.[2]

3. *His Voice.* All the evidence shows that he had an unusually good voice. It was powerful, rich in quality, well modulated, and very flexible.[3] Miss Florence Thorne, his research secretary for many years, has said that there was a suggestion of intense earnestness in his speech, which was captivating.[4] His articulation was good; one observer commented that he "spoke with a jerky and precise snap of his massive jaws."[5] Another criticized it for being too precise and noted that "a touch of the British creeps into his pronunciation."[6] Most of his speeches began slowly. As he worked toward the climax, his rate of utterance increased but never became rapid.[7]

4. *His Mentality.* By his own admission Gompers was not a scholar. He did not have the type of mind to do precise, objective thinking. "I worked intuitively," he wrote. "Some of my closest friends have frequently complained because it was not my custom to talk over and argue upon plans for action in advance. But that is something inherently impossible for me to do. My suggestions always grow out of situations."[8] Miss Thorne has said that his usual basis for decision, consciously or otherwise, was emotional.[9]

His reading was largely limited to newspapers, labor journals, and the like, publications from which he could get information and editorial comments about the immediate problems of labor. John R. Commons made the

---

[1] White, *op. cit.*

[2] These descriptions of his bodily action are based on answers to a questionnaire sent by the writer to John R. Commons, labor historian, University of Wisconsin; John P. Frey, president, Metal Trades Department, American Federation of Labor, and William Green, president of the Federation. All these men were closely associated with Gompers and heard him speak many times. There was a striking concord of opinion in their reports.

[3] Based on answers to a questionnaire sent to John R. Commons, John P. Frey, and William Green.

[4] Based on an interview with Miss Thorne.

[5] *New York Evening Sun*, Aug. 30, 1919.

[6] *Labor Advocate*, Nashville, Tenn., Dec. 22, 1905. A reprint of this statement appears in the Samuel Gompers scrap books, New York Public Library.

[7] Based on answers to a questionnaire sent to John R. Commons, John P. Frey, and William Green.

[8] Gompers, *op. cit.*, II, 1–7.

[9] Interview with Miss Thorne.

statement that he had not known any person more thoroughly grounded in the theories of Marx than Samuel Gompers.[1] It is likely, however, that his acquaintance with these theories came more from discussion with scholars than from reading. Benjamin Stolberg has written that Gompers admitted to him that he had never studied Marx or Kautsky or Lenin, "let alone the historical or theoretical implications of their thought."[2]

This quality of mind definitely affected his speaking. There are comparatively few references to literary or scholarly writing in his speeches. For materials of proof he relied mainly upon knowledge acquired from personal experience and observation.

In reading his speeches, one is impressed with the frequent use of the pronoun *I*, his many references to personal experiences, and superabundance of subjective expression as opposed to objective analysis and statement.[3] To work with self-abnegation was difficult for Gompers. He was almost constantly linking up issues and movements with himself, and it was only when the swirl of labor activities centered around him that his ego was satisfied.

With all his lack of scholarship there was a shrewdness about the man that should not be overlooked. He outwitted his opponents time and again in public discussion and debate. The Socialists in the A.F. of L. tried to upset his leadership but made little headway. They might present more complete philosophies of labor and politics, but they could not match his persuasive skill. While he might not fully understand their objectives, he knew their methods and could easily frustrate them. "For the Socialists alone he had no word of conciliation. . . . His method was always the same. He never began the attack. He waited patiently until every battery of the enemy had been unmasked. Then at the most effective moment he seized upon one point in his opponents' argument, and with remarkable adroitness turned, or seemed to turn, it against him. . . . "[4]

At the convention of the A.F. of L. in 1903, the radicals staged one of their grand offensives in an effort to capture control of the organization. Gompers waited until they had made their full charge, and then he counterattacked, using invective in a speech that has become famous in labor history and closing with a peroration that electrified his proletarian followers:

---

[1] John R. Commons, "The Passing of Samuel Gompers," *Current History* 21 (February, 1925): 670–676.

[2] Stolberg, *op. cit.*, p. 408.

[3] Gompers, *American Labor and the War* (New York, 1919). See also Samuel Gompers, Paul U. Kellogg, and William English Walling, *Addresses* delivered at the National Civic Federation (New York, 1918).

[4] *Outlook*, December, 1908, p. 755.

I want to tell you Socialists . . . I have heard your orators and watched the work of your movement the world over. I have kept close watch upon your doctrines for thirty years; have been closely associated with many of you and know how you think and what you propose. I know, too, what you have up your sleeve. And I want to say that I am entirely at variance with your philosophy. I declare it to you, I am not only at variance with your doctrines, but with your philosophy. Economically, you are unsound; socially, you are wrong; industrially, you are an impossibility.[1]

In this speech he made no attempt to analyze the doctrines of socialism, but the astute timing and the effective utterance of the invective achieved the desired results. Gompers sat down in the midst of prolonged applause, and the Socialists were defeated in the convention.

5. *His Style.* In the early years while he was struggling to get a foothold in the labor world, the speech of Gompers appeared stilted,[2] but as he grew older it lost this pompous quality and became direct and communicative. He seldom wrote out his speeches or prepared written outlines.[3] He spoke extemporaneously, usually without notes. This gave freshness and spontaneity to his style,[4] but Miss Thorne has pointed out that this lack of preparation often caused him to make "blundering introductions" and talk at random without having a clearly defined purpose. A reading of his speeches confirms this fact. There were times when his words did not flow smoothly, when the sentence structure was involved and the language not clear.[5] If, however, he was dealing with thoroughly familiar subject matter, these faults were less obvious. The evidence indicates that some of his First World War speeches were truly eloquent. John P. Frey has written about a speech that Gompers made in the summer of 1918 in London:

I watched him carefully. He gave no sign of being under any special stress; began his speech as was his custom, speaking slowly and with deliberation. He then analyzed the issues involved in war, one by one briefly and most pointedly. He then presented his conclusions based on the analysis he had made, and wound up with an appeal for human liberty which was outstanding in its effectiveness.

Lloyd George, who had opened the speech making, closed by reminding them he was not surprised at the substance of Mr. Gompers's remarks, for he had known him many years. He had often said that Mr. Gompers was one of the greatest of

---

[1] *American Federation of Labor Proceedings*, 1903, p. 198.
[2] Interview with Miss Thorne.
[3] Gompers, *Seventy Years of Life and Labor*, II, 331.
[4] Gompers, *American Labor and the War*, pp. VI–VII.
[5] *Ibid.* See also his speeches in debates at conventions of the A.F. of L., *Proceedings*, 1886–1924.

living orators and had now delivered what he considered to be the outstanding address up to that time delivered in England during the war.[1]

III. *Methods of Persuasion*

1. *Audience Adaptation.* The speaker has the problem of adapting his ideas to the thought patterns of his listeners. If his proposals tend to upset the more or less ordered concepts of life held by his audience, resistance is likely to be encountered. It is like making "an attack upon the foundations of our universe and, where big things are at stake, we do not readily admit that there is a distinction between our universe and the universe."[2] Gompers recognized this and was particularly careful not to run counter to the well-established beliefs of the workers.

Mark Sullivan has described the prevailing mood in America during the years preceding the nineties as one of irritation. It was a period when the average laborer had the feeling that his freedom of action and the attainment of his desires were being frustrated by an unseen enemy, which he personified as Invisible Government, Wall Street, etc.[3]

Gompers was able to catch and express this prevailing spirit. He had been a lowly cigar maker for many years; he had witnessed the horrors of an era that allowed extreme exploitation of labor; he had felt the sting of these conditions, and he was keenly aware of the sufferings of his fellow workers. He therefore came early to the conclusion that the labor movement was a struggle against the employer class. In this thinking was rooted the idea that labor must eternally struggle against the employer and through the development of its economic power be in a position to demand more of the good things of life. This attitude he clearly expressed in a speech to the 1892 convention of the A.F. of L. Referring to the trade-unionists, he proclaimed that "they have not been routed, they have merely retreated, and await a better opportunity to obtain the improved conditions which for the time they are deprived of. . . . What the toilers need at this time is to answer the bitterness and vindictiveness of the oppressors with Organization."[4] Six years later, speaking to the same convention, he contended that the trade-union movement was the crystalized expression of the discontent of the workers.[5]

Moreover, he was keenly aware of the traditional conservative attitude of the average American citizen.[6] For years Americans had been building

[1] Personal letter.
[2] Walter Lippmann, *Public Opinion* (New York, 1922), pp. 95–96.
[3] Mark Sullivan, *Our Times* (New York, 1926), I, Chap. 2, pp. 31–46.
[4] *American Federation of Labor Proceedings*, 1892, p. 12.
[5] *Ibid.*, 1898, p. 121.
[6] Selig Perlman, *A Theory of the Labor Movement*, pp. 154–233.

the stereotypes of "rugged individualism," "private property," "free enterprise," and other concepts associated with democracy "in the raw." William H. Sylvis, in the National Labor Union, T. V. Powderly, in the Knights of Labor, and Eugene V. Debs, in the Socialist party, in one way or another sought to upset these stereotypes but had little success, and all were cast aside as public enemies. Gompers did not make this mistake. While he made attack after attack against the capitalist, he favored the retention of private enterprise as an institution of the social order. He strongly and bitterly opposed socialism and other radical theories of his time. He insisted that labor and capital should be free to organize and develop their economic power.[1]

He was careful in his speeches to make it clear that his proposals were "natural" and "orderly" and not designed to upset the existing social order. He affirmed that trade-unionism and its program were consistent with conservative ideology. In 1904 he declared to the Federation members: "Brothers, the labor movement stands for the very best of which we can conceive. There is no institution that is worth maintaining that we propose to tear down or destroy. The labor movement is constructive in character, not destructive."[2]

Many businessmen vigorously fought Gompers, but they were less bitter toward him than they were toward the radical labor leaders who advocated upsetting the existing order to attain their ends. When he addressed the leaders of industry he was careful not to clash with their conservatism. In 1918 he spoke to the National Civic Federation, an organization with a membership representing the business, educational, and labor worlds:

There are some people who cannot think that there is such a thing as a constructive movement for the betterment and the protection of the conditions and the rights of the great mass of people of our country, unless they think in terms of political party. And because the American Federation of Labor declines to yield the direction of its affairs into the hands of the so-called intellectuals outside of the labor movement, we have mortally offended them: (laughter and applause). Our officers in our trade unions, local, central, national, international or our Federations, are our own men and our own women. The editors on our newspapers, official magazines, are our own men and our own women, those who have graduated from the industrial school of hard knocks, and they may not write with the finish of the intellectual giant, but they talk and write with the directness that cannot be misunderstood. In this we are somewhat different from the labor movements of several

[1] Louis Reed, *Labor Philosophy of Samuel Gompers* (New York, Columbia University Press, 1930); *Studies in History, Economics and Public Law,* edited by the Faculty of Political Sciences of Columbia University, No. 327.

[2] *American Federation of Labor Proceedings,* 1904, p. 7.

other countries. To any man or woman who has intellectuality and who has sympathy for our cause, we say, "Come, give us all the support you can," but when this movement of labor is to function, it will function according to the best judgment and interests of the great masses of the workers (applause).

There is one thing upon which all may rest assured, that this labor movement of America is going to be an American labor movement (applause), and a movement founded upon the conditions and situations which we find and which obtain here—not elsewhere. . . . Democracy . . . consists in an attitude of mind and the actions which follow that mental attitude.[1]

A basic characteristic of the American community that earlier labor leaders failed to take into account was a lack of class consciousness on the part of wage earners in this country. As Perlman has written, no other labor movement has ever had to contend with the fragility so characteristic of American labor organizations. In the main, this fragility of the organizations has come from the lack of class cohesiveness in American labor.[2]

This inability of American labor to stick together on principles and methodology was a strong factor militating against steady, substantial organization in early times. Gompers astutely discerned that the only consciousness that labor possessed was a "job consciousness." Within an individual craft, where the member or worker looked upon the jobs in the craft as common property, there might be potent solidarity. The workers had a common interest in their jobs and were willing to stick together and even fight to protect these jobs. This was quite different from a cohesion of all labor groups, which has its roots in a psychology of class consciousness. Gompers, therefore, always advocated simple craft unionism and vigorously opposed the formation of a labor party. As Louis S. Reed has stated:

> Probably the most important reason for Gompers's opposition to a labor party was one that he never expressed in public, and that was that he discerned no dominating sentiment among the rank and file workers for such a party, and that the majority of the leaders of the various unions were against this step. . . .
>
> One of Gompers's passions was to keep the presidency of the Federation till he died. To do this he had to keep close ideologically to the masses. . . . To receive their support and votes Gompers had to share and advocate their views.[3]

It should be pointed out that there were times when he spoke out in defiance of concepts and beliefs held by immediate audiences, particularly those made up of businessmen. In 1913, Gompers appeared before the National Civic Federation and flung defiance at those in the organization

---

[1] Gompers, Kellogg, and Walling, *op. cit.*, pp. 18, 19.
[2] Perlman, *op. cit.*, p. 7.
[3] Reed, *op. cit.*, p. 111.

who favored compulsory arbitration of labor disputes. His remarks were definitely contrary to the trend of discussion in the meeting. Gompers vehemently paced the floor, shook his fists, and said:

> The working men and women of the United States will fight rather than accept compulsory arbitration of their labor difficulties as proposed in a measure now before the New York Legislature.
>
> I should like to know what you gentlemen have in mind by model mediation and arbitration laws that will limit the rights to which workmen are entitled by God, by nature, and by the laws of the country. I agree with the National Civic Federation's worthy desire to avoid strikes, but do you gentlemen imagine that you can escape responsibility by making natural activities unlawful? You may compress steam, but as sure as nature's law, you will ultimately have an explosion.[1]

Other instances could be cited to show that Gompers did not always adapt his ideas to the mental pattern of the immediate audience. In all such cases, however, it is probable that he felt that such tactics, while they might not be popular with his listeners, would appeal to the larger audience upon which he mainly depended for support—that is, the rank and file of American labor.

The point that should be stressed is that Gompers tried to make himself a true spokesman of American labor, to make his utterances conform to the basic thoughts of the workers, and wherever he spoke to be careful that he did not do violence to their well-established beliefs.

2. *Use of Impelling Motives.* Modern rhetoricians are agreed that human desire is a basic factor in persuasion. Gompers fully recognized the importance of this principle and used it effectively in his speaking. Possessing no dictatorial powers in the Federation, he set about the task of developing a unified labor will through appeals to the impelling motives of the workers.

Soon after the creation of the Federation, Gompers made his first long trip into the Middle West, speaking in thirty-seven cities. In these speeches he assailed revolutionary labor organizations and argued for trade-unionism as the best means of satisfying the workers' wants.[2] A short time later he made his first speaking tour through New England. Again, in 1891 he made his first national tour, going as far west as San Francisco and Los Angeles and addressing labor groups in such cities as Rochester, Syracuse, Cleveland, Terre Haute, Kansas City, Denver, Salt Lake City, etc.[3]

---

[1] *The New York Times*, Jan. 30, 1913, p. 5.
[2] Gompers, *Seventy Years of Life and Labor*, I, 328, 336.
[3] *Ibid.*, p. 300.

He carried on these lecture tours from time to time for more than forty years. During the 4 months preceding his seventieth birthday, he traveled 15,000 miles and delivered 210 addresses.[1]

With the exception of one year, he spoke to each annual convention of the A.F. of L. In most of these speeches to the conventions and in those of his lecture tours he argued for trade-unionism on the grounds that it provided more of the "good things of life"—that is, more pay, shorter hours for labor, more leisure time, more healthful working conditions, etc., the basic wants of laborers everywhere. Radical social reformers might succeed for the moment in getting the attention of the rank and file of labor by talking of ultimate social ends and by arousing a "self-forgetful idealism" among laborers, but they could not compete for long with the astute Gompers, who talked of trade-unionism satisfying the basic wants of self-preservation, private gain, personal power, and pleasure.

At the convention of the A.F. of L. in 1904, some of the Socialist delegates proposed that the legislative committee of the Federation be abolished. Gompers pleaded for the retention of the committee on the grounds that it had brought real, tangible benefits to the workers, such as proper ventilation in mines, safety appliances in machine shops, and abolition of child labor in some states.[2] This appeal, needless to say, had more persuasive effect on the labor delegates than the argument of the Socialists that the Federation should devote its time and contribute its money to the "attainment of the cooperative commonwealth" so that proletarian rule ultimately would become absolute in American society.

Typical of his use of the impelling motives when speaking to laborers is the following excerpt from his annual speech to the 1910 convention of the Federation:

For what does organized labor contend if not to improve the standard of life, to uproot ignorance and foster education, to instill character and manhood and an independent spirit among our people, to bring about a recognition of the interdependence in modern life of man, and his fellowman? We aim to establish a normal workday, to take the children from the factory and the workshop and to give them the opportunity of the school, the home, and the playground. In a word, the unions of labor, recognizing the duty to toil, strive to educate their members, to make their homes and lives more cheerful in every way, to contribute an earnest effort toward making life the better worth living, to avail their members of their rights as citizens and to bear the duties and responsibilities and perform the obligations they owe to our country and to our fellow-men.[3]

[1] *The Washington Post*, Jan. 25, 1924.
[2] *American Federation of Labor Proceedings*, 1904, pp. 240–241.
[3] *American Federation of Labor Proceedings*, 1910, pp. 32–33.

For more than forty years Gompers defended the strike as one of labor's most effective weapons. During the famous Homestead steel strike of 1892, Gompers appeared in Homestead and made a speech to strengthen the morale of the strikers. He not only appealed to their pride but strongly suggested that their very lives and liberties depended upon their continued resistance to the alleged oppression of the Carnegie Steel Company.[1]

In his debate with Governor Allen, of Kansas, in 1920 he opposed compulsory arbitration on similar grounds:

It is unity which the workers must have and the freedom to exercise their normal activities so that the impress may be made upon the employer that their demands for a better life, their demands for a better return for the service they give to him and to society must be heard and heeded, that service which the workers give to society, without which progress would be meaningless and civilization a failure. . . .

That is the thing for which we are contending and will contend, no matter what may come. The men and the women of labor of America are sovereign citizens with all of you, and if it should come to pass that you can make labor compulsory for the working people, there is no reason why they should not turn upon all and say, "Well, if compulsory labor is right, then we shall be compelled to labor for society."[2]

In 1914 businessmen were urging the necessity of armament for the protection of American rights and interests, and the matter came up for serious discussion at a meeting of the National Civic Federation. Gompers agreed that America should arm to protect itself against "European Autocracy" and argued that if businessmen wanted good soldiers able to serve them efficiently and protect their interests, they should pay the laborers good wages:

All we ask is that you who are not workers realize that for war you need strong bodies and you can't get them if you give your workers starvation wages. That for war you need fever-resisting men, and that that kind of man doesn't come from the slums. The sledge-hammer will make such a man if he works with it, but only if the worker has ample food and clean surroundings. So more on your own account than on ours you have a reason to pay the American worker a liberal wage, give him reasonably short hours, and enable him to be an efficient human being.[3]

3. *Universality Argument.* As Hollingworth has pointed out, "the knowledge that the majority hold a given opinion inclines many individuals favorably toward the majority's decision."[4] Gompers recognized the potency

[1] *Pittsburgh Leader*, Aug. 14, 1892.

[2] Samuel Gompers and Henry J. Allen, *Gompers-Allen Debate*, May 28, 1920 (New York, 1920), p. 16.

[3] *The New York Times*, Dec. 6, 1914, Secs. 4 and 5, p. 4.

[4] H. L. Hollingworth, *The Psychology of the Audience* (New York, 1935), pp. 150–151.

of this type of suggestion and used it frequently in his speaking. In a speech at Salt Lake City on Aug. 22, 1911, he proudly referred to the growing interest of the public in the labor movement:

> The labor movement is growing in leaps and bounds. The newspapers are filled with it. No magazine is complete without a discussion of it. It has become a part of the curriculum of universities. The ministers are now giving their pulpits to a sympathetic discussion of the labor question, following the mandate of the carpenter of Nazareth. Which political party is there that dares leave its platform silent on the subject of labor?[1]

It is significant that Gompers took time in each one of his reports to the convention of the A.F. of L. to refer to the growth of trade-unionism. In his address to the convention of 1901 he pointed out the fact that the public was giving increasing support to labor, that the President of the United States had "set his seal of approval" upon organized labor.[2]

Here was the suggestion that the labor movement had arrived, was accepted and respected by the public at large. This use of "social suggestion," as James A. Winans has termed it, was one of Gompers's effective means of persuasion.

4. *Ethical Appeal.* As the A.F. of L. grew from year to year and Gompers was repeatedly re-elected president, his personal prestige progressively increased. In the National Civic Federation he was accorded hearings along with leading employers, educators, and other representatives of American life. The President of the United States sought his counsel and support. He traveled extensively over the country, making many contacts with important people both inside and outside labor circles.

This personal prestige in the latter part of his life added greatly to his persuasive power. Frank Tannenbaum, in his description of the last convention that Gompers attended, has suggested the hold that Gompers had come to have upon his followers. "It was interesting," wrote Mr. Tannenbaum, "to watch the absolute dominance that Mr. Gompers had, the absolute control of his followers, their complete surrender to his judgment and to his will."[3]

Gompers boasted of his unfailing devotion to labor, how he had refused bribes and intimidation by employers, and how he had refused large salaries offered him by business enterprises.[4] In a gesture of devotion to trade unionism he refused to wear a suit of clothes which had been made for him by a non-union tailor.[5] To avoid arousing suspicion among the

---

[1] *The Deseret Evening News* (Salt Lake City), Aug. 23, 1911, p. 5.
[2] *American Federation of Labor Proceedings*, 1901, p. 3.
[3] Frank Tannenbaum, "Samuel Gompers' Last Convention," *Survey*, 53 (Jan. 1, 1925) 393.
[4] Gompers, *Seventy Years of Life and Labor*, I, 34; I, 510–511.
[5] *The New York Daily Tribune*, Aug. 20, 1896, 1.

"rank and file" he refused to accept invitations at social functions without the assurance that other laboring men would be present.[1]

In the 1904 convention of the A.F. of L. he defended himself against the attacks of the Socialists, who charged that he was more interested in getting votes for re-election than in helping labor. This was striking at one of the pillars upon which his persuasive power rested. He was quick to reply:

> I know I need not expect any, but I ask for no quarter from you—and do not expect it from me; but I deny the right of any man . . . to insinuate . . . that if my election depended upon my changing my mind, I would change my mind. . . . I believe that there is no office, no position in the world more exalted or more honorable than the Presidency of the American Federation of Labor, but if the Convention shall now or at any time honor me with its confidence in any way, it must be because I have retained my self-respect, because I have not changed or played upon strings or thrown out a sheet anchor to catch every wind, so that votes might be cast for me.[2]

It is no overstatement to say that this quality of his character, which he freely advertised in his writing and speaking, gave him almost a necromantic influence over many labor audiences. Indicative of this power is the tribute paid him by one of his admirers at the last Federation convention Gompers attended:

> Two characteristics men admire, honesty and courage, and Sam has both of them. No one has ever been able truthfully to accuse him of having run under fire; no one can ever say that when he had been taken up by the spirit of evil onto the mountain top and shown all the kingdoms of the world and promised them if he would prove untrue to his trust, no one can ever say that he has not, in the language of the scriptures, said: "Get thee behind me, Satan." . . . Take him all in all, he was a man. We shall not look upon his like again.[3]

IV. *Special Rhetorical Devices*

As W. N. Brigance has said, style should be instantly intelligible to the hearer and requires more vividness in spoken language than in written.[4] It cannot be said that Gompers met this requirement as well as other American orators such as Wendell Phillips, Robert Ingersoll, or Henry W. Grady. He did possess some ability, however, to use speech detail, and at times his language was colorful and effective. There is noticeable improvement in his later speeches, especially those given during

---

[1] Gompers, *Seventy Years of Life and Labor*, II, 111.
[2] *American Federation of Labor Proceedings*, 1904, p. 201.
[3] *Ibid.*, 1924, p. 308.
[4] William Norwood Brigance, *Speech Composition* (New York, 1937), p. 200.

the First World War. The following excerpt, taken from one of these, seems to contain a degree of vividness not found in most of his earlier addresses:

Regardless of what may be the outcome of the war even the most inadequate attempt to picture conditions in those war-devastated countries causes one to grow sick at heart and mind. Suffering piled upon suffering; woe upon woe; horror upon horror. Picture if you can the Belgium over which armies have fought—Belgium that has been ravaged and burned and soaked in human blood. Picture a land with her industry and commerce destroyed and the flower of her young manhood slain in a needless and murderous war. Think of the starved minds and bodies of the women and children and old men—think of the natures warped and embittered by suffering and injustice. For decades and for decades the blight of this war will cast its shadow upon that land.

As for Germany, the devastating blight that followed in the trail of the Thirty Years' War will be but as the shadow in comparison with the terrible reality of the loss of her millions of young men in this carnage of unparalleled savagery. For the genius and power of trained minds have been prostituted to the service of war until now it is nothing but organized machine slaughter. Think of the artificial barbarous conditions existing under which men seriously assert that the holding of a particular geographic position by guns and armed forces is worth a million lives! Think of the power of a million minds. That the gaining of a single city is worth a million men is an assertion of strange values. What manner of civilization is this that assigns values with such barbarous disregard for human lives?

Whatever may be the outcome of the inevitable Waterloo that will close the conflict that is so incredibly brutal and stupid, may those who shall be charged with the responsibility of determining the terms of peace see the sorrowing faces and hear the lonely voices of the children and the helpless old, may they heed the lives of the young men wasted or sacrificed, may they have understanding hearts to learn the infinite wrongs of war.[1]

As a young man Gompers had trouble with composing his speeches. His sentences tended to be long and involved, and often he did not make his meaning clear.[2]

Later he became editor of the *American Federationist*, official publication of the A.F. of L., and his editorial writing for this journal during more than thirty years unquestionably improved both his written and spoken style. His sentences became shorter and his words more carefully chosen. Evidence of this is seen in his First World War addresses, to which reference has already been made.

An important technique in his persuasion was his use of "loaded words." In 1920 he wrote in the *American Federationist*:

[1] Gompers, *American Labor and the War*, pp. 27–29.
[2] Gompers, *Seventy Years of Life and Labor*, I, 250.

The labor movement of America does speak and it must be heard.
It speaks for progress.
It speaks for our established institutions.
It speaks for equality of opportunity.
It speaks for the rights of men and women and of children.
It speaks for the one thing that can save the world and bring solace to its weary spirit.
It speaks in measured denunciation of every vestige of autocracy.[1]

The words and phrases *progress, established institutions, equality of opportunity,* etc., are "yes-response" expressions used to unite the workers in support of organized labor. This multiplied repetition of short, positive statements, combined with a skilled use of "loaded words," was a factor in his persuasion.

He used this technique repeatedly in his speeches. In 1907 he declared to the annual convention of the A.F. of L.:

We meet on this historic ground representing the best general federated labor movement in the world, a movement founded upon the highest principles of justice, right and humanity; a movement which has for its mission not only the uplifting of the submerged, but the attainment of a higher and better life for all; a movement which aims to make the principles of the Golden Rule and of the Declaration of Independence the rule of conduct of our every-day lives.[2]

His use of these verbal sanctions was an effective means of getting favorable emotional response from many listeners. On the other hand, the scholar hearing or reading some of his speeches might justly criticize them on the grounds that they lacked substance and logical proof.

Gompers showed considerable skill in the use of the epigram. Some of his friends still quote verbatim some of his most striking utterances.[3] Typical of the terseness with which he could speak is the statement: "Some eat to work, some sleep to work, some dream to work, and it seems some are born only to work."[4]

Another example is this statement from a speech he made to a meeting of laborers in Salt Lake City in 1911.

There are national associations of manufacturers and anti-boycott organizations trying to crush labor. They've missed their chance. They can't do it. They missed their opportunity when they permitted the days of slavery and serfdom to end. The opportunity was lost when the men who labor began to learn the

---

[1] *American Federationist*, 27, No. 5 (May, 1920): 420–421.
[2] *American Federation of Labor Proceedings*, 1907, p. 17.
[3] Interview with John P. Frey.
[4] *Labor Advocate* (Nashville, Tenn.), Dec. 22, 1905, found in Gompers's scrap books, compiled by the A.F. of L., deposited in New York Public Library.

alphabet; when they learned that certain combinations of letters spelled man, woman, childhood, home, happiness, right, wrong, justice, freedom and humanity.[1]

In an address to a mass meeting in New York during the First World War, he proclaimed: "This was a war. Today, and since the entrance of the United States into this Titanic struggle, it is no longer a war—it is a crusade for freedom and justice!"[2]

Finally, Gompers's power to inveigh against his enemies was probably his most effective rhetorical weapon. When the enemy threatened to overpower him with argument, he often ignored the issue and relied on invective to win the battle. In his skirmishes with the Socialists, he used this technique many times. Daniel de Leon, a radical leader who sought to capture control of the Federation during the nineties, was one of the most vitriolic in his attacks against Gompers and the trade-unionists. Gompers, in his characteristic style, wrote of De Leon:

If Professor (?) De Leon, alias Loeb, leader of the Socialist Labor Party and editor of its official organ is not a paid agent of the mine operators and the money power generally he has certainly missed his calling. There is not an effort or a struggle made by the organized or unorganized workingmen of the country for some degree of justice which he not merely opposed but denounces in the most malignant and malicious manner; out-doing the most pronounced open enemies of the capitalist press which labor has. There is not a charge or insinuation which the skinflint employer, the corporation thug or apologist or villainous newspaper penny-a-liner has launched against labor organizations and their organizers which this *Agent Provocateur* has not rehashed, embellished and served up just at the time when it will serve the interests of the capitalist class best. The latest service which this creature, masquerading in the garb of a socialist, is rendering labor's enemy, is in the most virile abuse of the men placed in charge of conducting the desperate and heroic miner's struggle. No wonder the Professor (?) has not joined the New South African Colony of Hertzberg, Retzlaff and Co.; his pay must be larger and his game bigger; and then his style is not quite so vulgar as "stealing" the funds of a labor organization.[3]

Typical of his use of invective is the charge he made against William Randolph Hearst:

Did you ever know of a newspaper, or a chain of newspapers, owned by a multi-millionaire that devoted for more than four weeks, every day and twice a day, articles and editorials against a labor man? He has sent out his minions, his hirelings, to get in touch with some who might be gulled, bought, so that he might say something derogatory to my character.

[1] *The Deseret Evening News* (Salt Lake City), Aug. 23, 1911, p. 5.
[2] Gompers, *American Labor and the War*, p. 136.
[3] *American Federationist*, IV, No. 6 (August, 1897): 117.

And who did he get to say a word against me and my work and my character and my faithfulness? Who? A grafter of Boston, a shyster lawyer of Washington, one who was caught in the dragnet of the investigation by Congress of the National Association of Manufacturers, and whose chief operator was this man Mulhall; a lawyer, formerly a plate printer, repudiated and stigmatized by that magnificent organization as a man unworthy of belief or credit.

And who else? Some rag-tag, bob-tailed politician who was eating pap out of the millionaire bag of William Randolph Hearst. Where is there a recognized, respected trade unionist in America who has uttered anything of the character Hearst desired?[1]

Again, in 1910 he referred to Charles W. Eliot's book *The Future of Trades-unionism and Capitalism in Democracy* with these caustic words:

It reads, in fact, exceedingly like talk to the very young. It calls to mind the Sunday-school picture of a comfortable stall-fed old bossy cow, imparting her pious ruminations to a listening group of well-housed tender and meek-eyed veals. "Nothing serious is wrong in this world, children. Green pastures are within reach of all. So, be good. Don't horn one another. That's naughty. Take the feed your kind masters give you. Keep your hoofs clean. And, above all, never refer to the butcher. It's a very unpleasant subject, butchering. Forget it."[2]

V. *Conclusion*

While we cannot say with absolute accuracy how much influence Gompers wielded in the attainment of the ends that he set forth in 1886, it is safe to say that his influence was large, particularly if we bear in mind the fact that the sphere and impact of any individual human force is necessarily limited by external circumstances. Gompers started out with the simple premise that the main purpose of labor is to attain "more, more, here and now." When the curtains fell on his leadership in 1924, this objective, at least partially, had been attained. Labor conditions were much improved over what they were in the early days of labor organization. Membership in the A.F. of L. had risen from less than three hundred thousand in 1886 to more than three million in 1919. In 1865 the average working day was 11 hours, but by 1919 nearly 50 per cent of the wage earners of the country were working 8 hours or less.[3] In the eighties the exploitation of women and children in industry was widespread; by 1924 definite legislative attempts were being made to correct these conditions. Also by 1924 legislation for the restriction of immigration had been passed to aid domestic laborers, and by 1940 forty-two states had passed working-

[1] *American Federation of Labor Proceedings*, 1921, p. 401.
[2] *American Federationist*, 17, No. 11 (November, 1910): 961.
[3] Charles Ramsdell Lingley, *Since the Civil War* (New York, 1921), pp. 504–505.

men's compensation laws.[1] Finally, legislative enactment had brought about better working conditions, more sanitary and less hazardous.[2]

These improvements, for the most part, had come about during the leadership of Gompers. He by no means was responsible for all of them, but it is significant that he campaigned and agitated for all of them over a long period of time. One need only read his annual speeches to the Federation to be impressed with his enduring zeal for the attainment of these ends. He kept them before the public almost constantly for 40 years.

Miss Florence Calvert Thorne, his research secretary for many years, was at his bedside when he died. A few hours before his death she asked the nurse if he was sleeping. The nurse replied, "No, he keeps making speeches."[3] It was a fitting conclusion, a symbol of the important part that speaking had played in his life.

SELECTIVE BIBLIOGRAPHY

Biographies

Beard, Annie E. S.: "The Labor Statesman of the World," *Our Foreign-born Citizens*, New York, The Thomas Y. Crowell Company, 1922, pp. 109–117.

Cottler, Joseph: "The Grand Old Man of Labor," *Champions of Democracy*, Boston, Little, Brown, & Company, 1936, pp. 207–231.

Gompers, Samuel: *Seventy Years of Life and Labor*, 2 vols., New York, E. P. Dutton & Company, Inc., 1925. These two volumes, numbering more than a thousand pages, contain much specific information about Gompers's life to be found in no other source. Florence Calvert Thorne, who took her Ph. D. at the University of Chicago and was Gompers's research assistant for a number of years, helped assemble material for the work and wrote the Appendix, covering the last few months of his life.

Harvey, Roland Hill: *Samuel Gompers*, Stanford University, Calif., Stanford University Press, 1935. Contains an interesting account of important events in his life and is well documented.

General References

Andrews, Marietta Minnigerode: *My Studio Window*, New York, E. P. Dutton & Company, Inc., 1928. Includes some references to Gompers's speaking in Washington, D. C.

Beard, Mary: *The American Labor Movement*, New York, The Macmillan Company, 1931.

Buchanan, Joseph R.: *The Story of a Labor Agitator*, New York, The Outlook Company, 1903.

Carlton, Frank T.: *The History and Problems of Organized Labor*, rev. ed., Boston, D. C. Heath and Company, 1920.

Commons, John R., *et al.*: *History of Labour in the United States*, 2 vols., New York, The Macmillan Company, 1918. A monumental work containing detailed and authentic data on the history of the labor movement in America, with many references to Gompers and the A.F. of L.

Cummins, E. E.: *The Labor Problem in the United States*, New York, D. Van Nostrand Company, Inc., 1932.

[1] *Ibid.*, 506.

[2] *Ibid.*, pp. 507–508.

[3] Samuel Gompers, *Seventy Years of Life and Labor*, II, 552. Appendix written by Florence C. Thorne.

Eliot, C. W.: *The Future of Trade Unionism and Capitalism in a Democracy*, New York, G. P. Putnam's Sons, 1910.

Perlman, Selig: *A Theory of the Labor Movement*, New York, The Macmillan Company, 1928. A penetrating analysis of trade-unionism in terms of basic American attitudes. The author writes that Gompers succeeded because he adapted his labor ideas and methods to the American way of life.

———: *A History of Trade-unionism in the United States*, New York, The Macmillan Company, 1922.

Powderly, T. V.: *Thirty Years of Labor*, Columbus, Ohio, Excelsior Publishing House, 1889.

Reed, Louis: *The Labor Philosophy of Samuel Gompers*, New York, Columbia University Press, 1930. This is a Ph. D. dissertation and is a careful analysis of the subject. It has an excellent bibliography.

Stolberg, Benjamin: *The Story of the CIO*, New York, The Viking Press, 1938.

Ware, Norman J.: *The Labor Movement in the United States, 1860–1895*, New York, D. Appleton and Company, 1929.

———: Samuel Gompers, *Encyclopedia of the Social Sciences*, New York, 1930–1935, VI, 696–697.

Woll, Mathew: *The American Federation of Labor: Its Laws, Character, Strength and Manner of Working*, New York, Workers' Education Bureau of America, 1925.

Magazine Articles about Gompers

Signed Articles

Commons, John R.: "The Passing of Samuel Gompers," *New York Times Current History*, 21 (February, 1925): 670–676.

Greer, Hal W.: "Gompers and Competition," *American Law Review*, 42 (March and April, 1908): 277–282.

Hayworth, Donald: "Samuel Gompers, Orator," *Quarterly Journal of Speech*, 22 (December, 1936): 578–584.

Hendrick, Burton J.: "The Leadership of Samuel Gompers," *World's Work*, 35 (February, 1918): 381–387.

James, Alfred P.: "The First Convention of the American Federation of Labor," *Western Pennsylvania Historical Magazine*, 6 and 7 (1923–1924).

Simpson, G.: "Sam Gompers: Misleader of Labor," *American Mercury*, 33 (October, 1934): 185–188.

Stolberg, Benjamin: "What Manner of Man Was Gompers?" *Atlantic Monthly*, 135 (March, 1925): 404–412.

Tannenbaum, Frank: "Samuel Gompers' Last Convention," *Survey*, 53 (January, 1925): 391–394.

Weyl, Walter E.: "Samuel Gompers, Representative of American Labor," *Review of Reviews*, 31 (January, 1905): 44–47.

Wilhelm, D.: "Touchstone Mr. Gompers," *Independent*, 93 (January, 1918): 113.

Unsigned Articles

"Gomperian Forcefulness," *New Republic*, 12 (Aug. 11, 1917): 34–36.

"The Man between Two Millstones," *Current Literature*, 48 (January, 1910): 32–35.

"A National Storm Center," *Literary Digest*, 62, No. 10 (Sept. 13, 1919): 40–46.

"Plain Sam Gompers and His Empire," *Literary Digest*, 84 (Jan. 3, 1925): 31–36.

"Talk with Mr. Gompers," *Review of Reviews*, 10 (July, 1894): 27–29.

Writings and Speeches of Gompers

Addresses, New York, 1918; also contains speeches of Paul U. Kellogg and William English Walling.

American Federationist, Washington, D. C., American Federation of Labor. With the exception of 1 year, Gompers was editor of the official magazine from its beginning until his death in 1924. The editorials appeared over his name and often were reprints of his speeches.

American Labor and the War, New York, George H. Doran & Company, Inc., 1919. A collection of speeches made during the First World War.

Gompers, Samuel, collection of scrap books. The New York Public Library has forty-eight scrap books containing articles by and about Samuel Gompers, covering the period from 1902 to 1924. This material was collected by the A.F. of L. and consists of biographical sketches, addresses, press statements, and special magazine articles.

Labor and the Common Welfare, New York, E. P. Dutton & Company, Inc., 1919. Contains excerpts from Gompers's writings and speeches. Compiled and edited by Hayes Robbins.

Labor and the Employer, New York, E. P. Dutton & Company, Inc., 1920. Contains excerpts from Gompers's writings and speeches. Compiled and edited by Hayes Robbins.

Labor in Europe and America, New York, Harper & Brothers, 1910.

Organized Labor: Its Struggles, Its Enemies and Fool Friends, Washington, D. C., American Federation of Labor, 1904.

Out of Their Own Mouths, New York, E. P. Dutton & Company, Inc., 1921.

Proceedings American Federation of Labor, Washington, D. C. Gompers did a large amount of speaking at the annual conventions of the A.F. of L., and his speeches are recorded in the *Proceedings.*

Special Labor Documents

Forty Years of Action: Non-partisan Political Activity, n.d., Washington, D. C., American Federation of Labor.

Legislative Achievements of the American Federation of Labor, n.d., Washington, D. C.

Etten, Ida M.: *The Conditions of Women Workers,* Washington, D. C., American Federation of Labor, 1891.

"Report of Conditions of Employment in the Iron and Steel Industry in the United States," *Senate Document* 110, Sixty-second Congress, first session, Vol. III.

Reports of Industrial Commission, Washington, D. C., 1900 and 1901, Vols. V and XIX.

Unpublished Theses

Emery, Walter B.: Samuel Gompers: Spokesman for Labor, Ph.D. dissertation, University of Wisconsin, Madison, Wis., 1939.

Fisher, Margaret: Samuel Gompers' Influence in the American Labor Movement, B.A. thesis, University of Wisconsin, Madison, Wis., 1921.

Wagner, Virgil H.: Samuel Gompers and the Labor Radicals, Master of Philosophy thesis, University of Wisconsin, Madison, Wis., 1929.

Patrick Henry

by LOUIS A. MALLORY

Patrick Henry, born May 29, 1736, in Hanover County, Virginia, spent his boyhood at Mount Brilliant (afterwards known as the Retreat), some twenty-two miles from Richmond. He was educated until ten years of age in the country school; from tenth to fifteenth year was tutored at home by his father; in 1751 was placed by his father with a merchant of the county to receive mercantile training. He was set up in business in a country store by his father in 1752; business failed; married Sarah Shelton, 1754, and moved to Pine Slash, a 300-acre farm; tried storekeeping again and failed in 1758. After a very short period of study, he took the law examination at Williamsburg and passed, in 1760; emerged from obscurity, December 1, 1763, by his first great speech in The Parsons' Cause. He was elected to the House of Burgesses, 1765; assumed revolutionary leadership in Virginia after his If This Be Treason speech on May 29, 1765, and aroused resistance throughout the colonies. Between 1765 and 1774 he became a man of affairs, a leading lawyer and burgess, and head of the revolutionary democratic party in Virginia; was in First Continental Congress from September 5, 1774, until adjournment on October 26, 1774. He delivered the Give Me Liberty or Give Me Death speech in support of his resolutions to arm Virginia, March 23, 1775, and carried the resolutions by a small majority, but his plan for immediate military action was thwarted by the conservatives. He was in the Second Continental Congress from May 18, 1775, until adjournment on August 5, 1775; first governor of the state of Virginia, 1776; re-elected 1777 and 1778; declined election to fourth term, 1779; declined appointment to Continental Congress. From 1780 to 1784 he became the conservative leader in the Virginia Assembly; again governor, 1785 and 1786. Opposed adoption of the Federal Constitution, 1787–1788, and led fight for amendments, 1788–1791; argued British Debt Case, 1791–1793. He retired to Red Hill, Charlotte County, Virginia, 1794. Between 1794 and 1799 declined United States Senatorship, mission to Spain, offices of United States Secretary of State and Chief Justice of the United States, governorship of Virginia, and mission to France. Elected to the Virginia Assembly as a member of the Federalist party, 1799; died June 6, 1799.

Popular tradition has pictured Patrick Henry as a forensic genius who, overcoming the handicaps of obscure birth, poverty, lack of education, and natural inclination, rose as the champion of the people and, in an hour of grave social crisis, won a signal victory for democracy against the forces of aristocratic oppression. This concept contains some elements of truth but ignores many of the essential facts.

Patrick Henry

It is true that the circumstances and events of Henry's early life were not as a whole conducive to full development of his native powers. The frontier environment of western Virginia left much to be desired in the way of cultural and intellectual opportunity. Henry inherited no tradition of aristocratic superiority. He was of the people, if by "people" one means the substantial middle class from which the small planters and tradesmen of the Piedmont were recruited. The necessity of gaining his own livelihood forced him very early to turn his attention to practical affairs. He received no formal academic education and was what in a later period became designated as a "self-made man." He was subjected to the narrowing influences of class and sectional prejudice, unalleviated by broad social contacts or by extensive travel. When he took his seat in the legislative halls of Virginia, he came as an outlander, an inexperienced country lawyer taking his place among the wealthy and courtly aristocrats who had for decades wielded almost undisputed control of the colony. It is no wonder that popular tradition has seen in his sudden rise to leadership the flowering of some inexplicable genius.

As a matter of fact there are important circumstances in Henry's youth and early manhood that offer at least a partial explanation for his development both as a speaker and as a leader. In family, education, professional training, and opportunity, he was more fortunate than has frequently been indicated. His native endowments, important as they unquestionably are as an explanation of his character and career, are by no means the single explanation. Training played its part. Nor did he have to create the occasion for his success. Henry had the courage and the ability to take advantage of his opportunities. The opportunities, however, were created by the times.

Family Background and Early Training

In the first place, Patrick Henry came of a good family, respected for its cultural and intellectual attainments. Sarah Winston Henry, his mother, was a woman of recognized mental power and an unusual command of language. Other Winstons were noted for their ability in speech and music, and her brother William was considered one of Virginia's great orators.

John Henry, Patrick's father, who received a liberal education in Scotland, was enough of a classical scholar to cause the Reverend Samuel Davies to describe him as a man more familiar with his Horace than with his Bible. Many of John Henry's relatives in the mother country were noted for eminence in the pulpit, as educators, and as men of letters.[1]

[1] Moses Coit Tyler, *Patrick Henry*, in American Statesman Series (John T. Morse. Jr.. ed., Boston and New York, 1887), pp. 2-3.

Furthermore, Patrick Henry's early education, while undoubtedly limited, gave him very effective fundamental training, probably considerably more than was common among the families of his particular social group in Virginia. The exact quantity and quality of this early training can perhaps now never be stated with complete accuracy, for the evidence is meager and contradictory.[1] It appears certain, however, that Henry received considerable drill in Latin from his father and perhaps from his uncle, the Reverend Patrick Henry, for whom the speaker was named. He gained some knowledge of Greek, showed a definite aptitude for mathematics, was introduced early to ancient and modern history and somehow developed a marked proficiency not only in the use of words but also in the mechanics of writing. The letters of Patrick Henry consistently reveal the marks of effective fundamental training in the use of language.

Also, from the time Henry was twelve until he was twenty-four, he had the opportunity of observing the personality, delivery, and methods of composition of the Reverend Samuel Davies, a most effective public speaker, Davies preached in Hanover County from 1747 to 1759, when he became president of Princeton. There is insufficient evidence to enable one to say with assurance just how much Henry may have owed to Davies. That there was some influence cannot be doubted.

Henry's formal education, if it may be called such, was indeed a part of his early training, for he was but fifteen when he left his father's house to try his hand at practical affairs. From then on, so far as is known, the acquisition of knowledge and the development of skills were matters that he handled without direct assistance from others and in his own personal fashion.

Professional Training

After trying his hand unsuccessfully as a merchant and a farmer, Henry, in what may well have been a mood of desperation, made a decision that subsequent events proved to be a happy one: he determined to practice law. Accounts vary as to the time he spent in preparation for his legal examination, the times given ranging from 1 to 9 months. In any event, sometime in the early spring of 1760, Patrick Henry journeyed to Williamsburg, then the capital of Virginia, to seek admission to the bar.

Again accounts vary, but it is clear that Henry won his license to practice more through his power of practical persuasion than through any profound knowledge of the law. Another interesting fact that emerges is that at this time, when Henry was twenty-four, his appearance and manners

[1] *Cf.* William Wirt, *The Life and Character of Patrick Henry* (Philadelphia, 1817), pp. 23–24; Tyler, *op. cit.*, p. 13; and William Wirt Henry, *Patrick Henry: Life, Correspondence and Speeches* (New York, 1891), I, 8–10.

were such as to create an unfavorable first impression; but in conversation he revealed a powerful and commanding intellect.

If there can be little question that Henry was poorly qualified for the law when he took his examination, there can also be little question that he afterward qualified himself rapidly. In his study and in his practice he received invaluable disciplinary training. Also, some of his cases at least served to give him practical motivation for the development of his forensic powers. He had three years of this obscure but useful preparation before his first great opportunity presented itself.

The practice of law not only trained and developed Henry's intellectual and emotional powers but, more important, brought him into contact with the social and political issues that were assuming momentous proportions in the colonies. Henry was now a professional man, forced by his work into contact with other professional men, some of them leading citizens in their counties. Undoubtedly he heard much discussion of affairs.

The times were conducive to discussion. Already the struggle between Great Britain and her colonies was in the air. The first American Writ of Assistance had been issued in June, 1755, and had aroused the indignation of the merchants. The death of George II, on October 25, 1760, and the accession of George III to the throne foretold a more stringent enforcement of the various trade laws. In February, 1761, James Otis sounded a note of protest and of warning from the north. In Virginia an important controversy between the assembly and the home government was in progress. Economic, religious, and political questions were involved. The problem of taxation was not then of first importance, but issues no less significant were before the people.

The Parsons' Cause

In 1758 the Assembly of Virginia had passed the so-called Twopenny Act, which provided that debts and the salaries of officials, ordinarily payable in tobacco by legal regulation, be calculated in money at the rate of twopence a pound. This act particularly affected the ministers of the Church of England, the state church of the colony, for in 1755, the assembly had passed a similar law, and it now appeared that it was the intention to scale down the ministers' salaries when the price of tobacco was high, without providing any compensation for the frequent occasions when the price fell below normal. The clergy, naturally aroused by the threat of such a policy, protested vigorously.

Although the final stage in the passage of a Colonial law was the king's approval, the assembly put the Twopenny Act into effect as soon as the governor had signed it. The Bishop of London indicated that such action was very near to treason. Landon Carter and Richard Bland, leading Virginia lawyers, replied for the colony, and a merry war of pamphlets was on, in which John Camm, president of William and Mary College, supported the clergy.

The clergy did more than wage a war of pamphlets. Several of them instituted suits, after Camm, who had been sent to England with a petition, obtained the veto of the Twopenny Act under an order in council dated August 10, 1759. The most noteworthy of these suits became one of the most celebrated legal cases in American history.

It was instituted by the Reverend James Maury, of the parish of Fredericksville, in Louisa County, a man of good family, high character, and excellent reputation. On April 1, 1762, he brought suit in the County Court of Hanover. Peter Lyons, the leading lawyer in the county, was his counsel. John Lewis, another able advocate, appeared for the defendants. Lewis relied on the Act of 1758, with the provisions of which the defendants had fully complied. The plaintiff demurred to this plea as insufficient, thus raising the question of the validity of the act. When the demurrer was argued, on November 5, 1763, the court, with the evidence of the royal disallowance before it, "adjudged the act to be no law." John Henry, Patrick Henry's father, was the presiding justice.

This decision on the demurrer left nothing to be done in Maury's case but the determination by a jury of the damages to which he was entitled. These damages would naturally consist of the difference between the money actually paid him and the value of the tobacco to which he was entitled. Apparently the case had resolved itself into a question of mere arithmetic. Lewis, believing that there was nothing more to be done, expressed his desire to withdraw. The clergy had a right to be jubilant, for it appeared that in this test case the jury would be forced to give the full amount of damages claimed.

Now, however, came one of those dramatic occurrences occasionally to be found in history, in which, when the right setting has been provided by events and the right actor developed by circumstance, the two are brought together.

Far-reaching social, economic, and political forces had converged in the County Court of Hanover to produce a rare opportunity for anyone who was daring enough and capable enough to seize it. For three years an obscure young man had been steadily pushing his way to notice as a lawyer. When veteran and eminent counsel despaired, this young man was given his great chance. Patrick Henry was employed as counsel for the defense.

On December 1, 1763, the case was resumed, and after a jury that was far more satisfactory to the defendants than to the plaintiff had been selected, two gentlemen who were the largest purchasers of tobacco in the county were sworn as witnesses to prove the market price in 1759. Their testimony established the fact that the price was then more than three times as much as had been estimated in the payment of paper money actually made to the plaintiff in that year. When Patrick Henry rose to speak, in point of fact and in point of law he faced a lost cause.

In point of popular feeling, however, the cause was far from lost. Maury was on the unpopular side. In spite of the twenty or so members of the clergy who were present, the audience that packed the little court-house to overflowing was in the main hoping against hope that the new counsel might find some way of snatching victory from the already jubilant churchmen. Henry could not change the law. He could not overthrow the factual evidence on the price of tobacco. He could, however, influence the jury on the amount of damages to be awarded. This he proceeded to do.

For over an hour he talked. His own father was the presiding justice; the jury was made up of his friends and neighbors. He knew the temper of their minds. He knew their feelings on the issues of the day. Quickly he abandoned the letter of the law to connect the case with the broader social and political forces of the times.

The act of 1758, he said, had every characteristic of a good law; it was a law of general utility, and could not, consistently with the original com-pact between King and people, stipulating protection on the one hand and obedience on the other, be annulled. . . . A king, by disallowing acts of this salutary nature, from being the father of his people, degenerates into a tyrant, and forfeits all right to his subjects' obedience. . . . The only use of an established church and clergy in society, is to enforce obedience to civil sanctions, and the observance of those which are called duties of imperfect obligation. When a clergy ceases to answer these ends, the community have no further need of their ministry, and may justly strip them of their appointments. The clergy of Virginia, in this particular instance of their refusing to acquiesce in the law in question . . . had most notoriously counteracted those great ends of their institution. Therefore, instead of useful members of the state, they ought to be considered as enemies of the community; and in the case now before them, Mr. Maury, instead of countenance and protection and damages, very justly deserved to be punished with signal severity. . . . Excepting the jury were disposed to rivet the chains of bondage on their own necks, they would not let slip the opportunity which now offered of making an example of him as might, hereafter, be a warning to himself and his brethren, not to have the temer-ity, for the future, to dispute the validity of such laws, authenticated by the only authority which could give force to laws for the government of this

Colony, the authority of a legal representative of a Council, and of a kind and benevolent and patriot Governor.[1]

When Patrick Henry finished speaking the jury went out, and "in less than five minutes brought in a verdict for the Plaintiff, one penny damages."[2]

In the speech by which this remarkable verdict was secured, Henry's power as a speaker was for the first time released as a social force in a truly significant situation. The results were important both in their historical and in their personal aspects.

Historically, one important result was a weakening of the position of the state church in Virginia. The jury's action in the Maury suit set a precedent that directed the course of subsequent litigation and created a widespread public opinion unfavorable to the established clergy. A second important historical result arose from the fact that Henry's persuasive strategy had been to connect the issues of his case with the broader issues of the day. He not only kindled popular indignation against the clergy but directed public sentiment against the British overlordship as well. In his attack on the clergy Henry was serving the ruling powers in the colony no less than the people, but in his assertion of the common rights of man he struck a note that was to give the revolutionary movement in Virginia new direction. In arraying the people against the preachers he also began the process of leading them into revolution.

The personal result of Henry's success was to introduce a new conditioning factor into his development, the factor of a widespread public reputation. Up to this time he had been known by relatively few persons, who formed their opinions of him through direct observation of his person, his speech, and his behavior in social, business, and professional situations. Now his name spread through the colony. Judgments were formed by large numbers of persons who had to go on only what they heard. His name became a symbol. He began to experience the impact of forces, friendly and antagonistic, to which he had not hitherto been subjected. The fact that he had achieved success in a popular cause made the friendly forces overwhelmingly predominant. With his success in The Parsons' Cause the preparatory part of his life was completed. Patrick Henry the historical figure had emerged.

---

[1] Letter of the Reverend James Maury, the plaintiff, to the Reverend John Camm, Dec. 12, 1763; Ann Maury, *Memoirs of a Huguenot Family* (New York, 1853), pp. 418–424. This letter is, so far as is known, the only contemporary record of what Henry actually said. Wirt's account of the speech (*The Life and Character of Patrick Henry*, pp. 42–46) is a highly dramatic *description* written 50 years later from such reports as he was then able to gather.

[2] *Ibid.*

Patrick Henry

Henry *Assumes Political Leadership in Virginia*

In 1763 a political career offered a real opportunity to a capable and ambitious young man in Virginia. The public affairs of the colony had for years been under the control of a coterie of politicians from the eastern counties, representing the wealthy, conservative, and aristocratic ruling families of the tidewater. These men, while protesting strongly to the home government against any encroachment on their own economic, political, or social privileges, were thoroughly English in feeling and were of no mind to relinquish any of their prerogatives as a ruling class. The members from the newer western counties represented a group of colonists actually hostile to the imperial British government and no less hostile to the tidewater aristocracy. This sectional discontent provided a favorable political opportunity for any leader who was capable of utilizing it.

In 1765 William Johnson, burgess from Louisa County, resigned to accept another office. Patrick Henry, although then a resident of Hanover County, was elected to take his place. Three days after taking his seat he opened fire on the controlling political clique by making an attack on their cherished scheme of establishing a public loan office. Henry's attack was made on general principles rather than on any specific information, but it served to reveal a scandalous situation in the financial affairs of the colony and paved the way for his rise in popular favor.

Matters of greater importance than the loan-office episode almost at once gave Henry further opportunity. In May, 1765, the Virginia House of Burgesses received a copy of the Stamp Act. In spite of the protests that had been made, there can be little doubt that nothing very drastic would have happened if affairs had been left in the hands of the old leaders. But that is exactly where affairs were not allowed to remain. Patrick Henry, in one of the best timed moves of all his public career, took the floor and offered a series of defiant and inflammatory resolutions that he had written on the blank leaf of an old copy of *Coke upon Littleton*. He had shown these resolutions to George Johnston, of Fairfax, and to John Fleming, of Cumberland, and had obtained their promise of support. With this assurance he boldly proceeded to wrest the legislative leadership of Virginia from the shocked and scandalized conservatives.

No authentic complete account of Henry's speeches in support of his resolutions has ever been discovered. Several significant statements concerning the general effect he produced or in regard to the dramatic moment in which he was accused of having uttered treason have, however, been made. Thomas Jefferson wrote in his autobiography: "I attended the debate, however, at the door of the lobby of the H. of Burgesses, and heard the splendid display of Mr. Henry's talents as a popular orator. They were great indeed; such as I have never heard from any other man. He appeared to me to speak as Homer wrote."[1]

Henry biographers, relying either on an account given many years later by Judge John Tyler, who, when eighteen, had listened to the speech as he stood in the lobby by the side of Jefferson, or on a slightly differing version given by Edmund Randolph, agree in depicting Henry as being magnificently defiant as he uttered his famous reply: "If this be treason, make the most of it."

It is instructive to compare this high point in the debate as traditionally presented and as given by an anonymous French traveler, also an eye witness, whose diary was not discovered until 1921 and so has not been considered by any of the Henry biographers. The Frenchman wrote as follows:

> May 30th . . . I went imediately to the Assembly which was seting, where I was entertained with very strong debates concerning dutys that the Parlement wants to lay on the American colonys, which they call or stile stamp dutys. Shortly after I came in, one of the members stood up and said he had read that in former times Tarquin and Julus had their Brutus, Charles had his Cromwell, and he did not doubt but some good American would stand up in favour of his Country; but (says he) in a more moderate manner, and was going to continue, when the Speaker of the House rose and, said he, the last that stood up had spoke traison, and was sorey to see that not one of the members of the House was loyal enough to stop him before he had gone so far. Upon which the same member stood up again (His name is Henery) and said that if he had afronted the speaker or the House, he was ready to ask pardon, and he would shew his loyalty to His Majesty King George the third at the expence of the last drop of his blood; but what he had said must be attributed to the interest of his country's dying liberty which he had at heart, and the heat of passion might have lead him to have said something more than he intended; but, again, if he had said any thing wrong, he beged the Speaker and the House's pardon. Some other members stood up and backed him, on which that afaire was droped.[2]

The question involved in the differing accounts of this episode is one not so much of Henry's character as of his persuasive téchniques and of his relation to his audience. The traditional accounts present him as assuming aggressive and total command of the situation; the diary account

---

[1] *Writings of Thomas Jefferson* (collected and edited by Paul Leicester Ford, New York, 1892–1899), I, 6.

[2] Diary discovered in the Archives Nationales, Paris, in 1921. The writer, who has not been identified, wrote the preceding in English. Apparently he was an agent for the French government, possibly the Chevalier d'Annemours.—*American Historical Review*, 26 (1921): 726–747; S. E. Morison, *Sources and Documents Illustrating the American Revolution* (Oxford, 1923), I, 14–15.

indicates a more conciliatory method and a greater reliance on the support of friendly auditors. It is probably the more accurate.

The High Point of Henry's Career: The Liberty or Death Speech

The 9 years from 1765 to 1774, during which the policy of the British ministry progressively increased resentment in the colonies, gave Patrick Henry an opportunity to make good the position of leadership in Virginia that he had seized by forcing the adoption of his Stamp Act resolutions. He became an outstanding lawyer, legislator, and radical political organizer. During this period he laid the foundation for a considerable personal fortune, partly through his extensive legal practice, partly by a shrewd realization of the possibilities of investments in land. He showed his democratic and liberal tendencies by his support of religious toleration, his defense of dissenting ministers, and his opposition to the slave trade. It was the part he played in organizing the new democratic party in Virginia, however, which steadily increased his reputation with the common people of the colony.

In 1775 Henry was appointed a deputy to the Continental Congress. But it was in March of that year, after the Congress had adjourned, that he reached the high point of his career. The second Virginia convention met in St. John's Church, Richmond, on March 20. Peyton Randolph, the conservative leader, was elected president, and the convention at once took into consideration the proceedings of the Continental Congress, which were approved. On the third day of the session a copy of the petition and memorial of the Assembly of the Island of Jamaica, addressed to the king, December 28, 1774, was read. It was a bold vindication of the rights of the American colonies, but it also traced the grant of colonial rights to the king and held that the royal prerogative annexed to the crown was totally independent of the people, who could not invade, add to, or diminish it. This doctrine was not to the liking of the democratic leaders in the convention. It was nevertheless resolved that "unfeigned thanks and most grateful acknowledgments" be transmitted to the speaker of the Jamaica Assembly. Patrick Henry thereupon offered as an amendment three resolutions for putting the colony of Virginia into an immediate "posture of defense" through the raising and training of a "well-regulated militia."[1]

During the course of the bitter debate on these resolutions Patrick Henry delivered his most famous speech. His words have been printed over and over again in American histories, readers, and anthologies. The speech is presented as one of the great examples of American oratory, if not as an example of American literature. The phrase *give me liberty or give me death*

[1] Peter Force, 4 *American Archives* (1837–1843), I, 1072–1074; II, 167–168.

is the chief association with Henry's name today. Because of it the speech and the man have taken a place in American folklore and tradition.

The text of the speech as it has come down to us was written by William Wirt, Henry's first biographer, from the accounts of witnesses. It is this version that has constituted the chief source of information in regard to Henry's style of composition. So far as is known, no complete report of the speech existed prior to the publication of Wirt's *Life and Character of Patrick Henry*, in 1817, nor has any differing version since come to light. The wide popularity of Wirt's version has caused it to be accepted as the typical example of Henry's rhetorical style, and Wirt's account of the occasion and the speech has become the most influential single factor in determining Henry's popular reputation. None of Henry's other speeches has come to public attention in an edited form.

Wirt's description of the speech occasion gave the American public a dramatic, vividly written account in the popular, traditionally patriotic manner. Henry was given heroic proportions, set against the stereotype of British oppression of the colonies. It is significant that the text is at first in the form of an account of the speech rather than in the form of a direct report. It is also an interesting and significant fact that this reconstructed text is rhetorically superior to that of any other of Henry's reported speeches. It has a sustained literary quality that the others do not possess. There are a conciseness, a lack of repetition, a polish, a poetic quality, beside which much of the other texts seems almost commonplace. The speech rhythms of later texts reported in shorthand are for the most part much more those of ordinary conversation.

In his account of the effect of the speech Wirt idealizes the events and the men. He omits any mention of the narrow margin of five votes by which the resolutions were adopted. He ignores the existence of any significant party differences. A much more realistic account is contained in a letter written by James Parker, a merchant in Norfolk, Va., to Charles Stewart, under the date April 6, 1775.

The convention at Richmond is now over and you have the proceedings enclosed. Something very extraordinary was intended, but a disagreement amongst the Patriots put a stop to it. There was a motion made by P. Henry supported by T. Jefferson, G. Washington and R. H. Lee for referring to a committee the raising eighty-six men out of each county, and equipping them with arms, ammunition, etc. This was carried by a majority of 65 to 60 but the Committee could not agree upon the ways and means for their support. What flattened them all down was a hint of a Plea to be presented by P. Henry, no less than the taking of Government into their hands appointing Magistrates and levying money. The Treasurer, Coll. B. Harrison, Bland and Col. Ridduck [*sic*] saw into this and formed an opposition to this which overset the scheme. . . .

You never heard anything more infamously insolent than P. Henry's speech: he called the K— a Tyrant, a fool, a puppet and a tool to the ministry. Said there was no Englishmen, no Scots, no Britons, but a set of wretches sunk in Luxury, they had lost their native courage and (were) unable to look the brave Americans in the face. . . . This Creature is so infatuated, that he goes about I am told, praying and preaching amongst the common people.[1]

Parker was a Tory, and his letter must be evaluated in the light of this fact. It is probable, however, that his letter not only throws light on Henry's real purpose in submitting his resolutions but also suggests some of the less exalted and less restrained moments of the speech, moments that have not found their way into the traditional accounts.

All in all, it appears that although Wirt's version of this famous speech is not apocryphal, as has been sometimes asserted, it should be regarded as incomplete. He has taken the high points of the speech, those soaring moments when language, action, and emotion perfectly complement each other, moments that would naturally be fixed in the memory of the listener, and arranged them so as to give the impression that they alone constitute the speech. There is abundant evidence to show that Henry did not soar all the time in other speeches, and there is no reason to believe that he did so in this one.

Henry Elected the First Governor of the State of Virginia

Early in May, 1775, Henry led a large number of armed men in a march on Williamsburg and intimidated Governor Dunsmore into paying for some gunpowder that he had had removed from the magazine in the city. By this expedition Henry executed a striking *coup de main*, but he was once more thwarted by conservative opinion in his real object of seizing the government and inaugurating the Revolution without further delay.[2]

There is no question that Patrick Henry greatly desired to crown his revolutionary activities by service in the field. On August 5, 1775, it appeared as though this desire was to be consummated, for he was then appointed military commander in chief of Virginia. The granting of his desire was more of appearance than of reality, however, for although he was nominally given the supreme military command he was also required to be obedient to the Virginia Committee of Safety, a body of civilians, subject to the influence of party distrust and personal animosity. Henry's military ambitions were so completely checkmated by this committee that finally, on February 28, 1776, he resigned.

[1] *Magazine of History* (New York, 1906), III, 158.
[2] H. J. Eckenrode, *The Revolution in Virginia* (Boston, 1916), pp. 51–52.

There has been a good deal of discussion of this episode and what it revealed concerning Henry's abilities and character.[1] Its most significant aspect is probably what it revealed of the conservative fear of Henry's popularity. In order to understand this attitude it must be remembered that with the active participation of the common people in the revolution that movement had changed its character. Beginning as a mere commercial and political struggle with the mother country, it had now become a social revolution in America. Many of the Colonial leaders were no more favorably inclined to these new developments than were the British officials themselves. In all the colonies obscure but ambitious men of talent had seized the opportunity afforded by the quarrel with the mother country to advance their own interests by attacking special privilege at home. And in all the colonies there was no such man who had been more successful than Patrick Henry. His opponents were not, if they could help themselves, going to allow him to continue his progress by adding to his already tremendous reputation the renown that was then attached to a successful military career. His enemies, by denying him this final opportunity, were able to deal him a humiliating and a punishing blow.

In the Virginia convention of May, 1776, Henry advocated independence and a democratic constitution for Virginia. Independence was declared, but the constitution adopted was at best a compromise between liberal and conservative demands. It did, however, leave the door open to democratic development. Henry was elected governor of the newly created commonwealth over Nelson, his conservative opponent, by a vote of sixty to forty-five. With this election the overthrow of the old order was made dramatically apparent. Patrick Henry, the popular leader, a self-styled man of the people, was to take his place in the royal palace, symbol of kingly rule. Henry's election marked the passing of an old order and the beginning of a new. In addition, it came as a fitting reward to personal merit. It climaxed his career as a revolutionary leader, a career that had made him the most striking figure in Virginia politics.

Henry Changes from Radical to Conservative

During the War for Independence and the period of reconstruction that followed it, Henry sought steadily to make good the objectives he had had in mind during the period of revolutionary organization. As governor he worked industriously, under difficult conditions, to make the newly formed Virginia government function. From 1780 to 1785 he was active in the state legislature, taking the lead in securing legislation to wage the war successfully. Henry had never been a social reformer. His

[1] *Vide* William Wirt, *The Life and Character of Patrick Henry* (Philadelphia, 1818), pp. 178–208; Tyler, *Patrick Henry*, pp. 156–166; Henry, *Patrick Henry*, I, 333–357.

radicalism was directed primarily to the end of securing a limited type of political freedom for the members of his own social group in his own geographical section. The doctrinaire liberalism that actuated Jefferson had not touched Henry. He fought gallantly for the political and economic freedom of the yeomanry of Virginia, but he had little concern for the intellectual freedom of mankind. He opposed the liberating social influences that the Revolution set in motion. He became a leader of the conservative faction in the state legislature, even favoring a religious establishment in Virginia.

When the controversy over the Federal Constitution arose, Henry, taking a strictly sectional and states'-rights point of view, opposed its adoption. In so doing he was steadfast to the same principles and same interests that had governed his earlier policy toward Great Britain. He was still fighting for western agrarian and debtor groups against business and creditor interests.

From 1791 to 1799 the social conservatism that was a fundamental part of Henry's character became more and more dominant. Personal affairs and the social developments following the adoption of the Constitution shaped this change. During the six years between 1788 and 1794 Henry acquired enough of a fortune through his law practice and by successful land investments to enable him to retire in comfort, with the knowledge that not only were his remaining years provided for but he would be able to leave a considerable estate to his family. In 1794, when he was fifty-eight, he withdrew from professional life. Between 1791 and 1794 the new Federal government had not functioned too badly, and Henry, with his increased wealth, greater age, and the sense of having rounded out his career, was inclined to look at the new scheme of things with more kindly eyes. As Madison and Jefferson drew away more and more from Washington and began to form a party in opposition, Henry, who had always admired Washington greatly and who disliked Jefferson and Madison thoroughly, was swayed by these personal considerations. The Federalists, fully aware of his great influence, offered him a flattering series of appointments, all of which he declined. When, however, passage of the so-called Alien and Sedition Laws set Kentucky and Virginia in an uproar, Henry was prevailed upon by Washington to offer himself for election to the Virginia Assembly as a Federalist candidate. The transformation from radical to conservative was thus completed. Henry was successful in the election, but he died before he could take his seat.

Shorthand Reports of Henry's Speeches

The debates in the Virginia convention on the adoption of the Federal Constitution, reported in shorthand by David Robertson, have been preserved.[1] They reveal how Henry bore the brunt of the fight for 23 days against an imposing array of influence and talent, including such men as James Madison, Edmund Pendleton, and John Marshall. Robertson himself admitted that these reports were neither full nor entirely accurate, and some of the Henry biographers have made much of this admission.[2] They use the difference between the effect produced by a reading of the speeches as reported and their effect as related by witnesses as evidence of the great inadequacy of the reporting. Following Wirt, they suggest that Robertson was either unable to follow the speaker in his more emotional passages or that he was so spellbound that he simply laid down his pen. It is, of course, possible that this is true, but for the sake of accuracy it should be noted that it is also possible that Robertson merely recognized certain passages as flights, designed to give emotional reinforcement to the ideas presented, and, treating them as digressions from the serious business at hand, merely rested until the speaker again took up the delineation of his thought. William Wirt Henry, who, of all the Henry biographers, is least inclined to give weight to any evidence prejudicial to Patrick Henry, credits the reports with giving the views of the speaker truly and being, in the main, accurate as to diction.[3]

The full power of Henry's speaking is, of course, inadequately represented by any mere text of his speeches. It is unfair to judge any speaker by these rhetorical remains alone, for the preserved words are but a secondary record of one part of a total pattern of visible and audible symbols, constantly adjusted to the reactions of a particular audience. With a speaker such as Henry, who, by every account, relied very greatly on delivery, the written record is particularly inadequate to convey an impression of the total effect that he produced. The texts do, however, give us a good idea of the language he employed and the arrangement of his topics and ideas. These reports and the shorthand report of his speech in the case of the British debts, also reported by Robertson,[4] are the best available sources for the study of his methods and techniques of persuasion

Henry's Methods and Techniques of Persuasion

On Wednesday, June 4, 1788, the debate on the adoption of the Constitution began. Henry opened for the opposition with a speech that, in

---

[1] Jonathan Elliot, *The Debates in the Several State Conventions on the Adoption of the Federal Constitution* (Washington, D.C., 1854), Vol. III.

[2] See particularly Wirt, *Life and Character of Patrick Henry*, pp. 280–281n. and 330–332.

[3] *Patrick Henry*, III, 429.

[4] Presented in part, with an analysis, by Wirt; *Life and Character of Patrick Henry*, pp. 330 and 338–385. The original Robertson manuscript appears to have been lost.

spite of his impressive delivery, was too general, too rambling, and too purely emotional to be really effective.[1]

On the next day, however, following General Henry Lee, who had rather effectively pointed out the weakness of his opening, Henry made a general attack upon the whole Constitution in a speech that fills twenty-one pages of the *Debates*,[2] setting forth his objections with tremendous power.

Ignoring a taunt made by Lee but smoothly accepting a compliment, Henry referred disparagingly to his own talents, called attention to the importance of the subject, and came at once to his first point. His chief objection to the proposed system was that it endangered liberty. He appealed to the fear of loss of liberty, a powerful motivating drive in his audience. He urged strong resistance, throwing the influence of his personal reputation into the discussion. Through restatement he emphasized his point that liberty was in danger. He used the device of the rhetorical question. He sought to strengthen his influence by another reference to his reputation. He then attacked many particular points of the proposed Constitution. He followed no carefully drawn plan but carried his attack in general and along all fronts. He appealed to the popular fear of monarchy and despotism that was an aftermath of the Revolution, and, emphasizing the fact that the move for the Constitution was not a popular movement, he sounded another note of warning. He closed with a persuasive explanation for his method and a restatement of his central idea that the new system was dangerous.

The use of largely unsupported general assertion, even when employed by such a speaker as Patrick Henry, has its dangers, particularly on such an occasion as had brought the Virginia convention into being. Madison, who was Henry's most formidable opponent in the debates, quickly pointed out the weakness of Henry's method. "We ought not to address our arguments to the feelings and passions," he said, "but to those understandings and judgments which were selected by the people of this country, to decide this great question by a calm and rational investigation. I hope that gentlemen, in displaying their abilities on this occasion, instead of giving opinions and making assertions, will condescend to prove and demonstrate, by a fair and regular discussion."[3]

But throughout the debates Henry continued to rely primarily on an appeal to emotional drives rather than on proof and demonstration by any closely logical discussion of facts. Sectional differences were strong throughout the Revolutionary period and the period of reconstruction in which the debates took place. Henry, talking to a Virginia audience, was

---

[1] For text of this speech see Elliot, *Debates*, III, 21–23.
[2] *Ibid.*, pp. 43–64.
[3] *Ibid.*, pp. 86–87.

also working to gain the support of the fourteen Kentucky delegates. These Kentuckians, together with the men from the western parts of Virginia, were much aroused over the proposed plan of Congress to relinquish navigation rights on the Mississippi to Spain in return for trade concessions helpful to Northern interests. In speeches of June 7, 9, and 12, Henry made telling use of these sectional fears and prejudices.[1]

The majority of the people of Virginia were in the debtor group. The events of the period had developed a strong feeling against the wealthy and the aristocratic. In a few instances Henry utilized this feeling to strengthen the force of what he said.[2] The dispute with Great Britain had turned largely on economic differences, particularly those arising from taxation. Henry argued against the Constitution on much the same grounds that the American leaders had argued against British policies, thus appealing to the economic interests of his listeners.[3]

Henry was a practical man and a realist. He saw self-interest as the chief actuating force in human conduct, and he spoke accordingly. He knew also, however, the force of sentiments and ideals. His long speech of June 9 contained a most interesting passage revealing a combination of suspicious realism and hopeful idealism. He utilized both to strengthen the point he was making against the lack of checks in the Constitution.[4]

Throughout his speeches Henry expressed fears and forebodings of the future if the proposed change should be accepted. In the heat of debate on June 24 he made what amounted to a threat of force, thus making the most obvious use of an appeal to the fears of the audience.[5]

Henry's use of the lesser strokes of persuasive technique was highly skillful. His politeness to opponents, disparagement of his own powers, sincerity, recognition of the rights of others to hold opinions contrary to his own, use of repetition and amplification, occasional resort to sarcasm and ridicule all contributed materially to his effectiveness.

It is also abundantly evident that he had an effective oral style. His language was simple but vivid. His sentence structure was not involved. His ideas were made concrete and specific by images and figures drawn largely from common experience. His use of the first person and the rhetorical question gave directness to the style. He showed conversational quality that would be approved by modern speech theory. Movement, rhythm, and progression to a climax added to the effectiveness of his language.

At the opening of the convention the friends of the Constitution claimed that they outnumbered their opponents by at least fifty votes. When on

[1] *Ibid.*, pp. 141–142, 151–152, 325–326.
[2] *Ibid.*, pp. 139 and 148.
[3] *Ibid.*, pp. 56–57, 147, 156–157, 589–591.
[4] *Ibid.*, pp. 164–166.
[5] *Ibid.*, pp. 592–593.

Wednesday, June 25, the struggle for ratification was finally over, Henry was defeated; but by a majority of only ten votes. Considering the men who were opposed to him in the debates, the trend of events in the country, and the tremendous influence Washington's advocacy of the Constitution exerted, it is easily seen that Henry fought a gallant and a very effective fight.

Contemporary accounts of Henry's other speeches in deliberative assemblies and before the courts[1] indicate that he made little special preparation even for his important speeches. In the case of the British debts he is reported to have spent three days in the preparation of very complete notes and perhaps in writing out parts of the speech and committing them to memory. He seems usually to have relied on his general information and on his ability to adapt to the demands of a situation as they arose.

He took great pains to adapt his material and his delivery to each audience he faced. In doing so he utilized everything he knew of human nature in general and also what he knew of the special interests, beliefs, and emotional drives of the particular audience. He did everything he could to prevent unnecessary difficulties, being tactful both in manner and in subject matter, except in the comparatively rare instances where tact was no longer helpful.

His speaking was uneven, ranging from stumbling ineffectiveness to almost breath-taking brilliance. When fully engrossed in his subject, he exhibited a tremendous emotional intensity, which seemed to transform his person and to electrify his audience. His characteristic persuasive method was an emotional appeal based on skillfully selected and strongly asserted stereotypes. His reasoning, while frequently good, was never profound. At times it was obviously fallacious.

He relied greatly on delivery. He was so much a master of complete bodily expressiveness that frequently his presentation included no small part of the actor's art. He had a clear, powerful, flexible voice, which accounted for much of his effectiveness.

The tones of his voice, to say nothing of his matter and gestures, were insinuated into the feelings of his hearers in a manner that baffles description. It seemed to operate by mere sympathy, and by his tones alone it seemed to me that he could make you cry or laugh at pleasure. . . . He had a perfect command of a strong and musical voice, which he raised or lowered at pleasure, and modulated so as to fall in with any given chord of the human heart.[2]

[1] These accounts, in whole or in part, have been printed in the various biographies.

[2] Memorandum of Judge Spencer Roane, a significant manuscript source used by all the Henry biographers; printed in full in George Morgan, *The True Patrick Henry* (Philadelphia, 1907), pp. 435-454.

Henry was a man of medium height, slightly stooped in later years, with a lean, rather dark face, clear, blue eyes, and a wide, mobile mouth. He was bald, and always wore a wig in public. There was nothing particularly striking about either his appearance or his dress. He was frequently mistaken by strangers for some country parson. It was only when transformed by emotional intensity that he became a commanding figure. Then his weakest intonation and his smallest gesture seemed alive with significance.

In Appraisal

It is certain that no one man, or small group of men, caused the growth of the Revolutionary movement in America. The ideas, feelings, beliefs, prejudices, and opinions that were the subjective force behind objective events grew gradually from many sources. It is probable that some sort of break between the American colonies and Great Britain would have occurred even if Patrick Henry had never been born. It is equally true that so far as any single individual can cause a broad political movement, Patrick Henry was responsible for the American resort to force against Great Britain at the time and in the manner in which it occurred.

In 1765, when the British Parliament passed the Stamp Act in spite of the protest of the Colonial legislatures, American public opinion, even in its most radical aspects, did not contemplate actual resistance. It was Henry's bold resolutions, forced through the Virginia House of Burgesses against every opposition of the conservative leaders, that set the country ablaze. The resulting Stamp Act Congress showed the way to combined extralegal resistance to British policy. Rioting throughout the colonies prepared the people for a resort to force.

From 1765 to 1774 Henry did everything that lay in his power to strengthen resistance against British policy, and in the Continental Congress of 1774 he was an implacable foe to any compromise. On this point he probably shared his position with John and Samuel Adams, but these three were by far the most radical of the American leaders. If the meager reports of the debate on Galloway's compromise plan can be trusted, Henry was the principal cause for its defeat.

If Virginia had not supported Massachusetts in the resort to arms, the course of events might have been very different. By securing the passage of his resolution to arm the colony and by his actual resort to force in the gunpowder episode, Henry brought the fighting men of the colony into the conflict, roused the common people, and made a general war inevitable. Here again he was ahead of public opinion.

Henry had the virtues that a frontier environment fosters. His political career was largely built upon those virtues; his political faith expressed

598

them. The frontier also imposes limitations; and Henry was never able completely to throw them off. He distrusted the theoretical and the philosophical. He cared little for art or for letters. He had little concern for the emancipation of the human spirit, and he had no really broad humanitarianism. He was so sharply practical that at times the quality of his thought and feeling was seriously impaired. He deplored slavery but found it "impracticable" to do anything about it. He felt that it was righteous to forgive private wrongs but impolitic to forget a national grievance. On such points he was not behind other leaders of his time, but he also was not in advance of the conventional morality of his day. He was willing to risk his neck for the political liberty of freemen in America, but he made no move throughout his career to liberalize the suffrage requirements so that a greater portion of the citizenry might enjoy the right to vote. He fought valiantly for the right of dissenters to worship God as they saw fit, but he used his full power to keep church and state together. He surrendered his leadership of the liberal Democratic-Republican party largely because he could not brook the "infidelity" resulting from infiltration of French thought. He was a shrewd and effective political leader, but at no time was he a powerfully constructive social thinker. He was concerned more with immediate results than he was with future consequences, and his ethical and philosophic principles enabled him to accept easily the doctrine that the end justifies the means. He had the advocate's temperament and could quickly become convinced of the complete rightness of his cause and the complete wrongness of that of the opposition. He was not inclined to weigh and balance or to search for objective truth.

Yet Patrick Henry, judged by his effect on his own times and by the later results of his influence, must be recognized as one of the greatest of all political agitators. He became active in politics at a time when social and economic forces had come to a focus in such a way as to make some sort of historical crisis almost inevitable. In giving impetus and direction to events, however, he overcame tremendous difficulties: personal handicaps, social animosities, deep-seated customs and habits of thought and feeling, fears, interests, prejudices. He wrested political leadership from a group of capable and influential men who had exercised an almost undisputed control of his colony for years. He defied the power of the whole British Empire. He led in the organization of a radical political movement that imposed its views on the majority of the colonists, who were either indifferent or actually hostile to its purposes, forced America into a war with the mother country, and carried that war to a successful conclusion. Out of that bitter civil discord emerged a nation whose development to its present position of power and influence constitutes one of the marvels of history. Henry opposed the reorganization of government that to a considerable extent made the phenomenal development possible, but his very opposition produced useful modifications in the organic law. Rarely has a man so successfully influenced his own times, and rarely has a political movement had such tremendous results in so short a time.

Patrick Henry lives today in popular tradition as America's earliest and most eloquent advocate of the rights of the common man. He still is an inspiring symbol of that fierce love of liberty that is willing to risk all in the struggle against oppression. If critical accuracy demands a slight modification of the popular tradition, it nevertheless still reveals him as a man of courage, high purpose, and stupendous achievement. He carried his cause against what at the time must have seemed almost insuperable odds, and by his ability, force of character, and brilliant powers of public address earned for himself a place among the world's immortals. Friend and enemy alike would pay him tribute as the outstanding speaker of the American Revolution.

SELECTED BIBLIOGRAPHY

Manuscript Sources

The best manuscript material consists of the collection in possession of the Henry family at Red Hill, Virginia. This collection has been extensively used by the biographers, and the greater part of it appears in printed form in the various biographies.

The following sources furnish little material on Henry as a speaker but are useful in checking certain biographical details.

Council Journals, 1776–1796, Richmond, Virginia State Library.
Executive Communications, Richmond, Virginia State Library.
Executive Papers, Richmond, Virginia State Library.
Governor's Letter Book, Richmond, Virginia State Library.
Henry Papers, Washington, D.C., Library of Congress.
Henry Papers, Richmond, Virginia Historical Society.
Henry Papers, Charlottesville, University of Virginia.
Henry Papers, Draper Collection, Madison, University of Wisconsin.
Patent Books, Richmond, Virginia Land Office.

Official Printed Sources

Annals of the Congress of the United States, Washington, D.C., 1849.
A Calendar of Virginia State Papers and Other Manuscripts Deposited in the Virginia Library, W. P. Palmer, *et al.*, eds., 11 vols., Richmond, 1875–1893.
Correspondence of the American Revolution, Jared Sparks, ed., 4 vols., Boston, 1853.
Elliot, Jonathan: *The Debates in the Several State Conventions on the Adoption of the Federal Constitution, as Recommended by the General Convention at Philadelphia in 1787, together with the Journal of the Federal Convention*, 5 vols., Washington, D.C., 1854.
Force, Peter: *American Archives*, 4th series, a collection of authentic records, state papers, debates, letters, etc., prepared and published under authority of an act of Congress, Washington, D.C., 1837–1843.
Gales, Joseph: *The Debates and Proceedings in the Congress of the United States*, 42 vols., Washington, D.C., 1834–1856.

Journals of the Continental Congress 1774–1789, from the original records in the Library of Congress, W. C. Ford, *et al.*, eds., 15 vols., Washington, D.C., 1904–1909.

Journals of the Virginia House of Burgesses, 1761–1776, John Pendleton Kennedy, ed., 4 vols., Richmond, 1905–1907.

Journals of the House of Delegates of the Commonwealth of Virginia (from 1777 to 1790), 3 vols., Richmond, 1827–1828.

Official Letters of the Governors of the State of Virginia, Vol. I, The Letters of Patrick Henry, Richmond, 1926.

The Proceedings of the Convention of Delegates for the Counties and Corporations in the Colony of Virginia, Held at Richmond Town in the County of Henrico, on the 20th of March, 1775, prepared by a resolution of the house of delegates on Feb. 24, 1816, Richmond, 1816.

The Proceedings of the Convention of Delegates Held . . . in the City of Williamsburg in the Colony of Virginia . . . the 6th of May, 1776, Richmond, 1816.

The Writings of George Washington, from the original MS sources, 1745–1799, prepared under direction of the United States George Washington Bicentennial Commission, John C. Fitzpatrick, ed., 30 vols., Washington, D.C., 1931–1939.

Unofficial Printed Sources

Adams, John: *Works*, Charles Francis Adams, ed., 10 vols., Boston, 1856. Contains interesting references to Henry.

Foote, William Henry: *Sketches of Virginia, Historical and Biographical*, 1st and 2d series, Philadelphia, 1850 and 1855.

Howe, Henry: *Historical Collections of Virginia*, Charleston, 1852.

Jefferson, Thomas: *Notes on the State of Virginia*, Philadelphia, 1825.

————: *Writings*, collected and edited by Paul Leicester Ford, 10 vols., New York, 1892–1899. Jefferson greatly influenced the first biographical account of Henry. He is chiefly responsible for the tradition of Henry as a lazy, ill-spoken, uneducated child of nature, whose one ability was his power as a popular speaker. Jefferson's statements concerning Henry are important, particularly since the other evidence does not support them.

Madison, James: *Letters and Other Writings*, 4 vols., Philadelphia, 1865.

————: *Papers*, 3 vols., Washington, D.C., 1840–1841.

————: *Writings*, 9 vols., New York, 1900–1910.

Morison: S. E.: *Sources and Documents Illustrating the American Revolution*, Oxford, 1923.

Biographies, Memoirs, Etc.

Alexander, James W.: *The Life of Archibald Alexander*, New York, 1854. Contains interesting analysis of Henry's power as a speaker.

Arnold, Samuel G.: *The Life of Patrick Henry of Virginia*, New York, 1857.

Everett, Alexander H.: *Life of Patrick Henry*, in Sparks's Library of American Biography, 2d series, Boston, 1844, Vol. I.

Henry, William Wirt: *Patrick Henry: Life, Correspondence, and Speeches*, 3 vols., New York, 1891. The most complete of the Henry biographies. Contains many letters and except for Elliot's *Debates* is the best single source for the text of Henry's speeches. It is extremely biased. Facts are accurately presented, but interpretations are constantly forced to support thesis that Henry was the greatest man in Virginia.

Kennedy, John Pendleton: *Memoirs of the Life of William Wirt*, 2 vols., Philadelphia, 1856. Gives important information concerning the writing of the first Henry biography and of Jefferson's influence on Wirt's treatment of his subject.

Maury, Ann: *Memoirs of a Huguenot Family*, New York, 1853. Contains letter of plaintiff in The Parsons' Cause, the only contemporary account of Henry's speech.

Morgan, George: *The True Patrick Henry*, Philadelphia, 1907. Rather popular biographical treatment but prints Judge Spencer Roane's manuscript in full. This manuscript is one of the important source accounts.

Tyler, Moses Coit: *Patrick Henry*, in American Statesman Series, John T. Morse, Jr., ed., Boston and New York, 1887. A scholarly and unbiased study; probably the best of the Henry biographies.

Wirt, William: *The Life and Character of Patrick Henry*, Philadelphia, 1817. (Numerous subsequent editions.) The first Henry biography. Wirt chose to follow Jefferson rather than the facts. His striving after literary effect makes him very inaccurate in detail and in general interpretation.

Periodicals

American Historical Magazine (New York), 1895 to date.

The Magazine of History, with Notes and Queries, 26 vols., New York, January, 1905, to April, 1922. Publication discontinued.

Special Studies, Monographs, and Addresses

Ambler, Charles Henry: *Sectionalism in Virginia from 1776 to 1861*, Chicago, 1910.

Eckenrode, H. J.: *The Revolution in Virginia*, Boston, 1916. Excellent for an understanding of the social and political forces of Henry's time.

Grigsby, Hugh Blair: *The Virginia Convention of 1776*, Richmond, 1855.

Henry, William Wirt: *Character and Public Career of Patrick Henry*, Charlotte Court House, Virginia, 1867.

Mallory, Louis A.: Patrick Henry: Orator of the American Revolution, University of Wisconsin Ph. D. thesis, Madison, 1938. A detailed study of the life, character, and speaking methods of Patrick Henry; attempts to gather the evidence scattered through the manuscripts and biographies into one work; is the most complete study of Henry as a speaker; contains extensive bibliography.

Henry Clay

by ERNEST J. WRAGE

Henry Clay was born in Hanover County, Virginia, April 12, 1777. He was reared in the family home and attended a rural school; was left in Richmond when his family moved to Kentucky; successively clerked in a store, served as supernumerary in the High Court of Chancery, as amanuensis to George Wythe, Chancellor of the High Court of Chancery, and studied law under Robert Brooke. He was admitted to the Virginia bar, November, 1797; moved to Kentucky; admitted to its bar, March 20, 1798; elected to Kentucky legislature, 1803–1809; appointed to fill out unexpired terms in United States Senate in 1806 and 1809. He was a member of United States House of Representatives, 1811–1825, except for one term, and Speaker of the House for all but two years of his membership; member of United States Peace Commission at Ghent, 1814. Secretary of State, 1825–1829; member of United States Senate, 1831–1842 and 1849–1852. He was candidate for President, 1824, 1832, and 1844; died in Washington, D.C., June 29, 1852.

The winter of 1812–1813 was gloomy for the people and Congress of the United States. The war was going badly. Party spirit and sectionalism were rampant, and morale was low. Federalists were vaporing ·over the foreign policy, which, they insisted, resulted from the chicanery and ambitions of Jefferson, Madison, and jingoistic politicians. In an assault upon the Republicans, Josiah Quincy cried, "Nothing would satisfy them but blood." He recalled the legend of the giant who shouted:

> Fee, faw, fow, fum,
> I smell the blood of an Englishman;
> Dead or alive, I will have some!

He characterized the War Hawks as "young politicians, with the pinfeathers yet unshed, and the shell still sticking upon them—perfectly unfledged. . . . " He contemptuously referred to them as "sycophants, fawning reptiles, who crawled at the feet of the president, and left their filthy slime on the carpet of the palace." Thus Quincy placed before the country an excoriation of men and politics in a speech remarkable for its bitterness and abusiveness.

Sensitive and hot-blooded Republicans charged into battle, repelling insults and charges. On January 8 youthful Henry Clay stepped down from the Speaker's chair to pick up the gauntlet. For two days the house was tense with excitement, and the tall, colorful Kentuckian defended the war and flayed the opposition's lack of patriotism. He eloquently upheld Jefferson and Madison while indicting the fatuous policy of the Federalists. Warming up to his task, in an allusion to Jefferson and Quincy, he cried:

No; his own beloved Monticello is not less moved by the storms that beat against its sides than he hears with composure (if he hears at all) the howlings of the whole British pack, set loose from the Essex kennel! When the gentleman to whom I have been compelled to allude shall have mingled his dust with that of his abused ancestors; when he shall be consigned to oblivion, or, if he lives at all, shall live only in the treasonable annals of a certain junto; the name of Jefferson will be hailed as the second founder of the liberties of this people, and the period of his administration will be looked back to as one of the happiest and brightest epochs in American history.

Clay reviewed the causes of the war and the lack of success that had attended all efforts for an honorable peace. Now, he insisted, it was necessary to prosecute the war with vigor. He concluded in a lofty tone: "In such a cause, with the aid of Providence, we must come out crowned with success; but if we fail, let us fail like men—lash ourselves to our gallant tars, and expire together in one common struggle, fighting for 'seamen's rights and free trade.' "[1]

It was a brilliant argument, yet specious in parts. It combined eulogy and slashing derogation, and its pathos brought tears from the audience. While it drew fire from the opposition, it had the desired effect upon the country at large and contributed greatly to Clay's prestige. Such were the speaking capacities of the dashing Kentuckian, which contributed to party leadership during four decades of the nation's history. Yet this rankly partisan leader achieved still another and greater reputation, that of "the great pacificator." In a different temper he turned these capacities on three occasions to the purpose of compromise. Environment, philosophy, personality, and dialectical skill and versatility contributed to Clay's impress on his age. It is to a consideration of the interplay and influence of these forces that one turns to discover the nature and importance of the speaking and speeches of Henry Clay.

I. *Education and Development as a Speaker*

Henry Clay was born in the dark days of the Revolutionary War and was reared in an era of social and political ferment. His family lived in an area known as the Slashes in Hanover County, Virginia. His father,

---

[1] *Annals of Congress*, Twelfth Congress, second session, pp. 539ff; *ibid.*, pp. 659–676; George D. Prentice, *Biography of Henry Clay* (New York, 1831), pp. 90–91.

a Baptist preacher, established a reputation for being a loud if not particularly important enunciator of democratic and emotional religious doctrine. The Reverend John Clay died when Henry was but four years old, and the care of the seven children and small estate devolved upon Henry's mother, a spirited woman of exemplary qualities.

Henry shared the pleasures and duties common to the children of the neighborhood. His education was entrusted to Peter Deacon, a bibulous English schoolmaster. In a crude crib of logs he learned reading, writing, and arithmetic "as far as practice." The three years with Peter Deacon constituted the only formal education Clay ever received. Years later his biographers fondly related stories of his humble start in life, and Clay himself insisted that he had inherited only "infancy, ignorance, and indigence." More recent studies, however, disclose that by no means did the Clay family live in straitened circumstances, when measured by the yeomanry standards of the Slashes.[1]

The environment in which Henry was reared provided some compensations for a meager formal schooling. Hanover County was rich in traditions of the Revolutionary War and the postwar political revolution. Henry's earliest memories were of a raid by Colonel Tarleton, whose men ransacked Clay's home and thrust their swords into the fresh earth of his father's grave. The impressionable nature of the boy was stirred by thrilling stories of the Revolutionary War, which were related wherever people gathered, at Pamunkey gristmill, in Peter Deacon's school, at Hanover's courthouse, in taverns, or at firesides. Moreover, it was in Hanover County that Patrick Henry was born. The stories of Henry's eloquence stirred Clay's imagination and gave an impetus to his own ardent desires for expression.

Clay left the Slashes at the age of fourteen to clerk in a store in Richmond. About a year later, Henry Watkins, Clay's stepfather, secured for him an appointment as supernumerary in the High Court of Chancery. Here his keenness and personable qualities commended him to the attention of George Wythe, judge of the High Court of Chancery. Wythe needed an amanuensis, and for four years Clay remained with the chancellor, writing his decisions and letters. Young Henry could hardly have found a superior preceptor, for Wythe was one of the wisest, noblest, and most distinguished men in America. He was a liberal in social and political thought, as well as a profound classical scholar, who delighted his secretary by reading aloud from Homer and other authors of antiquity, although the youth understood not a word of the languages. Clay had the run of the chancellor's library, and Wythe directed his protégé's attention to Harris's

[1] For an excellent treatment of Clay's early life and background, see Bernard Mayo, *Henry Clay* (Boston, 1937), pp. 1–44; see also Zachary F. Smith and Mary Rogers Clay, *The Clay Family* (Louisville, *Filson Club Publication* 14, 1899).

Hermes, Tooke's *Diversions of Purley*, Bishop Lowth's *Grammar*, and other works. While this program did not afford the systematic instruction of a college, it gave Clay a taste of philosophy, literature, history, and law. In later years he spoke with gratitude of his intellectual improvement under the influence of Wythe's instruction, advice, and example.[1]

Then, as now, the legal profession afforded the most favorable opportunities for anyone with ambitions for public life. Clay was suited to the profession, and it was "Chancellor Wythe and Governor Brooke, who, by their joint advice, persuaded him, at the age of nineteen, to undertake the study of law." He left Wythe in order to enter not only the office but the home of Robert Brooke, formerly governor of the state and later its attorney general. Again it was Clay's good fortune to enjoy the personal interest of a distinguished and well-educated patron.

While in Richmond Clay became acquainted with such socially and politically important young men as John Marshall, Spencer Roane, and Bushrod Washington. His associations with Wythe and Brooke introduced him to cultured society; and the increasing permeability of a once rigid social structure made the personable youth highly acceptable to the elite. They held animated discussions on man, his rights, his government, its policies and proper limitations. Nor were the discussions confined to private conversations. Virginia's legal and political machinery was oiled by a variety of oratory that William Ellery Channing called the best he had ever heard. Political campaigns, *viva voce* election periods, court trials, and legislative sessions provided innumerable opportunities for public speaking, and it was a brand of oratory that contrasted sharply with that variety "which struts around the heart without ever entering it." The outstanding exponent of impassioned address was Patrick Henry. Clay heard him on two occasions and was greatly impressed by his voice, gestures, facial expression, and forcefulness. The spirited Virginians of that day shone with distinction in political circles. One explanation is that

Oratory was esteemed the first attribute of superior minds, and was assiduously cultivated. There were few newspapers, and the press had not attained the controlling power over the public mind as now. Political information was disseminated chiefly by public speaking, and every one aspiring to lead in the land was expected to be a fine speaker. . . . [2]

It is probably no overstatement, therefore, that Richmond's Rhetorical Society "was the pride of the community, and the gossip of all circles."

[1] Clay to B. B. Minor, May 3, 1851, a letter on his early associations with Wythe, in B. B. Minor, ed., *Decisions of Cases in Virginia by the High Court of Chancery* (Richmond, Va., 1852), pp. xxxii–xxxiv; *Annals of Congress*, Fifteenth Congress, first session, p. 1614.

[2] W. H. Sparks, *The Memories of Fifty Years* (Philadelphia, 1870), p. 22.

It was organized for the purpose "of exciting a spirit of mental improvement" among the young men by means "of recitation and debate." Clay was said to be not only chiefly responsible for the existence of the club but also "its animating spirit, and the star that gave it lustre."[1]

The excitement of the courts and legislative chambers that he visited, as well as that of the rhetorical society, was more congenial to Clay's temperament than the less ostentatious scholarly pursuits of Chancellor Wythe. After completing one year of legal training under Brooke, he decided to exchange the restrictions of a settled Virginia for the freedom and opportunities of a sparsely populated Kentucky. For a keen and industrious young man, Kentucky was a "lawyer's paradise."

Upon his arrival in Kentucky in November, 1797, Clay spent some time in study and establishing himself before beginning practice. He welcomed an opportunity to join a debating society as a means to both these ends. Shortly after his arrival he attended a meeting that proved to be particularly lively. Just as the vote was to be taken, Clay remarked *sub voce* that the subject had by no means been exhausted. The comment was overheard, and the chairman was urged to permit Mr. Clay to speak before putting the question to a vote. Clay did not have the presence of mind to resist the appeal, and he arose with extraordinary embarrassment. From what occurred it was apparent that he had been making speeches privately to imaginary juries, for in his confusion he began, "Gentlemen of the Jury." He was immediately aware of his mistake, which greatly increased his confusion. Several times he stammeringly repeated the address. Finally he collected himself and delivered an impromptu speech that delighted his audience and won for him the immediate and favorable attention of the community.[2]

Clay worked diligently to become an effective speaker. Years later he said to a class of law students:

I owe my success in life to one single fact—namely, that at an early period I commenced and continued for some years the practice of daily reading and speaking the contents of some historical or scientific book. These off-hand efforts were sometimes made in a cornfield; at others in the forest; and not infrequently in some distant barn, with the horse and ox for my only auditors. It is to this practice of the art of all arts that I am indebted for the primary and leading impulses that stimulated my progress and have shaped and moulded my entire destiny.[3]

[1] Calvin Colton, *The Life and Times of Henry Clay* (New York, 1846), I, 25.

[2] Prentice, *op. cit.*, pp. 8–9; Colton, *op. cit.*, I, 78–79.

[3] Charles H. Peck, *The Jacksonian Epoch* (New York, 1899), p. 17; Gilbert J. Clark, *Life Sketches of Eminent Lawyers* (Kansas City, 1895), I, 164; E. G. Parker, "Henry Clay as an Orator," *Putnam's Monthly Magazine*, 3 (1854): 499.

This statement and the subsequent events of his life show that Clay learned to speak by speaking. His program of self-improvement and his professional and political career provided practical experience in public speaking without reference to the metaphysics, logic, or rhetoric of the past. In later years Clay spoke with deep regret of his "neglected education," which "was improved by my own irregular exertions, without the benefit of systematic instruction."[1] He never acquired a reputation for being "a hard student," yet Amos Kendall, who tutored Clay's children, noted that the Clay library included "a multitude of miscellaneous books."[2] While Clay was never a profound student of history, he enjoyed reading it, drew from it in his speaking, and urged his sons to make a study of it. His respect for education is admirably revealed by the care with which he advised his sons in their educational programs and by his salutary efforts in behalf of Transylvania University.

From the time Clay began his busy professional and political career, his life was shaped primarily by influences and experiences that were practical rather than speculative and academic. While sensationally successful in law, his achievements were distinguished more by brilliance and persuasive appeal than by depth and breadth in legal knowledge.[3] The impact of his environment and his restless ambition exerted greater influence on his political thinking than did intellectual disciplines. He frequently expressed impatience with abstract and theoretical discussions on political matters. True wisdom, he felt "should look to what is practical in human affairs. . . . "[4]

Clay's development as a speaker, then, was stimulated and shaped by home and early environmental influences, associations and study with

[1] *The Works of Henry Clay* (Calvin Colton, ed., New York and London, 1904), IX, 362. Those volumes, which contain correspondence and speeches, will hereafter be cited as *Works of Clay.*

[2] *Autobiography of Amos Kendall* (William Stickney, ed., Boston, 1872), pp. 115, 122. A sales catalogue of a part of Clay's library lists books largely on law and history. There is one entry of a book on elocution: "#224. Early Western School Book. *The American Orator:* containing Rules and Directions to improve Youth and Others in the Ornamental and Useful Art of Eloquence (with Selections). By A Teacher. 12 mo. old half sheep and boards (some pp. discolored). Lexington (K.); Printed and Sold by Joseph Charles, and by all the Merchants in the Western Country, 1807 (*Rare Books, Broadsides, Autographs From the Library of the Eminent Statesman Henry Clay*, to be sold at auction Tuesday and Wednesday, April 5th and 6th, 1910 by the Merwin-Clayton Sales Company, 20–24 East 20th Street, New York)."
At the time this book was published Clay had already acquired a reputation as a speaker. It probably had no influence on his thinking and speaking, if he bothered to read it at all.

[3] Even Prentice, a devoted biographer, claimed no more for him. *Op. cit.*, pp. 11–12.

[4] *Register of Debates*, Twenty-fifth Congress, first session, p. 259; *Annals of Congress*, Sixteenth Congress, first session, p. 2048; Clay to Francis Brooke, Jan. 13, 1838, *Works of Clay*, V, 424.

distinguished Virginians, participation in debating societies, and by experiences of a long professional and political career. This background gave an eminently practical cast to his outlook on human affairs and to his speaking, a highly utilitarian purpose.

II. *Personality and Character*

Clay's remarkable personality contributed immeasurably to his success in politics and speaking. Not all were as circumspect as General Glascock, who, upon taking his seat in Congress, was approached by a friend: "General, may I introduce you to Henry Clay?" "No, Sir!" was the stern response. "I am his adversary, and choose not to subject myself to his fascination."[1]

It is worth repeating that Clay's early life was shaped by the eighteenth century romanticism of old Virginia. The liberal attitudes and customs of those among whom he lived were in marked contrast to the frosty puritanism of New England. The rustic youth had been impressed by the cultured manners of Wythe and his friends, manners that he studied and cultivated until they became second nature to him. He "inherited that Virginia geniality which, as it ripened with his years, made him an idol among Northern and Western multitudes who knew neither the source nor secret of his charm."[2] The chivalric elements of old Virginia united with bold frontier characteristics to produce in him "a sort of Kentuckyism."

Clay was not a handsome man. William Cullen Bryant, after a day at the Capitol, pictured him as "a tall, thin, narrow-shouldered, light-complexioned man, with a long nose, a little turned up at the end, and his hair combed back from the edge of his forehead." Clay's face mirrored every emotion he experienced. Harriet Martineau thought none of thirty portraits did him justice, and the suggestion was made to Joel Hart, since Clay's facial expression changed so rapidly and totally, that the artist should fix upon his mind one particular but striking expression and then paint it. Set deep in Clay's head were small but intensely "looking" gray eyes. On the lips of his large and rather unmanageable mouth there usually lurked an incipient smile. Years of social intercourse with distinguished people gave the effect of ease and nonchalance to his management of a loose-jointed and angular frame. He had the genial, jaunty air of Lord Palmerston. When aroused, he would draw himself up to his full height of more than six feet and tower majestically over his audience. Wiry and virile, he was by no means robust, and the effects of strenuous

[1] Horace Greeley, *Recollections of a Busy Life* (New York, 1868), p. 250.
[2] Henry Adams, *History of the United States* (New York, 1889–1891), I, 133–34.

living undermined his health early in his career. With regularity he played upon the sympathies of his hearers by references to fatigue and ill-health.

James O. Harrison studied Clay closely and attributed much of his effectiveness in speaking to temperament, referring to him as the most emotional man he ever knew. So sensitive was Clay that "a word, a touch, a memory" might operate on his nervous system to produce a response ranging from overwhelming impetuosity in expression to a lachrymose condition.[1] He loved the stage and thrilled to an audience. He derived intense emotional satisfaction from speaking, as is suggested by newspaper accounts, which frequently describe him as speaking with "visible emotion." It is interesting and significant that the warm-blooded and impulsive Kentuckian, once leader of the War Hawks, should later have gained a reputation as "the great pacificator." Often his hot temper provoked undignified altercations on legislative floors and twice it drove him to the dueling field; yet his cool calculations and unfailing patience made him an outstanding Speaker of the House of Representatives and a peer of parliamentarians. There were these antithetical characteristics in his kaleidoscopic personality.

Clay's mind was keen, agile, and resourceful. Even opponents conceded his brilliance. Colonel Richard M. Johnson, an erstwhile political ally, admitted that in those situations that tested mental resources, Clay appeared to advantage. "I have been associated with him on committees in connection with Calhoun, Lowndes, Cheves, Webster, and other distinguished individuals, but Clay was always the master-spirit."[2] His mind was "powerful but irregular," which is to say it had never been adequately disciplined by scholarly pursuits and that his brilliance did not always compensate for this deficiency. It is evident, however, that he was a man of many ideas, who at times showed vision and creativeness in grappling with practical problems of his age.

Clay's unquailing courage and self-confidence were asserted in a type of leadership that compelled party members to fall in line or quit camp. While the political frustrations that he and the Whigs experienced during the administrations of Jackson, Van Buren, and Tyler often made him peevish, fractious, dictatorial, and even insolent, as a rule his sense of humor prevailed, and he would delight associates with his urbanity. Young Thurlow Weed, for instance, after meeting Clay came away fascinated by the statesman and thoroughly pleased with himself. A chat with Clay was "almost enough to make a man think of 'running for Congress.'" It was

[1] From a photostat of a reply to James Parton, Clay MSS; James O. Harrison, Special Scrapbook, pp. 33–36, Harrison MSS.

[2] From the *Richmond Whig*, quoted in Epes Sargent and Horace Greeley, *The Life and Public Services of Henry Clay* (Auburn, 1852), p. 318.

said that "none knew better than he the wondrous power in seeming trifles; how much a word, a tone, a look can accomplish."[1]

Human and cordial though he was, Clay made all feel "that it was not the familiarity of a commonplace personage, but that of a high-bred gentleman who, from his own inherent graciousness and spirit of good-fellowship, chose to be thus affable." He insisted upon respectful distance and was accessible only "when approached through proper mediums."[2] In short, the social behavior of the high-spirited Kentuckian reflected his associations with gentlemen of the Old Dominion.

Clay's friends and admirers were legion. He was held in high esteem by men such as Lafayette, Jefferson, and Madison, and his every political misfortune was a source of deep personal grief to millions of Americans. He could exclaim with considerable truth: "Surely no man was ever blessed with more ardent and devoted friends than I am. . . . "

In light of his popularity, the disappointments and failures of his political career suggest an anomaly that invites explanation. The answers may be suggested by a consideration of other aspects of his character and of the vicissitudes of political life. His friends easily excused his faults as "*les plus beaux défauts de la nature humaine.*" Less charitable was a great and militant political opposition that spared no effort in giving publicity to his shortcomings or in manufacturing scurrilous charges. Clay was vituperatively denounced by press and speakers as "a profane swearer, a gambler, a sabbath breaker, a common drunkard, guilty of perjury, a robber, an adulterer and a murderer!"[3] This abuse continued for a quarter of a century until Clay bitterly complained, "I believe I have been charged with every crime enumerated on the Decalogue. . . . "[4]

As a circuit-riding lawyer Clay was known to be "a rather wildish fellow," and stories like the one of his "terpsichorean performance on the table" after the bottle had passed freely, for which he paid, without demur, the price of $120 for broken china, hardly improved his reputation.[5] Clay frankly enjoyed the social amenities of this world and was bent on having his share of them. His passion for cards was notorious. Especially in his early

[1] *Autobiography of Thurlow Weed* (Harriet A. Weed, ed., Boston, 1883), p. 181; James Parton, *Famous Americans of Recent Times* (Boston, 1879), pp. 5–6; Charles W. March, *Reminiscences of Congress* (New York, 1850), p. 42.

[2] Oliver Dyer, *Great Senators of the United States Forty Years Ago* (New York, 1889), pp. 218–219; George W. Bungay, *Off-hand Takings: Or Crayon Sketches of the Noticeable Men of Our Age* (New York, 1854), p. 22.

[3] For a summary of current charges leveled against Clay, see *Lexington* (Ky.) *Observer and Reporter*, Sept. 7, 1844.

[4] Clay to John M. Clayton, Aug. 22, 1844, Clayton MSS.

[5] R. T. Coleman, "Jo Daviess, of Kentucky," *Harper's New Monthly Magazine*, 21 (June–November, 1860): 352.

years he devoted much time to poker and brag. He once admitted winning as much as $1,500 in an evening and losing $600 in another.[1] As did other gentlemen in Kentucky, Clay owned race horses, and his interest in the tracks gave credence to tales of his gambling. There was a measure of truth in Adams's sharp criticism that "in politics, as in private life, Clay is essentially a gamester. . . . "[2] Being amazingly popular with women, it could be expected that he would be charged with irregularities, though no convincing evidence has been advanced to prove the claims. He deplored dueling, but his sensitiveness to personal honor and the conventions of his locale involved him in two encounters. In short, that which distinguished him for good fellowship and spirited living among broad-minded Kentuckians or Washington sophisticates was repeated, heightened in insinuation, or distorted to serve as political calumny to the nation at large. It is undoubtedly true that on election days there were thousands who voted against Clay on grounds of his moral delinquency.

Some animosity toward Clay developed from the personal nature of his speeches and from altercations into which his hot temper tricked him. For instance, he and venerable Senator Smith of Maryland once wrangled over the latter's position on the tariff question. Clay goaded the oldster by chanting doggerel:

> Old politicians chew on wisdom past,
> And *totter* on in business to the last.

"Totter, sir," cried Smith. "I totter. Though some twenty years older than the gentleman, I can yet stand firm, and am yet able to correct his errors. I could take a view of the gentleman's course, which would show how inconsistent he has been." "Take it, sir, take it—I dare you," shouted Clay. Adjournment was necessary to end the disorderliness of the scene.[3]

Clay had many a brush with Thomas Hart Benton and John C. Calhoun. In 1832 Benton upbraided Clay for a speech in which the latter's references to Jackson were said to be wanting in courtesy, to be indecorous and disrespectful. Clay responded with heat, observing that when "some Senators" rose to speak, "The galleries are quickly emptied, with whatever else the Senate chamber may then be filled." He added jeeringly, "I cannot at this period of my life, go with the member from Missouri and his Indian blankets to Boone's Lick, to be taught the rules and practice of politeness."

[1] *William Plumer's Memorandum of Proceedings in the United States Senate* 1803–1807 (Everett Somerville Brown, ed., New York, 1923), p. 608; *Memoirs of John Quincy Adams* (Charles Francis Adams, ed., Philadelphia, 1874), III, 32; William Henry Perrin, *The Pioneer Press of Kentucky* (Louisville, *Filson Club Publication* 3, 1888), pp. 15–16.

[2] J. Q. Adams, *Memoirs*, V, 59.

[3] *Register of Debates*, Twenty-second Congress, first session, pp. 296–297.

He reminded "Old Bullion" of the fight that had once taken place between Jackson and the Benton brothers: "I never complained of the President beating a brother of mine after he was prostrated and lying apparently lifeless." One taunt led to another, and it was with great difficulty that the chair finally restored order.[1]

Between 1837 and 1840 Calhoun broke his unnatural alliance with the Whigs. The process of separation was marked by sharp skirmishes between him and Clay. A head-on clash finally interrupted the *entente cordiale* between them for years. Calhoun had insisted that Clay came to him on bended knee, asking his support in the tariff compromise negotiations of 1833. He claimed that he once had Clay on his back and was his master. Clay was infuriated, and the punch line of his dramatic rejoinder created a sensation: "He my master! He my master! He my master! Sir, I *would not own him for my slave!*"[2] As Benton noted, Clay's frequent personal attacks delighted the galleries more than the Senate itself.

Fundamentally more damaging to his reputation and influence, however, was a general suspicion that Clay had strong personal ambitions that guided his political course. To a large part of the public this suspicion was confirmed by events attending the Presidential election of 1824. After having been eliminated from a four-way race, Clay was placed in the precarious position of president maker by virtue of his influence in the House of Representatives. When Clay decided to support Adams, the chagrined Jackson forces circulated the story that he had sold out to Adams and that his price was the office of Secretary of State. As it developed, Adams did offer the position to Clay, who accepted. This mistake in political judgment seemed to give credence to the charge. His opponents clamored "Bargain and Corruption" and for the rest of his days Clay was kept busy writing letters and giving speeches, denying the charge and explaining the circumstances that gave rise to it.[3] It haunted him in his dreams, impaired his health, and drove him to the dueling field to make John Randolph answer for a speech in which he referred to Adams and Clay as "the coalition of Blifil and Black George—the combination, unheard of till then, of the puritan with the black-leg."[4]

The masses were in no mood for any rational explanation of the affair and accepted without question the guileful story that "Old Hickory" had

---

[1] *Ibid.*, pp. 1293–1296.

[2] William Mathews, *Oratory and Orators* (Chicago, 1879), pp. 313–315; *Congressional Globe*, Twenty-sixth Congress, first session, p. 97.

[3] There is a vast amount of literature on this episode. *Cf.* Glyndon Van Deusen, *The Life of Henry Clay* (Boston, 1937), pp. 160–195, 211–229, and Marquis James, *The Life of Andrew Jackson* (New York, 1938), pp. 414–445.

[4] *Register of Debates*, Nineteenth Congress, first session, p. 401.

been robbed. The charge gave rise to a concerted attack on Clay's political principles and policies. Not only was he made out as one who cheated the wishes of the people in the Presidential contest, but his entire political career came under review. He was represented as having consistently opposed the best interest of the masses in favor of special interests and the classes. In the party division that followed, Jackson assumed the leadership of the proletariat, while Clay was left to champion the conservatives and other elements of the Whig conglomerate, the party that smugly claimed the support of " . . . nine tenths of the virtue, intelligence, and respectability of the nation. . . . "

Throughout his life Clay was the object of both unbounded affection and political obloquy, but wherever he went, crowds gave him every evidence of admiration and affection. There was, however, an element of ironic truth in Shepperd's hyperbole that Clay could get more men to listen to him and fewer to vote for him than anyone else in America.[1]

III. *The Kentucky Lawyer and Politician*

Clay's development and career as a speaker, lawyer, and politician should be viewed in relation to the character, temper, and institutions of the people of early Kentucky. After the Revolutionary War, the adventuresome and hardy folk of the Piedmont and mountain areas near the seaboard migrated to Kentucky "to see for themselves, as they could not think of being confined to the sterile mountains of Virginia where only small parcels of fertile land could be found in any one place."[2] It was the spirit, attitudes, and behavior of these people, generated in an environment of social ferment, that produced the distinctive traits often referred to as the "Kentucky personality." Travelers noted that among them there existed a spirit of "high independence" and "quick temper." They were a "choleric, vehement, tenacious" group of people with a "strain of fierceness" in their demands for personal democracy, and "the equality existing elsewhere in theory, exists here in fact." Curious, bold, assertive, and frequently objectionable in their behavior, the Kentuckians were also "frank, affable, polite, and hospitable in a high degree." Lexington, where Clay settled, was a thriving city with a population of 2,400 in 1800, the "emporium" of the frontier, the metropolis of the West, and an outpost of culture. Here the turbulence of frontier democracy in the persons of its hunters, boatmen, farmers, and tradesmen rubbed shoulders with the scions of the "most respectable families of Virginia" who had migrated to Kentucky. If, as it is

[1] Richard Malcom Johnston and William Hand Browne, *Life of Alexander H. Stephens* (Philadelphia, 1878), p. 184.

[2] Robert B. McAfee, "The Life and Times of Robert B. McAfee and His Family and Connections," *The Register of the Kentucky State Historical Society* (Frankfort, Ky.), 25 (1927): 13.

said, Clay's "culture was gained largely from the society of men with whom he came in contact," his Kentucky neighbors furnished a rich source book for the study of elemental and driving forces in a new America. A general insistence on personal democracy was expressed by a keen interest in the courts, political assemblies, hustings, and barbecues. Commenting on his trip through the West, James Flint thought here "the United States certainly opens an extensive school for eloquence."[1]

The Kentucky bar was remarkable for its many members and the brilliance of many of them. It seemed as though every man were intent on having at least one of his children "a disciple of Coke, or a fomenter of village vexation." The concentration of talent was not fortuitous. Endless land litigations and cases growing out of hard fights—"fist & skull-biting, gouging &"—made law a lucrative profession. In fact, the quality of the bar was superior to that of the bench. One explanation is that the Kentuckians took steps to limit professionalism in the courts. The legislature provided that two laymen should sit on the bench with the judge, and no decision could be reached without the consent of these assistants, an arrangement that Clay called a "buck-eye" judge and his associates. The intolerance of backwoodsmen for "men who split hairs, or scrupled over methods of reaching the right" permitted justice and equity to be meted out through common sense and the plausible.[2] The backwoods judges and juries could often be cajoled, persuaded, or bullied into making decisions and permitting outlandish practices.

In this setting Clay's talents shone brightly. As a fledgling lawyer, he whetted his talents on a Kentucky magistrate of little learning in a case in which he defended a man against a charge of stealing hogs. The evidence was against his client, but in a burst of inspiration Clay recalled an English decision dealing with a contested will, which he had once copied for Wythe. He recited it with such impressiveness that the befuddled magistrate freed the prisoner.[3] One of Clay's most remarkable coups was a defense of Willis, who was accused of a particularly atrocious murder. Clay succeeded in dividing the jury, and a motion was granted for a new trial. At the next trial, Clay pointed out that the decision of the jury would in no way affect the outcome of the case, since no man could twice be placed in jeopardy of his life for the same offense. This was a line of reasoning unfamiliar to the

---

[1] John Melish, *Travels in the United States of America* (Philadelphia, 1812), II, 208; Frederick J. Turner, "Contributions of the West to American Democracy," *The Atlantic Monthly*, 91 (January, 1903): 85–89; Charles A. Murray, *Travels in North America* (London 1839), I, 218ff.; James Flint, *Letters from America*—1822, in *Early Western Travels 1748–1846* (R. G. Thwaites, ed., Cleveland, 1904), IX, 277.

[2] Turner, *op. cit.*, p. 88.

[3] Joseph M. Rogers, *The True Henry Clay* (Philadelphia and London, 1904), pp. 28–29.

court, and it forbade his continuing it. Clay professed astonishment and indignation. If he were not permitted to defend a man's life in line of duty as he understood it, he would not continue the case. He picked up his bag and books and dramatically flounced from the courtroom. The judge was thoroughly bewildered and frightened by the awful responsibility Clay had plumped into his legal lap. He hastily sent a messenger who invited Clay to return and proceed with the case. Clay graciously consented and had little difficulty in securing an acquittal.[1]

There are many references to Clay's cases in biographies and newspapers, and many of the stories are sensational in nature. In all fairness it should be emphasized that Clay was not a mere pettifogger engaged in cheating the gallows. He was generous with advice and services to the poor and to slaves suing for freedom. At the hazard of his safety, and perhaps at the risk of his life, he broke up a gang of Kentucky "Regulators," who terrorized the community. A temporary commission as attorney for the state compelled him to ask the death penalty for a poor but high-minded slave. He won his case, but the episode opposed his natural sympathies, and he resigned his commission in disgust. Nor were Clay's talents limited to criminal cases. Two years after he began practice he won his case in a sawmill dispute, and "This event at once established Mr. Clay's practice and in a little time he was at the head of the Bar and was employed on one side of almost every suit in the Fayette courts."[2] His assiduity in prosecuting civil suits won for him a reputation as a shrewd and capable counselor. He merited the confidence and business of such men as John Breckinridge, Ninian Edwards, and Colonel Hart. While still under thirty, he was engaged by Aaron Burr in a trial in which the latter was acquitted of conspiracy.

Clay developed into a trial lawyer in the "grand tradition," and his fame became legendary throughout Kentucky and the Ohio Valley. In 1818, it was said " (Why) if we had a Roman Amphitheatre for a court-room, that would hold twenty thousand people, I think it could be filled just about these days, to hear a speech from the lips of Henry Clay!"[3]

When he appeared in defense of one of Kentucky's appellate judges, at an impeachment trial, "the lobbies were crowded with ladies and gentlemen to hear the defense of the judge's counsel," and even though the speaking was not his best ("yet by no means contemptible"), the spectators went

---

[1] Prentice, *op. cit.*, pp. 14–16; Daniel Mallory, *The Life and Speeches of the Hon. Henry Clay* (New York, 1843), I, 15. Later, Willis, when very drunk, hailed Clay on the street. Clay shook his head and commented: "Ah, Willis, poor fellow, I fear I have saved too many like you, who ought to be hanged."—Colton, *op. cit.*, I, 86, 96.

[2] McAfee, *op. cit.*, pp. 218–219.

[3] *Lexington* (Ky.) *Observer and Reporter*, Feb. 12, 1848.

away convinced that "he stands unrivalled in Kentucky, perhaps in the Western World—a happy growth, of his own happy soil."[1] In Ohio the lawyers would come from every part of the state to listen; and "such was the curiosity of members to hear him, that a quorum was not formed in either house of the Assembly, so the speakers of both houses adjourned their respective houses."[2]

While crumbling court records contain none of Clay's forensic speeches, the nature of his pleas to juries may be suggested by brief accounts of two cases. In 1829 Clay defended young Wickliffe, who had shot the editor of the *Kentucky Gazette*, after the latter had menaced him with a cane. In their eagerness to hear Clay, the spectators flocked to Lexington, and "by 8 o'clock every seat and every window was occupied, and the gallery crowded with ladies. . . . The press was so great in all the avenues leading to the bar, that it was with difficulty the sheriff could make way through the solid mass for the Judge and Jury." Particularly effective was Clay's insistence upon the natural right of self-preservation, a basic privilege of man, and his observation that the day of the trial was the anniversary of the Declaration of Independence, a day symbolic to all liberty-loving Americans. For 2½ hours he addressed the jury and then sent them away with a throbbing desire to extend special liberties to his client. In seven minutes they returned with an acquittal.[3]

In the latter part of his life, Clay defended a distant relative, Cassius M. Clay. Cassius had seriously carved up an antagonist with a bowie knife in a political brawl and was promptly tried for mayhem. His antislavery sympathies were extremely unpopular in Kentucky and augured ill for his chances with the jurors. Again Clay based his plea on those elemental rights that Kentuckians understood and respected. As he talked he stood close to the jury box, intense in voice and gestures, scarcely moving more than a step or two. Had not Cassius acted upon the "eternal laws of self-defense—which come only of God, and which none but He can annul, judge, or punish? Standing, as he did, without aiders or abettors, and without popular sympathy; with the fatal pistol of conspired murderers pointed at his heart, would you have had him meanly and cowardly fly? Or would you have had him to do just what he did do—there stand in defense, or there fall?" Clay drew himself higher and with great dignity looked directly, with flashing eye, at prisoner Cassius, and to the breathless court he delivered his final pronouncement. "And if he had not, he would not have been *worthy of*

---

[1] D. W. Wilson to George Wilson, Nov. 19, 1821, Durrett MSS.

[2] F. P. Blair to J. J. Crittenden, Jan. 6, 1821, Crittenden MSS; *Kentucky Reporter*, Jan. 28, 1822.

[3] *Kentucky Reporter*, July 8, 1829; Clay to J. S. Johnston, July 18, 1829, *Works of Clay*, IV, 240; Colton, *op. cit.*, I, 90–93; D. C. Humphreys to J. S. Johnston, n.d., Draper MSS.

6 1 7

the name which he bears!" The jury "had only to retire, write a verdict of not guilty, and return it to the court."[1]

During the early years Clay rode the circuit, engaged in arduous legal battles, and spent long evenings in conviviality. In these relationships he grew keen in sensing the impulses, desires, and forces that motivate men. He learned when "to confine himself to severe argument, when to indulge in the playfulness of humor," when to intimidate his victim with a "scorching blast of his indignation," and when to charm and placate juries with a beguiling fascination. He knew considerable law, as is attested by his competence before the United States Supreme Court,[2] but his extraordinary success was distinguished especially by the persuasive force he exercised on judges and juries. Conversely, each judge and jury served to provide experiences that contributed to his own development in speaking.

Despite his busy life as a lawyer, Clay soon won his spurs in political speaking. Kentucky was incensed by the enactment of the Alien and Sedition Laws in 1798. " . . . John Adams had scarcely a friend left in Kentucky, and few were more noisy than Mr. Clay against him, & Alien & Sedition Law . . . ," wrote McAfee.[3] One July day George Nicholas spoke on these obnoxious laws to a great crowd at Maxwell Springs. When he had finished, a shout went up for Clay, and the young lawyer, a resident of Lexington for less than a year, was hustled into a wagon. He plunged into a denunciation of "the hated laws with bold invectives." So successfully did he interpret the attitudes and emotions of his audience that the speech was received in deep silence. Slowly the applause developed, then increased to an ovation. Federalist speakers were refused a hearing. The crowd seized Nicholas and Clay and drew them through the streets in a carriage.[4] Two years later, Clay gave the principal address on the anniversary of American independence, and by 1803 he had become a likely candidate for public office.

Campaign and election days were of special interest to Kentuckians. Speeches were given at open air meetings and barbecues prior to and during the period of actual voting. The temper of public gatherings tested the ingenuity and resourcefulness of any speaker.

---

[1] Cassius Clay, *The Life of Cassius Mercellus Clay* (Cincinnati, 1886), I, 88–89.

[2] Webster spoke disparagingly of Clay as a lawyer. He thought Clay had talent and a "smattering of law." Justice Story and Chief-Justice Marshall, on the other hand, thought that Clay showed considerable ability at that bar. *Cf.* Peter Harvey, *Remininscences and Anecdotes of Daniel Webster* (Boston, 1877), pp. 214–218; Joseph Story to Mr. Justice Todd, Mar. 14, 1823, in *Life and Letters of Joseph Story* (W. W. Story, ed., Boston, 1851), I, 423; Sargent and Greeley, *op. cit.*, p. 315.

[3] *Op. cit.*, p. 219.

[4] Prentice, *op. cit.*, pp. 23–24; Mallory, *op. cit.*, I, 16–18; Robert McNutt McElroy, *Kentucky in the Nation's History* (New York, 1909), pp. 224–226.

Cock fighting was a *common* & favorite sport in those days—Horse racing was almost everyday business—The people indulged in almost all sorts of amusements— playing cards—fives or ball—throwing long bullets, & even pulling an old Ganders head off, was no uncommon sport—shooting, running foot races—wrestling— hopping–&c, &c. was practiced at all public gatherings—a *fist fight* followed as a matter of course—it must be a "fist fight" & nothing else.[1]

Such situations called for a "brand" of speaking that could successfully compete with counterattractions, rival candidates, and hecklers.

Clay was nominated for the state legislature in 1803, "without my knowledge or previous consent," as he put it. While voting was in progress, he staged a dramatic, last-minute appearance on the field. His "exceedingly pertinent" remarks delighted his audience and won the day. A part of the audience was made up of riflemen attending militia muster. "Young man," said one bushy hunter in buckskin, "you want to go to the legislature, I see?" Clay assented. "Are you a good shot?" asked the hunter. "The best in the country," boldly asserted Clay, who actually was a poor marksman. "Then you shall go; but you must give us a specimen of your skill; we must see you shoot." Clay hedged: "I never shoot any rifle but my own, and that is at home." "No matter," said the hunter, putting a rifle in Clay's hands. "If you can shoot any gun, you can shoot old Bess." For a moment Clay was nonplused, then "acted on the principle of Hoyle." "Well, put up your mark, put up your mark," he cried with an assumed bravado. He carefully aimed and fired. The bullet pierced the target near the center. The hunters were satisfied, and Clay was secretly astonished. "A chance shot," clamored some of his opponents. "Let him try again." Clay knew his advantage and also the improbability of another good shot. "Beat that, beat that," he noisily retorted, "and then I will."[2] Such boldness, spirit, and affability won for him a stock of popularity among the hunters and farmers of Kentucky. At the same time he was able to win the confidence of the influential people in Lexington. As William Littell put it in his biblical style:

Now Henry was an exceeding wise counsellor, the spirit of discretion & eloquence was in him; and when he spake, all the people marvelled at his wisdom: So the merchants and people of Lexington chose Henry to be their chief.[3]

Clay developed, as his brother-in-law noticed, "a rage for electioneering." Never was he denied the support of his Fayette district for any office he desired.

[1] Micah Taul, "Memoirs of Micah Taul," *The Register of the Kentucky State Historical Society* (Frankfort, Ky.), 27 (1929): 359.
[2] Mallory, *op. cit.*, I, 18–20.
[3] William Littell, *An Epistle from William, Surnamed Littell, to the People of the Realm of Kentucky* (Frankfort, 1806), p. 5.

Although the *Journals of the Kentucky House of Representatives* contain no reports of Clay's speeches, enough evidence is available to show that his ability in debate and in political tactics soon made him an outstanding member of that body. He fought successfully for the recharter of the Kentucky Insurance Company, an infant banking institution, against the opposition of coonskin democracy under the leadership of Felix Grundy. "Thus did Felix and Henry assail the chiefs of the people with cunning speeches for many days, insomuch that chiefs were astonished and confounded; and the *Wise Men* and all the people marvelled at their wisdom and subtlety."[1] He worked to have the capitol of the state moved to Lexington, and although he was unsuccessful, it was said of one of his speeches that "the effect, at the time, was great; and some good people conceded, that they saw the seat of government on the road to Lexington, where the orator resided."[2] In an effective speech he successfully resisted the hot-headed legislators who wished to prohibit the application of British law treatises in Kentucky courts. It is evident that the legislators appreciated his abilities, for he was appointed to fill out two unexpired terms in the United States Senate, as well as to the speakership of the lower house of the legislature.

The Kentucky environment proved congenial to Clay's background, temperament, interests, and ambitions. The free and easy manner in which courts were conducted and the vibrant and personal political democracy of the state afforded both unusual opportunities and a proving ground for developing power through speech. One is reminded of Ben Hardin's advice to Daniel Webster: "Sir, if you will come and settle in Kentucky, and learn our mode of speaking, you will be an orator equal to any Greece or Rome ever produced." Later Webster is said to have replied: "Would to God I had taken your advice."[3]

IV. *As a National Spokesman*

Clay's fame as a speaker was achieved in political address and debate. He once indicated his dislike for lecturing and ceremonial speaking, insisting he had " . . . neither time, taste, nor, perhaps, talents for compositions suited to such occasions." It is his career as a national spokesman, particularly, that invites inquiry into the questions with which he dealt and the types of speech situations he faced.

Clay's Premises. As has been stated, Clay's basic premises were drawn "from the world around him." In investigating this point, it should be noted that he was born and reared in an era when Colonial America was

[1] *Ibid.*, p. 6.
[2] Humphrey Marshall, *The History of Kentucky* (Frankfort, Ky., 1824), II, 9–10.
[3] Lucius P. Little, *Ben Hardin: His Times and Contemporaries* (Louisville, 1887), p. 355.

giving way to a changing order, optimistic in its point of view. Clay's early political attitudes are reflected in a passage that he declaimed with delight from Sir James Mackintosh's *Vindiciae Gallicae*.

It was time, (said the eloquent Scotsman) that the human powers, so long occupied by subordinate objects and inferior arts, should mark the commencement of a new era in history, by giving birth to the art of improving government, and increasing the civil happiness of man. It was time, as it has been wisely and eloquently said, that legislators, instead of that narrow and dastardly *coasting*, which never ventures to lose sight of usage and precedent, should, guided by the *polarity* of reason, hazard a bolder navigation, and discover, in unexplored regions, the treasure of public felicity.[1]

The events of Clay's long political career suggest the inspiration he gained from a point of view that he shared with the Scotsman.

Clay went to Kentucky a Jeffersonian, where his political sympathies were compatible with those to whom "Federalism (in the popular sense of the word) is of all political sins deemed the most mortal. . . . "[2] Throughout his life Clay articulated his fealty to Jefferson, but, viewed realistically, the vigorous and comprehensive program of nationalism that he sponsored did not comport with Jefferson's agrarianism. Clay's success in law, his overnight affluence, and his marriage in the family of Col. Hart, Lexington's leading businessman, led him to share the aspirations of frontier capitalists. Their economic interests were vested in the cultivation of hemp and in a surprising number of manufacturing industries.[3] From these enterprises sprang the need for protection against foreign competition and for roads and canals by which to transport goods to markets. In his first reported speech in the Senate, Clay explained, "The local interest, of the quarter of the country, which I have the honor to represent, will apologize for the trouble I may give you on this occasion."[4] He went to Congress a sectionalist, but it soon became apparent that the interests he represented could best be advanced by comprehensive national legislation. He was in the vanguard of those who developed faith in the possibilities of nationalism. When other young and aggressive Republicans were still showing sectional leanings, Clay exclaimed of the Union: "Diversified as are the interests of its various parts, how admirably do they blend together and

---

[1] Thomas Ritchie, *Thomas Ritchie's Letter Containing Reminiscences of Henry Clay and the Compromise* (Richmond, 1852), p. 2.

[2] William Littell, in an open letter to William Coleman, *Kentucky Gazette*, May 3, 1803.

[3] E. Merton Coulter, "The Genesis of Henry Clay's American System," *The South Atlantic Quarterly*, 25 (January, 1926): 45-54; Brent Moore, *The Hemp Industry in Kentucky* (Lexington, Ky., 1905).

[4] *Annals of Congress*, Eleventh Congress, second session, p. 626.

harmonize!"[1] As Henry Adams indicated, it was one of Clay's early speeches that "marked the appearance of a school which was for fifty years to express the national ideals of statesmanship. . . . In Clay's speech almost for the first time the two rhetorical marks of his generation made their appearance, and during the next half century the Union and the Fathers were rarely omitted from any popular harangue."[2]

The War of 1812 and subsequent events made for less rigid interpretation of the Constitution, and party lines between the Republicans and Federalists were softened by a common faith in the future of the nation. Clay rode the crest of the tide, and in 1816 he cried: "I love true glory. It is this sentiment which ought to be cherished; and in spite of cavils and sneers and attempts to put it down, it will finally conduct this nation to that height to which God and nature have destined it."[3] Of the politico-economic basis of nationalism, he remarked: "It has appeared to me, in the administration of the general Government, to be a just principle to inquire what great interests belong to each section of our country, and to promote those interests, as far as practicable, consistently with the Constitution, having always an eye to the welfare of the whole."[4] Late in life he wrote, "If anyone desires to know the leading and paramount object of my public life, the preservation of this Union will furnish him the key."[5] His speeches are convincing testimonials of his ardent belief in the nation in an era when the "compact theory" presented a serious threat to its perpetuity.

In Clay's bias for paternalistic nationalism may be discovered an explanation for his proposals and positions on domestic questions. His "American System" stemmed from this source. National self-sufficiency was to be attained by a protective tariff, which would develop agricultural and industrial markets at home. Economic reciprocity between sections was to be facilitated by the construction of internal improvements. Clay favored distributing among the states the proceeds obtained from the sale of public lands. Through internal improvements and a land policy that would develop a common economic stake in the national resources he hoped to bind the states into a consolidated whole. With reference to finance, he risked charges of political inconsistency to change from opposition to the Bank of the United States to the support of a nationalized fiscal policy.

Although Clay's attitudes on foreign policy were frequently derived from the economic interests he represented, in general they, too, reflect the

---

[1] *Ibid.*, Twelfth Congress, first session, p. 919.
[2] H. Adams, *op. cit.*, V, 190–191.
[3] *Annals of Congress*, Fourteenth Congress, first session, p. 784.
[4] Clay to Francis Brooke, Aug. 28, 1823, *Works of Clay*, IV, 81.
[5] Clay to Stephen F. Miller, July 1, 1844, *ibid.*, V, 491.

fervor of his nationalism. His jingoism in 1812 grew out of the clamor of the West with its insatiable greed for land and its desire to eliminate Indian troubles; yet it was during this episode that he developed into a full-blown nationalist, jealous of the nation's prestige and honor. He once urged our claims to Florida and Texas not only as being just but as being desirable for the enlargement of the nation. His enthusiasm for "The United Provinces of Rio de la Plata" reflected his confidence in his own American republic, as well as his wish for an "American System" with United States hegemony in establishing a "counter-poise" to reactionary European countries.

On questions of specific policy that give practical meaning to his great interest, Clay was not always consistent. As Morse expressed it, Clay "managed to get upon both sides of pretty much every question which arose in his day. . . . "[1] With respect to slavery, the Bank of the United States, the tariff, and territorial problems, this seems to be the case. He began his political career in Kentucky by urging emancipation of slaves; while in later years he continued to profess a dislike for slavery as an institution, he detested the abolitionists who risked the Union to serve their purpose. One of the difficult tasks of his life was to explain away his strong arguments of 1811 against the Bank of the United States, the institution that he came to support from 1815 until his death. He was the exponent of the protective tariff, yet in 1833 he compromised with the South Carolina Nullifiers on a bill that reversed the direction of previous protective legislation. He once urged claims to Texas as part of the nation; but in his Presidential campaign of 1844 he straddled the question of its annexation, and in 1847 he was bitter over expansion into the Southwest. To men who live by fixed principles, Clay's policies smack of shifting, temporizing, and opportunism. Much practical experience in politics, however, had convinced him of the expediency of compromise in implementing the democratic process and preserving the Union. In 1820 he was instrumental in negotiating the Missouri Compromise. Not only did this enhance his political reputation, but it convinced him of the efficacy of compromise as a legislative formula. Late in life he declared:

I go for honorable compromise whenever it can be made. Life itself is but a compromise between death and life, the struggle continuing throughout our whole existence, until the Great Destroyer finally triumphs. All legislation, all government, all society, is formed upon the principle of mutual concession, politeness, comity, courtesy; upon these everything is based. I bow to you today because you bow to me. . . . Let him who elevates himself above humanity, above its weaknesses, its infirmities, its wants, its necessities, say, if he pleases, I never will

[1] Introduction to Carl Schurz, *Life of Henry Clay* (reprint of 1899 ed., Boston, and New York, 1915), I, v–vi.

compromise, but let no one who is not above the frailties of our common nature disdain compromises.[1]

The influence that personal ambitions exerted on Clay's political thinking and behavior cannot be overlooked. Single motives, of course, cannot be assigned to explain his behavior. Patriot though he was, he was consumed by political ambition. Although always "most desirous not to seem anxious" for the office, actually he was a perennial candidate for the Presidency between 1824 and 1848. Critics point to his shifting of attitudes on the Bank of the United States, the tariff, the question of Texas, and other issues as evidence that Clay tacked with the winds to improve his political opportunities. While personal ambitions can hardly be discounted as a significant influence in his political life, his sublime self-confidence perfectly satisfied him that the good of his country was inextricably tied up with his personal advancement.

In brief, Clay's great interests were the vital questions of national well-being and the preservation of the Union itself. Within this framework it may be said that the impact of his environment and strong personal ambitions profoundly influenced his thinking and behavior.

The Audiences of a National Statesman. Turning from a consideration of Clay's premises to the speech situations he faced, it will be recalled that he entered the Senate in 1806 when yet below the legal age. He was not a bashful person, and three days after his entrance he gave his first speech. A short time later he lectured a member of the Senate on senatorial propriety. He excited immediate attention, and John Quincy Adams noted that the newcomer was "quite a young man—an orator—and a republican of the first fire." During his second short term in the Senate, his speeches on domestic manufacturing, internal improvements, the Florida question, and the Bank of the United States focused the political limelight on him.[2] These speeches were presented to small audiences of senators and spectators who met in a dingy chamber, one in such poor condition that it kept "the minds of the members, during every storm, in a state of fear & uneasiness, lest the wall, which is thick & high, should fall on them & either maim or kill them."[3] Clay was thoroughly impatient with the lethargy and inertia of the Senate, whose members spent their time "measuring tongues, and syllogistically cudgelling each other out of their unreasonable notions. . . ."[4]

[1] *Congressional Globe*, Thirty-first Congress, first session, p. 662.

[2] For reactions to his speeches, see the *Baltimore American*, quoted in the *Philadelphia Aurora and General Advertiser*, Jan. 8, 1811; the *Whig*, Feb. 15, 1811, quoted in the *Philadelphia, Aurora and General* Advertiser, Feb. 2, 1811; Washington Irving to his brother, Feb. 16, 1811 in *The Life and Letters of Washington Irving* (Pierre M. Irving, ed., New York, 1862), I, 271-72.

[3] Plumer, *Memorandum*, p. 527.

[4] Washington Irving, *Salmagundi* (New York, 1888), p. 202.

While speaking for a bill dealing with domestic manufacturing, he disclosed his impatience by asking sarcastically: " . . . and shall we close the circle of Congressional inefficiency by adding this also to the catalogue?"[1]

It might be argued that the most productive period of Clay's career was his years in the House of Representatives. Here he was the leader of that group of aggressive and ambitious young men who had been sent to cease "dastardly coasting" in politics and to supplant it with positive direction in legislative affairs. Lowndes, Cheves, Calhoun, Grundy, and Porter were representative of this group, and they made Clay Speaker of the House. His graciousness, affability, commanding qualities, and ready speech were popular with the members, which prompted John Randolph's caustic reference to the house as "Mr. H. Clay & Co." During his service, Clay's influence continued to extend with the growth of the house, whose membership increased to more than two hundred. Prior to the War of 1812, Clay and his fellow Republicans held a majority, and after the war the influence of the Federalists was negligible. Factionalism among Republicans, however, often presented obstacles to Clay and other party members.

Clay did not let the speakership keep him from giving speeches on such important issues as the War of 1812, rechartering of the Bank of the United States, internal improvements, the recognition of South America, the Missouri Compromise, protection of home industry, the cause of the revolting Greeks, and Jackson's invasion of Florida. On these occasions the chamber was packed by members, spectators, and senators, who deserted their business to hear him.

After serving in Adams's cabinet, Clay was in retirement until his return to the Senate in 1831. It had become rather common opinion that the Senate was vastly superior to the house in its make-up, interests, and speaking.[2] Between 1831 and 1852 Webster, Calhoun, Ewing, Crittenden, Clayton, Cass, and others gave brilliance to the body. It was an age when Thomas Hart Benton marshaled the victorious forces of Jackson against the most powerful array of speakers in the history of Congress, while Clay led the opposition to Jackson, Van Buren, and Tyler. Among the great problems on which Clay spoke were the public domain, finance, the expunging resolution, internal improvements, the tariff, and slavery. He retired in 1842 but returned in 1849 and was instrumental in effecting a compromise of sectional problems then agitating the country.

Printed copies of Clay's speeches were avidly sought after and read by the general public,[3] and his trips to and from Washington, his tours of the

---

[1] *Annals of Congress*, Eleventh Congress, first session, p. 630.

[2] Thomas Hamilton, *Men and Manners in America* (Edinburgh, 1833), II, 32–34.

[3] See J. T. Morehead to J. J. Crittenden, May 17, 1834, Crittenden MSS; *North American Review*, 25 (July–October, 1827): 431; *Daily Globe*, Feb. 9, 1850.

South, East, North, and West were scenes of tremendous demonstrations and repeated ovations in village and city. Enormous crowds gathered, many journeying from distant parts to hear him. Typical receptions included long and noisy parades, a dinner or barbecue, rounds of toasts and unrestrained eulogiums. Heightened by these preliminaries, such occasions provided settings in which Clay would rise with "visible emotion" and deliver an impassioned political speech, much to the satisfaction and delight of the audience. It is of incidental interest that during the trying years in which he felt compelled to refute the bargain and corruption charges he acquired the unenviable reputation of being a "table orator."

For nearly a half century, a speech from Henry Clay was an event of importance, whether in Washington, New York, Philadelphia, Boston, or some isolated hamlet. Of the hundreds of his speeches, one of the most significant was the "Compromise Speech" of February 5 and 6, 1850. In this and subsequent speeches Clay hoped to settle the sectional discord that troubled the country. The House of Representatives had passed a proviso, sponsored by David Wilmot, which prohibited slaves in the territory recently acquired from Mexico. The South was able to prevent its passage in the Senate, but the slavocracy, smarting under accumulated grievances, echoed Calhoun's insistence that "the day that the balance between the two sections of the country . . . is destroyed, is a day that will not be far removed from political revolution, anarchy, civil war, and widespread disaster."[1]

There was bad blood on both sides, and threats of disunion were freely uttered. Such was the state of the Union that lured Henry Clay, now seventy-three years of age, from the retreats of his beloved Ashland. He consented out of "a sense of stern duty" after the Kentucky legislature had taken the initiative in returning him to the Senate. Clay had studied carefully the resolutions and counterresolutions offered since the initial agitation on the various questions. From these he sifted and selected until he had incorporated into eight resolutions the urgent demands of both sections; and on January 29, 1850, he presented them in a short speech that was "talked of everywhere." The first reactions indicated that the North was more favorably disposed toward them than the South.[2] It was understood that in a few days Clay would speak at length on the resolutions, and the "magic wires" carried the news of the coming event to Boston, New York, Philadelphia, Charleston, the Lakes region, and across the Ohio River.

On the morning of February 5 the "little, cramped up, and wholly insufficient corner of the Capitol, known as the Senate chamber" was overflowing.

[1] *Congressional Globe*, Twenty-ninth Congress, second session, p. 454.
[2] Orlando Brown to J. J. Crittenden, Feb. 1, 1850, Crittenden MSS.

Before nine o'clock this morning, the galleries of the Senate were filled; by ten, all the approaches to the floor below were choked up; and in the principal ante-chamber a dense mass of ladies were crowded together, waiting for the chances of being admitted into the aisle and the single circle of seats outside the bar. The people, repulsed from the galleries for want of room, came down and filled up the rotunda.[1]

At 12 o'clock the main door of the Senate opened, and the ladies, presenting in their gay costumes all the colors of the long range of millinery stores of Division Street, "pressed forward in a solid phalanx," filling every cranny of the chamber. The tense audience waited expectantly.

"Whose seat is that?" goes in whispers around. "It is Calhoun's,—not well enough to be out yet." "Who is that sitting by Cass?" says one. "That is Buchanan, —come all the way from home to hear Clay." . . . "But where is Webster? I don't see him." "He is in the Supreme Court, where he has a case to argue today." "See Corwin, and Badger, and Berrien, and Dawson, all near Clay; all of them quiet while Clay pursues his writing. On the opposite side, Butler, and Foote, and Clemens, and Douglas."[2]

Clay had leaned heavily on the arm of a companion as he climbed the slippery steps to the Senate chamber that sparkling winter morning. "Old Hal" showed his age. His head, bald on top, was fringed with long gray hair, and his cheeks were sunken. But as usual his genial smile made its impression.[3] He worked at his desk in the Senate chamber until Mangum moved to proceed to the order of the day. Quietly, he put his papers in his desk, and arose with consummate ease and grace. The applause was deafening. The excitement carried over to those who were unable to obtain admittance, and they renewed their efforts at all entrances. Wild shouts, "mingled jargon of oaths, imprecations, and explosions of laughter" interrupted the speaker, and it was some time before officials were able to restore order. One reporter complained that these "vain efforts to force a passage, completely spoiled the force of his exordium."[4]

Clay opened the speech with a personal reference to impress his audience with the gravity of the crisis. "Mr. President, never, on any former occasion, have I risen under feelings of such deep solicitude. I have witnessed many periods of great anxiety, of peril, and of danger even to the country; but I have never before arisen to address any assembly so oppressed, so appalled, so anxious." He invoked God to still "the violence and rage of party" and prayed for aid in his efforts to this end. The source

---

[1] *New York Herald*, Feb. 7, 1850.

[2] Johnston and Browne, *op. cit.*, p. 249.

[3] Ben Perley Poore, *Perley's Reminiscences of Sixty Years in the National Metropolis* (Philadelphia, 1886), I 363.

[4] *New York Herald*, Feb. 7, 1850; Johnston and Browne, *loc. cit.*

of existing tensions he ascribed to "the violence and intemperance of party spirit." Then, to allay any personal prejudices that members might hold toward him or to remove suspicion that ambition plagued him, Clay assured the Senate that he would jostle no one "in the pursuit of these honors or that elevation" which any member might be seeking; but he still left the way open to preferment.

Clay remarked that he had cut himself off from all the pleasures of social life (amenities he thoroughly enjoyed) for the purpose of finding "some mode of accommodation, which should once more restore the blessings of concord, harmony, and peace to this great country." The purpose of the speech was "to settle all the controverted questions arising out of the subject of slavery" and to obtain from the two sections of the country some concessions, "not of principle, not of principle at all, but of feeling, of opinion, in relation to the matters in controversy between them."[1]

Most of the speech is concerned with the eight resolutions. California should be admitted into the Union without reference to slavery. The territories acquired from Mexico were to be organized without restriction or condition as to slavery. The boundary line between Texas and New Mexico was to be fixed in a specified manner, and the United States should assume the indebtedness Texas had incurred prior to annexation. It was inexpedient to abolish slavery in the District of Columbia, but it was desirable to eliminate slave traffic in that area. The Federal government should take effective steps to aid in the recovery of fugitive slaves. Finally, Congress had no power to interfere with slave trade between slaveholding states.

The discussion then moved to a detailed consideration of the Missouri Compromise, which demonstrated that "if we will only suffer our reason to have its scope and sway, and if we will still and hush the passion and excitement which have been created by the occasion, difficulties will be more than half removed. . . . " That the episode was introduced in part for its moral value is probable; but Clay also objected to the extension of the Missouri principle on the grounds that an interdiction of slavery north of the line 36° 30' would guarantee its preservation south of the line. He well knew that a vote for such guarantee could never be obtained. It should

---

[1] George Campbell's observations seem particularly relevant to the problem Clay faced in his speech situation. "But of all the prepossession in the minds of the hearers which tends to impede or counteract the design of the speaker, party-spirit, where it happens to prevail, is the most pernicious, being at once the most inflexible and the most unjust." Campbell suggests two possible ways to meet the difficulty. One way is to calm an unfavorable passion by annihilating or diminishing the object that raised it, and the other is to excite another passion to counterwork the undesirable emotional state.—George Campbell, *The Philosophy of Rhetoric* (Boston, 1835), I, 97, 101. This speech exemplifies Campbell's statement of the problem and his recommendations.

be added that this phase of the speech refreshed the minds of his hearers as to the speaker's role in those negotiations and thus further contributed to his prestige in the existing controversy.

Clay concluded with a fervent plea for the Union. He described its resources, reviewed the role that either section had played in its making, and portrayed the dire consequences that must result from secession. He emphasized the common stake that the sections had in the nation. "Mr. President," he cried, "I am directly opposed to any purpose of secession, of separation. I am for staying within the Union, and defying any portion of this Union to expel me or drive me out of the Union." He assured the South that they could better vindicate their rights by remaining within the Union than by being expelled without ceremony and authority.

The dissolution of the Union would be followed by war, Clay predicted. "Such a war, too, as that would be, following the dissolution of the Union! Sir, we may search the pages of history, and none so furious, so bloody, so implacable, so exterminating . . . —none of them raged with such violence . . . as will that war which shall follow that disastrous event—if that event ever happens—of dissolution." After war, he cried, "some Philip or Alexander, some Caesar or Napoleon, would rise . . . and crush the liberties of both the dissevered portions of this Union." He asked his audience to visualize "the extinction of this last and glorious light which is leading all mankind. . . . " Clay closed, as he had opened his speech, with a personal reference that emphasized the gravity of the crisis. "And, finally, Mr. President, I implore, as the best blessing which Heaven can bestow upon me upon earth, that if the direful and sad event of the dissolution of the Union shall happen, I may not survive to behold the sad and heart-rending spectacle."[1]

When the exhausted speaker finished his 2-day address, men and women rushed to congratulate him and shower on him evidence of deep personal affection. A reporter who heard the speech in its entirety commented: "Those who heard Mr. Clay's argument yesterday, and thought indifferently about it, were today irresistibly carried along by his peroration. . . . The orator was all animation, fire and impulse. . . . "[2] Conservative and influential papers predicted that the plan would find no favor with extremists but that it would pave the way for the acceptance of some plan not degrading to the different sections. Clay wrote to his son that "The speech has produced a powerful and salutary effect in the country and in Congress."[3] The demand for printed copies of the speech was great.

[1] Clay spoke 2½ hours the first day to deliver less than half of the speech. For the text, see *Congressional Globe*, Thirty-first Congress, first session, Appendix I, pp. 115-127.
[2] *New York Herald*, Feb. 8, 1850.
[3] H. Clay to James B. Clay, Mar. 6, 1850, *Works of Clay*, V, 601-602.

The *Daily Globe* announced that not less than 80,000 copies would be printed in Washington, and a notice of 2 weeks was required for all orders.[1]

The essentials of the eight resolutions were eventually passed as individual bills. This speech represented Clay's constructive case for his resolutions and may be considered the spearhead for subsequent debates. Considered in its broad aspects, the speech indicates two ways by which Clay hoped to reconcile the sections. In the first place, in a concrete, practical way he attempted to satisfy the urgent demands of both sections. It was necessary to disabuse minds, to obtain concessions, and to establish a degree of certainty that sectional demands would be met. In the second place, he brought home to his audience the common stake that the sections had in the Union, closing the speech with an ardent appeal to patriotism and sentiment. Throughout he pled for reason, mildness, temperance, and patriotism. It is a masterful case for his cause, replete in legal and historical arguments, revealing the heart of the patriot and hand of the artist. There remains, of course, the question whether Clay deliberately avoided any fundamental analysis of the forces that had produced the crisis or whether he was oblivious to the logic of events. Whichever may have been the case, there is much to be said for the thesis that in this and other speeches of the grueling compromise debates, Clay contributed significantly in postponing the war; and in this measure he helped ensure the Union he loved.[2] Looking back to this period, the Beards remark: "In every way the debate was a memorable forensic contest worthy of a place in the annals of oratory beside the noblest intellectual tourneys of ancient and modern times. It was significant on account of the men who participated, the eloquence and cogency of their arguments, and the results that flowed from their deliberations."[3]

V. *An Appraisal of Clay's Speaking and Speeches*

Clay is frequently referred to as an "orator by nature." In his own words, however, greatness lies "in preparation . . . I seem to speak off-hand, so does Mr. Webster; yet we both speak with preparation, and never without it on important subjects."[4] Yet Clay acquired no reputation for patient and tireless study devoted either to general background or specific preparation. As a lawyer he developed the capacity, "peculiar

---

[1] *Daily Globe*, Feb. 9, 1850.

[2] Clay is said to have spoken seventy times.—*Works of Clay*, III, 180.

[3] Charles A. Beard and Mary R. Beard, *The Rise of American Civilization* (New York, 1936), I, 713. By permission of The Macmillan Company.

[4] O. H. Smith, *Early Indiana Trials and Sketches* (Cincinnati, 1858), pp. 374–375; *cf.* Harrison, *op. cit.*, p. 43.

to himself," of bringing to bear on the matter before him his full power of concentration; but many contemporaries agree with Webster that Clay "was never a man of books—a hard student."

The materials for Clay's speeches were derived largely from personal experience and thinking related to political and economic problems, from general reading, conversations, and letters. Some of his speeches indicate considerable research, reflection, and attention to argument. For others he felt it necessary to apologize, while still others show little preparation and were presented without apology. In general Clay's speeches indicate attention to general plans and argument but do not bear the impress of meticulous care for details and minutiae of composition.

Clay delivered his speeches extemporaneously from notes.[1] Manuscripts were prepared by himself or under his direction but occasionally and then only as an assurance that he would appear correctly in print.[2] The available texts of his speeches, for the most part, are running accounts from reporters' pens. These reports probably maintain the arguments and general drift of his speeches with fidelity, but not until near the middle of the nineteenth century did they approximate the exact words of the speaker.[3] Clay spoke with regret that "many of his best speeches, made off-hand, were either not reported, or badly reported. . . . "[4] For instance, there are no satisfactory reports of his speeches on the Missouri question. Despite omissions and imperfections, along with related evidence the available accounts furnish a valuable basis for observations on his rhetoric.

Clay's extant speeches are almost entirely of the deliberative variety. They embrace practical political issues, and their basic motivation is to be discovered in the urgency of these issues. While the speeches are neither philosophical nor profoundly analytical, they possess the cogency of argument and breadth of appeal of the practical parliamentary speaker. In a campaign speech, Clay once candidly told his audience that he disliked all public speaking except in the courts and legislatures, where "there was a precise object to be pursued, by a train of thought and argument, adapted to its attainment."[5] In Clay's case, precept and practice unite to

---

[1] Thomas Hart Clay and Ellis Paxson Oberholtzer, *Henry Clay* (Philadelphia, 1910), p. 389; General William T. Sherman, quoted in Clark, *op. cit.*, pp. 164–166. Several people have informed the writer that they have seen notes from which Clay spoke. Only a few are included among the Clay MSS in the Library of Congress.

[2] Joel T. Hart to Dr. Thomas Nelson, Nov. 14, 1847, Durrett MSS; *Niles' National Register*, 73 (Nov. 20, 1847): 189.

[3] See Thomas Hart Benton's remark on reporting, *Congressional Globe*, Thirty-first Congress, first session, p. 1139; see also the *Daily Globe*, Feb. 9, 1850, for an appraisal of the *National Intelligencer's* report of Clay's "Compromise Speech."

[4] T. B. Stevenson to James B. Clay, Mar. 21, 1856, Clay MSS.

[5] From MS of speech delivered at Raleigh, N. C., 1844.

make the argument of first importance. The logical structure of the speeches consists typically of propositions of policy supported by enthymematic arguments. These are buttressed by examples, analogies, historical allusions, and references to authority. Much of the argument is refutative in nature and displays Clay's versatility as an extemporaneous debater. The chief merit of the speeches lies in the force of the argument and the dialectical skill that they display. While Clay derived ethos from the positions that he assumed, he also carefully identified his causes with such virtues as duty, patriotism, and respect for public welfare, frequently ascribing baser motives to opponents. He often dramatically represented situations as struggles between forces of evil and virtue. Moreover, his religious supplications and stock personal references to health, sacrifices, and service were intended to evoke ethical appeal. The emotional quality of his speaking was derived in great part from his delivery, but the speeches themselves are replete with distinct appeals to the emotions of his audiences. Clay was capable of both placating audiences and arousing them to an intense emotional fervor. Although his invention in general contributes to convincing cases for his propositions, individual arguments may be singled out as specious or challenged as stratagems. Moreover, ethical and emotional appeals are frequently put to questionable use in imputing motives and distorting judgments.

With respect to arrangement, the speeches demonstrate orderly presentations of material adapted to audiences. The introductions are personal in nature and usually stress the importance of the issue. The speeches are organized logically with attention to chronological and climactic development. The conclusions are in the nature of brief summaries, proposals of specific procedures, and appeals to emotions and higher motives. While the basic organization of each speech is clear, Clay's lack of meticulous attention to refinements of composition, as well as his extempore presentation, sometimes contributes to verbosity and discursiveness within the general framework. The fact that the texts represent only approximations of his actual words discourages a highly critical study of his oral style, but the available evidence indicates a surprising freedom from the ornateness and grandiloquence that characterize much of the oratory of Clay's time. On the whole it may be said that perspicuity and force are the chief characteristics of his style.

A convincing body of testimony left by those who heard Clay indicates a source of effectiveness not revealed by the printed vestiges of his speeches. "Intangible to delineation . . . " "he must be heard and felt" were the opinions of his auditors. His manner was prepossessing as he stepped onto the platform with a provoking smile on his genial face, human to the very core of his being. To be sure, to his enemies he appeared as a swashbuckling

Westerner, bold and insouciant. By and large, however, the Kentuckian fired the imagination and gripped the hearts of audiences.

As the speech progressed, Clay often achieved a state of "physical fever," of which he remarked: "I do not know how it is with others, but, on such occasions, I seem to be unconscious of the external world. Wholly engrossed by the subject before me, I lose all sense of personal identity, of time, or of surrounding objects."[1] One who observed the overt manifestation of this "self-absorption," described him in this way:

> His mode of speaking is very forcible—He fixes the attention by his earnest & emphatic tones & gestures—the last of which are however far from being graceful—He frequently shrugs up his shoulders, & twists his features, & indeed his whole body in the most dreadful scowls & contortions—Yet the whole seems natural; there is no appearance of acting, or theatrical effect—& you see in every motion & word the uncontrolled expression of violent feelings, & the result of a powerful but irregular mind—If there is any passion which he expresses with greater force than another it is contempt.[2]

He could lose himself with abandon in the intenseness of his feelings, but he also had a talent for histrionics, which he at times displayed with verisimilitude. He could make a dramatic event out of a pause for snuff or out of the use of his handkerchief and spectacles. Senator Cuthbert once taunted Clay with the question, "What part will Roscius next enact?" It was said that reporters sometimes would fling down their pens and exclaim: "He's a great actor, and that's the whole of it."[3] He could be bland, contemptuous, humble, indignant, disdainful, fierce, or amiable as the occasion demanded.

Clay had a magnificent voice. He once confided to a friend that nature "had singularly favored me by giving me a voice peculiarly adapted to produce the impressions I wished in public speaking."[4] It did not have a sonorous quality like that of Webster's, but it was a clear and powerful voice, resonant and organlike, with a certain passionate quality.[5] It was capable of subtle inflection in expressing feeling and meaning. He could

[1] Colton, *op. cit.*, I, 68; Mathews, *op. cit.*, p. 319. *Cf.* comments in the *National Journal*, quoted in *Kentucky Reporter*, Aug. 29, 1827; *Pennsylvania Whig*, quoted in *Lexington Observer and Kentucky Reporter*, Sept. 20, 1832.
[2] William Plumer to his father, Feb. 12, 1820, in *The Missouri Compromises and Presidential Politics 1820–1825* (Everett Somerville Brown, ed., St. Louis, 1926), pp. 8–9.
[3] Parker, *op. cit.*, p. 501; Parton, *op. cit.*, p. 5; Poore, *op. cit.*, I, 85, 148–149, 388–389.
[4] Sarah Mytton Maury, *The Statesmen of America* (London, 1847), pp. 437–438.
[5] The House of Representatives presented a serious acoustical problem. Of this Murray said, "I have been told, that Mr. Clay, when he was in that house, and some few others, could make themselves understood; but I think I never saw an apartment of the same magnitude in which the voice was so completely lost "—*Op. cit.*, I, 132.

compress into single words and phrases great intensity of force and significance.[1]

In general, Clay's delivery was marked by directness and communicativeness. He surveyed his audience "with watchful, shifting glances, taking in the field of vision, and making each one feel that he is seen and individually addressed." While a forceful speaker, he "did not like some quite popular declaimers indulge in violent contrasts of pitch. . . . " There were no obvious patterns of melody or rhythm, and the rate varied with his mood. He gave less attention to pronunciation and word order than the more meticulous Webster, for instance, might have approved.

Because of its source, one of the more interesting word pictures to present a general description of Clay's speaking was drawn by Daniel Webster.

Of what may be called the personal requisites for an acceptable public Speaker Mr. C. has an uncommon share. He has a tall & erect figure, with a general air & appearance such as prepossesses & strikes the audience. His voice is perhaps not equalled by that of any other public Speaker in the Country. It has not only great force, & compass, but is also clear, flexible, & susceptible of great variety of modulation. He has, no doubt, sometimes the common fault of the Country—at least the common fault of members of Congress—of speaking too loud; & his earnestness & ardor expose him to the danger of too much apparent vehemence. A northern audience, especially, would be likely to think that he speaks, even on ordinary topics, & under ordinary circumstances, with a degree of warmth, which, in our colder latitudes, is excited, or by our opinions justified, only by uncommon occasions. The result of all that belongs to his *manner*, is, that he is both an imposing & a persuasive Speaker. He fixes the attention, & holds it as long and as steadily, probably, as any man that has ever appeared in our halls of Legislation. Frank, lofty, & disinterested, with power to defend, & capacity to lead, he must necessarily be, & would always be, an important individual in any public assembly, to which he might belong.[2]

The essential character of Clay's manner of presentation was molded by the tastes and requirements of his Western audiences. They liked frankness of feelings and possessed an unbounded admiration for rousing oratory. With age and experience the pyrotechnics of his delivery underwent refinement, but without losing the dynamic qualities that made him compelling and almost never dull.

[1] See Sargent and Greeley, *op. cit.*, pp. 74–75; Joseph Packard, *Recollections of a Long Life*, 1812–1902 (Washington, D. C., 1902), p. 254. Lincoln thought Clay's effectiveness consisted of "that deeply earnest and impassioned tone and manner which can proceed only from great sincerity, and a thorough conviction in the speaker of the justice and importance of his cause." —Abraham Lincoln, "Eulogy on Henry Clay," in *Abraham Lincoln: Complete Works* (John G. Nicolay and John Hay, eds., New York, 1894), I, 170–171.

[2] From Ms in Dartmouth College Archives.

Clay's effectiveness in speaking can never be properly understood simply by reading the speeches for purposes of literary appraisal. As Abraham Lincoln put it, "All his efforts were for practical effect. He never spoke merely to be heard."[1] He was the advocate, speaking to living audiences on the rightness and wrongness of courses of action. William Plumer, who often listened to the triumvirate, once wrote to George Ticknor: "In popular address, in skillful adaptation of means to ends, in the contagious enthusiasm, which leaves no time for hesitation or doubt, in promptness, in confidence of power and of success, Clay possesses advantages over every person I ever saw, in the management of a popular assembly. . . . "[2] Three quarters of a century later, on the weight of the extant evidence of an earlier period, Professor McLaughlin concluded: "But if Clay's words do not now move us deeply, they did move and captivate the men to whom he spoke, and that is the aim of oratory. He was more nearly the great orator of his time than was any other; in power over a general audience and in ability to touch the chord of human sympathy, no one was quite his equal, at least in the field of politics."[3]

Clay's preeminence in the political life of his time cannot be understood or explained apart from his exceptional ability in public speaking. His speeches were his works, and through them he made an impress on his age. While his advocacy of many interests proved unsuccessful, the measure of his accomplishments and the words of contemporaries provide convincing evidence of his effectiveness as a public speaker.

SELECTED BIBLIOGRAPHY

A Selected List of Clay's Speeches

"Address to General Lafayette," a ceremonial speech, Dec. 10, 1824, United States House of Representatives, *Register of Debates*, Eighteenth Congress, second session, pp. 3-4.

"African Colonization," in support of the colonization of free Negroes in Liberia, Jan. 20, 1827, annual meeting of the American Colonization Society, Washington, D.C., *Works of Clay*, VI, 329—340.

"American Industry," for the tariff, Mar. 30 and 31, 1824, United States House of Representatives, *Annals of Congress*, Eighteenth Congress, first session, pp. 1962–2001.

"The American System," on the protective tariff, Feb. 2, 3, and 6, 1832, United States Senate, *Register of Debates*, Twenty-second Congress, first session, pp. 257–295.

"Bargain and Corruption," a refutation of charges, July 12, 1827, at a dinner in Lexington, Ky., *Niles' Weekly Register*, 32 (Aug. 4, 1827): 375–380; *Works of Clay*, VII, 341–355.

"The Compromise Resolutions," a plea for the adoption of eight resolutions to reconcile sectional differences, Feb. 5 and 6, 1850, United States Senate, *Congressioal Globe*, Thirty-first Congress, first session, Appendix J, pp. 115–127.

---

[1] Nicolay and Hay, *loc. cit.*

[2] Plumer to Tichnor, Apr. 2, 1853, Webster MSS.

[3] A. C. McLaughlin, "Publicists and Orators," *The Cambridge History of American Literature* (New York, 1931), II, 86. By permission of The Macmillan Company.

"The Compromise Tariff," for revision of tariff schedules, Feb. 12 and 25, 1833, United States, *Register of Debates*, Twenty-second Congress, second session, pp. 462–473; 730–742.

"Domestic Manufactures," first reported speech in Congress, Apr. 6, 1810, United States Senate, *Annals of Congress*, Eleventh Congress, first session, pp. 626–630.

"Emancipation of the South American States," for the recognition of South American colonies, Mar. 24 and 25, 1818, United States House of Representatives, *Annals of Congress*, Fifteenth Congress, first session, pp. 1474–1500.

"The Expunging Resolution," That the Senate's censorship of Jackson be not expunged from the journals, Jan. 16, 1837, United States Senate, *Register of Debates*, Twenty-fourth Congress, second session, pp. 429–440.

"The General Distress Caused by the Removal of the Deposits," an address to Van Buren, Mar. 7, 1834, United States Senate, *Register of Debates*, Twenty-third Congress, first session, pp. 829–832.

"The Greek Revolution," to recognize the independence of Greece. Jan. 20, 1824, United States House of Representatives, *Annals of Congress*, Eighteenth Congress, first session, pp. 1170–1178.

"Internal Improvement," for the construction of roads and canals, Mar. 13, 1818, United States House of Representarives, *Annals of Congress*, Fifteenth Congress, first session, pp. 1359–1380.

"The Mexican War," a critical review of the causes and objects of the war, Nov. 13, 1847, a Whig mass meeting, Lexington, Ky., *Niles' National Register*, 73 (Nov. 20, 1847): 197–200.

"The New Army Bill," A plea for the vigorous prosecution of the war, Jan. 8 and 9, 1813, United States House of Representatives, *Annals of Congress*, Twelfth Congress, second session, pp. 659–676.

"The Plan of the Sub-treasury," an attack on independent government depositories, Feb. 19, 1838, United States Senate, *Congressional Globe*, Twenty-fifth Congress, second session, Appendix, pp. 614–619.

"The Public Lands," for the distribution among the states of the proceeds from the sales of public lands, June 20, 1832, United States Senate, *Register of Debates*, Twenty-second Congress, first session, pp. 1096–1118.

"Our Relations with the Cherokee Indians," that treaties made with Indian nations be respected, Feb. 4, 1835, United States Senate, *Register of Debates*, Twenty-third Congress, second sessions, pp. 289–308.

"The Removal of the Deposits," an arraignment of Jackson for removing government deposits to "pet banks," Dec. 26 and 30, 1833, United States Senate, *Register of Debates*, Twenty-third Congress, first session, pp. 58–94.

"Renewing the Charter of the First Bank of the United States," Case against the First Bank, Feb. 15, 1811, United States Senate, *Annals of Congress*, Eleventh Congress, third session, 209–219.

"Reply to Mr. Mendenhall," a reply to a member of the Society of Friends who publicly presented a petition to Clay to liberate his slaves, Oct. 1, 1942, Richmond, Ind., *Works of Clay*, IX, 385–390.

"Retiring to Private Life," a campaign speech, June 9, 1842, a mass meeting, Lexington, Ky., *Works of Clay*, IX, 359–384.

"The Seminole War," An attack on Jackson's invasion of Florida, Jan. 20, 1819, United States House of Representatives. *Annals of Congress*, Fifteenth Congress, second session, pp. 631–655.

"Tyler's Veto of the Bank Bill," an attack on Tyler's veto of the proposed Bank of the United States, Aug. 19, 1841, United States Senate, *Congressional Globe*, Twenty-seventh Congress, first session, Appendix, 364–366.

"Valedictory to the Senate," upon his retirement from the Senate, Mar. 31, 1842, United States Senate, *Congressional Globe*, Twenty-seventh Congress, second session, pp. 376–377.

Manuscripts

Henry Clay Papers, Library of Congress.
John M. Clayton Papers, Library of Congress.
John J. Crittenden Papers, Library of Congress.
Robert T. Durrett Collection, University of Chicago.
James O. Harrison Papers, Library of Congress.
Daniel Webster Papers, Library of Congress.

Periodicals

Clark, L. G.: "Henry Clay—Personal Anecdotes, Incidents, etc.," *Harper's New Monthly Magazine*, 5 (June–November, 1852); 392–399.

Harrison, James O.: "Henry Clay: Reminiscences by His Executor," *The Century Magazine*, 33 (December, 1886–1887): 170–182.

Larned, W. A.: "Henry Clay; as an Orator," *The New Englander*, 2 (1844): 105–112. A critical account of Clay's speaking.

Parker, E. G.: "Henry Clay as an Orator," *Putnam's Monthly Magazine*, 3 (1854; 493–502. A descriptive account of Clay's speaking by one who heard him.

Peck, Charles H.: "The Speeches of Henry Clay," *Magazine of American History*, 16 (July–December, 1886); 58–67. A critical estimate of Clay's speeches.

"The Speeches of Henry Clay," *The North American Review*, 25 (July–October, 1827): 425–451. An interesting review of an early edition of Clay's speeches.

Books

Bradford, Gamaliel: *As God Made Them*, Boston, Houghton Mifflin Company, 1929. Contains a character study of Clay.

Clay, Thomas Hart, and Ellis Paxson Oberholtzer: *Henry Clay*, Philadelphia, George W. Jacobs and Company, 1910. A biography by Henry Clay's grandson, completed at his death by Oberholtzer.

Colton, Calvin: *The Life and Times of Henry Clay*, 2 vol., New York, A. S. Barnes and Company, 1846. A fulsome but extremely useful biography. Clay read the proof of the work.

———, ed.: *The Works of Henry Clay*, 10 vols., New York, G. P. Putnam's Sons, 1904. The set includes Colton's complete biography, more than two volumes of correspondence, and four volumes of speeches with introductory notes by the editor.

Dyer, Oliver: *Great Senators of the United States Forty Years Ago*, New York, Robert Banner's Sons, 1889. Dyer was a reporter and had an opportunity to study the great speakers in Congress.

Greeley, Horace: *Recollections of a Busy Life*, New York, J. B. Ford and Company, 1868. Contains interesting comments on the triumvirate.

Johnson, Gerald W.: *America's Silver Age*, New York, Harper & Brothers, 1939. An interpretation of the work of Clay, Calhoun, and Webster. Special attention is given to Clay.

Mallory, Daniel: *The Life and Speeches of the Hon. Henry Clay*, 2 vols., New York, R. P. Bixby and Company, 1843. A short biography of Clay and most of his important speeches up to Oct. 1, 1842.

Mathews, William: *Oratory and Orators*, Chicago, S. C. Griggs and Company, 1879. Contains descriptions of Clay's speaking by one who heard him.

Mayo, Bernard: *Henry Clay*, Boston, Houghton Mifflin Company, 1937. The first volume of a projected trilogy. An excellent biography; the best treatment available of Clay's life and work up to the War of 1812.

McLaughlin, A. C.: "Publicists and Orators, 1800-1850," *The Cambridge History of American Literature*, New York, The Macmillan Company, 1931, II, 86-88.

Parker, Edward G.: *The Golden Age of American Oratory*, Boston, Whittmore, Niles, and Hall, 1857. Parker heard Clay and studied his speaking.

Poage, George Rawlings: *Henry Clay and the Whig Party*, Chapel Hill, University of North Carolina Press, 1936. A study of the latter part of Clay's political career, with some reference to his speaking.

Prentice, George D.: *Biography of Henry Clay*, New York; John J. Phelps, 1831. A campaign biography by a brilliant journalist, fulsomely written. The first important biography of Clay.

Rogers, Joseph M.: *The True Henry Clay*, Philadelphia, J. B. Lippincott Company, 1904. Has some interesting information on Clay's speaking.

Sargent, Epes, and Horace Greeley: *The Life and Public Services of Henry Clay*, Auburn, N. Y., Derby and Miller, 1852. The authors were friends of Clay.

Schurz, Carl: *Life of Henry Clay*, 2 vols., Boston, Houghton Mifflin Company, 1888. The length of Clay's career and the brilliance of Schurz's writing made this study unique in that it is the only two-volume biography in the American Statesmen Series. A significant treatment of Clay for students of history and speech.

Van Deusen, Glyndon G.: *The Life of Henry Clay*, Boston, Little, Brown & Company, 1937. An excellent study of Clay.

Winthrop, Robert C.: *Memoir of Henry Clay*, Cambridge, John Wilson and Son, 1880. Contains valuable observations on Clay's speaking by a contemporary statesman and historian.

John C. Calhoun

by HERBERT L. CURRY

Born in the Abbeville district of South Carolina on March 18, 1782, John C. Calhoun was educated at Waddell's academy, 1795 and 1800–1802, and at Yale College, 1802–1804. Studied law with George Bowie at Abbeville, S.C., 1804–1805; at Judge Reeve's law school, Litchfield, Conn., 1805–1806; and with Henry W. De Saussure at Charleston, S.C., 1806–1807. He was admitted to the South Carolina bar in 1807 and to chancery-court practice in 1808; practiced law, 1808–1811; was a member of the South Carolina legislature, 1808–1810; married Florida Bonneau Calhoun, his second cousin, January 8, 1811. He was Representative in Congress, 1811–1817; Secretary of War, 1817–1824; nominated for the Presidency by the Pennsylvania delegates, 1822; Vice-President of the United States, 1825–1832; resigned the Vice-Presidency in 1833 to become a Senator representing South Carolina and maintained that office until 1843; Secretary of State, 1844–1845; Senator, 1845–1850; died in Washington, D.C., March 31, 1850.

The Great Nullifier, John C. Calhoun, left more than one hundred twenty major speeches as evidence of his endeavors to maintain the Union that he loved. The majority of these speeches were focused upon the issues which confronted the nation from 1830 to 1850, and they expressed the viewpoints of the man who was generally recognized as the spokesman for the South during that period. Hated by many in both areas of the country and loved by his friends and supporters, he attempted to stay the economic, political, and social forces that threatened to engulf his homeland. What manner of man was he? What were the defenses espoused by him for the South? How were they portrayed?

Backgrounds

The Calhoun family was of Scotch-Irish descent,[1] but both[2] John's parents, Patrick and Martha Calhoun, were of Irish origin. Patrick

[1] W. Pickney Starke, "Account of Calhoun's Early Life," as abridged by J. F. Jameson, "Correspondence of John C. Calhoun," in *The Annual Report of the American Historical Association* (Washington, D.C.) 1899, pp. 65–89; "Captain John Caldwell Calhoun," *National Register of the Sons of the American Revolution* (A. Howard Clark, ed., New York, 1902), pp. 721–723.

[2] John C. Calhoun, *Life of John C. Calhoun* (New York, 1843), p. 3.

Calhoun was a man of considerable financial acumen, high purpose, courage, and ability as a debater, who served in the Assembly of South Carolina for almost thirty years.[1] In his later years, John Calhoun credited his father with having encouraged in his son a "free spirit of inquiry and [an] intrepid zeal for truth. . . . "[2] Beyond this, we may only conjecture concerning the influence that Patrick Calhoun exerted upon his most famous son; the father, at least, had laid the foundations for an economic position that enabled the son to attend the best colleges of the day, to marry into the select circle of the aristocracy of the lowlands of South Carolina, and to become a member of the landed gentry, whose activities were limited to politics or planting or some combination of the two pursuits. John C. Calhoun's entry into politics and statecraft was probably determined not only by the example set by his father but also by the culture pattern of the society in which the elder Calhoun's acumen and ability permitted the son to move and live.

Young Calhoun's early education was obtained in the country schools of the upland areas of South Carolina—schools distinguished by the defectiveness with which the three R's were taught and by their sporadic, short sessions. At thirteen years of age he attended, for about a year, a school conducted by his brother-in-law, Moses Waddell, located in Columbia County, Georgia. When Waddell, after his wife's death, became an itinerant preacher, John Calhoun elected to remain on the Waddell plantation, where a lack of white companionship forced him to turn to the contents of a traveling library deposited in the Waddell home. In 14 weeks he had read Rollin's *Ancient History*, Robertson's *Charles V* and *America*, Voltaire's *Charles XII*, Cook's voyages, Brown's *Essays*, and Locke's *On the Human Understanding*.[3] His health declined under this regime, and his mother recalled him to the Calhoun homestead in South Carolina, which, since Patrick Calhoun's death, had lacked a male manager. These duties were gradually shifted to John's shoulders during the next four years, while at the same time he hunted, fished, and labored in the fields—an experience that partially explains his lifelong interest in agriculture. When Waddell, who had remarried, opened his school again, Calhoun began his formal education in earnest.

The curriculum at Waddell's school was severely classical, and it was here that the future Vice-President opened a Latin book for the first time in his life. The Friday-afternoon debating club probably provided him with his first formal training in public speaking. His work under Waddell was so thorough and so rapid that after two years of study he was able to enroll in

---

[1] *Ibid.*, pp. 1–9; Starke, *op. cit.*, pp. 2–7.
[2] Calhoun, *op. cit.*, p. 5.
[3] *Ibid.*, p. 5.

the junior class at Yale College, whose rules for admission as a freshman student included the ability to "read, translate, and parse Virgil, and the Greek Testament . . . to write Latin in prose . . . and to have learned the rules of Vulgar Arithmetic."[1] The curriculum for the junior year included English grammar, Greek, Latin, Hebrew, astronomy, navigation, surveying, and natural philosophy. The subjects studied in the senior year comprised rhetoric, ethics, logic, metaphysics, and the history of civil society. During both these years, theology was studied on each Saturday.[2]

Specific speech training was provided by disputations held twice each week during the junior and senior years. Such questions as: Ought foreign emigration be encouraged by the United States? Are novels beneficial? Are theatres beneficial? were discussed and decided in the negative—decisions that coincided with the expressed opinion of the tutor of the junior class, Benjamin Silliman. The senior disputations were heard by President Timothy Dwight, who discovered that young Calhoun did not accept the Federalist doctrines that Dwight attempted to implant in the minds of his students. The Carolinian maintained his Republican beliefs so adequately that Dwight is alleged to have thought the young man would one day be President of the United States.[3]

Extracurricular speech training was encouraged by the literary societies, the Linonian and the Society of Brothers in Unity, and in the meetings of Phi Beta Kappa. Calhoun seems to have been assigned to the Society of Brothers in Unity, which officially claimed him as a member,[4] but he became identified with the Linonian Society.[5] Phi Beta Kappa elected him to membership on July 11, 1803, at which time he also became treasurer of the organization.[6] Two weeks later, Calhoun and three other members of this organization debated the question: Is government founded on the social compact?—a question which the future Senator from South Carolina evidently answered in the affirmative, since this thesis later became the basis for his elaborate theory of government.

After graduation in September, 1804, Calhoun returned to Abbeville, S.C., where he spent the winter studying law with George Bowie, one of the

[1] The President and Fellows, *The Laws of Yale College* (New Haven, 1795), reprinted in 1860, p. 9.
[2] *Ibid.*, pp. 16–18.
[3] Calhoun, *op. cit.*, p. 6; see also John S. Jenkins, *The Life of John Caldwell Calhoun* (Auburn, N.Y., 1850), p. 31, or W. M. Meigs, *The Life of John Caldwell Calhoun* (New York, 1917), I, 67–68.
[4] Catalogue of the Society of Brothers in Unity, MS, Yale College Library, 1840, Preface.
[5] Records of Linonian, June 24, 1840, MS, Yale College Library, 1840.
[6] Records of Phi Beta Kappa, MS, Yale College Library. The author is indebted to Hollon A. Farr, graduate secretary of the Alpha Chapter of Connecticut of Phi Beta Kappa (1939) for this information.

ablest lawyers in the state. This experience seems to have confirmed his determination to enter that profession. By July 22, 1805, he had enrolled in the most famous law school of the day—Judge Reeve's school at Litchfield, Conn.

Studies at this institution were carried on by a combination of case methods, textbooks, and lectures. Municipal law, contracts, bailments, pleadings, private wrongs, real property, titles by deed, and constitutional law were considered. Moot courts, presided over by Judge James Gould, gave Calhoun an opportunity further to develop his talents for speaking. The debating society was credited by Calhoun with having added to his powers of extemporaneous debating.[1]

Even more important, perhaps, than his study and training was the influence exerted by Judge James Gould and Judge Tapping Reeve, the instructors at Litchfield during this period. Gould was lucid and was addicted to clear-cut rules and definitions[2]—a practice which later distinguished the speeches of the Great Nullifier. Judge Reeve and, to a lesser extent, Judge Gould were uncompromising Federalists. In fact, Reeve seems to have played a prominent part in laying the foundations for the proposal that New England should secede from the Union.[3] Perhaps there is more than a cursory connection between the attitude of New England, as represented by Reeve and Gould, and the nullification episode in 1833 than the apologists for that area would care to admit. From Gould the future Secretary of War probably acquired his love of simplicity of style and logical processes of thought, while Reeve provided a philosophy concerning the nature of our government which Calhoun deprecated—until he saw an opportunity to use it to enhance his fortunes and to defend the South from political aggression.

Late in 1806 Calhoun returned to Charleston, S. C., where he entered the office of Henry W. De Saussure in order to learn the specific legal practices of his home state. During the following year he was admitted to the bar and a year later was elected to the legislature of South Carolina—an honor that seems to have been at least partially produced by his speech on presenting his resolutions relative to the *Leopard-Chesapeake* affair. In 1810 he was elected to Congress and began his long career in national politics.

Calhoun—the Speaker

John C. Calhoun's speaking career was divided into two parts, the first covering the period from 1810 to 1817 and the second, from 1833 to 1850.

[1] Calhoun, *op. cit.*, p. 6; note also Meigs, *op. cit.*, I, 80n. quoting a reprint from the *United States Telegraph* that appeared in the *Charleston Mercury*, May 10, 1831.

[2] William Draper Lewis, *Great American Lawyers* (Philadelphia, 1907), II, 471–472.

[3] Henry C. Lodge, *Life and Letters of George Cabot* (2d rev. ed., Boston, 1878), pp. 442–443.

The policies and principles enunciated during these periods were not in agreement, and this inconsistency has led to the charge that he was willing to resort to any means or to adopt any principle which would further his personal political aims. The result was that he has been pictured as a scheming, unscrupulous politician who led the South toward the Civil War as the only means of achieving his ambition to be President.

But his contemporaries were unanimous in their opinion that he "differed from his great contemporaries in the possession of a private character above reproach."[1] Julian,[2] a political opponent, wrote, "in private life he was thoroughly upright and pure, and no suspicion of political jobbery was ever whispered in connection with his name." An abolitionist who had believed that the Senator looked like the incarnation of the devil indicated after further study that, "He impressed me as being deeply but unobtrusively religious and was so morally clean . . . that it was a pleasure to have one's soul get close to his soul. . . . "[3] These views were substantiated by Daniel Webster,[4] John Wentworth,[5] and Mrs. Smith[6] none of whom may be classed as an apologist for the Carolinian. If it is true that he was ambitious and therefore followed the drift of political expediency, it is equally true that he enjoyed a personal reputation among his contemporaries shared by few men of his time.

It is probable that such a reputation offers one explanation of the inability of the masses to appreciate and understand either the man or his principles. Henry Clay, the whisky-drinking poker player, or Jackson, the cock-fighting, horse-racing, former general of the army, were more likely to receive the support of the newly enfranchised farmers, tradesmen, mechanics, and laborers. As Parrington has written: "The early thirties [the period when Calhoun entered the Senate] . . . were robustious times when broadcloth in politics had suddenly gone out of style and homespun had come in. The new coonskin democracy had descended upon Washington."[7] The cotton planter from South Carolina was a "broadcloth" politician who had scant respect for the bourgeois who had so gleefully and uproariously descended upon Washington. The apostle of State Rights and Alexander Hamilton were one in their belief that government, even in a democracy, should be limited to those whose antecedents in terms of education, finances, social position, and breeding were of the best. The

[1] Benjamin Perley Poore, *Perley's Reminiscences* (Philadelphia, 1886), I, 136.

[2] George W. Julian, *Political Recollections, 1840–1872* (Chicago, 1884), p. 87.

[3] Oliver Dyer, *Great Senators of the United States Forty Years Ago* (New York, 1889), p. 178.

[4] Daniel Webster, *The Works of Daniel Webster* (New York, 1853), V, 370.

[5] John Wentworth, *Congressional Reminiscences* (Chicago, 1882), p. 25.

[6] Margaret B. Smith, *The First Forty Years of Washington Society* (New York, 1906), pp. 341–342.

[7] Vernon L. Parrington, *The Romantic Revolution in America* (New York, 1924), p. 174.

Greek city-state, with its aristocratic democracy, was Calhoun's ideal—an ideal at variance with the prevailing political opinion of the 1830's. The rapidity of the change and the extent to which Calhoun's philosophy lagged behind that of many of his contemporaries is indicated by Josiah Quincy's report that the Great Nullifier had said to him, "I think you will see that the interests of *gentlemen* of the North and those of the South are identical." Quincy later wrote, "I can quote no utterance more characteristic of the political Washington of twenty-six [1826] than this. The inference was that the 'glittering generalizations' of the Declaration were never meant to be taken seriously. *Gentlemen* were the natural rulers of America, after all."[1]

Coonskin democracy believed thoroughly in the "glittering generalizations" of the Declaration and came to Washington to ensure their application, regardless of the Calhouns, Adamses, and Websters, who represented the seaboard aristocracy. It seems probable that this conflict widened the breach, not only between Calhoun and his contemporaries in the Senate but also between the Nullifier and the masses, particularly those in the North.

Calhoun's use of logical methods and abstract principles did not encourage rapprochement between himself and the general public. Dyer characterized him as "speculative, theoretical, and philosophical"— a criticism so widespread that on one occasion, at least, the Senator defended himself against the accusation.[2] Mrs. Smith[3] and V. L. Parrington,[4] although writing about a century apart, came to the conclusion that personalities, rather than principles, appealed to the electorate during the 1830's.

Calhoun was not insensible to the role that personalities played in Washington, for he "was accustomed to make himself agreeable to young men appearing in Washington who might possibly rise to influence in their respective communities."[5] Senator Benton, of Missouri, informed John Wentworth that the Carolinian customarily procured "interviews with young men, and instill[ed] into their minds the seeds of secession, nullification, and treason."[6] It seems evident that the former Vice-President sought to impress his younger colleagues in Congress by personal appeals made within the confines of Calhoun's home in Washington.

The Senator's reputation as a conversationalist would suggest that the methods used to gain personal and political friends were partially success-

[1] Josiah Quincy, *Figures of the Past* (Boston, 1883), p. 264.
[2] "Speech on the Force Bill," *Congressional Debates*, Twenty-second Congress, second session, 1832–1833, IX, Part 1, 538; see also R. K. Crallé, *The Works of John C. Calhoun* (New York, 1888), II, 232. Hereafter this collection will be referred to as *Works*.
[3] Smith, *op. cit.*, p. 310.
[4] Parrington, *op. cit.*, p. 174.
[5] Quincy, *op. cit.*, p. 263.
[6] Wentworth, *op. cit.*, p. 20.

ful. Wentworth[1] and Dyer[2] had the highest praise for his abilities in this field. An English traveler commented that Calhoun was "remarkably free from that dogmatism which constitutes not the least of the social sins of Americans."[3] Harriet Martineau was not so favorably impressed. "He meets men," she wrote, "and harangues them by the fireside as in the Senate."[4] Her judgment was substantiated by a close friend and eulogist of the Carolinian, who said: "The colloquial powers of Mr. Calhoun have been highly lauded. But this is a mistake. Strictly speaking he had no uncommon endowment in that line. . . . The conversation in which he really shone was but a modified species of Senatorial debate."[5] We may conclude from these evidences that Calhoun had no uncommon endowment as a conversationalist but that he did have the power to impress some of his auditors.

His fondness for conversation and the means used to ensure auditors is an expression of the social nature of the man. This characteristic was also shown by the correctness with which his social duties in the capital were fulfilled. In addition, the Fort Hill home was "full of guests, who were welcomed with the open hospitality of the days of Southern prosperity."[6] But he was not a convivialist; he enjoyed meeting people and conversing with them, yet he never permitted himself to break the bonds of dignity and restraint. His many duties enforced long hours of labor alone, and his speeches indicate that much time was spent in reading and thinking. It is probable that he did not mix enough with people, but he certainly was neither unsociable nor reclusive.

A certain austerity was evident in the man. Perhaps the poor health which he had during most of his life and the stern Scotch Presbyterian beliefs of his parents were responsible for this quality. He lived an exemplary life, relatively free from the gambling and drinking that characterized many of the prominent men of the day. His political beliefs and talents were not for sale, as it seems was the case with Webster, for example. Although not a member of any denomination, he was religious to the extent of attempting to practice his Christianity.

Few instances of humor are to be found in Calhoun's speeches. Acquaintances remarked that they had never heard him make a jest or ridicule or

---

[1] *Ibid.*
[2] Dyer, *op. cit.*, p. 185.
[3] Thomas Hamilton, *Men and Manners in America* (2d ed., London, 1834), II, 146.
[4] Harriet Martineau, *Retrospect of Western Travel* (Cincinnati, 1838), I, 153.
[5] James Harvey Hammond, *An Oration on the Life, Character and Services of John Caldwell Calhoun* (Charleston, 1850), pp. 67–68.
[6] Mrs. Patrick Hues Mell, in the *Charleston Sunday News*, Apr. 30, 1905, quoted by Meigs, *op. cit.*, II, 84.

satirize a human being.[1] Levity simply was not a part of the character of the man. His failure to observe, appreciate, and use the lighter elements of life must stand as a defect of importance in his life.

That he was courageous is beyond question. Jackson's supposed threat to hang him for treason[2] left him unmoved and determined to proceed with his plan to resign the Vice-Presidency and return to Washington as a Senator—an act which established both his physical and his moral courage. Rarely was Calhoun to be found upon the popular side of a public question. He may have been obstinate, but he had the courage to fight for what he believed to be right, regardless of the consequences to him as an individual.

A pen portrait or two may enable us to visualize the man as some of his contemporaries saw him. Oliver Dyer wrote:

He was tall and gaunt. His complexion was dark and Indian like, and there seemed to be an inner complexion of a dark soul shining out through the skin of his face. His eyes were large, black, piercing, scintillant. His hair was iron grey, and rising straight from his scalp fell over on all sides. . . . His features were strongly marked, and their expression was firm, stern, aggressive, threatening.[3]

Miss Martineau described his head as "one of the most remarkable in the country."[4] These evidences suggest that he was a man of considerable stature, with characteristics that would catch and hold the attention of his auditors.

Opinions vary concerning the facility with which this physical mechanism was employed in a speech situation. In 1816 he was described as "the most elegant speaker that sits in the House. His gestures are easy and graceful, his manner forcible. . . . "[5] Dyer,[6] who heard him speak many times during the period from 1840 to 1850, was impressed by the "elegance of his diction, and the exquisite courtesy of his demeanor." But Wentworth was of the opinion that he "spoke like a college professor demonstrating to his class,"[7] and Miller[8] commented, "his gestures were stiff and like a pump handle. There was no ease, flexibility, grace, or charm in his manner." On another occasion the same critic described Calhoun's behavior in these words: "When he first rose to speak he almost always bent forward as if

[1] Mary Bates, "The Private Life of Calhoun," *International Monthly Magazine*, 4 (1851): 173–180.

[2] Marquis James, *The Life of Andrew Jackson* (New York, 1938), p. 617, quoting Poore, *op. cit.*, I, 138.

[3] Dyer, *op. cit.*, pp. 148–149.

[4] Martineau, *op. cit.*, I, 190.

[5] J. C. Jewett, *William and Mary Quarterly*, 17: 143.

[6] Dyer, *op. cit.*, p. 150.

[7] Wentworth, *op. cit.*, p. 21.

[8] Walter L. Miller, *American Law Review*, 33 (1899): 542.

from diffidence. But when fully aroused, he became stern and erect in his bearing. . . . " The stress under which the famous "Force Bill Speech" was given had caused Calhoun to push "the chairs out of his way, to the ends of the desks, and deliver . . . his speech, walking rapidly from side to side of his cage."[1]

It is evident that physically, Calhoun was active when he spoke, but the judgments concerning the effectiveness of this action varied according to the standards of the various observors.

Many critics, however, agree that the Senator's use of facial expression was a pertinent part of his speaking manner. One observed, "His eyes flashed, his brow seemed charged with thunder. . . . "[2] A second[3] believed that "His eyes indicated quick perception." Wrote Mathews, "His brilliant spectral eyes, his colorless cheeks, blanched with thought, and his compressed lips . . . riveted your attention as with hooks of steel."[4] Since other contemporaries[5] have made similar observations, we may conclude that his use of facial expression was sufficient to attract attention and cause favorable comment.

When we turn from the Great Nullifier's use of bodily action and facial expression to a consideration of his voice, inconsistencies again appear in the comments of his hearers. It was said that he had "only a poor voice which he had cultivated to make his utterances clear, strong, full and distinct; not musical but pleasant."[6] Some support[7] is given to this comment by an anonymous author, who stated that Calhoun, while at Waddell's academy, had an impediment or hesitancy in his speech. Oliver Dyer was "much impressed by the . . . bell-like sweetness and resonance of his voice . . . ";[8] Wentworth[9] believed that his voice "was silvery and attractive, but very earnest." Mathews[10] called his voice "harsh," and Miss Martineau[11] thought that it was "not sufficiently modulated . . . "; in fact, when he occasionally warmed into vehemence his "voice became almost a bark. . . . " From these conflicting reports, no valid statement

---

[1] Walter L. Miller, "Calhoun as a Lawyer and Statesman," *Green Bag*, 11: 275.

[2] Martineau, *op. cit.*, I, 194.

[3] Wentworth, *op. cit.*, p. 21.

[4] William Mathews, *Oratory and Orators* (Chicago, 1879), p. 312.

[5] Jenkins, *op. cit.*, p. 446; Miller, *American Law Review, op. cit.*, p. 542; Smith, *op. cit.*, p. 335.

[6] H. S. Fulkerson, *Random Recollections of Early Days in Mississippi* (Vicksburg, 1885), p. 63.

[7] *Measures, Not Men: Illustrated by Some Remarks upon the Public Conduct and Character of John C. Calhoun*, by a Citizen of New York (New York, 1823).

[8] Dyer, *op. cit.*, pp. 150–151.

[9] Wentworth, *op. cit.*, p. 21.

[10] Mathews, *op. cit.*, pp. 312–313.

[11] Martineau, *op. cit.*, I, 194.

concerning Calhoun's voice may be drawn, but his success as a speaker suggests that it was not unpleasant.

Speech Premises

The Nature of Our Government. It was Calhoun's belief that man's social nature brought him into association with other men. The selfish nature of some individuals in the group thus formed caused them to take advantage of other members. Governments were established to regulate this selfishness, but this institution contained representatives of the same selfish interests that were present in the group as a whole. Thus it, too, had a strong tendency toward disorder and abuse of its powers.[1] Therefore, constitutions were devised to check this tendency; governments based on such instruments had as their indispensable and primary principle the "responsibility of the rulers to the ruled, through the right of suffrage."[2] The rulers were but agents of the ruled, who retained complete sovereignty in themselves. Sovereignty could be neither delegated nor divided, but *powers,* one of its essential attributes, might be delegated by the people to their rulers.[3]

The government of the United States was, of course, founded on a constitution. In signing the Constitution, each state ratified that instrument for itself, and the citizens of the several states were bound to it only through the act of their respective state.[4] The Constitution, then, was a compact. Calhoun seems to have arrived at this concept after a study of the ratification documents of Massachusetts, New Hampshire, and Virginia[5] and the Virginia[6] and Kentucky Resolutions.[7] Webster could not accept this interpretation of these documents and declared, "The Constitution of the United States is not a league, confederacy or compact between the people of the several states in their sovereign capacities."[8] The Oracle from Massachusetts may have been sincere in this belief, or he may have been astute enough to see that this concept was virtually the keystone in the argument that the Carolinian had erected. Opinions varied in 1833 and have continued to vary concerning the interpretations to be placed on the documents

---

[1] *Works,* I, 1–7.

[2] *Ibid.,* I, 12.

[3] "Speech on the Force Bill," *Congressional Debates, op. cit.,* pp. 537–538; *Works,* II, 232.

[4] "Speech on the Force Bill," *Congressional Debates, op. cit.,* p. 532; *Works,* II, 221.

[5] "Documents Illustrative of the Formation of the Union of the American States," *House Document* 398, Sixty-ninth Congress, first session (Washington, D.C., 1927), pp. 1018, 1024, 1027–1034.

[6] James Madison, *Writings* (Gaillard Hunt, ed., New York, 1900–1908), VI, 326–331.

[7] Thomas Jefferson, *Writings* (P. L. Ford, ed., New York, 1894), VII, 289–309.

[8] *Congressional Debates,* Twenty-second Congress, second session, 1832–1833, IX, Part 1, 562.

Calhoun used. A. M. Schlesinger, of Harvard, is inclined to agree with the point of view expressed by the Great Nullifier.[1]

By ratifying the Constitution, the states renounced none of their sovereignty but delegated to the Federal government the right to exercise specific powers under certain conditions,[2] while reserving others to themselves. One of the powers so reserved was that of maintaining direct relationships with the electorate, and Calhoun protested sharply against the Force Bill on the grounds that it violated this reserved power, in that it treated the lawful resistance of a sovereign state as the "lawless acts of so many individuals, without possessing sovereignty or political rights."[3]

The parties to the compact retained the power to judge any infraction of their agreement, and in the case of a deliberate and dangerous exercise of power not granted to the Federal government, the states were empowered to nullify, within their own borders, the act of the government that assumed such power.[4] Perhaps the best statement of this concept of nullification is found in the famous "Letter to Governor Hamilton" and reads:

> I do not claim for a State the right to abrogate an act of the General Government. It is the Constitution that annuls an unconstitutional act. Such an act is of itself void and of no effect. What I claim is the right of the state, *as far as its citizens are concerned, to declare the extent of the obligation, and that such declaration is binding on them.* (Italics Calhoun's.)[5]

This is the essence of the doctrine with which Calhoun is so intimately associated and which he regarded as his finest achievement.

Nullification was a necessity, because no other means existed of settling disputes between the Federal and the state governments.[6] The Supreme Court could not be used in such instances, since the grant of such power would raise a mere department of the Federal government to a position superior to that held by one of the parties that had created the Constitution and thus invest it with the authority to alter the relative powers of the Federal and state governments.[7] The framers of the Constitution had specifically refused to grant such power to the Supreme Court, and it was never intended that this perogative should be granted. In fact, it was the

---

[1] A. M. Schlesinger, *Political and Social History of the United States,* 1829–1925 (New York, 1925), p. 30.

[2] "Speech on the Force Bill," *Congressional Debates, op. cit.,* pp. 537–538; *Works,* II, 231–233.

[3] *Ibid., Congressional Debates,* p. 536; *Works,* II, 228.

[4] *Ibid., Congressional Debates,* pp. 521, 532; *Works,* II, 200, 221; or *Works,* VI, 149.

[5] *Works,* VI, 149–150; see also *Works,* II, 200–201, 221; or "Speech on the Force Bill," *Congressional Debates, op. cit.,* pp. 521, 532.

[6] "Speech on the Force Bill," *Congressional Debates, op. cit.,* p. 550; *Works,* II, 256.

[7] *Ibid., Congressional Debates,* pp. 521–523; *Works,* II, 201–204.

Senator's belief that the Federal government had no power granted it by the Constitution for the control of a state by force, by veto, by judicial process, or by any other form.[1] Nullification was, therefore, a peaceful, effective, and practical means of settling disputes between the Federal and the state governments.

Secession was not contemplated in nullification, since the two differed in nature, object, and effect. Secession might result from nullification, if the other members of the compact attempted to grant the power in dispute. Used in conjunction with the concept of concurrent majorities, nullification would serve as a cement binding the parties to the compact into a cohesive unit.[2]

Calhoun further defended nullification by insisting that a return to the Articles of Confederation was not contemplated. Under the terms of the articles, one state could arrest the action of the Federal government, while under the Constitution, the action of more than one-fourth of the states was necessary to accomplish that result.

If an impasse was reached between the Federal government and a state or states, the former would have the choice of two lines of action: to abandon the contested power or to apply to the states, the source of all political authority, in one of two modes prescribed by the Constitution. An amendment to the Constitution, approved by a two-thirds majority in both houses of Congress and ratified by three-fourths of the states, would turn the trick, or an appeal could be made to the states convened in general assembly, in which case a three-fourths majority favoring the delegation of the contested power would settle the question.

But Calhoun's reputation as a political philosopher rests not upon nullification but upon his concept of concurrent majorities.[3] Stated fragmentarily in the "Letter to Governor Hamilton,"[4] the concept was brought to completion in the "Speech on the Force Bill"[5] and reiterated in the "Disquisitions on Government."[6] The presentation of this idea in the "Speech on the Force Bill" reads:

the community . . . shall upon all questions tending to bring the parts into conflict, the thirteen [states] against the eleven [states], take the will, not of the twenty-four as a unit, but of the thirteen and of the eleven separately,—the majority of each governing the parts, and where they concur, governing the whole,—and where they disagree, arresting the action of the government.[7]

[1] "Letter," *Works*, VI, 154.
[2] "Speech on the Force Bill," *Congressional Debates*, *op. cit.*, p. 550; *Works*, II, 257.
[3] Parrington, *op. cit.*, p. 72.
[4] *Works*, VI, 181–192.
[5] *Congressional Debates*, *op. cit.*, pp. 547–552; *Works*, II, 250–252, 254–255, 257–259.
[6] *Works*, I, 1–107, particularly 24–25, 28, 35, 59.
[7] *Congressional Debates*, *op. cit.*, p. 547; *Works*, II, 250.

The title given by the speaker to this concept may have been his own invention, but the principle had been in use in Rome when that state was governed by the tribunes; it formed a part of the machinery of the British Empire prior to and during Calhoun's life, and it had been applied to the reorganization of the government of South Carolina in 1808.[1] It is in operation today in the organization of the British Empire, in the French government, and in a limited manner in the U.S.S.R. Stripped of its State Rights appendages and modified in certain respects, it is the heart of the familiar principle of the referendum.

The most fantastic political idea which Calhoun produced was that of providing for two chief executives of the United States. The North and the South would each elect a president, and all measures passed by Congress would require signatures of both executives before becoming laws. Suggested vaguely in his speech on March 4, 1850,[2] and stated[3] more adequately in his "Discourse on the Constitution and Government of the United States," the concept achieved no fame and has been forgotten.

The gentleman from South Carolina was fearful of the power of a numerical majority. Nullification, concurrent majorities, and dual executives were all devices that were designed to protect a minority group from the will of a strong majority. The present methods of popular government, especially in the United States, would never have been accepted by the man from Fort Hill.

Protective Tariffs. The protective tariff seems to have had its origins in the tariff of 1816, passed from infancy to childhood by the enactment of 1820, grew to sizable adolescence through the bill passed in 1824, came to maturity in the "tariff of abominations" in 1828, and was officially fastened upon the nation as a permanent fixture by the Act of 1832.

The protective tariff was responsible for a number of the Senator's most important speeches[4] and writings.[5] In 1816 Calhoun was an advocate of "ample protection" for industry,[6] but by 1833 he had modified his position

---

[1] Meigs, *op. cit.*, I, 104–105.

[2] *Congesssional Globe*, Thirty-first Congress, first session, 1849–1850, XXI, Part 1, 451–455, especially 455.

[3] *Works*, I, 111–406; note especially 392–393.

[4] "Speech on the Tariff Bill," Apr. 4, 1816, *Annals of Congress*, Fourteenth Congress, first session, pp. 1329–1366, or *Works*, II, 163–173, where this speech is dated Apr. 6, 1816. See also "Speech on the Force Bill," *Congressional Debates, op. cit.*, pp. 519–533, or *Works*, II, 197–262; "Speech on Resolutions," Feb. 26, 1833, *Congressional Debates*, Twenty-second Congress, second session, 1832–1833, pp. 750–774, or *Works*, II, 263–309; "Speech on the Passage of the Tariff Bill," Aug. 5, 1842, *Appendix to the Congressional Globe*, Twenty-seventh Congress, second session, 1841–1842, I, 771–775, or *Works*, IV, 171–212.

[5] "Exposition and Address to the People of South Carolina," *Works*, VI, 124–144; and "Address to the People of the United States," *Works*, VI, 193–209.

[6] "Speech on the Tariff Bill," *Annals of Congress, op. cit.*, p. 1334; *Works*, II, 170.

by drawing a sharp distinction between tariffs for revenue purposes, which were entirely constitutional, and tariffs that raised duties "above the point of greatest revenue . . . ",[1] which were unconstitutional, oppressive, and unjust—in fact, they were an insidious perversion of the power granted to the Federal government to levy taxes for revenue purposes. In the "Exposition"[2] it was maintained that such power had been specifically denied that government by the action of the Constitutional Convention.

This constitutional objection was supported by materials which showed the unequal operations of a protective tariff upon the two main sections of the country. Reference to the commercial statistics of the period demonstrated that the value of the goods imported by the South was more than twice the value of those imported by the North. The duties on these imports were subtractions from the cycle of exchange which fell, in reality, upon the producer, because they reduced the amounts received by him from exported goods. These subtractions, then, were an export tax which oppressed the South more than they did the North. Economic laws indicated that imports were paid for by exports; such being the case, Southern products paid for the materials that the North imported and supplied about two-thirds of the total revenue of the Federal government. Only one-eighth of these funds were later returned to the South by Congressional appropriation.[3]

The belief that the consumer of imported goods, rather than the producer of exported materials, paid the import taxes was challenged by the fact that the protected market of the North forced the Southern consumer to absorb such taxes but that the world market, in which the South sold her goods, provided no such opportunity for the producer to relieve himself of this burden. In addition, protective tariffs reduced the amount and value of imports, thus making it more impossible to export the products of the South that paid for those imports. The whole scheme produced a limitation of the world markets upon which the prosperity of the country as a unit, and particularly that of the Southland, depended.

The undesirability of protective tariffs has been historically associated with the policies of the Democratic party, is in agreement with the tenets of conservative economic doctrines, and was the basis of the reciprocal tariff policy of the Franklin D. Roosevelt administration, particularly after 1936.

Currency and National Banks. Calhoun's name is most commonly associated with nullification and slavery, but the question which absorbed most

---

[1] *Appendix to the Congressional Globe,* Twenty-seventh Congress, second session, 1841–1842, I, 621; or "Speech on the Tariff Bill," July 28, 1842, *Works,* IV, 169.

[2] "The South Carolina Exposition," *Works,* VI, 15.

[3] "Address to the People of South Carolina," *op. cit.,* p. 80.

of his energies from 1833 to 1842 was the nation's financial situation. It is probable that he gave a greater number of speeches on this subject than upon any other, with the possible exception of slavery.

The subject was not a new one to this speaker, for he had introduced the bill which established the national bank in 1816. The charter of this institution permitted it to operate until 1836, but Nicholas Biddle, its commanding genius, thought, in 1832, that conditions were propitious for an attempt to renew it. The temporary closing of the tariff issue and the death of the threat of nullification permitted the bank issue to be brought before Congress. Clay and Webster joined forces with their late opponent in supporting the recharter of the bank.

The Great Nullifier was firmly opposed—as a matter of party principle—to anything but a complete divorce[1] between the government and private banks, yet in both 1816 and in 1834 he supported bills which united these two institutions. The explanation for this seeming inconsistency between policy and action is to be found in his thesis that a national bank provided the only means by which the government could extricate the nation from the difficulties which confronted it.[2] The most important factor that impelled him to support a national bank was that the government had been accepting bank notes in payment of taxes and using them to meet its bills. The two institutions were so closely connected by this means that any abrupt separation would disrupt the financial system of the nation. It is to be noted that the Senator supported the recharter of the bank upon the condition that the new charter should expire in 12 years and that the bank should systematically retire its bank notes and revert to specie circulation,[3] at least so far as its government operations were concerned.

Calhoun was a "hard-money" advocate, but he recognized the necessity of some medium of exchange that was less difficult to handle, especially for transactions carried on between parties at some distance from each other.[4] But he was perfectly familiar with Gresham's law, and after the demise of

[1] "Speech on the Bill to Recharter the United States Bank," Mar. 21, 1834, *Congressional Debates*, Twenty-third Congress, first session, 1833-1834, X, Part 1, 1057-1073, especially 1069; or *Works*, II, 344-376. This attitude is more pointedly stated in his "Speech on the Treasury Note Bill," Sept. 19, 1837, *Appendix to the Congressional Globe*, Twenty-fifth Congress, first session, V, 32-37; or *Works*, III, 60-93, especially 62-63. See also "Speech on the Removal of Public Deposits," Jan. 13, 1834, *Debates in Congress*, X, Part 1, 206-223, especially 217-218; or *Works*, II, 309-344, particularly 331.

[2] "Speech on the Bill to Establish a National Bank," Feb. 26, 1816, *Annals of Congress*, Fourteenth Congress, first session, 1815-1816, No. 29, pp. 1060-1066. Note especially pp. 1065-1066; cf. "Speech to Recharter," *op. cit.* or *Works*, II, 366-367.

[3] "Bill to Recharter," *op. cit.*, *Debates*, pp. 1067-1068; *Works*, II, 364-367.

[4] "Speech on the Treasury Note Bill," Sept. 19, 1837, *Appendix to the Congressional Globe*, Twenty-fifth Congress, first session, 1837, V, 32-37; *Works*, III, 83.

the national bank he advocated that only notes of specie-paying banks be accepted by the government in payment of taxes or purchase of public lands.[1]

As early as September 19, 1837, he was advocating a modified sub-treasury system[2] which would serve only as a bank of deposit, and five months later, on February 15, 1838, he denied the right of Congress "to make a general deposit of public revenues in a bank,"[3] or the right of the government to treat bank notes as money in its financial transactions.[4] The government, therefore, should collect its dues in specie, deposit it in an institution under Congressional control and separated from private banks, and pay its bills only under authorization by Congress from the specie deposited.

Neither Clay nor Webster supported Calhoun in these proposals; Webster preferred a national bank, while Clay proposed a league of state banks similar to that advocated by Jackson and his advisers.

Internal Improvements. The Carolinian did not limit his efforts to improve the business conditions of the country to a consideration of the banking problem. Always an ardent exponent of internal improvements, he had advocated, during his earlier years, that such improvements be made by the Federal government, because, "They require[d] the resources and the general superintendence of this Government to effect and complete them."[5]

Twenty-four years later he was to remark, "The experience of a quarter of a century had proved that this government was utterly unfit to carry on works of this kind."[6] Such improvements were within the power of the states[7] or were left to the initiative of private capital;[8] in case three or more states were involved[9] or where the improvements passed through public

---

[1] *Appendix to the Congressional Globe,* Twenty-fifth Congress, first session, V, 121–126; *Works,* III, 102–133; especially the amendment which this "Speech to Separate the Government from the Banks," Oct. 3, 1836, supports.

[2] "Speech on the Treasury Note Bill," Sept. 19, 1837, *Appendix to the Congressional Globe,* Twenty-fifth Congress, first session, V, 32–37; *Works,* III, 60–92.

[3] "Speech on the Independent Treasury Bill," *Appendix to the Congressional Globe,* Twenty-fifth Congress, second session, 1837–1838, VI, 188–195, especially 191; or *Works,* III, 202–243, especially 217.

[4] *Ibid. Appendix,* VI, 191; *Works,* III, 219.

[5] "Speech on the Internal Improvement Bill," Feb. 4, 1817, *Annals of Congress,* Fourteenth Congress, second session, 1816–1817, No. 30, pp. 851–858, particularly p. 852; or *Works,* II, 188.

[6] "Speech on the Cumberland Road Bill," Apr. 1, 1840, *Appendix to the Congressional Globe,* Twenty-sixth Congress, first session, 1839–1840, pp. 368–369, especially p. 368; *Works,* III, 491.

[7] "Address to the Memphis Convention," Nov. 13, 1845, *Works,* VI, 280.

[8] *Ibid.,* p. 280.

[9] "Report on the Memphis Memorial," June 26, 1846, *Works,* V, 275. This report states clearly Calhoun's philosophy concerning public improvements.

lands, the Federal government might be expected to finance them.[1] The Federal government could give indirect aid to such projects by granting portions of the public land to those interested in such schemes or by reducing the import duties on materials that were needed to carry on internal improvements.[2]

The Senator took more than a mere political interest in these improvements. He was a director of the ill-fated Louisville, Cincinnati, and Charleston Railroad[3] and took a leading part in the Memphis[4] convention of 1846, which was held to determine how trade in the Mississippi Valley could best be stimulated.

International Policies. As a youthful member of the lower house of Congress, Calhoun had been a wholehearted nationalist. He enthusiastically supported the War of 1812, since he believed that such action was necessary if the United States was not to sink into a state of acknowledged inferiority.[5] The depredations of foreign powers, especially those of England, on our trade, commerce, and seamen, could be met only by a firm attitude on our part.[6] The sectionalist protests[7] voiced by the representatives of New York and Massachusetts were given scant attention by the young War Hawk from South Carolina.

But three decades later, he had become a sectionalist whose opposition to the spirit of nationalism was intense. The compromise that was employed in closing the Oregon boundary dispute suggests that the war spirit did not flame so fiercely during Calhoun's later life. These two attitudes were fused during the years between 1837 and 1846, when his sectionalist spirit demanded that Texas be admitted to the Union, but he expected the annexation to be accomplished without war with Mexico.

Historical records indicate that Calhoun, as Secretary of State, carried on an involved intrigue with Mexico, Texas, and England in his effort to ensure annexation of the Lone Star state.[8] He believed, however, that this action could be accomplished by a display of generosity on the part of our government. In his "Speech in Reply to Mr. Benton of Missouri,"[9] the

[1] *Ibid.*, p. 289.

[2] "Address to the Memphis Convention," *op. cit.*, pp. 281–282.

[3] Meigs, *op. cit.*, II, 352–374, particularly 359.

[4] *Works*, V, 275; VI, 280.

[5] Calhoun, *op. cit.*, p. 9.

[6] "Speech on the Bill to Encourage Enlistments," Jan. 15, 1814, *Annals of Congress,* Thirteenth Congress, second session, 1813–1814, No. 26, pp. 994 *et seq.; Works*, II, 59; see also *Annals of Congress,* Thirteenth Congress, second session, No. 27, pp. 1673–1694, especially pp. 1674–1681, "Speech on the Loan Bill," Feb. 25, 1814; *Works*, II, 69–103, particularly 72–82.

[7] *Annals of Congress,* Thirteenth Congress, second session, No. 27, pp. 1686–1690.

[8] *Works*, V, 311–414, especially 330–356, 379–399.

[9] *Congressional Globe,* Twenty-ninth Congress, second session, 1846–1847, No. 16, pp. 498–501; or *Works*, IV, 362–382.

"Speech in Reply to Mr. Turney,"[1] and his "Speech on His Resolutions in Reference to the War with Mexico,"[2] he vehemently opposed the war which developed.

Defeated on this point by the action of President Polk, who seems to have desired a war,[3] Calhoun attempted to make the war defensive in character. He unsuccessfully opposed the granting of the funds necessary to carry on a war of conquest in his "Speech on the Three Million Bill"[4] and his two speeches on "The Ten Regiment Bill."[5]

His opposition to such a war was based not only on his belief that annexation could have been accomplished without a war but also upon the opinion that Mexico, with her vast territory and polyglot population, which possessed a culture pattern quite divergent from our own, could never be successfully made a part of the Union. The Mexicans would make but poor slaves and were incapable of self-government. Much as the Carolinian wanted Texas, he could see only disaster ahead for any attempt to incorporate Mexico itself into the Union.

A somewhat similar attitude was expressed when the proposal was made that Yucatan should be taken by force of arms.[6] An imperialistic policy or meddling in the affairs of other nations was discountenanced as dangerous to the peace, safety, and prosperity of the Union. It is interesting to note in this connection that the former Vice-President had quite a different interpretation of the Monroe Doctrine than that held by his contemporaries or statesmen of our day. As Secretary of War in Monroe's cabinet, he had participated in the discussions which led to the formulation of the proclamation, and he thought he knew what interpretation Monroe placed on the document. It was never intended that the Union should resist by armed force the intervention of any nation in Central or South America, unless such action obviously threatened the peace and safety of the Union.[7]

There can be little doubt that Calhoun feared foreign powers, especially England, whose commercial domination, sea power, and army he viewed

---

[1] *Ibid.*, pp. 395–399; or *Works*, VI, 328–339.

[2] *Appendix to the Congressional Globe*, Thirtieth Congress, first session, 1847–1848, pp. 49–53, especially pp. 52–53; or *Works*, IV, 396–424; see as well Meigs, *op. cit.*, II, 382–387. For an opposing point of view see R. T. Oliver, "Behind the Word: John Caldwell Calhoun," *Quarterly Journal of Speech*, 22, No. 3 (October, 1936): 424.

[3] James K. Polk, "Message to Congress," Dec. 2, 1845, *Appendix to the Congressional Globe*, Twenty-ninth Congress, first session, 1845–1846, p. 2; see also *House Executive Document* No. 60, Thirtieth Congress, first session, pp. 91, 108.

[4] *Congressional Globe*, Twenty-ninth Congress, second session, 1846–1847, No. 16, pp. 356–359; or *Works*, IV, 303–328, especially 304–306 and 316–328.

[5] *Congressional Globe*, Thirtieth Congress, first session, particularly pp. 630–633.

[6] "Speech on Yucatan," May 15, 1848, *Appendix to the Congressional Globe*, Thirtieth Congress, first session, 1847–1848, No. 17, p. 632; or *Works*, IV, 464–469.

[7] "Speech on Yucatan," *Appendix to the Congressional Globe*, p. 630; *Works*, IV, 458.

with apprehension.[1] His successful attempt to avoid war over the Oregon boundary was predicated upon these fears, as well as upon belief that historically our claim was weak and that time was a force which would react favorably for the Union, for it would permit the territory to be settled with Americans rather than English colonists. But he regarded France with some favor and raised his voice in protest when war against that nation was proposed in 1812 and in 1837.[2]

Calhoun's foreign policy was elastic. Every international situation affecting the Union directly was to be met in terms of its own particular needs. If our interests could be best served by a war—as in 1812—then that became his policy. But if the peculiarities of the situation suggested that a compromise settlement—as in the Oregon case—would suit our interests, that policy was adopted. The paramount objective was the peace and safety of the Union. Whatever policy seemed to offer a superior opportunity to ensure these desires was certain to be accepted by the statesman from South Carolina.

Slavery. The presence of a considerable number of slaves in the colonies, especially in those south of Mason and Dixon's line, had presented a problem to the Founding Fathers that they resolved by the well-known compromises in the Constitution. Theoretically, these compromises settled the question, but in reality, the struggle had just started. The formation of the Northwest Territory, the dispute which terminated in the Missouri Compromise, in an indirect manner the nullification episode, Abolition petitions, and the westward extension of the Union were all milestones along the road that led to the Civil War.

In his "Speech on the Force Bill"[3] and "Speech on Resolutions in Support of States Rights,"[4] Calhoun warned his Southern colleagues that the invasion by the Federal government of the reserved powers of the states was a threat to slavery. Three years later a second constitutional defense of the South's peculiar institution was established by maintaining that "Congress [had] no legitimate jurisdiction over the subject of slavery either here or elsewhere"[5] but that rather the institution[6] was "under the

---

[1] "Speech on the Loan Bill," *op. cit.*, Feb. 25, 1814.

[2] *Ibid.*, or *Works*, II, 85. See also his "Speech on the Relations of the United States and France," Feb. 14, 1837, *Congressional Globe*, Twenty-fourth Congress, first session, No. 3, p. 114, or *Works*, III, 14–27, particularly 26.

[3] *Congressional Debates, op. cit.*, p. 553; *Works*, II, 261.

[4] *Congressional Debates*, Twenty-second Congress, first session, IX, Part 1, 750–774, especially 774; *Works*, II, 308.

[5] "Speech on Abolition Petitions," Mar. 9, 1836, *Congressional Debates*, Twenty-fourth Congress, first session, 1835–1836, XII, Part I, 774; or *Works*, II, 483. See also "Speech on the Reception of Abolition Petitions," Feb. 6, 1837, *Congressional Debates*, Twenty-fourth Congress, second session, XII, Part I, 710–722; or *Works*, II, 625–634.

[6] *Ibid.*, *Debates*, first session, p. 1139; *Works*, II, 517.

sole and exclusive control of the States where the institution exists." Since this was the case, the South would be entitled to nullify any legislation by Congress which touched upon the subject—a rather empty threat in view of the fiasco of 1833.

The failure of Congress to heed these constitutional barriers to antislavery legislation would lead to civil war, for the South would resist with every drop of blood and every cent she possessed any attempts to eliminate slavery in that section of the country.[1]

When constitutional objections, threats of secession, and civil war failed to halt the antislavery agitation, the Senator shifted his defenses to meet the moral arguments of the abolitionists by declaring that slavery, instead of an evil "was a good—a positive good."[2]

This moral defense of the "peculiar labor" of the South was supported by two concepts: first, that a study of history indicated that in any civilized society, one portion of the community lived upon the labor of another portion; second, that since this was true, the real question was that of determining which labor system provided the greatest advantages for the laboring portion of the community. A detailed comparison of the living and working conditions of the slave and those of the laborer in the North and in Europe—where the industrial system was in full operation—showed that the slave possessed advantages which were not held by industrial workers. Slavery, therefore, fully justified its existence.

In his "Speech on the Oregon Bill," delivered in the Senate on June 27, 1848, Calhoun enriched this moral defense of slavery by adopting the political theory that some people are naturally and artificially inferior to others and should be expected to serve as "hewers of wood and drawers of water."[3]

It is probable that the Carolinian borrowed this concept from the Greek philosophers; but even these theorists were only restating a belief which has been traced by one authority to its expression by Confucius and from these writings back to its probable original source in the writings of Buddha.[4]

The Senator's constitutional defenses, threats of secession, and moral arguments for slavery were supplemented by attempts to persuade Congress that it could not prohibit the slaveowners from migrating into either free

[1] "Speech on Abolition Petitions," Mar. 9, 1836, *Debates*, first session, p. 777; *Works*, II, 488.

[2] "Speech on the Reception of Abolition Petitions," *op. cit., Debates*, p. 718; or *Works*, II, 631.

[3] *Appendix to the Congressional Globe*, Thirtieth Congress, first session, 1847–1848, XIII, 872; *Works*, IV, 507–511.

[4] E. S. Bogardus, *History of Social Thought* (2d ed., 3d printing, Los Angeles, 1929), p. 42, *passim.*

states or the various territorities. The struggle over the territories was particularly intense, for it was observed that the states which might be formed from such regions would either add to the dominant antislavery block in Congress or enable the proslavery forces more nearly to approach equality—if not superiority—of voting strength in the Senate. Such a condition would permit the South to block any legislation unfavorable to her "peculiar domestic institution." The historians Turner[1] and Channing[2] are of the opinion that the slave question was given force and direction by the successive additions of territory to the nation.

The careful reader may have noticed that on several questions Calhoun propounded varying policies during his career. In answer to the charge that he was inconsistent, the Senator defined inconsistency as "a change of conduct, when there is no change of circumstances to justify it."[3] He justified his seemingly inconsistent positions by insisting that the viewpoints that he expressed recognized and evaluated an issue in terms of the changing conditions which surrounded it.

Speech Methods

Most of Calhoun's speeches now available were presented before legislative bodies. In this characteristic he differs radically from Webster, who is as well known for his forensic and occasional addresses as he is for his legislative speeches, and Clay, who was regarded by some to have been without a peer in the field of occasional speaking.[4] None of the Great Nullifier's speeches before the bench nor any of those presented to popular audiences have achieved fame. Only a limited number of his occasional speeches are extant, and none of his legal efforts have been preserved. A legislative occasion preceded by adequate preparation seems to have been the speaking situation which he preferred.

This preference manifests itself in the structure and style of his speeches, which follow the classical pattern of organization. The introductions are of the short, factual, reference-to-theme type which are unemotional and lack attention-getting power. The thesis statement is likely to be found in the body of the speech rather than between the introduction and the body. They are not accurately stated and are dull. The body of the speech is generally organized on a deductive logical basis, although a combination logical-topical method may be employed. The conclusions are generally of

---

[1] F. J. Turner, *The Frontier in American History* (New York, 1920), pp. 201 *et seq.*

[2] Edward Channing, *A History of the United States* (6 vols., New York, 1905–1917), V, Chap. I.

[3] *Annals of Congress*, Thirteenth Congress, second session, 1813–1814, No. 27, 1065; *Works*, II, 109.

[4] Charles W. March, *Daniel Webster and His Contemporaries* (New York, 1852), p. 272.

the appeal-to-emotions type, but the simple rounding-out-of-the-thought type does occur. Much of the emotional appeal of the speech is likely to be found in the conclusion.

Almost every known logical device may be found in Calhoun's speeches. He consistently employed causal reasoning and showed a fondness for the cause-to-effect form. Enthymemes, particularly of the hypothetical and residual disjunctive type, were used frequently. Authority, specific instance, and analogy were employed upon occasion. Seldom is an argument supported by only one device; rather several are used.

Reductio ad absurdum, turning the tables, and the dilemma were his favorite forms of refutation, but counterargument was used frequently. These weapons may seem ponderous, but Calhoun was a constructive builder rather than a destroyer of arguments. A keen appreciation of both the proper position and the space allowed for refutation is evident. The technique was to state an opponent's argument, then to state its refutation. Neither the effect of the refutation nor its relation with the argument as a whole is considered, with the result that the refutatory technique does not compare with that used in constructive argument.

The pathetic proof is blunt, heavy, and abstract. Bald references to duty, honor, justice, right, truth, and fairness are frequently used and indicate that the classical scholars had considerable influence on Calhoun's technique. These proofs are poorly used; they do not even approach the facility which characterized his use of logical proof.

The same type of criticism applies to Calhoun's use of ethical proof. It is formal, stilted, obvious, and limited, in general, to the process of attempting to establish his character, intelligence, capacity, and vision. Severe criticism may be leveled at an opponent's argument, but rarely is the personality of an opponent subject to attack. His opponents were assumed to be gentlemen, in which class he placed himself, and among such persons name calling was deprecated.

The formal elements of unity, emphasis, and coherence are rigidly observed. A precise definition of position, a nice partition of his subject matter, a thorough analysis, and close adherence to his issues characterized the Carolinian's speeches. Issues and subissues are frequently stated as questions, answers are made, and summaries of the points given. This use of internal summaries is supplemented by external summaries. The whole process from analysis to final summary does produce rigidity, but there are few byways traversed in the process of making a speech.

Calhoun's speeches are a study in the use of language. Short, easily understood words thrown into simple, compound, and complex sentences make for ease of understanding. Figurative language, illustration, analogy, or words used merely for effect are rare. In this respect he offers a sharp contrast to the florid style which Webster displayed, particularly in his occasional addresses, and to the vituperative style which Benton employed. The total effect of Calhoun's methods was to produce speeches characterized by dry intellectuality. He seems to have been more interested in displaying intellectual processes than in moving men to accept his point of view.

Results of Calhoun's Speaking

For more than a quarter of a century the Great Nullifier was ranked as one of the nation's finest speakers. Yet he rarely achieved the ends which he sought, particularly when he spoke before the Senate. It must be admitted that as a good politician he probably asked for more than he expected to receive; his relative failure to achieve all that he demanded may have been more apparent than real. One can think of but few measures which resulted as Calhoun desired; he was defeated on nullification (the South claimed a victory on this one, since Clay's compromise reduced tariff duties), the banks, the Mexican War, internal improvements, abolition petitions, and the slavery issue. International affairs were settled as he advocated: war with England in 1812, a compromise agreement on the Oregon question, annexation of Texas, and a defeat of the Yucatan proposal.

His defeats, however, must not be charged against his speaking. In the nullification controversy he faced an embittered and hostile audience which because of personal and political affiliations could never have voted to support him. The Senate in 1850 was not so preponderantly in opposition as had been the case in 1833, but a strong majority was opposed—so opposed that the mighty Webster could do nothing with it.

Calhoun's function as a speaker was to present and keep alive a minority viewpoint. That he succeeded is indicated by the prominence which he achieved as a speaker and as a politician. The causes which he favored were doomed to defeat by the catastrophic changes produced by the impact of the Industrial Revolution upon the social, economic, and political patterns of American culture.

SELECTED BIBLIOGRAPHY

Primary Sources

Autobiography

Calhoun, John C.: *Life of John Caldwell Calhoun*, New York, 1843.

Reminiscences and Letters

Benton, Thomas H.: *Thirty Year's View*, 2 vols., New York, 1854–1858.
Dyer, Oliver: *Great Senators of the United States Forty Years Ago*, New York, 1889.
Fulkerson, Henry S.: *Random Recollections of Early Days in Mississippi*, Vicksburg, Miss., 1885.

Hale, Edward Everett: *Memories of a Hundred Years Ago*, New York, 1904.

Hamilton, Thomas: *Men and Manners in America*, 2 vols., 2d ed., London, 1834.

Hammond, James Harvey: *An Oration on the Life, Character and Services of John Caldwell Calhoun*, Charleston, S.C., 1850.

Julian, George W.: *Political Recollections*, 1840–1872, Chicago, 1884.

Martineau, Harriet: *Retrospect of Western Travel*, 2 vols., Cincinnati, 1838.

Mathews, William: *Oratory and Orators*, Chicago, 1879.

Nevins, Allan; compiler and ed.: *American Social History as Recorded by British Travellers*, New York, 1923.

Poore, Benjamin Perley: *Perley's Reminiscences*, Philadelphia, 1886.

Quincy, Josiah: *Figures of the Past*, Boston, 1883.

Smith, Margaret B.: *The First Forty Years of Washington Society*, New York, 1906.

Tyler, Lyon G.: *The Letters and Times of the Tylers*, 2 vols., Richmond, 1884.

Wentworth, John: *Congressional Reminiscences*, Chicago, 1882.

Wise, John S.: *Recollections of Thirteen Presidents*, New York, 1906.

Documents

Commons, John R., *et al.*: *Documentary History of American Industrial Society*, 11 vols., Cleveland, 1910–1911.

Correspondence between General Andrew Jackson and John C. Calhoun, Washington, D.C., 1831.

Register of Debates, Joseph Gales and William W. Seaton, 1824–1837.

U. S. Annals of Congress, 1811–1824.

U. S. Annual Report of the American Historical Association, 1898, 1899, 1911, 1913, 1914, 1929.

U. S. Congressional Globe, 1833–1850.

U. S. Documents Illustrative of the Formation of the American States, House Document 398, Sixty-ninth Congress, first session, Washington, D.C., 1927.

U. S. House Executive Document 60, Thirtieth Congress, first session.

Newspapers, Manuscripts, Magazines, Pamphlets

American Historical Review, 6 (1900–1901).

American Law Review, 33 (1899).

Catalogue of the Society of Brothers in Unity, MS, New Haven, Conn., 1840, Yale College Library.

Charleston Courier, 1803–1852.

Charleston Sunday News, 1879–1926.

Green Bag, 11 (1899).

Gulf States Historical Magazine, 1 (1902–1903).

Harper's Weekly, 1, 2, 3 (1857–1859).

International Monthly Magazine, 4 (1851).

Measures, Not Men, Illustrated by Some remarks upon the Public Conduct and Character of John Caldwell Calhoun, by a Citizen of New York, New York, 1823.

National Intelligencer, 1811–1853.

New York Daily Tribune, 1841–1866.

New York Morning Post, 1833.

Niles' Register, 1–54 (1811–1835).

The President and Fellows: *The Laws of Yale College*, New Haven, 1795, reprinted, 1860.

Records of Linonia, MS, New Haven, Conn., Yale College Library.

Records of Phi Beta Kappa, MS, New Haven, Conn., Yale College Library.

Southern Literary Messenger, 16 (1850); 20 (1854).

Washington Daily Union, 1845–1857.

William and Mary Quarterly, 18, 1st series (1900).

John C. Calhoun

Secondary Sources

Biographies

Bradford, Gamaliel: *As God Made Them*, Boston and New York, 1929.
Clark, A. Howard, ed.: *National Register of the Sons of American Revolution*, New York, 1902.
Cuningham, Clarence, ed.: *Ladies Calhoun Monument Association*, oration by L.Q.C. Lamar, Charleston, S.C., 1888.
Dodd, William E.: *Statesmen of the Old South*, New York, 1911.
Duyckinck, E. A.: *National Portrait Gallery*, New York, 1861.
Hunt, Gaillard: *John C. Calhoun*, Philadelphia, 1908.
Jenkins, John S.: *Life of John Caldwell Calhoun*, Auburn, N.Y., 1850.
Johnson, Gerald W.: *America's Silver Age*, New York, 1939.
Lewis, William Draper: *Great American Lawyers*, 8 vols., Philadelphia, 1907-1909.
March, Charles W.: *Daniel Webster and His Contemporaries*, New York, 1852.
Meigs, William M.: *The Life of John Caldwell Calhoun*, New York, 1917.
Phillips, U. B.: "John Caldwell Calhoun," *Dictionary of American Biography*, Vol. III, New York, 1929.
Pinckney, G. M.: *Life of John C. Calhoun*, Charleston, S.C., 1903.
Seitz, Don C.: "*The Also Rans*": *Men Who Missed the Presidency*, New York, 1928.
The South in the Building of the Nation, 13 vols., Richmond, 1909-1913, Vol. XI.
Starke, W. Pinckney: *Annual Report of the American Historical Association*, Vol. II, Washington, D.C., 1899.
Von Holst, Herman E.: *John C. Calhoun*, Boston and New York, 1899.

Theses and Criticisms

Curry, Herbert L.: An Evaluation of the Debating Technique of John Caldwell Calhoun in Representative Pro-Slavery Speeches, 1847-1850, unpublished M.A. thesis, University of Iowa, 1936.
Oliver, Robert T.: "Behind the Word: John Caldwell Calhoun," *Quarterly Journal of Speech*, 22, No. 3 (October, 1936).
Ritzman, Carl H.: A Critical Study of Four Representative Speeches on States Rights by John C. Calhoun, unpublished M.A. thesis, University of Iowa, 1935.
Schaper, Roxana: Southern Anti-Slavery Sentiment and Behavior, 1830-1860, unpublished M.A. thesis, University of Iowa, 1933.
Winters, Carolyn Z.: Defection of the Calhounites, 1832-1840, unpublished M.A. thesis, University of Iowa, 1923.

Speeches and Writings

Cralle, Richard K.: *The Works of John C. Calhoun*, 6 vols., New York, 1888.
Jefferson, Thomas: *Writings*. P. L. Ford, ed., 10 vols., New York, 1892-1899.
Madison, James: *Writings*. Gaillard Hunt, ed., 8 vols., New York, 1900-1908.
Webster, Daniel: *The Works of Daniel Webster*, 6 vols., New York, 1853.

General

Bancroft, Frederic: *Calhoun and the South Carolina Nullification Movement*, Baltimore, 1928.
Beard, Charles A., and Mary R. Beard: *Rise of American Civilization*, 3 vols., New York, 1927-1939.
Bogardus, Emory S.: *History of Social Thought*, 2d rev. ed., 3d printing, Los Angeles, 1929.
Bowers, Claude G.: *The Party Battles of the Jackson Period*, Boston, 1922.
Bruce, Harold R.: *American Parties and Politics*, 3d ed., New York, 1936.

Channing, Edward: *A History of the United States*, 6 vols., New York, 1905–1917.

Gettell, R. G.: *History of American Political Thought*, New York, 1928.

George, J. Z.: *The Political History of Slavery in the United States*, New York, 1915.

Holmes, A. G., and G. R. Sherill: *Thomas Green Clemson: His Life and Work*, Richmond, 1937.

Houston, David Franklin: *A Critical Study of Nullification in South Carolina*, New York, 1896.

James, Marquis: *The Life of Andrew Jackson*, New York, 1938.

Lodge, Henry C.: *Life and Letters of George Cabot*, 2d rev. ed., Boston, 1878.

McKenzie, Charles W.: *Party Government in the United States*, New York, 1938.

Parrington, Vernon L.: *Main Currents in American Thought*, 3 vols., New York, 1927–1930.

Pritchett, John Perry: *Calhoun—His Defense of the South*, Poughkeepsie, N.Y., 1937.

Schlesinger, A. M.: *Political and Social History of the United States*, 1829–1925, New York, 1925.

Turner, F. J.: *The Frontier in American History*, New York, 1920.

24

Daniel Webster[1]

by Wilbur Samuel Howell

and Hoyt Hopewell Hudson

Webster was born at Salisbury, N. H., on January 18, 1782, of Scottish ancestry. He was educated at village school, by private tutoring, and at Exeter Academy, whence he proceeded, after further private studies, to Dartmouth College in 1797. After being graduated in 1801, he entered a law office in Salisbury and then taught school and assisted the register of deeds in Fryeburg, Me., for most of 1 year. After further legal apprenticeship at Salisbury, he removed to Boston in 1804 and entered the office of the Honorable Mr. Christopher Gore. He was admitted to the bar in 1805 and practiced law at Boscawen, N. H., for 2 years and in Portsmouth for 9 years. In 1812 he was elected a member for New Hampshire of the Thirteenth Congress and 2 years later was re-elected. In 1816 he established himself in Boston and devoted himself to his legal practice, arguing the Dartmouth College case before the Supreme Court in 1818. A member of the convention called in 1820 to revise the constitution of Massachusetts, he was in 1822 again elected to Congress and in 1827 was chosen Senator. He remained in the Senate until 1841, when he became Secretary of State under President Harrison and kept the office when Tyler succeeded Harrison; in 1843, after completing negotiations for the important Ashburton treaty, he resigned. From 1845 to 1850 he was again in the Senate, and from midsummer, 1850, until his death on his farm at Marshfield, Mass., October 24, 1852, he was Secretary of State under President Fillmore.

He had continued his legal practice, more or less continuously, throughout his career. His national fame as an orator may be said to date from his Plymouth bicentennial speech (delivered 1820, published 1821), but this fame became international with the publication of his speech in the House, January 19, 1824, favoring the cause of Greek independence. In 1830, a few months after his debate with Hayne, he made his famous argument in the White murder case. From 1832 on he

---

[1] Although the authors have worked together in all stages of the preparation of this essay, advising each other and seeking consistency of method and judgment, they are aware that differences in their own interests have doubtless led to differences in emphasis within the body of this work. In an effort to explain what the reader may detect as changes in tone and spirit, they wish to say that Mr. Hudson has prepared the second and third sections of the essay and Mr. Howell, the fourth and fifth. To the first section both contributed. This acknowledgment, however, merely indicates lines of cleavage in style and manner. Each author endorses his colleague's results, and each wishes to express his pleasure in the collaboration.

was a hopeful aspirant to the Whig nomination for the Presidency, suffering disappointment in every election year, but perhaps most keenly in 1836, 1848, and 1852.

The best biographies of Webster are Claude Moore Fuess, *Daniel Webster* (2 vols., Boston, 1930), hereafter referred to as Fuess; George Ticknor Curtis, *Life of Daniel Webster* (2 vols., New York, 1872); John Bach McMaster, *Daniel Webster* (New York, 1902), referred to as McMaster; and Henry Cabot Lodge, *Daniel Webster* (Boston, 1883), referred to as Lodge. The best edition of Webster's works, including letters and much other material, is the National Edition, *The Writings and Speeches of Daniel Webster* (18 vols., Boston, 1903), hereafter referred to as *NE*.

I. *Portrait*

On July 4, 1800, the citizens of Hanover, N. H., on their own invitation, heard a Dartmouth College student, then eighteen years of age and in the third year of his college life, deliver a speech in celebration of American independence. Fifty-two years and 21 days later, on July 25, 1852, the same speaker, tired now and disappointed by a life that had brought him many rewards, but not the Presidency of his country, spoke at his estate at Marshfield, Mass., to a large group of his admirers, drawn together by his homecoming. These two dates mark the beginning and end of Daniel Webster's career as an orator. What lies between is familiar to most of us, despite a growing tendency to regard oratory of the past as one thing, at least, that may be safely forgotten. We know that Webster delivered oncefamous but now unread speeches at Plymouth, Bunker Hill, and Faneuil Hall. From our study of American history we remember the abstract of his "Reply to Hayne" and something about the "Seventh of March Speech," accepting upon the authority of the historians, if no longer upon our personal knowledge, the conviction that he possessed a sort of oratorical genius. We are even aware, in the midst of our indifference toward the forensic works upon which his reputation first came to depend, that he was a better than average speaker at the bar and an imposing advocate, before the Supreme Court, of Hamilton's and Marshall's theory of the Constitution. We accept his speeches, in short, as American classics and like to compare them with the orations of Demosthenes, Cicero, and Burke; but too easily we accept these and other classics as works so secure in reputation as to be safely ignored.

Although Webster's reputation thus has an existence quite apart from a general knowledge of its primary sources, we are nevertheless disposed to forget the extent of his activity as a speaker and the nature of the contribution that was peculiarly his own. He made many a speech famous in its own day and still associated with his name; but he made more speeches now unknown and unremembered, except by biographers and historians.

666

More than twelve volumes of the National Edition are devoted to full texts or short abstracts of his speeches. A rough compilation shows that he delivered more than five hundred public discourses (apart from brief speeches and rejoinders made in the Houses of Congress and many pleas in the courts), most of which have been preserved in whole or in part more or less as he delivered them, with some lost and a few still hidden from view in files of old newspapers.

This body of work is an impressive accomplishment, even in a country dedicated to the necessity and social utility of talk. On September 21, 1843, when Webster spoke at the State Agricultural Fair at Rochester, N. Y., he was introduced by James S. Wadsworth, who said of him that "the history of his life was the history of his country."[1] The remark equally applies to Webster's speeches. The subjects that he discussed from 1800 to 1852 were the chief subjects in the political and social history of that period, and to review his speeches in detail would be to travel across an epoch on a highway leading through the centers of a young nation's concerns. Had it been possible, indeed, to assemble, on July 25, 1852, all the persons who had heard him speak in the course of his life, the audience would have been the America of the first half of the nineteenth century. The inhabitants of the entire Atlantic seaboard, the settlers of the Ohio and the Mississippi valleys, judges of circuit court and Supreme Court, members of the House and Senate, the curious spectators of criminal trials, the old Federalists of New England, National Republicans and Whigs and Democrats, the slave-owners of the old South, invalids and pleasure seekers at Saratoga, farmers of the Genesee Valley, office workers in Baltimore, late and prodigious diners at the old Astor House in New York, frontiersmen at St. Louis, friends of Henry Clay in Kentucky, abolitionists, Quakers, Locofocos, Barnburners, Antimasons, vitriolic editors, parents who attended commencements at Hanover, men of letters, scholars at Harvard, mechanics, laborers, field hands, gamblers, horse traders, flatboat men—these would have been familiar with his voice, his appearance, his reputation. There would be present many men from thirty to forty years of age who had memorized, in their youth, passages from the "Bunker Hill Address" or from the "Reply to Hayne." Walt Whitman would be there, perhaps wondering whether he had been right when he had said that Webster was "indebted to the brandy bottle for his indignant eloquence" or nearer right when he was impressed by Webster's "grandeur of manner, size, importance, power—the breathing forth of these."[2] In the mind's eye some would see him from seats in the galleries of the House and Senate; others would

[1] *NE*, XIII, 174.
[2] *The Gathering of the Forces* (C. Rodgers and J. Black, eds., New York, 1920), II, 183, 184–185.

recall him as speaker at ceremonies attending the launching of steamboats or the opening of railroads; still others would remember that he addressed crowds waiting as his ship came to dock or shouting in the narrow streets under the balcony of his hotel. There would be memories of platforms under brown tents and in open fields; hazy memories of his voice half heard as the fumes of wine and the labor of digestion dulled the senses; bright memories of the slopes of Bunker Hill. The dignity of the old First Church in Plymouth, the chaste restraint of the Supreme Court chamber, the sting of mosquito bites at evening rallies, the smell of pine torches, the fatigue of the bystanders along Broadway, the excitement of the murder trial, the surge of crowds against rough board rostrums, the solemnity of the memorial service, the tension of the debate—recollections of all these would have been woven with the people's recollections of Webster. Their composite memory would mirror the image of the romantic-looking young man, 5 feet 10 inches tall, weighing less than 120 pounds, with black hair, massive forehead, eyebrows shaggy but not yet frozen into the stern frown of middle age, eyes quiet, steady, luminous, and dark, mouth large, chin slightly drawn into the collar as the head inclined forward; would mirror also the impressive man of forty-five, now weighing nearly 200 pounds, the brow more massive than ever, the eye stern and intense, the expression leonine, the chin grim and arrogant; would mirror finally the worn face of the man of seventy, his eyes curtained with the shadow of disappointment, his sense of superiority faded, his frown softened, his wisdom etched in lines of discouragement and resignation. The crowd would also have remembered the sound of his voice. It was a strong voice, though rarely raised in its full power, a masculine voice, deep and heavy, with none of the affected cadences or harmonies admired in schools of elocution. It was a voice that toward his later years would be hoarse with asthma and not always perfectly audible on the fringes of a meeting in the open air. It was a voice the pattern of which was the pattern of thought in the speaker's mind, emphasis being the external mark of feeling, pause, the interval when the thought formed, variety, the configuration of a lively and flexible imagination. Such a composite recollection was Daniel Webster the orator.

II. *Literature and Law*

Looking for a moment at Webster's oratory as a technique, apart from its specific content, we may tentatively say that it owed most to two disciplines—(1) a literary education and (2) the study and practice of law. Speaking before members of the Charleston bar in 1847, he said:

> If I am anything, it is the law—that noble profession, that sublime science which we all pursue—that has made me what I am. It has been my ambition, coeval

668

with my early manhood, nay, with my youth, to be thought worthy to be ranged under the banner of that profession. The law has been my chief stimulus, my controlling and abiding hope, nay, I might almost say, my presiding genius and guardian angel.

His successes in trials and suits conducted at Boscawen and Portsmouth gave him both the self-confidence and the reputation that carried him to local political leadership and made it possible for him to take a prominent position nationally as soon as he entered the House of Representatives. As is well known, in the early years at Portsmouth he learned from Jeremiah Mason, at first his legal opponent and competitor and then his close friend, many profitable lessons; principally he learned that simplicity, straightforwardness, even colloquialism were more effective in courtroom pleading than were the floridity and grandiloquence to which he had been addicted. As late as 1810 Webster was "not thought to be a deep read lawyer."[1] Yet his sharp contests with the best lawyers of New Hampshire were driving him, even then, to set greater store by exact knowledge, correct definition, and a study of precedents. Addressing hard-headed rural juries might well have cured him, even without Mason's example, of his youthful tendency to declamation.

In other respects, too, we can trace in his political speeches the influence of his legal work. When he was dealing with constitutional questions, his legal and political speaking were at one.[2] One notices as well that in his political and occasional speaking he usually traced the history of the question at issue; that often, in refuting an opponent's argument, he did so by examining the record and citing the historical basis of the argument and its refutation.[3] In all this we see the lawyer, accustomed to make a clear statement of the facts at the outset of his plea and also to cite precedents as the legal grounds of his arguments. At times he used, though playfully, the technical terms of the law in a political speech, as when he said of Southern secessionists, "their complaints and alleged grievances are like a very insufficient plea in the law; they are bad on general demurrer

---

[1] William Plumer, "Reminiscences of Daniel Webster," *NE*, XVII, 546.

[2] "Webster's arguments in *McCulloch* v. *Maryland* and *Gibbons* v. *Ogden* were the genesis of the Reply to Hayne," says Fuess, I, 373.

[3] An excellent example is Webster's answer to Hayne's question as to "*when*, and *how*, and *why* New England votes were found going for measures favorable to the West."—*NE*, VI, 26–27. Webster said that "to these questions retort would be justified; and it is both cogent and at hand. Nevertheless, I will answer the inquiry, not by retort, but by facts." In other words, he distinguishes between the usual method of the political speaker, "retort," and another method, which is essentially that of the lawyer. He goes on to cite dates and figures until he has answered all three parts of the question. Compare Lincoln's answer, at Cooper Union, to Douglas's argument concerning the attitude toward slavery of the framers of the Constitution.

for want of substance."[1] More important is the restraint that his legal experience imposed upon him in bringing charges against his opponents. It is difficult, probably impossible, to find an instance of Webster's imputing to anyone an action or even a motive without complete evidence for the imputation. Hence his personal relations with political opponents were always of the best, as had been and were his personal relations with opposing counsel in cases at law. Speaking in 1844 of President Jackson, he said: "It is hardly too much to say that he caused a revolution," but he immediately guarded himself by adding, "I do not so mean it in the strict sense of the word."[2] In his first Bunker Hill address he declared, "Let our object be our country, our whole country, and nothing but our country," thus using the pattern of the oath administered to witnesses in courts to express a sentiment that sounded deeply familiar and yet new. The sentence was widely quoted, admiringly passed from mouth to mouth, and frequently used as a toast and motto.

Webster's literary education was thoroughgoing almost beyond modern conception, though much of it was self-administered. His memories of childhood were as much of the books he read as of any other matters.[3] He says:

> I was fond of poetry. By far the greater part of Dr. Watts's Psalms and Hymns I could repeat *memoriter*, at ten or twelve years of age. . . . I remember that my father brought home from some of the lower towns Pope's Essay on Man. . . . I took it, and very soon could repeat it, from beginning to end. We had so few books that to read them once or twice was nothing. We thought they were all to be got by heart.

His father read the Bible with great force and expressiveness, and little Daniel imitated him. His qualifying examination for admission to Exeter Academy was the oral reading of Luke XXII. Pope, Addison, Shakespeare, Milton—these were the English authors with whom he had greatest and longest familiarity. He knew them rather better than a college teacher of English of today knows them, unless a "specialist" in one or the other of them. Similarly Webster mastered Latin literature[4] and knew it, to quote

---

[1] "Speech at Capon Springs," June 28, 1851, *NE*, XIII, 435.

[2] "Speech at Faneuil Hall," *NE*, XIII, 209.

[3] See his "Autobiography," *NE*, XVII, 6–9; the quotation is from p. 8.

[4] Excepting the playwrights and minor poets. Evidence for the rather strong and broad statements above is scattered through the works of Webster and can hardly be brought together in a single citation. Rufus Choate, "On the Death of Daniel Webster," *Modern Eloquence* (Philadelphia, 1900), VII, 216–229, dwells on Webster's learning and says that the "interior and narrower circle" of his familiarity consisted of Cicero, Vergil, Shakespeare, Bacon, Milton, Burke, Johnson. Choate went on to draw a comparison between Webster and Dr. Johnson.

and refer to, as well as does the teacher of classics. The habits of study in his youth and that eagerness for good reading which was engendered by a scarcity of books remained with him to the end. In 1823, upon receiving a set of Coke's *Reports*, he wrote:[1] "I shall certainly cultivate his [Lord Coke's] acquaintance in some interval or intermission of the Waverly Novels." In 1830 he is as curious about Byron[2] and as clear in his opinion of him as earlier he had been about Dr. Johnson or Edmund Burke. Late in life he quotes passages from Scott with delight, defends Pope against modern detractors, and discusses Hebrew poetry at great length, comparing the book of Job with the epics of Homer and criticizing both by reference to the *Poetics* of Aristotle.[3] In his most active period he kept on his table copies of Caesar, Vergil, and Livy, in Latin, and of Homer, in English.[4]

It is his address before the New York Historical Society, in February, 1852, "The Dignity and Importance of History," which displays Webster's learning to the greatest advantage. One may say, as has been said, that Webster went out of his way to "get up" his allusions to historical works in that address. He did not need any special study, however, to make his easy allusions to, and quotations from, Milton, Shakespeare, Dr. Johnson, and De Foe; and from good evidence found elsewhere we may say the same for whatever use he made of Livy, Sallust, Tacitus, Herodotus, and Thucydides. The proof of Webster's knowledge of literature is scattered through all the pages of his printed speeches and letters and indicates a degree of learning far superior to that of all but a very few of our statesmen. Adams and Jefferson he admired for learning; he imitated them, perhaps consciously, and probably surpassed the attainments of Adams. John Quincy Adams was a professor of rhetoric and oratory, with a good classical training, and Edward Everett was a professor of Greek, but neither showed the knowledge of English literature possessed by Webster.[5]

That Webster sometimes used literary or learned allusions by way of display, we have his own word in the following passage from a letter to his son, which also remarks upon the utility of a liberal education:

[1] *NE*, XVII, 327.

[2] *NE*, XVII, 533.

[3] *NE*, XIII, 566–577. The articles by Charles Lanman, "Daniel Webster's Social Hours," *Harper's New Monthly Magazine*, July–October, 1856, from which these extracts are taken, contain much additional comment upon Webster's literary interests.

[4] Edward G. Parker, *The Golden Age of American Oratory* (Boston, 1857), p. 112.

[5] It would be interesting, with more space at our disposal, to go into the matter of Webster's scientific studies. Agriculture, of course, he knew both practically and theoretically. He read books of geology and astronomy. In talking to Lanman, he said: "Life is too short for study. One life is required for a complete mastery of ancient classics, of Grecian and Roman lore—another for the full understanding and ready use of English poetry, from Chaucer down to the present time; while another should be devoted to modern sciences. I grow more convinced and more ashamed of my ignorance daily."—*NE*, XIII, 564.

. . . still save a little time, have a few *"horas subsecivas"* in which to cultivate liberal knowledge; it will turn to account, even practically. If, on a given occasion, a man can, gracefully, and without the air of a pedant, show a little more knowledge than the occasion requires, the world will give him credit for eminent attainments. It is an honest quackery. I have practised it, and sometimes with success. It is something like studying an extempore speech; but even that, done with address, has its effect. There is no doubt . . . that the circle of useful knowledge is much broader than it can be proved to be, in relation to any particular subject, *à priori.*

We find connections and coincidences, helps and succors, where we did not expect them. I have never learned any thing which I wish to forget; except how badly some people have behaved; and I every day find, on almost every subject, that I wish I had more knowledge than I possess, seeing that I could produce it, if not for use, yet for effect.[1]

This does not cancel, however, the proofs that Webster did have literary learning. It rather indicates, as do other expressions of his, that he felt humble when he contemplated the vast amount to be known. Whatever good conceit he had of his other accomplishments, he was always modest about this one.[2]

Webster's literary training also included practice in writing. He wrote considerable verse while in college and shortly afterward, some of which was printed in a newspaper. He published verse translations of some of the odes of Horace, though these have not been recovered. During his year in Fryeburg he got together a collection of original essays and verses, apparently with some idea of publishing it as a book to be entitled *Sports of Pequawket.* In other words, at this time, he was on the verge of authorship, and his story is not very different from that of some other American youths, such as Irving, Longfellow, Hawthorne, and Melville, who became authors. For the *Monthly Anthology*, a Boston literary magazine, he wrote four reviews and one essay in the years 1805–1808. Some of his verses show wit and ingenuity, and although neither they nor the prose writings we have mentioned deserve a place in literature, it must be observed that in such tasks of composition Webster learned much of grace and accuracy in expression. His large and ready vocabulary must have owed something to his labors in "elegant" writing. And in his letters as well as in his speeches we find passages of which any literary man would be proud. How better

[1] *NE*, XVIII, 16; the letter was written in 1836.
[2] Sarcasm, not modesty, dictated this sentence in the "Reply to Hayne," when Webster was about to deliver his crushing retort to Hayne's analogy concerning Banquo's ghost: "The honorable gentleman is fresh in his reading of the English classics, and can put me right if I am wrong; but, according to my poor recollection, it was. . . . " Yet it is to be doubted that Webster had actually looked into *Macbeth* during the previous evening, when he was planning his reply; he could probably trust his "poor recollection." The retort seems to have occurred to him when he was lying on a sofa in the presence of friends; see Fuess, I, 372*n.*

could one begin a letter to a lady than this: "I give to you the fresh thoughts of the morning, as I write this by candlelight, at six o'clock, A.M."[1]

If Webster had turned to writing at any period after his entry into public life, he would have emulated his younger contemporaries Bancroft and Prescott and written history. He did publish in the *North American Review* for July, 1818, a historical study, "The Battle of Bunker Hill and General Putnam," devoted to setting posterity right upon the character of Putnam and his actions in the battle. More than this, he hoped to write a history of the Constitution and of Washington's administration, to which he referred in 1848[2] as "an object which has engaged my contemplations for many years," to consist of about fifty chapters of fifty pages each. He made out in 1852 a full list of the topics to be covered in each of three projected volumes. Yet he also talked of preparing, for recreation, a book on the birds and fishes of Marshfield, and for his serious labors, a work on the evidences of Christianity, which was to include a translation of Cicero's *De natura deorum*, with annotations.[3] But he was in the last year of his life before he turned to any of these, and the last year was filled with other concerns.

The fact that Webster became the most distinguished speaker in his generation and allowed his purely literary talents to languish, reflects, in the realm of individual choice, a spirit and attitude not unlike that which, by his own admission,[4] made America neglectful of literary and artistic matters. Oratory itself is the embodiment of man's political and social interests. In a competitive society founded upon the principles of free speech and equality of opportunity, oratory is also an avenue to economic power. What Webster advanced in 1809 as causes of our neglect of literature are in reality the causes that explain his own youthful preference for an oratorical career. However much we may be biased against the orator and however much we may have been led by literary critics and aesthetes to believe that the main lights of national thought are reflected by creative artists and philosophers, it is well to temper our prejudice with the reflection that the American genius flowered in a very real sense before the advent of the literary movements of the nineteenth century and that this genius expressed itself in the Declaration of Independence, the Constitution, the *Federalist* papers, the fierce partisanship of political debates, the huge political meetings, the vitriolic editorials, the tactics

---

[1] *NE*, XVIII, 94; written Dec. 13, 1840, to Mrs. James W. Paige. The more famous letter about morning, written to the same lady from Richmond, "April 29, five o'clock, A.M., 1847" (*ibid.*, pp. 240–242) was a show piece, with some good passages and some that seem self-conscious. A part of it was put into school readers.

[2] *NE*, XV, 238*n.*

[3] *Ibid.*, p. 240.

[4] Principally in his Phi Beta Kappa Address at Dartmouth in 1809.

673

of political managers like Thurlow Weed, the Fourth of July orations. An American historian has remarked that "the American people have expressed themselves more fully in their political life than elsewhere, and more so than has been the case with most other nations."[1] Webster's choice was inspired by a realization that economic and political actions had their cultural no less than their selfish aspects and would lead a gifted man into an arena of historical as well as personal achievement. Webster's own words at Bunker Hill in 1825 show that, in preferring politics to literature, he was expressing the main interest of his generation:

Any adequate survey, however, of the prógress made during the last half-century, in the polite and the mechanic arts, in machinery and manufactures, in commerce and agriculture, in letters and in science, would require volumes. I must abstain wholly from these subjects, and turn, for a moment, to the contemplation of what has been done on the great question of politics and government. This is the master topic of the age; and during the whole fifty years, it has intensely occupied the thoughts of men.

We have said nothing of Webster's study of the art of speaking. The records of his academic training and exercises are available in the biographies. What is not so well known is the long letter of November 10, 1828,[2] to a clerical friend who had lent him a copy of Whately's *Elements of Rhetoric*, then a new book. Webster regretted that he had to return it before he had read it thoroughly, but he had "found in it twenty things which I have thought of often, and been convinced of long, but never before saw in print." He liked Whately's "hatred of adjectives, his love of Saxon words, and his idea of the true use of repetition." He suggested as an addition that "there is something which may be called argumentative repetition, that is capable sometimes of producing great effect." He was most interested in the question of general and specific language and wrote: "A book might be written on this little question, 'When is effect produced by generalization; when by particularization?' . . . An accurate writer should avoid generalities sometimes, not always; but when, it would require a treatise to expound." He analyzed examples from the Bible and Milton. He made this comment on one of his boyhood favorites:

Dr. Watts, who, by the way, I do not deem altogether a bad poet, somewhere speaks of the flight of an angel as being with "most amazing speed." But what idea is conveyed by this mode of expression? What is "amazing speed?" It would amaze

---

[1] C. R. Fish, *The Development of American Nationality* (New York, 1919), p. vii. The idea was expressed earlier by Parker: "Our people have been tauntingly asked, 'Where is your national literature?' Aside from our historical works, it is in our political speeches, state papers, and newspapers."—*The Golden Age of American Oratory*, p. 83.

[2] *NE*, XVII, 463–465.

us, if we saw an oyster moving a mile a day. It would not amaze us to see a grey-hound run a mile in a minute.

After college days, he seems to have made no special study of delivery, but, knowing as we do the attention he gave to fitting dress and to other details, we may be sure that he was not careless of how he spoke. It is difficult to know how any speaker really sounded who lived before the age of mechanical recording of sound and movement. Samuel L. Knapp wrote of Webster in 1830:[1] "Hear him, and you will say that his eloquence is founded on no model, ancient or modern—all his own excellences and defects. His voice has an extraordinary compass. His emphasis belongs to himself alone; it is founded on no rule, nor can it be reduced to any." Edward G. Parker is helpful concerning Webster's gestures and gives some hints as to how he seemed to a listener:[2]

> Webster's ordinary manner of speaking was that of a plain man, as would be natural to the expression of so practical a mind. It was strong, hearty, and down-right. His gestures were the gestures of enforcing rather than of describing; such gestures as a sturdy New England farmer under the shadow of the White Hills would use in dictating the tillage of his stubborn acres, or in exemplifying moral monitions to his son, by pointing to those mountains; the open palm of the hand, the pointing finger, the vigorous bringing down of the arm, the easy sidewise wave of all; these were pretty much his variety. . . . He seemed in no way bookish in speaking. He had the broad, deep-ringing tone of a son of the soil; a man who loved broad acres, great cattle, tall trees, and true men. A fresh, hearty, neighborly tone runs through his sentences.

Parker remarks that the attitude given Webster by Healy, in his painting of the "Reply to Hayne," is a "very unusual" one, and he implies that Webster never, or rarely, "assumed so melodramatic an air."[3] Repeatedly Parker testifies that on occasions or subjects that did not arouse his powers, Webster was disappointing. "On common themes, he either contented himself with brief statements as curt and clear as a good newspaper para-graph; or if he undertook more, he only floundered about, unwieldy." Elsewhere Parker refers to Webster as appearing "sluggish and torpid." Or again, "Lecture Committees have paid fabulous sums, to write the name of 'Daniel Webster' at the head of their Programme; but only to be stultified and paralyzed at the hard, drowsy periods, in which he pre-sented some views, intrinsically great, and insufferably dull." The same author tells of seeing an audience of ladies melt away as Webster delivered a constitutional argument before the Supreme Court, dealing with "prin-

[1] [S. P. Lyman], *Life and Memorials of Daniel Webster* (New York, 1853), II, 248–249.
[2] *Op. cit.*, pp. 114–115.
[3] *Ibid.*, p. 117; the quotations following in our text are from pp. 77, 91, 76, 199–200.

ciples as universal as the orb, and as profoundly interesting as the laws of a planetary system, and there was no want of historical allusion, and that general tone of grandeur which was inseparable from him"; and then, on the following day, Henry Clay, "on a cheap case, and with commonplace stuff of talk, packed up the fair crowd . . . and, what was more, he kept them there four mortal hours enchanted by his witchery of speech." But no one has spoken more enthusiastically than this same witness of Webster's impressive presence and varied, overwhelming displays of attractive power.[1]

We proceed from these general observations to the closer study of selected speeches. For two reasons we have not attempted to deal with any specimens of Webster's forensic oratory. (1) These are speeches that verbalize the speaker's sense of a complicated world of legal fact, testimony, indirect evidence, where oratorical truth can be established only by an elaborate study of common law, statute law, and constitutional law. Each particular case in which Webster appeared must receive special study and the speaker's role be judged upon its particular merits. Valuable as a new study of this subject might be, we are compelled to acknowledge its difficulty and to recognize that it cannot be brought within the limits of the present survey. (2) A volume, soon to be published by Professors James A. Winans and Howard A. Bradley, of Dartmouth College, will contain a detailed study of Webster's speeches in the White murder case and the Kenniston robbery case and will show not only the complexity and length of an examination of two forensic utterances but also the nature of Webster's contributions in this field.

III. *In Epic Vein*

Apart from his defense of the Union and his interpretation of the Constitution in the "Great Debate" and its aftermath, Webster's most solid service to America lies in a half-dozen speeches for special occasions—

---

[1] N. P. Willis confirms Parker. In the course of his account of Webster listening to Jenny Lind, Willis wrote: "We must remind the reader, here, that, to the cultivation of the voice, Mr. Webster's delivery shows that he has never paid attention. From other and sufficient advantages, probably, he has never felt the need of it. His ear, consequently, is uneducated to melody; and, in the rare instances when he has varied his habitual and ponderous cadences by a burst in a higher key, he has surpassed Art with the more sudden impassioning of Nature. Though, in *reading* a speech of Webster's, there are passages where your nostrils spread and your blood fires, you may have *heard* the same speech delivered, with no impression but the unincumbered profoundness of its truth. To use what may seem like a common-place remark, he is *as monotonous as thunder*—but it is because thunder has no need to be more varied and musical, that Webster leaves the roll of his bass unplayed upon by the lightning that outstrips it."—*Hurry-Graphs* (New York, 1851), p. 191.

the epideictic oratory of the Aristotelian classification. This statement may be disputable, but thought and study confirm it. Webster's occasional addresses, circulated widely in printed copies and drawn upon for school readers and books of declamation, gave to his youthful country what it most needed—heroes, shibboleths, and myths. Such intangibles as our common government and national heritage are possessed only so far as they are realized imaginatively. To this end symbols are necessary, even physical symbols such as the flag ("the gorgeous ensign of our Republic . . . not a stripe erased or polluted, not a star obscured"), the capito ("This is America! This is Washington! and this the Capitol of the United States"), battlefields ("You now behold the field . . . You see the lines of the little redoubt. . . . You see where Warren fell"), historic spots ("We shall not stand unmoved on the shore of Plymouth while the sea continues to wash it"), tombs of heroes and monuments ("on its banks repose the ashes of the Father of his Country, and at our side . . . rises to his memory the marble column, sublime in its simple grandeur, and fitly intended to reach a loftier height than any similar structure on the surface of the earth").[1] But behind and above these physical symbols there must be poetic symbols—myths, if you will—and symbolic concepts, which, as embodied in phrases, are but catchwords to those who live by catchwords but which are capable of a rich and more or less definite content. At the close of the Bunker Hill address of 1825, after saying that the preceding generation had won independence and founded the state, Webster said: "Our proper business is improvement," and a little later, "Let our conceptions be enlarged to the circle of our duties. Let us extend our ideas. . . . " This power to enlarge conceptions and extend ideas was peculiarly his. Calhoun could surpass Webster in subtlety and firmness of logical concatenation; Clay could always surpass either of them in attractive delivery and popular appeal. Webster's superiority lay in comprehensiveness and strength of intellect and, more particularly, in strength of imagination.

This last power shows at its purest in his epideictic oratory. The persuasive end of such oratory, according to Aristotle, is to establish honor or shame; that is, the epideictic speaker persuades an audience that some man or action or institution is to be praised or to be reviled. Yet such an

---

[1] How conscious early Americans were of their need of a current symbolism may be seen in the remarks of Gouverneur Morris concerning the national mint, in 1802: "I am far from wishing to overturn it. Though it be not of great necessity, nor even of substantial importance, though it be but a splendid trapping of your government; yet, as *it may, by impressing on your current coin the emblems of your sovereignty, have some tendency to encourage a national spirit and to foster the national pride*, I am willing to contribute . . . to its support."—S. C. Carpenter, *Select American Speeches* (Philadelphia, 1815), II, 76; [italics ours].

orator, as a rule, has no heavy task of changing people's minds. Most American listeners already believe that the American Revolutionists deserve honor. The orator's task is rather to objectify those deserts and that honor (just as the deliberative orator objectifies the expediency of a proposed action), making them have palpable reality and weight. He is working for the most part with intangibles, and his success depends upon the truth and force of his imagination. He will draw word pictures; he will dramatize; he will elevate, enlarge, and dignify. Above all he will stir and create emotions, knowing that imaginations are released by emotional disturbance and then act to heighten the very emotion that has set them free.

All this can be seen in Webster's first important occasional address, "First Settlement of New England," delivered in the First Church at Plymouth under the auspices of the Pilgrim Society. The date, December 22, 1820, marks the bicentennial of the landing of the Pilgrims. We have found little enough concerning the physical circumstances of the speech. We know from a reference in it that the weather was bitterly cold. One editor tells of "an immense concourse,"[1] but the church at Plymouth was of limited capacity. Most remarkable is the length of the speech; as printed, it would require at least 3 hours in delivery. It may have been expanded for the press by Webster (he kept it with him for a year before printing it), or it may be that the descendants of Pilgrims before whom he spoke were willing to listen to something matching the 3-hour sermons of their ancestors. Webster gave free play to his love of history, drawing vivid pictures of the departure of the Pilgrims from England, their arrival at the Rock, and the hardships they faced on the wintry coast. In depicting the landing, he skillfully alluded to the painting of the scene which Henry Sargent had just completed for the Pilgrim Society, and his own strokes of description gained vividness for auditors who recently had viewed the picture.[2] He went on to sketch, with easy mastery, the growth and progress that had occupied two centuries of New England's history and to compare in some detail the English colonies in America with colonies sent out by Greece and Rome. In a digression, but one having relevance to the Puritan principles that he had been discussing, he attacked the slave trade. Finally, he explained the American system of government and predicted the coming expansion and prosperity of the country. His emphasis upon the place of property in the American system was unfortunate. "It is probable that Webster would have been President of the United States," said E. P. Whipple, echoing many others, "had it not been for one short sentence

---

[1] *The Works of Daniel Webster* (Boston, 1851), I, 4.

[2] Compare his use of "the glorious statue by Houdon" to lend vividness to his portrayal of George Washington in "Addition to the Capitol," *NE*, IV, 316.

in this oration,—'Government is founded on property.'"[1] On the other hand, Whipple is wrong in calling this "the main political idea of the oration." Rather, it was seized upon as "main" by Webster's political opponents.[2] The general framework of the eulogy was something like this: New England is great, in its past, present, and future (and hence the United States is likewise great), because its founders and mode of founding were great; and these latter were great because of the courage and faith of the Pilgrims, who did not seek the New World for wealth but for religious liberty; the founding was great also because of the consequences that flowed from it.[3]

In style, tone, and the handling of rhetorical devices, "First Settlement of New England" suggests the orator in the first consciousness of his strength, somewhat pleased with himself and justifiably so; and yet he is in the happy situation of being able to utter sentiments that are deeply and authentically his own, so that amplification never endangers sincerity. The speech contains a number of passages that, for felicity of phrasing and for rhythmical movement, are hardly to be surpassed, whether by the later Webster or some other. The following paragraph will bear scrutiny:

Local attachments and sympathies would ere long spring up in the breasts of our ancestors, endearing to them the place of their refuge. Whatever natural objects are associated with interesting scenes and high efforts obtain a hold on human feeling, and demand from the heart a sort of recognition and regard. This Rock soon became hallowed in the esteem of the Pilgrims, and these hills grateful to their sight. Neither they nor their children were again to till the soil of England, nor again to traverse the seas which surround her. But here was a new sea, now open to their enterprise, and a new soil, which had not failed to respond gratefully to their laborious industry, and which was already assuming a robe of verdure. Hardly had they provided shelter for the living, ere they were summoned to erect sepulchres for the dead. The ground had become sacred, by inclosing the remains of some of their companions and connections. A parent, a child, a husband, or a wife, had gone

---

[1] *American Literature and Other Papers* (Boston, 1887), p. 159.

[2] McMaster's statement (McMaster, p. 97) concerning the speech made in the convention a few days before ("Basis of the Senate," *NE*, V, 8–25) that "he repeated it, word for word, to the crowd that gathered in the little church at Plymouth, as part of the oration on 'The First Settlement of New England,'" is simply not true, if we can judge from the speeches as printed. Not so much as a sentence is identical; and in the Plymouth oration he never mentioned the specific question of senatorial districts. But the subject is confused by some other tradition than that furnished by the printed speeches. Whipple's "one short sentence" does not appear in the Plymouth oration as printed; the nearest to it is: "It would seem, then, to be the part of political wisdom to found government on property."

[3] The touch of circular reasoning in such an outline is inherent in most historical eulogy: we are great because of our heroic ancestors; our ancestors were heroic because their actions produced us.

the way of all flesh, and mingled with the dust of New England. We naturally look with strong emotions to the spot, though it be a wilderness, where the ashes of those we have loved repose. Where the heart has laid down what it loved most, there it is desirous of laying itself down. No sculptured marble, no enduring monument, no honorable inscription, no ever-burning taper that would drive away the darkness of the tomb, can soften our sense of the reality of death, and hallow to our feelings the ground which is to cover us, like the consciousness that we shall sleep, dust to dust, with the objects of our affections.

Here is a remarkable amount of double construction, balance, antithesis, and yet no suggestion either of metrical singsong or epigrammatic crackle; and all reaches a climax in the fine, yet still subdued, antithesis of "Where the heart has laid down what it loved most, there it is desirous of laying itself down." The closing sentence may seem overelaborated, in comparison with the straightforwardness of what has preceded, yet the structure and length of this sentence are called for by its position and function. The finest bit of modulation comes in the three sentences beginning with "This Rock." The unobtrusive echoes of "hallowed . . . hills," "till the soil . . . traverse the seas . . . new sea, now open . . . new soil," are almost perfect. And if one goes a little farther and in pronouncing "New England" recalls the earlier "soil of England . . . new sea . . . new soil," one finds the structural tie beam of the paragraph.

One other passage, illustrating a different and perhaps more important power of the orator, should be examined. Early in the oration Webster is arguing that the founding of the Massachusetts colony was important because of its important consequences. He contrasts this event with most military victories, which cause temporary excitement but no permanent result. Yet "it is not always so." The Battle of Marathon is still memorable because there "Greece herself was saved." This introduces a brief catalogue of the glories of Greece, with special interest for the audience because in 1820 the patriotic nationalists of Greece were organizing and even fighting to throw off Turkish rule. Then comes a supremely skillful transition. Instead of baldly asserting that the landing of the Pilgrims was as important as the Battle of Marathon, Webster quotes the speech of the Athenian commander at the battle, as reported by Herodotus, "If we conquer, we shall make Athens the greatest city of Greece"; and against this prophecy he sets a longer speech of his own invention, "the more appropriate language of our fathers, when they landed on this Rock," prophesying that, with God's help, a great nation shall arise. It is an eloquent passage and may be viewed as a trial flight for the more famous invented speeches in the eulogy of Adams and Jefferson. But we cannot recount all the excellences of "First Settlement of New England," an attractive and persuasive composition that has been sufficiently acclaimed.

680

Webster later manifested more of strength, to be sure; whereas here he is frequently subdued and elegiac, he later displayed a vigorous and flashing style. But for an audience of the descendants of Pilgrims in Plymouth Church, the detonations of his full power, even if, at thirty-eight, he could have produced them, would have been out of place.

"The Bunker Hill Monument," usually called the "First Bunker Hill Address," was delivered in the open air at noon of a cool sunshiny day, June 17, 1825, the fiftieth anniversary of the Battle of Bunker Hill. It followed upon a procession from Boston Common, with 200 veterans of the Revolution (including 40 who had fought at Bunker Hill), riding in barouches, and upon the laying, by Lafayette, of the cornerstone of the monument. The audience that gathered on the north declivity of the hill and at its base, may have numbered 100,000. How many of these could hear Webster's voice and follow his words no one can say. From his opening phrases, "This uncounted multitude before me and around me," to the end, Webster showed his magnificent *sense of environment*, which served him in all his best efforts. He could always reach out, as it were, and find something within sight of his hearers from which to draw material for discourse.[1] On this occasion, besides the vast audience and the projected monument, he had about him the battlefield, the cities of Boston and Charlestown, the ships at mooring in the river, the Revolutionary veterans, and Lafayette. Add the fact that he was himself president of the Bunker Hill Monument Association, and by these immediate circumstances we have accounted for most of the speech. He went afield only by way of reference to the Greek struggle for independence and the similar movements taking place in South America. From these materials he made a speech that is unified in tone and emotion rather than in logical structure; for the apostrophes to the Revolutionary veterans and to Lafayette are removable units, and other topics come in no inevitable order. The first apostrophe constitutes the principal, almost the only, "purple patch" of the oration, and if ever an epideictic orator is justified in striving for the highest effects, Webster was justified in such a presence and on such a theme. The part that, to a modern reader, seems actually strained for is the tribute to Warren, with its elaborately prepared aposiopesis. Yet the testimony of hearers and the acclaim of succeeding generations would prove that the speaker brought it off successfully. More happy, it seems to us, is the

---

[1] Wendell Phillips's famous reference to the pictures on the walls, in his impassioned speech "The Murder of Lovejoy" in Faneuil Hall, Dec. 8, 1837, had been anticipated by Webster. Speaking at the same place on June 5, 1828, Webster said that if he had refused his vote for pensions for Revolutionary soldiers, "I could not have raised my voice in Faneuil Hall,—you would have awed me down; if you had not, the portraits of patriots which adorn these walls would have frowned me into silence."—*NE*, II, 16.

impressive use of the roll of names—"Prescott, Putnam, Stark, Brooks, Read, Pomeroy, Bridge! our eyes seek for you in vain amid this broken band. . . . You bring with you marks of honor from Trenton and Monmouth, from Yorktown, Camden, Bennington, and Saratoga"—a device in which the simplest of means on the part of the speaker awakens complex and freighted associations on the part of hearers.

The argument of "The Bunker Hill Monument" is similar to that of "First Settlement of New England." The battle was great (and the Revolution was great) because of its great participants and great consequences. After reviewing the story of the Revolution and of the battle and paying his tribute to the survivors, Webster says: "The leading reflection to which this occasion seems to invite us, respects the great changes which have happened in the fifty years since the battle of Bunker Hill was fought." More, perhaps, than in any other speech, he emphasizes that the American political system is an experiment, and some sentences seem to lie behind Lincoln's thinking as voiced at Gettysburg. Webster sounds modern here just because he is so near the heart of America's recurring problem and perennial hope:

> Our history hitherto proves, however, that the popular form is practicable, and that with wisdom and knowledge men may govern themselves; . . . If, in our case, the representative system ultimately fail, popular governments must be pronounced impossible. No combination of circumstances more favorable to the experiment can ever be expected to occur. The last hopes of mankind, therefore, rest with us; and if it should be proclaimed, that our example had become an argument against the experiment, the knell of popular liberty would be sounded throughout the earth. . . . Those who established our liberty and our government are daily dropping from among us. The great trust now descends to new hands.

These sentences, rather than the extravagant exclamations concerning Warren, represent the real tone of "The Bunker Hill Monument." By listening with the mind's ear to passages of this sort, we can understand why most contemporaries of Webster who left descriptions of his speaking emphasized its simplicity, weight, and manly directness. The rhythmical passages, the bold hyperboles, and emotional apostrophes belong, also, and have their own appeal, but they are not the staple of his utterance.

The best of the occasional addresses is "Adams and Jefferson," delivered in Faneuil Hall, August 2, 1826. Its excellence grew out of Webster's ability to recognize the strong persuasive resources that lay in the subject and occasion. John Adams and Thomas Jefferson had worked together as members of the Continental Congress; had been members of the committee chosen to draft the Declaration of Independence; had both signed that document, pledging to the accomplishment of its ends their lives, their fortunes, and their sacred honor; had both served the nation as ambassador, as Vice-President, as President. What was truly unique, however, among historical coincidences, was that both men had died on the same day, and that day was, of all days, July 4, the fiftieth anniversary of the Declaration.

Webster had enjoyed the acquaintance of both men. He knew that although they were diverse in political principles, opposed in personal tastes, antagonistic, even, to the point where they had been angry and embittered rivals, they yet had possessed a large area of common feeling and purpose, and this area provided a basis upon which partisan differences could at length be reconciled and a high national destiny be achieved. From the unique circumstance of the occasion, then, he drew the principles upon which partisanship, operating with friction and in opposing directions, might base its articles of agreement. Without principles of this kind, the end of partisanship is disunion: the country crumbles into fragments and fragments into unnumbered atoms. With principles of this kind, partisanship may operate and yet not damage the political organism. Webster's words in praise of Jefferson and Adams were to be remembered. Hayne misremembered them in the grand debate, when he sarcastically reminded Webster that he had recently assisted at the apotheosis of Jefferson, had fixed him as "a brilliant star in the clear upper sky," and would surely accord some respect to Jefferson's opinions. But others remembered without sarcasm the temper of Webster's eulogy, and in time the country itself was to emerge from a death struggle with the triumphant reassertion of the principle that partisanship should never be allowed to become the end, rather than the means, of social action.

The plan of the speech shows admirable symmetry and proportion. After an extended introduction, which dwells upon the coincidence of their deaths and traces the parallelism of their lives, Webster tells (1) the biography of Adams up to the meeting of the first Continental Congress and then (1') more briefly, the same portion of Jefferson's story. This brings him to the longest single section, (2) an account of the inception, drafting, and voting of the Declaration, with emphasis upon Jefferson's part in the drafting and Adams's part in winning the vote. After a brief digression praising four other signers, (3) the life of Adams after 1776 is recounted summarily, and (3') the same is done for Jefferson. Jefferson's founding of the University of Virginia leads to (4) an estimate of the scholarly and literary attainments of the two men, followed by (5) a judgment upon their administrations as President, with enforcement of the controlling idea, namely, that though opposed in policies and principles, the two were at one in serving their country and maintaining the Constitution; and this section is closed by a brief peroration to the eulogy proper. The speech could have ended here, but it would have lacked something of general application. After a short digression in praise of Charles Carroll, the only surviving signer of the Declaration, Webster delivers the peroration of the whole address, urging that Americans may appreciate their heritage and "resolve to maintain and perpetuate it." The speech took little more than two hours in delivery, with section 2, on the Declaration, occupying 45 minutes. The moving exposition of "true eloquence" comes exactly at the middle and is followed by the vivid dramatization of a session of the Continental Congress, with a speech by an unnamed opponent of independence and Adams's longer reply. Thus was the audience stirred and refreshed, in preparation for nearly fifty minutes of speaking yet to come. "The supposed speech of John Adams" was seized upon by compilers of readers and was probably memorized and declaimed more often than any other passage by Webster. Following upon Webster's own definition of true eloquence and his attribution of such eloquence to Adams,[1] its composition and delivery called for the orator's highest virtuosity. Webster decided that his imagined speaker and occasion would call for short sentences; of the fifty-seven sentences in the speech, thirty-seven run to fewer than twenty words, sixteen of them to fewer than ten words. Short, concrete words also prevail. It has more than once been observed that Webster's speaker against independence had a better basis in facts and logic than did his Adams. The only fact that Adams could cite was that George Washington had already been appointed commander by the Congress, and thus they had already committed themselves to resistance. His appeal is emotional, a plea to take a chance. By this dramatic propriety Webster was showing that the Declaration was an act of faith, that the signers could rest not on certainties but only on their own strength of resolution.

Although Webster here made the best use of the supposed speech in all rhetorical literature (unless one includes in that literature the classical historians from whom he learned the trick), we return to the suggestion that the real excellence of "Adams and Jefferson" lies in other passages—in the description of true eloquence, certainly; in the exordium, with its grave maxim, "The tears which flow, and the honors that are paid, when the founders of the republic die, give hope that the republic itself may be

---

[1] "He had been running along in his delivery tamely, when, suddenly, he came to the climax of his description of John Adams's oratory; raising his form, he brought his hands in front of him with a swing, and stepping to the front of the stage, he said with a broad swell and an imperious surge upward of the gruff tone of his voice, 'He spoke onward, right onward'; and into that single 'onward' he threw such a shock of force, that an auditor who sat directly in front of the stage, found himself involuntarily half rising from his seat, with the start which the words gave him. He was not surprised to observe, that the others in the pew with him also started, as by the push of one forward impulse."—Parker, *op. cit.*, pp. 93-94.

immortal"; in the preliminary peroration, drawn from the anthem sung by the choir before the speech began: "It was the last swelling peal of yonder choir, 'Their bodies are buried in peace, but their name liveth evermore.' I catch that solemn song, I echo that lofty strain of funeral triumph, 'Their name liveth evermore.'" Best of all, perhaps, and most truly Websterian, is such a passage as this from the close:

> It is not to inflate national vanity, nor to swell a light and empty feeling of self-importance, but it is that we may judge justly of our situation, and of our own duties, that I earnestly urge upon you this consideration of our position and our character among the nations of the earth. It cannot be denied, but by those who would dispute against the sun, that with America, and in America, a new era commences in human affairs. . . ′. If we cherish the virtues and the principles of our fathers, Heaven will assist us to carry on the work of human liberty and human happiness. Auspicious omens cheer us. Great examples are before us. . . . Washington is in the clear, upper sky. These other stars have now joined the American constellation; they circle round their centre, and the heavens beam with new light.

Above any particular passage, however, is the conception of the whole, the perfect matching of speaker and occasion.

On the centennial birthday of George Washington, February 22, 1832, Webster spoke for an hour at a public dinner in the national capital, and his speech was published under the title "The Character of Washington." With less of historical and biographical narrative than any other of the occasional addresses, this speech has a remarkable consistency of style; for in it Webster felt no need to quicken languishing interest or to balance matter of fact with flight of fancy. A passage near the opening alludes to that national symbolism that we have associated with all Webster's work in this kind:

> The recurrence of anniversaries, or of longer periods of time, naturally freshens the recollection, and deepens the impression, of events with which they are historically connected. Renowned places, also, have a power to awaken feeling, which all acknowledge. No American can pass by the fields of Bunker Hill, Monmouth, and Camden, as if they were ordinary spots on the earth's surface. . . . But neither of these sources of emotion equals the power with which great moral examples affect the mind. When sublime virtues cease to be abstractions, when they become embodied in human character, and exemplified in human conduct, we should be false to our own nature, if we did not indulge in the spontaneous effusions of our gratitude and our admiration. . . . The ingenuous youth of America will hold up to themselves the bright model of Washington's example, and study to be what they behold.

As in earlier addresses, Webster takes occasion to dwell upon the progress of America and of the world in the century that had passed, and he finds it easy to connect Washington with that progress. The body of the speech consists of a statement of Washington's doctrines and policies, especially as embodied in his "Farewell Address." Webster is speaking in the midst of Calhoun's agitations for nullification and dwells longest on Washington's "solicitude for the preservation of the Union." Again, with even more relevance than at Bunker Hill, he points to the experimental nature of the American system of government and the dire consequences that would flow from its failure. As at Plymouth, he had looked ahead to 1920, so here he predicts that in 1932 "other disciples of Washington will celebrate his birth" and "see, as we now see, the flag of the Union floating on the top of the Capitol." In this eulogy, somewhat more than in any of the other occasional speeches, Webster avails himself of the epideictic speaker's opportunity to persuade his hearers to a certain line of action. As Aristotle says, what the eulogist praises in his subject he may advise as the most expedient conduct for his audience. Webster commends the counsels of Washington in every instance as applicable to the United States of 1832. But the speech is a model of eulogy. Wholly without purple patches, it is chaste and yet earnest, dignified and yet expressive.

"The Completion of the Bunker Hill Monument," usually called the "Second Bunker Hill Address," was delivered on June 17, 1843, again after a procession from the Common and before an immense crowd, including President Tyler, in the open air. The speech occupied about an hour and a half. In it Webster again made use of the roll of names—this time giving the full names of the few surviving veterans of the Revolution who were present: "Gideon Foster of Danvers, Enos Reynolds of Boxford, Phineas Johnson, Robert Andrews, Elijah Dresser," etc.—the plain Yankee surnames and Biblical given names are impressive, as Webster knew. Again he gave free play to his sense of environment, perhaps to the best advantage in his career. In the midst of attending to the courtesies of the occasion, after mention of prominent Bostonians who had forwarded the construction of the memorial but before his tributes to the President and to the governor of Rhode Island, Webster said, "The Bunker Hill Monument is finished. Here it stands." He went on, turning toward the lofty tower as he spoke. Said Edward Everett, a member of the audience:[1] "The gesture, the look, the tone of the speaker, as he turned to the majestic shaft, seemed to invest it with a mysterious life; and men held their breath as if a solemn voice was about to come down from its towering summit." Webster was saying: "It is itself the orator of this occasion. It is not from my lips, it could not be from any human lips, that that strain of eloquence is this day to flow most competent to move and excite the vast multitudes

---

[1] *The Works of Daniel Webster* (Boston, 1851), I, lxvii.

around me. The powerful speaker stands motionless before us." Here he was interrupted by "long and loud applause."[1]

At first glance the topics drawn upon in this speech, and their order, show less of coherence and logical necessity than is usual with Webster. Everett says:[2] "This address does not appear to have had the advantage possessed by those of Plymouth in 1820, and of Bunker Hill in 1825, in having been written out for the press by Mr. Webster. It seems to have been prepared for publication from the reporter's notes, with some hasty revision, perhaps, by the author." Yet our text may for that reason bring us the closer to Webster; and once the amenities are taken care of and the battle has been vividly recalled, there is a well-knit argument. "If there was nothing of value in the principles of the American Revolution," said Webster, "then there is nothing valuable in the battle of Bunker Hill and its consequences. But if the Revolution was . . . an event which marked the progress of man all over the world from despotism to liberty, then this monument is not raised without cause." The remainder of the speech proves that the conditional clause in this last proposition is not contrary to fact. Characteristically, he first supports his proposition by showing that the Revolution was the culmination of two centuries or more of historical changes. For nearly ten minutes he reviews the causes that led to the settlement of Virginia and the sailing of the Pilgrims. Then, in order to isolate the important principles that animated the Revolution, he reviews the Spanish and Portuguese colonization of the New World, with its contrasted principles and results. This topic he dwells on for 20 minutes—and yet even here, by repeated reference, he keeps his hearers' attention upon his real subject. He passes to a summary of what the English colonists brought with them from the Old World: "The arts, sciences, and literature of England came over with the settlers." The common law came, the jury, habeas corpus, the Bible, the English language. Above all, self-government came. This passage leads to a brief listing of "the great elements of the American system of government." Yet the importance of the Revolution, Webster implies, cannot rest alone upon its achievements in and for the United States. What has this country returned to the Old World? The answer is brief but weighty and comes to a climax in the sentence: "America has furnished to the world the character of Washington!" This introduces a eulogy, 6 minutes in length, in which Webster gets back to the environment and the occasion by comparing the loftiness and uprightness of Washington's character with the physical characteristics of the monument. A peroration of 3 minutes urges that only high morality can ensure the perpetuity of political systems, even

[1] *Ibid.*, p. 82.
[2] *Ibid.*, p. lxvii.

687

of the best. One finds, on looking back, that this peroration had been foreshadowed in the early part of the speech when, after pointing to the monument as the orator of the day, Webster had introduced the subject of morality by saying that only a moral end can make significant any structure or memorial. Of the Great Pyramid of Egypt he said: "Without a just moral object, therefore, made known to man, though raised against the skies, it excites only conviction of power, mixed with strange wonder." The peroration echoes this passage.

The speaker was sixty-one years of age and was Secretary of State. The speech illustrates his ripened style, with less bravura than that of his early eulogies but with no less genuine, pervading energy. The few passages of pronounced rhythm or poetic image are wholly knit up into the texture of the whole. A deep earnestness underlies every part, except the somewhat perfunctory courtesies near the beginning; an earnestness whose cause was Webster's concern for the life of the Union. "Woe betide the man who brings to this day's worship feeling less than wholly American! . . . This column stands on Union." Thus his sentiments break out explicitly, but they animate the whole.

"The Addition to the Capitol," delivered July 4, 1851, at the laying of the cornerstone of the new addition, gives us the orator at the age of sixty-nine, for the second time Secretary of State. He indulges in lyrical flights as animated as those of his youth; but he also delivers a long table of statistics. The speech is something of a mélange, though not a disorderly one. Webster conceived his duty to be double: first he delivered a Fourth of July oration, 45 minutes in length; then he turned to "the particular occasion of our assembling," the celebration of the projected building, and talked for an hour and a quarter. The first speech defined American liberty and pleaded for Union. More than was his wont, Webster depended upon quotations—first Bishop Berkeley's prophecy for America, then a much longer prophecy, in prose, by another eighteenth century bishop, and last, Sir William Jones's answer to the question: What constitutes a state? The old master had not lost his touch, and such a passage as the following is as typically Websterian as anything he ever said:

This anniversary animates and gladdens and unites all American hearts. On other days of the year we may be party men, indulging in controversies, more or less important to the public good; we may have likes and dislikes, and we may maintain our political differences, often with warm, and sometimes with angry feelings. But today we are Americans all; and all nothing but Americans. As the great luminary over our heads, dissipating mists and fogs, now cheers the whole hemisphere, so do the associations connected with this day disperse all cloudy and sullen weather in the minds and hearts of true Americans. Every man's heart swells within him; every man's port and bearing become somewhat more proud and lofty, as he remembers that seventy-five years have rolled away, and that the great inheritance of liberty is still his; his, undiminished and unimpaired; his in all its original glory; his to enjoy, his to protect, and his to transmit to future generations.

Here we can see to advantage Webster's coupling or tripling of synonyms, a practice that appears consistently throughout his work but that may have increased in his latter years.

In the second part, concerning the capitol, Webster used statistics to establish the greatness and solidity of the young country's economic growth. He then addressed a series of challenging questions to the people of the South, asking whether they wished to destroy this national fabric. He showed that also in religion, literature, education, and science the country had made astounding progress. He dwelt upon the physical surroundings, hallowed as they were by association with the living and dead father of his country, and ended with another plea for the perpetuity of the Union.[1] It is noteworthy that once more he employed the device of the invented speech. After painting for his hearers the appearance of George Washington as he officiated at the ceremonies of 1793, he then imagined what Washington would say if he were to join them at their own ceremony. This imagined speech he followed with an emotional apostrophe, beginning, "Great Father of your Country! we heed your words." But the whole construction falls short of his earlier excellence and carries more than a suggestion of formula and catchword. "The Addition to the Capitol" is good only in scattered passages, though the age and authority of the speaker and the circumstance of the occasion gave it an effectiveness that, as late readers, we cannot measure.

Here we leave consideration of individual speeches upon special occasions.[2] Those to which we have called attention constitute a body of

---

[1] His last sentence may have suggested to Lincoln a famous phrase in the ending of his "Second Inaugural." Webster's more diffuse wording is: "And now, fellow-citizens, with hearts void of hatred, envy, and malice towards our own countrymen, or any of them, . . . "

[2] The principal ones left unconsidered are "Festival of the Sons of New Hampshire," delivered in the hall of the Fitchburg Railway Company in Boston, Nov. 7, 1849; "The Landing at Plymouth," Dec. 22, 1843, before the New England Society of New York; and "Pilgrim Festival at New York in 1850," on a similar occasion 7 years later; a brief eulogy upon Mr. Justice Story, pronounced before members of the Suffolk bar, met in the courtroom in Boston, Sept. 12, 1845; and a similar eulogy upon Jeremiah Mason in the Supreme Court of Massachusetts, Nov. 14, 1848. The third is the most spirited, and its eloquent Union sentiments are marred (for us) only by Webster's assurance that the Union at that time was safe beyond question. It contains another invented speech, this time put into the mouth of Elder William Brewster. The eulogy of Mason is largely and closely biographical, but its passages of tribute exhibit Webster's less formal style at its best. In the course of service in House and Senate, Webster had occasion often to pay tributes to deceased colleagues; several speeches of this sort are recorded, but none is especially distinguished, excepting the eulogy of Calhoun (*NE*, X, 100–102).

epideictic oratory not to be matched by any other speaker in modern times. Lincoln at Gettysburg surpassed Webster's best effort; Ingersoll at his brother's grave produced something unique and universally appealing; but for sustained and repeated excellence Webster stands alone. Whatever we may think of these speeches as we read them with tastes formed by the twentieth century, they accomplished what was expected of them, dignifying and making memorable the events, places, and men that called them forth. Their very length is a proof of the speaker's powers. On occasion we know that Webster disappointed his hearers by gruffly uttering perfunctory commonplaces and generalities, but the audiences of the great epideictic efforts felt no tedium though the speaker went on for a second, or even a third, hour. Here and there appears a touch of display, of sound above sense, of verbal fireworks; and yet we cannot be sure that even such did not contribute to the very real and solid effect of the speech in question. A speaker must have more than a few resources, if he is to succeed before audiences of varying temper. In the "Festival of the Sons of New Hampshire," Webster employed, early in the speech, the device of asking each one to shake hands with those next him, while he shook hands with those about him on the platform. At St. Louis, in a political address, he exclaimed, as he struck his palm on the shoulder of a "hardy yeoman" beside him: "This honest man, God bless him! is as truly my friend as though I clasped his hand as the descendant of John Hancock in Faneuil Hall!"[1] Not every weapon drawn will be effective; any one of them may prove to be a boomerang. But let the person who has never fought in the trenches discuss at his ease the niceties of armament; the orator must seize upon what he has at hand and strike.

This observation may remind us that at least two factors of Webster's style are left without illustration by a view of his epideictic oratory alone, namely, his humor and his colloquialism. To treat these at length is impossible here. He was not a humorous man, but he had a lively sense of the comic. This may be seen in his imagined picture of Senator Hayne marching, in his character as general, to seize the customhouse at Charleston. It may be seen to best effect, perhaps, in several passages of "Second Speech on the Sub-Treasury" or in the paragraph on patronage in "Objects of the Mexican War." Webster's light touches are often literary, depending upon the application of poetical sentiments to a political subject, as in this:

Sir, political partisans, and aspirants, and office-seekers are not sunflowers. They do not

"turn to their god when he sets
The same look which they turned when he rose."

[1] *NE*, XIII, 81–82.

He was capable of broader effects upon the hustings. An eye witness tells of a speech during the campaign of 1848, when Webster was attacking the nondescript party headed by Van Buren:

"Why, gentlemen," said Webster, to a gathering of sturdy and hard-featured people, "that Buffalo Platform is so rickety, it will hardly bear the fox-like tread of Mr. Van Buren"; and as he said "fox-like tread," he held out the palm of his left hand, and, with the other hand, played his fingers along his extended arm down to the hand, with a soft running motion, as if to represent the kitten-like advance of the foxy candidate upon his rickety "Platform." The answering shouts of laughter told that the shot was felt.[1]

His colloquialism appears in practically all his campaign speeches that are reported with any closeness whatever. Whether we choose to say that it was "put on" for effect or that it resulted from a sound sense of the occasion and from Webster's own homespun qualities depends upon our attitude toward Webster and our insight into his character.

To return to the epideictic oratory and to sum up, we have suggested that its effect was to furnish to Americans focuses for their imagination and loyal contemplation. This is the work that in other times and lands has been performed by the epic poet or prophet. Longfellow told of Paul Revere, Holmes of the *Constitution* and Bunker Hill, Bryant sang of Marion's men, Drake of the American flag, Emerson of Concord Bridge; but Webster contributed more than any of these to the American saga. He dramatized the nation's traditions and charged with power the less concrete symbols of our political life. This fact was observed by E. P. Whipple, in reviewing Webster's published speeches in 1844:[2] "He has done what no national poet has yet succeeded in doing,—associated his own great genius with all in our country's history and scenery which makes us rejoice that we are Americans. Over all those events in our history which are heroical, he has cast the hues of strong feeling and vivid imagination." In a later time, Senator George F. Hoar summed up the matter, having in mind, of course, Webster's work as a whole rather than merely the occasional addresses:[3]

[1] Parker, *op. cit.*, p. 115.

[2] In the July issue of the *North American Review;* we quote from the reprint in *Essays and Reviews* (2d ed., Boston, 1851), I, 180. Compare the tributes of members of the House of Representatives, published in S. M. Smucker, *The Life, Speeches, and Memorials of Daniel Webster* (Philadelphia, 1861), pp. 478, 486–487: (Mr. Chandler speaking) "His mind was moulded to the strong conception of the epic poet"; (Mr. Stanley speaking) "Daniel Webster was to the Revolutionary patriots of Massachusetts, to the founders of our Constitution in the Old Thirteen States, what Homer was to the ancient heroes."

[3] *The Proceedings of the Webster Centennial* (E. M. Hopkins, ed., Hanover, N. H., 1901?), pp. 270–272.

. . . the Republic is founded upon ideas. When those ideas lose their power over the minds and hearts of the people, the Republic will come to an end. It is the fortune of Daniel Webster, as of no other man except Jefferson, that the great ideas which lie at the foundation of the Republic clothe themselves to every man's understanding in his language, and rest for their sanction and vindication upon his argument . . . To the lover of constitutional liberty, there is nothing like the reply to Hayne since Pericles died, save only the dying speech of Chatham, and that of Patrick Henry at Williamsburg. . . . We cannot think of the Senate Chamber without him. We cannot think of the Supreme Court without him. We cannot think of Dartmouth College without him. We cannot think of Faneuil Hall without him. We cannot think of Boston, or Concord, or Lexington, or Bunker Hill, without him. . . . We cannot think of Massachusetts without him. We cannot think of America without him. We cannot think of the Constitution or of the Union without him.

IV. *The Great Debate*

Since a speech is a conscious attempt on the part of a speaker to overcome the various kinds of resistance of an audience to himself or to his beliefs and since oratorical ability is measured by his power to use the devices of oral discourse as the means of modifying or overcoming this resistance, we must, in formulating a critical opinion of Webster's genius, undertake to discuss the relation between his habits of procedure and the true opposition that he faced.

We have already seen him at work in the vein of eulogy, his commemorative speeches being designed to overcome the resistance offered by the native inability of man powerfully to feel accepted communal beliefs. This sort of resistance, as has been said, imposes upon the speaker no heavy task of changing people's minds, but rather the task of strengthening their hearts. The purely logical means of persuasion are of incidental value in the solution of this problem. The speaker prefers such other means as description and narrative, expressed in the vocabulary of feeling. His basic strategy is to present the familiar concept fired with imaginative insights, so that the old notion will regain the vigor of youth. The reason why Webster's occasional oratory achieved distinction is that, in addition to his powers of description and narration, he possessed the capacity to draw the highest inspiration from his sense that he faced an audience less convinced than himself. The spectacle of an America indifferent to the political significance of her historical position challenged him no less profoundly than religious leaders are challenged by man's unconcern for moral perfection.

Turning now to Webster's deliberative oratory, as Aristotle would have classified speeches in the Congress and during political campaigns, we see again that his moments of greatness come when the resistance that he faced aroused him to the point where he was willing to use his full powers.

At other times, his native indolence or his failure to recognize the extent and nature of opposition or his proud unconcern led him to deliver speeches that bore little relation to the persuasive problem before him.

In the so-called "Webster-Hayne Debate," the resistance encountered by Webster can be adequately explained in terms of the speeches that caused him to enter the combat, and his effectiveness can be measured only when that resistance is understood. Our first task, therefore, will be to describe not only what Hayne said as the debate on Foote's resolution gathered momentum and approached its climax but also what contributions were made by other members of the Senate during this historic episode and what large issues were at stake in the moves and countermoves of the debaters. Then we shall be prepared to see Webster's speeches in perspective and to answer the question whether his efforts deserve to be ranked among the most brilliant responses to opposition in legislative history.

The first session of the Twenty-first Congress opened December 7, 1829. Jackson's message was read next day, and the Senate occupied itself during the subsequent 2 weeks with the election of committees and the receipt of petitions. On December 29, the second day after its Christmas recess, Senator Foote, of Connecticut, presented a resolution "that the Committee on Public Lands be instructed to inquire into the expediency of limiting for a certain period the sales of the public lands to such lands only as have heretofore been offered for sale, and are subject to entry at the minimum price. And also, whether the office of Surveyor General may not be abolished without detriment to the public interest." This was the spark that kindled the flames of the famous controversy.

Foote's resolution was vigorously debated at intervals until the Senate adjourned on Monday, May 31, 1830. During these 5 months, twenty-one of the forty-eight men then in the Senate delivered, in all, sixty-five speeches upon the Connecticut Senator's proposal. Not only Hayne and Webster but Benton and Barton of Missouri, Holmes and Sprague of Maine, Livingston and Johnston of Louisiana, Rowan of Kentucky, Grundy of Tennessee, Clayton of Delaware, Smith of South Carolina, Woodbury of New Hampshire, and Foote himself joined the fray. "This debate," said Foote in a speech on May 20, "will form a compendious history of the policy of our Government, from its commencement for a half century, its progress in the arts as well as in arms, its trials and its triumphs."[1] No words more appropriately express the magnitude of the debate. As we read the documents of this legislative battle of a century

---

[1] Gales and Seaton, *Register of Debates in Congress* (Washington, D.C., 1830), VI, Part 1, pp. 438–439. Upon this volume we depend when we quote passages from, or otherwise refer to, the speeches on Foote's resolution.

ago, we see ambitious frontiersmen penetrating into forests and plains beyond the limits of the official survey, preempting the land of the magnificent interior, preparing for the assault upon the Rocky Mountains, dreaming of western slopes where a continent plunged into the Pacific Ocean. We see the growth of manufacturing in the Northeast, the slow formation of an industrial proletariat, the struggle of men for small freeholds. We see Indian wars and the spectacle of men swimming across the Tennessee River, pushing their arms before them on rafts, to attack the Cherokee town of Nickajack and drive savages from the Cumberland Gap. We are reminded of the negotiations with Spain over the free navigation of the Mississippi River. We hear the deliberations upon the Northwest Ordinance of 1787, the bickering of the original states under the Articles of Confederation, the accents of Jefferson and Madison in the Kentucky and Virginia resolutions. We remember that people are in the year 1830 swarming into the Mexican land of Texas. We are told of the War of 1812, when New England gave a dinner to the American soldier who surrendered Detroit and the better classes were displeased with the victory of a rough border captain at New Orleans. We catch glimpses of the interior of land offices in Missouri and Louisiana and of the daily tasks of surveyors dragging their chains through a wilderness never before bounded by the titles of law. We are menaced by talk of slavery, of disunion, of the sovereignty of states. We gather the sinister import of Senator Hayne's words when he talks of "the torches of discord" and "the glare of the weapon half-drawn from its scabbard."

Our chief concern, however, must now be limited to the first 29 days of the 5 months covered by the whole debate and to the first thirty-eight of the sixty-five speeches upon Foote's resolution. Webster withdrew from the debate on January 27, his "Third Reply to Hayne" on that day being the thirty-eighth speech of the series and his last in the controversy. Hayne spoke later, and so did the tireless Benton and others, but these speeches fall outside our present study.

On the day after he introduced his resolution, Foote, in response to a question by Benton, explained that the public lands then surveyed and on the market were more than adequate for the demand. He said that seventy-two million acres had been surveyed and were unsold, being on the market at the minimum price of $1.25 per acre. Since purchasers were buying the public lands at the rate of one million acres a year, he argued that the supply was adequate for some time to come. His figures were questioned by Benton and Kane, who said that the seventy-two million acres were mainly picked-over land, unfit for cultivation, and unenticing to prospective buyers. Holmes sprang to the defense of Foote, accepting his figures; but later he claimed that actually there were two hundred million acres ready for purchasers and that this area would accommodate a population of six million inhabitants, whereas the West at present had half that number. Holmes's figures were to be endorsed by Webster when he made his "First Reply to Hayne."

Foote's resolution involved two separate questions. In one sense, it seemed to say: Should the Senate instruct the Committee on Public Lands to initiate an inquiry into the present status of sales and surveys of the public domain, with the purpose of acquiring information upon which a sound policy could be based? Limited only to this question, the resolution would be difficult to attack, because an opponent would seem to be blocking an inquiry into an important subject. In another sense, however, the resolution seemed to recommend that the committee should be instructed to propose a limitation upon the sales of public land and a temporary termination of the surveys. If this were the import, then a supporter of the resolution would be in the position of saying that the opportunities of prospective purchasers of small farms in the West should be restricted.

Those who favored Foote's proposal in the early stages of the debate stressed that it was merely a resolution of inquiry, designed to elicit information, and that an attempt to block it was an attempt to block inquiry. They insisted that the resolution did not directly recommend a policy of restricted sales and surveys; such a policy, if proposed by the committee as a result of its investigation, could be debated when the Senate had received the committee's report. This position, however, was not maintained with any great consistency. Foote and Holmes, in particular, upheld the view that an inquiry was necessary; but in the same breath, they presented their figures upon the present status of the public lands, and these figures indicated that, so far as these two senators were concerned, no further inquiry was necessary, and the only question was whether a restrictive policy should be adopted.

The opponents meanwhile argued that Foote had offered a resolution of instruction, the purpose of which was to require the committee to recommend the limitation of sales and surveys of the public lands. The debate, they said, should not be upon the question: Should we order investigation? but upon the question: Should we order the committee to propose that sales be restricted and surveys discontinued? They held this to be the real issue. Benton was the chief spokesman for this view. He insisted that the Senate should consider this issue at once and not wait until the committee had made its dictated report.

In an effort to decide whether the resolution proposed an inquiry or a new land policy, Livingston made a brilliant speech, the twenty-eighth of the series, arguing that the two questions were obviously implicit in the resolution and that the proper thing to do was to limit the debate to the new policy contemplated by Foote. As a result of his speech and of other protests against the ambiguity of the resolution, Sprague moved an amendment, the force of which was to instruct the Committee on Public Lands to inquire whether sales should be restricted and surveys discontinued, on the one hand, or should be respectively accelerated and extended, on the other. Foote objected to the amendment, and it was not until January 20, after Hayne had made his first speech, that the Connecticut Senator, seeing how far afield the debate had progressed, agreed to Sprague's suggestion. Thus Webster's "First Reply to Hayne" was on the resolution as amended by Sprague and Foote. Webster's closing words of this speech moved an indefinite postponement of the amended resolution, and the rest of the debate was technically upon this motion, although by this time the question of inquiring into the status of the public lands had become a subject more honored in the breach than the observance. On Friday, May 21, 1830, 4 months after the clash between Webster and Hayne, the Senate concluded its discussion of Foote's resolution as amended, the immediate question still being Webster's motion to postpone indefinitely. No vote was ever taken upon this question or upon the resolution, both being before the Senate at the time of adjournment 10 days later.

We are now in a position to consider the most famous section of the debate. It is a mistake to suppose that even here Webster and Hayne were the only two protagonists. What Benton said is also of importance, if we wish to understand the purposes of the speakers. And only when we have a clear definition of these purposes are we able to appreciate the tactics of each man and the considerations that led each to select his topics of discussion. Benton and Hayne were allies during the debate. Their speeches led Webster to make his "First Reply," which was answered at some length by both opponents. For convenience, therefore, we may consider the speeches of Hayne and Benton as the affirmative case and Webster's three replies to Hayne as the negative.

These men were not debating a mere restricted proposition. They were, on the contrary, engaged in a struggle for power. Collectively they represented the America of 1830, each being the spokesman of a different one of the three major geographical sections of the country. But the struggle for power raised questions that were not to be answered by geography alone. Implied rather than stated, these questions are the terms that give emphasis and meaning to a discussion of the subjects covered by each of the speakers. (1) Could the conflicting interests of the three sections be reconciled within the framework of existing national political arrangements? If not, the future course of American history would be a tragic movement toward a victorious sectionalism, which at the end of the road would mean the triumph of the small independent sovereignty, the disintegration of the Federal structure, and the final collapse of a promising experiment in liberty and union. (2) If, on the other hand, these conflicting sectional interests could be reconciled, upon what principles would the reconciliation rest? Would the America of the future be an image of the Europe of the past, with continental security the object of a game of alliance and counter-alliance among geographical units, where today's friends were tomorrow's enemies, and where diplomats gambled in the hope that a lucky fall of the dice of power would always happen to guarantee order and prevent chaos? (3) Or would the history of America be the story of a new species of continental security, with liberty safeguarded within spheres of local and individual interests, but with social authority imposed in the regions where individual action became a matter of general concern? These questions define the respective positions of Hayne, Benton, and Webster and provide a clue to the specific aim of each speaker.

Space does not permit a complete analysis of the speeches of Benton and Hayne. Yet we must look briefly at the work of both men if we would establish a clear impression of the resistance to which Webster responded when he took the floor.

On the day after Foote's resolution was offered to the Senate, Benton sought postponement, arguing that the North was obviously intending to strike a blow at Western migration and that he wanted the Southern senators, who were then absent, to be on hand when the resolution was considered, so that they, as in the past, could come to the support of the young and struggling West in her battle against Northern selfishness. He saw Foote's resolution as part and parcel of attempts made over a period of 44 years to check migration into the empty interior, and he promised that later he would review the history of these attempts and show the resolution to be the manifestation of a settled and sinister hostility of the North to the West. These topics Benton developed in his speech on January 18, pointing out that limitation of sales and discontinuance of surveys would prevent the flow of population to the West and would confine the poor man to his position as journeyman in Northern industry. Safely ensconced behind the tariff wall, the North, Benton went on, wanted a cheap and degraded industrial proletariat to man her industries and was now bent upon restricting the opportunity of the humble workers. He shrewdly observed that the whole policy of the North toward the tariff and Western migration was a scheme that "taxes the South to injure the West, to pauperize the poor of the North." He went on to show how the North, in the negotiations with Spain, in 1786, upon the question of the free navigation of the Mississippi, had shown a tendency to yield to Spain's desire to prevent free use of the waterway and how the South had risen time after time during this period to check these Northern designs.

Even then, said Benton, the North was interested in blocking the flow of population westward. Northern opposition to appropriations for defense of the settlers against Indians and for extinguishing the Indian title to the land of the West was part of the same interest. In his reply to Webster's first speech on Foote's resolution, Benton reworked the material that he had used in these earlier remarks. He re-emphasized the West's case against the East. He attributed the benefits conferred upon the West to the loyal and friendly intervention of the South. He disclaimed an intention of attacking New England, which he admired; but New England was divided into the rich and well born, on the one hand, and the poor and humble, on the other, and his charge, he said, was leveled at the New England leaders who spoke, not for the people, but for the upper classes. He reverted to the negotiations with Spain upon the question of navigation of the Mississippi, to the circumstances of the passage of the Northwest Ordinance, to the appropriations for defense of the West against the Indians, in each instance showing that the North was the enemy, the South, the friend of the West.

Enough has been said of the content of Benton's speeches to show his tactics. Bent upon uniting South and West against North, he attempted to marshal evidence that would show how time-honored, how rich in history was the story of the association of the two allies. But he also attempted to divide the North into classes and parties by his appeals to the poor of New England, his praise of the Democratic party of Massachusetts, his castigation of the rich, selfish Federalists and manufacturers and capitalists. If we may borrow an illustration from diplomacy, Benton's position was that of an ambassador working in a foreign capital to cement an alliance between his country and a prospective ally, while at the same time he worked to divide against itself the country that the alliance was designed to thwart. These tactics are familiar to the student of modern propaganda. Like all attempts of the kind, Benton's was in one respect a propaganda of unity, in the other, a propaganda of disunity. The formation of a common front toward an enemy requires an emphasis upon the feelings that the members of the alliance have in common, and Benton's speeches did not go very far in this direction, possibly because he knew that the union of the South and the West was to be merely a marriage of convenience. But he was more emphatic in his attempt to divide and weaken the North. This purpose required a manipulation of jealousy, envy, bitterness, anger, fear—the motives that throw men into discord and confusion. To all these motives Benton appealed, as our analysis of his speeches has suggested.

Hayne's tactics were Benton's, purified, however, of any attempt to unite two sections against the third. His methods were directed toward the separation of the Federal organism into component states. No doubt he welcomed the fact that Benton, in the year 1830, was seeking an alliance between South and West against the North in an effort to prevent a limitation of the sales of the public lands. Such an alliance might prove useful to the South in her effort to relax the hold of the "abominable" tariff of 1828. But Hayne uneasily saw that the tariff was not unanimously disliked in the West. In fact, he openly mentioned in the debate the "murdered coalition" of 1824, when New England had supposedly bought Western support of the tariff and of the Presidency of John Quincy Adams, in return for Northern support of internal improvements and of Henry Clay as Secretary of State. Moreover, the tariff was linked to Clay's "American System," and Clay was from Kentucky. Facing these proofs of Western sympathy toward the tariff, Hayne realized that Benton might be a friend of the South only so long as the West would need help in the battle against Foote's resolution. The only policy that seemed to promise assistance to the South was to separate the West still farther from the North than Foote's resolution threatened to do and meanwhile to weaken the North by driving a wedge of party jealousy and class hatred between discordant segments of Northern opinion.

But Hayne was not interested in this policy merely because it offered a means of defeating the tariff. He feared the rising tide of criticism of slavery, and this came from the West and North. If these two sections were ever to unite against slavery, as they ultimately did in 1860, the South would be powerless to resist, short of outright war. Working to divide the West and the North from each other, seeking to deal in the merchandise of jealousy and suspicion, the South also saw that she needed a means of hardening separative tendencies into a permanent philosophy of government, and it was Calhoun, Hayne's alter ego and generalissimo, who devised this means, calling it the Carolina doctrine of nullification. Nullification was the philosophy of disunion, as Hayne's speeches were the strategy of disunion. Nullification was a theory of peaceful resistance under the Constitution to the power of the general government, whenever the exercise of that power conflicted dangerously with the welfare of the individual sovereign states. The philosophy of disunion, coupled with tactics that would divide the Union, made Hayne's speeches on Foote's resolution the most sinister force yet encountered by the American republic.

In his first speech, Hayne attacked, not the land policy proposed in Foote's resolution, but the policy already in operation. He pointed out how unfavorably this policy compared with that of the great colonial nations. The United States seeks, he said, to enrich herself from the sale of her public lands; she sells land at high prices, and the settlers have to send their money out of their state to pay the capitalists and the distant government. Hayne mentioned the poverty of the new sections, their constant need of relief from the burden of their debts; and he compared the condition of the small farmers in Missouri to that of the planters in the South, who also had to send their wealth to the North and East, in order to pay the revenue duties. The South, he added, stands in relation to the Federal government as Ireland stands to England. In a constructive vein, Hayne suggested what policy the United States should follow. The public lands should not be used as a source of revenue by the general government, for that would make the government independent of the people and would promote immense consolidation of Federal power and be fatal to state sovereignty. He deplored the apparent conspiracy to shut the common people out of the public domain, and make them dependent upon the industrialist who owned the cotton and woolen mills. He wanted the poor to find an asylum in the West. But he also deplored the tendency of Western states to come to Congress, hat in hand, asking for a grant of public lands for the establishment of this or that local improvement. These requests, he sternly insisted, give the Federal government the role of dispenser of largess and make the states suppliants and inferiors. He closed by outlining a tentative new policy, which would seek not to regulate industry and population or provide revenue but to create great flourishing communities and free and independent states.

Throughout this speech, Hayne referred to the Federal government as if he were speaking of a foreign power. His comparison of the South with Ireland under harsh English rule is merely one example. At another point, he strongly implied that the current method of disposing of public land was "your policy," not "our policy." His was a vein of detached, impersonal irony, with nothing to betray any loyalty to the idea of Union. Furthermore, he made no attempt to court the West. He thought, indeed, that their attitude toward the largess of the government was degrading. He even said that he did not seek to aggravate their discontent. "I do not know," he remarked, "that my voice will ever reach them." But despite this disclaimer, his speech did say that the West had a legitimate cause of complaint, and he did, in fact, try to aggravate discontent, his sympathy for the poor workers of the North being hardly a sentiment that would occur to a defender of slavery unless he had an ulterior purpose in dwelling upon it. The whole gist of his speech was that the general government was the enemy of local interests, the distant and tyrannous proprietor, the object of suspicion and fear, the source of poverty and hardship in Southern counties, frontier settlements, and Northern slums.

Hayne's second speech is one of the bitterest in American legislative annals. Here the philosophy and the tactics of disunion are brilliantly combined. He jeered at Webster for seeking to cement an alliance between

West and North. He recalled the "murdered coalition" of 1824. He utilized Burke's gibe at the English Tories, saying in effect that the West had grown great in spite of the protection of the general government. He accused Webster of inconsistency upon the policy toward the public lands. He remarked that the North's sudden interest in internal improvements was not dictated by constitutional scruple, as was Southern opposition, but by a selfish desire to gain Western votes for the tariff. Webster had said in his first speech that even the national debt tended to cement the seams of Union and was beneficial to that extent. Hayne retorted that Webster was interested in the welfare of those who held government bonds and whose attachment to the Union was a pecuniary attachment, not a devotion to freedom, virtue, patriotism.

He later defended slavery, charging Webster with an appeal to the passions and prejudices of those who believed that this institution weakened the South. He denied that slavery was a blight, in respect either to the physical power of the South or to her economic condition or moral character. He asked whether Webster's "significant hint of the weakness of slaveholding States, when contrasted with the superior strength of free States—like the glare of the weapon half-drawn from its scabbard—[was] intended to enforce the lessons of prudence and of patriotism." He remarked that, in a war, a large part of the population being of necessity engaged in agriculture and other pursuits behind the lines, the slaveholding states might well be able to maintain in the field a number of troops fully equal to what could be supported by a larger white population. He compared the wisdom, prudence, and humanity of the slaveowner with the inhumanity of the false philanthropists who allowed Northern Negroes to enjoy freedom in wretched, vile, and loathsome slums. He deplored the tendency of the North to light "the torches of discord" upon the question of domestic servitude. He said that the love of liberty was strengthened in the South by the existence of slavery. He raked the embers of old party feuds to start a fire of revulsion against the Federalists, represented by Webster; and he, contrasted their love of power with his own party's love of freedom. He exposed Webster's inconsistency upon the tariff. He reviewed the history of the early years of the Republic to show that South Carolina had been devoted to the true cause of liberty, while the political associates of Webster had held the Hartford Convention and threatened disunion. He reluctantly made these charges, he said, because they had the tendency "to excite sectional feelings, and sectional jealousies;" but Webster had "cast the first stone" and would find "that he lives in a glass house." Hayne emphasized that he intended these charges to apply to the peace party of New England during the War of 1812 and not to the Democrats and Antifederalists of that section.

He closed his speech with an exposition of the principle that gave his previous tactics a philosophical justification. He had sought to divide the West from the North, the poor from the rich, the Democrat from the Federalist, the slaveowner from the false philanthropist. Now he found the justification of a divided America in the doctrine of state sovereignty and the right of the small independent political divisions to nullify, and hence to destroy, the general government. He sought to show that this so-called "Carolina doctrine" was in reality the doctrine of Madison and Jefferson in the Virginia and Kentucky resolutions. In his last words, he said that if the South acted upon the sacred principle of resistance to unauthorized taxation and was animated by her great love of freedom, then, when she went beyond the limits of a cold prudence, her critics must, in the language of Burke, "pardon something to the spirit of liberty."

At one point in this speech, Hayne denied that the South had ever made professions of regard for the West in relation to appropriations for internal improvements. This was his declaration of purpose. He did not seek an alliance with the West; he sought, rather, to prevent sentiments of union from hardening into sectional alliances of any sort. His appeals were calculated to make the North suspicious of her leaders, the West distrustful of the friendship of the North, the slaveowners fearful of an attack upon their property, the poor envious and jealous of wealth and position. Every sentiment that disrupts unity, and sets men at each other's throats, was deftly encouraged by Hayne. Every fact and topic capable of prompting these sentiments were used in his speech. And the uglier side of disunity—strife, bitterness, hatred, selfishness—was concealed beneath the dignified and impressive philosophy of nullification.

The affirmative side of the debate now having been analyzed, we have a clear conception of the resistance to which Webster's speeches were a response, and we turn next to his presentation of the negative case. The word *negative* is misleading, for Webster took an affirmative position toward the attempt by Hayne to uphold a negative philosophy. But in the conventional terminology of debate, Webster was the defendant, in the sense that he replied to arguments already advanced. The fact that he used his technical position as an opportunity for the construction of a positive philosophy is an indication that his speeches approached the goal of an ideal rebuttal.

Webster's "First Reply to Hayne" began with the weak assertion that he was indifferent to the success or failure of Foote's resolution but was inclined to believe that the amount of public lands then on the market did not justify a policy that would accelerate the sale of lands or extend more rapidly the surveys. Had he continued in this vein, his tactics would have been suspiciously like those of Foote and Holmes, who sought to conceal a desire for the limitation of the sale of public land under an apparent attempt to seek information upon the subject. But Webster turned almost at once to the broader question of the policy of the general government toward the public domain, denying that this policy was harsh and oppressive. The general government has protected with blood and treasure those who went beyond the Alleghanies; and now she sells lands at a modest price, not so much to reimburse herself for the cost of the protection but rather because the terms of the original grants of the land to the general government had stipulated that the public domain was not to be given away but was to become the common property of all the states, to be used for the common benefit. Webster's defense of the general government was followed by an analysis of Hayne's objections to consolidation of powers. What, asked Webster, did Hayne mean by consolidation? If he meant only that the Union was strengthened by whatever induced the people of the states to hold together, then, of course, the public lands and everything in which the people had a common interest did tend toward consolidation, and to this species of consolidation every true American was attached. If he meant, however, that the Union was being consolidated by a gradual extension of the original powers granted to the general government, then it was obvious that no American favored that species of consolidation. The truth was, Webster went on, that consolidation of power was a rhetorical abstraction designed to disparage the Union, to magnify its evils, to reduce it to a mere question of expediency, and to fix its value by a bookkeeper's calculation of profit and loss. People who hold this view, said he, cherish no fixed and deep regard for the Union, and have no conception of its absolute and vital necessity to our welfare. "I deprecate and deplore this tone of thinking and acting," he avowed. " . . . I am a Unionist. . . . Far, indeed, in my wishes, very far distant be the day, when our associated and fraternal stripes shall be severed asunder, and when that happy constellation under which we have risen to so much renown, shall be broken up, and be seen sinking, star after star, into obscurity and night."

Soon Webster turned to the charge that the East had pursued a policy of settled hostility to the West, as part of a move to keep men in Eastern manufacturing cities and to harness the poor to the benches of a protected industry. Made first by Benton, this charge had been noticed and confirmed by Hayne; and Webster held that the endorser of the accusation was responsible for its truth. Webster's reply, richly documented from the history of the attitude of the East toward the public lands, furnished the rest of this speech and emphasized the justice and liberality of the policy consistently upheld by his state and section. The system of surveys ultimately adopted was a Northern idea; the Northwest Ordinance, excluding involuntary servitude from the Ohio country, was written by a Northerner, Nathan Dane, and had been "a great and salutary measure of prevention"; the North had also supported internal improvements like the Cumberland Road and Portland Canal, against which the constitutional scruples of the South had been set. A South Carolinian, said Webster, had once opposed Western migration and had proposed to limit sales of the public lands, on the grounds that the westward flow of peoples was impoverishing the South. And, Webster went on, I opposed those arguments then, and oppose them now. Webster concluded his speech by moving indefinite postponement of Foote's resolution.

Webster's defense of the general government and his expression of attachment to the Union were designed to allay sectional jealousies and hatreds. But it must be confessed that the concluding argument of his "First Reply" was not wholly devoid of the spirit of sectionalism. His remark upon the constitutional scruples of the South against internal improvements and upon the blessings of the exclusion of slavery from Ohio by the Northwest Ordinance were plainly meant to remind Benton that the West owed more to the North than to the South. Here, at any rate, he was replying in kind to his two opponents, and had the debate ended at this point, his speech would have been another incident in the history of sectional utterances. But Hayne was incensed, not only by what he called "the bitterest sarcasm" of Webster's manner of localizing the sentiment of disunion within South Carolina but also by Webster's references to the beneficent effects of the exclusion of slavery from the Northwest and to Southern objection to internal improvements. Perhaps, indeed, the remark about slavery rankled most. Perhaps this was the *casus belli*. At any rate, Hayne's reply to Webster produced the occasion for a speech that lifted the debate above its previous level.

Webster began his second speech with the request that the Secretary read Foote's resolution. When this had been done, Webster remarked that the subject under consideration had been almost the only topic in the whole range of national policy that had been overlooked by Hayne. Having thus focused attention upon the scope of the debate, Webster contrasted Hayne's tone of uneasiness, fear, anger, and personal bitterness with his own temperance and coolness. A few other observations upon Hayne's attempt to reduce the debate to a conflict of personalities and upon his own desire to avoid recrimination and to maintain good temper; a brief criticism of Hayne's allusion to Banquo's ghost; and a remark upon the bad taste of Hayne's sneer at Nathan Dane—these comments prepared the way for the main argument.

Hayne's defense of slavery had been so presented as to emphasize the irreconcilable opposition between those who merely sought in a spirit of humanity to administer an inherited social institution, and those false philanthropists who were bent upon interference with their neighbor's business. Webster replied that slavery was regarded in the North as a matter of local policy, left with the states themselves, and not subject to the interference of the Federal government. He said:

I regard domestic slavery as one of the greatest of evils, both moral and political. But, though it be a malady, and whether it be curable, and, if so, by what means; or, on the other hand, whether it be the *vulnus immedicabile* of the social system, I leave it to those whose right and duty it is to inquire and to decide. And this, I believe, sir, is, and uniformly has been, the sentiment of the North.

His immediate review of the Congressional history of this sentiment was designed to show the truth of his conclusion and to reveal that the only serious difference between him and Hayne was upon the question of the evil of slavery. He did not choose to complain that slave states calculated their Congressional representation upon the basis of their slave as well as free population; even that abuse was part of the original bargain. "The Union itself," he avowed, "is too full of benefit to be hazarded in propositions for changing its original basis. I go for the constitution as it is, and for the Union as it is." Thus Webster drew from the topic of slavery the tactics calculated to unite North and South. If the best way to divide people is to make them feel that their differences are fundamental and irreconcilable, then the best way to bring them together is to show, as Webster did, that the articles upon which they agree extend much farther than had been supposed.

Webster's next major argument concerned national policy toward the public lands. Hayne had wondered why Webster could believe that the lands should be sold by the government and could insist in the same breath that the government had the right to make free grants of land to states for canals, railways, and colleges. Webster replied that the conditions under which the lands had been granted to the government by the original states permitted the sale of lands for the common benefit of all the states and that gifts of land to states were justified upon the same premise. The states were not "in all main respects, separate and diverse." They were united, "having interests, common, associated, intermingled." They were one in respect to whatever was conducive to the common good. If the South objected to the appropriation of public land for a college in Ohio, the narrow-minded people of Massachusetts, said Webster, had quite a different attitude toward a local improvement in the South.

Sir, if a railroad or a canal, beginning in South Carolina, and ending in South Carolina, appeared to me to be of national importance and national magnitude, believing, as I do, that the power of Government extends to the encouragement of works of that description, if I were to stand up here, and ask what interest has Massachusetts in railroads in South Carolina, I should not be willing to face my constituents. These same narrow minded men would tell me, that they had sent me to act for the whole country, and that one who possessed too little comprehension, either of intellect or feeling; one who was not large enough, in mind and heart, to embrace the whole, was not fit to be entrusted with the interest of any part.

In these words, Webster answered Hayne's attempt to divide peoples of the West and South from their allegiance to the government. A land policy seen to rest upon dictates of politicians working always to secure benefits for their constituents might arouse suspicion and contempt; but a policy that came, as did Webster's, from a conception of common benefit would appeal to the altruistic dispositions in man's political character.

In the same vein, Webster justified a policy of internal improvements, showing that the North and South had both supported measures of this kind long before the time when Northern support had allegedly been purchased in return for Western support of the tariff. Political hopes and fears and party associations were not behind those early moves to benefit the citizens of all the states. As late as 1823, said Webster, Hayne's vote upon a certain bill indicated his acceptance of the constitutionality of internal improvements, and in 1816 the South had had an efficient hand in establishing a tariff. Was it not a little hard, argued Webster, to say that the tariff and internal improvements had been invented as part of a scheme to trade Northern selfishness against Western greed, to the end that the South would be ruined? Webster went on briefly to summarize his previous theory that the public debt was not an unmitigated evil, to the extent, at least, of its power to unite the people behind a common obligation; and he then touched briefly upon Hayne's objection to consolidation of the Union. Throughout these sections of the argument ran the theme of unity, of attachment to the common welfare, of loyalty to a government that had a decent degree of unselfishness, and a human concern for all sections and parties.

In one sense, Webster's argument on the tariff was weak. Hayne had accused him of inconsistency, and it is one of the most conspicuous facts in his political biography that he did in 1824 endorse the principle of free trade and in 1828, that of protection. But Webster, unsuccessful in his attempt convincingly to deny this inconsistency, did make the denial serve a useful purpose. New England had unavailingly opposed the tariff of 1824, Webster admitted, and his own vote had registered that opposition. But the tariff act carried. New England had either to submit or to prevent the operation of the tariff law by acting upon the Carolina doctrine of nullification. She submitted and found that she could profitably accommodate herself to the measure she had opposed. Webster asserted that his subsequent support of the tariff of 1828 was a vote to abolish the inequalities and to secure the degree of protection of the Act of 1824, his constituents being now adjusted to the operation of the law that they had previously disliked. The explanation did not acquit Webster of inconsistency; but it did reinforce the point that, when national laws worked hardship upon a section and caused temporary bitterness, the proper course was not to advocate dismemberment of the nation but to seek the elimination of the source of bitterness with an appeal to the common humanity of all people, or to give the laws a fair trial, with the possibility that they might produce advantage.

The first day's installment of Webster's reply came to an end in the midst of his discussion of the tariff.[1] Next day he spoke further upon this topic and then turned to the attacks made by Benton and Hayne upon New England. Here his words had a flexible and exact artistry. Commenting upon the nature of Hayne's attack, Webster said:

Why, sir, he has stretched a drag-net over the whole surface of perished pamphlets, indiscreet sermons, frothy paragraphs, and fuming popular addresses; over whatever the pulpit, in its moments of alarm, the press in its heats, and parties in their extravagance, have severally thrown off, in times of general excitement and violence. He has thus swept together a mass of such things as, but that they are now old, the public health would have required him rather to leave in their state of dispersion. For a good long hour or two, we had the unbroken pleasure of listening to the honorable member, while he recited, with his usual grace and spirit, and with evident high gusto, speeches, pamphlets, addresses, and all the *et caeteras* of the political press, such as warm heads produce in warm times; and such as it would be "discomfiture" indeed, for any one, whose taste did not delight in that sort of reading, to be obliged to peruse at any time. This is his war. This it is to carry the war into the enemy's country. It is an invasion of this sort, that he flatters himself with the expectation of gaining laurels fit to adorn a Senator's brow.

If he wanted to reply in kind, Webster went on, he could fill Hayne's ears with specimens of malice exhibited by spokesmen of other sections of the country. "Publications more abusive or scurrilous never saw the light, than were sent forth against Washington, and all his leading measures, from presses South of New England. But I shall not look them up. I employ no scavengers;[2] no one is in attendance on me, tendering such means of retaliation; and if there were, with an ass's load on [of?] them, with a bulk as huge as that which the gentleman himself has produced, I would not touch one of them." Webster added later:

[1] Fuess, I, 377.
[2] Woodbury, Senator from New Hampshire, had furnished Hayne with ammunition for the attack on New England, and Webster's reference is to him.

It is enough for me to say that if, in any part of this, their grateful occupation; if, in all their researches, they find any thing in the history of Massachusetts, or New England, or in the proceedings of any legislature, or other public body, disloyal to the Union, speaking slightly of its value, proposing to break it up, or recommending non-intercourse with neighboring States, on account of difference of political opinion, then, sir, I give them all up to the honorable gentleman's unrestrained rebuke; excepting, however, that he will extend his buffetings, in like manner, to all similar proceedings, wherever else to be found.

Denying that he had made an attack upon the honor or patriotism of South Carolina, Webster said that he had sought merely to answer those persons in the South "who speak of our Union with indifference, or doubt, taking pains to magnify its evils, and to say nothing of its benefits." "The honorable member himself, I was sure," said Webster of Hayne, "could never be one of these; and I regretted the expression of such opinions as he had avowed, because I thought their obvious tendency was to encourage feelings of disrespect to the Union, and to weaken its connection."

Webster's defense of New England was an attempt to show that love of the Union and loyalty to the whole country were more significant passions than was sectional bitterness. It was an attempt to unite what Benton and Hayne had torn asunder. Its whole intent and purpose made it a propaganda of unity, counteracting one of division. But Webster was not content with a mere display of tactics. He next sought to expound the philosophy of union. The last major argument of his speech was a reply to Hayne's theory of nullification. Hayne had said in effect that the end of consolidation of power was a complete centralized tyranny, with all individual liberty destroyed by the gradual encroachments of social authority. Webster's reply was calculated to show that the end of decentralization was chaos, with individual liberty destroyed by its unrestrained excesses. The lovers of liberty, among whom Hayne had numbered himself, and the lovers of union, represented by Webster, could gain their separate ends by realizing that true liberty could be preserved only by union, true union preserved only by liberty.

The most spectacular and effective statement of this argument came in Webster's final words, "Liberty *and* Union, now and forever, one and inseparable." But before he said this, he examined in detail the theory of the Constitution. He affirmed the extraconstitutional right of revolution as an ultimate remedy for tyrannous abuse of power on the part of any government but denied that a constitutional right of resistance to the general government existed in the basic law. Webster argued:

I say, the right of a State to annul a law of Congress, cannot be maintained but on the ground of the unalienable right of man to resist oppression; that is to say, upon the ground of revolution. I admit that there is an ultimate violent remedy, above the constitution, and in defiance of the constitution, which may be resorted to, when a revolution is to be justified. But I do not admit that, under the constitution, and in conformity with it, there is any mode in which a State Government, as a member of the Union, can interfere and stop the progress of the General Government, by force of her own laws, under any circumstances whatever.

Employing the disjunctive enthymeme, which he resorted to time and again in this part of the speech, Webster said that between submission to the law of the general government, when regularly pronounced constitutional, and open resistance to that law, which constituted revolution or rebellion, "there is no middle ground." Either Hayne rested his theory upon the right of revolution, which no one denied, or upon a constitutional right of resistance, which did not exist. In order to prove that the right of nullification was not a constitutional right, Webster examined the origin of the government, maintaining, not that the Federal authority was the creature of the states, but that it was the agent of the people. In words later to be echoed by Lincoln, Webster declared, "It is, sir, the people's constitution, the people's Government; made for the people; made by the people; and answerable to the people." The general government and the state governments derive their authority from the people. Neither can, in relation to the other, be called primary. The national government possesses those powers which can be shown to have been conferred upon it by the people; all other powers belong to state governments or to the people. So far as the Constitution gives the general government the right to make war, coin money and conclude treaties, so far do the people express their view of the limitation of the power of state sovereignty. So far as the Constitution reserves certain other rights to the states or to the people, so far do the people express their view of the independence of the states or of themselves. Whenever any congressional law can be shown to be within the powers of the general government, that law must be either obeyed or resisted by revolutionary means. Whenever any Congressional law transgresses the powers of the general government, that law can be declared unconstitutional, not by separate authorities existing in the states, but by the judicial arm of the general government. Under the Constitution, the people had recourse to the courts or to the process of amendment of the Constitution or to congressional repeal, whenever the law produced unendurable effects. Outside the Constitution, the people had the right of revolution. But between these two sets of remedies, there was no room for the remedy of constitutional rebellion endorsed by Hayne.

The day that marked the end of Webster's "Second Reply" was later devoted to a rejoinder by Hayne and by Webster, the latter's being, as we said above, his final utterance of the debate. These do not add to the materials already considered, and we may say that, so far as Webster is concerned, the debate ended with the famous words, "Liberty *and* Union, now and forever, one and inseparable."

The "Second Reply to Hayne" is rarely read nowadays in its entirety. Webster's peroration and his apostrophe to New England have been treated as removable units, as purple patches, and have been declaimed by schoolboys who never understood the context to which these eloquent periods belong. It is much rarer to find a reader who has studied the speeches of Benton and Hayne in the light of Webster's replies. Yet it is obvious that the true stature of these replies cannot be measured if we treat them as isolated events. What Webster did was to speak with his eye fixed upon the opposition that he faced, and what he as artist would have us do is to understand that opposition when we appraise his speeches. The great virtue of the "Second Reply" is that it accurately gauges and effectively meets the opponents' case.

Our analysis of Webster's strategy confirms this verdict. As we have seen, the strategy of Hayne and Benton, except for the latter's attempt to draw the South into an alliance with the West against Foote's resolution, was to secure sectional independence by creating a division of opinion at points where sectional differences, class hatreds, and partizan rivalries existed. This object called for speeches that created suspicion, fear, doubt, and distrust, justified, as all these attempts must be, by such a philosophical groundwork as the theory of nullification. Webster could have used materials of the same sort. He could have reminded Benton that internal improvements so dear to the West were opposed on constitutional grounds in the South; that the tariff, so hated in the South, was in part a Western measure; that slavery was not popular on the frontier. He could have commented upon the strange spectacle of Hayne, representative of slave-owners and defender of domestic slavery, espousing the cause of freedom and showing solicitude for the welfare of the humble worker of the North. But Webster chose to counteract the efforts of Benton and Hayne, not by easy invective, but by an appeal to the handsomer passions of the American people and by a philosophical argument that revealed that sectional independence was guaranteed in the basic law, and guaranteed in such a way as also to preserve national unity.

Balancing logical content against logical content, we see that Webster's reply was calculated to integrate Hayne's belief in individual liberty with the antithetical belief in social authority, very much as Mill was later to define freedom in terms of social responsibility. Thus Webster did not refute Hayne's contention but eliminated its weaknesses. When we weigh his basic appeals in the scale with Hayne's, we see the concept of common benefit in opposition to a concept of sectional jealousy, a belief in altruism in opposition to a belief in selfishness; in short, we see a high estimate of man's political character in opposition to a low estimate.

Although Webster and Hayne were ostensibly working to win support in the Senate, their real object was to win support with the people at large. They knew that their speeches would appear in newspapers, be circulated in pamphlets, be summarized in other speeches and in editorials. They did not speak to an audience of readers detached from the problems of that moment but to an audience that had to solve those problems. The oratorical critic must judge what was said in the light of its capacity to influence the immediate solution. He is interested in the speech not as a branch of literature but as a social implement. Considerations of history, geography, and economics had disposed the American audience of the year 1830 to accept Webster's position, but their belief was not so strong as to be immune to attack or so clear as to make eloquent restatement unnecessary. Webster's "Second Reply," at once eloquent and completely responsive to opposition, made it difficult for Hayne's doctrine to be anything but a counterstatement, an attempt to upset a richly documented belief. Webster may be said to have planted his conception so deeply in men's minds that a contradictory thesis like Hayne's could, as it were, take root only in the shadow of its great rival and could survive only by dint of the most laborious cultivation.

V. *Big Whig*

In the debate with Hayne, as we have seen, Webster's task was to overcome the resistance offered by the formidable argument of his opponent, and his speeches were dictated by that resistance. With his political speeches, he encountered a different sort of opposition, which, less easy to characterize, likewise determines his methods and explains his virtues and defects. Although Webster was an active political speaker throughout his maturity, his greatest efforts to achieve public leadership were made in the era between 1830 and 1844. Limiting ourselves to this period, we shall describe (1) the resistance that he encountered because he was a member of the Whig party and (2) the resistance that came from the public reputation fixed upon him by his opponents. Then we shall discuss the relation of his speeches to this resistance, our primary object being to measure his effectiveness as a political orator.

Could a national political party have been founded upon the doctrine that nullification was suicidal, while the other major party took the opposite view, and could elections have been held upon this issue alone in the period between 1830 and 1844, there is little doubt that nullification would have been defeated. There is also little doubt that Webster, after the retirement of Jackson, would have been the natural leader of the antinullification party and the strongest single candidate for the Presidency. But the issue of nullification did not divide the people along the lines of the existing political parties. Jackson, the pure Democrat, resisted the attempt by South Carolina to suspend the operation of the national tariff laws and thus made his party the defender of the Union, in every bit as real a sense as Webster was. The anti-Jackson faction could point to Webster as the champion of the Constitution, but in order to win a national majority, they had to have an argument that did not equally apply to the leaders of the opposition.

The story of Webster's party is the story of an attempt to find such an argument, powerful enough to command popular support, yet specific enough to be the property of nobody else. This argument had not been found in 1832, when old Federalists, Adams Republicans, and unattached conservatives of North and South and West joined together behind Henry Clay under the name of National Republicans. Four years later, with an issue, as they believed, in their conviction that Jackson had unconstitutionally extended the executive authority at the expense of Congressional government, they sought victory as the Whigs, a label conveniently borrowed from the English political opponents of the extension of the royal prerogative. It was true, of course, that Jackson had done many arbitrary things; yet Van Buren, his candidate, won the elections of 1836, while the Whigs divided their vote among three aspirants. At that period, the old conservative mercantilism of Boston and New York and Philadelphia seemed doomed as a political force. Thanks, however, to the depression of 1837 and the failure of recovery, the Democrats lost the elections of 1840 to the Whigs, under the nominal leadership of Harrison and Tyler. But almost at the moment of victory, the Whigs began to squander their substance in a riotous intraparty strife, and they became political outs in 1844. Their momentary recovery in 1848 proved to be a rally that but temporarily postponed their death. When the party succumbed after the elections of 1852, they could look back upon a strange record. They had won two national elections, had never named a President who served out his term, had never rallied as a party behind a constructive and adequate program, and had never been able to give their first-rate men, Clay and Webster, the highest office in the land.

As a political speaker, Webster had to face a difficult task. He had to recommend a cause that was successful only when depression, or quarrels in the opposite party, upset the course of nature and lent temporary effectiveness to the verbal persuasions of the Whigs. Identified with this party, he had to support a doctrine only partly his own. He was not the debater against Hayne, free to choose his own ground, free to define his own terms and draw up his own platform, free to assert rather than deny. On the contrary, the demands of his party forced him to be against Jackson and his successors rather than to be for anything in particular. This role was the harder because a valid constitutional opposition to Jackson's assumption of executive powers seemed always to suggest that the Whigs were not so much against executive authority as in favor of the unpopular things that Jackson had used that authority to abolish.

The Bank of the United States is the chief case in point. Jackson vetoed the bill which renewed its charter with the remark that the ownership of large blocks of bank stock by Europeans endangered our government, and that the bank was a device for making the rich richer and the poor poorer. Thurlow Weed, Whig editor of the *Albany Evening Journal*, felt that these two sentences would carry ten votes for every one influenced by a certain political speech made by Webster on the subject of Jackson's arbitrary attitude toward the bank, and accordingly Weed refused to publish Webster's speech in his newspaper.[1] There is no doubt that the question whether the bank should be re-established tormented and divided the Whigs. In the year 1840, for example, a political observer, writing from Saratoga Springs to the *Daily Albany Argus*, said that he had asked Whig leaders why they did not present boldly to the people the question of re-establishing the bank and let the people decide. The answer is, he sarcastically remarked, that many Whigs are "foolishly" opposed to the bank and would desert their party if an intention to reconstitute it were part of the Whig platform. In this dilemma, the Whig leaders, he concluded, are saying to themselves, "We will first get the power, and then do as we please."[2] As everybody knows, John Tyler's veto of the bill to revive the bank led to the split in the ranks of the Whigs after their victory in 1840 and was made the excuse for reading Tyler out of the party.

On another major question of the day, that of the annexation of Texas, the Whigs had a record which could be described as a timid mixture of hesitancy, opposition, and vacillation. Even the Democrats, in agreement elsewhere among themselves, divided upon this issue, which brought into headlong collision the desire of the country for westward expansion and the desire to prevent the growth of slavery. In fact, the division created by Van Buren's opposition to Polk upon this issue led to an open break among the Democrats in the elections of 1848, when the Whigs scored their second and last major victory.

Enough has been said to suggest what doctrinal difficulties faced the Whig party during the period when Webster was one of their chief spokesmen and what sort of reputation he had to assume merely because he belonged to that party. We must now turn to Webster's own public reputa-

---

[1] *Autobiography of Thurlow Weed* (Harriet A. Weed, ed., Boston, 1884), pp. 372–373.
[2] *Daily Albany Argus*, Aug. 24, 1840.

tion. The Whigs, we shall see, sought to make him a symbol with three clear meanings, each of which was calculated to have a favorable effect upon the public in connection with anything he might say; but to Democrats, he symbolized the unflattering predicament of the opponents of Jackson.

First of all, the Whig editors impressed upon their readers that Webster was a man with enlarged and liberal views of the Constitution. The dinner given in his honor at the City Hotel in New York, in 1831, was a tribute, said the *New-York Daily Advertiser* of March 25 of that year, not to the minor differences of party but to the broad principles of national character and national interest. Continued the *Advertiser:*

> The public services of Mr. Webster have extended through many years; but the great effort made by him during the first session of the late Congress, gave rise to this expression of public respect and gratitude. On that occasion . . . by a display of reasoning, of talents, and of eloquence, he displayed feelings of the purest patriotism, and views of the most enlarged and liberal description; at the same time supporting . . . the interests of the States, and the constitutional powers and jurisdiction of the federal government. But it was in the defence of the Judicial power, that he appeared to the highest advantage. By this great effort of his unrivalled abilities, he established, on a foundation not to be shaken, except by the hand of violence, the true principles of this important branch of the national government, and furnished to his country, for the use and information of all future ages, a constitutional argument that sophistry cannot weaken, nor the utmost ingenuity of false reasoning undermine.

At Saratoga, in 1840, Webster was saluted by the nearby *Albany Daily Advertiser* as "the great champion of the Constitution." Later that year, when he spoke at Patchogue, the *New York Herald* reported, in its issue of September 24, that the crowds gave "three cheers for the noble defender of the Constitution." By the year 1844, when Webster appeared at a large Whig rally in Albany, the slogans that associated him with the Constitution had become so firmly fixed in the public mind that even the Democratic *Daily Albany Argus* called him, not altogether admiringly, the "Great Expounder."

The second meaning that the Whigs attached to Webster as a political symbol was that his methods and characteristic procedures were those of a statesman. He appeals to the reason, not to the passions, said the *Morning Courier and New-York Enquirer* of his speech at Niblo's saloon. This address, continues the editor, "was a masterly effort; and if sound logic, clear conception, and historical accuracy, delineated by happy and beautiful metaphor, can add to the value or force of *truth*, then did Mr. Webster achieve such a triumph last night as will add even to his fame as a Statesman and an Orator." The *Albany Daily Advertiser* said of Webster's speech

714

at Saratoga that "we have never yet listened to an address which combined in itself so many varied excellencies—such clear illustration, such conclusive argument, such touching pathos, as this admirable address of Mr. Webster's." "Nor was there any thing about it," adds the writer, "to which the most fastidious opponent could object—no invective—no imputation of base motives—no torturing of facts or discoloring of opinions to strengthen his own or weaken his adversary's cause." In the same vein, Thurlow Weed's *Evening Journal* characterized Webster's speech in Albany in 1844 as one that

> with masterly power, explains the principles of our Government; describes, with all the clearness of demonstration, its workings for more than half a century; shows, with all the force of truth, that Loco Focoism is hostile to those principles and obstructs their progress; and then appeals solemnly to the People to decide, by their action in this great struggle, whether they will *preserve* or *destroy* the Political Institutions under which they have lived, notwithstanding the errors and defects of Administration, in the enjoyment of prosperity and happiness for fifty-six years.

The third meaning that Whig editors attached to Webster was that his speeches always held the audience in breathless attention. Perhaps the most extraordinary example of this aspect of his public reputation is furnished by the Whig journals that reported his speech at the Astor House on November 28, 1837. Dinner was served at 7:30 p.m., and was followed by a number of toasts and speeches. Finally, at 2 a.m., Mr. Hoffman, the toastmaster, proposed a toast to "Massachusetts and Daniel Webster—the Champion of the Constitution." Webster spoke until 3:20 a.m., and, said the *New-York Daily Express* next day, "enchained the attention of his audience." The *Morning Courier and New-York Enquirer* said of the same event that, when the toast was given to Webster, late as it was, none of the assembly had moved, "for they knew Daniel Webster was to speak." As he rose, "there burst forth such applause as belongs to few men to merit." When the cheering subsided, continued the editor, Webster spoke for nearly two hours and

> held the audience in unbroken admiration by a discourse which—touching almost all the prominent topics before the nation, as with a ray of light, and yet dwelling upon none so as to fatigue—constituted at once a review of the past, and an exhortation for the future—so clear, so eloquent and so patriotic, as to command the assent of all judgments and all hearts.

Scarcely less laudatory were the opinions expressed by other Whig editors upon the later speeches to which we have already referred. At Saratoga, in 1840, one passage in Webster's speech is said by the *Albany Daily Advertiser* to have had a profound effect. Writes the editor of this paper 2 days after the event:

There was an allusion which, falling naturally and in the most unstudied manner from his lips, suspended for the moment every breath, and brought tears to the eyes of the sternest among his auditors. It was when he spoke of the Log Cabin, half hidden in the snow drifts of New Hampshire, and looking out from her frontier hills upon a wilderness then unbroken by a single human habitation between itself and the walls of Quebec, which his father's hands had reared, and where in early life that father had toiled and struggled that he might give his children a better education and fit them for a higher station, than it had been his lot to enjoy.

One lady observed, after Webster's speech at Patchogue, that she could sit and hear Mr. Webster till sundown, day after day, and feel no fatigue. The *New York Herald*, which reports this testimony in its issue for September 24, 1840, also said of Webster that at Patchogue he had begun to speak soon after 12 and closed at 3 p.m., being listened to "with intense delight and profound attention." "One could," said the reporter, "have almost heard a pin drop on the green sward." Of Webster's 2½-hour speech at Albany in 1844, the local *Daily Advertiser* remarked next day that it had "kept in breathless attention an immense auditory."

The reputation given Webster by the Whig press of his day is not unlike his more recent fame in Whig histories and biographies. It may be a surprise to us, therefore, to know that when he spoke, many members of his audience would not necessarily think of his enlarged and enlightened views or his statesmanlike methods and would not inevitably accord him a profound and favorable attention. Yet if we wish to understand what resistance he encountered when he spoke, we must know what the citizens thought who were opposed to him and had the means to condition the public toward him. Our present concern is not to decide upon the truth or falsity of the Democratic view of Webster's character. What is important, rather, is to recognize that adverse opinions, whether true or false in the long perspective of historian or biographer, were freely expressed against him and accounted in part for the resistance that a voter of that day would have to his persuasions.

In the Democratic press, Webster's reputation had four related aspects. (1) The public was not allowed to forget that Webster had opposed the War of 1812, had once opposed the tariff, and perhaps even sympathized with the objects of the Hartford Convention. (2) There is a suggestion, running throughout newspaper comment from 1831 to 1844, that Webster and Clay were bitter rivals, bent in secret upon working each other's ruin, not upon presenting an adequate national program. (3) The Democrats often testify that his speeches were not effective, that he was cold, calculating, lacking in ardor and sympathy, preoccupied with appeals to the motives of gain or loss and that at times he resorted to pontifical quibbles or conscious artifice in order to produce effects. Finally, and most significantly, the charge persists that he was aristocratic in tendency, a friend of wealth and position, an enemy of the people, a hater of democracy, and a hired man of the capitalist and manufacturer.

Democratic editors made no attempt, as we have just done, to classify the charges against Webster. Sometimes one innuendo, sometimes another, sometimes a combination of two or three will appear in the same editorial. Accordingly, we shall give samples of the Democratic opinion of Webster, without sustained emphasis upon the nature of each particular charge, and allow the reader to judge of the adequacy of the classes just mentioned.

As a result of the failure of Henry Clay in the elections of 1832, the opponents of Jackson could only hope that their fortunes would improve before the next test of strength. Would Webster be nominated by his party in 1836? His trip to the West in the summer of 1833, where he spoke at Buffalo, Cincinnati, and Pittsburgh, indicates his interest in the answer to this question. But the Whigs entered the campaign of 1836 hopelessly divided in leadership, with Harrison representing the frontier, Webster the East, and White the South. Van Buren was elected with a reduced Democratic vote. Shortly after the inauguration, Webster made his speech at Niblo's saloon and that spring journeyed again to the West, calling publicly on Harrison in Ohio, appearing upon the speaker's platform with Henry Clay at St. Louis, meeting a young Whig named Lincoln in Illinois, and delivering speeches everywhere. These speeches represent his greatest effort to obtain the Presidency, and the one at Niblo's saloon is typical of the whole concerted move.

The *Evening Post*, staunch Democratic organ in New York, shows the nature of the antidote that was devised against Webster's campaign. Three days after he spoke at Niblo's saloon, the *Post*, as if to quiet the public enthusiasm with which his speech had been hailed by the Whigs, published a long editorial on Jackson, who was at the moment making his triumphal progress through the West on his way from Washington to retirement at the Hermitage. The substance of the editorial was that Jackson's great popularity rested upon his adoption of the wise maxim "that more advantage is gained by winning the confidence of mankind, than can ever be derived from deceiving them." A caustic parallel between Jackson and Webster was drawn by the editor to amplify his point. He wrote:

> There is in the mind, and genius of Andrew Jackson a generous ardor, which beautifully contrasts with the cold calculating frigidity of Daniel Webster, the champion of localities, and the opposite extreme of a liberal, widely extended patriotism. The reasonings and appeals of the latter, are always from self to self. They are addressed to the pockets rather than the principles of the People, and are exclusively based on calculations of loss and gain. Not one highminded, generous, or patriotic feeling, is invoked; and the measures of Government, are tested by their

anticipated influence on the price of domestic cottons or dumb fish. With him it is a question of arithmetic rather than logic; it is settled by cyphering rather than reasoning, and a penny in one scale outweighs a principle in the other.

Webster did not become the Whig candidate in 1840. Nor did Clay. It is well known, moreover, that Clay attributed his defeat to Webster, then absent on a trip to England. But while Clay was inclined to sulk and make little effort at first on behalf of Harrison, Webster, upon his return, engaged actively in the campaign and made a series of speeches in the summer and autumn of 1840, his object being to recommend the election of the "log-cabin" candidate. We have noticed that Webster's efforts were highly praised by his own associates; but his appearances caused acid to flow from Democratic pens. Of his speech at Saratoga, the *Daily Albany Argus* for August 24, 1840, said: "Mr. Webster labored long and hard on the bank question today; more openly than any other of their orators have dared to do. He has probably been better paid, or is more honest and consistent." Two days later, the *Argus* turned to open invective:

> Who is Daniel Webster? And where, politically, has he ever been? Let his opposi-
> tion to the war—his votes against every measure for its vigorous prosecution—his
> denunciations of Jefferson and Madison—his advocacy of every federal doctrine,
> and his opposition to every democratic administration—furnish the answer. And
> who is Gen. Harrison, and where politically has *he* ever been? Let Daniel Webster
> answer,—"WE have made William Henry Harrison the bearer of OUR standard."

As we have noticed, the Whig press declared that Webster's allusion at Saratoga to his father's log cabin had melted the vast audience into tears. The *Argus* for August 28 reprinted from the *Troy Budget* a Democratic view of the effectiveness of this part of Webster's speech. "We remember distinctly the allusion and noticed its effect," said the *Budget*, "and as we live we saw no one shed a tear, or appear to feel like it but Webster himself. There seemed to be so much affectation in the contortion of his countenance at the time, that a gentleman at our elbow remarked that his attempt to cry spoiled the beauty of the allusion." On August 29, the *Argus* discussed Webster as leader and orator of the "federal" or "modern whig" party during the past 30 years. Now, as during the dark days of the war and the Hartford Convention, it alleged, he is the "head" man. Then Webster's record throughout the war is cited, item by item, showing his systematic opposition to the nation's effort. Elsewhere in the same issue, Webster is hailed as "this blue-light federalist," "this uncompromising and steady opponent of the last war," "this cordial and undeviating hater of democracy." Webster is advised by the reporter who coined these epithets to learn the spirit of the American people and to tell the "dear people" of his fee of $5,000 from the house of Baring, British bankers.

Daniel Webster

When Webster spoke at Patchogue in September, 1840, the *Evening Post* for the twenty-fourth of that month commented upon Webster's declaration in the speech that he was not by birth an aristocrat. He forgets, said William Cullen Bryant, editor of the *Post*, that

there is a more narrow-minded, and in this country, more dangerous aristocracy, that of wealth. Of this aristocracy, we take leave to say, in spite of Mr. Webster's vulgar epithets and brutal threats, that he is a most serile [servile?] and thorough-paced champion, and that his whole public course has been an attempt to reduce the people of the United States under its dominion. Whoever would give by law peculiar privileges to associated wealth, whether in the shape of a Bank of the United States, or any other institution; whoever would impose a law for the benefit of a particular class to the injury of others, whether that law be a protective tariff or any other; whoever would accumulate patronage and concentrate power in the government, whether it be by a splendid system of what are called internal improvements, or by any other method, that man is an aristocrat, an adversary of the political rights of the mass; and such Mr. Webster has proved himself to be by a long series of public acts. Among the great leaders of the aristocratic party to which he belongs, we believe we make no mistake when we say that Mr. Webster, the future head of General Harrison's cabinet, is the rankest aristocrat of all. Struggle as violently and angrily as he may, the imputation will still cling to him; he might as well disown his own name.

Elsewhere in this editorial, the charge against Webster is given a different twist. He may possibly not be an aristocrat, conceded the editor, but may turn out to be a monarchist; he may not want the dominion of the few but may want to bring the nation under the rule of one. His speech at Patchogue, avowing himself a Democrat of the genuine Jeffersonian school, is an attempt to guard against suppositions such as these; but, said the *Post*, nothing is more impudent than Webster's intrusion among Jeffersonian Democrats.

When Webster spoke in Albany in 1844, he had behind him a term as Secretary of State and a reputation for having remained in John Tyler's cabinet when that unfortunate man had refused to permit his party to re-establish the Bank of the United States and had consequently been excommunicated from the congregation of the Whigs. Webster's immediate purpose in speaking at the rally in Albany was to advance the candidacy of his old rival Clay, who was once more the Whig nominee for the Presidency. The *Daily Albany Argus* for August 28, 1844, commented at length upon Webster's speech of the previous day, when, according to the Whig journals, the speaker had "kept in breathless attention an immense auditory." Admitting that the crowd at the rally had been large, but not so large as the Whigs said, the *Argus* observed that

Democrats were to be met with at every turn, who had come in even from the county towns hereabouts to hear the Great Expounder, and it is only to be regretted that there were not more of them present to see and hear this great gun of whiggery speak nearly three hours, and yet say nothing—if we except the subject of the tariff —on any of the great subjects of interest and discussion now before the public.

The *Argus* thought, furthermore, that the procession that had preceded the rally and, indeed, the rally itself had had little or no spirit. Even the live raccoons had not been animated. "'Excitement' there was none— nor any approach to it," said the Democratic voice. Then he continued:

We did not hear Mr. Webster until he had been speaking half an hour or more— such was the crowd and noise at that time. When we did hear him, he was hard at work at the Constitution—expounding it, as the phrase is, and detailing the practice under it from the foundation of things. . . . The leading idea of this portion of his speech seemed to be, that if locofocoism should obtain the ascendancy, an entire change in the Constitution and laws would be the result, and then where were we all to go? Mr. W. is always able; but this effort did not strike us as adding remarkably to his reputation as *the* expounder.

So of that part of his speech which treated of the practice of the government, his object was to show what nobody pretends to question, that the policy has been all along in laying duties, to discriminate with a view to protection. There was no need of half an hour's argument to prove this—but the point was labored with great industry. . . . The drift of this portion of his speech, as was apparent towards the close of it, was to show that the democratic party were for uprooting and changing the whole course of legislation on this subject—and he played upon the word in-ci-den-tal, as applied to protection by the democrats (and by Mr. Clay also,) and tried hard to show that it meant something different from "discrimination." He represented Mr. Polk as favorable to incidental protection . . . and undertook to draw a contrast between this kind of protection and that which results from discrimination, with the intent and design to protect. This struck us as poor quibbling for a great statesman. . . . On the subject of a Bank, Mr. W. said nothing, nor indeed on much else in agitation now, save the tariff.

But the Democratic view of Webster's ineffectiveness at Albany was not explained wholly in terms of his gratuitous arguments, his quibbles, his failure to mention the bank, and his possible disagreement with his own leader Clay on the subject of protection. It is the *Albany Evening Atlas*, the city's other influential Democratic paper, that stresses his most damaging omission of all and declares that the speech had an opposite effect to the one intended. Calling the rally a fruitless if not fatal display but admitting that a desire to hear Webster had prompted some to attend without being paid, the editor of the *Atlas*, in the issue of August 28, says:

Conspicuous in the procession, as if he had been a captive, gracing the triumph of a victorious enemy, rode Daniel Webster—and that "immedicable wound in the heart," which he attributes to "the dagger" of Henry Clay, was traced on his dark countenance. He was the prominent object of the spectacle, and though he was not greeted with any marks of good-will by the multitude, his presence was felt by them, and it damped the enthusiasm of the crowd in behalf of their leader. He was there ostensibly to speak in the cause of the man who had pursued him and his friends, and would pursue them "till they go to their graves, or he goes to his, with implacable resentment." But he disappointed those who thought he could so far forget himself as to speak in words of praise of his antagonist.[1]

The only topic of party politics, to which he alluded, was . . . Protection, and he chose this theme for his speech, while the proof he has produced that Mr. Clay had stood ready and offered to betray this policy, was fresh in the minds of his audience. During his whole speech, in which he reviewed the history of American politics, and made frequent allusions to the great men, distinguished in public history, he did not once mention the name of Henry Clay.

The object of the whole speech seems to have been, to appropriate to himself the question of protection, and to prove, what was once sneeringly alleged in reference to a distinguished democrat, that the history of the country could be given without a single recurrence to the name of Clay.

The day chosen for the display was a most beautiful one, and no accident marred the proceedings: but the speech and the speaking presence of Mr. Webster fell like a damp chill on the assembled multitude.

Space does not permit a more extended analysis of Webster's reputation in the Democratic press. Each comment that we have cited shows that he was the object of attack and that the charges mainly concern his past record, his active rivalry toward Clay, his ineffectiveness as a speaker for the Whigs, and his antidemocratic sentiments. If these indictments were allowed to pass unnoticed when he rose to speak, we could not doubt that his effectiveness would be diminished. Since the kind of reputation that he had in the Democratic papers is so obviously an extension of the kind of reputation his party had, we may, in speaking now of his habits of procedure, discuss his attempts to overcome the resistance that had been created against himself.

The speech delivered by Webster, March 15, 1837, in Niblo's saloon to an audience of 6,000 New Yorkers, exists in two versions, one a reporter's summary, published next day in the *New-York Daily Express*, and one the official text, prepared by Webster and published well over a month

---

[1] The three phrases in quotation marks are supposed by the editor of the *Atlas* to be from the pen of Webster himself and are chosen from two unsigned articles that had appeared sometime before in the *Madisonian*. These articles were, of course, an unfavorable appraisal of Clay, and the writer, be he Webster or another, had looked keenly at his subject. In order to show what Webster would have said at Albany, had he chosen to speak of Clay, the editor of the *Atlas* published on Aug. 29 the text of these two articles and commended them to the Whig editors as an important supplement to Webster's speech.

after he spoke.[1] The summary represents a speech of 2½ hours in length, the reporter tells us; and the official text would require about the same time for delivery. In substance, the two versions have also much in common. But a comparison of them indicates that the same purpose does not animate both discourses, that each has its own individual method, and that neither takes specific account of the resistance that has been described.

In the official text,[2] Webster's introduction surveys the common ground upon which all Whigs stand, promises frankness in the ensuing discourse, stresses that the audience is free to disagree with the speaker, and disclaims any disrespectful intention in criticizing the policies of Jackson. Then follows the body of the speech, in which Webster talks first of topics less urgently connected and then of those more urgently connected with the distressed state of the country. Under the first heading, he uses the words of the chairman of the meeting to indicate that freedom from local interests and prejudices and a devotion to a liberal and comprehensive view have been the aims of his public life. He next discusses briefly the theory of the Federal system, incidentally revealing his own approval of internal improvements and emphasizing that only by affection for the whole country can harmony be produced. This part of the speech concludes with a burst of eloquence, reminding the audience of the brotherhood of American liberty, the oneness of American hope, and the necessity of preserving the grand cause of liberty in the world by holding fast to the belief that "we have one country, one Constitution, one destiny."

Turning then to his second heading, Webster talks of the public lands, which, he says, should not become the property of the new states but should be for the common benefit and should be sold on liberal terms or donated at times for substantial improvements. The revenue of the government, Webster goes on, should not be such as to accumulate a surplus and should be maintained by duties on imports, administered according to the principle of protecting American labor and industry by means of discriminatory duties, while revenue from the sale of lands should be set apart for the use of the new states. Texas, says Webster, should not be annexed, the objections being that the acquisition of this territory was not justified by historical precedent and would dangerously arouse a community already dangerously excited by the prospect of the spread of slavery.

---

[1] The *Morning Courier and New-York Enquirer* for Mar. 17, 1837, says that Webster would proceed to Boston, where he would prepare his speech for the press and send it back to New York for publication. Not until Apr. 27 was the text received and published by the *New-York Daily Express*. This text was immediately circulated as a pamphlet and became the official version of the speech.

[2] *NE*, II, 193–230.

Webster's largest topic is the extension of the executive authority under Jackson. Conceding the goodness of Jackson's motives, Webster nevertheless deplores the principle behind the spoils system and attacks the argument that the President is a representative of the whole people. Then he reviews the history of Jackson's attitude toward the bank, showing that the currency, which had anciently been held to be outside the power of the executive, had become an example of executive interference. The bank's refusal to submit to Jackson's control was, says Webster, the cause that explained the veto of its charter, the removal of its deposits, and the present disordered state of the currency.

Webster's brief conclusion is devoted to an appeal to the Whigs to reveal their patriotism. He pledges himself to accomplish the duties that he has indicated and promises never to desert the principles of true liberty.

At several points, the reporter's summary of this speech differs from the official text. For one thing, the official text, as published in the *Daily Express*, bears the title "One Country, One Constitution, One Destiny." A reporter would probably have noted a phrase of this sort and other parts of the glowing period in which it occurs; yet the summary ignores the whole passage. Again, the official text and the summary differ in respect to Webster's argument that the President is not a representative of the people. The summary has Webster say that the general tendency of the age is toward elective monarchies and that, if a man is a representative of the whole people, and thus becomes the people, with the people's power transferred to him, then that man is made a despot and we have an elective monarchy in its worst form. The official text does not contain the words *elective monarchy;* but the reporter would hardly have used them if Webster had not. Nor does the official text reproduce at this point the outlines of the argument given in the summary.

Again, the summary has Webster say that the remedy for the surplus and justice to the country demanded, as he thought, the passing of Mr. Clay's land bill, which, of all the lucky hits of the great mind of that great man, he considered the happiest. This tribute to Clay and his land bill evoked "great cheering," says the reporter. But the official text omits the specific endorsement of this bill by Webster and also omits the tribute to Clay, who is not mentioned anywhere in the received text. It does not seem probable that the reporter would have invented this passage and the cheering that accompanied it. Again, when Webster discusses protection, and avows himself a moderate tariff man, the summary has him stress the advantage of protection to labor. "Capital," said Mr. W. (in the words of the reporter), "needs no protection,—it is lynx-eyed,—it can look out for itself—it asks of government only permanency and good faith in its pleasures [measures?], and it can shift itself at pleasure, for the capitalist alway [*sic*] has eyes wide open, as is now seen in New York,—but labor asks, and needs protection of the government, and it must have it, or it will pine away and starve."

At this point, continues the reporter, Mr. W. passed "a neat compliment" to John Hancock and the mechanics of Boston, headed in Revolutionary times by Paul Revere, after which he went on to the subject of Texas. In the official text, Webster discusses protection and then the annexation of Texas; but he makes no reference to "lynx-eyed" capital, no statement that capital can shift for itself, no allusion to John Hancock, the mechanics of Boston, or Paul Revere. Again, when Webster speaks of the source of Jackson's animosity to the bank, the summary resorts to direct quotation, making him say, "It is within my own knowledge that an attempt was made by the party in power, to make the Bank engage in the contests of the day; and, when it refused to engage in these contests, war was made upon it." As if to separate himself from the financial interests and to remove the affairs of the bank from the sphere of his own personal knowledge, he does not in the official text emphasize that the story of Jackson's struggle with the directors of the bank was anything but general historical knowledge.

The official text contains an illustration also found in the summary. Since the reporter devotes full space to it, we have the opportunity to compare his version with Webster's own later version. The official text says:

A character has been drawn of a very eminent citizen of Massachusetts, of the last age, which, though I think it does not entirely belong to him, yet very well describes a certain class of public men. It was said of this distinguished son of Massachusetts, that in matters of politics and government he cherished the most kind and benevolent feelings towards the whole earth. He earnestly desired to see all nations well governed; and to bring about this happy result, he wished that the United States might govern the rest of the world; that Massachusetts might govern the United States; that Boston might govern Massachusetts; and as for himself, his own humble ambition would be satisfied by governing the little town of Boston.

The summary reports the story thus:

A historian had written of an eminent citizen of Massachusetts, not with justice, perhaps, that he had the broadest and most patriotic view of human liberty. He wanted to see the whole world under the government of tree principles, and a free constitution: and for that purpose he wished the United States to govern the world. But to have the United States well governed, he thought it could be no where so well governed as by old Massachusetts, where he lived (a great laugh); but Massachusetts, even, might stray from the right path, and to bring the operations of government within reasonable bounds, he would let Boston govern Mass. (great applause and laughter) "For my own part, then," said the patriotic man, "I should be content with a very little power—I would not ask for much—I would only govern Boston, the city in which I live." (tremendous cheering) So, said Mr. W , it seems to be with some of the unambitious statesmen of the present day, who seek *liberty* for all mankind, but who seek to create it after their own way.

Having considered the important differences between the official text and the reporter's summary, we are forced to the conclusion that Webster, upon his return to Boston, prepared for publication a document that grew out of what he had said at Niblo's saloon but that was not a faithful version of the original speech. The necessity to condense a 2½-hour speech within the compass of two columns of newspaper space explains why the summary omitted things now found in the official text. But most of the differences between the two versions arise because things that are treated at some length in the summary are either omitted or substantially modified in the official text, and it is these differences which cannot be easily explained unless we conclude that Webster deliberately revised what he had originally said.

Both of the versions are respectable persuasive efforts. It is obvious, however, that they differ in purpose and in method. The official text, called by Lodge "the greatest purely political speech which he [Webster] ever delivered,"[1] must be regarded as a campaign document, intended to advance the Presidential aspirations of the author and to reach a vast national audience of readers, with various shades of political opinion. The original speech, as summarized, bears no less directly upon Webster's political ambitions, but is designed for a more localized audience of hearers. Differences in method grow out of this difference in fundamental intent. For one thing, the reporter's summary bears the stamp of oral presentation. Webster's story of the man who wanted to rule Boston is more effectively told for an audience of hearers in the reporter's summary than in Webster's own later text. His reference to "lynx-eyed" capital is another example of his greater liveliness and concreteness in speech than in writing. More-over, the original speech reflects the influence of the immediate audience upon the speaker, while the official text is adjusted to a generalized audi-ence. Webster's statement that "the capitalist . . . has eyes wide open, as is now seen in New York" is an example of a local reference that dis-appears from the official text. Finally, the original speech seems to bear some relation to the specific resistance that the Whigs and Webster so often encountered, while the official text, except in two passages, does not. Webster's generous tribute to Clay and his avowal that capital could shift for itself, while labor could not, were evidences in the original speech of personal generosity toward a rival and of a democratic concern for the

[1] Lodge, p. 238.

common man. When these statements disappear from the official text, something vital to the Whig cause has vanished. As if to compensate for these omissions, which told against him, Webster's text deletes the words *elective monarchy* and removes the imputation that he knew at first hand of the affairs of the Bank of the United States. But it cannot be doubted that what the official version gains by these two omissions is more than offset by what it loses when Clay is ignored, and the reference to the common man disappears.

The great weakness of both versions is that Webster did not take seriously the distrust that the majority of the community felt toward himself and his doctrines. Or rather, he conceived of that distrust as confined to what one said about particular issues and problems, like the currency, the tariff, and the public lands. The country did not care so much about the particular stand of a man toward a given issue; but it cared vitally about his spirit of approach, his respect for democracy, his capacity to humanize himself and his cause. Webster was at his best as speaker when his subject stirred him to great personal enthusiasm, as when he spoke at Plymouth and Bunker Hill and in praise of Adams and Jefferson. He also rose to great heights when he knew that he faced a formidable specific resistance, as in his debate with Hayne. When his subject did not fire him or when he did not feel challenged by that resistance, he delivered speeches that read well enough and are always above reproach but are not great, in the sense of being unique.

In 1837 Jackson, the redoubtable popular leader, was in retirement. Van Buren, his successor, had not shown an ability to hold the Democratic party in line. Depression threatened. The Whigs were gaining in strength. What was there in this situation to challenge Webster? Apparently nothing, judging by his speech at Niblo's saloon. He had simply, as he believed, to do the things that would not interrupt the swing of the country toward the Whigs. His weakness was the weakness of a great but indolent man who never really rose to the heights except under the pressure of personal enthusiasm or powerful opposition. Had he started to do in 1837 what he was later to do at Patchogue, where he belatedly responded to the resistance of the public toward himself, and responded brilliantly at that, his own personal career might not have been the story of thwarted ambition.

Webster's speech at Patchogue is altogether different from that just considered. It is different not so much in substance as in manner and spirit; for now Webster spoke to the popular audience with the deepest and fullest awareness of the popular resistance that he himself and the Whig party faced. This awareness, like that which had raised him to the heights of argument and imaginative power in his debate with Hayne, came once more with its magical inducements. He understood at last that the differ-

726

ence between the stand of the Whigs and Democrats upon specific issues was not so important as the assumed difference between them upon the major belief in democracy itself; and the result is a political speech of great persuasiveness.

The speech at Patchogue, delivered on September 22, 1840, does not present a textual problem, unless we attack the competency of the reporter who made a draft in shorthand as Webster spoke. The received text of this speech[1] is that which James Gordon Bennett first printed in the *New York Herald* for September 24, 1840, from the version made by his reporter at the scene.[2] As we consider it, we may be reasonably sure that Webster's own words, as he uttered them from the platform in the large tent at Patchogue to an audience of 2,500 men and 250 women, are forming again in our ears.

The speech is an open defense of the speaker himself against the charge that he is an aristocrat, and a powerful assault upon the Democrats for their failure to adhere in practice to their self-avowed democracy of principle. Webster says in effect that his own origin, his public record, and his innate character afford no evidence of aristocratic beliefs and that the public acts of Van Buren's administration are false to democratic ideals. But while the speech finds its unity in propositions like these, we cannot hope to explain its real structure unless we look beyond the requirements of formal organization. For a change, Webster does not inexorably conform to the pattern of a lawyer's brief. The pattern is there, of course—the central idea, the parts, the details. But when we have them before us, we have but imperfectly described the speech. Its richness, its color, its easy vitality, even, to a degree, its unity still await appraisal.

Perhaps the best way to describe the essential plan of the speech is to liken it to Mark Antony's speech to the Romans in Shakespeare's *Julius Caesar*. First are two preliminary themes, developed in alternation, each being repeated several times. "I come today, not with my rod and gun, but to take counsel with you, and to speak. The times are most extraordinary." Then come the two main themes. "You have been told that I'm aristocratic. Be it so. Yet, I did this and that, as you well know. Did this in Webster seem aristocratic? You have been told, 'Van Buren and the rest (whom I do not reproach) are lovers of the people.' Be it thus.

[1] *NE*, XIII, 114–142.

[2] In *The New York Herald* for Sept. 22, 1840, Bennett explained that he had arranged to report Webster's speech at Patchogue in full. "We have placed an express of blood horses on the whole line to Patchogue, and expect to have the speech from our reporter's hands by six o'clock this evening." Bennett was almost as good as his word. Part of Webster's speech was printed in the *Herald* on Sept. 23, the whole text next day, with the declaration, repeated in subsequent editions, that Webster had never been accurately reported until he fell into the hands of Bennett.

Yet they did this and that, and you must judge, if what they did shows love of you and yours." This paraphrase of the four themes suggests the structural pattern that Webster followed. We must understand, of course, that Webster spoke in the homely idiom of American politics, not in Elizabethan blank verse. We must also understand that the parallelism between his speech and Antony's is suggestive, not exact. Let us turn to the speech itself for a closer view of its structural rhythms.

After an introduction in which he skillfully alternates his two preliminary themes, Webster remarks, by way of transition, that party distinctions are transient, while the distinction that we are "the only true free people on the face of the earth" is the one "that shall ever be deeply prized by me, and by my children to the last moment of our lives." Then he turns to the first of his two major themes: [1]

Now, my friends, you know I have been some time in public life, and I have been too long in the councils of the nation not to be in some degree a marked character. Not 'marked down,' as you say of quail and partridges,—no, not just yet. But I am somewhat marked, and what I say will therefore be marked and commented upon by others than yourselves. You'll be addressed to-morrow by a gentleman of high talent—a distinguished supporter of the administration, one of the most distinguished, certainly in that portion of the councils of the nation to which I belong. He'll not say—but others will say for him—it will be said, and all the papers favorable to the administration will say—Don't believe Webster, that old aristocrat; he never tells the truth; he's an aristocrat, and you can't believe anything that he says. [The noble Brutus Hath told you Caesar was ambitious.]

Now, my friends, it would be very strange if I, who have grown up among the people, and as it were of the people, should, at my time of life, take to aristocracy. I have ploughed and sowed and reaped the acres that were my father's, and that now are mine. . . . I never held an office in the course of that life, except such an one as comes directly from the bestowment of the people; I have had no money out of the public treasury, except the pay as a member of Congress. . . . After all this, I shall still be told that I'm an aristocrat. Very well. Prove it. If I am one, I am quite false to my origin and connections, as well as to my nature. By what vote of mine in the public councils of the country, am I to be proved an aristocrat? [When that the poor have cried, Caesar hath wept: Ambition should be made of sterner stuff.] . . .

It was in 1832 or '33 that the great question of nullification excited so much attention. . . .

It was then that General Jackson came out with his proclamation. He said that one State ought not to resist all the States, and I thought so too. It was not democratic. Some persons, on the contrary, said it was the true meaning of the Constitution. You know who was at the head of that movement. It was Mr. Cal-

---

[1] The bracketed quotations are not part of Webster's speech. We have taken them from *Julius Caesar* and have inserted them here to suggest the parallelism between Antony's speech and Webster's.

houn, then also at the head of a great party. By a close vote, that great question was decided. Myself and my own friends were not favorable to Jackson's policy; we were unfavorable to his financial policy in relation to the Bank of the United States; but did we join those who were opposed to General Jackson in this great movement, in order to crush his administration? I could have done it in a single hour. In the position in which things then stood, if we could have consented to have seen the Constitution beaten down and trampled under foot, we had the whole play in our hands.

Was it for me, in a great contest like this, to say that we didn't like our leader, although he was upholding the Constitution, and therefore unite with the enemies of that Constitution, in order to crush both it and him? Oh, no. And I tell you, that when that affair was over, General Jackson, with a degree of grateful respect which I shall always properly remember, clapsed my hand and said, "If you and your Northern friends had not come in as you did, Calhoun and his party would have crushed me and the Constitution."

And yet I shall go for a very bad aristocrat. And echo will tell, in a thousand ways, from Brooklyn to Montauk Point, that Mr. Webster is a sad old aristocrat, and knows nothing of democracy, and particularly of the democracy of this country. [You all did see that on the Lupercal I thrice presented him a kingly crown, Which he did thrice refuse: was this ambition?]

Webster now introduces his second major theme, suspending for the moment the treatment of the first. He says:

On the other hand, our opponents know Suffolk well; they study it; they know that it was distinguished in the Revolution for its stern democracy, tried and proved. They remember that it produced the L'Hommedieus and the Floyds, and the Smiths and the Joneses—and they'll all come down here to-morrow as the Pharisees came of old—with their philacteries, and the garbs of Democracy. And the word "Democracy," "Democracy," "Democracy," will occur as often among them as "ditto," "ditto," "ditto," in a tradesman's bill (laughter), or five shillings and eight pence in an attorney's bill.

Now, all I have to say to you, my friends, is, look at facts! Words are cheap—promises easy and cost nothing. But there is an old adage among farmers, that "fine words butter no parsnips." [See what a rent the envious Casca made: Through this the well-beloved Brutus stabb'd.]

Soon he restates his second main theme:

I desire to put it upon that issue,—that if the measures of the present administration have been democratic, support them; if not, do not so. But do not take names for things, and professions for principles. By democratic measures, I mean such as the good old democrats of past times would have supported. Such measures as Chancellor Livingston would have supported; such as Mr. Jefferson would have supported; such as Virginia, the old pure school of democracy, would have sun-ported. [For Brutus, as you know, was Caesar's angel: Judge, O you gods, how dearly Caesar lov'd him.]

. . . Are the measures of the present administration democratic? Why the leading measure, and the only measure, is the Sub-Treasury. From Alpha to Omega, it's all "Sub-Treasury!"—"Sub-Treasury!"—"Sub-Treasury!" And its echoes have not yet ceased, and will not cease, till the administration go out of office. It puts one in mind of Orpheus going to seek Eurydice,—this cry:

> "Eurydice the woods,
> Eurydice the floods,
> Eurydice the rocks and hollow mountains rang."

and with our Government it is—

> "Sub-Treasury the woods,
> Sub-Treasury the floods,
> Sub-Treasury the rocks and hollow mountains ring."

[Then I, and you, and all of us fell down, Whilst bloody treason flourish'd over us.]

With the direct quotation from, and subsequent parody of, Pope's *Ode on St. Cecilia's Day*, Webster's recurrent rhythms sweep onward with increasing gusto and dexterity. He discusses the assertion, attributed to prominent Democrats, that the wages of American labor must be reduced to levels prevailing in Europe; he examines Van Buren's Militia bill; he further analyzes the principle behind the Sub-Treasury bill; he reviews the financial record of the administration in the war in Florida; he refutes the assertion that his party wants the Federal government to assume the debts of the states and that he himself went to England to see Baring Brothers and agree to a fee, in return for which he was to work for this policy. Throughout his discussion of these topics, his method is an enlargement of the pattern already described. "Here are their measures," he says, in effect. "Here are the sponsors of those measures. Here is what the measures provide. Now, does all this seem democratic? Judge for yourselves. Don't be deceived." Toward the end of the speech, he speaks feelingly and simply of Harrison:

And now let me observe that you have two men before you as candidates for the presidency, Mr. Van Buren and General Harrison. I shall not say much about them. We all know what General Harrison is. He is the son of one of the signers of the Declaration of Independence; he comes of a good stock; he was bred in a good school, where he early imbibed the true democratic principles of Mr. Jefferson; he has proved himself a brave man by his defence of his country against foreign and domestic foes; and he has well and ably filled several civil offices for his fellow citizens.

I believe, also, that he is a man who will practise what he professes. They say that he lives in the West. And they talk about what he eats,—I mean what he drinks,—and the house he lives in. They say he drinks hard cider and lives in a log-cabin. Well, I believe a man may be very honest for all that. And I think, too, that he is much better than they who are all talk and no cider.

I have been in his log-cabin. He lives in it still. And he has made an addition to it, as many of us do. He keeps a horse. Well, I found him to be a very hospitable gentleman; the string of his latch is not pulled in. And I give him my confidence.

And now I'll give you one other opinion, and you may judge of the values of the others by the accuracy of that. And it is that General Harrison will be the next President of the United States.

Enough has been said here of the speech at Patchogue to show that Webster, calculating accurately the resistance that he had to overcome, deserted his customary role of lawyer and debater before the select audiences of courtroom and Senate and made a truly popular speech, adapted to an audience of voters. As if by magic, a new Webster appears. His style has now great energy and simplicity; his sentences are short, his idiom homely and direct. His words are the words of the people, refined of ordinary coarseness, yet typical of ordinary life. Humor, sarcasm, irony replace the dignity and heaviness of the speech at Niblo's saloon. The structure is no longer that of formal proposition and proof but that of theme and countertheme, developed in robust variety by amplification, restatement, climax. The structure is even, as we have seen, Shakespearean. Small wonder, then, that this speech was hailed by Webster's contemporaries as an unusual and uncharacteristic speech. The *New York Herald* for Wednesday, September 30, 1840, expresses the astonishment that greeted Webster's effort at Patchogue and takes some of the credit for the change that had been wrought in his public manner. Says the *Herald:*

The recent brilliant public efforts made by the Hon. Daniel Webster at Wall street, Jamaica, and Patchogue, have set the whole community in a blaze. All are anxious to hear him speak, and all desire to read his speeches. The sole cause of all this, is the fact, that Mr. Webster never was reported at all until his celebrated Patchogue speech was reported accurately in the "Herald."

That effort, and that publication, has placed Mr. Webster in an entirely new light before the whole community. Previous to that, every one had merely considered Mr. Webster as a distinguished jurist—as a great constitutional lawyer. But his remarkable and brilliant speech at Patchogue has shown to the community that he possesses a truly Shakesperian mind.

The wonderful versatility of Mr. Webster's talents, as displayed in his speeches at Patchogue, Jamaica, and Wall street, within the last week, have stamped him more truly as a man of genius, than all the previous efforts of his life. His speech in Suffolk County shewed him to possess (in addition to his great legal and argumentative attainments) strong powers of biting sarcasm, rich bursts of humour, a spontaneous ebullition of wit, and withering satire, equalled by no one since the days of the ever memorable John Randolph, and scarcely excelled by that celebrated, talented, and extraordinary man, in his best days and brightest efforts. He possessed, however, besides his brilliant wit, withering sarcasm, and fine classic allusions, none of the argumentative and strong logical powers of Mr. Webster, and which he has displayed so strikingly within the last few days.

The fact is, that the speech of Mr. Webster, at Patchogue, display him more fully in the light of a man of genius, than anything else that he ever attempted. . . . it was a great effort. It evinced a wonderful adaptation of his extraordinary [*sic*] to the scenes, the circumstances, and the people that surrounded him.

We should dismiss the *Herald's* enthusiasm as the interested verdict of partizanship were it not for the fact that the text of the speech does, as we indicated, have a Shakespearean structure and, more than this, an almost perfect adaptation of words to the immediate attitudes of the people of the times. What explains the transformation wrought in Webster on this occasion? One clue is afforded by the *Herald's* statement that Webster had never been completely reported before, the reading public being acquainted with him only through speeches carefully revised and rewritten. Our own survey of the two texts of the speech at Niblo's saloon bears out the conclusion that the Webster who spoke to an audience was more robust and concrete in style than is the Webster who recast a speech for readers. The real Webster, then, so far, at least, as his oratorical reputation is concerned, lies concealed beneath his own formal literary habits and can be seen now, as in 1840, only when we give him no opportunity to superimpose his literary talents upon his actual persuasive technique. But this explanation goes only part of the way. It must also be admitted that the Webster who spoke at Patchogue, stimulated as he doubtless was by the knowledge that he was to be reported, and was to share in James Gordon Bennett's journalistic innovation, was more directly conscious of a resistance to be overcome, than he, for whatever reason, had usually been before, except in the debate with Hayne and in his occasional speeches.

What would have been the result, had Webster addressed himself as early as the year 1837 to the task of overcoming the resistance manifested toward him by the public? The answer is that he might easily have acquired the reputation as a popular speaker that his rival Clay always enjoyed, and Thurlow Weed might have worked behind the scenes at Harrisburg in 1839 for the nomination of Webster instead of Harrison. The Whig cause, of course, was never firm and statesmanlike, and Webster at Patchogue could not rectify its negations and compromises; but he could and did create for himself a new public reputation that, had it existed throughout Van Buren's administration, would have been far less of a barrier to his ambitions than was the reputation given him by political enemies or by extravagant admirers.

If space permitted, it would be possible to show that the great body of Webster's political oratory falls into position upon the scale already established. His speech at Saratoga in 1840, called by Fuess "perhaps his finest purely political address,"[1] illustrates many of the defects of the speech at Niblo's saloon and some of the virtues of that at Patchogue. At Albany, in 1844, he delivered a speech that was criticized, as we noticed earlier, for its labored attempt to distinguish between incidental and intentional protection, for its failure to discuss the question of Texas and the bank, and for its complete omission of any reference to Clay, the Whig candidate. In these and all other of Webster's political speeches, the critic is interested in the speaker's relation to the attitude of his audience and in his use of discourse as a means of intensifying or changing that attitude. Webster's greatest defect as spokesman of his party was that he habitually maintained an Olympian disregard of the undercurrents of opposition and sought usually to confine partisan differences within the realm of abstract political discussion. This strategy is successful only when a party is deeply entrenched in popular favor, as the result of historical accident or of a really enlightened public policy. But Webster's party, painful as it might have been for it to hear its plight so characterized, was not deeply entrenched. The Whig platform was a series of uncertain adjustments toward the positive issues and movements of the day. The history of that age was being made by Jackson, while the Whigs confined themselves to a succession of minority reports. Even if Webster had always spoken to the people as he spoke at Patchogue, his political strategy might have had little value in changing the settled course of events, for we must remember that Clay, with all the popular enthusiasm he created, could not win a national election. But at any rate, a strategy like that at Patchogue was required, and American political literature loses a large body of excellent speeches when a man of Webster's ability did not habitually respond, as he could so ably have done, to the real political dispositions of his audience.[2]

---

[1] Fuess, II, 86.

[2] For bibliography, see last paragraph of the biographical note at the beginning of this essay.

William L. Yancey

by REXFORD S. MITCHELL

William Lowndes Yancey was born at Ogeechee Shoals, Ga., August 10, 1814, the son of Benjamin C. Yancey, lawyer and political associate of John C. Calhoun, and Caroline Bird Yancey. His father died in 1817; his mother married the Reverend Nathan Beman, a Presbyterian clergyman, in 1822, and the family moved to New York, where Beman was actively identified with the antislavery movement. Yancey attended Williams College, 1831–1832; began the study of law in Greenville, S.C., 1833. He married Sarah Earle, daughter of a wealthy planter, in 1835; was an Alabama planter, 1835–1839; returned to the law in 1839. He was elected to the lower house of the legislature, 1841; upper house, 1843; Congress, 1844; re-elected but resigned September 1, 1846. He held no other public office until 1861 but became an outstanding leader of the Southern Rights movement. He was delegate to the Democratic national conventions of 1848 and 1860 and to the Convention of the People of Alabama in 1861; was Confederate Commissioner to England and France, 1861–1862; member of the Confederate Senate, 1862–1863; died July 27, 1863.

William Lowndes Yancey has been called the "Orator of Secession."[1] His constant theme, however, was not secession but the constitutional rights of the South. His first goal was "equality" in the Union; failing in that, he was for independence. He devoted relatively little attention to the theory of secession and much to the exposition of Southern rights and the manner in which they were being violated. He stressed, not the glories of independence, but the degradation of inequality within the Union. It is true that he early despaired of securing these rights and thought secession would result from an insistence upon them, yet this does not alter his fundamental point of view. Independence was a status desirable not in itself but only as an escape from inequality in the Union. Perhaps it is merely a matter of emphasis, but "Orator of Southern Constitutional Rights" seems to express more accurately his fundamental thesis.

In some respects such a title as "Arch-Enemy of Compromise" would characterize his career even better, for he spent his life fighting compromise. But this would describe his counterpart among the Northern extremists just as well, for although Wendell Phillips, the abolitionist orator, appealed

[1] W. G. Brown, *The Lower South in American History* (New York, 1902), p. 115.

to "a higher law" rather than the Constitution, he was just as relentless in his opposition to compromise.

Yancey was born in Georgia, of Virginia ancestry, but his boyhood environment was that of a New York Presbyterian parsonage, and he received most of his formal education in the North before going to South Carolina in 1833 to study law. Curiously, too, he began his speaking career as a *Unionist* orator. The nullification issue was still being bitterly contested in South Carolina when he arrived, and Yancey was inevitably drawn into the struggle. What determined his choice of camps is not clear. Perhaps his residence in the North and the predominant sentiment in his district were factors. In any event he soon became an ardent and uncompromising Unionist, and on July 4, 1834, when nineteen years old, made his debut as a political orator at a Unionist meeting in Lodi.

With unusual poise for a youth, he spoke for an hour, rapidly and very distinctly and without notes. They, he assured his Unionist audience, were the true patriots of South Carolina, for the "avowed object" of the nullifiers was "to dissolve the Union."[1] B. F. Perry, with whom he was studying law, reported that he spoke with "remarkable fluency and clearness" and thought his delivery "more conversational than might have been expected from one of his impulsive nature."[2] Many in the audience that day listened with peculiar interest, for they had known his father Benjamin Yancey, an eloquent young lawyer who had died when his son was but three. They thought they saw a strong resemblance to him in the youth and his manner of speaking. Much of the skill of the young orator, however, was the result of his mother's inspiration and careful training. Again and again she had recited to the boy the tale of his father's eloquence. And then, knitting in hand, she had heard him declaim, stressing poise and distinctness of utterance. His favorite declamation had been the old hymn "On Jordan's Stormy Banks I Stand."

The nullification controversy finally ended in a compromise that Yancey characteristically opposed to the last. Shortly after, the lure of rich new cotton lands drew him to Alabama, where he confidently anticipated a prosperous career as a planter. When an accidental poisoning of all his slaves destroyed his prospects, Yancey returned to law and eventually to politics. But during 5 years of plantation life his political views had undergone a radical change. In 1834 he had assailed John C. Calhoun and his doctrines; now he aligned himself with the Alabama followers of the South Carolinian, the State-rights wing of the Democratic party. What

---

[1] A summary of this address will be found in the *Greenville* (S.C.) *Mountaineer*, July 12, 1834; for a later Unionist address see *ibid.*, Oct. 4, 1834.

[2] John W. DuBose, *Life and Times of William Lowndes Yancey* (Birmingham, 1892), p. 33.

influenced him in this decision cannot be stated categorically. Plantation life may have provided opportunity for objective and more mature reflection concerning constitutional theory, as his biographer, DuBose, suggests.[1] It seems more likely, however, that the process was much like that which caused Calhoun and Webster to exchange positions between 1816 and 1832. Once convinced that the interests of one's section can be served best by the application of certain constitutional principles, it is not difficult to believe in the soundness of these principles. Economic interest has frequently determined attitude toward constitutional construction.[2] This need not imply that the individual is conscious of this influence; in most cases he is thoroughly convinced that the change is the result of objective thinking.

During the campaign of 1840 Yancey spoke at a number of Democratic rallies and participated in several joint debates. We have no record of what he said; we know only that Democratic leaders thought that they saw in the young man promise of unusual power before popular audiences. He was sent to the legislature. Here Robert Daugherty, an Irish Whig, whose withering sarcasm had made him a feared opponent, found in Yancey his equal.[3] Spirit and a ready wit made Yancey's invective especially effective and won for him the approval of delighted Democrats. He was elected to Congress in 1844, after a campaign in which he thoroughly covered the district on horseback and gave further evidence of effectiveness before Southern audiences.

Shortly after Yancey arrived in Washington, Thomas Clingman, tall and gaunt independent Whig from North Carolina, indulged with bitter sarcasm in an impassioned arraignment of Southern Democrats. This group, already incensed against Clingman because they thought he had betrayed Southern interests, were determined that he should be answered in kind. Yancey, whose reputation for invective had preceded him, was assigned the privilege of speaking for all. Impulsive Yancey was not averse to the task, nor did he disappoint his colleagues.[4] The result was a duel on the field of honor, in which neither contestant was injured but which Yancey had considerable difficulty explaining to many of his Baptist constituents.

He participated in the Congressional discussion of the Oregon question and other issues and attained general recognition as an effective debater. Newspaper correspondents and some of his colleagues began to refer to

[1] DuBose, *op. cit.*, p. 78.

[2] See A. M. Schlesinger, *New Viewpoints in American History* (New York, 1922), pp. 220–245.

[3] *Wetumpka* (Ala.) *Argus*, Feb. 14, 1844.

[4] *Congressional Globe*, Twenty-eighth Congress, second session, Appendix, pp. 85–90, 114–120; see also Thomas L. Clingman, *Speeches and Writings* (Raleigh, N.C., 1877), pp. 195–196.

him as "the Charles James Fox of America."[1] Certainly a fluent extemporaneous style, effective invective, and obvious sincerity and depth of feeling characterized the speaking of both. Moreover, they had a common weakness. Robert T. Oliver, student of Fox's oratory, says: "Under the excitement of debate he was swept into violence of language and an extremity of statement which he frequently had later cause to regret."[2] We have Yancey's confession that he labored under a similar difficulty. At one time he arose in the house to apologize for remarks he had made concerning Western Democrats who voted for internal improvements. "I regret," he said, "that I too frequently in the excitement of a general debate, use language that reflection convinces me were better left unsaid."[3]

Yancey may have regretted the language he employed to describe them, but as the session continued his impatience with Western Democrats who voted for internal improvements, as well as Eastern Democrats who favored higher tariff duties, increased. On June 30, 1846, he resigned his seat and in his final speech in the House, and later in an address to his constituents, charged Northern and Eastern Democrats with disloyalty to the party's historic principles. "If principle is dearer than mere party association," he declared, "we shall never again meet in common Democratic convention a large body of men who had vigorously opposed us on principle." The party, he said, must be brought back to the principles of strict construction, or the South must cease to rely on party and insist, regardless of platforms and party interests, upon all that it had a right to claim under the Constitution.[4] His no-compromise battle had begun.

As he returned from Washington, however, Yancey must have known that the tariff and internal improvements were not to be the primary issues. It was apparent that there loomed upon the political horizon a new issue that would soon overshadow these. The expansionist impulse in the South and West had made certain the acquisition of new territory through the Mexican war. Now a clash of interest between slaveholders and free farmers concerning this territory was inevitable, and with it would appear the question of the status of slavery in the territories. The storm broke, in fact, shortly after Yancey left Congress and months before the close of the war, when the Wilmot Proviso, which proposed to exclude slavery from all territory acquired, appeared in the house. Soon legislatures and mass meetings in North, West, and South were adopting resolutions, and petitions poured into Congress.

[1] DuBose, *op. cit.*, p. 148; *Greensboro* (Ala.) *Beacon*, July 9, 1856.
[2] Personal letter from Oliver, now at Bucknell University.
[3] *Congressional Globe*, Twenty-ninth Congress, first session, p. 499.
[4] *Congressional Globe*, Twenty-ninth Congress, second session, Appendix, pp. 993–997; for the address to his constituents see *Marion* (Ala.) *News*, July 13, 1846.

Yancey believed that the Constitution gave the slaveholders the right to take their slaves into territories and that it obligated Congress to protect them in this right. He thought this right to be fundamental. Only by forcing the free states, which, because of their greater population, now controlled the house, to recognize this constitutional guarantee could the South hope to maintain an equilibrium in the Senate for protection against legislation hostile to Southern institutions. The South could not afford to compromise as she had in 1820. She must insist on her full rights and refuse to cooperate politically with those who refused to recognize them.

As an initial step in furthering this program he proposed to persuade Alabama Democrats that they should insist that the national party take an unequivocal stand in the election of 1848 and refuse to support any Presidential candidate who did not do so. As a delegate to the state convention he carried in his pocket resolutions that committed Alabama Democrats to that position. When the resolutions committee reported a more moderate declaration, he obtained the floor and in a forensic triumph secured the unanimous adoption of his resolutions and election as a delegate to the national convention.[1] When he left shortly after on the spring circuit of the courts, his position appeared to be generally accepted by his party in the state, and there were indications that other Southern states might follow.

When he returned in April, however, he found to his bitter disappointment that he stood almost alone.[2] Political leaders and editors had begun to realize he had committed them to a position far in advance of the rest of the party and one to which the Northern and Western wings of the party could never agree. It was one thing to endorse enthusiastically in the excitement of convention an abstract right in which they believed, but it was an entirely different matter to insist on that right if it meant the disruption of the party and a Whig victory. At the convention their attention had been centered on the constitutional right; now they were thinking of the effect of insisting on that right.

But it was now certain that the country must face the territorial issue, for the Senate had ratified a treaty that provided for the cession of Mexican land, and Yancey fought on determinedly at the national convention. When a minority report embodying his position received but thirty-six votes and the convention proceeded to adopt a platform that entirely ignored the territorial issue, he announced that in accordance with his instructions he could no longer participate in the proceedings and with

---

[1] *Huntsville* (Ala.) *Democrat*, Mar. 8, 1848; *Journal of State Democratic Convention*, Feb. 15 and 16, 1848. The resolutions became the famous Alabama platform.

[2] C. P. Denman, *The Secession Movement in Alabama* (Montgomery, Ala., 1933), p. 11.

Wray of Alabama, withdrew.[1] He had failed to win even the Alabama Democrats to his position, but he had defined the issue that was to divide the party in 1860.

His course at the convention was vehemently condemned by Alabama party leaders, but his fight won him a popular following. No hall in Montgomery could contain the crowd that gathered to hear him upon his return; so he spoke from the porch of the Exchange Hotel. He addressed other mass meetings in central Alabama. He could not, he announced, support the Democratic ticket; he would refrain from voting and advised his hearers to do likewise. "We must let the Democrats of the free states know," he declared, "that when we use brave words they will be followed by determined acts."[2] The Democrats carried Alabama, but their vote was 6,000 less than in 1844.

The election of 1848 in no way settled the status of slaves in territories —the Whig party because of irreconcilable sectional differences had adopted no platform at all. Nor had Yancey's experience in the campaign altered his belief that the South must not compromise. It had, however, convinced him that if the South, or even Alabama, was brought to that position, it must be through a direct appeal to the people. The movement must grow from the bottom up, and he now determined to carry the issue directly to the people.

This decision marks the beginning of an 11-year crusade in which Yancey never faltered. It was in this crusade that he reached his full power as a speaker, a power that gradually won for him, without benefit of public office, a place of great influence in the lower South. First in Alabama and then, as his fame spread, in all the lower South, he proclaimed that compromise was submission with an effectiveness that brought him general recognition even in the North (where he was known as "the Prince of Fire-Eaters") as the most powerful spokesman of the Southern extremists.

Life in the lower South provided exceptional opportunity for such a crusade, for platform speaking was the most effective means of reaching the public ear. As Brown says: "But it was the spoken word, not the printed page, that guided thought, aroused enthusiasm, made history."[3] The people were extremely speech-conscious. They rode, or drove, for miles to hear some famous lawyer plead a case; party conventions were never without their gallery; and the mass meetings and barbecues during

---

[1] Proceedings of the Democratic Convention of 1848; W. L. Yancey, "Address to the People of Alabama" (pamphlet, Montgomery, Ala., 1848).

[2] *Montgomery Flag and Advertiser*, June 6, 1848; see also letter of Yancey to W. H. Lucas in *Flag and Advertiser*, July 29, 1848.

[3] Brown, *op. cit.*, p. 125.

political campaigns were veritable outpourings of the people. Some of the larger barbecues lasted two or three days, and there were races and games as well as speaking day and night.

There was a tendency, of course, under these circumstances for speeches to become exhibitions in which form became an end in itself. These audiences were susceptible to the charm of dramatic action, elegant diction, classical allusion, graceful gesture, and melodious voice. Frequently these, and not the arguments presented, were the matters the people discussed as they returned home, and often the graces of an orator were remembered long after what he had said was forgotten.

But Yancey seems to have made no effort to charm his hearers. Perhaps he was too intent on his purpose to give the matter a thought. Perhaps he consciously avoided qualities that would divert attention from his program of action. His biographer, DuBose, reports that he had a constant fear of being "a declaimer."[1] His speaking was characterized by strength rather than beauty, by directness rather than finesse.

Henry Hilliard, a talented Montgomery Whig, was Yancey's perennial opponent in joint debate. Perhaps a contrast of their speaking, written by a contemporary who heard both of them many times, will give a clearer idea of this aspect of Yancey's method. Wharfield G. Richardson, later president of Tuscaloosa Female College and professor of Greek at the University of Alabama, says:

> One [Hilliard] attracted you by the elegance of his diction; the other held you by the grip of his reason. One drew you by his bewitching rhetoric; the other drove you with his unsparing logic. . . . He [Yancey] was all directness, all earnestness, all determination, all fire. He did not have half the variety or vivacity of Hilliard; he was not half so picturesque, half so showy, but he was stronger.[2]

Thomas H. Watts, another Montgomery Whig who frequently opposed Yancey in court and on the political platform, says:

> When I say he was superb as an orator, I do not mean that he moved men by mere words, gorgeous metaphors, and poetic imagery. But I mean that his arguments were strong, arranged without apparent effort in logical order, his words apt, (without any surplus ones) to convey his exact meaning, and his manner, voice, and gesture, splendid for simplicity and earnestness.[3]

[1] DuBose, *op. cit.*, p. 148.

[2] W. C. Richardson, "Hilliard and Yancey—A Parallel," *Montgomery Advertiser*, Nov. 8, 1908. For contrasts that give the same impression, see G. F. Mellen, "Henry W. Hilliard and William L. Yancey," *Sewanee Review*, 17: 49–50; William R. Smith, *Reminiscences of a Long Life* (Washington, D.C., 1889), pp. 222–223; *Montgomery Advertiser*, July 24, 1855.

[3] Copy of letter from Watts to C. C. Clay, Jr., Sept. 11, 1880, found in the Yancey Collection of the Alabama State Department of Archives and History; original in the C. C. Clay, Jr., Papers at Duke University Library.

Yancey appears to have moved about the platform very little and to have employed relatively few gestures. Henry S. Foote, another of his political opponents, says: "His gestures were few, but these were most apt and impressive."[1] Richardson, a contemporary cited before, reports: "He did not nervously pace up and down the platform. His pose was firm and dignified, as if to remind his hearers that his position was impregnable. His gestures were few and impressive. They were employed to mark a climax or drive home a conviction."[2] DuBose, who heard him speak many times, says: "He seldom occupied more than a yard square of space through one of the longest of his addresses."[3] He reports that in a speech at a barbecue in Union Town in 1856, Yancey "stood with his right hand resting loosely on a table at his side, without reference to his scrap book lying before him, gesturing occasionally with his left hand, and without moving a yard's space, until in the peroration. . . . "[4]

At first thought this may seem strange for a man of Yancey's temperament. Yet his temperament may provide the explanation. He was a man of strong impulse and deep emotion. These he usually kept under control, but not without effort. His beliefs concerning the issues he discussed were emotionally re-enforced, and he reacted strongly as he spoke. He needed no profuse action to generate fervor; in fact, the generative effects of expansive bodily action might well have carried him beyond the point of control. DuBose says: "There was a visible suppression of feeling, a curbing of force latent in the man. . . . "[4]

He generally exercised restraint, too, in the use of his power in sarcasm and invective; perhaps experience had taught him it was best used sparingly. Foote says:

> In general he was able to keep the tempestuous feelings of his soul in a state of stoical suppression, but occasions sometimes arose when, either having lost his accustomed power of self control, or deeming it expedient to make some display of the stormier energies with which he was endowed, he unloosed all the furies under his command upon some noted antagonist, and did and said things which those who witnessed his sublime ravings never again forgot.[5]

Newspaper correspondents and other contemporaries, whether political friend or foe, seem to agree that much of Yancey's power lay in his ability to simplify complicated issues and in the manner in which he marshaled facts to the support of his position; in other words, in analysis and in the

[1] Henry S. Foote, *The Bench and Bar of the South and Southwest* (St. Louis, 1876), p. 238.
[2] Richardson, *loc. cit.*
[3] DuBose, *op. cit.*, p. 190.
[4] *Ibid.*, p. 331.
[5] Foote, *op. cit.*, p. 235.

use of logical proof.[1] There has been evidence of this in the statements of contemporaries already cited, but let us note the reports of two newspaper correspondents.[2] The Louisville correspondent for the *St. Louis Bulletin* says:

His power over the people lies in the fact that his speeches are masterpieces cf argument; that his logic is irresistible; and that you are unwilling to lose a single link in the chain of reasoning which leads you, whether you will or not, from his premises to embrace necessarily his conclusions. The argument, too, is done up, not in showy and sparkling dress, but in pure, simple and massive English, uncorrupted by the foreignisms which characterize the turgidity and bombast that modern writers and speakers consider the perfection of style.[3]

The *Mobile Daily Tribune* reports: "It was the simplest speech that we have heard this season, but full of the severest logic, expressed in the most appropriate language, the words falling exactly in the place the orator chose to marshal them. This is the beauty of Yancey's speeches."[4]

But make no mistake, in spite of his restraint in overt bodily action and the degree to which he appears to have employed logical argument, Yancey had no difficulty in stirring the emotions of his audiences. Watts says: "I have never heard anyone, who could stir a crowd to the height of enthusiastic fervor with as much apparent ease."[5] Watts thought the source of this power lay in his tremendous earnestness and sincerity. Yancey spoke, he says, "as if he felt, in the deepest recesses of his heart, the full measure of the words he used."[6] In other words, through a responsive voice and bodily action of the more covert type, Yancey not only revealed his own deep emotional reaction but kindled and aroused a similar response in his hearers.

Furthermore, much of Yancey's logical proof was employed to connect the course of action he proposed to the wants and desires of the people, to fit his proposal into their emotionally re-enforced beliefs and habits of thought. Unfortunately we shall probably never be able to study in detail Yancey's method of argument, for we have a verbatim record of not a one

---

[1] George F. Milton, Douglas biographer, in *The Eve of Conflict* (New York, 1934), p. 371, says: "He [Yancey] resembled John C. Calhoun in his restraint of statement and deliberation of speech: once grant his starting premise and the conclusion could not be assailed."

[2] See also *Greensboro* (Ala.) *Beacon*, July 9, 1856; letter of Levi W. Lawler, Sept. 19, 1856, quoted in DuBose, *op. cit.*, pp. 328–329; J. Hodgson, *The Cradle of the Confederacy* (Mobile, 1876), p. 260; and Henry Hilliard, *Politics and Pen Pictures at Home and Abroad* (New York, 1892), pp. 205–258.

[3] *St. Louis Bulletin*, Oct. 25, 1860.

[4] *Mobile Daily Tribune*, Nov. 2, 1860.

[5] Letter to Clay, *op. cit.*, Sept. 11, 1880.

[6] *Ibid.*

of the hundreds of speeches that he made before Southern audiences in those 11 years. Stenographers were not available at barbecues and mass meetings.[1] Moreover, we have few manuscripts. Yancey spoke extemporaneously and never wrote his speeches in preparation. He prepared carefully, however, thinking through and outlining each speech in advance. Occasionally he spoke without notes, frequently from his outline, in which he had inserted notes suggested by the occasion or his opponent's argument.[2] In a few cases he wrote out a speech after it had been delivered, but he was careful to say that it was prepared from his notes and that it represented only the "general tenor" of the argument. From these few manuscripts and a number of summaries of his speeches appearing in Southern newspapers we can, however, glean an idea of his general approach.

Although the great majority of them owned no slaves, the people of the Lower South were united in a fervid support of the institution of slavery. Basically this grew out of a dread of the social consequences of emancipation. If some satisfactory plan for removing the Negro could have been devised, it is likely that many of the nonslaveholders would have felt differently. But there was no such plan, and the people saw in slavery the only effective control of a black population that in many communities far outnumbered the whites. The rise of a militant abolitionist movement in the North, the strength of which was greatly overestimated in the South, served, of course, but to deepen the fervor of this conviction.[3]

Growing out of this conviction and economic interest was another belief whose roots lay deep in the emotional life of the Southern people. That was the doctrine of State rights, for this constitutional view provided the South, a minority, with the best means of protecting slavery as well as other interests. Moreover, the vast majority in all Yancey's audiences believed that the North and West had denied them rights that were constitutionally theirs. This had occurred, they thought, not only in a general misinterpretation of the Constitution but in the actual subversion of definite clauses, without which the Southern states would never have ratified that document—the fugitive-slave clause, for instance.[4]

[1] We *do* have stenographic reports of what he said at the Democratic convention of 1860 and to Northern audiences in the campaign that followed. It was not in these addresses; however, but in his direct appeal to the people of the lower South that he left his impress. Nor do these speeches indicate the nature of the Southern appeal; they were made to entirely different audiences.

[2] A part of his written preparation for one of his speeches, just which one is not clear, is among the Yancey Papers at the Alabama State Department of Archives and History.

[3] See U. B. Phillips, "The Central Theme of Southern History," *American Historical Review*, 34: 30–43; Paul A. Buck, "Poor Whites of the Old South," *ibid.*, 31: 41–55; W. B. Hesseltine, "Some New Aspects of the Pro-slavery Argument," *Journal of Negro History*, 21, No. 1: 1–14.

[4] Denman, *op. cit.*, pp. 17–18.

Yancey dwelt at length on the history of these "aggressions." They were, he declared, but the preliminary assaults of abolitionists, and in every case submission had brought, not peace, not a recognition of remaining rights, but further attacks upon them. If the Constitution had been administered in the spirit of the fathers, with a just view to the rights and equality of each section, the South would be powerful, happy, and contented. But upon the great issues affecting her prosperity and position in the Union, the Constitution, to all practical purposes, had been quietly and completely set aside. That venerable document had been rolled up and placed among the archives of the Republic, merely to be looked at and speculated upon occasionally as a curious thing. A new rule had been substituted for the Federal Constitution whenever the great question of slavery expansion had been an issue. That rule was called *compromise*. And in the name of compromise the rights of the South had been gradually taken away, in such a manner as to cause even a murmur of complaint to be looked upon as an act of bad faith. Compromise was nothing but a progressive surrender of rights. Further aggressions would come as rapidly as the South would bear them until the work of Abolition was complete. The South must cease to compromise.[1]

To a people quick in matters of personal honor and strong in sectional pride, he declared that the *honor* as well as the social security of the South was at stake and proclaimed that compromise was *submission*. When the colonies emerged from the Revolutionary War as independent states, he said, the states south of the Potomac were territorially in the ascendant. Yet through compromise that condition had been reversed. And now the South's great sectional rival, plethoric with the prosperity that compromise had conferred, complacently and triumphantly looked forward to the period, not far distant, when she would add to her numbers every new state admitted and completely dominate the Union.[2]

The alternative to compromise offered by Yancey, in case the North and West should refuse to recognize Constitutional rights, was, of course, *secession*. The right of secession was not, however, a new idea to Southern audiences, for the State-rights theory provided, not only the best means of protection within the Union but the way out of it. Neither Yancey's opponents nor his audiences doubted their right to secede, but his opponents and the majority in most of his audiences questioned the expediency of such radical action. They thought of secession only as a last resort and

---

[1] The wording of the argument in this paragraph follows closely that of a summary of Yancey's speech at a barbecue in Benton, Ala., July 17, 1858. The summary appears in the *Montgomery Advertiser*, July 28, 1858.

[2] The wording here also follows closely that of the summary of the Benton speech.

preferred to compromise.[1] In this they were influenced in part by a deep attachment to the Union.[2] Perhaps this is why Yancey advocated secession largely by implication. Except in the crises of 1850 and 1861, he devoted little time to urging secession, but he hammered unceasingly on the dangers of compromise, the only alternative to secession should the rights of the South be denied.

His opponents quickly recognized the most vulnerable point in his position; their constant and most effective attack was the charge that he was a *disunionist*. To this Yancey replied that those who were destroying the Union by refusing to abide by the compact under which it was formed were the real disunionists. If advocating the rights of all under the Constitution, never assailing a single provision of it, urging a policy of defense against the wrong done to Southern rights and equality meant being a friend of the Union, then, he declared, he should be universally acclaimed a Union man. But, he continued, neither Union or disunion was the paramount issue; it was the protection of Southern rights.[3]

Fundamentally Yancey's appeal was an attempt to summon to the support of his no-compromise position a galaxy of the strongest of motives. Perhaps this explains in part why his argument, when successful, stirred his audiences "to the height of enthusiastic fervor." Slavery and therefore, by inference, the social security, the homes, and the civilization of the South, as well as her rights, her honor, and her prosperity, were endangered by compromise. This argument his opponents met by denying the danger. Their appeal, in turn, was to the love of the Union. The motives to which Yancey appealed were potentially the stronger, for in spite of their devotion to the Union, all the people of the Lower South would have favored secession had they believed that remaining in the Union meant the destruction of slavery.[4] But Yancey faced the problem of convincing the people of this danger. To do this he must analyze the controversies of the past for trends and then project these trends into the future. This was a much more difficult task between 1850 and 1856 than that of his opponents, who needed but point to relative immediate security. That he succeeded as well as he did is an indication of his persuasive power. After 1856 the course of events raised in the South an increasing doubt of this security and provided him with more immediate support for his position.

In the crisis that followed the Mexican War, Yancey repeatedly urged that Alabama should secede if Southern states were denied their full rights

[1] Denman, *op. cit.*, p. 42.
[2] *Ibid.*, p. 44.
[3] Here the wording follows that of "Speech of Hon. W. L. Yancey delivered in the Democratic State Convention of 1860" (a pamphlet, Montgomery, Ala., 1860).
[4] Denman, *op. cit.*, p. 44.

in the new territory. But he knew that Alabama would never do so unless other states preceded her. His hope lay in Georgia. In Washington the congressmen of that state were freely threatening secession. Their chief purpose was to frighten Northern representatives into compromise,[1] but many of the people of the state, not sensing their underlying objective, were taking them at their word, and Yancey spoke at a number of Georgia mass meetings as the Southern radicals concentrated much of their effort on this pivotal state. When the Congressional battle finally ended in 1850, these representatives, Toombs, Stephens, and Cobb, in a whirlwind stump of the state, persuaded the people to accept the compromise that they had "wrung" from Congress as a "permanent settlement," with the definite proviso that the state would resist further aggression, "even to the disruption of the Union." This "Georgia plattorm" won general approval in the South, and although they fought on in some of the other states, Yancey and his colleagues knew that the immediate battle was lost.

His cause reached its lowest ebb, however, in 1854, with the repeal of the provisions of the Missouri Compromise in the Kansas-Nebraska Act.[2] Though Yancey warned that it involved a surrender of rights, it was generally approved in the South. When, however, the enactment of the law resulted in the rise of a party in the North opposed to the extension of slavery, the tide began to turn. When that party carried eleven free states in 1856, even conservative opinion in the South began to question the finality of the Compromise of 1850. This doubt increased as ten of the free states nullified the Fugitive Slave Law with "personal-liberty laws," and Western and Northern representatives, including Douglas, the author of the Kansas-Nebraska Act, refused to admit Kansas as a slave state under the Lecompton constitution, in spite of tremendous administration pressure. Then came a strange ally in John Brown, whose raid on Harper's Ferry brought a reaction almost hysterical in parts of the South. The logic of events was bearing out Yancey's predictions and supplying him with fresh and more powerful ammunition.

By 1860 a rampant Western Democracy was bent on sweeping Douglas, with his Freeport doctrine, to the Presidential chair, and Administration Democrats were glad to make common cause with the Southern-rights wing of the party in a desperate effort to prevent his nomination. Thus, at the historic Charleston convention, Yancey found himself the outstanding leader and recognized spokesman of the delegates of the lower

[1] U. B. Phillips, "Georgia and State Rights," *Annual Report of the American Historical Association*, 1 (1901): 164–165; U. B. Phillips, *Life of Robert Toombs* (New York, 1913), pp. 89–115 *passim*; M. J. White, *The Secessionist Movement in the United States* 1847–1852 (New Orleans, 1910), pp. 84–88.

[2] See P. O. Ray, *The Repeal of the Missouri Compromise* (Cleveland, 1909).

South. Moreover, these delegates were instructed to demand of the party the unequivocal stand for which Yancey had fought in 1848. It was Yancey who presented their cause in what Halstead, correspondent for the *Cincinnati Commercial,* termed "the speech of the convention."[1] And when their platform demands were rejected, the delegates of the lower South withdrew as Yancey had done almost alone in 1848.

He was a leading spirit in the organization of the Constitutional Democratic party and took an active part in the campaign that followed. The historian Fite calls him "the soul of the Breckinridge party."[2] In an invasion of the North he spoke at Cooper Institute, in New York, and at Faneuil Hall, in Boston, and in other cities. Northern newspaper reporters expressed surprise at his lack of bombast and the degree to which he employed logical argument,[3] but his tour probably had little effect otherwise.[4] Throughout the South he spoke to huge audiences. His only object, he declared, was to maintain the Constitution by electing the only candidate who could defeat Lincoln and avert the dangers that threatened the Union.[5]

The campaign that preceded the election of delegates to the Convention of the People of Alabama, in 1861, marks the last phase of Yancey's no-compromise appeal. Secession sentiment reached its height with the election of Lincoln, but it was by no means certain that the convention would vote to withdraw. Political leaders who had made common cause with Yancey in the Presidential campaign now counseled moderation and held out the hope that redress might still be secured within the Union. But in the words of John Forsyth, "The storm rages to such a madness that it is beyond the control of those who raised it,"[6] and urged on by

---

[1] Murat Halstead, *Caucuses of 1860* (Columbus, 1860), p. 49. The entire speech appears in *Charleston* (S.C.) *Mercury,* Apr. 28, 1860; *Florence* (Ala.) *Gazette,* May 23, May 30, June 2, June 13, 1860; *Mobile Weekly Register,* May 12, 1860. The report of the *Mercury* was reprinted in pamphlet form by Walker, Evans & Co., Charleston. For comments on the speech, see William Garrett, *Reminiscences of Public Men in Alabama* (Atlanta, 1872), p. 685; Hilliard, *op. cit.,* pp. 285–286; *Charleston Mercury,* May 1, 1860; *Florence Gazette,* May 21, 1860; *New York Times,* Apr. 28, 1860; *Chicago Press-Tribune,* May 1, 1860; *New Hampshire Gazette,* May 12, 1860.

[2] E. D. Fite, *The Presidential Campaign of 1860* (New York, 1902), p. 176.

[3] For reports of his speeches and comments concerning them, see *New York Times,* Oct. 11; *Philadelphia Press,* Oct. 12; *New York World,* Oct. 11; *New York Tribune,* Oct. 11; *New York Herald,* Oct. 15; *Boston Daily Courier,* Oct. 13; *Boston Post,* Oct. 15; *Washington Constitution,* Oct. 16; *Syracuse Daily Standard,* Oct. 17; *Rochester Democrat and American,* Oct. 18; *Central City Courier,* Oct. 18; *Cincinnati Enquirer,* Oct. 21; *Cincinnati Daily Commercial,* Oct. 22; all 1860.

[4] *Ibid.,* pp. 214–218.

[5] See Nashville speech, in *Nashvi.le Union and American,* Oct. 29, 1860, and New Orleans speech, in *New Orleans Daily Delta,* Oct. 30, 1860.

[6] Milton, *op. cit.,* p. 499, quoting letter from Forsyth.

Yancey and other Southern-rights leaders, the people of Alabama elected a narrow, but outright, majority favoring immediate secession.

George W. Vines, a member of Yancey's audience when he spoke at Dadeville during the campaign, reports:

> He used an earnest conversational tone—he told no ancedotes—he quoted no poetry—he paid no compliments to the fair ladies—his words and his demeanor were those of a strong, determined man discussing a very serious question. He declared that only two courses were open to the South,—separate secession or absolute submission. . . . Toward the close of his speech, taking his watch from his vest pocket and glancing at its face, then raising his eyes to the audience, still holding the watch in his right hand, he said: "By this time South Carolina has seceded from the Union." This was like Patrick Henry's "Why stand we here idle?" It was the spark that touched off the magazine of applause.[1]

Yancey was a leading figure at the convention, but he was too impatient with "cooperationists" to assist the more conciliatory leaders of his faction in securing the unity of action the occasion demanded.[2] In the end the South took the uncompromising action he had so long advocated but turned to more moderate leaders in the crisis it precipitated. The achievement of his goal marks the decline of Yancey's influence. Jefferson Davis, who, instead of leading the secession movement, appears to have been carried along with it,[3] was elected president of the Confederacy. Yancey was sent on a futile diplomatic mission to Great Britain and served for a time in the Senate. Death on July 27, 1863, spared him from witnessing the final collapse of the Confederacy that he had done so much to found.

What shall we say of William Lowndes Yancey in final appraisal? Dodd calls him "the greatest orator of the South since Patrick Henry," and Rhodes terms him "the most eloquent orator of the South."[4] Foote declares, "In my judgment, the South has contained within her limits, no such eloquent and effective speaker as William L. Yancey, since the death of George A. McDuffie"; and Hilliard, Yancey's perennial opponent, terms him "the most powerful advocate of the Southern rights doctrine in the whole country."[5] But our study has provided no opportunity for comparison. Brown and Adams declare he was among the half dozen men

[1] Letter of Vines to Thomas M. Owen, Dec. 27, 1909, to be found in the Yancey Collection of the Alabama Department of Archives and History.

[2] See W. R. Smith, *The History and Debates of the Convention of the People of Alabama* (Montgomery, 1861).

[3] W. E. Dodd, *Statesmen of the Old South* (New York, 1911), pp. 219–220.

[4] W. E. Dodd, *The Cotton Kingdom* (New Haven, 1921), p. 145; J. F. Rhodes, *History of the United States* (New York, 1906), II, 447.

[5] Foote, *op. cit.*, p. 237; Hilliard, *op. cit.*, pp. 250–258.

William L. Yancey

who had most to do with shaping our destiny in the nineteenth century.[1] Perhaps this is putting his influence too strongly. His oratory played a leading part in winning a large number, but still a minority, of the people of the lower South to a no-compromise position, but it was only when more moderate leaders made common cause with him that a majority was attained. Let us be conservative and say that Yancey, through his power as a speaker, achieved a position of great influence in the critical period just preceding the Civil War. Let us emphasize the fact that this position was attained without the benefit of public office, without legislative hall or executive mansion as a sounding board. And then let us add that if the South had been victorious, tradition might have made him the Patrick Henry of the Confederacy.

SELECTED BIBLIOGRAPHY

Biography and Historical Background

John W. DuBose, *Life and Times of William Lowndes Yancey* (Montgomery, 1892), is the only biography. It is voluminous and obviously partisan but is valuable if carefully used. DuBose, who heard Yancey speak often, records his own firsthand impressions and quotes verbatim portions of many primary sources not easily found elsewhere. The private papers of Yancey used by DuBose are now at the Alabama State Department of Archives and History. They consist of several large scrapbooks, filled with personal and political data for the entire period of his life; several bound files of newspaper clippings, usually a summary of one of his speeches or an account of some political meeting; and a number of manuscript letters and political documents.

In addition to the standard general histories of the period, a number of secondary works are helpful with different aspects of the historical background. Many of these have been cited; see footnotes on pages 736, 738, 743, 746, 747, 748, and 749. A. C. Cole, *The Whig Party in the South* (Washington, D.C., 1913) should also be mentioned. Of the primary sources readily available, "*Correspondence of Robert Toombs, Alexander Stephens, and Howell Cobb*," U. B. Phillips, ed., *American Historical Association Report*, 1911, is valuable. Of the biographies of contemporaries the author has found A. Craven, *Edmund Ruffin, Southerner* (New York, 1932); L. A. White, *Robert Barnwell Rhett: Father of Secession* (New York, 1931); G. F. Milton, *The Eve of Conflict: Stephen A. Douglas and the Needless War* (New York, 1934); and U. B. Phillips, *Life of Robert Toombs* (New York, 1913) most helpful.

Yancey's Speaking

As has been indicated, many valuable primary sources will be found in the Yancey Papers. Numerous summaries of Yancey's speeches and comments concerning them are to be found in newspaper files, especially those of Alabama. A number of these have been cited; a more complete list, as well as verbatim quotations from a large number, will be found in the author's Doctoral dissertation, William Lowndes Yancey: Orator of Southern Constitutional Rights (Wisconsin, 1937). Murat Halstead, *Caucuses of 1860* (Columbus, 1860) contains all the reports of Halstead, correspondent of the *Cincinnati Commercial*, concerning the Charleston convention.

[1] Brown, *op. cit.*, pp. 146–152; J. T. Adams, *America's Tragedy* (New York, 1934), p. 126.

The sources for other contemporary reports—those of Lawler, DuBose, Richardson, Hilliard, Foote, Vines, and Smith—have been cited. See footnotes on pages 735, 740, 741, 742, and 748. Others of interest are *Memoirs of Colonel John S. Mosby* (Charles W. Russell, ed., Boston, 1917); James M. Stewart, My Recollections of William L. Yancey 1845–1863, manuscript at Alabama Department of Archives and History; W. Garrett, *Reminiscences of Public Men in Alabama* (Atlanta, 1872), p. 685; S. S. Scott, "Recollections of the Alabama State Convention of 1860," *Alabama Historical Society Transactions*, 4: 313–320; and W. R. Smith, *Reminiscences of a Long Life* (Washington, D.C., 1889). The *Congressional Globe*, of course, contains reports of all Yancey's speeches in the house, and W. R. Smith, *The History and the Debates of the Convention of the People of Alabama* (Montgomery, 1861) includes summaries of all speeches at the convention of 1861.

The best secondary accounts of Yancey's speaking are W. G. Brown, *The Lower South in American History* (New York, 1903); G. F. Mellen, "Henry Hilliard and William L. Yancey," *Sewanee Review*, 27: 32–50; and G. Petrie, "What Will Be the Final Estimate of Yancey?" *Alabama Historical Society Transactions*, 4: 307–312.

26

Charles Sumner

by R. ELAINE PAGEL and CARL DALLINGER

Born in Boston, January 6, 1811, Charles Sumner was educated in the Boston Public Latin School, Harvard College (class of 1830), and Harvard Law School (class of 1833). He was admitted to the bar in 1834 and set up practice in Boston. From December, 1837, to April, 1840, he was in Europe, visiting England, France, Italy, and Germany. Upon his return he contributed frequently to various legal publications. He first came to public attention as city orator of Boston, July 4, 1845, in a forthright speech against war, "The True Grandeur of Nations." Several other notable orations followed: the Phi Beta Kappa oration at Harvard, 1846, "The Scholar, the Jurist, the Artist, the Philanthropist"; "White Slavery in the Barbary States," before the Mercantile Library Association, 1847; "The War System in the Commonwealth of Nations," before the American Peace Society, 1849. He was elected to the United States Senate in 1851 and served until his death in 1874. There he became one of the outstanding advocates of the abolition of slavery, climaxing his career with an attack upon this institution in a speech in the Senate May 19 and 20, 1856, "The Crime Against Kansas." This attack, particularly that part directed at Senator Butler, of South Carolina, created such feeling that Sumner was assaulted and seriously injured by Preston Brooks, a Representative from South Carolina. He was not able to resume his seat in the Senate for 3 years, during which time he became by reputation the hero and martyr of the North and its cause. He served as chairman of the Senate Committee on Foreign Relations from 1861 to 1871; died March 11, 1874.

"I have now but one solicitude,—it is to print a revised edition of my speeches before I die. . . . These speeches are my life. . . . "[1] These words, written in 1869, were the testimony of a man who, 25 years earlier, had protested his aversion for public life. Yet the hundreds of speeches Charles Sumner delivered did become his *life*, and through them he made his impress upon American life.

Sumner moved suddenly into prominence upon the public platform at the time when "fifty-four forty or fight" was the current slogan in the Oregon dispute and when some of our leaders were urging the intervention of the United States in the Texas dispute. Although these tensions had

---

[1] Letter to S. G. Howe in 1869, published in Edward L. Pierce, *Memoir and Letters of Charles Sumner* (London, 1893), IV, 370.

arisen, in 1845 the nation was celebrating 30 years of uninterrupted peace. On July Fourth of that year the citizens of Boston had assembled at Tremont Temple to hold their seventy-fifth annual celebration, originally initiated to commemorate the Boston Massacre but changed in 1783 to an anniversary of the Declaration of Independence.[1] On that occasion, Sumner began his speaking career in an address that literally shocked fellow Bostonians. Part of his audience threatened to walk out during the speech, and at a banquet that followed he was bitterly criticized for some of his remarks.[2]

Ideology

In that first important address, "The True Grandeur of Nations," which had such a startling reception, Sumner made an uncompromising attack upon the war system. He championed this cause most strenuously during the first 5 years of his public life. After defining war as "*a public armed contest, between nations, in order to establish justice between them;* as for instance, to determine a disputed boundary line, or the title to a territory,"[3] he asserted, "*In our age, there can be no peace that is not honorable; there can be no war that is not dishonorable.*"[4] It was this stand that drew the storm of criticism. Then, after discussing what he labeled the "character of war," "the miseries it produces," "its insufficiency, as a mode of determining justice," and the "prejudices by which war is sustained," he suggested a Congress of Nations or Arbitration as substitutes for war and concluded that true grandeur "*is in the moral elevation, sustained, enlightened, and decorated by the intellect of man.*"[5]

The "War System of the Commonwealth of Nations," Sumner's address before the American Peace Society, in Park Street Church, Boston, May 28, 1849, gives the most complete development of his ideas on war and peace. In this speech he advocated more definitely than in "The True Grandeur of Nations" the adoption of a Congress of Nations with a "High Court of Judicature" as the "most complete and permanent substitute" for war, with a secondary suggestion of a system of arbitration by formal treaties between two or more nations.[6] He made no allowance for the use of any type of force to enforce the decisions of the Congress of Nations or to maintain the system of arbitration. In other words, as compared to

---

[1] *Ibid.* (Boston, 1877), II, 338.
[2] Letter from Adjutant General Henry K. Oliver to Pierce, *ibid.*, pp. 345–346.
[3] Charles Sumner, *The True Grandeur of Nations* (Boston, 1845), p. 7.
[4] *Ibid.*, p. 4.
[5] Charles Sumner, *Works* (Boston, 1870), I, 124.
[6] *Ibid.* (1872), II, 262–263.

the League of Nations of 1919, Sumner's suggestions did not include even the use of sanctions against miscreant nations.

He was not a complete pacifist, however, admitting the right of self-defense in the most extreme circumstances. The weight of his argument was thrown toward the elimination of the war system, which, if accomplished, he maintained would automatically eliminate the question of self-defense. Sumner believed that since war was included in the law of nations, it was therefore approved by the nations. In his opinion the principal objective to be accomplished was to have war as an arbiter eliminated from the law of nations. This could be accomplished by arousing the "public will." The means by which Sumner would arouse the public will was to educate people to the true character of war, its cruelties and inadequacies. Thus he held that the practical thing to be accomplished was to secure the comprehension of the true character of war.[1]

Although he made no definite predictions, Sumner believed that the world-wide abolition of war and the establishment of permanent peace could be accomplished soon. He spoke at length of signs that augured the overthrow of the war system, thus giving the impression, if not the assurance, that war was rapidly becoming a thing of the past.[2] Offering no hint as to whether he was speaking in terms of years or centuries, he predicted to his brother that "this cause [peace] is destined to triumph much earlier than many imagine."[3] In this prophecy he was at least naïve.

The hope of universal peace had been alive for centuries. Sumner first crystallized his convictions on the subject soon after leaving college, when he heard an address by William Ladd.[4] Many of his ideas were borrowed from Noah Worcester and William Ellery Channing, who, as founders and active members of the American Peace Society, were also ardent advocates of peace.[5] The inspiration for the creation of a congress of nations came mainly from Abbé Saint-Pierre and William Ladd, according to Sumner's own testimony.[6] For the ideology in his speeches on peace, therefore, Sumner merits no distinction for originality, and in his predictions of the imminent abolition of the war system he proved himself to be a poor prophet.

In 1845 the dynamic question in the public mind was not peace but slavery. The issue, supposedly closed in 1820 by the Missouri Compromise, was being reopened by the prospect of acquiring new slave territory in

[1] *Ibid.*, II, 261–262.
[2] *Ibid.*, pp. 223–258; also, I, 111–116.
[3] Letter to George Sumner, July 17, 1849, in Pierce, *op. cit.*, III, 44.
[4] Charles Sumner, *Addresses on War* (Boston, 1902), p. xv.
[5] Sumner, *Works*, I, 293–297; II, 247–248.
[6] *Ibid.*, II, 235–237, 264.

Texas. Soon the issue took first place in Sumner's thoughts. The importance it assumed in his thinking is indicated by the hopes that stimulated him to make a final revised edition of all his speeches: "As a connected series they will illustrate the progress of the great battle with slavery, and what I have done in it."[1]

Stimulated by the antislavery sympathies of William Ellery Channing, Sumner became a radical abolitionist even when Abolitionism was unpopular in Massachusetts. He opposed the annexation of Texas and vigorously denounced the Mexican war because, as he asserted, they were designed "to extend and strengthen Slavery. . . . "[2] Not only did he contend that slavery was inconsistent with the Declaration of Independence and the Constitution but that, under the Constitution, Congress had the power to legislate slavery out of existence.[3] He particularly decried the fact that the "Slave Oligarchy" determined the national policy by contriving to maintain its power in Congress through the extension of slave territory, in spite of the fact that the South contained a minority of the population. He urged upon the North the practicability of overthrowing this Congressional power of the South as a means of abolishing slavery by legislative acts.[4]

The intensity of Sumner's antislavery feeling is revealed by the fact that he joined those who denounced Daniel Webster with betraying Massachusetts in supporting the Compromise of 1850. When charged with failing to keep his oath to uphold the Constitution by rebelling against the Fugitive Slave Act, Sumner replied that he had sworn to uphold the Constitution as he saw it, not as the South interpreted it.[5]

Sumner's most scathing philippic against slavery, "The Crime Against Kansas," is part of the debate in the Senate upon a bill introduced by Seward for the admission of Kansas into the Union. There had been frequent clashes between slavery and antislavery interests in Kansas, and on May 19 and 20, 1856, Sumner denounced the South for its "latest outrage upon freedom." His principal argument was that the crimes committed against the people in the Territory of Kansas by the slavery interests were in violation of the Constitution, especially the Bill of Rights, against nature itself, and against the Missouri Compromise, which was supposed to guarantee forever freedom in the remaining Louisiana Territory north of 36' 30". Even the right of Popular Sovereignty had been violated, he asserted. This, in his opinion, represented an attempt on the part of the

---

[1] Pierce, *op. cit.*, IV, 370.
[2] Sumner, *Works*, I, 152; 317–329; 333–351.
[3] *Ibid.*, pp. 309–313.
[4] *Ibid.*, IV, 42–48.
[5] Pierce, *op. cit.*, III, 381–386.

South to impose slavery upon the entire nation and constituted a threat to our constitutional government itself. The solution to the problem, as Sumner saw it, was the immediate admission of Kansas as a free state, as provided by Seward's bill.[1]

After the election of Lincoln, when attempts at compromises were made in an effort to prevent a complete rupture between the two sections of the country, Sumner continued adamant toward slavery, urging the North to remain "firm."[2] He was impatient in demanding immediate, not gradual, emancipation and the arming of Negroes, maintaining that these two policies were essential to the successful prosecution of the war because of the demoralizing effect that they would have on the South and the opposite effect that they would have in the North, because of the improved foreign relations that he believed would result, particularly with England, and because of an unwavering conviction that slavery should be abolished as soon as possible.[3]

Sumner's attitude toward Reconstruction was based upon the principle that the states participating in the rebellion had committed "state suicide," thereby reverting to the status of territories and thus putting their reconstruction under the power of Congress, not in the hands of the President.[4] The two particular conditions that Sumner wished to impose upon the seceded states as conditions for their reincorporation into the Union were complete emancipation and impartial suffrage. On these two points he was unequivocating.

It is apparent that Sumner was uncompromising rather than original in his ideas on slavery. In his attitude toward slavery as well as toward war he had been influenced greatly by William Ellery Channing. The slavery debate was thirty years old when Sumner took his seat in the Senate. But where Lincoln was patient Sumner was impatient. Where Lincoln appeased Sumner demanded. And history questions the wisdom of this severe policy of Reconstruction which finally prevailed, for it produced more chaos and vindictiveness than amelioration and rebuilding in the South.[5] In this struggle Sumner was a champion more of the Negro than of the Union. He was guided by one goal, complete Abolition.

The question might be asked: How did Sumner reconcile his attitude toward war with his support of the Civil War? We should imagine that one who had declared that " . . . *there can be no peace that is not honorable; there can be no war that is not dishonorable*" would have followed a policy of

[1] Sumner, *Works*, IV, 127–256.
[2] Pierce, *op. cit.*, IV, 9, 16, 64.
[3] Sumner, *Works*, VI, 64; VII, 191–236, 262–265, 266–277.
[4] *Ibid.*, VI, 301–318, 397; VII, 14.
[5] J. S. Bassett, *A Short History of the United States* (New York, 1937), pp. 619–638.

compromise and appeasement with the South to prevent an outbreak. In the last analysis Sumner did not reconcile these two points of view. His idealism on war retracted before his dogmatism on slavery, and he was forced to justify a war for Abolition.[1] It was unfortunate that he lived in a time when the two humanitarian causes that he espoused had to conflict.

Structure and Arrangement of Ideas

This insight into Sumner's ideas and convictions invites the inquiry: How did he present his ideas in attempting to implant these same convictions in his audiences? Unfortunately, in answering this question, we are hampered by unreliable texts of a number of his speeches. For example, a study of the various available texts of "The True Grandeur of Nations" reveals extensive and important inconsistencies in both style and content. The changes in style are extensive enough to result in a reduction of those elements which adapt the speech to the audience. Even the original manuscript, as it now stands, appears to be a revision prepared for the first printer of the address, about which Sumner makes the following admission: "I now place at your disposal a copy of the Oration, much of which was necessarily omitted in the delivery, on account of its length."[2] Further evidence is available on this and other speeches showing that they are not thoroughly trustworthy records of what he actually said at the time they were delivered. We must keep in mind, therefore, that our judgments concerning Sumner's skill as a speaker are based upon texts of questionable validity.

The disposition of Sumner's ideas is best described by the arrangement of *exordium*, *narration*, *partition*, *proof*, *refutation*, and *peroration*. The main point of deviation from this plan of organization is found in his use of refutation. In the "War System of the Commonwealth of Nations," what refutation there is appears between the narration and partition, where he replies to the critics of the peace cause.[3] A different arrangement of rebuttal materials is displayed in "Crime Against Kansas," where, between the partition and proof, Sumner digresses to respond to his opponents, Senator Butler of South Carolina and Senator Douglas of Illinois, and then returns to his direct attack upon these two adversaries after the recapitulation at the end of his main argument.[4] But for the exception of his use of refutation, Sumner's principal addresses follow the outline described above.

[1] Letter to Duchess of Argyll, in Pierce, *op. cit.* IV, 134.
[2] Sumner, *The True Grandeur of Nations*, Introduction, letter to T. A. Davis.
[3] Sumner, *Works*, II, 181–186.
[4] *Ibid.*, IV, 144–151, 239–244.

One of the most distinctive characteristics of his speeches is the partition. It appears with but one exception[1] in all of his best known efforts. Just before launching into his proof he sets up in numerical form the main points to be developed in the body of the speech. "Crime Against Kansas" provides a typical example where we find: "My task will be divided under three different heads: *first*, THE CRIME AGAINST KANSAS, in its origin and extent; *secondly*, THE APOLOGIES FOR THE CRIME; and *thirdly*, THE TRUE REMEDY."[2] With similar explicitness, although frequently with greater detail, he sets forth the partition in his other addresses.

Almost equally unique is the recapitulation that Sumner incorporated with considerable consistency at the end of his body of proof. This is of special interest because of the peculiar treatment he gives it. Modern speech principles teach us that summarization is one method of developing a conclusion. However, evidence seems to indicate that he considered the summary a separate unit of the speech distinct from the proof and peroration. This factor can best be observed in "Crime Against Kansas."[3]

We are given some insight into Sumner's own opinions concerning the disposition of the body of the speech. Just before presenting the *partition* in his address entitled "Our Foreign Relations," he says, "There is always a natural order in unfolding a subject. . . . "[4] Again, in "The Crime Against Kansas," he considers that to expose the crime against Kansas is "logically . . . the beginning of the argument" and later in the speech that the "Remedies four-fold . . . range themselves in natural order."[5] Sumner does not define his term *natural order*, but it implies either a logical development or some form of chronological development. An examination of his speeches verifies this interpretation. In all his outstanding addresses he follows one of these two types of development in the general structure of the proof, excluding what is familiarly known as a *topical* or *selective* arrangement.

As one would imagine, the following of a "natural order" resulted most frequently in a logical disposition of the main argument. Notable examples at this point are his two outstanding peace orations, "The True Grandeur of Nations," in which he develops his argument by showing "*first*, the character of war, *secondly*, the miseries it produces, . . . *thirdly*, its utter and pitiful insufficiency, as a mode of determining justice, . . . *fourthly*, . . . the various prejudices by which it is sustained. . . . "[6]

[1] "White Slavery in the Barbary States," *ibid.*, I, 386.
[2] *Ibid.*, IV, 144.
[3] *Ibid.*, pp. 236–237.
[4] *Ibid.*, VII, 334.
[5] *Ibid.*, IV, 151, 208.
[6] *Ibid.*, I, 17.

and the "War System of the Commonwealth of Nations," in which he first unfolds "the true character of War and the War System . . . " and, second, "the means by which this system can be overthrown."[1] In this relationship we have already referred to "The Crime Against Kansas" and "Our Foreign Relations." Additional illustrations could be drawn from "Fame and Glory" and "White Slavery in the Barbary States," which extends the list of those speeches following a logical pattern of development to a majority of his best efforts.

The outstanding example of his use of a chronological outline is "The Scholar, the Jurist, the Artist, the Philanthropist." It is particularly interesting because, governing himself by the dates on which the four men died, he reverses " . . . the order in which they left us . . . " taking the last first.[2] In doing so, Sumner was probably not so much interested in maintaining a time sequence as he was in propounding his pet ideas. Thus a eulogy of the "Philanthropist," William Ellery Channing, was a convenient climax to the speech, because it provided him with the best opportunity to impress upon his audience his views on war and slavery.[3]

Sumner also uses a chronological arrangement extensively in marshaling his evidence. Because he uses so much historical material he finds it convenient to follow a time sequence in presenting his examples and illustrations. Thus, in following a "natural order," Sumner develops his speeches in a logical form in a majority of instances, with a secondary preference for a chronological scheme.

He seemed to be weakest in the development of his conclusions. Apparently he had a failing for talking overtime and then extending his peroration by introducing a point that he could not seem to forbear discussing.[4] At the present time he would be criticized for introducing new material in his conclusion. Even in the absence of this defect some of his endings seem burdensome in length.

Seldom may a speaker be criticized for having his speeches too well outlined, yet Sumner may be arraigned justly on this point. He seems to have overdone the suggestion of his former teacher in "having his points fixed and always visible, his statements almost laboriously distinct. . . . "[5] A detailed enumeration of his main points in the partition rigidly adhered to in the proof, which, in turn, is followed by a detailed recapitulation, contributes to a "blockiness" in the total pattern of his speeches. The skeleton shows, destroying the artistic smoothness so desirable in an ora-

[1] *Ibid.*, II, 185–186.
[2] *Ibid.*, I, 249.
[3] *Ibid.*, pp. 249, 289–298.
[4] *Ibid.*, II, 272.
[5] E. T. Channing, *Lectures on Rhetoric and Oratory*, (Boston, 1856), p. 71.

tion. It was this fact which prompted Cassius M. Clay to make the following comment about "The Crime Against Kansas": "Perhaps the only drawback . . . is the studied arrangement of your speech, which, although assisting the memory in the public mind, savors too much of the pulpit, and 'smells too much of the lamp.'"[1] Thus we may conclude that Sumner displays a little too much fastidiousness in framing his ideas for his audiences.

Methods of Proof

Naturally our interest next turns to the arguments Sumner employed in these carefully organized speeches. What were his tools of persuasion? Aristotle says there are three types of proof among the means of persuasion: *ethical, pathetic,* and *logical.* Using this classification, we shall direct our analysis, first, to Sumner's use of ethical proof.

Ethical Proof. In those forces of persuasion arising out of and resulting from the man himself, Sumner presents a picture of contrasts. In certain intrinsic qualities of manhood he possessed great appeal. Chief among these was high moral character. From the beginning to the end of his career Charles Sumner was known as a man whose word could be neither bought nor sold. His character was unimpeachable. Even his enemies testified to his forthrightness and integrity. In addition, he possessed those physical characteristics which increase a speaker's attractiveness. He was a large, handsome man, standing over six feet in height, described as one "whom you would notice amongst other men. . . . "[2] Character and physique were leading factors in Sumner's personal appeal.

Two events also served to increase materially the force of his ethical proof. The first was his sojourn abroad from December, 1837, to April, 1840, during which time he achieved considerable fame for his success in English social and political life. The friendships he cultivated with all the leaders in England gave him great prestige in this country. The second event was the famous assault upon Sumner by Preston Brooks in the Senate chamber May 22, 1856. This attempt upon his life by slave interests raised Sumner to the rank of a martyr in the eyes of the North, with the result that a romantic or heroic appeal enhanced his later speeches. These two experiences increased his influence as an individual upon his audiences.

Unhappily, in that other area of ethical argument, namely, that which the speaker invents, Sumner was particularly weak. One of his closest friends confessed: "he was sometimes so earnest and persistent in what was regarded as extreme views as seriously to annoy his friends."[3] This

[1] Letter from Cassius M. Clay to Sumner, in Sumner, *Works,* IV, 133.
[2] Description by E. R. Hoar, Pierce, *op. cit.,* IV, 85ff.
[3] Letter from Peleg Chandler to Pierce, *ibid.,* II, 254.

characteristic is illustrated in his first important address, "The True Grandeur of Nations." The occasion was a celebration of the Declaration of Independence, featured by a military parade from the courthouse to Tremont Temple, where the day was climaxed by an oration, in this instance, "The True Grandeur of Nations." To this patriotic, Bostonian audience, proud of the sacrifices that their fathers had made at Bunker Hill, a large section of which was composed of men dressed in uniform, Sumner bluntly declared: "*In our age, there can be no peace that is not honorable; there can be no war that is not dishonorable.*"[1] Later he denounced soldiers as "lazy consumers of the fruits of earth who might do the state good service in the various departments of useful industry."[2] Such an attack upon the respected members of his audience enrolled in national defense was as needless as it was undiplomatic. And when, a few moments later, he compared the militia to galley slaves in the streets of Pisa, "who are compelled to wear dresses stamped with the name of the crime for which they are suffering punishment . . . "[3] the soldiers in the audience threatened to walk out in a body and were deterred only by the good graces of their commander.

Another example is "The Crime Against Kansas." Although political tension was high at the time and men took offense easily, much of the cause for the assault upon Sumner, which resulted from this speech, may be traced to this same type of untempered invective. The comparison of Senator Butler to Don Quixote and his harlot is not only embarrassing but insulting.[4]

If paragraphs could be found that would partially counterbalance the effect of the contempt expressed in the sections referred to above, we could perhaps be less critical of Sumner's use of ethical proof. It does not seem that he intended to be malicious. The sincerity and high moral tone of his speeches are admirable. The very boldness of Sumner's stand appealed to large groups of his listeners. But he seemed to rely almost solely upon his personal integrity to establish his own character as a speaker with his audiences. His speeches do not demonstrate a sufficient sensitiveness to audience reactions to credit him with an effective use of ethical appeal.

Pathetic Proof. If Sumner did not possess the skill of winning the friendship of his audience he did understand the value of emotional appeals in persuasive speaking. Basing his speeches upon moral foundations, through the power of language and direct pathetic appeals, he runs the

[1] Sumner, *The True Grandeur of Nations*, p. 4.
[2] *Ibid.*, p. 60.
[3] *Ibid.*, p. 63.
[4] Sumner, *Works*, IV, 143–151.

gamut of emotions that impel men to action. Writing to John Bright, Sumner said: "I am always sure, if my feet are planted on a moral principle, that I cannot be permanently defeated,—such is the providence of God; and I am sure that those whose feet are not planted on a moral principle cannot stand permanently."[1] Here lies the strength of his speeches. The main currents running through all his attacks upon war are that war is utterly insufficient as a mode of determining *justice*, that by its very character it degrades man and produces untold misery (an appeal to *self-preservation* and *humanity*), that war is an extravagant waste of *wealth*, that war is completely incompatible with *national honor*, and that "*The True Grandeur of Humanity is in moral elevation, sustained, enlightened and decorated by the intellect of man.*"[2] In "The Crime Against Kansas" the opening sentence directs the entire speech toward an appeal to *justice* by calling upon the Senate to "redress a great wrong."[3] Likewise, the virtues of *knowledge, justice, beauty,* and *love* are the motivating factors in "The Scholar, the Jurist, the Artist, the Philanthropist."[4] Were we to draw illustrations from Sumner's other orations we should observe the same characteristics. It was this quality in Sumner which won for him the title "the great reformer."

Not only in the moral undergirding of his ideas but in his very use of language he seeks an emotional effect. He designs each sentence with a view to its emotional as well as its intellectual appeal. This is revealed in his frequent use of strong adjectives. The crowning example of this practice is found in "The Crime Against Kansas," where he labels the apologies for the crime as the "*Apology tyrannical,*" the "*Apology imbecile,*" the "*Apology infamous,*" and the proposed remedies for the crime as "*the Remedy of Tyranny,*" "*the Remedy of Folly,*" "*the Remedy of Injustice and Civil War,*" and "*the Remedy of Justice and Peace.*"[5] Obviously these epithets have more than descriptive implications. Sumner's attention to the motivative value of language can be observed throughout all his speeches and is also evidenced in the fact that most of the textual inconsistencies in his speeches result from word substitutions.

As one might expect, two parts of Sumner's orations are more specifically devoted to pathetic appeals than others, the exordium and the peroration. He followed not only the Ciceronian pattern but also the classical uses for these several parts of a speech. Since, as we have already observed, he used very little direct ethical proof, this left the exordium and peroration

---

[1] Letter from Sumner to John Bright, in Pierce, *op. cit.*, IV, 146.
[2] Sumner, *Works*, I, 124.
[3] *Ibid.*, IV, 137.
[4] *Ibid.*, I, 248.
[5] *Ibid.*, IV, 185, 208.

almost entirely open to pathetic appeal. The way is further cleared in the peroration by Sumner's unique treatment of the summary as a separate unit of the speech. So we find the introductions and conclusions of these addresses charged with "impelling motives."

A rather obvious criticism of Sumner's use of pathetic proof is his lack of subtlety. In the main the appeals are obvious and direct. Through the use of exaggerated style in presenting his illustrations it frequently becomes apparent that he is working for an effect. But the lofty appeals to duty, beneficence, justice, freedom, and Christianity won for Sumner, if not acceptance, at least respect. And the variety of appeals he used not only evidence how much he relied on them for persuasion but also convince us that they are the main strength of his power.

Logical Proof. The variety that Sumner displayed in his use of pathetic proof does not carry over into the logical arguments he employs. An early habit he developed of retreating to the world of books for the support of his ideas manifests itself in his orations. William Story, who knew Sumner intimately for many years, observed: "When he could steady himself against a statement by an ancient author he felt strong. His own moral sense, which was very high, seemed to buttress itself with a passage from Cicero or Epictetus. He seemed to build upon them as upon a rock, and thence defy you to shake him."[1] Thus we find arguments from authority, illustration, specific example, and statistics predominating among the types used.

A typical illustration of the type of argument Sumner employs is found in "The True Grandeur of Nations," where he develops his first main point. He begins: "First, as to the essential character and root of war, or that part of our nature whence it proceeds. Listen to the voice from the ancient poet. . . . "[2] and then follows a series of illustrations and quotations from ancient authors. These, in turn, are followed by "similar illustrations" from "early fields of modern literature."[3] The result is more of a literary and historical exposé than a closely knit chain of reasoning. In all his attacks upon war, not once does Sumner mention the Revolutionary War. He does attack the Mexican War and alludes to the War of 1812. But most of the time he remains safely within the confines of history and literature. In this connection it is interesting to note that Sumner referred to his arguments in some of his speeches as expositions.[4] The same scholarly approach is maintained in most of the arguments in most of his speeches.

[1] Letter from William Story to Pierce, in Pierce, *op. cit.*, I, 106.
[2] Sumner, *Works*, I, 18.
[3] *Ibid.*, pp. 19–20.
[4] *Ibid.*, II, 215, 259.

In some of his speeches on slavery we find some relief from this classical erudition. For example, in "The Crime Against Kansas" the very nature of the subject forced him to draw upon contemporary events and documents for evidence. This Sumner does with great thoroughness and thus builds his most convincing arguments. Even so, these arguments are frequently embellished with literary and classical allusions.

As can be readily seen, the general form of argument that Sumner used was the inductive process, and in this he showed most strength. He felt that if he could build up a preponderance of authorities and examples his conclusions would be inevitable. Both in the development of the main points of his argument and in his attempt to establish his main proposition, Sumner put his trust in inductive reasoning.

There are several notable weaknesses in Sumner's logical proof. One occurs in "The True Grandeur of Nations." Since the oration is an invective against war, the definition of war by which he sets the limits of the institution he is attacking is of primary importance. At this point some of his audience disagreed with him, and thus his argument was weakened at its foundation, the definition of terms.

An attempt at deductive reasoning betrays another weak argument in Sumner's attack upon war. He reasoned that since war is carried on against public property and military objectives, to remove these objectives (forts, navy yards, and arsenals) would lessen the chances of war.[1] The error here is in the assumption that it is the arsenals that provoke war. Obviously a nation lays itself open to attack by being weak as well as by being strong. This example illustrates Sumner's weakness in handling deductive causal relationships. He was inclined to warp his reasoning to suit the conclusion he desired.

Thus we see that Sumner is more of a scholar than a logician, buttressing his arguments principally from the world of books. His wealth of illustrative material seemed to dictate his method of argument more than his argument dictated his use of examples. Relying upon inductive reasoning, his logical proof became most effective when he drew his evidence from contemporary affairs rather than from the classics.

Style

To complete our analysis of Sumner's speaking practices, as revealed in the speeches themselves, we turn our attention now to his style. What language skills did he display in composing these carefully ordered ideas on war and slavery?

We modern believers in the conversational mode of speaking would have criticized Sumner severely for his studied, flamboyant style. He does

---

[1] *Ibid.*, I, 90.

not use the language of conversation but rather a type of expression that would have been more at home in the days of Cicero and Quintilian than in contemporary life. Here again we see the influence of Sumner's scholarly leaning. He loved the classics, and he spoke in the language of the classics. A typical passage from his speeches is found in the opening sentence of the "War System of the Commonwealth of Nations": "We are assembled in what may be called the Holy Week of our community, not occupied by pomps of a complex ceremonial, swelling in tides of music, beneath time honored arches, but set apart, with the unadorned simplicity of early custom, to anniversary meetings of those charitable and religious associations from whose good works our country derives such true honor."[1] If the source was not known, the style might lead us to mistake this for an excerpt from some Greek or Roman orator.

Not only in word choice but in sentence structure the elements of directness are lacking. In the majority of instances Sumner's sentences are long and involved. Complex and compound sentences abound to the extent that we may safely say that his speeches possess more of a written than of a spoken style. This perhaps is a result of Sumner's habit of writing out and memorizing his speeches before delivering them.[2] The result was that they had lost the quality of spontaneous utterance. When his critics could find no other point of attack they would malign him for his "vapid rhetoric." And we may legitimately criticize him for not keeping his style subordinate to his ideas, frequently letting it become so evident as to call attention to itself.

Among the special stylistic devices, Sumner seemed to display his favoritism for two. One, undoubtedly the result of his love of books, was the use of allusions. These were drawn particularly from the Bible, the Greek and Roman classics, and European history. Sometimes he did not confine them to the status of allusions but invoked them as authorities.

The second device, in which Sumner displayed his greatest skill, was in his use of epithets. He displayed his greatest adeptness in name calling in "The Crime Against Kansas."[3] But his insistence in referring to war as a *system* and the frequent use of the terms *slave-mongers* and *slave oligarchy* are further illustrations of this factor in his speeches.

Quite prominent also is his use of direct quotation. Frequently these are in Latin, which again shows the influence of Sumner's scholarship. He runs the gamut of authors, well known and obscure, displaying the wide range of his reading for which he was so well known.

[1] *Ibid.*, II, 177.
[2] G. W. Haynes, *Charles Sumner* (Philadelphia, 1909), p. 386.
[3] See p. 761.

The general picture one receives of Sumner's speeches is best described in his own words, when he wrote to Theodore Parker concerning "The Crime Against Kansas": "I shall pronounce the most thorough philippic ever uttered in a legislative body"[1] or in his letter to Agassiz, where he referred to one of his speeches as a *disquisition*.[2]

Physical Aspects

Physically Sumner was attractive, 6 feet 4 inches tall, powerfully built. Until the time of the Brooks assault, his strong health and athletic habits kept him "the impersonation of manly beauty and power . . . ,"[3] so that, as one senatorial associate remarked, "He was a man of such mark in his mere exterior as to arrest at once the attention of a stranger and make him a chief among ten thousand."[4]

Sumner had, besides, a finely cut face, which some even called handsome, and an additional quality, constantly remarked upon by his contemporaries, which they termed a *commanding presence*. Evidently this was his manner—somewhat aloof and a trifle haughty—which seemed to give him the appearance of one of importance. Such qualities combined made the man quite an imposing figure. His appearance alone, says Higginson, "marked him as a leader and ruler among men. . . . "[5]

Likewise was Sumner's voice of a type that added force to the words he uttered. It was clear and powerful enough to be heard distinctly yet of sufficient flexibility to allow changes in quality and tone. There is evidence that Sumner used his voice effectively, both to retain the interest of an audience through a long speech and to enforce the ideas he was presenting.

Very little has been written about Sumner's gestures and movements as such, but almost every commentator remarks upon the fervor and vigor of his delivery. Evidently this was the quality that most impressed his listeners. Naturally of a strong and strenuous nature in the way he applied himself to any task he felt worth doing, Sumner spoke in the same manner. When aroused by the occasion and the subject, he became fiercely vehement.[6] His movements, though generally graceful, followed no rules save that of power, the most frequent gesture being that of swinging an arm over his head.

[1] Letter to Theodore Parker, in Pierce, *op. cit.*, III, 439.
[2] *Ibid.*, IV, 327.
[3] *Ibid.*, II, 342.
[4] D. D. Pratt, quoted in *ibid.*, IV, 85.
[5] Thomas Wentworth Higginson, *Contemporaries* (Boston, 1899), p. 284.
[6] Justin McCarthy, *Reminiscences* (New York, 1899), I, 215.

Such strenuous delivery may even have overcome some of the deficiencies apparent to those who read Sumner's speeches. One contemporary remarks that his "long chains of rhetoric, of accumulated facts, of erudite illustration, . . . might have been cumbrous and tedious had they not been sustained by vigor such as his."[1] Henry Ward Beecher has remarked that he commanded rather than persuaded his audience,[2] which impression is probably due in part to the force with which Sumner presented his ideas to his listeners.

The picture is therefore drawn of a man of such striking appearance, both in physique and manner, as to draw attention to himself even in a crowd, speaking in a clear and flexible voice, with such fervor and vigor as to hold the attention of a large audience through a somewhat cumbrous speech lasting several hours. This was Charles Sumner in his prime.

This vigorous delivery was applied to speeches that had been carefully written and generally were fully enough in Sumner's mind to enable him to deliver them practically from memory. It was this aspect of his speaking which drew the following caustic criticism from Stephen A. Douglas regarding "The Crime Against Kansas": "the Senator from Massachusetts had his speech written, printed, committed to memory, practiced every night before a glass, with a negro boy to hold the candle and watch the gestures. . . . "[3] It must be remembered that Sumner had delivered a scathing denunciation of Douglas in this speech, which undoubtedly stimulated Douglas to reply in equal terms. But Ralph Waldo Emerson, Richard Henry Dana, and others friendly to Sumner testify that it was his habit to write out his speeches preparatory to their delivery.[4]

After the Brooks assault the picture of Sumner speaking must be retouched. Physically, he was weakened, and his ardour, except on rare occasions, was gone. Even his voice lacked the strength it once had. In a tone of regret, Sumner admitted his power to master his manuscript was weakening when he wrote to Dr. Lieber, after his address of September 10, 1863, on "Our Foreign Relations": "I had intended to speak without notes; but I found my brain, exhausted perhaps by labor, did not grapple with the text, so I read for the first time before such an audience."[5]

But Sumner had already built his reputation upon his earlier speeches, and perhaps his listeners still saw the powerful orator they had once heard. If not, it may be that the "martyrdom" Sumner had suffered now served

[1] Higginson, *op. cit.*, p. 287.
[2] Henry Ward Beecher, *Lectures and Orations* (New York, 1913), pp. 16–17.
[3] Sumner, *Works*, IV, 250.
[4] *Ibid.*, pp. 299, 317, 319; also, Anna Laurens Dawes, *Charles Sumner* (New York, 1898), p. 128; also, Pierce, *op. cit.*, III, 442.
[5] Pierce, *op. cit.*, IV, 166.

as the device for gaining respectful attention in place of the powerful delivery he had previously been able to employ.

At any rate, Sumner, in his important speaking days, must be remembered as strong and imposing in appearance, powerful and controlled of voice, and strenuous in manner.

Impression on Immediate Audience

Without discovering what his audiences thought of Sumner's speaking ability, a clear picture of his effectiveness would be impossible. But the answer to such a question is somewhat hard to ferret out of the available writings. Almost any contemporary writer was bound to be influenced by several less objective factors—the general public opinion about the ideas touched upon; the writer's own feelings concerning the subject of the speech; and to or for whom he was writing his observations. Impressions of the speaker's ability are particularly likely to be colored when he speaks upon such deeply controversial subjects as those on which Sumner spoke. That the picture of contemporary opinion of Sumner as a speaker is built from scanty and questionable material should therefore be remembered, even though an effort to weigh sources against each other has been made.

It is evident first of all that Sumner's speaking soon began quite consistently to draw large audiences. When it was known that he was to speak, the Senate Chamber was usually well filled, sometimes even the anterooms being packed. This fact in itself seems to indicate popular appreciation of the speaker beyond interest in the subjects that called forth his addresses.

The written opinions of the listeners as to the ability of the speaker naturally vary as does the quality of the speeches. It does appear, though, that in general the audience felt, when listening to the speeches recognized today as among Sumner's best, that they were hearing a man of unusual ability. Their comments seem to fall into two general categories: that he was "eloquent" and that he was courageous.

The conception of Sumner's "eloquence" was early established. Even on his first appearance as a public orator, the newspapers, although many of them questioned either his stand or his wisdom in taking it, generally recognized the "eloquence and power" of the oration.

After "The Scholar, the Jurist, the Artist, the Philanthropist," the impression of Sumner's ability grew. Edward Everett told Felton that he had never heard the speech surpassed and that he didn't know that he had "ever heard it equalled."[1] Longfellow wrote in his journal concerning the same address, mentioning its "ease and elegance" and saying that it was

---

[1] Quoted in *ibid.*, III, 20.

"from beginning to end triumphant."[1] Edward Everett Hale wrote to Sumner that he had entirely "commanded and swayed your audience."[2]

Even after "The Crime Against Kansas," which aroused all sorts of censure, as well as praise, of the man and his ideas, his reputation for eloquence evidently was unshaken. The Northern newspapers, in general, highly applauded Sumner's superior exhibition of speaking, even while many correspondents assailed him for being so outspoken on so threatening a subject, while the Southern papers, though violently flaying his ideas, had little to say in criticism of the quality of their presentation.

The second general opinion concerning Sumner was that he was a speaker of courage. Very few men, indeed, had the boldness to speak out as Sumner did about slavery and militarism. Even though some may have thought such outspokenness a long-lacking necessity, as Henry Ward Beecher expressed it,[3] while others believed it harmful to the cause for which it was aimed, all recognized that Sumner possessed it.

Thus it appears that the people of Sumner's day, recognizing him essentially as a speaker of "eloquence" and courage, flocked to hear him, from either admiration or curiosity. If Sumner himself had been asked, probably he would have said that the controversy that his speeches aroused among his contemporaries was in itself an indication of the power of his speaking. The compliments, he felt, showed that he was efficiently representing the lovers of liberty and justice, while the calumnies proved "that his blows . . . were telling . . . against the enemies of freedom and right."[4]

At least, if the amount of controversy aroused by a speaker does indicate the greatness of his influence, then Sumner could certainly be said to have had great effect upon his immediate audience.

Speech Training and Education

Because of the rather unusual way in which Sumner entered upon his speaking career, his training and preparation perhaps deserve more attention than would that of some others. For Sumner almost became a speaker overnight, it seemed. Although recognized as a young man of intellectual ability and a certain proficiency at law, he was almost completely unknown as a speaker on July 3, 1846. But on July 4, even those who violently disagreed with him were forced to admit that here was a man of unusual speaking ability.

[1] Quoted in *ibid.*, p. 17.
[2] Quoted in *ibid.*, p. 18.
[3] Quoted in the *National Anti-Slavery Standard* (New York), May 31, 1856, p. 3.
[4] Edwin Percy Whipple, *Recollections of Eminent Men* (Boston, 1896), p. 205.

One does not simply "open his mouth and speak" in such a fashion. Training and education, even though possibly not planned for that end, must combine with what innate abilities the man may have to enable him to make such a maiden speech as "The True Grandeur of Nations." Sumner's first 33 years should be examined, therefore, to find the important factors influencing his development and to determine how each may have contributed to the formation of the orator.

The Sumners could not be called a *speaking family*, even though some of them had made occasional speeches. So all thought of this orator having been "born," in the sense that Pitt the younger "inherited" his speaking career, is dispelled. Nevertheless, Charles Pinckney Sumner, the father, must be given at least indirect credit for part of his son's accomplishments.

The elder Sumner, who was comparatively well educated and, by occupation, was a county sheriff most of his life, had an unusual devotion to studies and research. He loved books and read many of them. History, in particular, was intriguing to him, and besides reading it avidly, he liked to assemble detailed tables and charts.[1] So strong was his love for this subject that he may have influenced the development in his son of his liking for it also. It will be noted what an important trait, in its effect upon his speaking, this characteristic came to be in the son.

Other influences of the father seem to have taken root in the younger Sumner's personality. C. P. Sumner was known for his earnestness and steadfastness of purpose, his conscientousness, courage, and independence. One is impressed that these same traits were outstanding in the son and assumes that the father's example may have contributed to their establishment. If so, Charles Pinckney Sumner must be given credit for his son's speaking ability to the extent that these traits characterized his ideology and style.

More than this indirect influence cannot be said to have come to Sumner by parental influence, however, for his gloomy, extremely formal father offered him little understanding or encouragement, even though he did set the example in scholarly taste, earnestness, tenacity, and courage.

Sumner's elementary education was of the typical New England classical sort common in the first half of the nineteenth century. He first attended a dame school, kept by his aunt, where he studied geography along with the Three R's. Later he went to the West Writing School for a short time and then changed to another private writing school.

In the meantime, the boy bought with his own pennies some Latin grammars, which he studied privately, at the knowledge of which his father allowed him to enroll concurrently in the Boston Public Latin School. This famous school had just undergone a broadening curriculum change,

[1] Pierce, *op. cit.*, I, 28.

so that Charles Sumner learned history, geography, and arithmetic, as well as Latin and Greek, even though the ancient classics were still by far the largest part of the course. Sumner's rank is said to have been only respectable, although his general readings were wide and careful.[1]

Although Sumner's higher education in reality continued throughout his entire life, the formal part of it came within the years 1826–1834 and falls into three periods.

The first was that of his attendance at Harvard College, where, although the curriculum was being extended, the course was still highly classical, centered around ancient languages and mathematics, with some science and philosophy and incidental English and history courses. Of these, Sumner neglected science and mathematics, because he did not like them, and devoted even a greater share of his time to classics, history, and literature. As a result, his rank was never very high, but his knowledge in selected fields was greater than that of any student in the school at the time.[2]

Graduated in 1830, dissatisfied with his accomplishments and undecided as to what profession to enter, Sumner resolved to spend some time with his books—to learn more of the history and literature he liked so much and to make up his neglected mathematics. For a whole year, therefore, Sumner arose at 5 and worked usually until after midnight, completing a schedule of study amazing in its thoroughness.

Finally deciding that law should be his profession, Sumner entered the new Harvard Law School in 1831, determined to become a good lawyer by knowing "every thing," as he expressed it—"law, history, philosophy, human nature . . . and . . . literature."[3] He therefore laid out a strict schedule of study—morning, law; afternoon, classics; evening, history and subjects collateral to law—which he followed closely during his 2 years at law school. As a result, his reputation at law school was very high. On receiving his degree and studying for a year in a law office, he was admitted to the bar in 1837. He had obtained a predominantly classical education, which provided the foundation for his later pursuits, and, in addition, a specialized training for his chosen profession.

Sumner really had two professions, though he probably would have admitted only one of them—law. But schoolteaching also came to be a profession to him through circumstance. His friend and former instructor, Judge Story, of Harvard Law School, asked him to substitute for him while he attended Supreme Court in 1835 and was so pleased with Sumner's work that he called upon him frequently thereafter, once for several months

[1] *Ibid.*, p. 37.
[2] *Ibid.*, p. 48.
[3] Letter to Jonathan Stearns, quoted in *ibid.*, p. 110.

during an illness. Sumner's name is therefore listed in the Harvard University Register as a law instructor.[1]

This incidental profession seems important to his speech preparation, because his teaching was done almost entirely by the lecture method, and in this lecturing Sumner had his first taste of trying to influence an audience. As he wrote, "I endeavor to stimulate them as much as possible. . . . "[2]

Law was more to Sumner's liking, but even so, he was never very successful in it. This may have been because of his interest in its literature and science rather than its practice. However, this professional experience seems to have had direct influence upon his later speaking, for from it he learned the important habit of careful preparation and gained some experience in speaking to convince.

His professional life thus gives the first direct training for speaking. One occupation taught him to influence audiences; the other, to convince them. Both helped found his characteristic of thorough speech planning.

Of the experiences of his early life most observably affecting his speaking, Sumner's acquaintance with literature is perhaps paramount. His speeches were filled with quotations from and references to it. He began to set the background for these references as early as his days at Harvard, where he read not only more widely than most of the students but more thoughtfully. He kept a notebook of the passages he liked, condensed statements of books and the philosophy of the authors, and committed to memory many passages. Such a practice seems to have continued through his life as his acquaintance with literature broadened. By the end of his year of private study he had read most of the principal Latin classics, and when he left law school he had digested other Latin as well as many Greek classics, Shakespeare, and the British poets.

During his stay in Europe, much of his time was devoted to reading. While in Rome, for instance, he read from 6 in the morning to 5 or 6 in the afternoon each day, so that when he left Italy he could write: "there is hardly a classic in the [Italian] language of which I have not read the whole, or considerable portions."[3]

This wide acquaintance with literature provided Sumner with a wealth of illustration when be began to make his addresses. It may be that he sometimes used this wealth unwisely by too many long quotations and analogies, but literary illustrations were often used to advantage in his important speeches.

His rather wide experience in writing was another influence that affected Sumner's speaking. His aptitude for this activity had developed

[1] *Historical Register of Harvard University*, 1636–1936 (Cambridge, 1937), p. 424.
[2] Letter to Professor Greenleaf, quoted in Pierce, *op. cit.*, I, 188.
[3] Letter to George Greene, quoted in *ibid.*, II, 116

771

as early as his college days, when his essays won the Bowdoin Prize in literature twice and won other contests, also, including one sponsored by the Boston Society for the Diffusion of Useful Knowledge.

While in law school Sumner began to write for the *American Jurist*, to which he contributed for several years and of which he finally became an editor. At the same time, critical and expository articles by Sumner were appearing in the *American Monthly Review*, the *North American Review*, and the *Law Reporter*. Peleg Chandler, editor of the *Law Reporter*, said Sumner's writing was "usually apposite, full of learning, and very interesting."[1]

Sumner was meantime engaged in another sort of writing—an elaborate correspondence. All through his life he habitually wrote many long letters, containing both description of places and events and expression of his beliefs on all sorts of subjects. These letters were almost uniformly carefully worded and organized and represent a rather high quality of literary effort.

Some rather extensive legal writing was also taking part of Sumner's time, including the editing of a voluminous work by Francis Vesy, Jr., on *Equity Reports*, which received acclaim among jurists of the time.

All such writing, was, however, probably less important than some writing aimed to persuade, which Sumner also produced. He wrote, at the request of the American minister to France, a presentation of the argument of the United States in the Northeastern boundary dispute, aimed to acquaint Englishmen with the American point of view, an article that received praise for its clearness and tone. The success of this writing caused requests to write other articles of the same type, including one in defense of a ship's commander who had hanged as a mutineer the son of a government official and one defending the British right to search American ships.

The approbation that these articles received indicates that Sumner had developed the ability successfully to use language and logic in writing to convince. If so, this writing, since it contained many of the same basic factors as would persuasive speaking, may be assumed as important in preparing Sumner for the type of speeches he later made.

In the meantime, although Sumner made no outstanding speeches before 1845, his education and profession were providing chances for some speechmaking, if of a different sort.

At the Boston Public Latin School and at Harvard at this time, declamation was part of the curriculum; so Sumner, learning essays and reciting them, began his speech experience in school. Included in the required curriculum at Harvard at the time was also a course in rhetoric and oratory,

---

[1] Quoted in *ibid.*, p. 252.

taught by Edward T. Channing. It was a lecture rather than a performance course, but in it the students were given theories of speechmaking. Channing evidently taught his students that ideas rather than "the graces of address, or sweetness and variety of tones" were the important features of good speaking[1] and therefore said very little about delivery, which may have been one of the causes of Sumner's early speeches being rather dull, though full of "strong manly sentiments . . . , solid facts and statements of principles. . . . "[2]

While still in college, Sumner did some other formal speaking, including parts in class exhibitions and commencement exercises. Perhaps of more importance to his speech training, however, were the discussions and debates in which he must have participated as a member of the famous Harvard Hasty Pudding Club, where enthusiastic participation in such exercises was the order of most meetings.

After college, Sumner's few speeches were mainly law lectures, didactic and essaylike in style. Only one was a speech before a more popular audience. It was delivered before the Boston Prison Discipline Society, in 1843, criticizing a committee report during a debate within the society.

Of seemingly more importance as speech experiences than those few formal addresses, however, were the amount and kind of conversation in which Sumner engaged. He loved to talk with learned men and sought them out whenever possible and conversed with them upon almost every topic. There are records of his associations with outstanding Americans— Webster, Ingersoll, Longfellow, William E. Channing, Chancellor Kent, and Rufus Choate, among others. Especially during his European journey the number of notables with whom he conversed is amazing. In England, he was received by important judges, lawyers, divines, statesmen, noblemen—an acquaintance with English society said to be wider than any American had previously enjoyed. In Germany, Austria, France, and Italy he likewise met on friendly terms important and learned men.

Thus, although Sumner's formal speeches were few in number, combined with the perhaps more important informal speech experiences, they did at least introduce him to the problems of oral language use, audience adaptation, and delivery.

Coupled with his own scattered appearances as a speaker, however, were numerous experiences in listening to others speak. Since the first half of the nineteenth century was an era of frequent and some great oratory, Sumner heard many important orators during his youth. The fact that he listened quite critically to such speakers may be considered important to his speech preparation.

[1] Channing, *op. cit.*, pp. 23–24.
[2] Pierce, *op. cit.*, I, 106.

Sumner heard Webster's famous "Eulogy on Adams and Jefferson" when he was fifteen; later he listened to John Quincy Adams, and from 1830 on his letters and journals contain references to having heard such speakers as Clay, Calhoun, Webster, Josiah Quincy, Carlyle, Everett, Garrison, as well as European orators, including Lord Brougham, Lord Lyndhurst, Sir Robert Peel, and Lord John Russell. And whenever Sumner mentioned hearing an orator he almost always made remarks about his effectiveness—his manner, his action, his voice, his wording—showing that he had grown conscious of the power of delivery and had learned what made speaking effective.

It is said that the 3 years spent in Europe from 1837 to 1840 added "the finishing touches to his great preparation."[1] True, it did provide knowledge of European laws, institutions, and customs, which gave him the ability to speak authoritatively and use illustrations aptly when referring to that continent.

He went to Europe with a serious purpose in mind—" . . . self-improvement from the various sources of study, observation, and society . . . "[2]—and it must be admitted that he put forth unusual efforts to reap every possible experience.

First, in France, he went sightseeing, then spent a month or more learning the language, heard over one hundred fifty lectures at the Sorbonne, the College of France, and the Law School, on all sorts of subjects, attended the courts regularly, conversing with judges, lawyers, and studying the French code, going to the museums, Chamber of Deputies, theatre, historic places, and, in general, packing his months with every sort of experience.

He went next to England, where he remained over a year, studying courts and the system of laws, traveling the circuits, invading English society to a wider degree than even most natives, attending Parliament, and becoming thoroughly acquainted with English policies and ideas.

Leaving England for a brief return to Paris, Sumner went on to Italy for a period of intense study of the classics and Italian art, also to meet people. Then to Germany, where he learned the language, studied the literature, met important men, and observed the courts. A brief 3 weeks renewing friendships in England, and Sumner returned home with his purpose—to add to his education—most certainly accomplished.

To his speech preparation the trip had contributed, as well as material for illustration, a broader plane of thought and a ground of authority on which to base arguments on foreign affairs.

---

[1] Archibald H. Grimke, *The Life of Charles Sumner* (New York, 1892), p. 58.
[2] Letter from Sumner to Professor Greenleaf, quoted in Pierce, *op. cit.*, I, 209.

The background from which emerged the orator of the day of July 4, 1846, was thus one of classical education and wide experience. By understanding his preparation, it is easier to account for Sumner's leaning toward historical and classical references in his speeches, his authoritative concepts of the problems of foreign affairs, his effective delivery, to some extent his ideas, and, in particular, his ability to make a first speech of the quality of "The True Grandeur of Nations."

SELECTED BIBLIOGRAPHY

Biographies

Caldwell, Howard W.: *Great American Legislators*, Chicago, J. H. Miller, 1900.

Dawes, Anna Laurens: *Charles Sumner*, New York, Dodd, Mead & Company, Inc., 1898.

Grimke, Archibald H.: *The Life of Charles Sumner*, New York, Funk & Wagnalls Company, 1892.

Haynes, George H.: *Charles Sumner*, Philadelphia, George W. Jacobs and Co., 1909.

Higginson, Thomas Wentworth: *Contemporaries*, Boston, Houghton Mifflin Company, 1899.

Lester, C. Edwards: *Life and Public Services of Charles Sumner*, New York, United States Publishing Company, 1874.

McCarthy, Justin: *Reminiscences*, New York, Harper & Brothers, 1899.

Pierce, Edward L.: *Memoir and Letters of Charles Sumner*, Boston, Roberts Brothers, 1877, Vols. I, II; London, Sampson Low, Marston and Co., 1893, Vols. III, IV.

Storey, Moorfield: *Charles Sumner*, Boston, Houghton Mifflin Company, 1900.

Whipple, Edwin Percy: *Recollections of Eminent Men*, Boston, Houghton Mifflin Company, 1896.

Speeches

Executive Document 15, Twenty-eighth Congress, first session.

Morris, Charles: *The World's Great Orators and Their Best Orations*, Philadelphia, John C. Winston Company, 1902.

Sumner, Charles: *Addresses on War*, Boston, Ginn and Company, 1902.

————: *Orations and Speeches*, 2 vols., Boston, Ticknor, 1850.

————: The True Grandeur of Nations, the original MS, Harvard Library, Cambridge, Mass.

————: *The True Grandeur of Nations*, Boston, J. H. Eastburn, 1845.

————: *Works*, 15 vols., Boston, Lee and Shepard, 1870 to 1877.

General References on the Man and His Speeches

The Albion, New York, May 24; June 7, 1856.

Beecher, Henry Ward: *Lectures and Orations*, Newell Dwight, ed., New York, Fleming H. Revell Company, 1913.

Boston Daily Advertiser, Aug. 28, 1846.

Brougham, Henry Lord: *Life and Times of Henry Lord Brougham*, 3 vols., Edinburgh, William Blackwood and Sons, 1871.

Channing, Edward T.: *Lectures on Rhetoric and Oratory*, Boston, Ticknor and Fields, 1856.

Channing, W. H.: *The Life and Times of William E. Channing*, Boston, American Unitarian Association, 1899.

A Citizen of Boston: *Remarks upon an Oration Delivered by Charles Sumner before the Authorities of the City of Boston, July 4, 1845*, Boston, William Crosby and H. P. Nichols, 1845.

Clarke, James Freeman: *Autobiography, Diary, and Correspondence*, Edward Everett Hale, ed., Boston, Houghton Mifflin Company, 1919.
Dallinger, Carl A.: Inventio in the Speeches of Charles Sumner, M. A. thesis, University of Iowa, 1938.
The Evening Post, New York, August 31, 1846; July 9, 1845.
Frothingham, O. B.: *Memoir of William Ellery Channing*, Boston, Houghton Mifflin Company, 1886.
Johnson, A. B.: "Recollections of Charles Sumner," *Scribner's Monthly*, 8 (1874): 475–490; 9 (1874): 101–114; 10 (1875): 224–229.
The Liberator, Boston, July 11, 1845.
Morning Courier and New York Inquirer, Aug. 29, 1846; May 24, 1856.
National Anti-Slavery Standard, New York, May 22, 24, 26, 31; June 14, 21, 1856.
The National Era, Washington, May 29, 1856.
New York Daily Times, May 22, 24, 26, 1856.
New York Daily Tribune, May 20, 21, 22, 1856.
New York Dispatch, May 25, 1846.

27

Stephen A. Douglas

by FOREST L. WHAN

Born April 23, 1813, to Sarah Fiske Douglas and Stephen Arnold Douglas, a physician in Brandon, Vt., Stephen A. Douglas was educated in the Canandaigua Academy, New York. He was cabinetmaker apprentice at Middlebury, Vt., and later a schoolmaster at Winchester, Ill., 1833–1834; admitted to the bar, 1834; state's attorney for Illinois, 1834; one term in Illinois legislature, 1836; register of Federal Land Office at Springfield, Ill., 1837; became a Mason, 1840. He was Secretary of State of Illinois, 1841; associate justice, Illinois Supreme Court, 1841; House of Representative, United States Congress, 1843–1847; chairman of House Committee on Territories. He married Martha Martin, 1847; United States Senate, 1847 until his death; was chairman of Senate Committee on Territories, 1847–1858; regent to Smithsonian Institute, 1854–1860. He donated land for establishment of the Baptist Institute (which later became the University of Chicago), 1856. He aided in the Compromise of 1850, the passage of the Kansas-Nebraska bill and the repeal of the Missouri Compromise, the defeat of the Lecompton Constitution; Presidential nominee for the Democratic party, 1860; died June 3, 1861.

The Problem

Stephen A. Douglas is still the subject of controversy. Although his biography has been written many times and historians recognize him as a great persuader, the prevailing judgment on his speaking ability has been in the light of post-Civil War philosophy. This study attempts a more objective evaluation.

The task of examining the entire speaking career of Douglas would be gigantic. For 11 years he was a prairie politician, during which time he stumped the state of Illinois and followed the varied occupations of schoolmaster, state's attorney, legislator, Secretary of State, and justice of the Illinois Supreme Court. He was elected as Representative from Illinois to the United States Congress three times and was for 16 years United States Senator. As chairman of the most important Congressional committee of the period in both House and Senate, Committee on Territories, he brought into being a dozen new territories and states. He made thousands of speeches on the stump throughout the United States and hundreds of others in committee meetings and on the floor of both houses of Congress.

777

It is generally agreed, however, that the campaign for the Illinois senator-ship in 1858 was the most important in his career. In it he stumped Illinois from end to end in typical Douglas style. In its effort to evaluate Douglas as a speaker, this study limits itself to an examination of that one campaign.

Much has been written concerning the historic campaign. Indeed, no other for a minor office has received as much attention by historians, most of them giving more space to this local canvass than to any of the Presidential races. Every biographer of the two participants, as well as biographers of other politicians of the day, devotes a chapter or more to the speeches given by Lincoln and Douglas during these 4 months. But only one[1] of these has dealt with the speaking ability of Stephen A. Douglas as evidenced in this campaign. Following the example set by historians and biographers, this critic dealt with only the seven famous joint discussions, ignoring the remaining forty-seven scheduled addresses, delivered in forty-one additional counties.[2] Although all have agreed that Douglas owed his career to his ability to persuade audiences, most have condemned him harshly as a sophist and a trickster, lacking in originality and constructive logic.[3] They have so condemned him seemingly without examining more than the ten published speeches of the campaign and without analyzing the basic beliefs and attitudes of the audiences he faced.[4] Historians have been content, in the light of their knowledge of political affiliations in Illinois, to examine the speeches and criticize their author.

We are justified, then, in re-examining this campaign, in making a careful study of speaking situations, and in applying the principles of rhetorical criticism to it. Was Douglas, the great persuader, insincere and incon-

---

[1] A. M. Barnes, A Rhetorical Analysis of the Speeches of Stephen A. Douglas in the Lincoln-Douglas Debates (M.A. thesis, Department of Speech, State University of Iowa 1937).

[2] The clipping from the *New York Times* (reported in the *Illinois State Register*, Nov. 23 1858), usually quoted by historians, erred in reporting Douglas to have spoken in fifty-seven counties. Fifty-eight of the fifty-nine "set speeches" were made in forty-eight counties; one has not yet been traced.

[3] Such usually dispassionate historians as Henry Wilson, Hermann von Holst, and James Ford Rhodes have claimed Douglas to have been "selfish," "to disregard the rights of man, the enduring interests of the country and the sacred claims of the Christian religion," to believe that "moral ideas had no place in politics." These historians seemingly allowed subjective feeling to influence their judgment. Wilson became Vice-President through the Republican party, von Holst was a rabid abolitionist, Rhodes was forced to pay the Douglas heirs $30,000 because the senior Rhodes had mismanaged Douglas's estate.

[4] A. J. Beveridge (*Abraham Lincoln*, 2 vols., Boston, Houghton Mifflin Company, 1928) and A. C. Cole (*The Era of the Civil War*, 1848–1870, Springfield, *Centennial History of Illinois*, Illinois Centennial Committee, 1919, Vol. III) are the only two historians who have made a careful study of the various audiences. Neither condemns Douglas for his ideas, his arguments, or his plan of campaign; but neither has made a careful rhetorical study.

sistent? Was he lacking in originality and constructive logic? Were his logical and emotional arguments basically dishonest?

This study will be made and existing speeches of the campaign appraised from the standpoint of the influence upon them of the audiences, the occasion, the speaker, and the issues. It posits the responsibility of the great speaker to choose the best possible means of logical and emotional persuasion, without becoming insincere or inconsistent. It posits his responsibility to determine with care the validity and reliability of evidence and argument. The study is based upon the philosophy that oratorical criticism should be made in the light of the psychology of the audience, the occasion, and the speaker and not merely from the standpoint of the amount of argument, evidence, or emotional materials found in the printed speech. On the basis of this philosophy the study evaluates Douglas's effectiveness in using the various methods of proof open to him, and in adapting his arguments to the audiences he faced.

The Audience

The audiences that Douglas faced in the campaign of 1858 were a product of many trends that influenced the people of Illinois during the preceding decade. In order to understand fully what was in the minds of the people during the summer and fall of 1858, it is necessary to understand these trends.

The first influencing trend was that of a shift in population toward the West. The year 1848 marked the beginning of a new epoch in Illinois history. Before that date the state was filled largely with frontiersmen, most of whom came from the South; by 1858 these early settlers had moved on to California, Kansas, and Nebraska, leaving Illinois to the great influx of settlers from the East and abroad, who quadrupled the population of the state in 10 years.[1]

Whereas early colonization had been largely in the central and southern sections of the state, with the most thickly populated counties found in the former, the new immigrants settled in the north.[2] They came seeking a land of opportunity for their sons—cheap land, rich land; and many sought in addition an escape from economic or religious oppression.[3]

[1] The best single history of this movement is found in Cole, *op. cit.*, pp. 1–50. See also J. M. Peck, *Gazettier of Illinois* (2d. ed., Philadelphia, Griggs & Elliott, 1837); *New York Semi Weekly Tribune*, Oct. 12, 1858, quoting Illinois census reports of 1855 and 1858; *Illinois State Register* for the decade.

[2] Lillian Foster's *Wayside Glimpses*, reprinted in *Illinois Historical Society Journal*, 5, No. 3, hereafter referred to as *Journal; Belleville Advocate*, Apr. 25, 1850; Cole, *op. cit.*

[3] Charles Lanphier to R. G. Lanphier, May 3, 1844, Patton MSS; *Journal*, 11: 271. Economic and religious oppression abroad, together with the potato famine in Ireland, sent millions of Europeans to other lands. Throughout the world the forties and fifties were periods

The new populace was composed largely of Yankees from New England, fortune seekers from other Eastern states, and refugees from oppression in the Old World.[1] The Yankees settled in the northern part of he state,[2] the fortune seekers scattered over the central portion,[3] and the immigrants from abroad settled in certain counties: the Scandinavians in the northern counties, in Galesburg and near Chicago,[4] the Irish in the cities,[5] the Germans in and around Chicago, Belleville, Galena, Alton, Peoria, and Peru.[6] The English were so scattered that they were relatively unimportant politically; the French were politically important only in Chicago, Kankakee, and Ottawa. The vast majority of the aliens, then, settled in the northern third of the state, along the Illinois River, across from St. Louis, or near Quincy. The rest of central and southern Illinois was comparatively free from foreign born.[7]

The location of the new population was extremely important in the 1858 campaign, for the influx of Eastern and foreign born exerted a strong influence toward the acceptance of the ideas of the new Republican party. The French and Scandinavians were strongly inclined toward Abolitionism, the Irish were staunch Democrats but inclined to favor Buchanan's stand, and the Germans were switching to the Republican party because of anti-slavery beliefs. Thus the people to whom Douglas was to speak in 1858 were

---

of social, political, economic, and emotional revolution. In 1845 Great Britain abandoned her corn laws, and her party system was shattered. In 1846 Karl Marx wrote against capitalism. In 1848 nationalism flared in Hungary; Germany experienced revolution; France installed her third Napoleon; revolutions occurred in Austria, Lombardy, Venice, Denmark, and Schleswig-Holstein. In 1849 the Roman National Assembly divested the Pope of all temporal power and proclaimed a republic. Japan was opened to American ships in 1853; the Crimean War ended in 1855; India revolted in 1857. Old habits were being overthrown and new ones acquired in this restless age. The product of such revolution filled Illinois and drove out the frontiersmen.

[1] *Chicago Magazine*, 1: 94–96; *Journal*, 15: 592–599; 11: 271, reporting that 76 per cent of the people in Illinois in 1850 had been born elsewhere, although only 23 per cent of the people in the United States were born in other than the states in which they lived.

[2] Beveridge, *op. cit.*, I, 177; Cole, *op. cit.*, p. 14.

[3] Beveridge, *op. cit.*, I, 221; *Illinois State Historical Society Transactions*, hereafter referred to as *Transactions*, Vols. 27, 85.

[4] *Chicago Democrat*, Aug. 15, 1859; *Chicago Press and Tribune*, Sept. 4, 1858; Cole, *op. cit.*, p. 19. Cole claims that this immigration stopped after 1854, but records of Galesburg show that while its American-born population increased less than 25 per cent between 1860 and 1865, the Swedish population increased over 95 per cent.

[5] *Chicago Democrat*, Dec. 17, 1849; *Chicago Tribune*, Dec. 23, 1853.

[6] Cole, *op. cit.*, p. 23; *Journal*, 7: 7–33; *Chicago Daily Journal*, July 5, 1849; *World Almanac* (1935), p. 257, showing Illinois to have more foreign born than other states, excepting New York. Later immigrants tended to settle where earlier countrymen had gone before.

[7] Only one county in the northern third of the state contained less than 30 per cent born abroad. In the southern part of the state five counties had less than 1 per cent.

not those to whom he spoke, with whom he worked and played, by whom he was acclaimed during his residence in Illinois before he left for Washington in 1843.[1] This change in population during the decade preceding 1858 meant new ideals, new concepts, and new methods of living and was the cause of the tremendous development that made the state fourth in rank in the Union by 1860.[2]

A second trend of the fifties that affected the beliefs, attitudes, and emotional character of the people in 1858 was the great development in agriculture and industry.[3] The number engaged in agricultural pursuits doubled, acreage increased 73.7 per cent, and the value of farm property quadrupled.[4] Illinois became first in wheat production, fourth in oat production, first in corn production, fourth in rye, fifth in barley, and third in hay and forage. She became second among Northern states in area of improved land. Yet only 50 per cent of the land was in farms in 1858.[5] Although farming was not diversified, Illinois began high-class livestock raising and trebled the value of her farm machinery.[6]

Such advancement caused the agriculturist to realize the necessity of providing for his future needs. More agricultural societies sprang up than existed in any other state,[7] and a realization grew of the value of education.[8] So strong did the farm consciousness develop that for the first time in Illinois a political party recognized the need of education for farmers and mechanics, and in places wholesale purchasing cooperatives were formed.[9]

Industrially the state lagged behind agriculture, but manufacturing in this period advanced about 30 per cent.[10] The value of raw materials was

[1] Historians have failed to note that Douglas did not live in Illinois after 1843. From that time on to his death he held office in Washington, D.C. Although his legal residence was established in Chicago, he merely visited the city and state between sessions of Congress.

[2] *Transactions*, 42: 135.

[3] Only ten incorporated cities existed in 1850, all but Springfield and Bloomington in counties containing foreign born to the extent of 22 per cent or more by 1860. Many other towns were incorporated during the decade. See E. E. Calkins, *They Broke the Prairie* (Charles Scribner's Sons, 1937), p. 206; C. J. Sellong, *A Review of the Commerce, Manufactures, and the Public and Private Improvements of Galesburg*, Galesburg, J. H. Sherman, Printer, 1857; *Chicago Magazine*, March, 1857, pp. 94–96; May, 1857.

[4] Cole, *op. cit.*, p. 85; *Transactions*, 26: 101 and Vol. 31; H. L. Busch, The Fortune of Stephen A. Douglas (M. A. thesis, Department of History, University of Chicago, 1936), p. 28.

[5] *Transactions*, 26: 101; 34: 107.

[6] "Auditor's Report," *Reports Made to the General Assembly of Illinois* (Springfield, Bailhocke and Baker, 1859), pp. 45–53; *Transactions*, 26: 102–103.

[7] *Oquawka Spectator*, Mar. 22, 1854; *Knox Republican*, Aug. 11, 1858; Cole, *op. cit.*, p. 79.

[8] *Transactions*, 23: 157, reprinting John Reynolds, "The Agricultural Resources of Southern Illinois."

[9] *Chicago Tribune*, Sept. 7, 1854; *Our Constitution*, June 26, 1858.

[10] Peck, *op. cit.*, pp. 16–35, for list of factories; *Transactions*, 28: 57–63; Sellong, *op. cit.*, pp. 42–47, for factories in Galesburg; *Transactions*, 42: 135.

still not recognized by the populace. But the trend toward centralization of industry had already begun about Chicago. And although the panic of 1857 affected the farming portion of the state during the campaign year, Chicago remained relatively free from its influence.[1]

Closely allied to economic development, and affecting it, was the increased speed of communication and transportation. Two hundred six of the 783 newspapers started before 1860 were in operation in 1858.[2] Every important town was in telegraphic connection with Chicago and Eastern cities, linking more closely to Eastern sentiment the citizens of Illinois. But transportation trends were of even more importance in influencing the beliefs of the Westerners. In 1850 the West was closely linked with the South by river trade; traffic with the East was toward the West only. Therefore, the economic interests of Illinois lay with the South.[3] After the building of the railroads and the increase of immigration from the East and abroad, however, the hold of the South over the West was greatly lessened. Trade routes were all-important in shaping the political faith of the time. Until the late fifties no party that was sectional in nature was able to gain dominance in Illinois. Before that time a national party, with at least tolerance for Southern institutions (such as Whig and Democratic parties), was essential. Transportation in this manner greatly influenced the acceptance of the issues of the 1858 campaign. And transportation facilities developed more rapidly during the decade preceding 1858 than in any other like period of years in American history.[4]

Other trends of an economic nature were municipal development, the beginning of public-utility development, and the establishment of a free school system.

The economic beliefs of the people of Illinois that resulted from the trends just mentioned seemed to be as follows. (1) They seemed to place security above comfort and to look upon poverty as the inexcusable result of laziness or extravagance, although economic misfortune was beginning to be recognized as such.[5] (2) They were breaking away from their indif-

---

[1] *Banker's Magazine*, 12: 1857, as reported by Cole, *op. cit.*, p. 100; *Transactions*, 28: 78, 82.

[2] F. W. Scotte, "Newspapers and Periodicals of Illinois, 1814–1879," *Illinois Historical Collections*, Vol. VI, *Bibliographical Series* 1, pp. lxiii, lxix (hereafter referred to as *Collections*, VI).

[3] Guy Stevens Callender, *Economic History of the United States* (Boston, Ginn & Company, 1909), Chap. IV. Beveridge believes this to be the chief reason for Alton's anxiety over Lovejoy's Abolition paper in the thirties.

[4] *Journal*, 10, No. 1: 17–85, carries a detailed discussion of the development of railroads in the fifties; *Chicago Magazine*, 1: 159; Cole, *op. cit.*, pp. 5, 51.

[5] This conclusion is drawn from editorials in the *Dubuque* (Iowa) *Daily Times*, Nov. 5, 1857; *Washington* (Iowa) *Press*, Aug. 25, 1858; *New York Semi Weekly Tribune*, June 30, 1858; *Illinois State Register*, Aug. 18, 1848; *Iowa City Weekly State Reporter*, Apr. 14, 1858; *Rockford Register*, July 19, 1858. Also, from conversations with Max Speulda, who recalls his boyhood

ferent attitude toward a tariff and beginning to accept the thesis of tariff for revenue only.[1] But they inconsistently maintained a mercantilistic philosophy toward trade with the East because of the scarcity of metallic money.[2] (3) The fever of speculation overcame an inherent suspicion of corporate enterprise and centralization of economic control and aided in the rapid advance of industrial speculation.[3] (4) Although indirect taxation was desired for the Federal government, direct taxation of the most vicious type was advocated for local revenue.[4] (5) Prices were accepted as important because they determined the amount of sale and not because high prices were believed to bring prosperity; the result of low prices on debtors was understood; and the people did not theorize on price determination or the possibility of price control.[5] (6) The populace believed the purpose of banks to be (*a*) acceptance of deposits, (*b*) providing large loans for capital improvement, (*c*) the concentration of small sums into large amounts, (*d*) the providing of short time loans, (*e*) the issuing of currency, and (*f*) the providing of safety to note holders. But they deemed dollar-for-dollar backing of notes by liquid bonds as providing this safety. Banks should pay interest on deposits and should be more closely supervised than private lenders.[6] (7) Although recognizing money as a medium of exchange, the

in Illinois in this period. Also, from reprints found in *Transactions*, 17: 52; 26: 102. Also, Patton MSS (deed to sale of land) and B. H. Hibbard, *History of Public Land Policies* (New York, The Macmillan Company, 1924), Chap. VI.

[1] Callender (*op. cit.*, p. 487) reports that tariff was chiefly a political issue in the fifties; Douglas claimed that it was no longer a political issue, men in both parties taking differing views. Newspapers of the period, votes of Congressmen on tariff bills, and ballots cast on "tariff for revenue only" campaigns seem to bear out Douglas rather than Callender. Therefore, the tariff question could not be raised by either party during the campaign in Illinois.

[2] *Weekly State Reporter*, Apr. 14, 1858 (editorial); Sept. 14, 1858 (editorial), reporting a meeting in Des Moines advocating the boycotting of Eastern goods and condemning Wall Street. The scarcity of money in Illinois explains Western philosophy, which was the reverse of Western attitude toward international problems.

[3] The Whig party had inherited an antagonism toward central authority.—*Transactions*, 32: 109. But economically the distrust disappeared, as was evidenced by growth of stock-company railroads; other privately developed internal improvements; and toll roads, financed by corporations.

[4] *Journal*, 12: 41–44 for history of the poll tax. See *Transactions*, 32: 118, reporting that the Whig poll tax of 1847 passed; but the Whig leaders (Lincoln, Logan, and Bledsoe) in 1848 condemned direct Federal taxation.—Beveridge, *op. cit.*, I, 357.

[5] *Semi Weekly Tribune*, Jan. 12, 1858, for article by Carey; *Weekly State Reporter*, Apr. 14, 1858; *Fulton Democrat*, Aug. 29, 1858; *Semi Weekly Tribune*, June 30, 1858.

[6] This conclusion is drawn after a study of banking history in Illinois as indicated by bank legislation (*Transactions*, 32: 109–129). Other source material included Patton MSS (W. B Lanphier to father, June 6, 1840); *Weekly State Reporter*, Apr. 14, 1858; *Laws of 1851*, pp. 163–175; *Chicago Daily Journal*, Oct. 21, 1850; auditor's report in *Oquawka Spectator*, Feb. 5, 1858; *Bankers' Magazine*, 6, New Series: 995–1000; 7: 239–240, 681–995; *Chicago Magazine*, June, 1857, p. 371.

populace was interested in obtaining a medium that would have a value of its own. Gold was considered the best medium because it represented wealth aside from its ability to purchase. The people seemed to realize that cheaper money drives out dearer money. And although paper inflation was a reality, the populace did not speculate upon its advantages or disadvantages.[1] (8) The people accepted the idea of "free trade in money"; they believed that restriction of interest charges would make money scarce and therefore dear; they held that the fixation of interest was not dependent upon either "repayment for abstinence," "time-preference," or "productivity" of capital, but upon the scarcity of money.[2] (9) They believed that rent should be fixed on the principle of getting all the traffic would bear.[3] (10) The people of Illinois did not accept the "wage-fund" or "marginal-productivity" theories of wages. They believed that wages were determined by the productivity of labor alone. They encouraged immigration, believed in the dignity of labor, accepted child and woman labor without question, and did not recognize moral or social obligations to the worker. They did not theorize on the evils of technology but welcomed laborsaving devices. Their problem was one of conserving labor, not one of providing more employment.[4] Finally, the majority of Illinoisans accepted wholeheartedly the theory of the value of internal improvements, being willing to subscribe heavily for them individually and accepting huge government debt to make them possible.[5]

[1] Patton MSS, Harris to Lanphier, Apr. 11, 1850, showing worry over a draft being honored; Beveridge, *op. cit.*, p. 556n.; *Oquawka Spectator*, Oct. 24, 31, 1854, listing bankrupt banks (forty-one in all). Conversations with Max Speulda brought out many tales of the counterfeiting trouble.—*Fulton Democrat*, Aug. 1, 1857, for long editorial on the evils of counterfeiting; *Semi Weekly Tribune*, New York, Jan. 1, Feb. 2, 1858, for arguments of economists; *Weekly State Reporter*, July 14, 1858, for dangers of free bank paper in Illinois and Indiana; Beveridge, *op. cit.*, I, 556, for scarcity of hard money. C. B. Johnson, *Illinois in the Fifties* (Illinois Centennial Ed., Champaign, Ill., Flanigan-Pearson Co., 1918), pp. 62–67, has discussion of money and description of "counterfeit detectors"; Douglas MSS, Ward to Douglas, Jan. 13, 1858, wanting a new law on money.

[2] *Semi Weekly Tribune*, Sept. 3, 1858, publishing a letter from Minnesota; P. E. Angle, *New Letters and Papers of Abraham Lincoln* (Boston, Houghton Mifflin Company, 1930) Lincoln to Hay; Tracy, *op. cit.*, p. 63; *Chicago Magazine*, 1: 371; Cole, *op. cit.*, p. 92; *Transactions*, 42: 59; Calkins, *op. cit.*, pp. 213–214; *Weekly State Reporter*, Apr. 21, 1858—all showing that people accepted free trade in money in spite of laws against usury.

[3] Cole, *op. cit.*, pp. 2–3, quoting newspapers to show that shortage of dwelling places in Chicago caused $500 houses to bring between $300 and $400 a year in rent.

[4] American economists attack the European concepts of labor, their attacks being carried in many Illinois newspapers in 1858. And although some labor unions were formed, labor was still largely unskilled. Long years of apprenticeship, together with hordes of immigrant labor, made it possible to keep wages down. Newspapers continually carried stories of the "honor of labor," "honest sweat," and the like but showed no inclination to champion the cause of labor reform.

[5] The willingness with which people subscribed for railroads is shown clearly by a study of railroad advancement, road building, etc.

These, then, seem to be the economic beliefs held by the people of Illinois during the fifties, particularly toward the end of the decade. The horror of extravagance, the new attitude toward tariff, the belief in the dignity of labor, and the experience with unemployment during the panic all had a vital influence on the 1858 campaign issues. Attitudes toward taxation, banking, and corporate enterprise, the acceptance of high rents and usury, and the lack of a feeling of moral and social responsibility toward labor all typifies stereotypes that affected acceptance of various arguments in the campaign.

Concepts that linked poverty with extravagance and scarcity of money with the greedy East prepared the way for Republican attacks upon Douglas as a waster and an agent of Tammany. An apathetic attitude toward tariff kept that issue from the campaign. Concepts of labor and wages probably strengthened the desire for freedom for the blacks, yet prepared the populace for appeals to fear of black-labor invasion. Beliefs concerning free trade in money, interest rates, and rents typified the growing enthusiasm for freedom in all things. Although acceptance of corporate enterprise and universal support of internal improvements represented a growing tolerance for centralized economic control, attitudes toward taxation, banks, issuance of currency, interest rates, and rents showed that the people of Illinois were still subject to State-rights appeals—very important items to Douglas in the 1858 campaign.

A third major trend, which must be understood to appreciate the beliefs and attitudes of the people of 1858, is that of increasing interest in and development of free educational opportunities. In 1835 the Southern counties were instrumental in repealing an inoperative free-school law passed in 1825. The South favored private schools and academies, and the state as a whole was unwilling to support free education.[1] From then on until the fifties, and the arrival of a new population, nothing was done by the state and little by towns in behalf of education, in spite of the urging of a small minority.[2] But in 1854 the state legislature gave way to renewed agitation[3] and established the office of superintendent of public instruction; and the present Free School Law of Illinois was established. By 1858 the superintendent was instrumental in building 3,000 schoolhouses, organizing 2,000 school districts, enrolling 440,000 students, or 14 out of every 15 children of school age, for an average term of almost 7 months.[4] Free

---

[1] *Journal*, 11: 358–369.

[2] George W. Smith, "The Old Illinois Agricultural College," *Journal*, Vol. 5, gives a history of the minority fight. An editorial in *Illinois Monthly Magazine*, 1: 114–117, gives a good picture of the attitude of the period toward education.

[3] *Illinois Laws of* 1854, pp. 13–14.

[4] *Transactions*, 42: 132.

public high schools were established in the larger towns and cities,[1] and no less than two dozen institutions of higher learning were incorporated. Although the fight for a state university failed and President Buchanan vetoed the land-grant bill of 1859, the struggle for free schools was indicative of the growing belief in democracy and equal opportunity for all, which was so important to Lincoln in the 1858 campaign.

But formal education, coming late in the decade, does not provide a good index of the mental attainments of the adult voters. It merely shows the greatness of the trend and that these people were bringing West with them the institutions they had known in the East. Over 75 per cent of the populace had been born elsewhere, and it is possible that this percentage included the vast majority of voting adults in the state. A study of the books they are known to have read, the flood of pamphlets reaching all parts of the state, and the famous lecturers to whom they are known to have listened in 1857 and 1858 give a better index to the voters' level of education. The books dealt with either travel or very emotional subject matter;[2] pamphlets were mostly political in nature and emotional to the extreme;[3] lectures, too, were largely political but, whenever held, were attended by huge crowds. Although little evidence of what is commonly called *culture* has been handed down to us from the period, that a desire for more cultural attainments was prevalent is evidenced by the establishment of a state natural history society in 1858 and Chicago's first formal art exhibition for Illinois pieces in 1859.

Thus we see that belief in educational and cultural development was crystallizing throughout the fifties and resulted in a school system, libraries, and various types of societies for intellectual advancement. The people were intellectually alert, extremely interested in politics, emotional in nature, and desirous of better education for their children. These things symbolized their sincere belief in the manifest destiny of the state, the Union, and democracy and represented a growing tendency in Illinois to accept Republican philosophy.

[1] Belling lists fifty high schools established in these years, thirty in towns and cities in which Douglas spoke during the campaign of 1858.—*Journal*, 11: 523-524.

[2] For example, books in demand at Galesburg (Calkins, *op. cit.*, p. 254) were as follows: Bayard Taylor's *Cyclopedia of Modern Travel*; H. B. Stowe's *Dred*; Fowler's *How to Travel*; Mrs. Stowe's *Journey to Italy*; *Letters of Madame de Sévigné*; Colton's *American Atlas*; *Waverley Novels*; *Little Dorritt*; Rice's *Mabel or Heart Histories, A Tale of Truth*; De Witt's *Kate Weston*; Starback's *Missionary Heroes and Martyrs*; Brownell's *The New World*; and H. S. Taylor's *The Family Doctor*. Add to this list *Uncle Tom's Cabin* and the novels of Bulwer-Lytton (published in most Illinois newspapers).

[3] They were broadcast by the hundreds of thousands. See Patton MSS, letter from Harris to Lanphier, Feb. 1, 1850, together with other letters mentioning the number of political pamphlets to be published. Douglas MSS contains thousands of letters from all parts of Illinois and surrounding states, requesting copies of his speeches.

Another institution experiencing great development during the decade was that of religion. The number of churches doubled during the decade; the value of church property quadrupled.[1] To such an extent was church attendance considered necessary to good character that both Lincoln and Douglas were attacked in some quarters for their negligence in that matter. But churches were not the only evidence of religious fervor. Revival meetings made Illinois second only to New York in the number of converts gained, second or third in the Union in the Bible cause, and second to none in the number experiencing hypnotic "jerks" brought on by fanatical fervency.[2] Religious fervor typified the emotional character of the people, an element that strongly influenced Douglas and Lincoln in building their speeches for the 1858 campaign.

Other emotional reforms, such as Nudism and Free Love, were also widely supported. Among the strongest was the anti-Catholic, antiforeign Know-Nothing movement, which led the Irish and Germans to fear other than the Democratic party. The movement and the reaction to it were important in determining acceptance of the doctrine that "all men are created equal"—an important issue of the campaign. The Barnburners believed in "free opinion, free speech, free discussion, free soil, and free labor." The ladies began campaigns for women's rights: the right to vote, the right to retain their own last names in marriage, and the right to dress reform.

But although the movements just mentioned, together with others, were the result of an almost universal desire for freedom from restraint and domination, other movements of equal strength were based upon a plea for more restraint. The hand-in-hand movement of such radically opposed doctrines was one of the great paradoxes of the Illinois people in 1858.[3]

The rise and fall of the "Order of the Star Spangled Banner" exemplifies this paradox. In a land of reforms for freedom, the Know-Nothing society, as it was more often called, through its mystic appeal of secrecy and its fight against all Catholics and foreign born, achieved a balance of power in 1854. Still more surprising, blue laws were becoming popular.[4] And most

---

[1] *Transactions,* 42: 131–132; *Journal,* 15: 477–500.

[2] Patton MSS, Diller to Miss Lanphier, Mar. 13, 1848; *Chicago Daily Democratic Press,* Mar. 16, 1858; *Semi Weekly Tribune,* July and August, 1858; and *Oquawka Spectator,* Feb. 26, 1858, all have editorials on the "jerks."

[3] Lincoln saw and felt this inconsistency.—Lincoln to Owen Lovejoy, Aug. 11, 1855, reprinted in Tracy, *Uncollected Letters of Abraham Lincoln* (Boston, Houghton Mifflin Company, 1917), pp. 59–60.

[4] Jelliff reported city ordinances in Galesburg against keeping stores open after 11 p.m. on Saturday; Chicago objected to running the Horse Railway on Sunday; the president of Knox College tried to stop the railroad from running through Galesburg on Sunday (Centennial Paper, Galesburg Public Library MSS).

important of all, the temperance movement became a great stumbling block to the Democratic party during the decade. Agitation for prohibition proved a vexing problem for all political parties until it collapsed following the referendum on the "Maine Liquor Law" in 1855.

Closely allied to these reforms was that of Abolitionism, the radical antislavery movement. Until late in the decade, abolitionists were looked upon with displeasure, to say the least.[1] It was not until the repeal of the Missouri Compromise, the publication of Mrs. Stowe's *Uncle Tom's Cabin*, the attempt at a more stringent Fugitive Slave Law, the Kansas-Lecompton Constitution fight, the Dred Scott decision, and the triumph of the Republican party in 1860 had each in turn influenced Northern and Western thought against slavery that Abolitionism ceased to be a curse to the hopeful politician, either Democratic or Republican, in Illinois.

A review of Illinois legislation on the slavery problem bears out this fact. Early laws were those of the slave states in spite of the state constitution. Early antislavery societies in Illinois made little headway. In 1825 the governor of Illinois actually was indicted for freeing his slaves without paying the bond due under the law. And it was only after a Supreme Court of Illinois reversal of a second trial that he was freed of his fine. In 1836–1837 the general assembly of Illinois adopted a resolution by a vote of seventy-seven to six, resolving that the "General Government cannot Abolish Slavery in the District of Columbia, against the wishes of the citizens of said District."[2] And although the courts held existing laws to be illegal in 1839, it was not until the Yankees and foreign born replaced the pioneers that the legislature took notice of the situation.[3] In 1848 the legislature rebuked Douglas by instructing Illinois Congressmen to work for laws that would make Texas a free state but rescinded the resolutions at the next session.[4] The legislature ignored the 1847 referendum vote of the people, demanding prohibition of immigration of blacks, until such a bill was passed in 1853.[5] The bill adopted that year showed a greater desire to keep black labor from competing with white than it did a desire to see justice done to the Negro. Illinois was still far from Abolitionism or

---

[1] Lincoln took pains to deny Abolitionism as late as 1861 (Beveridge, *op. cit.*, II, 17–18), and both parties declared, "Abolition is an odius ephithet among us. . . . —" *Ibid.*, II, 273.

[2] *House Journal*, session 1836–1837, pp. 241–244, 309, 311. The legislature also resolved: "We highly disapprove of the formation of Abolition Societies. . . . "

[3] *Kinney v. Cook*, 1839.

[4] *Laws of Illinois*, Springfield, Lanphier & Walker, 1853, reprinting the laws of 1846, 1847, and 1849, p. 234.

[5] *Public Laws of 1853*, pp. 57–60; heavy fines were imposed on every Negro entering the state, free or slave. If the fine ($100 to $500) could not be paid, the Negro was auctioned to the person bidding the shortest period of servitude in return for paying the fine. The act called the auction a *sale*.

from believing the whites and blacks "equal," the antislavery forces being outnumbered two to one.

The early "Black Laws" were finally repealed in the 1853–1854 session, but the Negro remained a persecuted group. Although northern Illinois was more charitable to the black man than was the southern part of the state, race hatred was so strong in the latter that in 1857 the whites attempted to drive all Negroes from Mound City, and kidnapers in Cairo made a business of selling slaves to the Missourians.

However, all through the decade the antislavery sentiment was growing, especially in the northern part of the state, which was rapidly filling with Yankees and foreign born. In 1858 election returns showed southern Illinois overwhelmingly proslavery in sentiment, northern Illinois overwhelmingly abolitionist in sentiment, and the great central part of the state either in favor of following out the principles of popular sovereignty in territories as well as states or merely against the extension of the evil. But the trend was definitely toward Abolitionism. Although Douglas could not hope to win the Abolition voters of the North, he could strive so to discredit them in central Illinois that no more votes would be lost.

Thus the decade was marked by strong emotional trends in Illinois. And if one is truly to appreciate the emotional feeling of the time, the emotional character of the people whom Douglas faced, he must remember that these movements were not mere passive undercurrents. They were the moving spirit of political and social life. They swept the state! Men did not merely believe or disbelieve in these things, as do men of today. They felt keenly! They fought mortal duels over these abstractions—even in the United States Congress. The strength of their beliefs was evidenced by their willingness to travel a hundred miles by ox cart in wet weather to hear a single debate on one of these subjects—days of hard, primitive travel. It was further evidenced by men's willingness to give up friends, money, business, or chance at personal gain in order to settle Kansas to make it free or slave. It was evidenced in growth of political parties on moral and emotional issues alone. It was an emotional decade!

Finally, to understand the reasons for the mind-set of the audiences that faced Douglas in 1858, we must examine briefly the political trends of the period. Women had made no move as yet for suffrage rights in Illinois.[1] Politically, the picture of the decade is one of waning Democratic supremacy. The Germans, Irish, English, and Scandinavians had joined its ranks

[1] *Journal*, 13: 145–179, the movement started in the 1860's. Women took no part in politics. Out of over three thousand letters received by Douglas during the early months of 1858, commenting upon his recent Lecompton fight or asking for his speeches, only two were from women; see Douglas MSS.

upon their arrival, no doubt because of the magic of the name.[1] When the Whigs in 1840 and the Know-Nothings in the fifties ran on a platform of nativism, these foreigners were more closely knit to the Democratic party. The first break occurred with the repeal of the Missouri Compromise. Strongly opposed to slavery and to the Clayton amendment, which denied to foreigners any political rights in the new territories, the German press fought repeal of the compromise.[2] However, their opposition was not strong enough to send them to the Whig party, traditionally nativistic. In 1856 they stood solidly behind Buchanan, but the slavery issue split them during the following 4 years. In 1858 Douglas's anti-Lecompton battle swung many of the puzzled Germans back to the Douglas camp and aided greatly in his election.[3] But the desertion of the German leaders Schneider, Koerner, and Carl Schurz left the Germans a very doubtful element in the 1858 election. Both parties fought for this vote.[4] It was not until 1860 that the rank and file of the Germans followed their leaders into the Republican camp.

On the other hand, the French were solidly behind the Republicans from the beginning, and the Irish remained staunchly Democratic and were opposed to nativism throughout the decade.[5] Thus the decline of Democratic power in this period was caused in part by the switch of the foreign vote from the Democratic to the Republican party, resulting primarily from hatred of slavery that characterized the emigrants who had fled their native lands to escape oppression.

A second political development was the decline and death of the Whig party between 1836 and 1853. During those years it did not win a single election, but any year after 1848 a fusion of Whigs with the American party would have ousted the Democrats. However, the Whigs were not radical enough on the slavery issue for the Americans, and no fusion resulted. Strongly and traditionally conservative, many Whigs in 1854 and 1856 joined the Democrats rather than join the new, seemingly radical Republican party.[6] Although the majority of Whigs were antislavery, they were

[1] Frank E. Stevens, "Life of Stephen A. Douglas," *Journal*, 16 (Springfield, 1923–1924): 333; *Journal*, 7: 7–33; Cole, *op. cit.*, p. 150.

[2] *Illinois Journal*, Mar. 15, 1854; Beveridge, *op. cit.*, II, 228; Cole, *op. cit.*, p. 123.

[3] Lincoln to Berdan, July 10, 1856, in Paul M. Angle, *New Letters . . .* , pp. 161–162, discussing the problem of the Germans. See also Freeport letter, typical of many, to Douglas, Mar. 1, 1858, enclosing resolutions of a German meeting endorsing Douglas's actions.

[4] Smalley to Douglas, Jan. 20, 1858; Bach to Douglas, Apr. 10, 1858; and A. V. Hofer to Douglas, July 1, 1858, Douglas MSS.

[5] Harris to Douglas, July 7, 1858, Douglas MSS; Cole, *op. cit.*, pp. 176–177.

[6] *Transactions*, 32: 109. The foundation of Douglas's charge of conspiracy between Lincoln and Trumbull dates back to Whig trouble with the radical element. Douglas seemed to have enough reason to believe the charge. Lincoln's Whig friends and supporters were outraged at

not ready to consort with abolitionists, whom Clay had taught them to fear. Some joined the Republicans, others the Democrats, but a great number were unaffiliated. With the Germans they created the real audience to whom the two parties were forced to plead for votes. These two groups would decide the 1858 election. Unaffiliated Whig strongholds were for the most part in central Illinois; the Yankee and Scandinavian Whigs of the north had gone Republican.

In Illinois the Republican party was born in 1856, after an unsuccessful attempt by abolitionists to form such a party in 1854. It was a fusion of many elements—Know-Nothings, strongly antislavery Whigs, abolitionists, renegade Democrats, and Free-Soilers. These groups fused on the antislavery issue but did not agree on the solution to the problem. Because of the abolitionary character of the 1854 organizers, the Democrats and many unaffiliated Whigs and Germans had been led to believe that the Republican party was in truth a party of abolitionists.[1] Previous parties had been strongly united and national in nature. The conservative Whigs, the Germans, and the Democrats could not understand that a great political party could be united against a common enemy, though divided in opinion as to the proper solution of the evil it fought. Therefore, these groups did not believe that the 1856 platform represented the true aim of the party. The Democrats believed the mild platform a clever attempt at concealment, a dishonest bid for votes. The sectional nature of the party, together with incompatible arguments advanced by leaders in different parts of the state, lent credence to this belief. The political trend of the decade was a shifting of party affiliation. It was a shifting of power to the hands of the more radically inclined, but the shift was not completed until the end of the decade. The campaign of 1858 was unlike either that of 1856 or that of 1860. In 1856 the Democrats were still dominant; in 1860 the Republicans were certain to win. In 1858, however, each party had a chance to win, and each party was determined to get control of the legislature and send its representative to the Senate of the United States.

Trumbull's election in 1855.—*House Journal* (Illinois), Feb. 10, 1855, pp. 391–392. The *Illinois State Register* chuckled that for weeks the Whigs had flirted with the radicals in order to get votes and that the Whigs had been skinned instead (Feb. 12, 1855). This undenied argument came back to trouble Lincoln in 1858. Trumbull felt his obligation to Lincoln.—Trumbull to Palmer, June 19, 1858, *Journal*, 16: 120–141; Beveridge, *op. cit.*, II, 383, 525, 555.

[1] In Abolition-controlled communities, the Republican party was frankly abolitionist; in Whig-controlled communities, the Republican party stood against extension of slave territory (*e.g., cf.* the "Resolutions adopted at . . . Rockford, Aug. 30, 1858," found in Douglas MSS, with those adopted at Whig Springfield). For statements of radical leaders, see Beveridge, *op. cit.*, II, 411–453. Douglas and other Democrats honestly believed Lincoln and other Republicans to be abolitionists at heart.

One other item should be noticed. It was the day of joint debate, with campaigns extending over seven or eight months and stump speaking playing a major role. When joint debates were scheduled, rigid rules of timekeeping were kept, and the audiences of from a few hundred to 15,000 remained listening for two or three hours—often in the rain. Caravans of listeners would travel 50 miles or more by ox cart or horseback to hear some of these discussions. The people of Illinois were tremendously interested in their politics.

Certain other beliefs of the people of Illinois have been indicated by the foregoing discussion. The very character of the people and the manner of their living made them love a fighter. They liked the man who would carry the fight to his opponent, not the man who was content to defend himself.[1] Democratic people that they were, they insisted that their orators speak a democratic language and disliked eloquence if it seemed to them to be showy or affected. They understood and appreciated local slang, forceful phrases, and language that was highly declarative.[2] "Manifest Destiny" was a fixed belief. It had guided the earlier settlers in their actions and still influence the people of the state. Just as strong was the belief of many in the strength and glory of the Union. The disunion element of Ohio and the Eastern abolitionists was not reflected in the masses of Illinois,[3] as the continual championing of the Union on the part of both parties indicated. These, then, were the people to whom Douglas spoke.

The Occasion

Speaking generally, the occasion for the campaign speeches made by Douglas in 1858 is so well known that it demands little explanation here. Douglas, a member of the Senate of the United States for nearly twelve years, was seeking re-election. Lincoln, a local politician and lawyer, who 10 years earlier had served one term in the United States House of Representatives and who had left that body to find himself in disrepute at home,

---

[1] That the Republicans realized this tendency to despise the defender and uphold the aggressive man was shown by their continued advice to Lincoln to keep Douglas from getting him on the defensive. It may account for Lincoln's questions to Douglas at Freeport and no doubt accounts in part for the more aggressive stand Lincoln took in the later debates. Judd, for example, wrote Trumbull, "The only trouble will be that (as I told him) he will allow Douglas to put him on the defensive. . . . "—Beveridge, *op. cit.*, II, 609.

[2] *Illinois Monthly Magazine* was forced to move to Ohio because it was too literary for the people of Illinois. The slang used by nearly all orators, even preacher Lovejoy, in Illinois, during the period, together with similar slang found in most of the existing private letters and newspapers, bears out the conclusion.

[3] *Illinois State Register*, Aug. 12, 1856. Almost no instance of disunion sentiment can be found in the letters or newspapers of the period in Illinois. What disunion sentiment existed in the North was to be found further east.—*Fulton Democrat*, Oct. 24, 1857.

was opposing as the "unanimous choice" of the newly created Republican party. These men were not canvassing for votes for themselves but were working for votes for their colleagues, who were running for seats in the Illinois legislature. The legislature, in turn, would elect the Senator, the procedure followed in 1858. The issue was basically that of "popular sovereignty" for the newly created territories on the issue of slavery, versus the determined stand of the Republicans—"No more slave territory."

But beneath the surface of these well-known facts were many and varied matters that made the occasion of each speech a new and varied problem. If the occasion in general and the specific occasions discovered in different sections in particular are to be truly appreciated and evaluated, much more must be explained.

First of all, the battle was not a simple battle of campaign speeches between Douglas and Lincoln. Much of the actual work of the campaign was of necessity carried on by the newspapers. Further, each man could count upon the support of local men who were candidates in each district, and upon powerful allies brought in from outside the State.[1] Lincoln and Douglas could also depend upon their unseen audiences in every section of the state reading their more telling arguments. They could depend upon allies in unvisited sections and could depend a great deal upon party ballyhoo.

A second factor, which added to the concern of Douglas and the joy of Lincoln, was the split within the Democratic party. Douglas's anti-Lecompton fight in the Senate, which he had just won against unbelievable odds, had embittered an already unfriendly administration toward him. Buchanan was determined to kill the Little Giant, even though it meant the election of a Republican Senator from Illinois.[2]

A third factor that influenced a decision in preparing the campaign was that of the apportionment basis under which local legislators were elected and the location of what both parties knew to be "doubtful"

---

[1] Lincoln had more of this type of support than did Douglas. Senator Trumbull stumped the state, causing more trouble than Lincoln.—Cole, *op. cit.*, p. 173; Beveridge, *op. cit.*, II, 587; see Douglas's speeches. Bright, Fitch, Willard, Carpenter, and Leib campaigned against Douglas at Buchanan's request.—Douglas MSS, Sheahan to Douglas, Feb. 10, 1858; Ryan to Douglas, Jan. 27, 1858; Ezra Reed to Douglas, Jan. 21, 1858. The Democrats brought in German speakers to offset the work of Schurz, Koerner, Koffman, and others.—Douglas MSS. Breckenridge and Pugh refused to aid Douglas.—Douglas MSS.

[2] *Washington Union*, Dec. 23, 1857; Binmore to Douglas, July 22, 1858; S. W. Randall to Douglas, Feb. 26, 1858; J. J. Harvey to Douglas, July 11, 1858; W. D. Bien to Douglas, Jan. 18, 1858; and many other letters to Douglas reporting "Head Lopping," Douglas MSS; *Illinois Daily State Journal*, Jan. 30, Mar. 24, Apr. 30, May 8, June 7, 30, July 23, 1858; Harris to Lanphier, Jan. 30, and May 27, 1858; Douglas to Lanphier, Dec. 3, 1853, and Apr. 3, 1855, Patton MSS.

districts. The 1850 apportionment basis was still in use, thus nullifying a part of the tremendous increase in anti-slavery vote in the northern part of the state. The two candidates knew that the "pivotal counties would be Scott, Morgan, Sangamon, Macoupin, Madison, St. Clair, Randolph, Bond, Mason, Champaign, Logan, Macon, Peoria, Woodford, Marshall, Putnam, and Coles."[1] The Republican party believed itself certain of winning enough legislative seats to elect Lincoln. It listed its assets as (1) growth of Republican strength, (2) disorganization and split of the Democrats, (3) the belief that Illinois Republicans knew Douglas to be "Ambitious, Unscrupulous, Desperate."[2]

A fourth factor in the campaign that Douglas recognized and attempted to meet was that of newspaper affiliation. Through newspapers the candidates must reach the unseen audience. By 1856 most of the leading papers in northern Illinois were Republican. In other sections the Republicans had the advantage. But many new papers were established, most of them Democratic, supported financially by Douglas.[3] Newspapers played a dual role. Both sides printed only the speeches of their own candidates, unless an editor believed that printing both speeches would be damaging to the enemy.[4] Second, newspapers made almost every charge against an opposing candidate that the originality of the editor could devise.[5]

The fifth element of importance was that of the issues involved. Through its own organ each party stated the issue as it saw it. Douglas's paper[6] claimed the issue was:

> Mr. Lincoln is recommended for senator, and however unusual such an issue may be, it is now plainly and squarely one before the people of the State for United States Senator—Stephen A. Douglas on the one side and Abraham Lincoln on the other. The Democracy of one against the black republican principles of the other. For one we accept the issue in this shape, and shall so fight the battle—popular sovereignty against congressional sovereignty—democracy against federalism.

On the other hand, Lincoln's Chicago organ saw the issue as one based upon the right of the people of a territory to exclude slavery in the light

[1] Parmenias Bond to Trumbull, June 28, 1856, Trumbull MSS; Harris to Douglas, July 7, 1858, Douglas MSS. Douglas's speaking itinerary shows that he followed Harris's advice, speaking twenty-four times in the counties named and twenty-one times in neighboring towns, ignoring pleas for speeches from other counties.—Douglas MSS.

[2] *New York Semi Weekly Tribune*, Oct. 12, July 20, 1858; Herndon to Parker, Aug. 31, 1858 (reprinted in Newton, *op. cit.*, pp. 202–203).

[3] *Collections*, VI, lxxix, for list of papers and affiliation. For Douglas's financial support of papers, see Douglas MSS, letters of 1857 and 1858.

[4] For example, *Knox Republican*, June to December, 1858, and *Fulton Democrat*, July to December, 1858.

[5] The writer has itemized thirteen major charges made by the Republican press and six major countercharges by the Democratic press.

[6] *Illinois State Register*, June 17, 1858.

of the Supreme Court decision concerning Dred Scott.[1] Both parties accepted the issue as that of territorial popular sovereignty on slavery. But as in most arguments, the opponents placed different construction on the definition of the issues and the actions of opposing candidates. Because the people of the State were familiar with the issues, the latter element became dominant in the campaign. It was, then, a campaign in which the people must be taught to interpret the motives behind past happenings, doings, and sayings that were well known to those people. Each candidate must make the people accept his own interpretations.

Thus, although the apparent issue between the two parties was that of popular sovereignty versus the demand of the Republicans for no more slave territory, the actual issue between Lincoln and Douglas was the ethical one of their relative consistency and honesty. Each was trying to build his own prestige in order to win the votes of the suspicious Germans and Whigs. Douglas fought the suspicion that he was in league with the South; Lincoln fought the suspicion that he was in league with the abolitionists. Douglas's Nebraska bill had aroused the ire of all antislavery elements in Illinois; the Dred Scott decision had added fuel to the flames; but Douglas's anti-Lecompton fight had partially allayed the fears of the unaffiliated Whigs and Germans. All the arguments of the campaign were directed toward establishing or destroying prestige. In reality, the issue was the single one of the motives of the candidates.

The Man

In evaluating Douglas as a speaker, the first questions to be answered are: Did he make an attempt to analyze his audience? Was he familiar with, or did he make an attempt to discover, the basic beliefs and attitudes of the listeners? Did he familiarize himself with the trends that influenced them?

It must be remembered that Douglas spent the 15 years preceding 1858 in Washington, D. C. During that time a great change took place in the people of Illinois, the political character of the state, and the basic beliefs and attitudes of the populace. That Douglas was conscious of these changes, that he made repeated and varied efforts to analyze the trends and their results, and that he was in closer touch with the pulse of his constituents than any other man in Illinois is now quite obvious. Not only did he take a number of Illinois newspapers,[2] not only did he rely on his huge cor-

---

[1] *Chicago Daily Journal*, Aug. 24, 1858, listing eight questions for Douglas to answer, all based on this fundamental issue.

[2] See Douglas MSS for many letters telling of the placing of Douglas's name on subscription lists. See Patton MSS for letters from Douglas to Lanphier, asking for Illinois papers so that Douglas might keep in touch with events in Illinois.

respondence,[1] not only did he place lieutenants and research workers in the field[2] but he took part in every campaign in the state, speaking hundreds of times, in every section.[3] Further than this, he spent much time, when not on duty in Washington, quietly traveling over Illinois, meeting and talking with every class of people.[4] It is doubtful if any man could have done more to analyze his audience during the 10 years preceding 1858. As a result of this analysis and because of his remarkable memory for names and personal interests, Douglas was in an excellent position to analyze his seen and unseen audiences during the campaign.[5]

A second question of importance concerns the method used by Douglas in preparing his speeches. Little positive evidence remains on this point. But it seems certain that he spoke extemporaneously in every instance during the campaign of 1858. Stevens tells us that Douglas frequently admitted that he could not write a speech for delivery.[6] The conclusion is further borne out by the lack of speech notes found in the Douglas manuscripts. Although the manuscripts contain many personal items, such as receipts for hotel bills, not a single speech outline or page of notes taken during the debates is to be found for the year 1858. One thing is certain; like all local campaigns in which Douglas participated for 25 years, that of 1858 was far too strenuous to allow either contestant to write out his speeches in full, even had he been so inclined. Lincoln claimed that he trusted to the inspiration of the moment; the more experienced Douglas may have done likewise.

More positive evidence that the speeches were not written lies within reported speeches themselves. Douglas was often interrupted by members of his audience or by an opponent on the platform. In every instance he replied to his questioner, and after his reply,[7] worked back smoothly into

[1] Douglas MSS. There are over twenty thousand letters in this group, more than one-third of which are from people in Illinois. Many contain clippings and other information about events and people in the state or express opinions on political issues.

[2] Harris to Douglas, July 7, 1858; Dunn to Douglas, Jan. 16, 1858; Thornaz to Douglas, Jan. 12, 1858; Lanphier to Douglas, Aug. 26, 1858; Drum to Douglas, Sept. 20, 1858, Douglas MSS. See also many letters from Douglas to Lanphier, Patton MSS, asking the Illinois editor to obtain and forward information.

[3] Beveridge (*op. cit.*, II, 162) concluded that Douglas came in contact with more people in more places than any other politician, learning at first hand the state of public opinion.

[4] *Fulton Democrat*, Oct. 3, 1858 (reprinting the *Newburyport* [Mass.] *Herald's* Illinois correspondent); Hatch to Trumbull, Sept. 11, 1857; Douglas to Lanphier, July 7, 1855.

[5] Douglas's disputed action in repeating his explanation of the "Freeport Doctrine" becomes significantly obvious in the light of his knowledge of his audience.

[6] Frank E. Stevens, "Life of Stephen A. Douglas," *Journal of the Illinois State Historical Society*, 16 (Springfield, 1923-1924): 266.

[7] In the "Joliet Speech" of Aug. 31, 1858, for example, Douglas was interrupted fourteen times by members of his audience. In the same speech he was interrupted six times by Lovejoy, Republican Congressman, seated upon the platform.—*Joliet Signal*, Sept. 7, 1858.

the stream of thought that had been interrupted. We must conclude that Douglas carried the outline of his speech in mind and delivered that speech extemporaneously.

A third question of importance concerns the source of Douglas's ideas. The first and principal source seemed to be that of observation and experience. As one of the major actors in the Compromise of 1850, as the leader of the Democratic party in the Senate for 6 years preceding the campaign, as adviser to the party leaders in the House of Representatives, as a tireless stump speaker in all parts of the Union in support of Democratic nominees, as chairman of the Senate Committee on Territories, as author of the Kansas-Nebraska bill, and as the leader in the fight against the Lecompton constitution, Douglas's knowledge of the history of the campaign issues was as sound as that of any man in the country at that time. He had been one of the moving spirits in the political events of the preceding 10 years. Standing high in the councils of the party, he was in a position to know what went on behind the scenes.

One vital influence of this nature on Douglas's argument was that of the Democratic party. Douglas arrived in Illinois and began to take part in politics at the very time the Jackson men were forming the Democratic party. The basic principle of party organizations was that of the convention and party regularity. The convention idea was new; never before had party representatives met, defined the party creed, and selected party candidates. The resulting conception of party regularity demanded that party members must vote only for candidates selected by the convention, that the candidate must subordinate his own opinion to the principles drafted by the convention, and that officeholders must carry out only the measures approved by the convention. Douglas took part in this movement from the first. For 25 years, preceding 1858, Douglas was schooled in the philosophy of the Democrats. Party fidelity as outlined in the platform was the ruling principle of his political life. It came before the principle of personal gain and before the principle of fidelity to the dictates of the President. After 25 years under this principle, it was natural for him to believe that the Danites were no longer true Democrats, because they deliberately attempted to violate the Cincinnati platform plank of popular sovereignty. It was just as natural for him to fail to understand that a great political party could develop without unity of thought and purpose. His political life had been spent under a system of national parties, whose elements agreed on all their political aims. In the light of his past experiences with the Whig and Democratic parties, Douglas could only believe that the middle-of-the-road statements of the Bloomington Republican platform and the denials of Abolitionism made by the Republican candidate Lincoln were clever attempts to disguise the true Abolition doctrines of the party

797

in order to win votes. His experiences with abolitionists, his observations of Lincoln's actions, and his experiences with party regularity influenced him in accepting the belief that Lincoln and the Republicans were at heart abolitionists.

Douglas's attitude toward the institution of slavery was likewise a product of his environment. An Eastern Yankee by birth and education, a Westerner by adoption and training, a Southerner by marriage, Douglas was in an excellent position to appreciate the many and varied attitudes of the different sections of Illinois on the slavery question. Although he repeatedly declared his indifference to the fate of the Negro in other sections of the Union and stoutly maintained his belief in the sanctity of popular sovereignty as more important to civilization than all the Negroes in the South, he nowhere declared in favor of slavery extension. His actions and words lead us to believe that he would have voted against slavery in any locality in which he lived, had he been required to vote as an ordinary citizen. Douglas sympathized with the South, understood its philosophy, and battled for the constitutional rights of that section. His Yankee training had been tempered by the relatively disinterested attitude of early Illinois and still further by his contact with his wife's people and his political and social friends in the South. He could not accept slavery as a moral good;[1] neither could he accept it as an intolerable wrong. Instead, he seemed resolutely to refuse to consider the moral aspect in connection with his political duties. Popular sovereignty was a principle of expediency. Under its dictates peace would reign. As the 1850 agitation showed, under any other policy the Union was endangered or lost. The hope of the white race depended upon preservation of the Union and came before moral or religious considerations for the blacks. Douglas's attitude toward the institution of slavery was a product of his environment.

Another basic belief that Douglas accepted because of environmental training was that of the manifest destiny[2] of the United States. This belief prompted one of the strongest arguments of his campaign—the argument that Lincoln's evasion of the "no more slave States" question was an evasion of future certainty. And his belief in manifest destiny clearly underlay the necessity for the preservation of the Union, the basis for arguments in behalf of popular sovereignty.

Two other philosophies that developed from experience were clearly evidenced in the campaign. First, Douglas came to believe early in life

---

[1] *Congressional Globe*, Thirtieth Congress, first session, Appendix, pp. 506–507; Thirty-second Congress, first session, Appendix, p. 66; *Transactions* (1901), pp. 48 *et seq.*; Douglas to Lanphier, Aug. 3, 1850, Patton MSS.

[2] See Douglas's speeches made at Freeport, Ottawa, Quincy, Alton, Charleston, Jonesboro, and Joliet; see also his speech on Cuba, quoted by Howland, *op. cit.*, p. 172.

that it is well to "admit nothing and require my adversary to prove everything material to the success of his case."[1] This philosophy lay behind his determination to keep his opponent always on the defensive and was evidenced by his shrewd guess that Lincoln's and Trumbull's charges were attempts to place Douglas on the defensive. It also was evidenced in his refusal to admit that the Rockford resolutions did not represent the Republican party in 1858. He promised his Northern audiences that he would look into the matter of his error when he arrived in Springfield, but he did not completely capitulate until the necessity of debate made it profitable.[2] This philosophy was one of Douglas's strongest debate techniques.

Second, Douglas early decided that "indiscriminate abuse of political opponents, whose humble condition or insignificance prevents the possibility of injury, and who may be greatly benefited by the notoriety thus acquired" was "foolish and impolitic."[3] It accounted for Douglas's attitude toward Lincoln during the campaign.[4]

Still another set of beliefs that was influenced strongly by his experience, tempered slightly by his reading, was Douglas's religious concept. A Congregationalist by birth, he acquired a distaste for all Northern preachers because of their interference in politics. But he allowed his Catholic wife to raise their children as Catholics, and he himself read books on religion. It was political experience that affected his religious ideas.

Douglas's belief that popular sovereignty would rule in spite of Congressional law also grew from experience and observation. This doctrine of the power of local legislation, as outlined at Freeport and elsewhere, became the ruling principle of his life and was the basis upon which all his arguments rested in the 1858 campaign. During the years in Illinois he observed the practical operations of popular sovereignty and the effectiveness of unfriendly legislation in many and varied instances.[5]

---

[1] Stephen A. Douglas, *Autobiography*, written in 1838, reprinted from the *Journal of the Illinois State Historical Society*, October, 1912, by the Illinois State Journal Co., State Printers, Springfield, 1913, pp. 19–20.

[2] This refusal cost Lincoln much time and trouble in repeating the charge of "fraud," and it allowed Douglas to draw into every discussion a reference to Lincoln's earlier and unfortunate war record. It also allowed Douglas to take a strong offensive on the matter of Lincoln's Abolition tendencies.

[3] Douglas, *Autobiography*, pp. 15–16.

[4] In the early part of the campaign he spoke "kindly" of Lincoln and confined his adverse remarks to inference and mild ridicule. Not until Trumbull's charges were made and widely printed did Douglas believe the time had come for strong invective.

[5] Douglas had witnessed the practical operation of this law in Illinois under the "Black Laws" during the thirties and forties, subsequent black legislation in the fifties, helplessness of courts in face of local antipathy to liquor-interest property rights, the failure of prohibition laws, the acceptance of usury in the face of illegality, the operation of underground railroads and refusal to support the Fugitive Slave Law, the failure to convict those who aided runaway

Thus it appears that experience and observation influenced Douglas greatly in the acceptance of certain beliefs and philosophies that dictated his actions and arguments in the 1858 campaign. Environmental influences accounted in part for his anti-Lecompton fight, which rested on his acceptance of the theory of support of party principles as outlined in the convention platform. They accounted for his arguments against the Danites, who were running counter to his philosophy of party regularity. They accounted for his conviction that Lincoln and the Republican party were hiding their Abolition purposes behind a mildly worded platform and accounted for his refusal to accept that platform as the official position of the Republican party. Experience and observation influenced him greatly in his attitude toward slavery, caused him to accept and practice his "admit nothing" philosophy, gave him his philosophy concerning invective, accounted for his lack of active religious affiliation in the face of popular criticism, and accounted for his firm conviction in the manifest destiny of the United States, the basis for the principal arguments of the campaign. Experience and observation likewise offered a foundation for his belief in, and arguments in behalf of, the primacy of popular sovereignty in territories as well as in states; and they accounted for his acceptance of, and his insistance in, the strength and justice of the theory of "unfriendly legislation."

Douglas was also influenced by certain of his contemporaries, by certain fathers of the Republic, and by certain British and American orators. Chief among his contemporaries in their influence upon him were Cass and Clay: Cass, in his advocacy of popular sovereignty;[1] Clay, in his attitude of compromise in 1850.[2] Second to these in influence upon Douglas were famous British and American orators: Burke, with his philosophy of ultimate good of the decision of the masses, Chatham, the master of invective, Calhoun, with his demonstration that extreme philosophy on slavery was disastrous.[3] From boyhood Douglas was an inveterate reader of the Congressional debates, a practice that he continued during the 1858 campaign.[4] His wide reading of Congressional debates, of the Constitutional Convention debates, and of those of the several states on the adoption of the Constitution must have done much to convince him that the fathers

---

slaves, the failure to guarantee free speech to abolitionist Lovejoy, duels taking place in spite of law, cities denying circuses and theatres the right of doing business, etc. His life in Illinois had proved that popular sovereignty ruled, regardless of Congressional action.

[1] McClernand to Lanphier and Walker, May 30, 1848, Patton MSS; and Shields to Douglas, Apr. 25, 1848, Douglas MSS.

[2] Douglas referred to Clay and his attitude toward compromise in nearly every speech of the campaign.

[3] *Congressional Globe*, Thirtieth Congress, first session, Appendix, pp. 507–508; Douglas speech of Feb. 23, 1859, quoting Calhoun, Douglas MSS.

[4] Douglas, *Autobiography*, pp. 10, 15; Douglas to Lanphier, August, 1858, Patton MSS.

of the Republic did not include the Negro in the "equality clause" of the Declaration of Independence.[1]

These readings, together with his study of law, gave Douglas a basis for his attitude toward the courts. Although no narrow constructionalist, Douglas believed firmly in the necessity of recognizing the supremacy of court decisions. He did not deny the right of man to differ with the court[2] but insisted that a war upon the court was a war upon one of the foundations of democracy. It is quite clear that on this issue Douglas rationalized on a basis of expediency, unless we conclude that he completely reversed his philosophy of 18 years before, when he fought the Supreme Court of Illinois on the issue of "bias."[3]

Douglas's philosophy of unfriendly legislation was probably influenced by a number of his contemporaries. It was no new doctrine. Calhoun, Webster, Seward, Theodore Parker, Orr, of South Carolina, and others had advocated or admitted the truth of the principle, each in his turn.[4] Both the abolitionists of the North and the extremists of the South had advanced the theory at one time or another. The Republican party of the state of Illinois advanced the doctrine in regard to states, refusing to admit its operation in territories. And even Lincoln, in his "Bloomington Speech," in 1856, had argued that the time would come when only local laws could "shelter a slaveholder" in defiance of the Constitution. Further, two justices of the Supreme Court and the conservative press throughout the land had argued at the time of the Dred Scott case that it was an abstraction that could not re-establish slavery in free territory.[5] That Douglas was acquainted with, noticed, and was influenced by these statements is shown by his letter to Lanphier and Walker.[6] Hence the second great source of Douglas's ideas was that of the arguments of great statesmen, both past and contemporary.

A third source of influence was that of contemporary public opinion as expressed in newspapers and in letters from his constituents. Thousands of letters from all parts of the country poured in upon him, reporting

---

[1] Madison Cutts, *A Brief Treatise upon Constitutional and Party Questions* (New York, D. Appleton & Company, 1866), pp. 50–51, quoting Douglas. The campaign speeches show familiarity with the lives and thoughts of these men.

[2] Cutts, *op. cit.*, pp. 11, 53–54, quoting Douglas.

[3] Douglas, *Autobiography*, pp. 17–18; Stevens, *op. cit.*, p. 334.

[4] For Calhoun's statement, see his Fugitive Slave Law speech, *Congressional Globe*, Thirty-first Congress, first session, 21, Part I: 483–484; for Seward's statement, see *ibid.*, Thirty-first Congress, first session, 22, Part II, Appendix: 260–269. Webster argued it again and again, as did Parker.—Beveridge, *op. cit.*, II, 101; II, 27, 131. Douglas referred to Orr's statement again and again in 1858.

[5] Beveridge, *op. cit.*, I, 439; II, 377, 571, 486; *Chicago Tribune*, Mar. 14, 1857.

[6] Patton MSS, Jan. 7, 1850. (Douglas asked that they burn the letter.)

popular sentiment, criticizing, or offering advice. They offered a barometer of public opinion and probably had their influence on Douglas the politician. Together with other influences, they must have affected him in his apparent disregard of Southern sentiment during the anti-Lecompton fight in the Senate and in his freedom from worry over the effect of his "Freeport Doctrine" on Southern voters.[1]

Another important question concerning the man Douglas regards his sincerity and consistency of argument. One of the major charges against him has been that if his popular-sovereignty and unfriendly-legislation arguments were sound, his earlier arguments in favor of rigid enforcement of the Fugitive Slave Law were of necessity unsound. History has argued that, since Douglas advanced both, he must have been insincere in his support of one. Because historians agree that the fugitive-slave enforcement philosophy was sound, they argue that Douglas was guilty of sophistry in advancing the "Freeport Doctrine." Could Douglas consistently and honestly hold refusal to uphold the constitutional guarantee of returning fugitive slaves to be "nullification" and at the same time uphold the right of localities to refuse to protect the slaveowner's property in the territories? Douglas argued that he could, and an examination of his arguments of earlier years seems to prove him sincere in this declaration.[2]

Our question resolves itself into a determination of the method of rationalizing the two beliefs; evidence is conclusive that he was sincere in both. Douglas insisted that slaves were property under the Constitution and that they could therefore be *taken into* the territories. But he argued that that was as far as the constitutional right went with any property; the Constitution could not guarantee the free use and enjoyment of that property in any state or territory. The use and enjoyment of property must of necessity depend upon local law. If the majority of people were against any type of property, the mere right to carry it into the territory was a barren right. He believed the whole question of slavery extension to be "academic." On the other hand, the Fugitive Slave Law was a compromise gesture, which guaranteed the return of runaway slaves to their owners. To withhold legislation in this case was to break a contract the North had made with the South—was to break an express guarantee of the Constitution itself. Had the Constitution guaranteed to the slaveholder that the *use* and *enjoyment* of slavery would be protected in the territories, Douglas would have been forced to uphold that guarantee, as he did the Fugitive Slave Law. As it was, Douglas could see no incon-

---

[1] The full evidence on this point, as gathered and documented by the author, fills six typewritten pages, and obviously cannot be reproduced here. But it is definite and conclusive.

[2] Again the full documented evidence cannot be reproduced here for lack of space, as it fills five typewritten pages.

sistency; he was the product of his environment. Both philosophies were philosophies of expediency, and he believed in both with sincerity and honesty. Douglas saw no more inconsistency in these two beliefs than did the judges in the 1930's who upheld labor's right to strike but denied labor the right to enforce its demands by use of the sit-down strike.

Another charge of inconsistency, and therefore of insincerity, was that Douglas's anti-Lecompton fight was inconsistent with the Kansas-Nebraska bill. However, this charge was based on the false assumption that the Kansas-Nebraska bill was an endeavor to make Kansas and Nebraska slave territory.[1] Both campaigns were actually based on the philosophy of popular sovereignty, and the charge may be quickly dismissed as a political move.

A second and tangent set of charges against Douglas became important in the campaign and later led historians to accept the Republican charge that Douglas was at heart a sophist. One of the best known of these grew out of Douglas's unfortunate use of a set of local Republican resolutions during the Ottawa debate. He erred in naming the place at which the resolutions were drawn. Lincoln charged Douglas with forgery; historians have charged that Douglas did not always make a reasonable effect to assure the authenticity or validity of his evidence before using it.[2] Recently discovered evidence substantiates Douglas's claim that he acted in good faith and that he made a serious attempt to determine the authenticity of the materials he used.[3]

Historians have also charged that Douglas was willing to draw "conclusions only half warranted by fact"[4] because he claimed that the Nebraska bill was based on the fundamental principle involved in the Compromise of 1850. They hold that his real motive for introduction of the bill was that it opened the territory for a transcontinental railroad.[5]

[1] *Chicago Daily Journal*, June 30, July 26, 1858; *New York Tribune*, Sept. 21, 1858.

[2] J. W. Burgess, *The Middle Period* (New York, Charles Scribner's Sons, 1897), p. 385; Stevens, *op. cit.*, p. 329; Barnes, *op. cit.*, p. 29.

[3] Douglas was in the midst of his campaign and could not travel to Springfield to check on the statement of Major Harris. Hence he wrote to Lanphier (Patton MSS), asking his friend and political advisor to check Harris's evidence. Lanphier supplied Douglas with the false information he used. Douglas again wrote (Aug. 26, 1858), and again Lanphier replied. The letters are not those of a careless man; rather they are those of the very careful speaker. He refused to rely on the *Register's* report of Harris's speech in the *Congressional Globe*, attempting to check the evidence further. The letters bear out in every detail Douglas's explanation during the campaign.

[4] Barnes, *op. cit.*, p. 29, 163; see footnote 3, p. 778.

[5] George F. Milton, in *The Eve of Conflict* (Boston, Houghton Mifflin Company, 1934), p. 101, believes this the most convincing reason for the repeal of the Missouri Compromise but adds to it the "pleas of the land-hungry for virgin soil; the desire of the Wyandotte Indians for a share in the prosperity of the pale-face, the complexities of Iowa politics and the Missouri

There seems to be little doubt that the railroad issue had its influence upon the repeal of the Missouri Compromise. But it does not follow that Douglas was dishonest in his assertion that he was consistent and sincere in his belief that the Nebraska bill was based upon the principle established by the Compromise of 1850. It would seem that an honest belief in the universal acceptance of the principle of popular sovereignty was a natural conclusion to the experiences we have enumerated elsewhere in this study. Twice before as chairman of the Senate Committee on Territories, he had introduced a bill opening Nebraska. Although he found his new bill profitable to himself, it does not follow that this discovery changed his opinion concerning the universality of the acceptance of popular sovereignty. Douglas, as well as others, had argued before 1854 that the Missouri Compromise had never been operative, that popular sovereignty would have kept the slaves out as surely had no Missouri Compromise been in existence. The charge of insincerity or "of drawing conclusions only half warranted by fact" does not seem to be valid in this instance.

One of the chief, if not the most effective, arguments used by the Republicans to kill Douglas's prestige in 1858 was Senator Trumbull's charge that Douglas had conspired to "defraud and cheat the people [of Kansas] out of their right, and then claim credit for it."[1] Subsequent historians have argued that the charge was untrue.[2]

The various charges of inconsistency made against Douglas during the campaign and since by historians seem to have been unfounded. However, these charges were valuable to the Republicans in bringing again before the people of Illinois the question raised by the "Appeal of 1854." Could Douglas be trusted? The charges forced him to the defensive, the weaker position with the audience he had to convince. How well he handled himself on the defensive we shall presently see. Coupled with other and minor attacks of dishonesty, these charges increased and redeveloped the suspicions engendered by the Kansas-Nebraska bill and the Chase "Appeal."

The final question of importance concerns Douglas as a public speaker. Although he studied the classics as a boy and debated in apprentice shop and academy debates before he left New England,[3] he received his major training in speech from the school of experience. Almost from the time he

---

Democratic War. . . . " Douglas gave the first of these tangent reasons outlined by Milton as the true one.—Cutts, *op. cit.*, pp. 85-101.

[1] Most of the Illinois newspapers in 1858 gave more space to Trumbull's charge than to any single Lincoln argument. Lincoln devoted one of the debates with Douglas to this charge.

[2] Beveridge, *op. cit.*, II, 420, 527-529, 578; Cole, *op. cit.*, pp. 173-174; Milton, *op. cit.*, p. 334; *Congressional Globe*, Thirty-fifth Congress, first session, Part I, pp. 21-22, 112, 113-122, 127.

[3] Douglas, *Autobiography*, pp. 9-10.

reached Illinois until the day of his death, Douglas took part in extremely arduous political campaigns and in every major debate while he was in Congress.[1] He supplemented this practical training by reading all the records of Congressional debates, records of many debates of state legislatures, speeches of such men as Burke, Chatham, Webster, Calhoun, and other famous orators.

His delivery was extremely effective. Both friend and foe paid tribute to his ability to hold his audience.[2] All agreed that he used a staccato style of utterance, and most evidence indicates that his voice had great carrying power.[3] It was a deep bass, with an interesting, "explosive quality," yet his enunciation and pronunciation were clear and distinct. He often spoke without using notes of any kind, although he carried much manuscript material to read when the occasion demanded.[4]

In appearance he often was described as "majestic." Short in stature, his head was large, his eyes spirited, his bearing assured. He moved little when he spoke and seldom gestured, depending upon his extremely expressionable features and his able voice to put across the meaning, with little aid from bodily activity.[5] He always dressed in the latest fashion, believing that his constituents liked to see their public servants well dressed.

There is a great deal of evidence to show that honorable, well-read, moral, and courageous Douglas was a good loser, a modest winner, a patriot, a true friend, and a believer in education. Such was the man Douglas, who came to handle the speaking situation before the people we have described earlier.

The Speeches

The preceding analysis shows that a courageous and able speaker, who believed firmly in the necessity for popular sovereignty in the territories, was to address a divided audience in an effort to win approval and confidence. How and with what effectiveness this man handled this situation is the chief concern of the rhetorical critic.

[1] C. E. Carr, in *Stephen A. Douglas* (Chicago, A. C. McClurg & Company, 1909), p. 11, points out, for example, that at twenty-seven Douglas spoke 207 times during a 7-month campaign.

[2] *Oquawka Spectator*, Oct. 17, 1854; *Illinois State Register*, Oct. 31, 1858.

[3] *Republican-Register*, 1908; *Evening Mail*, 1908 (clippings found in the Galesburg Public Library MSS).

[4] *Transactions*, 4: 41–50; *Chicago Times*, July 11, 1858; Milton, *op. cit.*, p. 311.

[5] Carr, *op. cit.*, pp. 41–42, quoting the *New York Times;* William H. Herndon and Jesse W. Weik, *Abraham Lincoln* (D. Appleton & Company, Inc., 1901), p. 94; Louis Howland, *Stephen A. Douglas* (New York, Charles Scribner's Sons, 1920), p. 234, quoting Mrs. Stowe, an enemy. Volk's life-sized statue of Douglas stands today on the capitol grounds at Springfield, Ill. See also, *Transactions*, 4: 41–50.

Because Douglas was pleading for election, one would expect to be able to classify the speeches of the 1858 campaign as *deliberative* in character. Theoretically, he was pleading for future action to an audience of "judges of the future." One expects to find "advice and counsel" predominant in the speeches of "exhortation and dissuasion." Any consideration, other than those of "advantage and injury" to the state upon the outcome of the election, would be expected to be subsidiary considerations. However, an examination of existing speeches shows that the chief methods used by Douglas were those of the *forensic* speaker, that is, praise and blame or attack and defense. Rarely is future action mentioned. Without exception the speeches subordinate the elements of *deliberative* speaking and leave *deliberative* ends to inference. The "elements of Forensic speaking," justice and injustice, are the ruling themes. He treats his audiences as "judges of the past" and uses the devices of accusation and defense. According to Aristotle's classification, they are clearly *forensic* speeches, with *deliberative* ends inferred.

The reason for this change in aim and method is quite clear. The issues were well known; the aims and motives of Douglas were under a cloud of suspicion in the important counties. Douglas was in a sense on trial before the great jury of foreign-born and ex-Whigs, upon whom the result of the election largely depended.

Subordinate to these arguments of attack and defense ran a strong "exhortation" for belief in the principle of popular sovereignty, but advice as to the actual vote for local Democratic nominees was left to inference.

In form the speeches fell into two general classes. On seven occasions Douglas entered into formal joint debate with his opponent. On the other occasions he addressed an audience to which his opponent was not to speak immediately. In the latter instances Douglas used the first part of the speech in developing his major arguments and the last part in refutation of arguments made against him previously in the campaign.[1] In formal debate he used two methods of arrangement, according to his place on the program. When he spoke first, he followed the general pattern of speeches given to audiences gathered to hear him alone, his second address being entirely rebuttal in nature. When he followed Lincoln in speaking, Douglas usually "took up where Mr. Lincoln left off," giving the first part of his time to rebuttal arguments and using the latter part for developing arguments not

---

[1] On one or two occasions Lovejoy replied immediately after Douglas had spoken, and at the start of the campaign Lincoln talked a few hours after Douglas's meetings had broken up. But repeated objection to this procedure by the Democratic press made Lincoln believe it advisable to delay his arrival and answer for a day or two. See *Illinois State Register*, Aug. 2, 1858; *Daily Chicago Times*, Oct. 1, 1858; *Chicago Daily Journal*, July 21, 1858; *The Writings of Abraham Lincoln* (A. B. Lapsley, ed., New York, P. F. Collier & Son, Inc., 1906), V, 9; Buckner to Douglas, July 30, 1858, Douglas MSS.

mentioned by his opponent—for a constructive case. Excepting the latter occasions, then, the form of the speeches consisted of a short introduction (designed to put the audience in a receptive frame of mind), an absence of a statement of thesis, constructive arguments, refutation of opponent's arguments, and a short appeal for belief in the major theme of the speech.

The authenticity of the texts of the printed speeches is in no doubt so far as ideas and methods of presenting them are concerned. Because this study is not concerned with style, the printed speeches are authentic enough for its purpose.

The first question of importance concerning the effectiveness of Douglas's speaking in this campaign is whether he was able to adapt his arguments and materials to the stereotypes or mental attitudes of the different audiences he faced.

One of the best indications of his ability so to adapt lies in a comparison of the first three speeches of the campaign, delivered on July 9, 16, and 17 at Chicago, Bloomington, and Springfield, respectively. The three audiences differed greatly, ranging from Abolition Chicago, through Whig Bloomington, to friendly Springfield. These three speeches use approximately the same evidence and are based on the same philosophy, but great differences are to be found in the way these arguments are framed and in the implication of the conclusions that are drawn.

It is important to remember the differences existing among the three audiences. Chicago had a population of nearly one hundred thousand, 50 per cent of which had been born on foreign soil; 13 per cent of Bloomington's 8,000 inhabitants had been born abroad; and 17 per cent of those in Springfield had migrated from Europe. In Chicago the foreign born were of all nationalities, but the majority was divided fairly evenly among Irish, German, and Scandinavian.[1] In Bloomington and Springfield the great majority of foreign born were German. In Chicago Douglas faced very strong opposition and did not expect to win the majority of votes. Cook County was strongly "Free Soil," the marine vote was against Douglas, the Scandinavians were abolitionists, the Germans were suspicious, even the Democratic Irish were against him in July,[2] and many strong Democrats had left the ranks of the party to support the Republicans. In Bloomington, however, Lincoln feared the loss of Republicans to the Douglas cause.[3] The Danites had no power there, there were no marine workers, no Scandinavians, and the city had proved itself conservative.[4] McLean County was

[1] *Chicago Magazine*, March and May, 1857.

[2] Cole, *op. cit.*, p. 161.

[3] Lincoln to Trumbull, Dec. 28, 1857, reprinted in Tracy, *op. cit.*, pp. 83–84.

[4] Bloomington was the site of the state Republican convention in 1856 and placed a restraining hand on the Northern abolitionists present. The county had refused to endorse abolitionist Lovejoy.—Cole, *op. cit.*, p. 150.

one of those marked by Douglas as questionable. It was possible to win this county. In Springfield, on the other hand, Douglas was certain of victory.[1]

An examination of the speeches shows how Douglas varied his ideas before these three audiences, one of which could not be won, one of which might be won, and a third of which was already considered in the Democratic fold.

The introductions differed to fit the audiences: in Chicago Douglas commented upon the strength of the belief in popular sovereignty that would draw such a huge crowd; in Bloomington he acknowledged his recognition of the split in the Democratic party and the alliance between the Danites and Republicans; in Springfield he declared himself happy to believe that the large audience signified approval of his own actions in supporting popular sovereignty.

The theses of the three speeches also differed. At Chicago he argued that popular sovereignty is the dearest and most sacred principle in free government; at Bloomington he stated his thesis to be that of "vindicating" his own actions in the Senate; at Springfield (not clearly stated) the thesis seemed to be that popular sovereignty is the principle upon which the institutions of democracy rest. The second thesis differed widely, then, from the other two; it was at Bloomington only that Douglas believed that a strong defense would influence the election. At Chicago he placed emphasis upon the sacred character of popular sovereignty, the argument that had won that city in 1850 and the philosophy least likely to antagonize the great mass of foreign born who had fled their fatherlands because of oppression. At Springfield he placed emphasis upon the *vital* character of the principle; his audience was more likely to worry over a threat to the existence of the Union.

The first body of proof used in each of the three speeches concerned the anti-Lecompton fight in the Senate and House of Representatives. In each city the majority of voters had been against the Lecompton constitution. But at Chicago Douglas used this body of evidence to prove that he had devoted his best energies to the vindication of popular sovereignty; at Bloomington he used three times as many words in bringing out the same evidence to prove that Douglas had "acted in good faith" with his constituents; at Springfield he used these facts to prove that he would *always* lead the fight against that which threatened the most vital element in the existence of the Union.

[1] Lincoln to Trumbull, Dec. 18, 1857, in Tracy, *op. cit.*, p. 83. Harris, a Douglas man, was elected from Springfield in 1856. Roberts to Douglas, Jan. 7, 1858, Douglas MSS; *Illinois State Register*, Jan. 14, 1858. Springfield never gave its vote to Lincoln; even in the campaign of 1860 the county cast 55 per cent of its vote for Douglas.

The second body of evidence was used at Chicago to prove that the Republicans had recently endorsed popular sovereignty "manfully"; at Bloomington, to prove that the Republicans had "changed over" to popular sovereignty; and at Springfield, to prove that the Republicans had gone over to Douglas, not Douglas to the Republicans.

The third set of evidence was used at Chicago to prove that the principle of popular sovereignty had been vindicated as a permanent rule; at Bloomington, to prove that Douglas had acted in good faith; and at Springfield, only a part of the evidence was used to prove that his "predictions have come true."

The fourth body of proof was used to attack Republican principles of uniformity and Negro equality. At Chicago Douglas said that his "opponent's" theory was less desirable than popular sovereignty; at Bloomington the evidence proved that "Mr. Lincoln's" principles were "less in accordance with the genius of our free institutions, the peace and harmony of the Republic, than those I advocate"; at Springfield the evidence proved Mr. Lincoln's ideas to be "monstrous revolutionary doctrines." Douglas gave more than twice as much time as he used in Chicago to an attack upon Lincoln in both Bloomington and Springfield.

The fifth argument used in Chicago was the unsupported assertion that his fight was against an alliance between the Republicans and the Danites. It is possible that Douglas had the Irish vote in mind when he made the charge; but little or no appeal for either sympathy or action was contained in it. The argument was rather, a warning statement that Douglas would fight whomsoever he found attempting to split the Democratic party, be he Republican or Federal officeholder. At Bloomington, however, the argument became a strong appeal for a solid Democratic front against the Republicans. In Springfield the split in the party was merely mentioned as Lincoln's one chance to win.

In concluding at Chicago, Douglas thanked the audience for the splendid reception it had given him, announcing that it repaid him for his past efforts and offered inducement and incentive for the future. There was no appeal for future action; there was no appeal for belief. It was the summary of a man who had given his arguments, knew that they were not enough, and recognized the uselessness of appealing for votes. At Bloomington, however, the conclusion was nearly three times as long. A strong appeal to the Whig element was made by identifying himself with Webster and Clay and by the use of an appeal to "Union" men. He summarized his two main arguments by instructing those present to vote for Lincoln if they believed his principles more conducive to peace and harmony and perpetuity of the Union He added, however, that he would be grateful for their support if they believed Douglas had been faithful. At Springfield Douglas concluded much as he had at Bloomington but added that the voters of Sangamon owed him nothing for all his efforts in their behalf; they had more than paid for those efforts with the splendid reception and welcome.

Thus did Douglas vary his arguments at Chicago, Bloomington, and Springfield. His evidence was the same in each case, so much so that he has been charged with having given the same speech at each place. But with audiences with widely different political stereotypes, the inferences and conclusions he drew from his evidence changed to meet the needs of the situation. In Republican Chicago he seems to have made no attempt to win the vote but spent his time in explaining the wisdom of popular sovereignty as compared to Lincoln's principle. At Bloomington he justified his own course, flayed Lincoln's principles, and appealed for the vote of both the "Union Whigs" and the Democrats present. At Springfield he justified popular sovereignty, attacked Lincoln's principles as monstrous in character, and asked that the best man might win. In no case, however, did he draw conclusions that he did not believe to be true. He was able to adapt his material to meet the needs of the situation without becoming insincere or dishonest.

The question naturally arises: How would the speeches affect the great unseen, reading audience that Douglas knew he would have? Douglas left no clear explanation of his attitude toward his reading public. But the speeches were admirably planned and timed to fit that audience. The first speech was a fair and clear explanation of the issues of the campaign as he saw them—almost expository in nature. He did not attack his opponent strongly, choosing to leave to inference the more severe things he believed of Lincoln. It was not a speech that would lose him the undecided vote of the questionable counties. It was hardly a speech to which the Republicans could object. They might disagree with his arguments, but they could find little that rankled.

The second speech was stronger. It was aimed at the voters he knew he must win if he was to succeed. His attacks upon Lincoln still were not attacks upon "sincerity," but they were much stronger than at Chicago. In Springfield the ridicule became harsher, although Douglas ignored the question of Lincoln's sincerity in his beliefs. The three speeches build up nicely toward the goal that Douglas was to reach later in the campaign, without scaring "off" the timid voters in the questionable counties. Later Douglas was to attack Lincoln strongly, to accuse him of deceit, a thing Douglas already believed of his opponent.

The preceding analysis shows how Douglas adapted his material to audiences differing in political faith. An examination of other speeches shows that he was able to adapt his arguments to the individual differences of audiences that were alike in political affiliation. On August 25 and 31 he spoke in Galena and Joliet. Although both audiences were for the Republican party, they differed in other respects. By the time these places were reached, the campaign was a month and a half old, and all the important issues and charges of the campaign had been brought to the attention of the reading public. With the exception of two minor arguments, the evidence and reasoning used in the two speeches were the same. Again the order of arguments was nearly identical. The speaker, the occasion, the time element, and the issues were the same in each case; only the audiences differed.

Both audiences were located in what was conceded to be Republican territory, and both were located in areas in which about 33 per cent of the population had been born abroad. But there the similarity ended. Galena was located in a mining district; Joliet in an agricultural. Galena had been settled from the South in early days and had increased its population largely from German immigration; Joliet, growing rapidly during the thirties and forties, had of late attracted Yankees and Scandinavians. Joliet had a strong Abolition element but also contained many old-line Whigs not yet ready to embrace those doctrines.[1] It might be partially swung to the Democrats. No Senator was to be elected from Joliet's district in 1858, however.

Galena, on the other hand, offered little chance of Democratic success in the senatorial race. Its district included Jo Daviess and Stephenson counties, the former going anti-Nebraska by 55 per cent and the latter by 65 per cent in 1854. Although the city of Galena, with its Southern and German element, might be won, it was impossible to hope to win the senatorial vote.

The two representative districts were even less inclined to go Democratic. Previous elections indicated that Joliet offered a slightly better opportunity than Galena,[2] but both seemed impossible to win. The location of the two cities within their districts changed the complexion of the speaking problem, however. The Joliet district stretched for over one hundred miles from north to south, and Joliet was located in the northern third, near Chicago, from which it would draw heavily via railroad. The French of Kankakee held the balance of power in the central third of the district for the Republicans; only the southern third of the district might be won. Galena, however, lay on the extreme western and northern edge of its district, forty or fifty miles from the Scandinavian Whig stronghold in Carroll county.

From the foregoing analysis it is seen that Douglas must appeal to former Democrats, both foreign-born and old residents, in Galena. He might well take a strong anti-abolitionist stand. He must plead for popular sovereignty and peace. In Joliet Douglas must appeal to both Whigs and

[1] Wilcox to Douglas, Mar. 3, 1858, Douglas MSS.
[2] *Illinois State Register*, Nov. 6, 1858; Cole, *op. cit.*, p. 132.

former Democrats, but the Yankee-Scandinavian element made extreme ground against abolitionists inadvisable.

An analysis shows that one general technique was used in adjusting every argument, almost every paragraph of the printed speech. A few examples will make the technique clear; there is no need of considering every argument.[1]

The introductions were nearly identical in length, subject matter, and organization. But in Galena the introduction was purely explanatory, with no effort made to link up the facts presented with the past experiences of the audience. On the other hand, in Joliet, Douglas made his first bid for Whig support in the introduction itself, reminding the older residents of the facts he presented and eulogizing the Whig candidate and party of 20 years before.

In discussing the fight over the Compromise of 1850, Douglas argued at antislavery, ex-Democratic Galena that Whigs and Democrats were forced to substitute the principle of popular sovereignty for the Missouri Compromise, because the Free-Soil abolitionists would not carry out the earlier principles in good faith. In Joliet the same evidence proved that the Whig and Democratic parties had stood together under the leadership of the immortal Clay to fight the schemes of the abolitionists of the North *and* the disunionists of the South by adopting the compromise measures of 1850. However, Douglas took care at Galena (with its Southern heritage) to say, "The Abolitionists caused all the agitation . . . " and at Joliet (with its abolitionists), to speak kindly of the early-day abolitionists as "philanthropists."

Again, discussing the reaction of the abolitionists to the compromise as typified by the action of the Chicago City Council, Douglas told his audience at Galena, "I thought it my duty to defend them [the measures] from the fanaticism of the people of that city." At Joliet, only 30 miles from Chicago, Douglas took three times as much time in making the argument, saying in part, "I considered it my duty . . . to meet the excited people . . . ," and he linked the argument with Clay and Fillmore. He went on to glorify Chicago for its action in repealing the resolutions.

Similarly, in Galena Douglas reviewed the action of the Illinois legislature in 1851 in upholding popular sovereignty and concluded that only four abolitionists voted in the negative against a united front of Whigs and Democrats. But in Joliet he took much more time to point out that the action remained the standing instruction of the people to that day,

[1] For copies of the speeches see *Galena Daily Advertiser*, files in office of the *Galena Gazette* (the author was furnished with a stenographic copy by H. J. Grimm, business manager of the *Gazette*); *Jo.iet Signal*, Sept. 7, 1858, files in possession of Florence L. Ketcham, Minooka, Ill., who furnished the author with a stenographic copy of the speech.

adding that Whigs and Democrats has stood on that platform ever since, while abolitionists stood unanimously committed against the principle.

In concluding his argument at Galena on the history of popular sovereignty to 1854, Douglas merely stated the thesis upon which he had shown Whigs and Democrats alike to stand. But at Joliet he asked his audience how it had come that so many Democrats and Whigs had "strayed away, and following false lights and false leaders until they have got off this platform, and wandered into the center of the Abolition camp."

The basic philosophy of the speeches was the same, the organization of the arguments was the same in each speech, and even the conclusions drawn were practically the same. But in Galena Douglas directed his arguments at the puzzled Germans and former Democrats of Southern origin who had wandered away from the party. At Joliet he directed his arguments at former Whigs and at antislavery Democrats who had joined the Republican party, taking care to refrain from unduly angering abolitionists present.

This technique was used in every paragraph of the speeches; every argument could be examined as has been that on popular sovereignty. The evidence is overwhelming in proof that Douglas was adept at fitting his evidence and arguments to the needs of the situation, and all without becoming insincere and dishonest.

The next question to consider, concerning Douglas's effectiveness in speaking in this campaign, has to do with his methods of proof and the way he adapted those methods to the different audiences he faced. As has been suggested earlier, basically the speeches rested upon a desire to build prestige and to tear down the prestige of an opponent. It is quite natural, therefore, to discover that, basically, the arguments rested upon the ethical mode of proof. Most of the logical and pathetic arguments were directed toward the end of building or destroying prestige.

But the important element of Douglas's method was the way in which he varied it to fit the different audiences to whom he spoke. Two different methods were used. One was to dispose the audience favorably toward the speaker; the other was to undermine the prestige of his opponent. In some speeches Douglas used only the latter; in others he employed both methods. This difference has caused some confusion among historians and speech critics who have examined only the seven joint debates. Historians and critics have noted that Douglas gave emphasis to the method of attack at Ottawa, Freeport, and Jonesboro and that he gave some attention to defense at Quincy and a great deal of attention to defense at Charleston, Galesburg, and Alton. The first three debates were held in the first towns mentioned above. Two of these were located in admittedly Republican territory, and the latter was an admittedly Democratic stronghold.

Historians and critics have concluded[1] that Douglas was driven to the defensive by Lincoln's arguments.

However, an examination of the whole campaign belies this conclusion. The campaign was nearly six weeks in progress before the first of the debates was held and nearly ten weeks old before the Jonesboro debate took place. All the charges and countercharges, the arguments, and the evidence used in the debates had been given space in the newspapers before the first joint debate was held. Lincoln added no new and stronger arguments after the debates began. Second, an examination of Douglas's speeches given at Clinton, Beardstown, Bloomington, and Springfield shows that he used strongly defensive ethical proof at those places, all visited before the first joint debate. Third, the Quincy debate was scheduled nearly a week after the Galesburg discussion and within 2 days of the Alton contest, yet it drew fewer defensive arguments than did the other two. Clearly, the difference in use of ethical proof depended upon something other than mere time of delivery. If Lincoln's forcefulness caused the change, there is no way of accounting for the differences that existed between the speeches given at Galena, Joliet, Chicago, Ottawa, Freeport, Jonesboro, and Quincy and those given at Bloomington, Clinton, Beardstown, Charleston, Danville, Henry, Alton, and Springfield. This difference becomes clear, however, when the speeches are analyzed in terms of the attitude of the audiences toward the speaker and issues.

An analysis of the speeches and audiences shows that in localities which were clearly Democratic and in which Douglas's friends were quite certain to carry the election, emphasis was placed on attacks upon Lincoln and other Republicans, with little or no attempt being made deliberately to dispose those audiences more favorably toward Douglas. The larger the Democratic majority the stronger this emphasis.[2] Even in rebuttal, his answers to attacks upon him seem to have been given not so much in order to reply to Lincoln's charges as to take advantage of an opportunity further to destroy the opponent's prestige.

In clearly Abolition or Republican counties, Douglas again refused to spend much time in building his own prestige, devoting the greater part of his ethical proof to tearing down that of Lincoln. At Chicago, Ottawa, Freeport, Joliet, and Galena, ethical proof designed to build prestige was

---

[1] For example, Barnes, *op. cit.*, pp. 117, 134, 158, 176, and 196.

[2] For example, in strongly Democratic Jonesboro Douglas offered no defense of himself nor mentioned his fight with the Democratic administration. The entire emphasis of the ethical mode became an attempt to discredit Lincoln, Trumbull, and the Republican party. Nowhere did he believe it necessary to defend his own consistency, his patriotism, his courage, or his veracity; always he charged Lincoln and the Republicans with the desire to conceal, cheat, and mislead. The same methods were used at Quincy, another Democratic stronghold.

subordinated to that which attacked the prestige of opponents. In short, when in territory that was conceded to be either Democratic or Republican, his ethical mode ignored the method of disposing the audience more favorably toward the speaker. Attack was used instead of defense; and the time element did not enter the picture.

In questionable counties, however, Douglas was careful to re-establish his own prestige, as well as to attack that of Lincoln. The date on which the speech was given seemed to have little to do with the use of this method. Further than this, examination shows that the more questionable the support of his audience the more clearly did he attempt to use ethical proof in support of his own prestige.

This shift in ethical mode is apparent in every speech of which we have record, made in counties that were admittedly doubtful, no matter on what date they were given.[1]

Thus Douglas changed his ethical mode according to the degree of support he believed the audience to typify. When the audience was strongly in favor of one candidate and could not be won by the other, he used chiefly the method of destroying the prestige of his opponent. When the audience was doubtful in its allegiance, when it appeared possible for either candidate to win the vote of that county, Douglas used both the methods of attack and defense. The more doubtful the allegiance of the audience the stronger became the device of defense.

The question of the effectiveness of this method cannot be answered with any degree of accuracy, for the amount of the total success of the campaign due to this device cannot be estimated. But it seems the best possible method to use. Douglas was on trial in the doubtful counties, not in the others where he had already been either approved or condemned beyond hope of change. In Democratic counties attacks on Republicans and Lincoln were more likely to win votes than a reiteration of the point of Douglas's honesty, an item in which the audience already believed. It was only in the questionable districts that Lincoln and Trumbull were weaning votes from Douglas by their charges. The method of varying ethical arguments probably proved effective.

A second question of importance, concerning effectiveness of the methods of proof used by Douglas, has to do with the emotional appeals he made before different types of audience. Rhetoricians generally concede that the problem of the speaker is to analyze properly the specific interests of a given audience and sound those emotional notes that produce the maximum desired effect.

Normally the ethical mode is used to dispose an audience more favorably toward the speaker and more strongly opposed to an opponent, so

[1] Galesburg, Danville, Henry, Clinton, Beardstown, Bloomington, and Charleston.

815

that logical and emotional arguments will be more quickly accepted or rejected, as the case may be. Because of the nature of this campaign, however, ethical proof became an end in itself. The logical and emotional arguments used by Douglas were largely developed to strengthen or destroy prestige. Therefore, the emotional appeals used by Douglas were subordinate to and parallel with, and were used to strengthen, the ethical purpose.

When attacking Lincoln, Trumbull, or other Republicans, Douglas's chief appeal was to indignation: indignation at dishonesty, desire to cheat constituents, unfairness, willingness to sacrifice party and patriots for personal gain, willingness to destroy faith in American institutions, and willingness to endanger the very Union itself.[1] He made this appeal for "indignation" through the various subordinate appeals of "pride" in country, race, patriots, national institutions and accomplishments; "fear" of disunion; "anger" at sacrilege, unfairness, and indecent actions. The basic appeal to indignation was used in every speech, no matter what the political tendency of the audience, in support of the parallel ethical appeal for unfriendliness toward Lincoln.

But although the basic emotional appeal remained the same for each audience, Douglas was careful to base his subordinate and supporting appeals on the individual stereotypes of the different audiences. For example, in Abolition Joliet, Douglas's appeals sustained the abolitionists who took philanthropic or religious views of slavery but decried the demagogues who made use of these high ideals for purposes of getting into office. In such old Whig strongholds as Bloomington and Charleston, Douglas identified himself with, and appealed to, the Whig pride in that party's former leader Clay. In Democratic Jonesboro and former Democratic Alton, he appealed to pride in the Democratic party and the Union, warning against a split in both if Lincoln should win.

When disposing the audience more favorably toward himself, Douglas's chief emotional appeal was to the desire for justice and fair play. At times he played upon his auditors' sympathy; at others he identified himself with the things they revered—party, patriots, and national accomplishments. But the major plea was for justice and fairness. Appeals to other emotions were used to support this basic plea.[2]

---

[1] For example, see the Joliet speech, *Joliet Signal*, Sept. 7, 1858; Beardstown speech, *Fulton Democrat*, Aug. 27, 1858; Jonesboro speech, in G. H. Putnam, *The Political Debates between Abraham Lincoln and Stephen A. Douglas* (New York, G. P. Putnam's Sons, 2d printing, 1924), pp. 321–322.

[2] For example, see the Clinton speech, in the *Fulton Democrat*, Aug. 6, 1858; the Bloomington speech in Putnam, *op. cit.*, Part I, pp. 108–109; the Beardstown speech in the *Fulton Democrat*, Aug. 27, 1858; the Galesburg speech, Putnam, *op. cit.*, pp. 142–143, 151.

Stephen A. Douglas

Although every motivating appeal included in the list of human wants, with the possible exception of "profit," was used by Douglas during the campaign, these appeals were subordinated to, and used to strengthen, the ethical purposes on which the speeches were based. In a few cases appeals to "self preservation," "personal and social convenience," and "necessity" were used. "Pride" in, and "loyalty" to, race, country, national accomplishments, institutions, party, patriots, and reputation; "duty"; and "ambition" were appealed to. But all were subordinate to, and used in support of, the two major appeals of the campaign: "indignation" toward Lincoln and the Republican leaders, "fair play" and "justice" toward Douglas. Because of this subordination of pathetic to ethical mode, one finds these two basic pathetic appeals paralleling the two major ethical devices. Before audiences that were either strongly opposed to or strongly in favor of Douglas, his emotional appeals were nearly all directed toward "indignation."[1] Before audiences of doubtful allegiance, strong appeals to "indignation" were used, but similarly strong appeals to "justice" and "fair play" were made.[2]

The effectiveness of Douglas's method of subordinating pathetic to ethical mode seems to lie in the unity that it gave the speeches. With an ethical purpose in mind, the subordination of pathetic appeals, so that they paralleled and strengthened this purpose, caused the entire argument to center about the characters of the two principals of the campaign. So closely did the two methods of proof coincide that it is nearly impossible to illustrate one without illustrating the other. Although the motive of "indignation" or "anger" is not a "high" one in itself, the supporting appeals of "pride" and "loyalty" upon which it depended were so strong that it is hard to condemn continued appeal to "indignation."

Again it is impossible to determine accurately the effectiveness of the use of pathetic appeals. Newspaper reports of immediate response by the audience were too biased to allow an examination on that score. But the appeals were well adapted to the purpose Douglas had in mind and were adjusted in excellent fashion to meet the needs of the immediate audience and occasion.

One possible criticism of Douglas's use of the pathetic mode is that at times he antagonized parts of his audience. At Joliet, for example, he was interrupted by members of the audience no less than twenty times and was led to apologize toward the end of the address for treading on "corns." But when it is remembered that Douglas's chief concern was the winning of the wavering Germans and the "timid" Whigs, these examples of bold-

---

[1] See the speeches made at Galena, Joliet, Ottawa, Freeport, and Jonesboro.
[2] See the speeches made at Charleston, Galesburg, Quincy, Alton, Beardstown, and Clinton.

ness and courage probably strengthened his prestige. Such tactics could cost him few votes; they might win many for him.

A third question, concerning the effectiveness of the methods of proof used in this campaign, deals with the evidence and reasoning used. Douglas's sources of material have already been examined. Of that material he relied partly upon direct evidence, quoting from printed speeches and occasionally from a letter. More often he relied upon circumstantial evidence that was hearsay but was known by the audience to be true. So often did he rely upon the common knowledge of his audience of recent political happenings that he rarely felt compelled to establish the validity of his evidence by stating its source. Exceptions to this rule were those instances in which he quoted directly from a printed speech or letter and those instances when he used himself as authority for things he had witnessed in Congress. Even when quoting directly, Douglas did not always believe it necessary to explain where he had got his evidence or the exact date of its occurrence.[1]

The major attack upon Douglas's evidence during the campaign was that upon his use of the so-called "Springfield Resolutions." Because of Douglas's error in this instance, the authenticity of the remainder of his evidence lay open to attack. Lincoln took advantage of his opening by often casting doubt on other evidence the Little Giant used. However, this development did not cause Douglas to vary his method of presenting evidence. He probably believed that a mere statement of source would not defend him from these attacks. And he may have believed that a more careful statement of source would call additional attention to his error at Ottawa. Since Douglas's honesty was already doubted by many Whigs and Germans, upon whom the election depended, this refusal to state the source of evidence more carefully may be accepted as a weakness which limited Douglas's effectiveness. But his use of known facts as circumstantial evidence in support of conclusions he argued to be logical must have been effective with an audience that prided itself upon its interest in and knowledge of political events.

[1] For example, at Ottawa he merely told the audience that he held in his hand the resolutions adopted at Springfield in 1854. Another example was his use of Matheny's speech, explaining the 1854 alliance between Trumbull and Lincoln. Douglas reported what Matheny had said and supposed that even Mr. Lincoln would not deny it, since there were "many witnesses" to the truth of the matter. After Lincoln's denial, Douglas again quoted Matheny from "one of the numerous speeches of the same tenor that was made about that time . . . 1856." Although Lincoln often denied the authenticity of the evidence, Douglas never explained its source. Either he did not know the source, a doubtful conclusion, in view of the care he took in determining the authenticity of the "Springfield Resolutions," or he did not believe it necessary to answer Lincoln's insinuations.

Douglas's reasoning was usually inductive in form, including many instances of generalization and much causal reasoning. His attacks on Lincoln and Republicans were usually of the latter type; his defense of self was more often of the former. Only in his concluding appeals for preservation of the Union, for the necessity of popular sovereignty, and for belief in manifest destiny did syllogistic reasoning play an important role.

From the standpoint of logic, Douglas was often guilty of one type of fallacy—that of arguing "beside the point." Because his purpose was ethical in nature, many of his arguments seem to have rested upon the *ad hominem* basis. Often was he found linking Republican doctrine with abolitionists, with the inference that the very linkage disproved the doctrine.[1] As has been seen, Douglas had been a careful student of the classics and of the logic of Burke and other great orators. He must have known that such reasoning does not always lead to sound conclusions. One must infer that Douglas deliberately used this type of reasoning because he believed it to be effective on the occasions when he used it. But one must remember that Douglas was sincere in his distrust and hatred for abolitionists. Further, he knew that the Whig and German element held a fear or hatred of abolitionists only second to his own. His *ad hominem* arguments were used to strengthen in his audience a belief that Douglas already held. The ethical nature of the campaign seems to justify the use of such methods of reasoning.

Another fallacy of the same nature, so far as pure logic is concerned, was Douglas's frequent use of *ad verecundiam* reasoning. In nearly every speech he argued that the Union could always exist half slave and half free because it had in the past. In nearly every speech he likewise argued that a divided Union was desirable and workable because the fathers had made the Union half slave and half free. From the standpoint of pure logic, these two arguments are fallacious; but from the standpoint of rhetorical proof, they should not be condemned. Both arguments dealt with probable future happenings. Proofs from example and authority were all that were possible. His opponent had offered Biblical testimony in support of opposite conclusions. What better example could Douglas cite than 50 years of history? What better testimony could he offer to patriotic Americans, in a period when patriotism was one of the moving spirits of social life, than the testimony of the authors of the Constitution and the signers of the Declaration of Independence? To condemn such arguments is to condemn argument from authority and example. Although they may be condemned by the logician, they should be upheld as effective and permissible by the

[1] Putnam, *op. cit.*, I, 198–199; II, 181, for Ottawa and Quincy examples. *Galena Daily Advertiser* for examples in that city.

rhetorician who defines his art as "finding the best possible means of persuasion."

Douglas's evidence and reasoning seem to have been effective in the campaign of 1858. His chief fault lay in neglecting or refusing to establish the source of his evidence before an audience already suspicious of his motives. But his strength lay in the use of evidence already known to be true by an audience vitally concerned and interested in past political happenings. Although he often used reasoning that logicians may condemn as "beside the point," the ethical nature of the campaign, together with the character of popular attitudes and beliefs, made such methods acceptable to the rhetorician.

A further question to be asked, concerning effectiveness of the speeches of the campaign, deals with the special methods of refutation used. Douglas made use of all the six special methods of rhetoric. Unusually good use was made of two of them. Before an audience that was strongly opposed to him, Douglas made unusually good use of the "method of dilemma." For example, at Joliet he gave the audience no less than six dilemma questions to ponder over, repeating each again and again.[1] Unusually good use was also made of the method of *reductio ad absurdum* before all types of audiences. Especially was the device effective in attacking Lincoln's philosophies as impractical, in ridiculing Lincoln's answers to the questions put at Ottawa, and in discrediting Lincoln before doubtful audiences. Every speech of the campaign of which we have record contains this device.

"Douglas's ability to use "methods of residues" was typified by his argument at Clinton, Freeport, Charleston, and Galesburg in reply to Lincoln's charge of conspiracy between the Supreme Court, President Pierce, President Buchanan, and Douglas. One by one he eliminated the first three, leaving only Douglas to be accounted for—"leaving the public to say whether I, by myself, without their concurrence, could have gone into a conspiracy with them."[2] Again and again he "exposed inconsistencies" and irrelevant arguments made by Lincoln, often through the use of analogies, dilemmas, or ridicule. His method of "adopting opposing arguments" is typified by his answer at Charleston to Lincoln's refutation of a Douglas attack on Trumbull.[3]

The question of the effectiveness of the use of these methods of refutation leads to the observation that Douglas was seldom content to apply a single method of refutation to an opponent's argument. This was especially true of arguments he proved to be "irrelevant." For example, in counterrefutation, after showing that Lincoln's Jackson argument was an

---

[1] *Joliet Signal*, Sept. 7, 1858.
[2] Putnam, *op. cit.*, II, p. 38.
[3] *Ibid.*, II, p. 24.

evasion of the point at issue, Douglas went on to prove the Jackson argument wrong in fact. Again, after attacking Lincoln's repetition of the Trumbull charge as irrelevant to the campaign, Douglas went on to prove the charge untrue. This habit of spending time in refuting arguments that he had showed to be irrelevant has been criticized. The critic inferred that Douglas actually believed the argument relevant; otherwise he would not have wasted time in answer to it.[1] However, the critic confused relevancy with effectiveness. In *forensic* speaking irrelevant arguments may be as effective as pertinent ones, swaying an audience although an opponent has proved their irrelevancy. Douglas realized that the charges had been printed again and again. He needed to answer them in order to nullify their effect. Examination shows that Douglas used time in disproving irrelevant arguments only when he faced an audience of doubtful allegiance, an audience with whom he must build his own prestige by taking the defensive. For example, Douglas ruled out Lincoln's entire speech at Charleston as irrelevant to the campaign, but he afterward spent over a third of his time in answering the charge thus ruled out. He also attempted to disprove the charge at Beardstown, Havana, Lewistown, and Jacksonville, before audiences of doubtful allegiance. But he did not attempt to disprove the argument at Ottawa, Freeport, Jonesboro, Galena, or Joliet, before audiences of definite allegiance, although the charge had been widely published before these speeches were given. It would seem, therefore, that Douglas was willing to answer irrelevant arguments if he believed that those arguments were likely to prove effective before a given audience. This willingness does not prove that he was insincere in his charge that the arguments were irrelevant. It is another illustration of Douglas's awareness of his audience and the needs of the situation.

It is clear that Douglas was extremely effective in rebuttal. His answers to the arguments advanced by Lincoln must have carried a great deal of weight in the doubtful middle counties. It was around the stereotypes of the people in these counties that Douglas built his rebuttal arguments. The evidence he presented was known by them to be true. The conclusions he drew must have sounded logical to a people who were suspicious of politicians and jealous of their ballot power.

General Effectiveness

Although it is impossible to allot to the speeches the exact part they played in determining the results of the election, certain things should be noted that tend to support the conclusion that Douglas's speaking was extremely important in keeping the Illinois legislature Democratic in 1858.

[1] Barnes, *op. cit.*, p. 203.

As has been noted, reports of applause, cheers, and other marks of approval given by an immediate audience cannot be accepted as evidence of effectiveness. Not only were newspapers partial and biased to the extent of falsifying reports but a small minority of determined supporters might account for the interruptions and applause recorded. It was the day of intense rivalry, staunch support of candidates, and noisy interruptions. On the other hand the skill shown in the use of the various methods of proof and refutation would lead a present-day critic to suspect that the speeches were very effective.

In analyzing the campaign, historians have arrived at conflicting conclusions in answering the question: Who won the debates? By far the majority have noted that the Republicans polled more votes than did the Democrats,[1] concluding that this proved that the better speaker, Lincoln, was cheated out of a hard-earned victory by an antiquated apportionment system. However, others have pointed out that the Democrats gained more votes over the 1856 total than did the Republicans,[2] and Cole[3] had invalidated this argument by pointing out that the 1856 vote was not a fair indication of previous Republican strength. Still others have concluded that the question is "still unanswered."[4]

No attempt will be made here to answer the question conclusively, but certain new evidence should be noted. The foregoing description of trends, affecting the people of Illinois, indicates that the state was rapidly drifting toward Republican-party philosophy. Although the anti-Nebraska vote of 1854 gives an indication of what the Republicans could expect in 1858, a mere comparison of total votes gained gives no indication of the relative effectiveness of the speaking ability of the two candidates. It does not take into account the rapid growth in population and other trends before mentioned. More importantly, it does not take into account the fact that the speeches of these two candidates represented only one element of the campaign. To assume that the speeches of Lincoln and Douglas accounted entirely for the shift in vote is questionable, causal reasoning.

However, there is one method of comparing votes that does indicate the relative effectiveness of the two speakers in this campaign. No historian has yet compared the shift in votes in counties in which the two men spoke with the shift in vote in counties in which they did not speak. Assuming

---

[1] Putnam, *op. cit.*, p. xvi: John A. Logan, *The Great Conspiracy* (New York, A. R. Hart and Co., 1886), p. 83. See also, nearly any biography of Lincoln, with the exception of that of Beveridge.

[2] Allen Johnson, *Stephen A. Douglas* (New York, The Macmillan Company, 1906), p. 392; D. W. Lusk, *Illinois Politics and Politicians*, Springfield, N. W. Roper, 1884.

[3] Cole, *op. cit.*, p. 164.

[4] Barnes, *op. cit.*, p. 207.

that other influencing factors were operative in all counties, such a comparison should give a better basis for judging the effectiveness of the two speakers. Lincoln, in nearly every instance, spoke where Douglas had spoken previously. He had, as he admitted, an advantage in having "a concluding speech on him"; it "is the very thing."[1] The comparison is possible.

Dividing the state arbitrarily, as most historians have divided it, into the north (twenty-three counties), the central (forty-nine counties), and the south (thirty counties), the following gains of 10 per cent or more over the 1854 vote are discovered for the two parties.[2] *In the Republican counties in which the two men spoke in the north, Douglas gained in 4; Lincoln, in 3. In those in which they did not speak, Douglas gained in 1, and Lincoln gained in 7. In the great, doubtful, central section, where the two men spoke, Douglas gained in 18; Lincoln did not gain in a single county. Where they did not speak in this area, Douglas gained in 5 and Lincoln in 4. In the Democratic strongholds of the south, Douglas gained in 2 in which they spoke; Lincoln gained in 2. Where they did not speak, Douglas gained in 2 and Lincoln in 8. For the state as a whole, then, Douglas gained strength of 10 per cent or more in 24 counties in which the two men spoke; Lincoln gained in 5. In counties where they did not speak, Douglas gained in only 8 and Lincoln in 19.*

It must be remembered that Douglas shunned counties that were admittedly Democratic, speaking only twice in those places. He chose to speak nine times in admittedly Republican strongholds. Both men spent the remainder of their time in the doubtful counties of the state. It is also interesting to note that ten counties that had gone anti-Nebraska in 1854 went Democratic in 1858; only three that had been Democratic went Republican in the latter year. This was true in spite of the trends of the decade and the split in the Democratic party. Douglas spoke in eight of the ten Republican counties that became Democratic; Lincoln spoke in but one of the three Democratic counties that became Republican.

The foregoing analysis bears out our earlier conclusion that the state was rapidly drifting toward Republican philosophy. The Republicans seem to have had good reason to believe that Lincoln's election was certain.

It is impossible to conclude that the great difference in shift in vote between counties in which the men spoke and counties in which they did not was entirely due to their respective speaking abilities. But it seems

---

[1] Lincoln to Dr. Fifthian, Sept. 3, 1858, reprinted in *The Writings of Abraham Lincoln* (A. B. Lapsley, ed., New York, P. F. Collier & Son, Inc., 1906), V, 9.

[2] See election charts in Cole, *op. cit.*, pp. 132, 178, for report of vote by counties. To determine in which counties the two men spoke, see schedules of speaking engagements published in the *Illinois State Register* and the *Illinois State Journal* for the duration of the campaign.

logical to believe that speaking ability played an important part in bringing about this difference. To assume otherwise is to place an unusual reliance on coincidence or to argue that neither man had the ability to determine in which counties speaking would influence the election. Such a large difference in shift in votes in the two types of counties indicates that the oratory of Stephen A. Douglas was one of the sustaining factors in keeping the Democratic legislature in Illinois in 1858. It indicates that Douglas's campaign speeches were very effective.

We may conclude, then, that history has sadly misjudged Douglas as a speaker. The charges of inconsistency, insincerity, trickery, and carelessness have been made in the light of post-Civil War philosophy, after an examination of only a few of the printed speeches. Historians and critics have ignored the need to understand thoroughly the four elements that go into every speaking situation before judgment may be passed; they have failed to realize that it is dangerous to criticize isolated speeches that appear in print until the conditions under which the speeches were given have been reconstructed.

An examination of the individual audiences to whom Douglas spoke, the various influences that accounted for his beliefs, and the total number of campaign speeches now in existence shows conclusively that Douglas was not driven to the defensive by a superior opponent. It shows conclusively that his arguments were basically honest, sincere, and consistent. In fact, many of the things that have drawn the critics' disapproval prove to be masterly techniques of an unusually fine speaker, who was a past master at audience analysis and adaptation. Douglas should be remembered as one of the ablest speakers the United States has produced.

SELECTED BIBLIOGRAPHY

The sources listed below comprise only a small per cent of the hundreds of documents bearing upon this subject. All government documents, general works, newspapers, biographies, and reminiscences have been omitted. They may be easily located by interested scholars who examine recent biographies of Lincoln and Douglas.

Manuscripts and Interviews

Sidney Breese MSS. Some papers and letters of Sidney Breese, located in the Illinois Historical Library, Springfield, Ill.

Chicago Historical Society MSS. Letters and papers in the possession of the Chicago Historical Society, Chicago, Ill.

Douglas MSS. An estimated twenty thousand letters received by Douglas from constituents, friends, and enemies, located in all parts of the United States and in many foreign countries. The letters for the years 1854 to 1858 were the most valuable single collection of source material. Owned by the University of Chicago.

Galesburg Public Library MSS.

Illinois State Historical Library MSS, Springfield, Ill. Many letters and papers of contemporaries of Douglas, including some letters from Douglas to other Illinois politicians. Many pamphlets are included.

David King MSS. Letters and papers written between 1820 and 1846. Nearly three hundred private letters are included. Property of Mrs. B. K. Mason, placed in safekeeping of the Morgan County Historical Society and, in turn, in the Jacksonville, Ill., Public Library.

B. K. Mason MSS. Includes many letters, pictures, and some books and papers belonging to Mason. Placed in safekeeping of the Morgan County Historical Society and, in turn, in the Jacksonville, Ill., Public Library.

Ensley Moore's Estate MSS. In safekeeping of the Morgan County Historical Society.

Morgan County Historical Society MSS. Consists of a large library of books, pamphlets, newspapers, and other source materials. Is valuable in establishing audience beliefs and attitudes. Located in the basement of the Public Library in Jacksonville, Ill.

Newberry Library MSS, Chicago, Ill. Includes letters, pamphlets, and newspapers written in Illinois during the fifties. A few letters from Douglas to other politicians are included.

Patton MSS. The private letters and papers of Charles N. Lanphier, editor of the *Illinois State Register* during the fifties. Besides certain family letters, it contains a great number of letters from Douglas, Harris, and other Illinois politicians. Next to the Douglas MSS, the most valuable single source collection for the purposes of this study. Owned jointly by Charles Lanphier Patton and William Lanphier Patton, Springfield, Ill., who kindly placed them at the disposal of the author. Part of the manuscripts are deposited with the Illinois State Historical Library for safekeeping; remainder in the possession of the owners.

Max Speulda, 1328 Holmes Ave., Springfield, Ill. Mr. Speulda is the son of an old Springfield resident. In an interview with the author he recalled life in Springfield in the fifties and sixties and some interesting incidents concerning Lincoln and Douglas, part of which he personally experienced and part of which were told him by his father.

Douglas's 1858 Campaign Speeches

Aside from the speeches given in joint debate and those usually published with the debates, those listed below are the only ones reported in any of the newspapers whose files are known to exist today.

Clinton, July 27, 1858, *Fulton Democrat*, Aug. 6, 1858 (incomplete).

Beardstown, Aug. 11, 1858, *Fulton Democrat*, Aug. 27, 1858 (incomplete).

Galena, Aug. 25, 1858, *Galena Daily Advertiser* (files in 1936 in offices of *Galena Gazette*); *Fulton Democrat*, Sept. 6, 1858 (incomplete).

Joliet, August 31, 1858, *Joliet Signal*, Sept. 7, 1858 (in 1936 in possession of Florence Ketcham, Manooka, Ill).

Jacksonville, Sept. 6, 1858, Putnam's *Lincoln Douglas Debates*, Part II, pp. 80–91; *Fulton Democrat*, Sept. 24, 1858 (incomplete in both cases).

Sullivan, Sept. 20, 1858, *Illinois State Register*, Sept. 23, 1858 (incomplete).

Danville, Sept. 21, 1858, *Fulton Democrat*, Oct. 8, 1858 (incomplete).

Henry, Oct. 5, 1858, *Daily Chicago Times*, Oct. 5, 1858 (incomplete).

Springfield, Oct. 20, 1858, *Illinois State Register*, Oct. 27, 1858 (incomplete).

Thirteen other files of papers, located in towns in which Douglas spoke, are in existence. But Douglas's speeches in those towns were not reported by the local papers.

Contemporary Accounts

Angle, Paul M.: Lincoln, *Day by Day Activities*, 1854–1861, *New Letters and Papers of Lincoln*, The Abraham Lincoln Association, 1933; Springfield, Boston, Houghton Mifflin Company, 1930.

Black, Bessie M.: "Green Vardiman Black," diary, *Illinois Historical Society Transactions* (Springfield), 38 (1931).

Boulton, Archibald L.: *Lincoln and Douglas Debates*, New York, Henry Holt and Company, Inc., 1905.

Breese, Judge Sidney: "Some Old Letters," *Illinois State Historical Society Journal* (Springfield), 2 (1909).

Cairnes, J. E.: *The Slave Power: Its Character, Career, and Probable Designs*, New York, Carleton, 1862.

Carey, H. C.: *Principles of Political Economy*, Philadelphia, Carey, Lea and Blanchard, 1837–1840.

Democratic Press, *Rock Island and Surrounding in* 1853, Chicago, 1854.

Documentary History of American Industrial Society, Vol. V, Part I, "*Plantation and Frontier*, 1619–1863," U. B. Phillips, ed., Cleveland, Ohio, The Arthur H. Clark Co., 1909.

Douglas, Stephen A.: *Autobiography*, 1838, reprinted in *Illinois State Historical Society Journal* (Springfield), October, 1912, 1913.

Cutts, Madison: *A Brief Treatise upon Constitutional and Party Questions as I Received It Orally from the Late Senator Stephen A. Douglas of Illinois*, New York, D. Appleton and Company, 1866.

Foster, Lillian: *Wayside Glimpses, North and South*, New York, 1859, reprinted in *Illinois State Historical Society Journal* (Springfield), 5 (1912).

Glover, L. M.: *Gratitude to God: A Thanksgiving Discourse*, Jacksonville, 1858; *Our Country Vindicated*, Jacksonville, 1860.

Hubbard MSS, published in *Illinois Historical Society Transactions* (Springfield), 40 (1933).

Illinois Republican State Central Committee, "A Political Record of Stephen A. Douglas on the Slavery Question," campaign pamphlet, 1860.

Lincoln, Abraham: *The Writings of Abraham Lincoln*, A. B. Lapsley, ed., New York, P. F. Collier & Son, Inc., 1906, Vol. V.

Logan, John A.: *The Great Conspiracy: Its Origin and History*, New York, A. R. Hart and Company, 1886.

McKee, Thomas Hudson: *National Conventions and Platforms of All Political Parties*, 1787–1900, 3d rev. ed., Baltimore, The Friedenwald Company, 1900.

Olmsted, F. L.: *Journey in the Seaboard Slave States*, New York, Dix and Edwards, 1856.

Peck, J. M.: *Gazetteer of Illinois*, 2d rev. ed., Philadelphia, Griggs and Elliott, 1837.

Putnam, G. H., ed.: *The Political Debates between Abraham Lincoln and Stephen A. Douglas*, New York, G. P. Putnam's Sons, 1924.

Reynolds, John: "The Agricultural Resources of Southern Illinois," *Transactions of Illinois State Agricultural Society*, 2 (1856); part reprinted in *Illinois State Historical Society Transactions* (Springfield), 24 (1917).

Root, O. F.: *Root's Peoria City Directory*, Peoria, Benjamin Foster, 1856.

Sellong, C. J.: *A Review of the Commerce, Manufactures and the Public and Private Improvements of Galesburg*, Galesburg, J. H. Sherman, 1851.

Sparks, E. E., ed.: "The Lincoln-Douglas Debates of 1858," *Collections of the Illinois State Historical Society* (Springfield), 3 (1910).

Tracy, Gilbert A., compiler: *Uncollected Letters of Abraham Lincoln*, Boston, Houghton Mifflin Company, 1917.

Turner, J. B.: "A Plan for an Industrial University for the State of Illinois," pamphlet, 1850.

United States Politics, Vol. I; 23 pamphlets published between 1852 and 1860, bound by Newberry Library, Chicago, Ill.

Walker, Amasa: "The Wage Fund Theory," *North American Review*, 120.

Weston, George Melville: *Progress of Slavery in the United States*, Washington, D.C., Weston, 1857.

Monographs and Special Works

Ashby, W. T.: The Oratorical Technique of Stephen A. Douglas in Defense of the Union, 1860–61, M.A. thesis, typewritten, Department of Speech, State University of Iowa, 1935.

Baird, Glenn Earl: The Southern Tours of Stephen A. Douglas, M.A. thesis, typewritten, Department of History, University of Chicago.

Baringer, William E.: "Campaign Technique in Illinois in 1860," M.A. thesis, printed in *Illinois State Historical Society Transactions* (Springfield), 39 (1932).

Barnes, A. M.: A Rhetorical Analysis of the Speeches of Stephen A. Douglas in the Lincoln-Douglas Debates, M.A. thesis, typewritten, Department of Speech, State University of Iowa, 1937.

Barton, William E.: *Lincoln and Douglas at Galesburg*, Chicago, University of Chicago Press, 1921; *Lincoln and Douglas at Charleston*, Chicago, University of Chicago Press, 1922.

Brown, Caroline Owsley: "Springfield Society before the Civil War," *Illinois State Historical Society Journal* (Springfield), 15 (1922).

Fishback, Mason M.: "Illinois Legislation on Slavery and Free Negroes, 1818–1865," *Illinois State Historical Society Transactions*, 11 (1904).

Glenn, John M.: "The Industrial Development of Illinois," *Illinois State Historical Society Transactions* (Springfield), 28 (1921).

Jelliff, Fred R.: Municipal History of Galesburg as Shown by Town and City Records, typewritten analysis of all laws, Galesburg Public Library.

Johnson, Charles: "Every Day Life in Illinois Near the Middle of the Nineteenth Century," *Illinois State Historical Society Transactions*, 19 (1912).

King, Adema Ruth: "The Last Years of the Whig Party in Illinois, 1847–1856," M. A. thesis, Department of History, printed in *Illinois State Historical Society Transactions*, 32 (1925).

Kofoid, Carrie P.: "Puritan Influences in the Formative Years of Illinois History," *Illinois State Historical Society Transactions*, 12 (1905).

Pooley, W. V.: "Settlement of Illinois from 1830–1850," *University of Wisconsin Bulletin* 220, Madison, 1908.

Taylor, Florence Walton: "Culture in Illinois in Lincoln's Day," *Illinois State Historical Society Transactions* (Springfield), 42 (1935).

Whan, F. L.: Invention in the Speeches of Stephen A. Douglas in the 1858 Campaign for Illinois Senatorship, Ph. D. dissertation, typewritten, Department of Speech, State University of Iowa, 1938.

Abraham Lincoln: His Development in the Skills of the Platform

by MILDRED FREBURG BERRY

Abraham Lincoln was born February 12, 1809, near Hodgenville, Ky. His family moved to Indiana in 1816 and to Illinois in 1830; he attended schools of Kentucky and Indiana less than one year; served in Illinois legislature, 1834–1842; admitted to the bar, 1837. He failed to secure nomination for Congress, 1843, 1844; member of House of Representatives, 1847–1849; returned to practice of law. He was defeated in the race for United States Senator, 1855; nominated by the Republican party for the United States Senate, 1858, and engaged in a series of debates with Douglas; defeated in the election by Douglas. He delivered the "President-making" address at Cooper Institute, New York, February, 1860; nominated by the Republican party for the Presidency of the United States, May, 1860; elected President, defeating Douglas, Bell, and Breckinridge; re-elected president, 1864, defeating McClellan. Died April 15, 1865.

If speakers are born, not made, Abraham Lincoln[1] was not destined to be a speaker, for he had few of the obvious natural graces of an orator. Indeed, if native physical equipment determines one's bent, Lincoln should have shied away from the public platform. When he evinced his first interest in speaking as a boy of eleven years, he was a tall, thin, ungainly, awkward lad, and the years wrought no transformation in this respect. "He never knows where or how to place his hands or his feet," complained one reporter

[1] Until his election to the Presidency Lincoln's first name appeared commonly in the press as "Abram." ("A. Lincoln," "Abe Lincoln," and "Mr. Lincoln" also were used.) As late as 1860 the *New York Times* referred to him as "Abram Lincoln." [" . . . Abram Lincoln, of Illinois, is declared candidate for President of the National Republican Party."—*New York Times*, 9, No. 2703 (May 19, 1860)]. A popular campaign song in 1864 began, "We are coming, father Abra'm, 600,000 more!"—*Lincoln Campaign Songster for the Use of Clubs* (Philadelphia, Mason and Co., 1864). See also *Milwaukee Daily Sentinel*, Oct. 1, 1859; *New York Spectator*, May 28, 1860; *Cincinnati Daily Commercial*, Sept. 19, 1859; *Boston Daily Journal*, Sept. 23, 1848. Lincoln attempted to settle the question by advising George Ashmun in a letter on June 4, 1860: "It seems as if the question whether my first name is 'Abraham' or 'Abram' will never be settled. It is 'Abraham,' and if the letter of acceptance is not yet in print, you may, if you think fit, have my signature thereto printed 'Abraham Lincoln.' Exercise your judgment about this."—John G. Nicolay and John Hay, editors, *Complete Works of Abraham Lincoln* (12 vols., New York, Francis D. Tandy, 1905), VI, 38.

after hearing him speak. "They are always in his way and he has not learned to reduce them to his service."[1]

Not only did he lack grace in posture and bearing but the fine muscular coordination necessary for vocal articulatory flexibility also was wanting. I am "compelled by nature to speak slowly,"[2] admitted Lincoln, and his hearers must have agreed, for no reporter ever characterized Abe's speech as "an uninterrupted flow of felicitous language." There was little evidence of the muscular agility of a fluent speaker.

His physiognomy, moreover, was such as to attract attention only for its peculiarity and homeliness. In the campaign of 1864, the *Comic Monthly* found Lincoln's platform appearance a favorite subject for derision and jest.

His anatomy is composed mostly of bones, and when walking he resembles the off-spring of a happy marriage between a derrick and wind-mill. When speaking he reminds one of the old signal-telegraph that used to stand on Staten Island. His head is shaped something like a ruta-bago, and his complexion is that of a Saratoga trunk. His hands and feet are plenty large enough and in society he has the air of having too many of them.[3]

Nor could his voice be likened to the silver tones of Calhoun or Clay or Webster, men whose speaking style was the accepted mode of the day. Lincoln's voice was high-pitched, with a nasal tenor quality. His sole likeness to his models in voice lay in its intensity; he could make himself heard. He evidently did not possess a good tonal memory or pitch discrimination so essential to fine vocal control, for all his contemporaries agreed that he could not carry a tune.[4]

Yet if he possessed none of the "outward natural graces," he had inherited other qualities, less obvious, which may have compensated well for his deficiencies. In the first place, he had a highly sensitive nervous system, which exhibited itself through a curious, inquiring, retentive mind and heightened sensory appreciation. Dennis Hanks, who lived with the Lincoln family and who was Abe's companion on many a jaunt, said, "We learned by sight, scent and hearing."[5] Whenever a stranger passed by

[1] *The Dover Gazette* (N. H.), Mar. 3, 1860; also in Elwin L. Page, *Abraham Lincoln in New Hampshire* (Boston, Houghton Mifflin Company, 1929), p. 80.

[2] William H. Herndon and Jesse W. Weik, *Herndon's Lincoln: The True Story of a Great Life* (3 vols., Chicago, New York, Belford, Clarke and Co., 1889), II, 338–339.

[3] *Only Authentic Life of Abraham Lincoln (alias "Old Abe," 1864, A Son of the West)*, published by the *Comic Monthly*, 109 Nassau St., New York. Copy in Newberry Library, Chicago.

[4] "Abe was fond of music, but was himself wholly unable to produce three harmonious notes together."—Ward H. Lamon, *Life of Abraham Lincoln* (Boston, James R. Osgood and Co., 1872). (Authorship now credited to Chauncey F. Black).

[5] Herndon and Weik, *op. cit.*, I, 67.

their farm Abe was always the first to break in to ask questions, a habit for which he was often punished by his father.[1] If a visitor's or neighbor's remarks were incomprehensible to him, Abe said that he

> would spend no small part of the night walking up and down and trying to make out what was the exact meaning of some of their, to me, dark sayings. I could not sleep, although I tried to, when I got on such a hunt for an idea until I had caught it; and when I thought I had got it, I was not satisfied until I had repeated it over and over; until I had put it in language plain enough, as I thought, for any boy I knew to comprehend. This was a kind of passion with me, and it has stuck by me; for I am never easy now, when I am handling a thought, till I have bounded it north and bounded it south, and bounded it east and bounded it west.[2]

Here is evidence of a true intellectual curiosity, which was satisfied only by the sternest kind of mental exercise.

It was a curious mind and a retentive mind. Those things which he had learned, albeit he learned them slowly, he remembered with great accuracy. When Brooks asked him how he could repeat verbatim from Seward's speech, which he had just heard, Lincoln replied that he "couldn't help remembering."[3] When he went to Springfield from New Salem, Joshua Speed said that Lincoln "could recite more poetry than any other man in Town."[4] Not only was his retentive power exercised on words; he remembered accurately and could reproduce facial expressions, tones, and gesticulations. Nat Grigsby told Lamon that Abe would attend the "preachings" at Pigeon Creek Church "with a view to catching whatever might be ludicrous in the preacher's air or matter, and making it the subject of mimicry as soon as he could collect an audience of idle boys and men to hear him."[5] He frequently reproduced a sermon with the same "nasal tones, rolling eyes, and all manner of droll aggravations, to the great delight of Nat Grigsby and the wild fellows whom Nat was able to assemble."[6]

He had social qualities, too, which put him in the way of "preachings" and other less formal gatherings. He was, by nature, gregarious and like many great orators got his inspiration and much of his learning from his friends, in Abe's case, from the "gang" at William Jones's store at Gentry-

---

[1] Hanks to Herndon, Jan. 26, 1866. Weik MSS, Jesse W. Weik Collection, Greencastle, Ind.

[2] Interview of the Reverend J. P. Gulliver with Abraham Lincoln, in 1860, in New England, *New York Independent*, Sept. 1, 1864; also in *The Century Magazine*, 34 (1887): 527. Herndon questioned the accuracy of Gulliver's report of his interview. See Emanuel Hertz, *The Hidden Lincoln* (New York, The Viking Press, 1938), pp. 401-402.

[3] Noah Brooks, "Glimpses of Lincoln in War Time," *The Century Magazine*, O.S. 49, N.S. 27, (1894-1895): 457-467.

[4] Speed to Herndon, Dec. 6, 1866; Weik MSS.

[5] Lamon, *op. cit.*, p. 55.

[6] *Ibid.*

ville or on their expeditions to logrollings, shooting matches, or frontier weddings. "Hunting was entirely too 'still' an occupation for him," says Lamon. "All sorts of frolics and all kinds of popular gatherings, whether for work or amusement, possessed irresistible attractions for Abe. He loved to see and be seen, to make sport and to enjoy it."[1] And Lamon might well have added "to hear and to be heard." This "irresistible attraction" to people Lincoln never lost. When J. H. Buckingham, of Boston, took a trip through Illinois following the Rivers and Harbors Convention in Chicago, in 1847, he wrote in his diary:

We were now in the district represented by our Whig Congressman [Abraham Lincoln], and he knew, or appeared to know, everybody we met, the name of the tenant of every farm-house, and the owner of every plot of ground. Such a shaking of hands—such a how-d'y-do—such a greeting of different kinds as we saw, was never seen before; it seemed as if he knew everything, and he had a kind word, a smile and a bow for everybody on the road, even to the horses, and the cattle and the swine. . . . We started in a grumbling humor, but our Whig congressman was determined to be good natured and to keep all the rest so if he could; he told stories, and badgered his opponent . . . until we all laughed, in spite of the dismal circumstance in which we were placed.[2]

Herndon never actually complained of Lincoln's desire for company, but he did say that Lincoln was rarely in his office, always on the street or circuit "beating the bushes for more business."[3] Life on the circuit was attractive to him particularly because of the camaraderie of the lawyers and judge who traveled with him. His native equipment, uneven and lacking in some respects, nevertheless threw him early in the direction of public speech.

He might not have exercised his talent, however, had not the very nature of his environment placed a premium on public speaking. When people met in this frontier community for a sociable or barn raising, the event turned out to be a contest in wit and merriment. The crowds gathered around the one who could tell the best yarns or recite the raciest jingles, often of his own composition. That one in the Gentryville neighborhood was Abe Lincoln. "He was the only man or boy within a wide compass who had learning enough to furnish the literature for such occasions. . . . "[4] Talk was the medium, too, by which information was disseminated and public opinion mobilized. There were few newspapers, infrequent

[1] *Ibid.*, p. 54.

[2] J. H. Buckingham, *Illinois as Lincoln Knew It: A Boston Reporter's Record of a Trip in 1847* (Harry E. Pratt, ed. of reprint, reprinted from papers in *Illinois History and Transactions for 1937*, for members of the Abraham Lincoln Association, Springfield, Ill., 1938), pp. 30–33.

[3] Jesse W. Weik, "Lincoln as a Lawyer," *The Century Magazine*, 66 (June, 1904): 279–289.

[4] Lamon, *op. cit.*, p. 54.

travelers, and a very occasional post. Politics, nevertheless, was a live question, and he who could lead the discussion won the acclaim of the community. "We had political discussions from 1825 to 1830, the year Lincoln left for Illinois. We attended them, heard questions discussed, talked everything over and over, and in fact wore it out. We learned much in this way."[1] Herndon reports one of Abe's companions as saying, "Lincoln would frequently make political speeches to the boys. . . . He would keep them til midnight. Abe was a good talker, a good reasoner, and a kind of newsboy."[2]

Jury speaking, too, came in for its share of fame. "It supplied the place of theaters, lecture and concert rooms . . . ," said Arnold (a close personal friend of Lincoln for 25 years). "The leading lawyers and judges were the star actors and had each his partizans. Hence crowds attended the court to see the judges, to hear the lawyers contend with argument, and law, and wit for success, victory and fame."[3] The county trials were held in Boonville (15 miles from Gentryville), and Lincoln often was an interested spectator. It was there that he heard a famous trial lawyer of southern Indiana, John A. Brackenridge.[4] Abe sat entranced. It was the best speech he had heard up to that time. Many years later he recalled this incident and remarked, "If I could, as I then thought, have made as good a speech as that, my soul would have been satisfied. . . . "[5] Again the power of the spoken word had been impressed upon him. Little wonder that he later urged lawyers to "practice and cultivate extempore speaking. It is the lawyer's avenue to the public."[6]

How much pulpit eloquence contributed to the regard of this community for speech is conjectural. When a traveling preacher stopped at Pigeon Creek to conduct services, the whole neighborhood turned out to hear him. It was a flamboyant, ministerial style of speaking: "The preacher would take his stand, draw off his coat, open his shirt collar, commence service by singing and prayer; take his text and preach till the sweat would roll off in great drops,"[7] said Mrs. Crawford, wife of Josiah Crawford, for whom Lincoln worked. We know that on Monday morning Lincoln often "would mount a stump and deliver with wonderful approach to exactness

---

[1] Nat Grigsby's statement, Sept. 12, 1865, Gentryville, Ind., in Hertz, *op. cit.*, p. 356.

[2] Herndon and Weik, *op. cit.*, I, 58.

[3] Isaac N. Arnold, *Life of Abraham Lincoln* (Chicago, Jansen, McClurg and Co., 1884), pp. 56–57.

[4] Spelling doubtful. Herndon and Weik give Breckenridge; Barton, Beveridge, M. H. Houser, John Iglehart (*Indiana Historical Society Publications*) give Brackenridge.

[5] Herndon and Weik, *op. cit.*, I, 59.

[6] John G. Nicolay and John Hay, ed., *Abraham Lincoln: Complete Works* (2 vols., New York, D. Appleton and Company, 1894), I, 163.

[7] Lamon, *op. cit.*, p. 42.

the sermon he had heard the day before."[1] Whether he did it in a serious mood or only as another piece of clowning one does not know. It was, at any rate, one more activity in which speaking was the *sine qua non* of success.

Another environmental factor worked in a negative way to push Abe further along the path of public speech. Manual labor was the only means of livelihood in his community, and he had a positive dislike for this type of work. He must have realized early in his life that if he were to escape the fate of his father and his relatives, he must turn to some calling physically less strenuous and more rewarding. Politics was the road and the spoken word the best vehicle of transportation. "Abe was not energetic," says his stepsister, "except in one thing—he was active and persistent in learning—read everything he could."[2] Both John Hanks and John Romine, a neighbor for whom Abe worked, stated openly that Abe was lazy when it came to manual labor. "He worked for me," says Romine, "but was always reading and thinking. I used to get mad at him for it. I say he was awful lazy. He would laugh and talk—crack his jokes and tell stories all the time; didn't love work half as much as his pay. He said to me one day that his father taught him to work but never learned him to love it." Immediately upon his return from the field "he would go to the cupboard, snatch a piece of cornbread, sit down, take a book, cock his legs up as high as his head and read," and, adds John Hanks, "whenever Abe had a chance in the field while at work, or at the house, he would stop and read."[3] The distasteful toil incited him to find other pursuits more congenial to his temperament.

Preparation for the Platform

As far as one can learn, no teacher of elocution ever wandered into the neighborhood in Indiana offering to give lessons in his art. The brief period of schooling that Abe enjoyed did not include public speaking or declamation, although there were oral exercises that might be considered as a very rudimentary preparation had Abe gone to school regularly.[4] The whole school session, in fact, was conducted orally. His teachers, Dorsey, Crawford, and Sweeney, in Indiana all conducted "blab" schools; studying as

---

[1] Chapman to Herndon, Weik MSS, and Lamon, *ibid.*, pp. 39–40.

[2] Mrs. Moore's statement, Weik MSS.

[3] Romine's statement, Weik MSS, and Herndon and Weik, *op. cit.*, I, 42–44.

[4] Lincoln's total schooling in Kentucky and Indiana amounted to less than one year. See John Hanks to Herndon, June 13, 1865, Weik MSS; also, J. L. Scripps, *Life of Abraham Lincoln* (Chicago Press and Tribune Co., 1860), p. 2: "The aggregate of all the time thus spent [in school] both in Kentucky and Indiana did not amount to one year."

well as reciting was done aloud. This evidently became a lifelong habit with Lincoln, for Herndon complained, "Singularly enough Lincoln never read any other way but aloud," a habit that annoyed Herndon "almost beyond the point of endurance."[1] The school possessed no readers, if Senator Henderson's account of his interview with Lincoln at the White House is accurate. Lincoln is reported to have said on this occasion that "reading books and grammars were unknown" in the log schoolhouse that he attended. "All our reading," he said, "was done from the Scriptures, and we stood up in a long line and read in turn from the Bible."[2,3] There were special days, however, when "exhibitions" of reading and speaking were staged. When Herndon asked Mrs. Crawford what books Abe read she replied: "Can't say what books Abe read, but I have a book called The *Kentucky Preceptor*, which we brought from Kentucky, and in which and from which Abe learned his school orations, speeches, and pieces to recite. School exhibitions used to be the order of the day, not as now however. Abe attended them, spoke, and acted his part always well, free from rant and swell."[4] The *Kentucky Preceptor* is not listed as one of the textbooks of the three schools that Abe attended, but since he worked for the Crawfords and had access to the book, it is highly probable that he used some of the declamations he found in it for school exhibitions.

When the young Lincoln reached New Salem and sought the services of Mentor Graham, the "Bunker Hill school master on Rock Creek," in the study of surveying and grammar, he also may have received some tutorial training in speaking. Elocution was Mentor Graham's hobby, and since Abe not only studied with him but also boarded at his cabin it is unlikely that he would not have taken advantage of the training for which the schoolmaster was famous. "One of his fads was the teaching of elecution [*sic*]," writes J. Q. Primm, one of Graham's pupils. "He used a stump about twenty yards in front of the school house door as a platform for the pupils to stand on. The stump was flat on top. The tree having been sawed down. He would stand in the door and give instructions as to just what to say, and how to say it, this being the lesson in elecution."[5] That such training actually did take place is suggested in Graham's interview with Herndon some years later: "He studies to see the subject matter clearly and to

[1] Herndon and Weik, *op. cit.*, II, 332.
[2] William E. Barton, *Abraham Lincoln and His Books* (Chicago, Marshall Field and Co., 1920).
[3] There were passages for oral reading in Thomas Dilworth's "speller and pronouncer," *A New Guide to the English Tongue*, which was a text in Dorsey's school in Indiana. *Aesop's Fables* and maxims and sentences in prose are included.
[4] Elizabeth Crawford's statement to Herndon, in Hertz, *op. cit.*, p. 366.
[5] Reminiscences of J. Q. Primm, Lincoln, Ill., in collection of Oliver R. Barrett, Chicago.

express it truly and strongly. I have known him to study for hours the best way of three to express an idea."[1]

"Good boys who to their books apply
Will all be great men by and by"[2]

The boy who composed these lines must have believed in their teaching, for he scoured the countryside for books. Among others, he found two books devoted exclusively to public speaking and reading, the *Kentucky Preceptor*[3] and Scott's *Lessons in Elocution;*[4] there is indirect evidence, too, that he also read another book that gave some attention to elocution: Lindley Murray's *English Reader.*[5]

In a sense, these books represented something more than textbooks in reading and speaking. The compiler had a secondary purpose in mind, namely, to present to the reader the best passages in political and moral philosophy that were available in abbreviated form. "A Teacher," the anonymous author of the *Kentucky Preceptor*, explains that "the compiler has endeavored to fix upon those subjects only, which are calculated to engage the attention, and improve the heart."[6] *The English Reader* likewise is "designed to assist Young Persons to read with propriety and effect; to improve their language and sentiments; and to inculcate some of the most important principles of piety and virtue."[7]

The highly moral tone is evident in the selection of the passages that exalt patriotism, courage, honesty, friendship, self-sacrifice, etc. The *Preceptor* differs from Scott and Murray in the substitution of American forensic literature for the traditional British addresses. Here the young Lincoln found such examples as "The Inaugural Speech of President Jefferson," "The Baccalaureate Address of President Nott of Union College," and "The Funeral Oration by 'Governeur Morris.'" These books, taken as a whole, made up a fairly comprehensive manual of the philosophy of government, education, religion, and personal and group living.

[1] Mentor Graham's statement.—Herndon and Weik, *op. cit.*, I, 121.

[2] "During my visit to Indiana I met Richardson, who showed these two lines which Abe had prepared for him."—Herndon and Weik, *ibid.*, p. 41.

[3] Borrowed from Josiah Crawford. This copy is now in the collection of Oliver R. Barrett, Chicago.

[4] Lincoln found this book in the library of David Turnham.—Lamon, *op. cit.*, p. 37n.

[5] "Mr. Lincoln told me in later years that Murray's *English Reader* was the best school book ever put into the hands of an American youth. I conclude, therefore, that he must have used that also."—Herndon and Weik, *op. cit.*, I, 36.

[6] *Kentucky Preceptor* (3d ed., Lexington, Ky., Maccoun, Tilford and Co., 1812), Preface, p. ii.

[7] Lindley Murray, *The English Reader* (10th ed., Haverhill, Mass., Burrill and Tileston, 1817), title page.

Did these books furnish any comparable aid in learning the techniques of public speaking? To what extent did the young speaker find instruction, for example, in bodily action, diction, and voice? Murray, in his *English Reader*, devotes only a sentence to bodily action. He advises the student to "accompany the Emotions and Passions which your words express by correspondent tones, looks and gestures," adding that any description or rules of gesture are "ineffectual."[1] The *Kentucky Preceptor*, likewise, gives no explicit directions, suggesting principles only indirectly in a passage "On Elocution":

> Cicero . . . even maintains, that a good figure is necessary for an orator; and, particularly, that he must not be overgrown and clumsy. He shews by it, that he knew mankind well, and knew the powers of an agreeable figure and a *graceful manner*. Men are much oftener led by their hearts than by their understandings. The way to the heart is through the senses: please their eyes and their ears, and the work is half done . . . if a man has parts, he must know of how much consequence it is to him to have a *graceful manner of speaking*. . . . [2]

Scott's aim, by his own admission, is something of an innovation. It is his purpose to present a complete "system of gesture." He deplores the fact

> that boys . . . stand motionless, while they are pronouncing the most impassioned language . . . and that they should sprawl into an awkward, ungain [*sic*], and desultory action, is still more offensive and disgusting. What then remains, but that such a general style of action be adopted, as shall be easily conceived, and easily executed; which, though not expressive of any particular passion, shall not be inconsistent with the expression of any passion; which shall always keep the body in a graceful position. . . . [3]

This system, he assures the reader, has been taught "with abundant success . . . in one of the most respectable academies near London."[4] A single example will suffice to indicate the particularity with which Scott describes his "system of Gesture." This, says the author, is

> the attitude in which a boy should always place himself, when he begins to speak . . . : [The speaker] should rest the whole weight of his body on the right leg; the other, just touching the ground, at the distance at which it would naturally fall, if lifted up to show that the body does not bear upon it. The knees should be straight, and braced, and the body though perfectly straight not perpendicular, but inclining as far to the right as a firm position on the right leg will permit. The right arm must then be held out with the palm open, the fingers straight and close, the thumb

[1] Murray, *ibid.*, Sec. VI, p. xii.

[2] *Kentucky Preceptor*, pp. 52–54.

[3] William Scott, *Lessons in Elocution* (Hartford, Lincoln and Gleason, 1806), Prefix, Sec. I, On the Speaking of Speeches at Schools.

[4] Scott, *ibid.*, Prefix, p. 16.

almost as distant from them as it will go, and the flat of the hand neither horizontal nor vertical, but exactly between both. . . . When the pupil has pronounced one sentence, in the position thus described, the hand, as if lifeless, must drop down to the side, the very moment the last accented word is pronounced; and the body, without altering the place of the feet, poise itself on the left leg, while the left hand raises itself, into exactly the same position as the right was before, and continues in this position till the end of the next sentence, when it drops down on the side, as if dead; and the body poising itself on the right leg, as before, continues with the right arm extended, till the end of the succeeding sentence; and so on, from right to left, and from left to right, alternately, till the speech is ended.[1]

In the succeeding pages Scott describes meticulously other gestures that may be made during the full tide of the address.

How much attention Lincoln paid to these passages on action can be judged best by the descriptions of him on the platform in Illinois, to be related in the next section. It is safe to conclude that he may have emulated the mobile facial expressions in his early stump speaking, but it is also certain that he copied neither the posture nor the elegant gestures described by Scott, nor was he the picture of grace that the lecturer on elocution painted in the *Kentucky Preceptor.*

There are some rules in these books, however, to which Abe must have given greater thought. The importance of clarity of enunciation and correct pronunciation were lessons never to be forgotten by him. From Walker's *Speaker*, Scott extracts such serviceable principles as these: "Let your articulation be distinct and deliberate"; "Pronounce your words with propriety and elegance"; and "In every Sentence, distinguish the more significant Words, by a natural, forcible and varied emphasis."[2] "What is the constant and just observation as to all actors upon the stage?" asks the *Preceptor.* "Is it not, that those who have most sense always speak the best, though they may not have the best voices? They will speak *plainly, distinctly,* and with a *proper emphasis,* be their voices ever so bad."[3]

If Murray made a particular contribution to Lincoln's understanding of diction, it must have been his reiteration of the simple, conversational style in reading and speaking:

Return to the various, natural expressive tones of conversational speech. . . . Many persons err in this respect. When they read to others, and with solemnity, they pronounce the syllables in a different manner from what they do at other times. They dwell upon them and protract them; they multiply accents on the same word;

[1] *Ibid.*, pp. 3–5.
[2] *Ibid.*, pp. 33ff.
[3] *Kentucky Preceptor*, pp. 53–54.

from a mistaken notion that it gives gravity and importance to their subject, and adds to the energy of their delivery.[1]

Lincoln's insistence on testing his speech by reading aloud has been mentioned earlier. The value of such practice may have been enforced upon him by these authors. "The learner should daily read aloud by himself," says Scott, "and as often as he has an opportunity, under the direction of an instructor or friend. He should also recite compositions memoriter."[2] "You will read aloud to yourself, and tune your utterance to your own ear; and read at first, *much slower* than you need to, in order to correct that shameful habit of speaking *faster* than you ought. In short, you will make it your business, your study, and your pleasure, to *speak well*, if *you think right*."[3] Lincoln's justification of this practice is based on another and, perhaps, sounder educational theory: "When I read aloud two senses catch the idea: first, I see what I read; second, I hear it, and therefore I can remember it better."[4] The "Propriety of pronunciation," calling, as it did, for a "living demonstration," could scarcely have much value to this student;[5] but if the reports of the speaker in action are reliable, the lessons in enunciation, rate, and emphasis stood him in good stead.

Did Lincoln get any instruction in voice from these textbooks? The *Preceptor* includes only the most incidental advice in a short passage entitled "The Bad Reader"; Scott warns against "bellowing" and explains in some detail how to "acquire a compass and variety in the Height of your Voice." The greatest help is found in Murray, who devotes a section to "Proper Loudness of Voice" and one to "Tones." Did Abe remember that Murray said, "It is a great mistake, to imagine that one must take the highest pitch of his voice, in order to be well heard in a large company. This is confounding two things which are different, loudness or strength of sound, with the key or note on which we speak."[6] Evidently not, or if he did, nervous tension and the demands of an outdoor audience conspired often to nullify the teaching.

Here, then, are the known books[7] that taught Abram Lincoln the techniques and much of the content of speech. If they are compared with

---

[1] Murray, *op. cit.*, p. viii.

[2] Scott, *op. cit.*, p. 42.

[3] *Kentucky Preceptor*, p. 54.

[4] Herndon and Weik, *op. cit.*, II, 332–333.

[5] "The teachers were, for the most part, ignorant, uncultivated men, rough of speech, uncouth in manners, and rarely competent to teach beyond the simplest rudiments of learning. . . . "—J. L. Scripps, *Life of Abraham Lincoln* (Chicago Press and Tribune Co., 1860), p. 1.

[6] Murray, *op. cit.*, Sec. I, p. vi.

[7] This assertion is based on the research of the following authors: William E. Barton, *Abraham Lincoln and His Books* (Chicago, Marshall Field and Co., 1920); Albert J. Beveridge, *Abraham Lincoln 1809–1858* (2 vols., Boston, New York, Houghton Mifflin Company, 1928), I, 62–77; Herndon and Weik, *op. cit.*, I, 40ff; Rufus Rockwell Wilson, *What Lincoln Read*

other books of their kind and time, it is no exaggeration to say that Lincoln had the advantage of instruction not available to a great many boys of that day.

It might well be claimed that all the books that Lincoln read contributed to his education as an effective speaker. True, but certain ones had a closer bearing on his training than others. In addition to the books devoted exclusively to oral reading and speaking and the Bible, which was used as a text in school, one should mention other works containing speeches that enabled the young Lincoln to catch the form and spirit of forensic literature. By his own acknowledgment, Weems's *Life of George Washington* was such a book.[1] It is written in a highly embellished, forensic style, the author frequently addressing the reader directly in order to enforce lessons of humility, courage, and generosity.[2] Others written in a similar style are Ramsey's *Life of Marion*, Ramsey's *Life of Washington*, Grimshaw's *History of the United States*,[3] and *Sermons and Speeches of Theodore Parker*.[4] Other students might include the *Revised Laws of Indiana*,[5]

(Chicago, Pioneer Publishing Co., 1932); M. L. Houser, *The Books That Lincoln Read* (Peoria, Edward Jacob Print Shop, 1929). Houser notes that Lincoln also had access to A. T. Lowe's *Columbian Class Book* (4th ed., Worcester, Dorr and Howland, 1829), a reader "consisting of Geographical, Historical and Biographical Extracts."

[1] In addressing the Senate of the state of New Jersey, Feb. 21, 1861, Lincoln said, "May I be pardoned if, on this occasion, I mention that away back in my childhood, the earliest days of my being able to read I got hold of a small book, such a one as few of the younger members have ever seen—Weems' *Life of Washington*. I remember all the accounts there given of the battlefields and struggles for the liberties of the country. . . . I recollect thinking then, boy even though I was, that there must have been something more than common that these men struggled for."—*New York Spectator*, Feb. 25, 1861.

[2] The following is typical of Weems's style: "Young reader: go thy way; think of Washington; and Hope. Though humble thy birth, low thy fortune, and few thy friends, still think of Washington; and Hope. Like him, honour thy God; and delight in glorious toil. Then, like him, 'thou shalt stand before kings. Thou shalt not stand before common men.'"—M. L. Weems, *The Life of George Washington* (Philadelphia, J. B. Lippincott Company, 1860), p. 232.

[3] In a denunciation of slavery Grimshaw pleads with the reader: "Let us not only declare by words, but demonstrate by our actions 'That all men are created equal; that they are endowed, by their Creator, with certain inalienable rights; that amongst these, are life, liberty, and the pursuit of happiness.'"—William Grimshaw, *History of the United States* (Philadelphia, Grigg and Elliott, 1833), p. 301.

[4] "On Herndon's return from the east [in 1858] he brought with him additional sermons of Theodore Parker; one, a lecture on 'Effect of Slavery on the American People.' Lincoln read and returned marked with a pencil the following: 'Democracy is direct self-government, over all the people, for all the people, by all the people.'"—Herndon and Weik, *op. cit.*, II, 396.

[5] Lamon, *op. cit.*, p. 37, entitles the volume *The Revised Statutes of Indiana*, as do Francis F. Browne, *The Everyday Life of Abraham Lincoln*, p. 86; Herndon and Weik, *op. cit.*, p. 45; E. L. Masters, *Lincoln The Man* (New York, Dodd, Mead and Company, 1931), p. 22. Masters says: "Lincoln gained his succinct phrasing from a study of the *Statutes of Indiana*." Later researchers, Beveridge, Wilson, Howser, and others, refer to the *Revised Laws of Indiana*.

which contained the Declaration of Independence, the Constitution of the United States, and the first twelve amendments; and several books that Lincoln read while living in New Salem: Gibbon's *Decline and Fall of the Roman Empire* and Rollin's *Ancient History*. If one disregards, however, their contribution to the substance of Lincoln's speeches and limits oneself to their form, they can scarcely be designated as specific contributions to his oral style.

Books, however, were not the sole purveyors of literature in the oral style in that day. Lincoln's most regular forensic mentors in his last years in Indiana and throughout his residence in New Salem were the newspapers on which he could lay his hands.[1] Indeed, if he had not realized earlier the power of speech in political leadership, it was forcibly impressed upon him as he read these journals: The *Louisville Journal*,[2] The *Telescope*,[3] the *National Intelligencer*, the *Cincinnati Gazette*, the *Missouri Republican*, and the *Sangamo Journal*.[4] Newspapers then gave prominence to the text of the speech; it was printed in its entirety on the front page. If it were too long for one issue it was continued in the next. In these papers he had the opportunity to read Webster's famous "Liberty and Union" reply to Hayne;[5] Clay's speeches in the Senate on the American system of tariffs,[6] on the reduction of duties,[7] on the sale of public lands,[8] and on Abolition;[9] Andrew Jackson's message to Congress;[10] and Calhoun's debate

---

[1] "Newspapers were [to be] had" and "Abe was a constant reader of them. I am sure of this for the years 1827-28-29-30."—Mrs. Sarah Lincoln, Weik MSS.

[2] Beveridge, *op. cit.*, I, 97, states that Lincoln's friend, William Jones, the storekeeper in Gentryville, who was a staunch Republican, took the *Louisville Journal* and that Lincoln read these papers. The *Louisville Journal*, however, was not founded until 1831, the year after Lincoln's departure for Illinois. It may have been the *Louisville Public Advertiser* that Lincoln read in Indiana; in New Salem he read the *Louisville Journal*.

[3] William Wood's statement, Sept. 15, 1865: "I took newspapers, some from Ohio, Cincinnati, the names of which I have now forgotten. One of these papers was a temperance paper. Abe used to borrow it, take it home and read it, and talk it over with me . . . I took the *Telescope*."—Hertz, *op. cit.*, pp. 363-364.

"Absalom Roby is authority for the statement that even at that early day Abe was a patient reader of a Louisville newspaper, which someone at Gentryville kindly furnished him."—Herndon and Weik, *op. cit.*, I, 39-40. .

[4] Later changed to the *Sangamon Journal*. "The final syllable of this name was then pronounced to rhyme with 'raw.' In later days the letter 'n' was added, probably for euphony's sake."—Herndon and Weik, ibid., p. 87 n. It became the *Illinois Daily Journal*, Sept. 2, 1848.

[5] *Louisville Public Advertiser*, Feb. 10, 1830.

[6] *Sangamo Journal*, Apr. 5, 1832.

[7] *Sangamo Journal*, Jan. 11, 1832.

[8] *National Intelligencer*, Dec. 29, 1835.

[9] *Sangamo Journal*, Mar. 2, 1839.

[10] *National Intelligencer*, Dec. 10, 1835.

in the Senate on the abolition of slavery in the District of Columbia.[1]
Reading aloud these speeches, as was his wont, Lincoln had an excellent
opportunity to absorb the spirit and style of contemporary American
oratory.

There was no auditorium or speech laboratory in Gentryville or New
Salem in which Abe could practice public speaking. Save for the possible
lessons in elocution by Mentor Graham in New Salem, the schools that
Lincoln attended gave only the most occasional opportunity for exhibitions
of declamation and oratory.[2] Where, then, did he try out the precepts he
had learned in these books and journals dealing directly or indirectly
with public speaking? The countryside was Abe's auditorium. Wherever
he could find one or two eager listeners he practiced his art. He found
them at home, the country store, the neighborhood sociables, the blacksmith's shop. "He kept his audiences at the country store until midnight,
listening to his shrewd wisdom, native wit and vivid recitals."[3] "He was
so odd, original and humorous and witty that all the People in town
would gather around him," said Dennis Hanks to Herndon. "I would get
tired, want to go home, cuss Abe most heartily."[4] Sometimes he would
entertain his companions "by repeating to them long passages from the
books he had been reading."[5] At other times he was the neighborhood
"preacher." His stepsister, Matilda Johnston, relates that "when father
and mother would go to church Abe would take down the Bible, read a
verse, give out a hymn, and we would sing. Abe was about fifteen years of
age. He preached and we would do the crying."[6] "But this practice of
'preaching' and political speaking into which Abe had fallen, at length
became a great nuisance to old Tom [Lincoln]. . . . When it was announced that Abe had taken the 'stump' on the harvest field there was an
end to work. The hands flocked around him, and listened to his curious
speeches with infinite delight."[6] Finally, his father had to forbid his
speaking during working hours, said Mrs. Sarah Lincoln, for "when Abe
begins to speak, all the hands flock to hear him."[7] He also would practice
without an audience. Many a day, says Nicolay, Lincoln could be found
"mounting a lonely stump and making a mock harangue to nodding corn

---

[1] *National Intelligencer*, Jan. 29, 1836; *The Globe*, Jan. 9, 1836.

[2] Lincoln attended three schools in Indiana for a period totaling less than a year. They were
conducted by Andrew Crawford (1818), Azel Dorsey (1823), Mr. Sweeney (1826). See Nat
Grigsby's statement in Hertz, *op. cit.*, p. 354.

[3] Arnold, *op. cit.*, p. 43.

[4] Hanks to Herndon, Mar. 22, 1866, Weik MSS, and Beveridge, *op. cit.*, I, 87.

[5] Lamon, *op. cit.*, p. 39.

[6] *Ibid.*

[7] Arnold, *op. cit.*, p. 43.

rows and the stolid pumpkins that lay between them."[1] Sometimes he wrote his "lectures," declamations, fragments of speeches that he had learned or had composed himself. "Frequently," relates his stepmother, "he had no paper to write his pieces down on. Then he would put them with chalk on a board or plank, sometimes only making a few signs of what he intended to write. When he got paper he would copy them, always bringing them to me and reading them."[2] It was a practice that he kept up while working at the home of Josiah Crawford;[3] here he wrote his ideas on "Temperance" and on "American Government," "the best form of government for an intelligent people."[4] Nicolay believed that this was a valuable exercise in oral style, for "he learned to appreciate the value of the pen as an instrument to formulate and record his thought, and the more clearly, forcibly and elegantly to express it."[5]

Abe's first serious efforts at stump speaking began almost immediately with his removal to Illinois. In the summer of 1830, while working for a farmer near the village of Decatur, he was attracted to the village square, where "A backwoods orator was on the wagon ranting against the 'Old Line Whigs,' for which principles Lincoln then held strong sympathies. The moment the speaker finished, young Lincoln mounted a stump and in the first political speech of his life he so vigorously refuted the charges of the speaker that he was roundly cheered for his earnestness and pluck."[6] Whether this is the same speech that John Hanks remembered is not clear: " . . . a man by the name of Posey came into our neighborhood and made a speech. It was a bad one, and I said Abe could beat it. I turned down a box and Abe made his speech. The other man was a candidate—Abe wasn't. Abe beat him to death, his subject being the navigation of the Sangamon River."[7]

When the young politician moved to New Salem he joined a debating club that held regular meetings devoted to political questions. He made a speech soon after his admission, in which he "pursued the question with reason and argument so pithy and forcible that all were amazed." They had heard him entertain the boys at Offut's store, but they realized from

[1] John G. Nicolay, "Lincoln's Literary Experiments," *The Century Magazine*, 25 (1894): 824.

[2] Herndon and Weik, *op. cit.*, I, 43.

[3] "He spent his evenings as he did at home—writing on wooden shovels or boards with a coal, or keel, from the branch."—Lamon, *op. cit.*, p. 50.

[4] Herndon and Weik, *op. cit.*, I, 61; Lamon, *op. cit.*, p. 69.

[5] John G. Nicolay, "Lincoln's Literary Experiments," *The Century Magazine*, 25 (1894): 825.

[6] "Lincoln and the Illinois Central," *Illinois Central Magazine*, 15, No. 8 (February, 1927), 5–11.

[7] Hanks to Herndon, in Herndon and Weik, *op. cit.*, I, 71.

this occasion that "there was more in Abe's head than wit and fun; that he was already a fine speaker."[1]

When he announced his candidacy for the state legislature in 1832 the stump assumed an added importance for him. Here was a real test of his power and a platform for practice. People did not flock to hear him, for he was comparatively unknown.

The aspiring local candidate of those days was lucky if he found a gathering of twenty or thirty settlers at a shooting match, a raising, or other neighborhood occasion to whom he could propose his reforms in State legislation, or his national views on tariff and internal improvement. Sometimes it was an evening meeting assembled in a district log school house, lighted by two or three tallow candles, with an audience of ten or fifteen persons. Only those who have been through experiences of this kind can appreciate the chilling effect of such surroundings upon oratorical enthusiasm. Here the speaker needed all his epigrams, and anecdotes, to dissipate the expectant gravity, the staring solemnity of his auditors in the ghostly half-light inside, and the dismal darkness and loneliness outside the little cabin. They needed to be seasoned with pithy argument and witty illustration and rendered in a vocabulary that had the flavor of the cabin and the energy of the frontier.[2]

There is scanty record of the practice in speaking that he received in this campaign, probably because of his three-months' absence from New Salem as a member of the militia in the Black Hawk War.[3] "The Speach hee made was at Paps Vill," James A. Herndon reports an old settler as saying, "thar was a large gathering thar on account of a sale of goods hee was the only candidate thar and was called on to make a speach."[4] Not a single report exists of his speaking in his second campaign, and in the 1834–1835 session of the legislature he "was a *working* member . . . but did not attempt the *role* of speaker."[5] By 1836, however, several made note of the young legislator's campaign for re-election. He even appeared in Springfield and made a speech in answer to George Forquer, a Jackson Democrat. Joshua Speed, who heard Lincoln for the first time on this occasion, remarked, "I was then fresh from Kentucky, and had heard

[1] Lamon, *op. cit.*, pp. 121–122.
[2] John G. Nicolay, "Lincoln's Literary Experiments," *The Century Magazine*, 25 (1894): 825.
[3] Lincoln must have continued his practice in speech, for "Father Dixon said that while the little army was encamped at Dixon's Ferry, 'every evening, when off duty, Lincoln could be found sitting on the grass, with a group of soldiers, eagerly listening to his stories. . . .'" —Isaac N. Arnold, "Address to Chicago Historical Society," Nov. 19, 1868 (Chicago, Fergus Printing Co., 1877).
[4] James A. Herndon to William H. Herndon, Weik MSS, May 29, 1865; also Lamon, *op. cit.*, p. 125. The speech begins, "Fellow citizens, I presume you all know who I am—I am humble Abraham Lincoln."—Herndon, *op. cit.*, I, 104.
[5] Scripps, *op. cit.*, p. 12.

many of her great orators. It seemed to me, then, as it seems to me now, that I never heard a more effective speaker. He carried the crowd with him and swayed them as he pleased."[1]

When Lincoln journeyed by stagecoach to Vandalia to take his seat as a floor leader in the Assembly on December 5, 1836, his apprenticeship was over. He had earned a reputation as an accomplished speaker.

"I Introduce . . . an Eminent Citizen of the West—Abram Lincoln of Illinois" [2]

When the speaker at Cooper Institute stepped forward to acknowledge this introduction by William Cullen Bryant, did he put into practice the principles of speaking that he had found in his textbooks in Gentryville and New Salem? He may have remembered Scott's opening exhortation that "Resistless Eloquence Wielded at will the fierce Democracy," but he was a poor example, indeed, of Scott's descriptions of the speaker in action on the platform. At no time in his career, in fact, did he even faintly resemble in posture, bearing, or movement the elegant pictures drawn by Scott in his *Lessons in Elocution*. If a "man is first seen, then heard," Lincoln created an adverse impression when he rose to address an audience. " . . . crooked-legged, stoop-shouldered, square-built, and anything but handsome in the face," wrote the editor of the *Amboy Times*, who had just heard Lincoln for the first time at Dixon, Ill., in 1856; and then in a softer vein he adds, "It is plain that nature took but little trouble in fashioning his outer man, but a gem may be encased in a rude casket. . . . His first remarks were not of a character to overcome the unfavorable impression which his uncouth appearance made."[3] More tactful, perhaps, is the description by the reporter following Lincoln's speech in Janesville, Wis.: "Many present saw Mr. Lincoln for the first time; and as his person is tall, lean and wiry, his complexion dark, his physiognomy homely, and his phrenological developments peculiar, he attracted much attention."[4] The "assemblage" in Cincinnati in the fall of that year, 1859, were able by the aid of a "few jets of gas at the sidewalk" to get "a good view of the speaker." "It is not wonderful that he is called 'Old Abe,'" says the *Commercial* reporter, "for his personal appearance is odd enough, and eminently suggestive of kindly nick-names."[5] Rollins, who presided at a Republican

[1] Joshua F. Speed, *Reminiscences of Abraham Lincoln* (Louisville, Ky., John P. Marton and Co., 1884), p. 17.

[2] *New York Times*, Feb. 28, 1860.

[3] *Amboy Times*, July 24, 1856.

[4] *Janesville Morning Gazette*, Oct. 4, 1859.

[5] *Cincinnati Daily Commercial*, Sept. 19, 1859.

rally at Concord, N. H., which Lincoln addressed in 1860, called him "a unique specimen of the human family. Long, lank and awkward . . . the real Yankee." Yet he believed that "these oddities and peculiarities which would seem to detract from the efficiency of an orator all go to gain the sympathy of his hearers . . . "[1]

Less ready were the reporters to mention his mode of dress—evidently doubtful taste even in those days! From other sources one gathers that his clothes served to high-light his ungainly, awkward appearance. At the beginning of his political career in the canvass of 1832, he was clad in "a mixed jeans coat, clawhammer style, short in the sleeves and bobtail—in fact it was so short . . . that he could not sit on it; flax and tow-linen pantaloons . . . and potmetal boots."[2] At the Rivers and Harbors Convention in 1847 in Chicago he appeared in "a short-waisted, thin swallow-tailed coat, short vest of the same material, thin pantaloons scarcely coming down to his ankles, straw hat, a pair of brogans, and woolen socks."[3] He had not improved his dress materially by the summer of 1858, when he shared the platform with the fashionably attired Douglas. Lincoln was a strange contrast in "baggy trowsers so short that they showed his rough boots," a long linen duster blotched with perspiration stains, sleeves always too short and an old stove pipe hat."[4] This was political capital for his bitter opponent, the *Chicago Times* reporter, who saw him as "the most. abject picture of wretchedness we have ever witnessed. His knees knocked together, and the chattering of his teeth could be heard all over the stand."[5] It is doubtful if he ever found a suit that did not accentuate his long arms and legs. Henry Whitney, who traveled the circuit with him in Illinois, remembered, "His coat and vest hung loosely on his giant frame. His trousers were invariably too short."[6]

When he went to New York for his engagement at Cooper Institute he carried with him a new black frock coat and trousers purchased for the occasion, but they ill became him. They "showed the creases made while packed in the valise"; the low collar accentuated the prominent Adam's

---

[1] Page, *op. cit.*, p. 39.

[2] Statement of A. Y. Ellis, who heard his speech at Pappsville.—Herndon and Weik, *op. cit.*, I, 103.

[3] Elihu B. Washburne, "Abraham Lincoln in Illinois," *North American Review*, October, 1885, reprinted in B. B. Gernon, *The Lincolns in Chicago* (Chicago, Ancarthe Publishing. Co., 1934).

[4] Statement of William H. Porter, Le Roy, Ill., to William E. Barton, at Bloomington, Ill., Feb. 9, 1923 (in Barton Collection, University of Chicago); and report of eye witness at Freeport debate; in *Sixty-fourth Anniversary of Lincoln-Douglas Debate*, F. A. Fulwider, ed., privately printed, Aug. 26, 1922.

[5] *The Daily Chicago Times*, Oct. 9, 1858.

[6] Statement of Henry C. Whitney, in Jesse W. Weik, "Lincoln as a Lawyer," *The Century Magazine*, 68, No. 1 (June, 1904), 285.

apple and long "head-stock"; and Lincoln for the first time was conscious of his dress.

> On his return home . . . [he] told me that . . . he was greatly abashed over his personal appearance . . . for a long time after he began his speech and before he became 'warmed up' he imagined that the audience noticed the contrast between his Western clothes and the neat-fitting suits of Mr. Bryant and others who sat on the platform. The collar of his coat . . . had an unpleasant way of flying up whenever he raised his arm to gesticulate. He imagined the audience noticed that also.[1]

It probably deserved the description that the *Boston Daily Journal* accorded it, the dress of a "Connecticut deacon."[2]

Such attire could only have accentuated the strange posture and gestures of this "prairie orator . . . who followed no rules of declamation." Reaching the front of the platform, "he always stood squarely on his feet, toe even with toe";[3] and if Lamon is correct in his description of Lincoln's tendency to be pigeon-toed and flat-footed,[4] such a posture would be the most natural one, albeit a direct contradiction to Scott's exhortation to "rest the weight of the body on the right leg; the other, just touching the ground."[5] As he arose to address political rallies, juries, his body, "thin through the chest, and hence slightly stoop-shouldered . . . inclined forward to a slight degree."[6] He must have paid little heed to Scott's command to hold the right arm out "with the palm open . . . neither horizontal nor vertical, but exactly between both."[7] "After having risen," Herndon says, "he generally placed his hands behind him, the back of his left hand in the palm of his right, the thumb and fingers of his right hand clasped around the left arm at the wrist. . . . [In truth he] played the combination of awkwardness, sensitiveness and diffidence."[8] As he began to speak, his face, too, seemed dull and lifeless. "Aside from the sad, pained look due to habitual melancholy, his face had no characteristic or

[1] Herndon and Weik, *op. cit.*, III, 454–455.
[2] " . . . tall, slim, lank, rather queer, with an unmistakably Yankee look—dresses like a Connecticut deacon— . . . "—*Boston Daily Journal*, Feb. 29, 1860.
[3] Herndon and Weik, *op. cit.*, II, 408.
[4] Lamon, *op. cit.*, p. 470.
[5] Scott, *op. cit.*, p. 3.
[6] Herndon and Weik, *op. cit.*, II, 405.
"In the spring term of the Tazewell County Court, in 1847, which at that time, was held in the village of Fremont, I was detained as a witness an entire week . . . Mr. Lincoln slowly got up, and in his strange half-erect attitude . . . began. . . . "—Statement of George W. Minier, *Lincoln Memorial Album* (O. H. Oldroyd, ed. Springfield, Lincoln Publishing Co. 1890), p. 187.
[7] Scott, *op. cit.*, p. 4.
[8] Herndon and Weik, *op. cit.*, II, 406.

fixed expression."[1] At first there was "a curious, introspective look in his eyes,"[2] a mental indirectness, which defeated the words he uttered.

Such opponents as the *Illinois State Register* played up his unimpressive manner: " . . . he commenced with embarrassment and continued without making the slightest impression."[3] At the Ottawa debate he "gazed over the audience as though at a loss for words, and when at last he began speaking another disappointment chilled his supporters' hopes . . . his opening sentences, commonplace enough in themselves, were uttered hesitatingly, as though he were groping for words."[4]

Lincoln evidently suffered throughout his career from that bugbear of all students of public speech, stage fright. For the first few moments of every address his facial and bodily expressions were those of fear. He "froze in his tracks"; "he had a far away prophetic look in his eyes";[5] his face became lifeless, his figure inert, his speech hesitating; "it seemed a real labor to adjust himself to his surroundings";[6] a poor representation, indeed, of the "bold and commanding figure" depicted by Scott in his *Lessons!* Lincoln freely admitted this problem. Writing to Herndon from Washington, in 1848, he said, "I find speaking here [House of Representatives] and elsewhere about the same thing. I was about as badly scared, and no worse, as I am when I speak in court."[7] On his return home from his speech in New York, in 1860, he remarked to an associate in his office that "he had never felt more embarrassed for the first few minutes."[8]

The stage fright, however, wore off after five or ten minutes, and then occurred a transformation in his action.

As he warmed up to his subject the dull, listless features dropped like a mask. His face lighted up as with an inward fire. The eye began to sparkle, the mouth to smile, the whole countenance was wreathed in animation. His body began to move in unison with his thought. He straightened up; his form expanded; . . . a splendid and imposing figure. . . . [9]

To keep in harmony with his growing warmth his hands relaxed their grasp and fell to his side. . . . He did not gesticulate as much with his hands as with his

---

[1] *Ibid.*, p. 405.

[2] Joseph Medill, "Lincoln's Lost Speech," *McClure's Magazine*, 7, No. 7 (1896): 321.

[3] *Illinois State Register*, Nov. 23, 1839.

[4] Fred Hill, "The Battle of the Giants," *Abraham Lincoln* (Lincoln Farm Association, Feb. 12, 1907), p. 13.

[5] Statement of Oliver Crissey, of Avon, Ill., who attended the debate in Galesburg, Oct. 7, 1858.—*Evening Mail* (Galesburg), Oct. 8, 1908.

[6] Herndon and Weik, *op. cit.*, II, 405.

[7] *Complete Works*, I, 100, Jan. 8, 1848.

[8] Statement of Henry B. Rankin, *Illinois State Register*, Feb. 11, 1917.

[9] These descriptive phrases are repeated in various ways in Horace White, *Abraham Lincoln in 1854* (Illinois State Historical Society, January, 1908); Noah Brooks, *Abraham Lincoln* (New York, G. P. Putnam's Sons, 1894), pp. 199–200; Herndon and Weik, *op. cit.*, II, 405–408.

head.[1] He used the latter frequently, throwing it with vim this way and that. This movement was a significant one when he sought to enforce his statement. It sometimes came with a quick jerk, as if throwing off electric sparks into combustible material.[2]

He had, however, certain typical gestures that the audiences were wont to recall with delight. When Lincoln dropped into explanation, he "frequently caught hold with his left hand, of the lapel of his coat, keeping his thumb upright and leaving his right hand free to gesticulate."[3] At moments of great intensity his arms swung into action. When he cried out, "The advocates of the extension of slavery into the new States will soon find themselves squelched!" he "raised his right arm to the right, bringing his hand down almost to his feet."[4] This sweeping gesture he used often, "stooping forward almost to the ground to enforce some point . . . "[5] At other times, "to dot the ideas in the minds of his hearers," he extended the long, bony index finger of his right hand.[6] When he wanted to show thorough detestation of an idea, he would throw both arms upward, with fists clenched in determination.[7] At other times, " . . . his clinched hand came down as if he were a blacksmith striking on his anvil. . . . "[8] They were jackknife gestures, quick, incisive, unpredictable in their suddenness, accompanied often by a "quick turn of the body to right and left as he drove home a red-hot rivet of appeal."[9] Although Horace White claimed that when Lincoln reached the climax of his speech a stranger might say, "Why, this man . . . is really handsome," it is doubtful if his action ever became truly graceful.[10]

---

[1] Horace White, who was with Lincoln throughout the debates in 1858, confirms this statement by Herndon: "His gestures were made with his body and head rather than with his arms."—*Abraham Lincoln in* 1854, pp. 10–11.

[2] Herndon and Weik, *op. cit.*, II, 406.

[3] *Ibid.*, p. 408.

[4] Memory of Delia A. Varney of Lincoln's speech at Dover, N.H., Mar. 2, 1860, in Page, *op. cit.*, p. 85.

[5] *The Daily National* (Milwaukee), Oct. 1, 1859.

[6] Ben Perley Poore's statement, in William Eleroy Curtis, *The True Abraham Lincoln* (Philadelphia, J. B. Lippincott Company, 1903), p. 98; C. H. Brainerd's statement, in Joseph H. Barrett, *Abraham Lincoln and His Presidency* (2 vols., Cincinnati, Robert Clarke Co., 1904), I, 98; Herndon and Weik, *op. cit.*, II, 407.

[7] Herndon and Weik, *op. cit.*, II, 406.

[8] Henry M. Field, "Mr. Lincoln at The Cooper Institute," *The Independent*, No. 2418 (Apr. 4, 1895).

[9] Statement of John B. Stevens, who heard Lincoln at Dover, N.H., March, 1860, in Elwin L. Page, *op. cit.*, p. 81.

[10] Horace White, in Introduction to William H. Herndon and Jesse W. Weik, *Abraham Lincoln* (2d ed., 2 vols., New York, D. Appleton and Company, 1892), p. xxvi.

Abraham Lincoln: His Development in the Skills

It is strange that a face as lifeless as was Lincoln's in repose[1] could suddenly become so mobile on the platform; no picture of his action as a speaker is quite complete without some special mention of this talent. Always something of a mimic, he bettered Scott's teaching of the "Rules for Expressing . . . the various Passions" and perfected his technique by practice on the boys at the store in Gentryville and New Salem. In the canvass of 1840 so successfully did he mimic the facial expression of his opponent, Jesse B. Thomas, that the crowd cheered and yelled for more.[2] The newspapers, on the other hand, were not agreed upon the merits of such talent. A paper politically opposed to him issued a warning:

> Mr. Lincoln, another Federal candidate for Elector, followed in the evening. His argument was truly ingenious. He has, however, a sort of *assumed clownishness* in his manner which does not become him. It is *assumed*—assumed for effect. Mr. L. will sometimes make his language correspond with this *clownish* manner, and he can thus frequently raise a loud laugh among his Whig hearers; but this entire game of buffoonery convinces the mind of no man, and is utterly lost on the majority of his audience. We seriously advise Mr. Lincoln to correct this *clownish* fault, before it grows upon him.[3]

That he did not correct it at once is fairly certain, for he was still indulging in "mock-clownish" expressions while a member of Congress: He would "stride down the alley towards the speaker's chair, holding his left hand behind him so that he could now and then shake the tails of his own dress-coat, while he earnestly gesticulated with his long right arm, shaking the bony index finger at the Democrats on the other side of the Chamber."[4] Some writers believe that Lincoln abandoned this unusual style after his participation in Whig rallies in New England, following the close of Congress in 1848.[5] Perhaps the close association with Whig men of culture and the example of restrained public speech of such men as Seward[6] did have some tempering effect on Lincoln's speaking manner. In the following months he toned down, somewhat, the grotesque and boisterous mimicry in which he was wont to indulge, but these same New Englanders were remarking as late as 1860 that Lincoln's was a "new type of delivery . . .

---

[1] M. S. Snow, "A Personal Reminiscence," *The Magazine of History*, Extra No. 145 (1928), p. 44. In speech at Exeter, N.H., "it seemed absolutely like another person speaking to us, from the man who had sat upon his chair looking as if he hadn't a friend in the world."

[2] William H. Herndon and Jesse W. Weik, *Herndon's Lincoln: The True Story of a Great Life* (3 vols., Chicago, New York, Bedford, Clarke and Co., 1889), I, 197.

[3] *Illinois State Register*, Nov. 23, 1839.

[4] Curtis, *op. cit.*, p. 98 (Lincoln's speech on "General Taylor and the Veto," July 27, 1848).

[5] Beveridge holds this opinion; see Beveridge, *op. cit.*, I, 476.

[6] Lincoln heard Seward at Tremont Temple, Sept. 22, 1848.

worth a long walk to see the man."[1] It is safe to say that he always made some use of this talent in his persuasive speeches. At Jonesboro, an eye witness remembered that when he desired to make a point, he

produces a shrug of his shoulder, an elevation of his eyebrows, a depression of his mouth, and a general malformation of countenance, so comically awkward that it never fails to bring down the house . . . the peculiar characteristic of his delivery is the remarkable mobility of his features, the frequent contortions of which excite a merriment his words could not produce.[2]

Of that "countenance full of humor or frowning with scorn," the Janesville audience will always "have a vivid recollection."[3] The reporter for the *New York Tribune* presents "herewith a full and accurate report of this Speech [Cooper Institute] . . . yet the tones, the gestures, the kindling eye and the mirth-provoking look defy the reporter's skill."[4] From memories such as these grew the tales of Lincoln's buffoonery, until many a bitter Southern paper in 1861 dubbed him "the strong man on the stump . . . the country clown with a nose of wax."[5]

The prairie audiences of the fifties saw Lincoln in his most vigorous and telling delivery on the stump. Unfortunately, he did not carry over this intensity in facial and bodily expression to occasions calling for impressive or informative speeches. It was an integral part only of his forensic style. His informative lectures and eulogies, often excellent in substance, were great disappointments because they were delivered in a dry, unimpassioned manner. Possibly the inherent limitations of a manuscript conspired to defeat him, for he read most of these addresses. One of his earliest efforts, his speech to the Springfield Temperance Society, is a bombastic piece, and this may account, in part, for its failure. Lincoln himself later recognized its inadequacies; he told one of his companions that "the people understand him better when he comes down from his stilts, and talks to them from their own level."[6]

His later nonpolitical addresses, however, are restrained in style, yet they, too, miss fire. "Clay's eloquence," said Lincoln, consisted in an "earnest and impassioned tone and manner,"[7] yet Lincoln delivered these very words in the driest "tone and manner"; " . . . in no part of it was he more

[1] Page, *op. cit.*, p. 39.

[2] *Life and Martyrdom of Abraham Lincoln* (Philadelphia, T. B. Peterson and Bros., 1864), pp. 45–46.

[3] *Janesville Morning Gazette*, Oct. 4, 1859.

[4] Editorial, *New York Daily Tribune*, Feb. 28, 1860.

[5] *The Charleston Mercury*, Mar. 5, 1861.

[6] Lamon, *op. cit.*, p. 230.

[7] Eulogy of Henry Clay, July 16, 1852. *Abraham Lincoln: Complete Works* (2 vols., New York, D. Appleton and Company, 1894), I, 167–169.

than ordinarily animated . . . cold phrases and a tame style."[1] Lincoln realized that it was a failure, acknowledging that "he lacked the imagination necessary for a performance of that character."[2] Similarly, his lecture on "Discoveries and Inventions," which he read on several occasions,[3] "died aborning . . . a dull dead thing . . . no spirit and no life"—so wrote Herndon, who heard him on that occasion.[4] His lecture on "Man" proved to be a "flat and ignominious failure . . . delivered to . . . small and gradually waning audiences."[5] The contrast in these styles the *Milwaukee Daily National* sums up with extraordinary clarity. The crowd at the state fair knew that usually on such occasions "the dryest mess of platitudes" was served up, and "the appearance of the speaker is always a sign for a general dispersion of the visitors to the floral halls, the cow pens, and the side shows. But the fame of Mr. Lincoln attracted at least two-thirds of all upon the Fair grounds to his immediate vicinity." They expected the dynamic delivery about which they had heard so much. What a disappointment!

Except, however, the ungainly form, the homely face, and the clear, powerful voice, nobody yesterday saw the "Abe" Lincoln of the political arena. There was, to be sure, the evidence of profound thought in the address, for he always displays that, but the master strokes of his backwoods and homespun oratory, the wit, pungency, and sharpness were wanting, together with the *awkward gesticulation, the contortions of countenance,* and *the stooping forward almost to the ground to enforce some point of argument, or add vigor to some invective.* [Italics the author's.] The Hon. Abraham Lincoln instead of plain "Abe" was the speaker.[6]

In the field of persuasion, when the issues were sharp, the contest keen, Lincoln knew no peers in vigorous action on the platform; when the end of the speech was to inform or to impress, there was little in his manner to suggest the dynamic quality of his forensic style.

One cannot fairly include any criticism of the bodily action that accompanied Lincoln's delivery of his speeches following his election to the Presidency. Many factors conspired to make them compositions, superb literary efforts rather than speeches. The customs of office combined with

---

[1] Lamon, *op. cit.*, p. 339.

[2] J. G. Holland, *The Life of Abraham Lincoln* (Springfield, Mass., The Republican Press, Samuel Bowles & Co., 1866), p. 133.

[3] "One night during Court week I heard Lincoln give his address on 'Inventions'. He read the address. . . . "—Statement of Dean Charles E. Capen, at Bloomington, to William E. Barton, Feb. 9, 1923, in unpublished notes, Barton Collection, University of Chicago.

Letter of Herndon to Jesse Fell, Feb. 21, 1891: "I was not mistaken in the lecture which Mr. Lincoln read."—Hertz, *op. cit.*, p. 262.

[4] Hertz, *op. cit.*, p. 262.

[5] Whitney, *op. cit.*, p. 209.

[6] *The Daily National* (Milwaukee), Oct. 1, 1859.

the criticism of his colloquial language in informal remarks[1] to force him to read from a manuscript all his formal and many occasional utterances. As was his habit, his reading was accompanied by very little overt action,[2] and what little there was, was lost in the attention of the audience to a greater concern, the doctrines that Lincoln expounded. Moreover, by the

[1] In a speech to serenaders in Washington on July 4, 1863, Lincoln, said, " . . . and on the fourth the cohorts of those who opposed the Declaration that all men are created equal *'turned tail'* and *run.*" (Italics the author's.) Helen Nicolay says that after that time, "although a ready impromptu speaker, he made for himself a rule to which he adhered during his Presidency. This was to say nothing in public that he had not first committed to writing."—Helen Nicolay, *Personal Traits of Abraham Lincoln* (New York, D. Appleton and Company, 1913), pp. 370–371.

Nicolay and Hay comment on Lincoln's speech to serenaders at White House, Nov. 10, 1864: "Not wishing to speak extempore on an occasion where his words would receive so wide a publication, he sat down and hastily wrote a speech."—*Op. cit.,* IX, 379.

Lincoln reminded serenaders at Gettysburg, Nov. 18, 1863, that "in my position it is sometimes important that I should not say foolish things. It very often happens that the only way to help it is to say nothing at all. Believing that is my present condition this evening, I must beg of you to excuse me from addressing you further."—*New York Tribune,* Nov. 20, 1863.

The reaction of *The Round Table* to his impromptu speeches en route to Washington, Feb. 11–23, 1861, is typical: "Where is American Oratory? One of the most surprising of the phenomena of this wonderful war is the decadence of American oratory. At few periods of the world's history have there been such grand opportunities for eloquence; but our orators have been dumb or have uttered only uncertain sounds . . . President Lincoln journeyed the country on his way to Washington. At every station, at every city, he paused to make a speech. What speeches they were! A joke; a story; inquiries for the little girl who had advised him to wear whiskers; and a declaration that there was 'nobody hurt!' Good enough jokes; good enough stories; good enough off-hand speeches; but not the speech that every thoughtful citizen waited to hear."—*The Round Table* (New York), 2, No. 30. (July 9, 1864). (Nonpartisan journal devoted to "a weekly record of the notable, the useful and the tasteful.")

[2] "I stood near enough to the speaker's elbow not to obstruct any gestures he might make, although he made but few. . . . " [First Inaugural Address, Mar. 4, 1860].—Henry Watterson, *Abraham Lincoln* (Louisville, Ky., Courier-Journal Printing Co., 1899), p. 21.

"The address was read in an easy, unaffected manner, without the least effort at effect. . . . [He] made no pretence of doing anything else than reading it."—J. B. Remensnyder, "With Lincoln at Gettysburg," *Hearst's Magazine,* February, 1914; also, *The Magazine of History,* 32, No. 1 (1926), p. 10.

"There was no gesture except with both hands up and down, grasping the manuscript. . . . " [Gettysburg Address, Nov. 19, 1863.] Statement of Professor Philip M. Bilke, Gettysburg, Pa. (in collection of Albert H. Griffith, Fisk, Wis.).

"Abraham Lincoln, rising tall and gaunt among the groups about him, stepped forward and read his inaugural address, which was printed in two broad columns upon a single page of large paper." [Second Inaugural Address, Mar. 4, 1865.]—Noah Brooks: "Lincoln's Reelection," *The Century Magazine,* 49 (1895): 865–872.

"There was no effort at oratorical display, no endeavour to be impressive, not the slightest mannerism of any kind whatsoever." [Second Inaugural Address.]—Ervin S. Chapman, *Latest Light on Abraham Lincoln* (New York, Fleming H. Revell Co., 1917), p. 286.

time Lincoln reached the Presidency, he was too well known to necessitate any detailed description of his speaking manner in the reading of such formal utterances as the inaugural addresses. After the First Inaugural the "Public Man" notes in his diary only this—that "Mr. Lincoln was pale and very nervous, and did not read his address very well. His spectacles troubled him [and] his position was crowded and uncomfortable. . . ."[1] His "Dedicatory Remarks" at Gettysburg (so listed on the program), following upon an "Address by Edward Everett," did not warrant on the basis of either importance or length any special comment on the movement or gestures of the speaker. Merely by way of introduction to the speech, the newspapers made such a statement as this: "The President rises slowly, draws from his pocket a paper, and, when commotion subsides, in a sharp, unmusical treble voice, reads the brief and pithy remarks."[2] Southern newspapers, which might have been expected to seize upon every possible point of criticism, including action, contented themselves, in the main, with flaying without mercy his doctrines, occasionally throwing in such general epithets as these: "a canting, ill-bred, indecent old man"; "Puritanical, vulgar, slang-whanging speech"; "blatant old ass"; "a baboon."[3] Of his action on the platform they gave no specific account.

"Let Us, Therefore, Give the Voice Full Strength and Swell of Sound; But Always Pitch It on Our Ordinary Speaking Key"[4]

Did Lincoln take cognizance of this precept from his mentor? If Murray intended the "full swell and sound" to mean a rich, sonorous voice, Lincoln lacked this primary attribute. His "ordinary speaking key," always somewhat high, was raised in pitch as he began his public speeches. It was no "natural orator's" voice, this, but a thin, high-pitched voice, carrying distinct nasal overtones and having to commend it only a conversational rhythm and a strong intensity—so strong that it could be heard to the farthest limits of the crowd.

A complex of factors, aside from the main determinant, the physiological milieu, assisted in establishing his characteristic pitch and quality. His teachers, Murray, Scott, and the anonymous author of the *Kentucky Preceptor*, advocated imitation as the best method of learning vocal control;

---

[1] Carl Sandburg, *The War Years* (4 vols., New York, Harcourt, Brace and Company, 1939), I, 123.
[2] *The Cincinnati Commercial*, Nov. 21, 1863. For similar accounts from newspapers, see Sandburg, *op. cit.* I, 468–475.
[3] *The Charleston Mercury*, Feb. 16, 1861; Mar. 7, 1861; Nov. 9, 1863. *The Chattanooga Rebel*, Nov. 2, 1863.
[4] Murray, *The English Reader*, vi.

he may have imitated the vocal pattern all too common in that section, a nasal twang. Another consideration to be reckoned with was the "auditorium of the prairies." The great contests in speaking were outdoors, and anyone who has met this trial of an acoustic infinitude knows the natural tendency to enhance the carrying power by nasal reinforcement and a higher pitch. In all winds and weathers, amid distractions, Lincoln fought for the attention of his auditors. "Yesterday a high wind combined with the dust rendered the day somewhat unfavorable."[1] "It commenced raining before the speaking began and continued to rain a perfect torrent during the whole time of speaking."[2] "At ten o'clock the streets and sidewalks around the public square were almost impassable, and those who essayed out doors anywhere in the vicinity were well nigh stifled with dust for the pains."[3] "Ottawa was deluged in dust . . . the accommodations were of the most wretched character. Two or three times the surge of people on the platform nearly drove the reporters off . . . "[4] "The inevitable brass cannon was there [The Fair Grounds where the debate was held] before them, filling the yard with a loud noise and a bad smell."[5] "An arctic frost accompanied by a sour, northwest wind" lasted during the whole day.[6] Add to the noise, dust, confusion, wind and rain, an audience of five to fifteen thousand people, standing through 3 hours of debate, and one has a fair idea of the effect of these physical factors on the vocal pitch and quality of a speaker intent on being heard.

His voice, never deep, became "fifey and shrill"[7] under the tension of the hour. Murray's warning against raising the pitch instead of increasing the intensity was lost in the hurly-burly of a great bout. "He had a thin, tenor, or rather falsetto voice," said Horace White, "almost as high pitched as a boatswain's whistle."[8] As Lincoln proceeded with his speech Herndon remembered that "the exercise of his [Lincoln's] vocal organs altered somewhat the tone of his voice, . . . [it] mellowed into a more harmonious and pleasant sound."[9] Brooks, who heard him at Cooper Institute, said that Lincoln began "with a voice that was high pitched and rather disagreeable with a nasal twang," but he too found the voice less "disagreeable" as he

---

[1] Address at Wisconsin state fair, Sept. 30, 1859, *Milwaukee Daily Sentinel,* Oct. 1, 1859.
[2] *Illinois State Journal,* Sept. 14, 1858 (report of speech by Lincoln at Hillsboro, Montgomery County).
[3] Debate at Charleston, *Chicago Daily Press and Tribune,* Sept. 22, 1858.
[4] Debate at Ottawa, *Chicago Daily Press and Tribune,* Aug. 23, 1858.
[5] Debate at Jonesboro, *Chicago Daily Press and Tribune,* Sept. 17, 1858.
[6] Debate at Galesburg, *Chicago Daily Press and Tribune,* Oct. 9, 1858.
[7] *Boston Daily Journal,* Feb. 29, 1860.
[8] Horace White, *The Lincoln and Douglas Debates* (Chicago, University of Chicago Press, 1914), p. 20.
[9] Herndon and Weik, *op. cit.,* II, 407.

progressed.[1] Probably as Lincoln became more at ease the pitch was lowered and consequently the twang was less noticeable, although at no time could his voice be described as pleasant in pitch or quality.[2]

Granted that Lincoln's voice was not impressive for its beauty, still it had one attribute which did commend it to audiences: "it could be heard farther and . . . had better wearing qualities than Douglas's rich baritones. . . . "[3] Here was a signal talent and one that Lincoln had acquired by the time he entered politics. His reading and practice in Indiana had stood him in good stead; he tried out on "the nodding corn rows" the principle emphasized in every textbook that he had picked up. In spite of dust and wind and moving crowds, Lincoln's voice penetrated to the fringe of the audience, " . . . a clear trumpet tone that can be heard at an immense distance. Except N. P. Banks, I never heard a man who could talk to a large crowd with such ease," declared the editor of the *Beloit Journal*.[4] The crowd in the market place in Cincinnati did not settle down to listen until they "discovered there would be no difficulty in hearing Mr. Lincoln. . . . [They] were satisfied with the voice."[5] He continued to make himself heard when, as President, he resorted to reading his speeches. At the First Inaugural many testified to "a clear and emphatic voice [which] reached nearly to the outskirts of the vast throng. . . . I think fully thirty thousand persons heard him throughout," says the *New York Tribune*.[6] One who heard him at Gettysburg thought that "the speaker's voice was not loud, but its clear and tenor tones made it heard distinctly to the furthest limits of the audience."[7] Noah Brooks, who heard Lincoln deliver his Second Inaugural Address, wrote: "Every word was clear and audible as the somewhat shrill and ringing tones of Lincoln's voice sounded over the vast concourse."[8]

[1] Brooks, *op. cit.*, pp. 199–200.

[2] See also John H. Littlefield, "Recollections of One Who Studied Law with Lincoln," *The Independent*, Apr. 4, 1895; statement of Judge Thomas Drummond, in Holland, *op. cit.*, pp. 131–132; Fred Hill, "The Battle of the Giants," in *Abraham Lincoln*, p. 13.

[3] Horace White, *The Lincoln-Douglas Debates, op. cit.*, p. 20.

[4] *Beloit Journal*, Oct. 19, 1859.

[5] *Cincinnati Daily Commercial*, Sept. 19, 1859.

[6] *New York Daily Tribune*, Mar. 5, 1861.

Confirmatory evidence is found in the following: *National Intelligencer*, Mar. 5, 1861: " . . . the address of Mr. Lincoln, which he read with a clear, loud, and distinct voice, quite intelligible by at least *ten thousand* persons below him." L. E. Chittenden, *Recollections of President Lincoln and His Administration* (New York, Harper & Brothers, 1904), p. 88: "Mr. Lincoln's ordinary voice was pitched in a high and not unmusical key. Without effort it was heard at an unusual distance."

[7] J. B. Remensnyder, "With Lincoln at Gettysburg," *Hearst's Magazine*, February, 1914, p. 15.

[8] Noah Brooks, "Lincoln's Reelection," *The Century Magazine*, 49 (1895): 865–872.

Brooks, in this statement, has suggested another quality of Lincoln's speech. Not only could he be heard; he could be understood at great distances. A slow rate, a peculiar emphasis, and a perfect enunciation conspired to produce this effect.

> *"Learn to speak slow, all other graces*
> *Will follow in their proper places"* [1]

Was it this lesson expressed in various ways in the *Preceptor* and in Scott and Murray or a slow neuromuscular synergy or the leisurely tenor of life and speech in Kentucky and Indiana that accounts for Lincoln's rate of utterance? Lincoln, we know, believed that he could not speak rapidly. When Herndon urged him "to speak with more vim" in addressing a jury, Lincoln protested, "I am compelled by nature to speak slowly, but when I do throw off a thought it seems to me, though it comes with some effort, it has force enough to cut its own way and travel at a greater distance." [2] If the *Evening Post* was correct in its assertion that "Mr. Lincoln speaks at the rate of one hundred words in a minute," it was, indeed, deliberate utterance. [3] In the debates with Douglas he increased his rate slightly as he warmed up to his subject; but at no time did he have a smooth-flowing, rapid utterance. [4] His manner was always "very deliberate," says Littlefield [5] and, adds many a reporter, "impressive." [6] Lincoln must have realized that it was impressive, for he cautioned Conkling, who was to read his last stump speech for him at the meeting of the "Unconditional Union Men," in Springfield, in 1863: "You are one of the best public readers. I have but one suggestion—read it very slowly." [7] The deliberate rate enabled him also to place strong emphasis on the important words. He had a habit of "duly punctuating every sentence as he uttered it," wrote the *Cincinnati Com-*

---

[1] Scott, *Lessons in Elocution.*

[2] Herndon and Weik, *op. cit.,* II, 338–339.

[3] *The Evening Post* (New York), Mar. 4, 1861.
"Some of the reporters state that Dan'l Webster speaks at the rate of from eighty to one hundred and ten words per minute; Gerritt Smith from eighty to ninety; Dr. Tyng from one hundred and twenty to one hundred and forty; . . . Mr. Clay, one hundred thirty to one hundred and sixty; Mr. Choate and Mr. Calhoun, from one hundred sixty to two hundred."—*Beardstown* (Ill.) *Gazette*, Dec. 6, 1848.

[4] Horace White, *The Lincoln and Douglas Debates,* (Chicago, University of Chicago Press, 1914), pp. 20–21.

[5] John H. Littlefield, "Recollections of One Who Studied Law with Lincoln," *The Independent,* Apr. 4, 1895, p. 447.

[6] *New York Daily Tribune,* Mar. 5, 1861; also, Philip M. Belke, statement to Albert H. Griffith, Fisk, Wis. (copy in Barton Collection, University of Chicago).

[7] Letter to The Honorable Mr. James C. Conkling, Aug. 27, 1863.—John G. Nicolay and John Hay, *Complete Works of Abraham Lincoln* (12 vols., New York, Francis D. Tandy, 1905), IX, 102.

mercial.[1] Sometimes he heightened the emphasis by pause, mainly at the beginning and the climax of his speech. Men recalled that at Cooper Institute in the silence at the climax, the tension was so great one could hear the sizzling of the gas burners. When he left Springfield for Washington, he "turned toward the people, . . . paused for several seconds, 'till he could control his emotions" before beginning his farewell speech.[2] On March 4, 1865, after raising his arm in "token that he would speak, . . . he paused a moment, and, looking over the brilliant scene, still hesitated."[3] One can imagine the dramatic emphasis that such moments of silence gave to his words.

A clear, emphatic utterance suggests the perfect enunciation for which Lincoln was noted. An auditor at the Galesburg debate, who complained that he could not hear Douglas and attributed his difficulty to the wind, said, "When Lincoln got up to speak his articulation was so perfect that I knew immediately that it was not the wind that made it hard to hear."[4] White, Nicolay, and Herndon corroborate the opinion of many a reporter that "he spoke with singular clearness of enunciation. . . . "[5]

Did Lincoln have a pronunciation peculiar to his native state, Kentucky? The record is scanty, but it is conceivable that his speech did attract some attention for this reason. He had had little or no teaching in pronunciation. Dilworth, *A New Guide to the English Tongue*, which was his text in spelling at Dorsey's school[6] was designed for British rather than American children[7] and was an inaccurate guide at best.[8] Springfield had been settled largely by an influx of people from Kentucky, Indiana, and the South; so Lincoln's peculiarities in pronunciation might not have been noticed, even in Illinois. Many of his contemporaries designate his speech as "quaint" but fail to describe it in any detail, White, alone, stating definitely that Lincoln "had the accent and pronunciation peculiar to his native state, Kentucky."[9] It must have been a consistent practice of his to substitute the vowel [ɪ] for [ɛ] in such words as *chair, care, chairman,* and *again.* When he

[1] *Cincinnati Daily Commercial,* Sept. 19, 1859.

[2] *Illinois State Journal,* Feb. 12, 1861.

[3] Arnold, *op. cit.,* p. 402. (Arnold was a member of Congress from Chicago during the whole of Lincoln's first term.)

[4] Statement of J. N. Carson, of Gerlaw, who stood near the speaker's stand at the debate.— *Evening Mail* (Galesburg, Ill.), Oct. 8, 1908.

[5] *Cincinnati Daily Commercial,* Sept. 19, 1859.

[6] M. L. Houser, *The Books That Lincoln Read,* p. 3; also, Beveridge, *op. cit.,* I, 62.

[7] Note, for example, the warning against the addition of *h* in certain words beginning with a vowel, a characteristic of cockney speech.

[8] For example, "Words pronounced alike but spelled differently: 'reddish' and 'radish,' " etc.

[9] Horace White, *Abraham Lincoln in 1854* (Illinois State Historical Society, January, 1908), pp. 10–11.

arose to address the audience at Cooper Institute, in 1860, he drawled "Mister Cheerman," says Brooks, and many, I venture, said with Brooks, "You won't do; . . ."[1] In a poem, "The Bear Hunt,"[2] which Lincoln wrote after a visit to Indiana, in 1844, *again* and *skin* are rhymed. Capen, who heard him in his "Lost Speech," at Bloomington, remembered, "He pronounced 'only' as 'unly' and the numeral 'one' as 'own.'"[3] Commenting on the Inaugural, the unfriendly *Cincinnati Enquirer* reported that

though externally Mr. Lincoln has been the subject of a marvellous metamorphosis, his address and conversation remain unchanged. . . . he said when introduced "I've *heern* of you often and always took you to be a tall man. . . . When the Illinois delegation paid their respects to him, he turned to his Secretary, and accosting him by name said, "you must know these *fellers*."[4]

There is no direct report of his use of *outen* (out), *fit* (fought), *caise* (because), *tuck* (took), *sot* (sat), and *whar* (where); but Beveridge, finding that these words were native to Indiana, assumed that Abe so pronounced them.[5] One would expect the antiunion papers, particularly in the South, to seize upon any peculiarity of pronunciation and make capital of it; no such report is contained in the files of the *Charleston Mercury* or the *Richmond Enquirer*. They called his speech "vulgar," "indecent," "ill-bred," "profane," "slang-whanging," but they filed no "bill of particulars." The *Chicago Times* set upon him for his grammar, his "inelegant language, distorted sentences and mixed-up phraseology" but refrained from any specific allusion to his pronunciation.[6]

Here, then, is Abram Lincoln on the platform: no silver-tongued orator but an unpretending, direct, unmusical, articulate speaker, suffering from most of the problems of action, voice, and language that beset young politicians on the stump. Aided by the knowledge he had gained from his textbooks on elocution and from general reading and by his constant practice in speaking and writing, he rose in rare moments to unparalleled heights of simple eloquence.

[1] Brooks, *op. cit.*, pp. 199–200.

[2] Paul M. Angle, ed., *New Letters and Papers* (Houghton, Mifflin Company, 1930), p. 28.

[3] Statement of Dean Charles E. Capen, Wesleyan University, to William E. Barton, unpublished letters, Barton Collection, University of Chicago.

[4] *Cincinnati Daily Enquirer*, Mar. 6, 1861.

[5] Beveridge, *op. cit.*, I, 53–54.

[6] "Any man who ever heard Abraham Lincoln speak, knows that he cannot utter five distinct sentences in succession,—knows that his language is inelegant, his sentences distorted, and his whole phraseology so mixed up that it is tenfold more difficult to render what he says in intelligible English than it would be to report what any other speaker would say."—*The Daily Chicago Times*, Oct. 12, 1858.

Abraham Lincoln: His Emergence as the Voice of the People

by EARL W. WILEY

Had Lincoln died prior to 1854 not a syllable of his utterances would have survived him. But in that fateful year the United States Senate, by a vote of nearly three to one, passed the Kansas-Nebraska bill. Immediately the cry arose throughout the North that the Missouri Compromise had been repealed, that all precedent in the adjudication of slavery in Federal territories had been upset. Whereupon North and South glared at one another more hatefully than ever, and the quandary persisted of whether the control of slavery in the territories rested with the Congress of the United States or with the people of any territory affected.

It was the eve of a political revolution. But any revolution remains inarticulate so long as the mob speaks for it. It falls to the lot of someone among them to define it, and having defined it, he becomes their logical leader. When that man raises his voice social action becomes integrated, and the masses take step, prone to follow the one who can phrase the situation that lies beyond their own power of expression. It was the fate of Abraham Lincoln that he learned to speak well. It was his fortune to speak under the pressure of a crisis that baffled his countrymen.

Eloquence[1] is something more than the knack of saying the right thing in the right way. It is the knack of saying the right thing in the right way to the right people met at the right time and place. Because a speech is an experience put to utterance, it takes a great experience to make a great speech. At best, speech is national and institutional in its implications, and the artistry of the speaker is but one of the factors involved in the process. In the case of Lincoln, the imponderables favored him. The year 1809, for example, was an exciting hour for his birth, because the child born to Nancy Hanks in that year reached the fullness of his maturity at the moment when secession menaced the Union.

[1] The terms *eloquence, oratory, persuasion, effective speech,* and the like are utilized interchangeably in this study.

859

Lincoln's Emergence as an Orator of Rank

It happened that Lincoln's emergence as an orator of rank occurred in 1854. The hour fell on the afternoon of October 4. The locale was the Hall of Representatives, in Springfield, Ill. The *right* people were in attendance, that is, influential Democrats and Whigs and abolitionists of all hues of radicalism, as well as remnants of anti-Nebraska persuasion assorted from sundry loyalties. Stephen A. Douglas himself was present.

Anecdotes and quips crackled from Lincoln's lips as he sought in a prologue to blend into a stream of attention the mixed interests of his listeners.[1] Smiles, chuckles, and laughter greeted his preliminary sallies. Several times in the course of these informal remarks Douglas rose to his feet and heckled him, and each time Lincoln met these interruptions with good grace. Finally, Douglas made one thrust too many, and immediately Lincoln became stern and forbidding toward him. Thereupon, the air in the stuffy hall grew tense, and presently the great throng became quiescent under the spell of an argument that marshaled the tradition of the past, the need of the present, and the hope of the future against the slavery statesmanship of Stephen A. Douglas, as represented in the Kansas-Nebraska bill.

That day Lincoln transcended the partisan. He breathed into his tones something of the spirit of the Declaration of Independence, something of the humanism of Thomas Jefferson. Nor was he the rough-and-ready stump speaker of the invective type he had been in years past. He cast no stones at the South. He challenged no man's motives. In the analysis of his text he was strangely impersonal toward Douglas, a rival he had delighted to strafe at the hustings for 15 years. Withal, he was the keen strategist in debate, the master of aggression in argument. And he stood on high moral grounds, on the thesis that slavery was wrong in principle and, being wrong in principle, its introduction into free soil should be resisted. Years later, January 30, 1908, Horace White, an eye witness to the events, addressing the Illinois State Historical Society, remarked, "The speech of 1854 made so profound an impression on me that I feel under its spell to this day." The *Chicago Journal*, October 30, 1854, observed, "The impression created by Mr. Lincoln on all men, of all parties, was, first, that he was an honest man, and second, that he was a powerful speaker."

Society placed before Lincoln a grave issue in 1854. It created for him a great occasion and made available a passionate auditory. But it was Lincoln who supplied the expression that symbolized the national perplexity. That brings us face to face with our problem, because at final analysis it is the individual who mounts the platform and states the case for

[1] The *Illinois State Register*, Oct. 6, 1854, called these jests *Lincolnisms*.

the many. Accordingly, we ask: How came it that in 1854 Lincoln was recognized by men of antirepeal leanings as "a powerful speaker"? What forces had combined to make him eloquent? The design of this study is to venture an answer to these queries and their implications. Our method will be to piece together experiences—specific and general—which (in addition to those given in the preceding study on Lincoln by Mildred Freburg Berry) appear to have contributed substance to his effectiveness as a speaker.

Repression as a Factor in Lincoln's Training

The Mexican War speech has interest for us in this particular. Lincoln made that argument from the floor of the House of Representatives, in Washington, D.C., January 12, 1848. It was a Whig's rejoinder to President Polk's Mexican War policy, an argument in which, point by point, Lincoln sought to rebut every contention the President had advanced in his message justifying the war. Logically, it was a brilliant partisan performance. Yet that performance appears to have contributed mightily to Lincoln's voluntary withdrawal from politics in 1849.

Not that Lincoln pronounced anything discreditable to himself on the occasion in question. Actually, he evaluated the entry of United States troops into Mexico with historical accuracy. But only fanatics like Socrates talk so bluntly as Lincoln talked that day into the teeth of a rugged nationalism. Had not Stephen Decatur recently remarked something about my country, right or wrong? Lincoln was rebuffed summarily for dissenting from the popular enthusiasm for the war, his clients in Illinois failing to approve candor of this species on the part of their elected representative in Congress. At public meetings held in his own district, for instance, he was branded as a Benedict Arnold on the face of it.[1] The worshipful Herndon threw up his hands despairingly at the strangeness of his words, and the Whig and the Democratic newspapers in Springfield fought the issue over in many a partisan edition.

This experience presumably served Lincoln as a lesson in mass psychology. Not only did he learn from it that truth must sometimes truckle to expediency in bargaining for votes, that syllogisms are but slender reeds with which to stop the flow of a rising nationalism, but also he perhaps learned that there is an element of timing involved in oratory fundamental to the art, that there is a tide in the affairs of eloquence, even, that leads on to fortune. Following the event, for 5 years Lincoln inclined to a policy of

---

[1] For example, the *Illinois State Register*, Feb. 11, 1848, cited that at a public rally held in Clark County, "without distinction of party," Lincoln had been *rebuked* for the "stain he inflicted on their proud name of patriotism and glory, in the part they [his constituents] have taken in their country's cause."

861

silence on national issues. Even the great crisis of 1850 did not move him to words. In 1854, as shown, he finally broke silence, recognizing that the hour of utterance had struck. Men marveled at his new-found eloquence, but Lincoln realized that the key to the miracle lay within the hearts of his own auditors.

Let us call attention to an incident fated to play a part in the senatorial debates of 1858, which appears related to Lincoln's growing sense of caution. As described, Lincoln made his first ranking utterance on the afternoon of October 4, 1854, in Springfield. That night he was invited to address a group of extremists. He avoided that engagement as he would the plague, sensing that the time had not yet come for him so much as to touch hands with the radicals. Instead, he hitched up his driving horse and departed from town,[1] deciding that he had legal business to attend to in Tazewell County. That deliberate action represented one of the most momentous decisions Lincoln ever made. Four years later, at Ottawa, in the first of the Lincoln-Douglas joint debates, Douglas mistakenly assumed that Lincoln had attended that meeting of Black Republicans in 1854 and on the strength of that assumption went on to fashion a series of questions seeking to make Lincoln appear as a dangerous radical. When the facts finally came out, the accusation fell to the ground, and Lincoln earned the reward that goes to the man whose judgment is equal to the delicacy of the occasion involved.

Lincoln's ingenuity in finding the time and the place for uttering a vivid period is shown in his voicing of the celebrated house-divided-against-itself paragraph, June 16, 1858. At every turn he met with opposition in his intention to cite the passage. Leonard Swett, one of his ablest advisers, declared the reference wholly inappropriate for the event. Elihu Washburne took the same position. Judge T. Lyle Dickey declared the passage was little short of suicide as a political utterance, and only Herndon sensed the expediency of citing it at the beginning of a campaign.[2] Convinced that the public was prepared to analyze the slavery issue in terms of the sentiment implied in the reference, Lincoln challenged all opposition and on it posed his startling accusation that Democratic leaders, including Pierce and Buchanan and Taney and Douglas, had *conspired* to make the Union all slave. Immediately the eyes of the nation looked toward Springfield.

Two and two are always four in the world of science. But the common denominator of group opinion is always changing, and so it becomes important to the man speaking to identify the propitious moment for uttering what lies in his heart; and granted the gift of identification, the

[1] William H. Herndon and Jesse W. Weik, *Abraham Lincoln* (New York, 1926), II, 40–41.
[2] *Ibid.*, pp. 66–69.

speaker must be prepared to analyze his theme in accord with the dominant intellects among his auditory. Thought of that sort springs from objective behavior.

Lincoln's Objective Approach to Public Address

By 1860 Lincoln had achieved an approach to political events that was commandingly intellectual. The Cooper Union argument holds proof of that assertion. An appreciation of this claim can best be observed by tracing the evolution of the Cooper Union theme in Lincoln's discourse from 1854 to 1860. Let us note this phenomenon in his thinking in terms of his logic.

Resolved to its lowest terms, the Cooper Union argument comes to this: Did the statesmen who founded the Republic believe (with Lincoln) that the control of slavery in Federal territories rested with the Congress? Or did they believe (with Douglas) that this authority rested with the territories? In terms of partisanship it came to this: Did the Republican or the Democratic party represent the policy of the founders of the Constitution in dealing with slavery in Federal territories? In terms of personalities the question came to this: Who stood closer to Washington and Jefferson, politically, as regarded the claim that Congress possessed the authority to control slavery in Federal territories, Lincoln or Douglas?

Lincoln found his Cooper Union text in remarks Douglas had made in Columbus, Ohio, in September, 1859: "Our fathers," Douglas there declared, "when they framed the government under which we live, understood this question just as well, and even better, than we do now."[1] Summarized Lincoln at Cooper Union:

> The sum of the whole is that of our thirty-nine fathers who framed the original Constitution, twenty-one,—a clear majority of the whole—certainly understood that no proper division of local from Federal authority, nor any part of the Constitution, forbade the Federal Government to control slavery in the Federal Territories; while all the rest had probably the same understanding. Such, unquestionably, was the understanding of our fathers who framed the original Constitution; and the text affirms that they understood the question "better than we."[2]

At Cooper Union Lincoln adduced the direct, documentary evidence to prove his own contention. Thereby he sustained the fundamental republicanism of the Republican party. In the past he had not been so successful because he had approached the issue on the basis of probabilities. Cooper Union shows Lincoln in the role of the Olympian. The interesting thing is

[1] John G. Nicolay and John Hay, *Complete Works of Abraham Lincoln* (New York, 1905), V, 294.
[2] *Ibid.*, p. 304.

that it took him 6 years to get to the task of proving the moot issue by a method proper to the situation. That takes us to the story of the theme that led Lincoln to New York City.[1]

The issue—so far as Lincoln was concerned—originated in the Kansas-Nebraska bill, 1854. Douglas was the man who had maneuvred that legislation through the United States Senate, as stated; and in response to the bill arose the cry that the Missouri Compromise had been repealed, that a new national policy toward slavery in the territories had been foisted on the nation by scheming men.

Not at all! averred Douglas confidently. The Kansas-Nebraska bill gives renewed sanctity to the statesmanship of the early patriots of the Republic. Those venerable men recognized that the people of a state should be unhampered to determine their own domestic affairs free from outside meddling. That principle of self-determination was called *popular sovereignty!* Thus he postulated his rejoinder to dissentients in 1854.

At Peoria, October 16, 1854, Lincoln submitted his first recorded rebuttal to Douglas on the issue.[2] Prior to that event, however, he had built up his case through a series of addresses and debates made in central Illinois, including the Springfield speech, October 4, made 12 days prior to the Peoria event.[3] *But in all these trials his material of proof was circumstantial.* And so it was inadequate. He cited, for instance, how the founders had purposely shunned the word *slavery* in phrasing the text of the Constitution. From that circumstance he inferred, accordingly, that the founders both had anticipated the extinction of slavery in the Union and opposed any policy that contributed to its enlargement.

To bolster his position further Lincoln cited how the founders had legislated to abandon the African slave trade. From that he inferred that they worked on a theory contrary to that on which the repeal policy was predicated. But principally he postulated his contention on the antislavery clause of the Ordinance of 1787. That clause prohibited slavery from ever penetrating the Northwest Territory or any of the states to be carved

---

[1] As the Cooper Union argument the author arbitrarily designates only that division of the entire address which dealt with the personal testimony of the Revolutionary statesmen. It includes the first thirty-five paragraphs. See *ibid.*, pp. 293–309.

[2] The Springfield address of Oct. 4 is known to history as the "Peoria Address." Following the delivery of the Peoria speech, Lincoln wrote it out carefully and had it printed. See Nicolay and Hay, *op. cit.*, II, 190ff.

[3] Lincoln made his first public attack on the repeal policy at the Scott County Whig Convention, in Winchester, Aug. 26. Two days later he debated the proposition with Thomas L. Harris, in Carrollton. He continued to argue the issue up to the time of the state fair, in Springfield, held during the first week in October. This series of discussions shows perfectly how Lincoln altered and improved his argument in the open forum. For particulars of these speeches, see Paul M. Angle, *The Day-by-day Activities of Abraham Lincoln*, 1854–1861 (Springfield, Ill., 1933), pp. 34–40.

out of it. Lincoln perceived in that clause an instance in which Federal authority had asserted control of slavery in the territories. But 1787 was not 1789; and the controversy definitely concerned the men who drafted the Constitution, and their labors materialized in 1789.

Lincoln continued to argue the issue in the same groove in the Buchanan-Fremont-Fillmore campaign of 1856. The second phase in the enlargement of the controversy came with the announcement of the Dred Scott decision, 1857. Some claimed that that decision altered the legal status of the Negro, among other things, from that of man to that of chattel. Others declared that it nullified the authority of the people of a territory to banish slavery from its borders once it had been introduced. That development militated against one aspect of popular sovereignty as Douglas defined it, Lincoln was quick to note. When rumors of a *proposed* decision designed to prohibit any of the states from ridding themselves of slavery went into circulation, Lincoln began to dream of a Democratic *conspiracy* to abrogate the slavery policy of the founders in respect to the control of slavery in Federal domain. With this alarming prospect Lincoln identified Senator Stephen A. Douglas, Chief Justice Roger Taney, former President Franklin Pierce, and President James Buchanan. He announced his accusation in Springfield, June 16, 1858, as stated. *The case he made in support of his indictment was entirely circumstantial.*

During the early days of the senatorial campaign of 1858, Douglas kept his hands discreetly off the charge. Bu the was especially violent toward the introductory words with which Lincoln had led up to the accusation. Those words constituted the notable house-divided-against-itself passage. "Why cannot the nation stand as half-slave and half-free?" Douglas thundered; "has it not so stood since its founding?" Obviously, the two protagonists were diametrically opposed on the assumptions underlying their reasoning. Each man was logical in his conclusion if granted the truth of his premises.

The joint clashes between Lincoln and Douglas in 1858 contributed nothing fundamental to the enlargement of the argument on the vexing issue. But those debates represented an incubation period in which each man thought through every ramification of the matter a thousand times. And both of them came out of the debates aware of some gross flaw in their proof designed to show just what the founders actually believed concerning the proposition at stake. In 1859 Douglas ransacked the files of history, seeking material to prove that he stood with the fathers on the issue. He published his data in the September issue of *Harper's Magazine*, 1859.

Lincoln took hold of that *ex parte* article in Columbus, Ohio, September 16, 1859. But having nothing new to offer in support of his own case, he sought to give the *coup de grâce* to Douglas's findings. Facts of the matter, meanwhile, continued to lie buried in musty volumes. Then came the invitation to speak at Beecher's Church, in Brooklyn. We can believe that his own misgivings on the issue came flashing to mind on the receipt of that invitation. And so he went—at long last— to the old chronicles and letters of the statesmen of the Revolution to discover the facts of the matter. How well Lincoln succeeded in his quest at Cooper Union (the meeting was transferred from Brooklyn to New York City) has already been shown.

Society gains a friend whenever a man learns to think public issues through objectively. It gains a showman if this person can time his utterances to the mood of the crowd addressed..But society does not gain an orator until this man is prepared to utter his ideologies effectively. This leads us to another aspect of Lincoln's rhetoric, perhaps to its most artistic aspect.

Building the Text of the First Inaugural Address

By 1861, on a trial-and-error basis, Lincoln had mastered a medium of expression suited to the tastes of the crowd. This claim is supported by the story that lies behind the invention of the First Inaugural Address. Let us trace the high lights of that development to prove our claim. Lincoln began the actual composition of the address during the anxious days of January, 1861, in Springfield, when the pulse of the Republic trembled with disunion. Streets of the tiny prairie village resounded with the foot beats of big-time politicians, and farmer folk on street corners nodded to the President-elect in easy familiarity. Metropolitan newsmen dogged his steps, office seekers fell across his path at every turn, and at the State House Mrs. Lincoln served tea to a motley line of guests.

One day Lincoln broke loose from the grip of hangers-on and climbed the three flights of stairs leading to a room in a brick office building standing across from the rugged old State House, the scene of many of Lincoln's political speeches. On the shiny surface top of a hardwood table he wrote out the original draft of the address.[1] But he had first compared his own sentiments with what other men, in positions similar to that in which he now found himself, had said. He had reviewed the Republican platform and the much-discussed speech Alexander H. Stephens had recently made. He had arranged with Herndon to furnish him copies of Henry Clay's "Speech of 1850," Andrew Jackson's "Proclamation against Nullification," the "Constitution," and, later, Daniel Webster's "Reply to Hayne."[2] (He regarded this latter argument as a model of American eloquence and had

[1] "The first draft of the Inaugural Message is now being made by the President elect. . . . It will not be finished until after consultation with the Republican leaders in Washington."— *New York Tribune*, Jan. 29, 1861.

[2] Herndon and Weik, *op. cit.*, II, 188.

been much influenced by it in composing his speech of June 16, 1858.) Guided by these strong minds, he revised his own version of the address before putting it in the hands of W. H. Bailhache, to be set up and printed on the press of the *Illinois State Journal*.[1] Friends advised him on matters of syntax in the copy.

Lincoln showed a copy of the proposed address to Judge David Davis, who approved every word in it. Senator-elect O. H. Browning recommended that the tone of one passage in it be softened. Francis P. Blair[2] approved of it in its entirety, but William H. Seward suggested no fewer than thirty-six items of revision.[3] Stephen A. Douglas probably proposed one point of revision in it. These three latter men studied the manuscript in Washington.

Seward's criticism of the text was searching and constructive. He admitted the generic strength of the logic,[4] but he thought the composition lacked finesse and subtlety. Seward thought, for example, that the manuscript reference to the Republican platform was impolitic and proposed that the second and third paragraphs be deleted.[5] Lincoln agreed to this recommendation. Seward thought the ending was cold and lifeless as Lincoln had written it and submitted two passages for substitution. The first of these Lincoln discarded as inappropriate to the end sought.[6] The second passage read as follows:

I close. We are not, we must not be, aliens or enemies, but fellow-countrymen and brethren. Although passion has strained our bonds of affection too hardly, they must not, I am sure they will not, be broken. The mystic chords which, proceeding from so many battle-fields and so many patriot graves, pass through all the hearts and all the hearths in this broad continent of ours, will yet harmonize in their ancient music when breathed upon by the guardian angel of the nation.[7]

Lincoln rewrote this passage to read as follows:

I am loath to close. We are not enemies, but friends. We must not be enemies. Though passion may have strained, it must not break our bonds of affection. The mystic chords of memory, stretching from every battlefield, and patriot grave, to every living heart and hearthstone, all over this broad land, will yet swell the chorus of the Union, when again touched, as surely they will be, by the better angels of our nature.[7]

---

[1] John G. Nicolay and John Hay, *Abraham Lincoln: A History* (New York, 1890), III, 319.
[2] *Ibid.*, p. 319; also, pp. 333–334, footnote 12.
[3] For Seward's suggestions, see *ibid.*, pp. 327–344, footnotes.
[4] *Ibid.*, p. 321.
[5] *Ibid.*, p. 320.
[6] For this version, see *ibid.*, p. 343, footnote 42.
[7] *Ibid.*

Lincoln had improved Seward's passage in rhythmic notation. Some of Seward's modifications Lincoln rejected in full. Some he recast, and others he adopted in full. He wrote in the original draft, for example, "A disruption of the Federal Union is menaced, and, as far as can be on paper, is already effected. The particulars of what has been done are so familiar and so fresh that I need not waste any time in recounting them." For this rendition he substituted Seward's wording, to wit: "A disruption of the Federal Union, heretofore only mentioned, is now formidably attempted."[1] Possibly because of Seward's influence Lincoln introduced minor phrasal changes. He made "current experiences" to read as "current events and experience"; and "greater practice" became "different practice." One sentence he rewrote entirely, eliminating all reference to particular Southern states.[2] The passage dealing with the question of *tinkering with the Constitution* he revised entirely, although the hand of Douglas appeared in this alteration quite as much as Seward's.[3]

Seward aside, Lincoln made nine alterations of the original draft independently, although unnamed persons may have influenced him in this. He substituted, for instance, "our national fabric" for "Union,"[4] and "constituted" for "constructed."[5] The original text underwent a grand total of at least forty-five modifications. Argumentatively, the significant emendations were Browning's suggestion that nothing explicit be said about the retaking of Government property and Seward's recommendation to omit all mention of the Chicago platform. Ethically, the salutary modification was Lincoln's revision of Seward's proposed ending. The ultimate aim of all modifications was to soften the tone of the underlying declaration of the address, *that the Union would be maintained inviolate regardless of resistance.*

Argument of the address stands out as a composite of century-old Union tradition. The note of firmness sounding in it bespoke Jackson. The spirit of compromise in it recalled Clay. Stephens revealed himself in the argument that the South lacked justification for secession.[6] Webster is suggested in the contention that the principle of secession is unsound in logic. Browning struck a note of friendship. A hint of self-determination betrayed the hand of Douglas, and the bubbling spirit of optimism, the high sense of persuasion and the tenderness reflected Seward. And behind it all appears dimly a shadowed image of old Independence Hall and the intent

[1] *Ibid.*, pp. 330–331, footnote 5.

[2] *Ibid.*, p. 337, footnote 23.

[3] Louis Howland, *Stephen A. Douglas* (New York, 1920), pp. 362–363.

[4] Nicolay and Hay, *Abraham Lincoln: A History*, p. 335, footnote 16.

[5] *Ibid.*, footnote 18.

[6] Before the Georgia legislature, Nov. 14, 1860, Alexander H. Stephens made a strong "Union Speech." It was the talk of the country at the time.

faces of Madison and Jefferson and Hamilton. Yet essentially, the argument was Lincoln's, an examplar of his craftmanship in his maturity.

Gettysburg Address as the Product of Democratic Procedures

It is a fair inference that Lincoln's art of expression, judged by the way the First Inaugural Address was pieced together, word by word, was paraphrastic rather than spontaneous. The array of argument as shown in the building of his Cooper Union Address, already cited, also indicated studied and deliberate methods. Slow, cautious, groping, such were the marks of Lincoln's speech composition in the mature years of his career. Slow, cautious, groping, such are the marks of democratic processes. Lincoln, representative democrat, trained in the folkways of democracy, had identified these processes with his speech technique. Indeed, the great orator is always the Great Commoner, and he who would talk with the gods must first learn to walk with the humblest citizen. The Gettysburg Address stands as a token of this phenomenon.

Lincoln's intent at Gettysburg was to say something to stimulate his countrymen to preserve a government boasting the ideal that *all men are created equal.* As a barefoot boy in Indiana Lincoln became enthralled by the sentiment in that proposition directly out of the Declaration of Independence. Weems's *Washington* had impressed him with the doctrine of the rights of man. As a young man in Illinois, under the influence of Paine and Webster and Clay, he continued to meditate on the philosophy of that doctrine. Eulogizing Henry Clay in 1852, he paid tribute to the sentiment for the first time in a public address. When the Kansas-Nebraska bill became law he believed his concept of the doctrine to be challenged; when the Dred Scott decision was announced he feared it to be threatened with extinction; and when whisperings of a new Dred Scott decision arose, one that would make it impossible for even the free states to keep slavery outside their borders, he sensed a movement among the Democrats to abandon the doctrine altogether. In that spirit he spoke on June 16, 1858, charging his opponents with a *conspiracy* to make the Union all *slave.* In the same spirit he debated Douglas during the long summer that ensued, opposing Douglas's conception of popular sovereignty with the theme afterward immortalized at Gettysburg.

The nub of the Gettysburg theme was the nub of Lincoln's lifelong political philosophy and the counterpart of the philosophy promulgated by the Confederacy. Lincoln, as President, was prepared in principle to exploit that philosophy whenever the opportunity presented itself. The immediate occasion occurred on the night of July 7, 1863, when serenaders assembled on the White House lawn to celebrate two Union victories in the field, Gettysburg and Vicksburg. The fact that the achievements fell on the

Fourth of July carried an occult meaning to the man saturated with the liberalism of the Déclaration of Independence and trained to a belief in the magic of dreams and the efficacy of madstones.

The unexciting words Lincoln addressed to serenaders on the night of July 7 may be properly regarded as the tentative draft of the Gettysburg Address:

"How long ago is it?" he asked, "eighty-odd years since, on the Fourth of July, for the first time in the history of the world, a nation, by its representatives, assembled and declared, as a self-evident truth, 'that all men are created equal.' That was the birthday of the United States of America." Coming nearer to his argument, he added,

. . . and now on this last Fourth of July just passed, when we have a gigantic rebellion, at the bottom of which is an effort to overthrow the principle that all men are created equal, we have the surrender of a most powerful position and army on that very day, . . . and on the fourth [day] the cohorts of those who opposed the Declaration that all men are created equal "turned tail" and run. Gentlemen, this is a glorious theme, and the occasion for a speech, but I am not prepared to make one worthy of the occasion.[1]

Let us now turn to the story of the phrasing of the historic words spoken at Gettysburg. Between the time of the utterance of these plain words and November 19, the "glorious theme" of July 7 flashed to Lincoln's mind as a fitting theme for the memorial event. Antecedents of the composition of the remarks made at Gettysburg are unknown to us with any degree of certainty.[2] John G. Nicolay and James Speed thought that Lincoln wrote out a portion of the address in Washington and finished it in Gettysburg.[3] Judge Wills believed the text was composed at his residence, in Gettysburg, on the night preceding the ceremonies.[4] Wayne MacVeigh declared that he observed Lincoln writing something in the coach en route to Gettysburg.[5] Others corroborated that version. A more recent essayist, writing romantically, has described Lincoln as asking for a piece of brown wrapping paper that lay in the aisle of the coach and then, using the stub of a pencil, as writing the speech on it; after finishing the task he is said to have dropped the paper to the floor and looked away disconsolately, as if distressed with the results of his effort.[6] Major James B. Frey, on the other hand, who attended Lincoln throughout the journey from Washington

[1] Nicolay and Hay, *Complete Works*, IX, 20–21.
[2] William E. Barton, *The Life of Abraham Lincoln* (Indianapolis, 1925), II, Chap. XV.
[3] *Ibid.*, pp. 201–202.
[4] *Ibid.*, pp. 198–199.
[5] *Ibid.*, pp. 196–197.
[6] *Ibid.*, p. 198.

to the battlefield, declared that to his knowledge the President did no writing on the trip.

Text of the address found in our anthologies was composed 3 months following the event, at the solicitation of George Bancroft.[1] At that time he recast whatever phraseology he had pronounced on the battlefield, to provide a copy of the speech for the Baltimore Soldier's and Sailor's Fair. But this recasting itself was the culmination of prior revisions Lincoln made in Washington following the trip to Gettysburg. It was the belief of Robert Lincoln that the first rewriting of the address was probably made for John Hay. The President wrote another copy of it at the request of Judge Wills, who desired that Lincoln send him the original draft of the address, to be preserved with other mementos of the event.[2] In February, 1864, Lincoln wrote yet another copy for a sanitary fair held in New York City.[2] Finally he wrote for the Baltimore occasion the draft already mentioned; but finding this manuscript unsuited for lithographing purposes, both sides of the paper having been written on, he made yet another copy of it.[2] This final version, representing Lincoln's most mature reflection and artistry, has generally been accepted as the standard text of the address.

Revision and yet more revision characterized Lincoln's composition method. The few score words he spoke at Gettysburg were months in the making. In a sense, the composing of that address had no beginning that we can identify, for the concepts that stimulated those words had long been in Lincoln's heart. The process of recasting tended to purge his style of its impromptu crudities and embellish it with the craftsmanship of vivid extemporaneous expression. This is an important consideration, refuting the all-too-popular fallacy heard that the Gettysburg Address was the offhand utterance of a man inspired.

Lincoln as Bombastes

At Gettysburg, Lincoln voiced the humility of a people crushed by civil strife. By the same token he captured the expression geared to the sentiment defined. But Lincoln had not always played the lofty role of nationalist in public address. There had been times when he voiced above all else his own desire to achieve place and position in politics. There had been times when he was the spokesman of Whiggery. When so motivated, he had failed to pitch his tone to elevated expression. Turning the calendar back 25 years from Gettysburg, we can glimpse the manner of style when geared to the tempo of commonplaces. The bit of exuberance that follows is found in his declamation to the Springfield Lyceum, January 27, 1838:

[1] *Ibid.*, p. 205.
[2] *Ibid.*

Let reverence for the laws be breathed by every American mother to the lisping babe that prattles on her breast; let it be taught in schools, in seminaries, and in colleges; let it be written in primers, spelling-books, and in almanacs; let it be preached from the pulpit, proclaimed in legislative halls, and enforced in courts of justice. And, in short, let it become the political religion of the nation; and let the old and the young, the rich and the poor, the grave and the gay of all sexes and tongues and colors and conditions, sacrifice unceasingly upon its altars.[1]

In the following passage, taken from the same address, Lincoln leaned toward fustian:

They, [Revolutionary fathers] are gone. They were a forest of giant oaks; but the all-restless hurricane has swept over them, and left only here and there a lonely trunk, despoiled of its verdure, shorn of its foliage, unshading and unshaded, to murmur in a few more gentle breezes, and to combat with its mutilated limbs a few more ruder storms, then to sink and be no more.[2]

Note that in this passage "a lonely trunk" is empowered "to murmur in a few more gentle breezes." In the following passage, taken from Lincoln's address to the Washingtonian Temperance Society, February 22, 1842, the speaker vies with Bombastes:

Turn now to the temperance revolution. In it we shall find a stronger bondage broken, a viler slavery manumitted, a greater tyrant deposed; in it, more of want supplied, more disease healed, more sorrow assuaged. By it no orphans starving, no widows weeping. By it, none wounded in feeling, none injured in interest; even the dram-drinker and dram-seller will have glided into other occupations so gradually as never to have felt the change, and will stand ready to join all others in the universal song of gladness. And what a noble ally this to the cause of political freedom; with such an aid its march cannot fail to be on and on, till every son of earth shall drink in rich fruition the sorrow-quenching draughts of perfect liberty. Happy days when—all appetites controlled, all poisons subdued, all matter subjected—mind, all conquering mind, shall live and move, the monarch of the world. Glorious consummation! Hail, fall of fury! Reign of reason, all hail![3]

Passages like these indicate the student seeking mastery of his tools. As late as in 1850, Lincoln pronounced periods more dithyrambic than sober. These Gorgian flourishes took the form of antitheses, epithets, violent metaphors, exclamations, and parallelisms, in particular. It may be said that between 1838 and 1850 Lincoln experimented with words as if eager to test the strength of each stylistic artifice, and in the dim world of panegyric he gave full play to that urge. It took the cogency of the Kansas-

[1] Nicolay and Hay, *Complete Works*, I, 43.
[2] *Ibid.*, p. 49.
[3] *Ibid.*, pp. 208–209.

Nebraska bill, 1854, as stated, to wrench his attention irrevocably from the sign to the concept.

With Malice toward None

Patently, Lincoln sought a skill in words to enable him the better to satisfy his political ambition. But speech utilized for designs grossly subjective promotes an earth-bound rhetoric. Events came that menaced the Union, and Lincoln began to look outside himself, outside his party for objectives. At Gettysburg, looking over new-made graves into the skies of another day, he was detached, repressed, and rhythmic in mood and word. It was detachment from himself that he had achieved, from his own whims and caprices. It was repression from his own wayward enthusiasms for Whiggery that he had achieved under the spur of a greater cause. Ancient critics wrote that an orator was a *good* man skilled in speaking. Lincoln met those qualifications at Gettysburg. He was a *good* man in the sense that he was willing to give up something of himself in order to make room for others in his thought. Concession of that sort is the core of a true rhetoric.

On the occasion of his Second Inaugural, Lincoln was Father Abraham, the gentle sire who chided his children for engaging in a quarrel that netted them pain and death. Ethically, the address glitters alongside the harangue directed at Lewis Cass, let us say. Gladstone reflected that crushing responsibilities had made Lincoln tolerant. Like a passage from Greek tragedy sounded his peroration:

> With malice toward none; with charity for all; with firmness in the right, as God gives us to see the right, let us strive on to finish the work we are in; to bind up the nation's wounds; to care for him who shall have borne the battle, and for his widow, and his orphan—to do all which may achieve and cherish a just and lasting peace among ourselves, and with all nations.[1]

Now to sum up our study. We have sought to show how particular speech experiences taught Lincoln lessons contributory to his speech development. The Mexican War argument, for example, taught him the need of caution and repression in utterance. The speech of June 16, 1858, revealed his high sense of timeliness in getting his charges before the public. Antecedents of the Cooper Union argument revealed the evolutionary nature of his greatest political argument from a subjective to an objective strategy. The story behind the First Inaugural Address describes the refining process by which Lincoln's expression grew to aptness. The Gettysburg Address represents the voicing of a sentiment long in the hearts of his

---

[1] Nicolay and Hay, *Complete Works*, II, 657. For Biblical allusions see Matthew VII:1; Psalms: XIX, 9.

people. The Second Inaugural Address shows that he had learned to subordinate much of himself to make room for others in his heart.

A thought from Hesiod occurs to us as we seek to catch the deeper significance of our inquiry into Lincoln, the man of words. Hesiod tells us that he was given a leaf or two from Helicon, and forthwith he became a poet instead of a shepherd—and so he sang the praises of the gods. Lincoln's elevation in oratory is not so easily explained.

Rather, Lincoln is the purest product of American eloquence, a speaker cradled to his art in the bawling forum of court and lyceum, of parliament and stump—and so he sang the praises of the crowd that sired him. He was at times rough, biased, unlovely in his expression. But that development stems from the democratic process, for the crowd itself is sometimes ugly. Yet every decline in Lincoln's expression is balanced by an amazing passage of beauty; for deep in the hearts of the people are the beatitudes awaiting the word that will release them. And so throughout his speech progression runs a thread of ordered regularity.

Our study is virtually that of a plowman who learned to speak the minds of many men. First Lincoln learned to speak for himself and next, for a faction. Then he learned to speak for a Republic beset by disunion. Finally, he learned to speak for mankind, voicing as his own the lost causes of the generations. Provincial, partisan, nationalist, humanist, Lincoln became, in turn, the spokesman of many men. The trend of his development veered from the personal and partisan to the impersonal and universal. Growth of this sort comes only to men of vast capacity for improvement.

Our study implies how any man, aware of the privileges of the American way, will attain an aim in life, will become apt in rhetoric in seeking the fulfillment of that aim. If endowed generously by nature, he will become unusually apt in expression. Granted the advantages of a major issue and a throbbing sympathy for mankind, he will become the voice of the people. At least, it was so of Lincoln.

SELECTED BIBLIOGRAPHY[1]

Letters and Manuscripts

Angle, Paul M., ed.: *New Letters and Papers*, Boston, Houghton Mifflin Company, 1930.

Hertz, Emmanuel: *Abraham Lincoln: A New Portrait*, New York, Liveright Publishing Corporation, 1931, Vol. II.

Nicolay, John G., and John Hay, eds.: *Abraham Lincoln: Complete Works*, 2 vols., New York, The Century Company, 1894.

—— and ——: *Complete Works of Abraham Lincoln*, 12 vols ,New York, Tandy, 1905.

Tracy, A. Gilbert: *Uncollected Letters of Abraham Lincoln*, Boston, Houghton Mifflin Company, 1917.

[1] Prepared jointly by Mrs. Berry and Mr. Wiley.

Lincoln: His Emergence as the Voice of the People

Books

Arnold, Isaac N.: *Life of Abraham Lincoln*, Chicago, Jansen, McClurg and Co., 1884.

———: *Reminiscences of the Illinois Bar Forty Years Ago*, Chicago, Fergus Printing Co., 1881.

Barrett, Joseph H.: *Abraham Lincoln and His Presidency*, 2 vols., Cincinnati, Robert Clarke Co., 1904.

Barton, William E.: *Abraham Lincoln and His Books*, Chicago, Marshall Field and Co., 1920.

———: *The Life of Abraham Lincoln*, 2 vols., Indianapolis, The Bobbs-Merrill Company, 1925.

Beveridge, Albert J.: *Abraham Lincoln: 1809–1858*, 2 vols., Boston, Houghton Mifflin Company, 1928.

Brooks, Noah: *Abraham Lincoln*, New York, G. P. Putnam's Sons, 1894.

Browne, Francis F.: *The Every Day Life of Abraham Lincoln*, New York, N. D. Thompson Pub. Co., 1886.

Chapman, Ervin S.: *Latest Light on Abraham Lincoln*, New York, Fleming H. Revell Company, 1917.

Chittenden, L. E.: *Recollections of President Lincoln and His Administration*, New York, Harper & Brothers, 1904.

Curtis, William Eleroy: *The True Abraham Lincoln*, Philadelphia, J. B. Lippincott Company, 1904.

Gillespie, Joseph: *Recollections of Early Illinois and Her Noted Men*, Chicago, Fergus Printing Co., 1880.

Grimshaw, William: *History of the United States*, Philadelphia, Grigg and Elliott, 1833.

Herndon, William H., and Jesse W. Weik: *Herndon's Lincoln: The True Story of a Great Life* 3 vols., Chicago, New York, Belford, Clarke and Co., 1889.

Hertz, Emanuel: *The Hidden Lincoln*, New York, The Viking Press, 1938.

Holland, J. G.: *The Life of Abraham Lincoln*, Springfield, Mass., The Republican Press, Samuel Bowles and Co., 1866.

Houser, M. L.: *The Books that Lincoln Read*, Peoria, Edward Jacob Print Shop, 1929.

Kentucky Preceptor, 3d ed., Lexington, Maccoun, Tilford and Co., 1812.

Lamon, Ward H.: *Life of Abraham Lincoln*, Boston, James R. Osgood and Co., 1872. (Authorship now credited to Chauncey F. Black.)

McMurtrie, D. C., ed.: *Lincoln Group Papers*, Chicago, Black Cat Press, 1936.

Murray, Lindley: *The English Reader*, 10th ed., Haverhill, Mass., Burrill and Tileston, 1817.

Nicolay, Helen: *Personal Traits of Abraham Lincoln*, New York, The Century Company, 1913.

Nicolay, John G., and John Hay: *Abraham Lincoln: A History*, New York, The Century Company, 1890.

Oldroyd, O. H., ed.: *Lincoln Memorial Album*, Springfield, Lincoln Pub. Co., 1890.

Page, Elwin L.: *Abraham Lincoln in New Hampshire*, Boston, Houghton Mifflin Company, 1929.

Pratt, Harry E., ed.: *Illinois as Lincoln Knew It*, reprinted from *Papers in Illinois History and Transactions for* 1937, for members of the Abraham Lincoln Association, Springfield, Ill., 1938.

Ramsay, David: *The Life of George Washington*, New York, Hopkins and Seymour, 1807.

Sandburg, Carl: *The Prairie Years*, 2 vols., New York, Harcourt, Brace and Company, 1926.

———: *The War Years*, New York, 4 vols., Harcourt, Brace and Company, 1939.

Scott, William: *Lessons in Elocution*, Hartford, Lincoln and Gleason, 1806.

Scripps, J. L.: *Life of Abraham Lincoln*, Chicago, Chicago Press and Tribune Company, 1860.

Sparks, Edwin E.: *The Lincoln-Douglas Debates of* 1858, Illinois State Historical Library Collections, Springfield, 1908, Vol. III.

Speed, Joshua F.: *Reminiscences of Abraham Lincoln*, Louisville, John P. Marton and Co., 1864.

Tarbell, Ida M.: *The Life of Abraham Lincoln*, 2 vols., New York, Doubleday and McClure, 1900.
Watterson, Henry: *Abraham Lincoln*, Louisville, Courier Journal Printing Co., 1899.
Weems, M. L.: *The Life of George Washington*, Philadelphia, J. B. Lippincott Company, 1860.
White, Horace: *Abraham Lincoln in 1854*, Illinois State Historical Society, January, 1908.
———: *The Lincoln and Douglas Debates*, Chicago, University of Chicago Press, 1914.
Whitney, Henry C.: *Life on the Circuit with Lincoln*, Boston, Estes and Laurist, 1892.
Wilson, Rufus Rockwell: *What Lincoln Read*, Chicago, Pioneer Publishing Co., 1932.

Collections of Letters and Manuscripts

Oliver R. Barrett Collection of Letters, Chicago.
William E. Barton Collection of Letters and Manuscripts, Chicago, University of Chicago.
Albert H. Griffith Collection of Letters and Manuscripts, Fisk, Wis.
Jesse W. Weik Collection of Letters and Manuscripts, Greencastle, Ind.
Collection of Letters and rare Lincolniana: (1) by Illinois Historical Society; (2) by Indiana Historical Society; (3) by Chicago Historical Society; (4) by Wisconsin Historical Society.

Periodicals

Brooks, Noah: "Glimpses of Lincoln in War Time," *The Century Magazine*, O. S., 49 (N. S., 27) (1894–1895): 457–467.
———: "Lincoln's Reelection," *The Century Magazine*, 49 (1895): 865–872.
Field, Henry M.: "Mr. Lincoln at the Cooper Institute," *The Independent*, Apr. 4, 1895.
Fulwider, F. A.: "Sixty-fourth Anniversary of Lincoln Douglas Debate," privately printed, Aug. 26, 1922.
Hill, Fred: "The Battle of the Giants," *Abraham Lincoln*, Lincoln Farm Association, Feb. 12, 1907.
Littlefield, John H.: "Recollections of One Who Studied Law with Lincoln," *The Independent*, Apr. 4, 1895.
Medill, Joseph: "Lincoln's Lost Speech," *McClure's Magazine*, 7, No. 4, (1896): 319–331.
Nicolay, John J.: "Lincoln's Literary Experiments," *The Century Magazine*, 25 (1894): 824.
Remensnyder, J. B.: "With Lincoln at Gettysburg," *Hearst's Magazine* (February, 1914); also, *The Magazine of History*, 32, No. 1 (1926): 7–15.
Weik, Jesse W., "Lincoln as a Lawyer," *The Century Magazine*, 66 (June, 1904): 279–289.
———: "Lincoln and the Illinois Central," *The Illinois Central Magazine*, 15, No. 8 (February, 1927): 5–11.
———: "The President on the Stump," *The North American Review*, 102 (1866): 530–544.

Newspapers

Files of newspapers, 1820–1860, were consulted in the following places:

Illinois newspapers: Journals of Central and Southern Illinois, Illinois Historical Society, Springfield. Chicago journals, Newberry Library, Chicago, Chicago Historical Society, Chicago.
Kentucky, Ohio, and Indiana newspapers, Library of the University of Chicago.
Wisconsin newspapers: Wisconsin Historical Society, Madison.
Amboy Times, July 24, 1856.
Beardstown (Ill.) *Gazette*, Dec. 6, 1848.
Beloit Journal, Oct. 19, 1859.
Boston Daily Journal, Feb. 29, 1860.
The Charleston Mercury, 66: 11092; Mar. 5, 1861; Feb. 16, 1861; Mar. 7, 1861; Nov. 9, 1863.
Chattanooga Rebel, Nov. 2, 1863.

Lincoln: His Emergence as the Voice of the People

Chicago Daily Press and Tribune, Sept. 22, 1858; Aug. 23, 1858; Sept. 17, 1858; Oct. 9, 1858; Oct. 18, 1858.

Cincinnati Daily Commercial, 20: 170; Sept. 19, 1899; Nov. 21, 1863; Sept. 19, 1859.

Cincinnati Daily Enquirer, 24: 109, Mar. 6, 1861.

The Daily Chicago Times, Oct. 9, 1858; Oct. 12, 1858.

Daily Illinois State Journal, Sept. 14, 1859; Feb. 12, 1861.

The Daily National (Milwaukee), 1 (Oct. 1, 1859): 18.

The Dover (N. H.) *Gazette*, Mar. 3, 1860.

Evening Mail (Galesburg), Oct. 8, 1908.

Evening Post (New York), Mar. 4, 1861.

The Globe, Jan. 9, 1836.

Illinois State Register, Nov. 23, 1839; Oct. 6, 1854; June 22, 1858.

The Illinois Statesman, July 3, 1843.

Janesville Morning Gazette, 3 (Oct. 4, 1859): 179.

Louisville Public Advertiser, Feb. 10, 1830.

Milwaukee Daily Sentinel, Oct. 1, 1859.

National Intelligencer, Dec. 29, 1835; Dec. 10, 1835; Jan. 29, 1836; Mar. 5, 1861.

New York Daily Tribune, 19: 5880; Feb. 28, 1860; Mar. 5, 1861.

New York Independent, Sept. 1, 1864.

New York Spectator, May 28, 1860; Feb. 25, 1861; Mar. 7, 1861.

New York Times, 9: 2633; Feb. 28, 1860.

The Round Table (New York) 2 (July 9, 1864): 30, 2.

Sangamo Journal, Apr. 5, 1832; Jan. 11, 1832; Mar. 2, 1839.

James G. Blaine

by HENRY G. ROBERTS

Born in West Brownsville, Pa., January 31, 1830, James G. Blaine was graduated from Washington College (now Washington and Jefferson), 1847. He taught mathematics and ancient languages at Western Military Institute, Georgetown, Ky., 1848–1851; English and literature at the Pennsylvania Institute for the Blind, Philadelphia, 1851–1853; was editor of the *Kennebec Journal* (Augusta, Me.), 1854–1857, and editor in chief of the *Portland* (Me.) *Advertiser*, 1857–1860; delegate to the Republican national convention, 1856. Member of the House of Representatives of Maine, 1858–1862; Speaker of the House, 1861–1862; chairman of the Republican State Committee of Maine, 1859–1881. Member of the United States House of Representatives, 1863–1876; Speaker of the House, 1869–1875. Member of United States Senate, 1876–1881; Secretary of State, 1881. He was Republican nominee for President, 1884; defeated by Cleveland; Secretary of State, 1889–1892; president of the First International American Conference, 1889–1890; died January 27, 1893.

If James G. Blaine had not entered politics, he might never have made a public speech. At college, where he excelled in mathematics and did well enough in languages and literature to share the honors at his graduation, Blaine did not distinguish himself as a public speaker.[1] Although he impressed his classmates with his passion for political argument,[2] he never took part in a public exhibition[3] and rarely, if ever, joined in the debates of his debating society.[4] The reason for his hesitancy was his inability to face an audience without the most acute embarrassment because of a defect in his speech, an impediment that he later overcame by patient drilling but that persisted for years as a slight lisp.[5] But when

[1] However, Blaine did deliver the English salutatory at his graduation exercise. His subject was "The Duty of an Educated American."—Willis Fletcher Johnson, *Life of James G. Blaine* (Philadelphia, Atlantic Publishing Co., 1893), p. 44.

[2] Hugh Craig, *The Biography and Public Services of Hon. James G. Blaine* (New York, H. S. Goodspeed & Co., 1884), pp. 34–35.

[3] E. K. Cressey, *Pine to Potomac: Life of James G. Blaine* (Boston, James H. Earle, 1884), p. 63.

[4] Craig, *op. cit.*, p. 30; Edward Stanwood, "James Gillespie Blaine" (*American Statesmen*, 2d series, Boston, Houghton Mifflin Company, 1905), p. 17.

[5] Craig, *op. cit.*, pp. 29–30; Theron C. Crawford, *James G. Blaine: A Study of His Life and Career* (Philadelphia, Englewood Publishing Co., 1893), pp. 48, 66. Crawford, long-time Washington correspondent and intimate friend of Blaine, probably wrote with authority.

as editor of the politically potent *Kennebec Journal,* of Augusta, Me., he emerged from obscurity, and a career in politics opened before him, the ability to make a speech became a practical necessity. Returning from the Philadelphia convention of 1856 and being asked to give an account of the proceedings, the young editor "turned pale and red by turns, and almost tottering to the front, he stood trembling until the generous applause which welcomed him had died away, when, by a supreme effort, he broke the spell, at first by the utterance of some hesitating words of greeting and thanks, and then gathering confidence, he went on. . . . "[1] Blaine forced himself to make other speeches in that first campaign,[2] but he had difficulty in becoming accustomed to the sound of his own voice, and as late as 1858 his distrust of his ability to face an audience was so real that only the most persistent urging of his friends prevailed upon him to stand for the legislature.[3] In the State House, however, he found it easier to make a speech.[4] Facing a smaller audience—many were his intimate friends—Blaine finally put aside his trepidation, and by 1861, when he was elected Speaker, he was as ready a debater as any of his colleagues.[5]

That he had been forced to speak in public only from political necessity, that learning to speak had been a most unpleasant business, and that what he had learned had been learned in a practical school where votes rather than artistic consideration were important—all this had a marked effect upon Blaine as a public speaker. To him speechmaking was then and always remained a practical, never a fine art.

At thirty-two Blaine was elected to Congress and took his seat in the House of Representatives on December 7, 1863. For 6 years he served in the House, rapidly gaining prestige on the floor, in the committee rooms, and in the higher councils of his party. Elected Speaker of the House in

---

[1] Eye-witness account quoted by Cressey, *op. cit.,* pp. 124–125.

[2] One, probably typical, is a speech delivered in Litchfield, Me., June 28, 1856. See James G. Blaine, *Political Discussions: Legislative, Diplomatic, and Popular* (Norwich, Conn., Henry Bill Publishing Co., 1887), pp. 1–8.

[3] J. P. Boyd, *Life and Public Services of Hon. James G. Blaine, the Illustrious American Orator, Diplomat, and Statesman* (Philadelphia, Publishers' Union, 1893), p. 135.

[4] As a part of his editorial duties on the *Kennebec Journal,* Blaine had reported the debates of the Maine Senate and thus was perfectly familiar with legislative procedure. His custom was never to watch the speakers but to sit in his favorite chair before the fire in the Senate chamber, gazing into the flames and framing a running answer to every argument brought forward. Although he never made notes, he was able to return to the Journal office and write a full and accurate synopsis of the speeches.—Gail Hamilton (Mary Abigail Dodge), *Biography of James G. Blaine* (Norwich, Conn., Henry Bill Publishing Co., 1895), p. 107. Miss Dodge, for many years a member of the Blaine household, wrote the authorized biography of Blaine.

[5] Blaine's most notable speech in the Maine legislature was "Confiscation of Rebel Property," delivered Feb. 7, 1862. See Blaine, *op. cit.,* pp. 18–36.

1869, he ruled that tumultuous body with firmness and impartiality[1] and so consolidated his position as generalissimo of the Republican majority that in 1875, when the Democrats returned to power in the House, he seemed the man most likely to succeed Grant to the Presidency. Rebuffed at Cincinnati in 1876, he was immediately elevated from the House to the Senate and served there until 1881, when he joined Garfield's cabinet as Secretary of State. After those few months that ended with the assissination of the President, Blaine, at fifty-one, retired to private life. With the exception of his campaign for the Presidency in 1884 and his service as Harrison's Secretary of State, that is the story of Blaine the politician; and it is, in large measure, the story of Blaine the orator. In the comparatively brief period between 1863 and the eulogy of Garfield in 1882, Blaine acquired his reputation as one of the great speakers of his generation and made all the speeches that are remembered in this later time.

In the House, Blaine carved his niche as a debater rather than as an orator. Already a practiced professional politician, his experience as speaker of the house in Maine had taught him that the business of a legislative body was to get legislation enacted, and he was impatient with colleagues who slowed up the process with rambling, inconsequential speeches. While Blaine did make occasional set speeches, particularly when the interests of Maine were involved or new legislation was to be introduced, the real measure of his effectiveness on the floor lay in the searching questions and well-timed interruptions, the points of order, and the spirited rebuttal that cut through the maze of parliamentary meanderings and brought back the discussion to the point at issue.

In debate Blaine proved to be a formidable antagonist. To a keen mind and a wide background of knowledge was added a truly remarkable memory.[2] Always a hard worker, he made it his rule never to speak on a bill until he had mastered it thoroughly.[3] With that initial advantage it was difficult to trap him; yet time and again he was able to confound the opposition by calling up a neglected, though crucial, piece of information.

---

[1] As Speaker, Blaine almost never took part in the debate on the floor. On one of the rare occasions, he said, "Mr. Speaker, in old times it was the ordinary habit of the Speaker of the House of Representatives to take part in debate. The custom has fallen into disuse. For one, I am very glad that it has. . . . The Speaker should, with consistent fidelity to his own party, be the impartial administrator of the rules of the House, and a constant participation in the discussions of members would take from him that appearance of impartiality which it is so important to maintain in rulings of the Chair."—*Congressional Globe*, Forty-second Congress, first session, p. 125.

[2] When asked, "How can you remember so?" Blaine's only explanation was, "How can you help it?"—Hamilton, *op. cit.*, p. 107.

[3] Charles Edward Russell, *Blaine of Maine: His Life and Times* (New York, Cosmopolitan Book Corporation, 1931), p. 101.

His remarks were clear, closely reasoned, and to the point. Argumentative rather than persuasive in tone, they relied upon a wealth of facts and figures rather than upon emotionalism for their effectiveness. Their style was plain, almost severe; the virtual absence of so-called "flights of oratory" was characteristic. Blaine's manner on the floor matched his words. He spoke there exactly as he talked in the cloakroom—simply, directly, in a sort of animated conversation.[1] He spoke very rapidly,[2] and his voice, always somewhat metallic,[3] rang with earnestness. Unlike many of his colleagues, this young man from Maine was really intent on convincing someone of something, and once the issue was joined the House felt the full impact of his vibrant personality, his "magnetic manner," as Thaddeus Stevens put it.[4]

However, personal magnetism alone could not have carried the argument against such opponents as Stevens. Blaine had both the ability to reach down into a complicated situation plucking out the core, and the knack of fastening upon the weakest point of an adversary's argument. He could not be fussed; he could not be drawn off by a red herring; and, most important of all, he rarely lost his temper. Likewise, it was difficult to outmaneuver him; Blaine was the best parliamentarian in the House. Most disconcerting, perhaps, was his favorite strategy of unexpected attack. Rarely taking the defensive, he cultivated a reputation for impetuosity and daring. Actually, he coolly and carefully calculated his chances and then moved with such dramatic suddenness as to surprise and overwhelm his opponent. Not only did such tactics win victories upon the floor but in the public mind they added color to his personality and laid the foundation for the legend of the Plumed Knight.

During his first term in Congress Blaine spoke on a number of minor issues, but he attracted the most attention in a series of clashes with Stevens on financial questions. Much to Stevens's surprise the House eventually sided with Blaine in every instance. As he rose to prominence in the House, his preoccupation with routine matters increased; and, although he frequently took the floor, he spoke usually upon matters that had come

[1] Hamilton, *op. cit.*, p. 156.
[2] Blaine sometimes spoke as rapidly as 240 words per minute in the heat of debate. New York *Tribune*, Feb. 28, 1882, p. 1.
[3] Crawford, *op. cit.*, pp. 23, 179.
[4] In a futile attempt to bring back the Gold bill, which the House, following Blaine, had laid on the table, Stevens said, "My excellent friend from Maine, in an alarmed and excited manner, informed the House that the bill was fraught with innumerable mischiefs; . . . The House, partaking of the magnetic manner of my friend from Maine, . . . and wishing to escape the evils of this gunpowder plot, immediately laid it on the table."—*Congressional Globe*, Thirty-eighth Congress, second session, p. 117. It was the characterization most frequently applied to Blaine in later years.

before his two major committees, Military Affairs and Appropriations. Except for the debates on the Fourteenth Amendment and on his own amendment to the Reconstruction Act of March, 1867, Blaine took a comparatively small part in the debates on Reconstruction, but on the currency question he took a firm stand. In a strong speech on November 26, 1867, he was the first in the House to attack the repudiation theories of Pendleton and Butler.

Ten years later in the Senate, where he never became the leader he had been in the House,[1] he did not relent in his opposition to "soft money," denouncing the Bland bill on the floor and giving over the greater part of his speeches on his swing through the West in the campaign of 1878 to advocacy of "honest money." While his interest in domestic affairs—particularly in the plight of the remnant of Southern Republicans—did not diminish, Blaine became increasingly interested in foreign affairs, as his vigorous speeches in the Senate on South American trade, Chinese immigration, and the Halifax award testify. It is probable, however, that "during his senatorial years Blaine exerted more influence by his correspondence and his addresses in various parts of the country than he did by his speeches on the floor."[2]

From his earliest years in Congress until his health broke in 1891, Blaine was one of the foremost stump speakers of the Republican party. Always effective before popular audiences, in campaign years he was deluged with calls for assistance. Fortunately, he found campaigning no real labor. Blaine genuinely liked people, loved the excitement of a political rally, and considered speaking in the open air better exercise than gymnastics.[3] Facing an enthusiastic audience exhilarated him, and since the same thread of argument ran through all of his speeches, speaking four or five times a day seemed an excellent way to spend a vacation.[4] His speeches were much like his speeches in Congress—vigorous, full of information, aimed at the head rather than the heart. Blaine was no spellbinder like Conkling or Ingersoll, but he had a certain clearness of statement, directness of argument, and plain and understandable way of putting things that

[1] Serving only 4 years in the Senate, Blaine always was considered a comparative newcomer by veteran members. Accustomed to the running fire of debate in the House, he had difficulty in adjusting himself to the slower and more formal procedure of the Senate. In particular, his persistent habit of asking questions, correcting mistatements, and interjecting little speeches of his own into the speeches of his colleagues was resented. Finally, he was hostile to the Hayes administration, yet he could not bring himself to join the opposition group led by Conkling and Morton.

[2] David Saville Muzzey, *James G. Blaine: A Political Idol of Other Days* (New York, Dodd, Mead & Company, Inc., 1934), p. 130.

[3] Hamilton, *op. cit.*, p. 192.

[4] During his swing around the country in the campaign of 1884, Blaine spoke more than four hundred times in 6 weeks. A representative selection of these speeches is included in his *Political Discussions, Legislative, Diplomatic, and Popular.*

carried his audience with him. His forte was to make a short speech and to focus the whole of the speech upon a single issue.[1] Equally characteristic was his willingness to give a good-natured answer to sincere questions from the crowd.[2]

But more important than anything he said or did on the platform was the personality of the man himself. Blaine was the perfect campaigner who never forgot a name or a face and had the rare faculty of generating enthusiasm in everyone who came in contact with him. He was always a notable figure; when he entered a room his vitality, his air of good fellowship, and his natural dignity drew all eyes toward him. When he came to the front of the platform and stood there grasping the corners of his reading desk—tall, straight, with piercing eyes and rapidly whitening hair and beard framing a face so pallid as to be almost colorless—he seemed to be the personification of everything that was real and good and true in American political life.

Actually, however, Blaine's fame as an orator does not rest on his power as a debater or on his persuasiveness as a campaign speaker, although both give background and add substance to it. Rather, the tradition of his greatness springs from four highly dramatic speeches that made history in their own time and that quicken the imagination of this later generation.

The first was his spectacular tilt with Conkling in 1866. Both Blaine and Conkling were young men, both ambitious, and each recognized in the other a stumbling block in Republican councils; but their rivalry went deeper. The arrogant and insolent Conkling was the antithesis of the cool, cautious, and courteous Blaine, whose charm and good nature were winning him many friends in the House. Personal relations between the two had become strained, and, on the part of Conkling at least, antagonism had ripened into animosity

On the afternoon of April 24, 1866, Blaine was in the diplomatic gallery chatting with a constituent when Conkling rose to attack the provost general of the army, General James B. Fry. Conkling had not taken his seat before Blaine was on the floor in Fry's defense. Taking Conkling to task for traducing a distinguished officer who would have no opportunity to defend himself, Blaine vigorously refuted the charges against the provost general, attributing the whole incident to "the quarrels of the gentleman from New York with General Fry, in which quarrels it is generally understood the gentleman came out second best at the War Department."[3] Conkling, with characteristic arrogance, gave the lie to Blaine, and a bitter personal quarrel developed. It was renewed by Blaine on the following day, and on the thirtieth he asked to have read from the

[1] Interview with Chauncey M. Depew, quoted in *New York Tribune*, Jan. 28, 1893, p. 12.
[2] Cressey, *op. cit.*, pp. 232–234, 193.
[3] *Congressional Globe*, Thirty-ninth Congress, first session, p. 2152.

clerk's desk a letter from General Fry, a letter that substantiated Blaine's statements *in toto* and added an even more damaging charge—that Conkling, in violation of the law, had accepted a fee of $3,000 as judge advocate while he was also receiving pay as a member of Congress.[1] Badgered by the sharp-witted Blaine, Conkling steadily gave ground, and as the debate went against him he began to rely more and more upon that withering sarcasm that had beaten down so many other opponents. Finally, angered beyond endurance, he lashed out at Blaine: "If the member from Maine had the least idea how profoundly indifferent I am to his opinion upon the subject which he has been discussing, or upon any other subject personal to me, I think he would hardly take the trouble to rise here and express his opinion."[2] Blaine, cool and collected, moved in for the kill. Turning directly toward Conkling and taking a step in his direction, Blaine flung at him this unforgettable retort: "The contempt of that large-minded gentleman is so wilting; his haughty disdain, his grandiloquent swell, his majestic, supereminent, overpowering, turkey-gobbler strut has been so crushing to myself and all the members of this House that I know it was an act of the greatest temerity for me to venture upon a controversy with him." The House roared with laughter, but Blaine raised his hand for quiet. Referring to a chance statement in the *New York Independent* that the mantle of the late Henry Winter Davis had fallen upon Conkling, Blaine continued: "The gentleman took it seriously, and it has given his strut additional pomposity. The resemblance is great. It is striking. Hyperion to a satyr, Thersites to Hercules, mud to marble, dunghill to diamond, a singed cat to a Bengal tiger, a whining puppy to a roaring lion. Shade of the mighty Davis, forgive the almost profanation of that jocose satire!"[3]

Blaine had made a name for himself by thrashing the young bully of the House, but events proved that he had committed a prime political blunder. Conkling could neither forgive nor forget, and it was Conkling who blocked Blaine in the conventions of 1876 and 1880 and whose disaffection was a major factor in Blaine's defeat in 1884. "It rarely happens," Champ Clark wrote years later, "that a piece of sarcastic oratory, only thirty-one lines long, prevents two men from reaching the Presidency of the United States, and turns one political party out of the possession of the national government by putting another in."[4]

---

[1] See James B. Fry, *The Conkling and Blaine-Fry Controversy* in 1866 (New York, A. G. Sherwood & Co., 1893).

[2] *Congressional Globe*, Thirty-ninth Congress, first session, p. 2298.

[3] *Ibid.*, p. 2299.

[4] Champ Clark, *My Quarter Century of American Politics* (New York, Harper & Brothers, 1920), II, 312.

The next two great personal triumphs took place 10 years later in those few months in the spring of 1876 when Blaine was the spectacular leader of the minority in the House and the outstanding candidate for the Republican nomination for the Presidency.

Early in the session Samuel Randall, of Pennsylvania, a veteran Democrat, introduced a bill to restore full political rights to all former Confederate officials who were still under the ban imposed by the Fourteenth Amendment.[1] Blaine then gave notice that he would offer an amendment that would exclude Jefferson Davis from its privileges—a most embarrassing move, for there were many Northern Democrats willing to vote for general amnesty who would think twice before going on record as opposing an amendment specifically excluding the unreconstructed Confederate President. When, on January 10, 1876, Randall called up his bill he most unwisely refused to admit the amendment and to allow the measure to be debated. Outgeneraled by Blaine, the Democrats were unable to rally the two-thirds majority required by the Constitution, and the amnesty bill was defeated. Blaine immediately moved to reconsider the vote and, having snatched control of the measure from Randall's hands, took the floor to make what "was perhaps the most effective appeal to partisan solidarity in the name of righteous indignation that has ever been made in Congress."[2]

Reviewing the "imperishable record of liberality . . . magnanimity, and mercy" of Republican Congresses in granting amnesty to all but about seven hundred fifty of the conquered leaders and maintaining his willingness to extend it to all save one of them, Blaine continued: "It is not . . . because he was personally or especially of consequence, that I except him. But I except him on this ground: that he was the author, knowingly, deliberately, guiltily, and willfully, of the gigantic murders and crimes at Andersonville." Since this bill had been introduced, Blaine had reread some of the historic cruelties of the world. "And I here, before God, measuring my words, knowing their full extent and import, declare that neither the deeds of the Duke of Alva in the Low Countries, nor the massacre of Saint Bartholomew, nor the thumbscrews and engines of torture of the Spanish Inquisition begin to compare in atrocity with the hideous crime of Andersonville." Citing the inflammatory report of the Congressional investigating committee of 1867, quoting the eye-witness

---

[1] It must have been presumed that the bill would pass with little opposition, for an identical bill had passed the Republican House in 1873 by a vote of 141 to 29, without the formality of a roll call, but "it was one thing for Republicans to extend amnesty to the South by an act of grace; it was quite a different thing for Democrats to remove disabilities as a simple matter of justice."—Muzzey, *op. cit.*, pp. 76–77.

[2] *Ibid.*, pp. 77–78.

account of a Catholic priest of Georgia called to the prison to administer the last rites of his church to naked and vermin-ridden men,
reading an infamous telegram from the military commander of the district, he piled high the indictment against the one man "who by a wink
of his eye, by a wave of his hand, by a nod of his head, could have stopped
the atrocity at Andersonville." "Some of us," he concluded dramatically,
"had kinsmen there, most of us had friends there, all of us had countrymen
there, and in the name of those kinsmen, friends, and countrymen, I here
protest, and shall with my vote protest, against their calling back and
crowning with the hours of full American citizenship the man who organized
that murder."[1]

Such unexpected demagoguery came as a stunning blow to the Southerners in Congress; the more so since Blaine had made many friends in the
South by his generally conciliatory attitude. Many scented a trap, but
Benjamin H. Hill, of Georgia, played into Blaine's hands with a bitter
speech in defense of the South. Hill had blundered indeed. Throughout
the North, Southern Democrats were promptly branded "unrepentant
rebels," and the standard of the Bloody Shirt was raised anew.

From a political point of view, Blaine's had been an exceedingly clever
maneuver. By a brilliant flanking attack, he had both· disconcerted the
Democratic majority and diverted attention from the scandalous record
of the Grant administration by giving his party a really popular issue for
the campaign of 1876. Some of Blaine's friends doubted the wisdom of his
course in stirring up old hatreds,[2] and Carl Schurz predicted that it would
cost Blaine the Presidency;[3] but William Lloyd Garrison and Wendell
Phillips joined multitudes of others in writing letters of effusive praise.[4]
However, the greatest response came from the rank and file of the Republican party. Men who previously had merely admired Blaine now claimed
him as their hero, and state after state began to instruct its delegates to
vote for Blaine in the Cincinnati convention.

Blaine had not been seriously involved in the Crédit Mobilier scandals,
but now that he had captured the attention of the nation ugly rumors
began to circulate that he had been involved in a shady transaction with
the directors of the Union Pacific Railroad. On April 24, he read to the
House a carefully prepared and documented denial of the charges that

[1] *Congressional Record*, Forty-fourth Congress, first session, pp. 323–326.

[2] Whitelaw Reid, editor of the *New York Tribune* and later Blaine's foremost editorial
backer, felt that the speech had greatly damaged Blaine in Pennsylvania and New England.—
Royal Cortissoz, *The Life of Whitelaw Reid* (London, T. Thornton Butterworth, Ltd., 1921),
I, 333–334.

[3] Carl Schurz, *The Reminiscences of Carl Schurz* (New York, The McClure Co., 1908), III,
365.

[4] Hamilton, *op. cit.*, pp. 426, 381.

seemed to vindicate him completely and that raised even higher the popular clamor for his nomination. Nevertheless, an investigating committee was appointed, and under the guise of a railroad investigation, it began to ransack Blaine's private and public career in the hope that something damaging might be uncovered. The committee turned up little of interest until May 31, 1876, when one James Mulligan, a bookkeeper, appeared to testify. He claimed to have with him certain incriminating letters written by Blaine to Mulligan's former employer, Warren Fisher, a Boston broker, but before the letters could be read the committee recessed. That evening Blaine visited Mulligan at his hotel, got possession of the letters, and carried them away with him. When the committee met the following morning, Blaine refused to hand them over, maintaining that they were private letters that had nothing to do with the investigation. Although his position was sustained by two eminent lawyers, one of them the Democrat Jeremiah S. Black, Blaine's situation was far from comfortable. Not only had he violated the prerogatives of the House but reasonable men throughout the country were asking why, if there was nothing incriminating in the letters, Blaine should refuse to make them public.

Word leaked out that he would break his silence, and on June 5, just 9 days before the Cincinnati convention, the floor and the galleries were packed as Blaine rose to make a personal explanation. Instinctively dramatic, he opened by reading the resolution authorizing the investigation. Becoming more heated, he alleged that he had been the victim of persecution at the hands of a partisan committee intent on investigating not the Pacific railroads but James G. Blaine. As to his refusal to surrender the letters, he had been perfectly within his rights. Then, with every eye fixed upon him, he went on:

But, sir, having vindicated that right, standing by it, ready to make any sacrifice in the defense of it, . . . I am ready for any extremity of contest or conflict in behalf of so sacred a right. And while I am so, I am not afraid to show the letters. Thank God Almighty, I am not ashamed to show them. There they are, [holding up a package of letters.] There is the very original package. And with some sense of humiliation, with a mortification that I do not pretend to conceal, with a sense of outrage which I think any man in my position would feel, I invite the confidence of 44,000,000 of my countrymen while I read those letters from this desk.[1]

As soon as order could be restored, Blaine proceeded to read the letters—not, however, in their regular order—and their contents seemed innocuous enough.

But Blaine had not finished; his strategy was always one of attack and surprise. There had been one witness, Josiah Caldwell, who had not been

---

[1] *Congressional Record*, Forty-fourth Congress, first session, p. 3604.

available for questioning, and Blaine had asked that a cablegram be sent to him. Now, advancing down the aisle toward Proctor Knott, he asked if the dispatch had been sent. Knott tried to parry the question by saying that he had not been able to get Caldwell's address. The verbatim report of this exchange is illuminating:

Mr. Blaine. Has the gentleman from Kentucky received a dispatch from Caldwell?
Mr. Knott. I will explain that directly.
Mr. Blaine. I want a categorical answer.
Mr. Knott. I received a dispatch purporting to be from Mr. Caldwell.
Mr. Blaine. You did?
Mr. Knott. How did you know I got it?
Mr. Blaine. When did you get it? I want the gentleman from Kentucky to answer when he got it.
Mr. Knott. Answer my question first.
Mr. Blaine. I never heard of it until yesterday.
Mr. Knott. How did you hear of it?
Mr. Blaine. I heard you got a dispatch last Thursday morning at eight o'clock from Josiah Caldwell completely and absolutely exonerating me from this charge, and you have suppressed it. [Protracted applause upon the floor and in the galleries.] I want the gentleman to answer. [After a pause.] Does the gentleman from Kentucky decline to answer?[1]

The legions of Blaine supporters were ecstatic in their jubilation, and—for the moment, at least—the great preponderance of sentiment was that Blaine had freed himself from any stigma of corruption. Even the hostile and skeptical *New York Times* paid him a backhanded compliment by saying that never before in American politics had there been a man "capable under similar circumstances of conceiving and executing so brilliant and dashing a *coup*."[2] As the dramatic impact of the speech wore away, Blaine's evasions, inconsistencies, and subterfuges became more evident, and in 1884 the "Mulligan Letters" would not be downed. It would have been better strategy to make a clean breast of the matter, admitting that although he had done nothing illegal or dishonest he had erred in having any connection whatever with railroad speculation.

The last of Blaine's great speeches was, of course, the eulogy of Garfield. Blaine had made Garfield President by breaking the deadlock in the convention of 1880, had dominated his administration as Secretary of State, and had been at his side when the President was shot down. Needless to say, Garfield's death had come as a terrific blow to Blaine. Not only had an intimate friend been murdered but Blaine's own plans for the future had been ruthlessly shattered.

[1] *Ibid.*, p. 3608.
[2] *New York Times*, June 6, 1876, p. 1.

At first, Blaine hesitated to accept the invitation of Congress to deliver the memorial address,[1] but having accepted, he entered upon the task wholeheartedly and lavished more care upon it than he had ever given to a state paper or public address.[2] It was first written in a careless draft[3] and then written and rewritten, read and reread. Every superfluous word was struck[4] and every statement weighed for its effect.[5] After 6 weeks of exhausting labor, the manuscript was ready to be copied on black-bordered paper, in a hand so large that it would not be necessary for the orator to use his spectacles.[6] On February 27, 1882, it was delivered with great effect before a distinguished audience in the hall of the House of Representatives. Blaine was invited to deliver the oration in New York at the Academy of Music, "but it had been written for one occasion and was never repeated."[7]

The address itself is well known, but the complexities of Blaine's position are not always fully realized. He had to satisfy the demands of two audiences: the hypercritical audience in the House which was well aware of Garfield's weaknesses, and the larger audience, throughout the country, which by that time had idealized the dead President as a hero and a martyr. Furthermore, he faced an audience divided into bitter and warring factions—one with wounds still raw from the buffeting it had received at the hands of Blaine and Garfield. Finally, there was Blaine himself. He, as much as Garfield, had been responsible for the policies of the administration; and although these policies had been reversed by Arthur, Blaine was still the leader of one strong wing of the Republican party and was its potential candidate for the Presidency in 1884. His situation was precarious, yet he told the story of Garfield's life without shrinking from any issue, but with such good taste and simple dignity that neither Halfbreed nor Stalwart nor Democrat could take offense. That, far more than any felicity of style or depth of sentiment,[8] entitles the

---

[1] Harriet Stanwood Blaine, *Letters of Mrs. James G. Blaine* (New York, Duffield and Co., 1908), I, 271–272.

[2] Thomas H. Sherman, *Twenty Years with James G. Blaine* (New York, The Grafton Press, 1928), p. 89.

[3] H. S. Blaine, *op. cit.*, I, 313.

[4] Some three thousand words were cut from the original manuscript.—Crawford, *op. cit.*, p. 552.

[5] H. S. Blaine, *op. cit.*, I, 307–308.

[6] *Ibid.*, I, 310.

[7] Hamilton, *op. cit.*, p. 523.

[8] The most frequently quoted passage is the conclusion: "As the end drew near, his early craving for the sea returned. The stately mansion of power had been to him the wearisome hospital of pain, and he begged to be taken from its prison walls, from its oppressive, stifling air, from its homelessness and hopelessness. Gently, silently, the love of a great people bore the pale sufferer to the longed-for healing of the sea, to live or to die, as God should will,

eulogy to its reputation as one of the masterpieces of American oratory. As Mrs. Henry Adams, Blaine's irreconcilable critic, wrote to her father, "Blaine won laurels for his oration and even his opponents must admit that it was a difficult thing very skillfully done."[1]

It would be idle to insist that James G. Blaine be ranked as one of America's very greatest orators. Rather, he should be remembered for what he was—a great political leader who made brilliant use of public speaking as a tool for the attainment of ends he believed to be desirable.

BIBLIOGRAPHICAL NOTE

Blaine was careless of his correspondence, was accustomed to write in his own hand, and rarely made copies of his letters. As a result, there is little manuscript material available. The Blaine Papers in the Library of Congress contain something less than a thousand items.

Among the numerous popular biographies that appeared during the campaign of 1884 and after Blaine's death in 1893, T. C. Crawford's *James G. Blaine: A Study of his Life and Career* (Philadelphia, 1893) is the most useful. The *Letters of Mrs. James G. Blaine* (New York, 1908) and Gail Hamilton's *Biography of James G. Blaine* (Norwich, Conn., 1895) give the best intimate pictures of Blaine, while Edward Stanwood's *James Gillespie Blaine* (Boston, 1905) is a short, judicious biography whose usefulness is limited, since it is without notes on critical apparatus. The two most recent biographies are Charles Edward Russell's *Blaine of Maine: His Life and Times* (New York, 1931) and David S. Muzzey's *James G. Blaine: A Political Idol of Other Days* (New York, 1934). Russell's account is stimulating but biased. Muzzey's biography, although it is marred by innumerable minor errors, is definitely the most satisfactory treatment of Blaine's life and career now available.

The best sources of Blaine's speech texts are the files of the *Congressional Globe* and *Congressional Record* and Blaine's own collection of his speeches, *Political Discussions, Legislative, Diplomatic, and Popular* (Norwich, Conn., 1887).

---

within sight of its heaving billows, within sound of its manifold voices. With wan, fevered face tenderly lifted to the cooling breeze, he looked out wistfully upon the ocean's changing wonders; on its far sails, whitening in the morning light; on its restless waves, rolling shoreward to break and die beneath the noonday sun; on the red clouds of evening, arching low to the horizon; on the serene and shining pathway of the stars. Let us think that his dying eyes read a mystic meaning which only the rapt and parting soul may know. Let us believe that in the silence of the receding world he heard the great waves breaking on the farther shore, and felt already upon his wasted brow the breath of the eternal morning."—Blaine, *op. cit.*, p. 525.

[1] Marion Hooper Adams, *The Letters of Mrs. Henry Adams*, 1865–1883 (Boston, Little, Brown & Company, 1936), p. 359.

31

William Jennings Bryan

by MYRON G. PHILLIPS

William Jennings Bryan was born in Salem, Ill., March 19, 1860; A.B. (highest honors and valedictorian) Illinois College, 1881; LL.B. Union College of Law, Chicago, 1883. Admitted to Illinois bar, 1883; practiced Jacksonville, Ill., 1883–1887; then at Lincoln, Nebr. He was a member of the Fifty-second and Fifty-third Congresses (1891–1895), first Nebraska district; defeated for United States Senator, 1894; editor, *Omaha World Herald*, 1894–1896. He wrote silver plank in Democratic party platform in 1896 and was nominated by the Democrats for the Presidency but was defeated by McKinley. He lectured on bimetallism, 1897–1898; raised Third Regiment Nebraska Volunteer Infantry for Spanish-American War, May, 1898; became its colonel; was again nominated for President, 1900, this time by the Democrats, Populists, and Silver Republicans, but was again defeated by McKinley. Established a political magazine, *The Commoner*, at Lincoln. Made tour of world, 1906, and contributed to newspapers; was nominated a third time for the Presidency at Denver, 1908, and was defeated by Taft. Served as Secretary of State in Woodrow Wilson's cabinet, March 4, 1913, to June 9, 1915; died, July 26, 1925, Dayton, Tenn. at the close of the Scopes trial, in which he was engaged as counsel for the prosecution.

Public Issues

On a winter morning in 1888, William Jennings Bryan, then twenty-seven years of age, stepped from a train in Lincoln, Nebr., following an all-night ride in a day coach from a small town in a western part of the state. He walked home, climbed the stairs, and quietly entered the bedroom where his wife was asleep. He wakened her, sat on the edge of the bed, and said: "Mary, I have had a strange experience. Last night I found that I had power over the audience. I could move them as I chose. I have more than usual power as a speaker. I know it. God grant I may use it wisely." He then fell on his knees and prayed.

For the next 37 years Bryan was to have an influential voice in every public issue before the American people. A fair evaluation of his influence can be made only after consideration of the political and economic background of the time.

Bryan had been born in 1860. The tremendous influence of the great triumvirate—Webster, Clay, and Calhoun—was still fresh. Phillips and Beecher were rousing the North against slavery. Toombs and Yancey were firing the South to defense. The debates of Lincoln and Douglas were still echoing. Seward and Sumner were in their prime, and Ingersoll was fast approaching his. As Bryan reached manhood slavery was no longer an issue, the question of State Rights had faded from popularity, but with their passing new issues occupied the public mind, to which Bryan gave his voice.

In 1887 he moved from Illinois to Nebraska, and in 1890 he was elected as a Democrat to Congress from a normally Republican district. Disowned by the old guard of his state, he toured the Middle West in 1896, aroused the masses to white heat over silver, and captured the Democratic nomination for the Presidency. To understand this surprising rise to leadership, we must look behind the man to the social and economic background of the era.

By 1887 the United States was assimilating the recently won West. No longer were there ox wagons and prairie schooners to dot the horizon of the unchanging plains. The middle half of the nineteenth century had witnessed a parade to the West and in its wake a trail of scattered graves. But sun and wind and rain had obliterated these, for the march into the West had stopped.

This situation is understandable when it is recalled that the Industrial Revolution, accelerated in 1865, had reached a peak, and that the free land of the West, made available to settlers by the government, had given out. The nation was reacting to the truth of Macaulay's statement: "When free land gives out America will be put to the test."

And so at the three-quarter post of the century there had arisen a wave of discontent, best exemplified with the rise of a political party known as the Populists.

This party had its origin in the coalition of three important organizations: the Grangers, the Greenbackers, and the Farmers' Alliance. Each of these had its own issues, some overlapping in intent, but when they united in 1891 they had gained control of the legislatures of Kansas and Nebraska and held the balance of power in Illinois, Minnesota, and South Dakota. Briefly, the party demanded the free coinage of silver; the abolition of national banks; an issue of gold and silver currency sufficient to permit the business of the country to be worked on a cash basis; loan of money to the people at 2 per cent on the guarantee of agricultural crops; government ownership of canals, railroads, telephones, telegraph; direct election of Senators; adoption of initiative and referendum; and the prohibition of alien ownership of land. Two of these became outstanding: free and unlimited coinage of silver at sixteen to one and the establishment of a graduated Federal income tax.

During the eighties, the farmer found himself in a position adequately summed up by the phrase "ten-cent corn and ten per cent interest." He found himself spending more money to produce staple goods than he could get from its sale. The market prices of the day showed 4-cent eggs, 5-cent butter, 10-cent corn and 50-cent wheat. The market would not buy his hogs, and interest on borrowed money was prohibitive. The farmer, pushed to desperation, turned to politics for relief. Thus began the great agrarian revolt that was to last for a quarter of a century.

This agrarian revolt was in opposition to Eastern capitalism and was an attempt to nullify the law of concentration. The ideal of plutocracy, now dominant, was naturally repugnant to people who were drenched in Jeffersonian and Jacksonian democracy. Poverty was augmented as wealth increased—"the rich got richer and the poor grew poorer."

Vernon L. Parrington, literary historian, tells that Mary E. Lease, of Kansas, "struck from the common bitterness a phrase that embodied the militant spirit of Populism. Week after week she travelled the prairie country urging the farmers to 'raise less corn and more hell,' and at her call the sunburned faces settled into grim purpose." Parrington continues:

> The farmers had become class conscious. . . . They used the vocabulary of realism, and the unctuous political platitudes and sophistries of county-seat politicians rolled off their minds like water from a duck's back. They were fighting a great battle—they believed—against Wall Street and the Eastern money-power; they were bent on saving America from the plutocracy; and they swept over the county-seat towns, burying the old machine politicians under an avalanche of votes, capturing state legislatures, electing Congressmen and Senators, and looking forward to greater power . . . . It was the last mortal struggle between agrarianism and capitalism, and to understand it one must turn back to the long agitation over the money question.[1]

Briefly the money dispute was this: since 1878 there had been an authorized limited coinage of silver: first under the Bland-Allison Act and second, under the Sherman Silver Act of 1890. These had limited and defined the coinage of silver. The agrarians demanded that these restrictions be lifted, and President Cleveland opposed it. When the panic of 1893 developed, Cleveland secured the repeal of the Sherman Law and so forced the acceptance of gold as the sole standard of value. This act, prompted by a Democratic administration, aroused indignant protests but no more than those aroused when the Supreme Court declared unconstitutional the Federal Income Tax Law, which had provided for a Federal income tax.

By 1896 this clouded and willfully submerged issue was brought out into the open. As Oberholtzer said: "We at last had reached the climax of the long conflict with silver which for weary years had infested our politics and blocked so many movements in Congress for the public welfare."[2]

[1] Vernon L. Parrington, *The Beginnings of Critical Realism in America, 1860–1920* (New York, Harcourt, Brace and Co., 1930), III, p. 266.

[2] Ellis Paxson Oberholtzer, *A History of the United States Since the Civil War* (New York, The Macmillan Company, 1937), V (1888–1901), p. 421.

During the period 1896–1900 another issue was precipitated. The free land of the West that the government had offered to those who would settle it had given out. The country was experiencing growing pains, and there developed a movement that led to territorial expansion overseas. The war with Spain brought the issue to the fore, and it was the banner of anti-imperialism that Bryan waved aloft during his Presidential campaign of 1900.

Bryan's Background

Silas Bryan, William's father, was a lawyer and judge in Salem, Ill., who knew and respected the power of the spoken word. William's mother, Mariah Bryan, was in accord. So early in Bryan's career he developed a respect for good speaking. His own recollections, reported by his wife, are that "The first recorded efforts of declamation show that at the age of seven or eight he committed to memory his geography lesson, and then was placed on a little table where he declaimed the same."[1] Bryan himself speaks of how the "child of a public speaker has the influence of his father's example . . . the devotion and diligence of a mother who, like my mother, encouraged the tendency, . . . "[2]

The training started at home continued when he entered high school. "In the high school I . . . went a step forward in the art of declamation in the literary society work. We had a debating club in the high school and I recall taking a part in what we called The Senate, . . . "[3]

After his graduation from high school Bryan entered Whipple Academy and, later, Illinois College, at Jacksonville. Here he gave himself to an intensive effort at improving his speaking. If he was not particularly successful in all of it, he was at least persistent, for he set his hand to take advantage of every opportunity for improvement. He took an active part in the meetings of the literary society at Illinois College by engaging in debate and discussion, even though his first appearance in the group "called forth more applause from my trembling knees than from the audience."[4] The records of Sigma Pi, the literary and debating society at Illinois College, bear testimony to the active part that Bryan took in it.

He was made a member of Sigma Pi while still a student in Whipple Academy. Membership in the society was limited to approximately twenty-five men. In spite of that, Bryan's name was placed before the group, and

---

[1] William Jennings Bryan and his wife, Mary Baird Bryan, *Memoirs of William Jennings Bryan* (Philadelphia, John C. Winston Company, 1925), p. 241.

[2] *Ibid.*, p. 41.

[3] *Ibid.*, p. 42.

[4] *Ibid.*, p. 59.

he was accepted either because of excellent recommendations of some member or because of literary ability demonstrated while a student at Whipple.

An examination of the minutes of the organization for the period of Bryan's membership (1876–1881) shows that he was one of its most devoted and active members. The roll book shows him to have been absent but six times and only once without excuse. The society met more or less regularly every 2 weeks, and about every other meeting Bryan was on the program. It is significant to note that his participation was always in the form of platform speech, and in no instance is it recorded that he engaged in "Selected Reading." As he grew older and more experienced he was given a place on the program for open meetings, a distinct honor, since only the better performers were chosen for those nights.

Debate was one of his major activities, and the minutes show that he was a "responsible" in twelve debates before the society during his career there. Not always is it indicated, but whenever it is, Bryan was on the negative side. This man, who in later years refused to drink a toast in champagne, who campaigned so vigorously for national prohibition, once took the negative on the proposition: Resolved: That the traffic in alcoholic beverages be prohibited by law![1]

Of the twelve debates participated in, the judgment of the critic for the evening and the audience were divided six and six. Not in every instance was there agreement.

The recording secretaries of the society did not always comment on the performance of the members, but scattered through the records are to be found such comments as: "The essay was well received eliciting but little criticism."[2] " . . . compared favorably with any that the society had listened to at any of its previous meetings."[3] "Then came Bryan who spoke well as he always does."[3b] "Bryan in the course of the debate brought down the house. . . ."[4] "Bryan's pathetic address moved all to tears."[5] " . . . rendered in the usual striking and entertaining manner and style."[6] " . . . one of the most fiery and at the same time logical debates of the year."[7]

---

[1] Sigma Pi Minutes, Feb. 21, 1879, Archives of Sigma Pi, Illinois College, Jacksonville, Ill. This society is not to be confused with the social fraternity of the same name that was founded several years later.

[2] *Ibid.*, Jan. 21, 1876.

[3] *Ibid.*, Oct. 20, 1876.

[3b] *Ibid.*, Oct. 27, 1876.

[4] *Ibid.*, Feb. 16, 1877.

[5] *Ibid.*, Sept. 21, 1877.

[6] *Ibid.*, Oct. 25, 1878.

[7] *Ibid.*, May 16, 1879.

Other evidence of Bryan's worth and achievements as a member of Sigma Pi can be found outside the cold records of the meetings. The college newspaper, the *College Rambler*, for April, 1880, when commenting on Bryan's performance in one of the society's open meetings, tells of one of his orations, entitled "Master Motives." The writer called it "the crowning exercise of the evening . . . The delivery and general arrangement of his thoughts were good and deserving of much praise."

Added to the training in the society was the usual academic training available from tutors and regular faculty instructors.

. . . I received the usual training in public speaking. Professor Hamilton was our instructor. . . . He rather leaned to the dramatic and recommended dramatic pieces to us. I rather preferred the oratorical style. He complimented me by saying that I declaimed the oratorical pieces so well that he could not be of much assistance to me along that line. He trained us in modulation of the voice, gesticulation, etc., and I presume that his instructions were beneficial to me, although I have been so much more interested in the subject matter than in the form of presentation that my use of his advice has been unconscious rather than intentional.

. . . I do not know to what extent I am indebted to him for the settled opinions which I have formed on public speaking . . . . But the training that one receives, both in . . . voice and in action, finally becomes a part of him—a second nature, so to speak—and he obeys the suggestions he has received without a thought.[1]

Local and intercollegiate oratorical contests likewise lured young Bryan. As early as prep-school days, in Whipple Academy, he engaged in forensic competition. A review of the commencement exercises as set down in the college annual for 1877 lists Bryan as one of the competitors in the "annual contest for the Whipple Prizes which are offered for excellence of Declamation."

The *College Rambler*, the minutes of Sigma Pi, newspapers of the period, and his *Memoirs* all attest to Bryan's participation in contests of various sorts. The *College Rambler* for June, 1878, lists Bryan as the winner of second place in freshman declamation. The same issue states that he tied for second in Latin prose composition.

In his junior year he won the oratorical contest that entitled him to represent his college in the Illinois state contest held in October, 1880, at Galesburg. Bryan, using as his subject "Justice," received second place. Not all agreed with the final result. The *College Rambler* for November, 1880, quotes a writer in *The Illini:* "In the writer's opinion the orator who was given the second should have had the first. That this was also

[1] See *Memoirs*, p. 87. The "Professor Hamilton" mentioned here undoubtedly was Professor Hamill, for the catalogues from Illinois College for that period do not list Hamilton but do list Hamill. This Professor Hamill and his work are referred to in an article by T. C. Trueblood in the *Quarterly Journal of Speech*, February, 1926, pp. 1–11.

the opinion of a majority of the judges is shown by the fact that two of them marked him highest. But the other judge, for some unimaginable reason, marked him fifth, and so dropped him to the second place."

The failure to win first honor did not deter him from entering another contest in his senior year, even though this one was a thesis contest and not an oratorical contest. " . . . there I came second," he again recorded.[1]

He strove to improve his speech in other ways. For example, he learned the wisdom of making a conscious effort to get attention in an introduction, and he tells how he had observed that Wendell Phillips, when he spoke in Jacksonville, had done so in his famous lecture "The Lost Arts." Bryan made the observation that Russell H. Conwell employed the same art.

Opinions differ as to the books that Bryan read during the years of his formal education. The accurate facts cannot be completely known, but an examination of the records and conversation with individuals who are familiar with the reading facilities of Illinois College in Bryan's time can give at least a partial picture.

When Bryan was a student there the college library was more of a museum than a place of study. A "No Trespassing" sign was on the lawn in front of the library, and the building itself was open but one hour during the day. A thirst for knowledge and a desire to read on the part of the ambitious student had, perforce, to be satisfied in other ways. For members of the debating societies the problem was somewhat simplified, since in their meeting rooms were shelves, which still stand, 30 feet long and higher than a man can reach, all filled with books. It was a circulating library for the use of society members. The minutes book carries records, however incomplete, of books withdrawn by the members. The page of records kept by W. W. Ross and headed "W. J. Bryan" indicate that he withdrew twenty-five books, and the titles and dates were as follows:[2]

Nov. 5	Quadroon
Mar. 8	Lowell's Poems, vol. 2
Mar. 17	Samuel Black in England
Dec. 8	Cooper Sea Tales
Mar. 30	Hist. Greece, Grote, 8 vol.
Oct. 5/77	Vol. I History U.S.—Bauer
Oct. 12/77	Vol. II " " "
Jan. 4	Vol. 2 History U.S.
Apr. 26	British Poets (Shelley, vol. 3)

[1] *Ibid.*, pp. 92–93.

[2] Sigma Pi Records. The preceding list is set down just as it was found, with dates copied as entered in the records. Note that but one year date is indicated—1877. It is fair to assume that all listings above that are for the academic year 1876–1877 and that all below Apr. 26 are for the academic years 1879–1881. However, there is no proof that the extant records are complete. Neither do the records indicate what books were used in the rooms of the society.

Sept. 19	Students Manual—Todd
Mar. 5	Gilded Age, Mark Twain (Rogers)
Oct. 22	French Revolution, Lamartine
Mar. 4	Mary Queen of Scots
Mar. 4	Queen Elizabeth
Mar. 21	History of Greece, Grote, vol. XI
Apr. 16	Mary Queen of Scots
Apr. 29	Queen Elizabeth
Mar. 28	Nicholas Nickleby

Nor do the bare records tell the whole story. During Bryan's 6 years in Jacksonville he made his home with Dr. Hiram K. Jones, a physician of prominence, head of the literary circle of the city and for some years a lecturer at Concord (Mass.) School of Philosophy. Mr. and Mrs. Jones had no children and so made a home for Bryan and other students of the college, who were given access to one of the largest private libraries in the city.[1] Bryan himself found it difficult to calculate the influence that association with Dr. and Mrs. Jones had upon his ideas and ideals.[2] One can hardly imagine that Bryan, living in such an environment, with a man whose interests ran the gamut of medicine, philosophy, literature, and kindred subjects, did not avail himself of the opportunity to read and study in the quietude of his own quarters and thus compensate for inadequate library facilities that the college afforded. Indeed, the positive evidence disproves the statement that "during his attendance of six years, Bryan drew eighteen [books],—largely works of fiction";[3] and bare records plus reasonable inference discredit Paxton Hibben's opinion that "young Bryan did little of what he called 'indulging in reading.'"[4] It is true however, that in spite of Bryan's interest in oratory, he had not been a genuine student of orators of an earlier day.[5]

Of course, it must be remembered that young Bryan was called upon to read certain works that were required by curricular study. When it is remembered that he was graduated as valedictorian of his class and when Illinois College records show that he had an average of 87 to 92, one cannot doubt that he was a reasonably careful student of required work. The college catalogue of the period indicates what courses were offered and

[1] Mrs. C. H. Rammelkamp, wife of a former president of Illinois College, to the author.

[2] *Memoirs*, p. 53.

[3] George R. Poage, "College Career of William Jennings Bryan," *Mississippi Valley Historical Review*, 15 (September, 1928): 170.

[4] Paxton Hibben, *The Peerless Leader*, (New York, Farrar & Rhinehart, Inc., 1929), p. 70.

[5] At his death, four volumes on Burke and Erskine, which Bryan had bought during his college and law student days, were presented by Mrs. Bryan to W. Norwood Brigance, who states that in some the folios were still uncut and none had been opened enough to relieve the binding of its original stiffness.

only a few—such as "Surveying," "Meteorology," and "Differential Calculus"—were optional. The list follows, giving insight to the background that Bryan had when he was graduated and went on to the study of law:

Freshman Class

First Term

Algebra	Selection from Greek Authors
Elocution	Greek Prose Composition
Latin Prose Composition	

Second Term

Geometry	Livy
Elocution	Selection from Greek Authors

Third Term

Geometry	Livy, finished
Selection from Greek Authors	Exercises in Declamation through the year

Sophomore Class

First Term

Plane Trigonometry and Mensuration	Horace
Homer	Composition
	Rhetoric

Second Term

Navigation, Spherical Trigonometry & Conic Sections	Homer, finished
	Rhetoric, finished
German	Composition

Third Term

Physics, commenced	German
Tacitus	Composition

Junior Class

First Term

Physics, completed	German
Greek Tragedy	Composition

Second Term

Astronomy	Tusculan Disputations
Chemistry, with lectures	Composition

Third Term

Thucydides	Geology
Tacitus	Composition
	English Literature or History

Senior Class

First Term

Logic	Political Economy
Porter's Elements of the Human Intellect	History or English Literature
	Written Orations

Second Term

Porter's Elements, finished	Demosthenes
Moral Science	DeTocqueville's Amer. Democracy
Written Orations	

Third Term

DeTocqueville, finished	Demosthenes, finished
Evidences of Christianity	International Law

The college records indicate that Bryan led the composition class with a grade of 96; the classes in mechanics, economics, psychology, and logic, with a grade of 97; and the classes in moral philosophy and American government (De Tocqueville) with a grade of 100. Lower grades in German and geology decreased the general average.

To all this must be added the significant fact that Bryan was not only a reader but a careful student of the Bible. Even a cursory examination of his speeches reveals his dependence upon the Bible for texts, morals, and allusions. "Naboth's Vineyard" and "The Prince of Peace" are familiar titles of his speeches. The "cross of gold" and "crown of thorns" allusions, together with hundreds of others that dot speeches, indicate that its pages were used as a well from which he drew more frequently than from any other single source.

So, as young Bryan moved from the elm-lined streets and ivy-covered buildings of Jacksonville and Illinois College on to reading of law in Chicago under the guidance of Lyman Trumbull, Lincoln's friend of Civil War days, and soon on to the sparsely settled plains of Nebraska, it may be an understatement to say that he was fairly well read and sufficiently prepared to identify himself with the issues of the day and to make his voice the voice of the passions of people who soon were to become his ward to the end of his life.

Bryan's Ability to Project His Ideas

Bryan's greatness as a speaker lay mainly in two sources: his extraordinary delivery and his ability to identify himself with the mass sense of need.

He appealed to the common man. The farmer, the laborer, the man in the street looked to him as a political messiah. It was an age of economic and political ills, which were confounding and distressing to those who were not privileged to share a just portion of worldly goods. They chafed under the bridle of economic royalty, and when Bryan took the platform to speak out against those ills and practices with disturbing effect, the common man heard a voice that made his own thoughts articulate. Bryan spoke for what men *wanted*.

He probably saw clearly the danger in more aspects of public policy than any public man of his day. His ideas and utterances on gold, taxation, and imperialism have been vindicated by history.

However, having seen the faults and having sifted facts until he saw the evil, he was careless and inadequate in effecting remedies. More often than not he simply never saw the problem through. In other words, he was sensitive to the felt difficulties in national life, was precise in locating and defining them, but did not reason the validity of possible solutions.

His deficiency lay in the broad scope of argument and in his utter lack of a fecund imagination, in a lack of ability to synthesize a program. He was not constructive or creative, but he was an effective orator.

With such a premise confronting the observer there must, of necessity, be conflicting opinions as to the ability of Bryan to project his ideas on an audience. There is no foot rule to measure either his influence or his ability, but it is possible to make an objective examination of evidence. Such evidence as contained in his speeches, in critical comments of historians and contemporaries, and from it, with the personality and character of the man ever cutting across the whole, reasonable conclusions may be reached.

It is common belief that Bryan's closing speech at the Chicago convention in 1896 marked his first great triumph as an orator. As a matter of fact, it was the culmination of a series of triumphs. While a delegate to the Democratic state convention in Omaha, 1888, he had been called on for a speech, which he gave. It was on the tariff and was received with wild enthusiasm. It marked him as a speaker of ability and eventually led to the nomination for Congressman from the first Nebraska District in 1890. It was during this campaign that he challenged his opponent W. J. Connell to a series of debates. Connell accepted, and Bryan overwhelmed him. The district was strongly Republican; in 1888 Morton, the Democratic candidate, had been defeated by 3,400 votes, whereas Bryan had been victorious, with a majority of 6,700.

Bryan went on to triumph in Congress. His maiden effort was another speech on the tariff on March 16, 1892. He overcame repeated interruptions from the floor and won a complete victory. The following day the speech and the speaker were acclaimed by the press. One hundred thousand copies of the speech were circulated, and Congressman W. L. Wilson chose Bryan as his lieutenant in the tariff fight the following year. It was with this that the "boy orator of the Platte" gained for himself a place in the political sun.

While in Congress he gave several other speeches on issues of importance. One of the best of them was on the income tax. It and his maiden speech demonstrate that Bryan *could* argue effectively. These were speeches directed almost solely to the intellect, for they contained reasoning that was hardly refutable. They are unlike his speeches before popular audiences in which he was more of an emotionalist.

Bryan's reputation as a speaker was further heightened during the debates with Thurston as part of the campaign of 1894, when the men were campaigning for the office of Senator of the United States. Thurston was elected, but these debates, held before audiences numbering as high as 15,000, helped to establish Bryan as one who gave voice to the thoughts of the common man.

In the interim between his defeat for Senator and the Chicago convention, Bryan went on speaking. He toured the country in behalf of bimetallism, and it was he who was largely responsible for the success of the Silver Democrats as they swept into power at the convention of 1896.

Thus when Bryan went to the convention, he was not unprepared for the chance that was to be his. He had gone ready to meet the arguments that arose out of the split over the silver issue. He had made a rough draft of the now famous "Cross of Gold" speech; he had the support of the Nebraska delegation; and had even conversed with his wife in the quiet of their hotel room about the possibility of becoming the choice of his party.

Two reports had been submitted to the convention: the majority favoring free coinage of silver and the minority favoring the gold standard. Compromise could not be reached within the committee, which made it necessary to present the issue to the convention floor. Bryan was asked to take charge of the debate for the bimetallists. It was agreed that Tillman, of South Carolina, would open for that group and that Hill, of New York, Vilas, of Wisconsin, and Russell, of Massachusetts, should follow with the case for the gold standard. Bryan was then to close the debate.

At the conclusion of the speeches favoring the gold standard, the convention was weary from hours of discussion. Acoustics were poor in the old Coliseum. The delegates had not been able to hear the speeches adequately, and they were confused as well as weary.

Bryan then took the floor. He spoke deliberately. His penetrating voice carried to the far corners of the hall. The tired delegates became aroused: "I would be presumptuous, indeed, to present myself against the distinguished gentlemen to whom you have listened if this were mere measuring of abilities. . . . I come to speak to you in defense of a cause as holy as the cause of liberty. . . . "

As Bryan concluded each sentence, the 20,000 people before him rose as a unit in applause. As he raised his hand for silence, the crowd dropped as a unit to await his next words. Indeed, Emerson would have found in him the sublime example of his ideal orator as one "who plays upon the assembly of men as a master upon the keys of a piano."

Bryan continued to speak. "Serene and self-possessed, and with a smile upon his lips, he faced the roaring multitude with a splendid consciousness of power." With glowing eloquence, "perfect clearness, and simplicity of language," he "was the absolute master of the multitude . . . it was as Bryan willed." On he spoke until he reached the memorable conclusion: "You shall not press down upon the brow of labor this crown of thorns; you shall not crucify mankind upon a cross of gold."

There was a pause. Then 20,000 men and women gave vent to an irresistible enthusiasm. Bryan had met their mood. They had found a spokesman for their cause—a spokesman who had given voice to the feelings that welled within their hearts.

No description of the scene at the conclusion of Bryan's speech can be adequate. Phrases that dot the press of the period and speak of a "delirium of excitement," "hysterical frenzy," tumult like that of a "great sea thundering against the dikes" give but a hint of the complete picture.[1] One thing is certain: Bryan had dominated the convention completely. Had he been willing, he could have been nominated then by acclamation, but he chose not to change the order of the regular proceedings. The silver platform was adopted, and he was nominated the next day.

Critics have said that the speech contained no argument. In the main this is true, though not wholly so, for it did contain some argument and some answers to arguments that had been presented by Hill and others before him. Another criticism is that what argument was used was nothing new. That, too, cannot be denied. But what these critics overlooked was that here was a situation that did not call for argument. Here was a crowd in an emotional and suggestible state. The majority of the crowd felt as Bryan did. They were bitter over "ten cent corn and ten per cent interest." They needed someone, not to argue for them but to articulate their resentment. They wanted a leader, and in Bryan they found him.

Bryan's rise to international prominence had come within the period of 8 short years. The Democratic National Committee, backed by Cleveland, had bent every effort to check that rising power, but to no avail. In speaking of Bryan's triumph in Chicago, one newspaper said that his "impassioned speech . . . overthrew the diligently organized work of

---

[1] *The Lincoln (Nebr.) News*, July 10, 1896, p. 8, gives the most vivid picture. "Ten acres of people on the sloping side of the Coliseum yesterday saw the silver-helmeted gladiators in the arena overpower the gold phalanx and plant the banner of silver upon the ramparts of Democracy . . . amid scenes of enthusiasm such as, perhaps, never before occurred in a national convention. They saw 20,000 people, . . . swayed like windswept fields; they heard the awful roar of 20,000 voices burst like a volcano against the reverberating dome overhead; they saw a man carried upon the shoulders of others intoxicated by enthusiasm, . . . The applause was the spontaneous outburst of enthusiasm kindled by the torch of magnetic eloquence. . . . His audience . . . was full of pentup enthusiasm. The powder magazine needed but the spark and Bryan applied it with the skill of genius . . . Marc Antony never applied the match more effectively. The convention took fire with enthusiasm. It crackled as though it was aflame. Hill was forgotten; all else was forgotten for the moment. Every chair in the valley of the Coliseum and every chair in the vast wilderness of the hillsides became a rock upon which frantic men and women were wildly waving handkerchiefs, canes, hats and umbrellas—anything movable. Some, like demented, divested themselves of their coats and flung them high in the air . . . Old political generals were stupefied."

months and weeks. . . . "[1] The control of the East over the Democratic party was not completely broken. The West and South had taken command and made Bryan its standard bearer. "If the election had been held that July day," said William Allen White, "Bryan would have been chosen President. Indeed, all his opponents did in the three months following his speech was to arouse the people from their trance . . . "[2]

But the election was nearly four months away. There was work to be done, and knowing that the press, bankers, industrial leaders, and even the Eastern Democratic organization were opposed to him, Bryan turned to the only availing weapon, his power of speech. He toured the country, travelling 18,000 miles, speaking fifteen to twenty times a day to a total of nearly 5,000,000 people. The West he easily captured, and he roused even the East until great corporations, frightened as they never had been before, opened their bulging money bags and poured funds by the millions into the Republican pot at the nod of Mark Hanna, one of the most adroit political managers that the world has seen. In this way the Republicans spent $7,000,000 to Bryan's paltry $300,000. Hanna sent out speakers, house-to-house campaigners, with money in their pockets, and organized voters to vote on election day in doubtful districts. Every available means was used to create a feeling of panic. Factory workers were told "if Bryan is elected Tuesday, you needn't come back to work on Monday." Mrs. Henry Cabot Lodge after the election wrote to Cecil Spring-Rice:

The great fight is won. It was a fight conducted by trained and experienced forces, with both hands full of money, with the full power of the press and prestige— on one side; on the other, a disorganized mob at first, out of which burst into sight, hearing and force—one man, but such a man! Alone, penniless, without backing, without money, with scarce a paper, without speakers, that man fought such a fight that even those in the East can call him a Crusader, an inspired fanatic—a prophet! It has been marvelous. Hampered by such a following, such a platform,— and even the men whose names were our greatest weapon against him deserted him and left him to fight alone,—he almost won . . . . We had during the last week of the campaign 18,000 speakers on the stump. He alone spoke for his party but speeches which spoke to the intelligence and to the hearts of the people, and with a capital P. It is over now but the vote is seven millions to six millions and a half.

He reached the climax of his career in this year 1896 and lived out a long and slow anticlimax from 1896 to 1925. Many times his enemies thought he was dead politically, and sometimes even his friends feared that he was, but just as many times he arose to remind them that he was still a power in public life and was dangerous to those who stood in his path.

[1] *Omaha Daily Bee*, July 11, 1896, p. 1.
[2] *McClure's Magazine*, 15 (July, 1900): 234.

William Jennings Bryan

After the Spanish-American War, when the issue of imperialism arose, Bryan organized the forces against it. When he declared, "Imperialism has no warrant in the Bible" and "The command, 'Go ye into all the world and preach the gospel to every creature' has no Gatling gun attachment," he precipitated an issue upon which he was again nominated by his party in 1900. His opponents were certain that this defeat, sharper, more clear-cut than the previous one, would mark his final exit from the political scene. Little did they know that 4 years later, they would hear from him in St. Louis as he defeated every political plank to which he was opposed.

As he toured the world in 1905 and 1906, speaking as he went, vast crowds went to hear him. Inspired by Kipling's famous poem "The White Man's Burden," his lecture on the same theme thrilled thousands. The year's absence from America did not dull the ardor of his admirers, as was attested upon his return to New York, when thousands of people, representatives from every state in the Union, jammed Madison Square Garden to hear him speak. The forecast of the press following that occasion proved to be correct, for in Denver, in 1908, on the first ballot, he received 90 per cent of the total votes. For the third time he had become the Democratic party's choice for President of the United States. His absence from the political arena only served to let him gird his loins for future battles.

Taft's victory over Bryan in 1908, following McKinley's victories in 1896 and 1900, ended Bryan's career as a candidate for public office, but it did not mark the end of his hold on the Democratic party. In 1909 he launched his effort to write a prohibition plank into the platform. He was defeated, of course, but 9 years later his plank was written into the Federal Constitution. His power, too, carried to the 1912 convention.

Champ Clark had been installed as the favorite, but Bryan opposed him, claiming that Clark represented the moneyed interests. Bryan thus took up a fight for Wilson. With the same irresistible power that had ever been his, he waged the fight and saw Wilson nominated on the forty-sixth ballot.

Bryan was appointed as Secretary of State by Woodrow Wilson and went on lecturing during that period. He resigned the office in 1915 because he could not see eye to eye with his President over the European situation. He immediately toured the country, speaking in behalf of peace; and on one instance 12,000 people jammed Madison Square Garden, and altogether 100,000 in and out of the hall came to hear him.

In the convention of 1916 Nebraska refused to send him as a delegate, but he was there as a newspaper reporter. He was espied in a corner, where he had gone to escape public notice. Convention delegates demanded that he speak, and, under suspension of rules, he did so. He again roused the convention with a discussion of issues of the hour, placing greatest emphasis on the issue of peace. After America's entrance into the war, Bryan spoke in behalf of the government, urging support and cooperation.

The Democratic convention of 1920 again found Bryan a delegate, and though he was an important figure, he lost his fight for the dry plank, which he had hoped would be incorpo₁ated in the platform.

It was following this that he changed his legal residence from Nebraska to Florida and the people of that state sent him as a delegate to the convention in 1924. It was he who kept the Ku Klux Klan plank out of the platform. He supported McAdoo, and there arose a deadlock, and the choice was about to fall on John W. Davis. Bryan was opposed to Davis, and so powerful was Bryan and so needed was his support that the convention felt it imperative to nominate a man favorable to Bryan; so it selected Charles Bryan, a brother of William Jennings, as the Vice-Presidential candidate.

As one recounts the actions and influence of Bryan in these conventions, it cannot be doubted that Bryan's power as a speaker was the chief factor in the maintenance of his hold on the party for 30 years.

But the political arena was not the only place where Bryan's power as a speaker made itself felt. About 1915 his political power declined, but with that decline his influence in the field of religion rose. Throughout his life he had been a man of staunch religious views. He forever applied religious principles to politics and national affairs. The most popular of all his lectures, delivered scores of times, in hundreds of cities, towns, hamlets, was that in which he presented Christ as "The Prince of Peace." It is not surprising, therefore, to find Bryan, in his declining years, turning to activity within the church.

It was this strong feeling, augmented by a thorough grounding in fundamentalism, that prompted him to assume the prosecution of the Tennessee schoolteacher, Scopes, when on trial for teaching the theory of evolution in the schools of Dayton, Tenn. The details of the trial are unimportant. It is enough to say that Bryan pitted himself against a clever adversary, Clarence Darrow; that technically Bryan won his case and, with the eyes of the world centered upon him, died at the close of the trial, as eloquent in death as he had been in life.

Thus closed the career of one of the greatest orators of modern times. For 37 years his eloquence had influenced millions, until his name became a synonym for the power of the spoken word. It is impossible to estimate how many speeches he gave or how many millions of people had heard him. Single audiences were known to have numbered 15,000. Fifteen speeches a day was a common occurrence, and, so far as is known, the record for a single day was thirty-six. A newspaper correspondent once estimated that, during Bryan's speaking career, he spent one-third of his nights at home, one-third in hotels, and one-third on trains. Only the day before his death he traveled 200 miles and gave two formal addresses.

Because Bryan was defeated three times for the Presidency, because the issues for which he fought were not immediately accepted, critics often maintain that he was therefore ineffective. To answer those critics one needs but to point to the direct election of Senators, the adoption of a graduated Federal income tax, and the Prohibition Amendment, which even Bryan lived to see become a part of our Federal law. Even a study of monetary reform would reveal that we were nearer to Bryan's position 40 years later than to that of his opponents. In that we might say that he was "born thirty years too soon."

Such a man was William Jennings Bryan. When the masses of American people first chose him as their spokesman, the national monetary situation was acute. The abandonment of silver and the adoption of gold had created an economic distress, particularly in the farmer group. Bryan foresaw the danger of welding currency to the gold standard, and his foresight was vindicated 30 years later.

But one searches his speeches in vain to find a rational explanation of how free silver, or its 16 to 1 parity with gold, would eliminate national distress. Having sensed the danger of the gold standard, he simply *assumed* that abandoning it in favor of the free coinage of silver would be the cure-all for the country's ills. His method was to dramatize the national need and to offer a patent-medicine solution.

So it was when he carried the torch against imperialism. The smoke from the gunpowder had scarcely lifted from Santiago harbor when Bryan raised his voice against the imperialistic tendencies of American statesmen. With almost clairvoyant sense he foresaw the international complications that would arise out of the war. Cuba, Puerto Rico, the Philippines—these meant "danger!" to Bryan. But again one searches his speeches in vain for logical argument in opposition to a policy of territorial acquisition. His voice was raised, rather, in passionate appeal that it was " . . . the voice of the serpent, not the voice of God, which bids us eat."[1]

Nor did the passing years change him. At the close of his life he sensed that something was causing a decline in religious influence, and it was by instinct rather than analysis that he laid the blame on the teaching of evolution. The Scopes trial in Tennessee afforded him a chance to articulate his views, but again he resorted to the same method. His argument was centered not on the evidence of evolution but on its danger as a heresy.

---

[1] "Naboth's Vineyard," *Speeches of William Jennings Bryan* (New York, 1913), II, 8.

All his life, excepting perhaps his 4 years in the House of Representatives, where his speeches show their nearest approach to full logical consistency, to inquiring minds that might want a bill of particulars, he responded by asking for a vote of confidence. He *could* argue, as his earlier speeches well show. But from the moment he stepped on the national platform in 1896 the ruling passion of his life was to touch the hearts of the people. He believed that "Persuasive speech is from heart to heart, not from mind to mind."[1]

It is true perhaps that he did not misjudge the mass mind, that they were more influenced by his dramatization of ills than they would have been by an analysis of remedies, but to discerning minds this remained the weakness of his method. Typical of their reaction was that of Old Jules, hero of the biographical novel by Mari Sandoz.

The Panhandle always took an active interest in politics . . . The local orator's words fell loud and lifeless . . . Then the imported man arose, a mere stripling, an unknown young lawyer from Lincoln. He opened his generous mouth and the noisy audience before him quieted. Words flowed over them in a flood swift and clear as the Niobrara. Jules pushed his cap back. The older heads began to nod approval to one another. The speaker established the issues, swung into the tariff and ended on free silver, and when he sat down the crowd was still as a lull in a dry-land thunderstorm. Then in a frenzy of applause the audience arose, climbed to the benches, and swept forward upon the prophet come to them. Never would these men see another such day as when the Panhandle first heard the young Bryan.

Jules watches the Lincoln attorney leave the building with the local bigwigs of his party. . . . A wonderful speech, yet Jules knew that nothing he said was remarkable, new, or particularly sound. It was the way he said those things, as a fine young crusader, armed with a voice that swayed the emotions of the crusted skeptic. What couldn't a man with true vision do with such a gift![2]

Such a viewpoint as that of "Old Jules" becomes significant when it is understood that the character was Miss Sandoz's father. To the writer Miss Sandoz added further that "Old Jules," upon his return, was telling his wife and family of his experience. "He convinced *me* while I was listening to him. But on the long ride home I had time to think and I realized that he really hadn't said anything."

To get even a clearer picture and better understanding of this rare individual, there must forever be, cutting across the things he did, his personality and character. Photographs and comments by contemporaries give us an accurate account. The *Lincoln* (Neb.) *News* of July 10, 1896, describes him as one with a "clean-cut, firm mouth, a strong Roman nose

[1] William Jennings Bryan, *In His Image*, (New York, Fleming H. Revell Company, 1922), p. 251.

[2] Mari Sandoz, *Old Jules*, (Boston, Little, Brown & Company, 1935), p. 113.

and a head of black hair brushed back from his forehead and falling over his collar in short curls." He was a large man, broad-shouldered, heavy-limbed, clear-eyed, and was able to carry his 200 pounds in commanding fashion. He was a clean liver; a total abstainer from the use of tobacco or intoxicants in any form. Tremendous energy and reserve power made it possible for him to be up at 5 a.m., speak from fifteen to thirty times each day, and to be on the stump continuously through three campaigns.

His sense of humor has been a matter of controversy. Oberholtzer says his character was devoid of humor.[1] Charles Willis Thompson, who had better opportunity to know, states:

> . . . It will probably astonish ninety-nine one-hundredths of Bryan's followers and foes to be told that in private he was full of humor, but it is true. In public he never permitted a hint of this damning fact to escape, but in a small circle of friends he exuded humor at every pore. He had wit, too . . . and this dark secret he also concealed.
> In public he was always as solemn as a sexton . . . .[2]

In scattered writings through *The First Battle* Bryan explains why he withheld his private sense of humor in political addresses. He desired, he said, that his audiences attend seriously to the business at hand, and humor in a political speech was likely to set the speaker up as an entertainer not qualified to hold office or to speak for those who desired to hold office.

Added to these characteristics, probably towering above all others, was one that marked him as a man apart, which contributed more to his phenomenal power over an audience; that was—his absolute sincerity, his unswerving faith in whatever cause he might espouse. "He dodged none of the issues," admits the ever critical Hibben.[3] Whether one agreed with Bryan or not, one was convinced of that steadfastness of purpose and his absolute honesty. "There is no doubt that, next to a good voice and a keen histrionic instinct, what has done most for Bryan's success in the worldly sense has been his faith in himself."[4]

Bryan saw the religious and political problems of his day as crises, and as ever has been the case, these crises produced great oratory. As one examines his speeches on the silver question, on prohibition, on evolution, one cannot but sense that the words were inspired by a terrible earnestness that lifted him to planes of eloquence beyond the men of weaker convictions. He believed in his preachment with the unswerving faith of an evangelist, and like the evangelist he believed himself called to be the

---

[1] *A History of the United States since the Civil War*, V, 424–425.

[2] Charles Willis Thompson, *Presidents I've Known and Two Near Presidents* (Indianapolis, The Bobbs-Merrill Company, 1929), p. 64.

[3] *The Peerless Leader*, p. 149.

[4] Anonymous, *The Independent*, 56 (June 9, 1904): 1301–1320.

savior of the people. He spoke not as the scribes and Pharisees but as one having authority.

But the picture is still incomplete without giving consideration to his delivery. Bryan's voice was a marvellous organ of expression, unequaled by that of any speaker of his generation. It was not a deep voice, but it had power and a carrying quality that made it possible for 15,000 people, seated in the open air, to hear him without the aid of modern-day loud-speaker systems. It was a rich voice, sometimes mellow with tenderness, then flashing with indignation. Yet purity rather than richness was its outstanding element.

His inflections and modulations were superb, and though his hearers were captured by the silver music of his voice rather than being aware of specific elements, these elements, like overtones in music, enriched the whole. Carl E. Seashore, authority on the psychology of music and speech, recorded and analyzed Bryan's voice with a "phoneloscope" just before his death. Said Seashore:

> The picture of Bryan's voice shows all the peculiarities of his inflection, stress, intonation, rhythm, and scores of other factors. . . .
>
> . . . In general we may say that his voice is characterized by a wide range of inflection, great carrying power, similarity to conversational tone, and rhythmic flow. . . .
>
> . . . If the ideal of oratory is that it be based on conversation, then in this particular Bryan's voice and oratory came very near to it.
>
> His inflections were those of everyday speech, and not in an artificial form, adopted only for effect.[1]

Another distinction of Bryan's voice was his perfect articulation. Every essential speech sound was given its full value. Under his touch there was no weakening or slurring of sounds. He spoke always of his party as the "Democra*t*ic Par*t*y," never, as with most speakers, was it the "Dema-cra*d*ic Par*d*y." This accounts in a large measure for his extraordinary range of audibility. How extensive this was is suggested by Mrs. Bryan, in reference to one of her husband's appearances in Corpus Christi, Tex. She had remained in the hotel while he was speaking and on opening her window could hear each word and syllable he uttered, though he was three blocks away.

The press, biographers of his time, friends, and foes alike agree that his voice was phenomenal. He was the "silver-tongued orator," the "lute-toned speaker." His was "a voice as sweet as when a master hand touches the keys of a perfect musical instrument."

Coupled with this marvelous voice was an attitude of poise and bearing that never overstepped the bounds of temperance. People who have heard

[1] Carl E. Seashore, *Emerson Quarterly*, November, 1925, p. 7.

him agree that he spoke without haste, strain, or flurry and that his gestures were simple and spontaneous. Photographs of him on the speaker's platform indicate that his gestures were never expansive but nevertheless were strong and graceful. An index finger raised above his head or both hands outstretched before him were commonly used.

Contemporary judgment of Bryan's ability to project his ideas on his hearers is plentiful and varied. Mark Sullivan tells of violent partisans such as Henry Watterson, who called Bryan a "political faker,"[1] and Oberholtzer, the historian, called him "a rare bigot."[2] But the voice of judgment in America does not come alone from the press or from Whig historians. It comes also from the farms and factories, the Main Streets of America. It is the voice made eloquent by Edwin Markham:

> Bowed by the weight of centuries he leans
> Upon his hoe and gazes on the ground,
> The emptiness of ages in his face,
> And on his back the burden of the world.

To this group Bryan was the messiah of politics. A quarter of a century after his last futile effort to gain the Presidency they still remembered him wistfully. "The big fellows crucified him on that cross of gold," said one of the jobless as late as 1938. It is this group that compels the critic to render favorable judgment of Bryan's ability to project his ideas.

Speech Preparation

Bryan's method of speech preparation was not consistent throughout his 45 years of speaking but changed to suit the circumstances and experience of the speaker. During his twenties he wrote and memorized his speeches. Some evidence exists to show that he rehearsed them as his wife listened.

I think I am able to give you the information which you wish. As a young man, Mr. Bryan wrote out his speeches with great care, but abandoned the practice before many years. Often he spoke entirely without notes, when his subject was one with which he was entirely familiar and upon which he had spoken before. If the subject was a new one, he was apt to make brief notes of the heads of paragraphs. These he did not expand but simply used them to direct his thought at the time.[3]

This seems to bear out the fact that as Bryan gained experience he made scant outlines and used no notes while speaking.

[1] Mark Sullivan, *Our Times: The Turn of the Century*, 1900–1904, (New York, Charles Scribner's Sons, 1926), I, 292.

[2] *A History of the United States Since the Civil War*, p. 410.

[3] An excerpt from a letter dated Oct. 27, 1925, from Cocoanut Grove, Fla., written by Mrs. Bryan to W. Norwood Brigance. A facsimile of some of Bryan's sample notes may be found in an article by Brigance "In the Workshop of Great Speakers," *American Speech*, August, 1926.

When a copy of one his public lectures was desired for publication and he had no stenographic copy of the speech as actually delivered, he would dictate it to his secretary. J. R. Farris, his secretary for many years, gives an interesting account of Bryan's method of dictation. He never paced the floor, never had an outline or note before him. He would rather sit in a chair, lean forward, usually have the finger tips of one hand touching those of the other. In this position he would dictate at an even rate as rapidly as a stenographer could follow him. "I could take him at an average rate of speed, and he set a pace comfortable for me," said Farris. "If he had a less experienced stenographer, he would speak at a slower rate; but if he had one who could take him at high speed he spoke faster." Farris also added that he "seldom changed a word that he dictated. I might almost say that he never did. He seemed to know exactly what he wanted to say."[1]

There are so many versions of how Bryan prepared the "Cross of Gold" speech that the record should be cleared. Paul L. Haworth, historian, states that he "had brought to the convention a carefully prepared speech, which he had committed to memory."[2] Oberholtzer, another historian, classifies it as "an old speech warmed over." Both are partially true but essentially misleading.

The genesis of this speech began with the rise of the silver question two decades previous. Bryan had spoken on it in Congress. He stumped Nebraska on the issue in 1894–1895. He had toured the West speaking on it prior to the convention in 1896. He had arranged a debate in Crete, Nebr., with John Irish, of Iowa, to be held between the preliminary conference at Chicago and the opening of the convention and after attending the early sessions of the convention in Chicago, returned to Nebraska to engage Irish and sped back to Chicago. " . . . In the debate with Irish I used the sentence with which I closed my Chicago speech. . . . I had used it a few times before that time, recognizing its fitness for the conclusion of a climax, and had laid it away for a proper occasion."[3] Meanwhile, he had been using every means at his disposal to get a chance to speak at the convention and planned the details for such a speech. "While I spent all my spare time in arranging the arguments for any speech that I might deliver at the Convention, I prepared only one new argument. . . . "[4]

"The speech that I expected to make was not different from the speeches that I had been making except in the setting, . . . "[5]

---

[1] As given to W. Norwood Brigance in private interview, Lincoln, Nebr., August, 1925.

[2] Paul L. Haworth, *The United States in Our Own Times*, (New York, Charles Scribner's Sons, 1920), p. 227.

[3] *Memoirs*, p. 103.

[4] *Ibid.*, p. 104.

[5] *Ibid.*, p. 110.

When at last the chance came to close the debate for the free silver forces, he was prepared, not with a written manuscript, but with a speech that had grown out of scores of previous addresses on the subject. To say that the whole structure was written and memorized is an absurdity that ignores the fact that he matched his topics against the speeches of Russell, Vilas, and Hill, who had spoken just previously against the silver coinage. Bryan himself says:

> . . . I had spent three years studying the question from every angle and I had time and again answered all the arguments that the other side had advanced. All that I had to do was to analyze the speeches of Hill, Vilas and Russell as they were made and then present the answer as effectively as I could. . . . I was prepared to answer in an extemporaneous speech the arguments which had been presented. . . . [1]

Criticism of Speeches

Just as Bryan kept his appeals on the plane of the common man, so did his style fit the intellect of the common man. His style was for the hearer rather than the reader, and it is not difficult to detect certain devices and concepts that he employed in keeping it so. The distinguishing characteristic of his style is its concreteness. To achieve it Bryan used analogy, antithesis, allusion, illustration, and figures of speech.

Analogy and antithesis abound throughout all his speeches. When he sought a means of conveying to his audience the high motives of the silver Democrats he did so with analogy: "With a zeal approaching the zeal which inspired the Crusaders who followed Peter the Hermit, our silver Democrats went forth from victory unto victory." When he wished to point out the danger of annexing the Philippines, he said:

> History is replete with predictions which once wore the hue of destiny, but which failed of fulfillment because those who uttered them saw too small an arc of the circle of events. . . . When Napoleon emerged victorious from Marengo, from Ulm, and from Austerlitz, he thought himself the child of destiny, but destiny was not revealed until Blucher's forces joined the army of Wellington and the vanquished Corsican began his melancholy march toward St. Helena. When the

---

[1] *Ibid.*, p. 114. Bryan's versatility in extemporaneous debate would be sufficient answer to the rumor circulated by his critics that Mrs. Bryan wrote many or most of his speechs—if any answer at all were needed. The rumor, of course, is preposterous. There is no evidence to sustain it, not a note or outline of one of Bryan's speeches has ever been found in the handwriting of Mrs. Bryan, or any testimony from a single person who ever saw such a document or ever heard any verbal coaching. It is simply a rumor blown before the wind of political criticism. To anyone who has studied Bryan's career—his early debates with Connell, Thurston, and in Congress, his stump speaking between 1894 and 1896, and his debates in the political conventions from 1896 to 1924—the idea of Bryan declaiming speeches written for him by another is amusing.

redcoats of George III routed the New Englanders at Lexington and Bunker Hill there arose before the British sovereign visions of colonies taxed without representation and drained of their wealth by foreign-made laws, but destiny was not revealed until the surrender of Cornwallis completed the work begun at Independence Hall and ushered into existence a government deriving its just powers from the consent of the governed.

The examples of antithesis are manifold. The following, from the Tennessee case, is selected at random: "Christians desire that their children be taught all sciences, but they do not want them to lose sight of the Rock of Ages while they study the age of rocks; neither do they desire them to become so absorbed in measuring the distance between the stars that they will forget Him who holds the stars in his hands."

Bryan used illustrations and allusions extensively. In their subject matter he showed a distinct preference for certain fields over others. Classical allusions and illustrations are seldom found. He states in his introduction to his *World Famous Orations* that when they are familiar to the audience they ornament a speech, but since he used so few in his own speeches, we can assume that he considered the average popular audience unacquainted with classical literature. Literary references find a scant place in Bryan's speeches except for a few uses made of poetry. One finds no reference to Shakespeare, Dryden, Pope, Swift, Byron, Keats, Shelley, Hawthorne, Jonson, and the like. He preferred Scott, Burns, Longfellow, and Kipling.

The bulk of his illustrative material comes from history, from nature, and from the Bible. Again and again in the advocacy of popular reform he drew from past epochs in the rise of individual rights, as the *Magna Carta*, the Bill of Rights, the Declaration of Independence. Demosthenes, Alexander, Caesar, Napoleon, and the French Revolution provided him with many illustrations. To an even greater extent he drew from American history, with frequent references to Jefferson and Lincoln. The Colonial and Revolutionary eras were his favorite periods.

The Bible, of course, was his chief source of allusions and illustrative material. He once wrote that lessons drawn from the Bible reinforce a speech because people are more familiar with it than with any other book. He used it as a source for entire speeches. In his lecture on "Man" he began: "The Psalmist asks Jehovah, 'What is man that thou art mindful of him, and the son of man that thou visitest him?'" His lecture on "The Price of a Soul" was woven around this reference: "What shall it profit a man if he gain the whole world and lose his own soul?" One of his early speeches against imperialism, "Naboth's Vineyard," opened with the story of King Ahab and Naboth, the vineyard owner, and closed with an allusion to the serpent and the Garden of Eden.

Much illustrative material was also taken from nature. The following example from a speech delivered at the University of Nebraska and addressed to the religious skeptics who wanted to understand everything says: "Let him find out, if he can, why it is that a black cow can eat green grass and then give white milk with yellow butter in it." In a lecture, "In the Beginning—God," he uses these illustrations drawn from nature:

> If they find a piece of pottery in a mound, supposed to be ancient, they will venture to estimate the degree of civilization of the designer from the rude scratches on its surface, and yet they cannot discern the evidence of design which the Creator has written upon every piece of His handiwork.
> On lofty mountain summits He builds His mighty reservoirs and piles high the winter snows, which, melting, furnish the water for singing brooks, for the hidden veins, and for the springs that pour out their refreshing flood through the smitten rocks. At His touch the same element that furnishes ice to cool the fevered brow furnishes also the steam to move man's commerce. . . . He imprisons the roaring cataract's exhaustless energy for the service of man: He stores away in the bowels of the earth beds of coal and rivers of oil; He studs the canyon's frowning walls with precious metals and priceless gems. . . .

Another of Bryan's stock in trade was his figurative language. Walter Dill Scott, former president of Northwestern University, was one of many who state that Bryan was a master in the use of figures of speech. The famous "cross of gold and crown of thorns" is but one of hundreds. Though metaphor was his favorite, he used similes, hyperboles, and personifications. If irony or sarcasm be considered figurative language, he used them but slightly. One excellent example to show his deftness and skill in its use without letting it degenerate into abuse is one from his speech on the "Income Tax:" "They call that man a statesman whose ear is turned to catch the slightest pulsations of a pocket-book, and denounce as a demagogue anyone who dares to listen to the heart-beat of humanity."

To understand the secret of Bryan's power and charm one cannot avoid giving attention to his choice of words. It can be summarized by saying that he used words spoken by people rather than words read in books. In lectures to students interested in learning how to speak well he gives that advice and cites the Bible as authority in the following example of Paul, as found in I Corinthians XIV:9: " . . . Except ye utter by the tongue words easy to be understood, how shall it be known what is spoken? for ye shall speak into the air."

Bryan certainly practiced what he preached. He exhibited a preference for such words as:

tell rather than *inform*.
war rather than *conflict*.

rich rather than *wealthy*.
hide rather than *conceal*.
climb rather than *ascend*.
pay rather than *compensation* or *remuneration*.
work or *toil* rather than *labor*.
make or *build* rather than *create* or *erect*.

Bryan used no foreign phrases, even though he had been a careful student of Latin. We know, of course, that he had been a poor German student, but here again we can explain his non-use of them on the ground that he wanted the style to be instantly intelligible to the hearer.

He preferred specific to general words. One example from his "Prince of Peace," as he speaks on the immortality of the soul, is sufficient to illustrate:

If the Father deigns to touch with divine power the cold and pulseless heart of the buried acorn and to make it burst forth from its prison walls, will He leave neglected in the earth the soul of man made in the image of his Creator? If He stoops to give to the rosebud, whose withered blossoms float upon the autumn breeze, the sweet assurance of another springtime, will He refuse the words of hope to the sons of men when the frosts of winter come? If matter, mute and inanimate, . . . can never die, will the imperial spirit of man suffer annihilation when it has paid a brief visit like a royal guest to this tenement of clay?

Finally, in considering Bryan's words, one cannot miss seeing the use made of loaded or highly emotionalized words. In an examination of three representative speeches, one political, one religious, and one lecture, one is struck by the repeated use of the following highly emotionalized words:

duty	*human*	*peace*
blood	*love*	*spirit*
flag	*justice*	*right*
God	*man*	*life*
heart	*ideals*	

His sentences were, in the main, short. Or if he used a long sentence he frequently relieved it by following with a short one, often of two or three words. Consider these typical examples from the "Cross of Gold":

. . . The income tax law was not unconstitutional when it was passed; it was not unconstitutional when it went before the Supreme Court for the first time; it did not become unconstitutional until one of the judges changed his mind, and we cannot be expected to know when a judge will change his mind. *The income tax is just.*

And they had good reason for their doubt, because there is scarcely a State here today asking for the gold standard which is not in the absolute control of the Republican party. *But note the change.*

These are typical, too, of the length of his sentences. Generally, his sentences did not exceed forty words, and frequent use was made of the very short sentence—one of four or five words.

He showed a preference for Anglo-Saxon words over Latin at the ratio of about two or three to one. He would not sacrifice clarity in order to use a word of Anglo-Saxon origin. His chief guide was to use a word that expressed the idea precisely.

Bryan made some use of the question. At times he literally laid down a barrage with them until those who would assault his argument had to work their way through them. But these were used when he had time to contemplate. When he was in the heat of argument he seldom used the device. It is for that reason that the question is most frequently found in introductions and conclusions of his speeches.

And now to the most controversial topic of all in the criticism of Bryan's speeches. Earlier in this study it was stated that Bryan was lacking in the broad scope of argument, that he chose to speak from "heart to heart and not from mind to mind." Some have gone so far as to say that his speeches were utterly devoid of argument, that "you could drive a prairie schooner through any one of them." Generally, his speaking was highly emotionalized. That was his strength. A fair and objective conclusion is that he *could* argue when he felt argument to be necessary, but he knew that an argument may often confirm others in their opinion rather than move them to change it. For that reason his appeals were to patriotism, justice, and reverence. Perhaps he carried the tendency too far, but his preference was from choice, not from necessity, and if one criticizes his choice, one must remember that in his choice lay his tremendous power as a speaker.

If one doubts his ability to argue let him read Bryan's earlier speeches on the "Income Tax" and the "Tariff." These are packed with hard, jolting arguments. Also, in the speech "America's Mission," on the issue of imperialism, delivered before the Virginia Democratic Association, his appeals were alternately to the head and to the heart.

Bryan's strength also lay in the simplicity of his style and the directness and precision of his diction. The cold print of Bryan's words, posterity's sole legacy, reveals, above all things, its imagery, its vividness, its simplicity. It reveals much of the man himself, but it falls far short of revealing the powerful eloquence that came from the utterance of these words by the man himself.

As to the impact of Bryan's speaking on the generation in which he lived, James Truslow Adams, a dispassionate critic, has given perhaps the most penetrating evaluation. Samuel Adams, wrote James Truslow Adams

917

in his *Epic of America,* was "the greatest master in manipulating the masses whom America has ever seen except possibly Bryan."

SELECTED BIBLIOGRAPHY

Books

Bryan, Mary Baird: *Life and Speeches of the Hon. William Jennings Bryan,* Baltimore, R. H. Woodward Co., 1900.

Bryan, William Jennings: *The First Battle,* Chicago, W. B. Conkey Co., 1896.

———, and his wife, Mary Baird Bryan: *Memoirs of William Jennings Bryan,* Philadelphia, John C. Winston Company, 1925.

Herrick, G. F., and J. C. Herrick: *The Life of William Jennings Bryan,* Chicago, Buxton Publishing House, 1925.

Hibben, Paxton: *The Peerless Leader,* New York, Farrar & Rhinehart, 1929.

Long, J. C.: *Bryan: The Great Commoner,* New York, D. Appleton Company, 1928.

Parrington, Vernon L.: *The Beginnings of Critical Realism in America,* 1860–1920, New York, Harcourt, Brace and Company, 1930.

Speeches of William Jennings Bryan, revised and arranged by himself; biographical introduction by Mary Baird Bryan, 2 vols., New York, Funk & Wagnalls Company, 1913.

Sullivan, Mark: *Our Times,* New York, Charles Scribner's Sons, 1926.

Thompson, Charles Willis: *Presidents I Have Known and Two Near-Presidents,* Indianapolis, The Bobbs-Merrill Company, 1929.

Werner, W. R.: *Bryan,* New York, Harcourt, Brace and Company, 1929.

Williams, Wayne C.: *William Jennings Bryan,* New York, Fleming H. Revell Company, 1923.

Newspapers

The Commoner, Lincoln, Nebr. Entire file.

The Conservative, published in Nebraska City; editorial each Thursday by J. Sterling Morton, Secretary of Agriculture under Cleveland; Vols. 1–4 (complete), July 14, 1898 to May 29, 1902.

Lincoln (Nebr.) *Daily Star,* 1903–1925.

Lincoln (Nebr.) *Evening News,* 10 (Mar. 2, 1891 . . .).

Morning World Herald (Omaha), 1890–1925.

Nebraska State Journal, 1890–1925.

Omaha (Nebr.) *Daily Bee,* 1890–1925.

College Rambler, 1875–1881. The student newspaper of Illinois College.

Miscellaneous

The Minutes of Sigma Pi, 1878–1881, Illinois College.

Albert J. Beveridge

by Herold Truslow Ross

Albert J. Beveridge was born in Highland County, Ohio, October 6, 1862; reared in Moultrie County, Illinois; graduated from Sullivan, Ill., high school in 1881 and from DePauw University in 1885. He was a lawyer in Indianapolis, 1886–1899; United States Senator, 1899–1911; political speaker in every national and Congressional campaign from 1884 to 1924 except one (1918), a total of twenty in all; chairman of the Progressive national convention, Chicago, 1912; candidate for the United States Senate, 1922. He was engaged in historical research and writing, 1913–1927, especially the *Life of John Marshall* (Vols. I–II, 1916; III–IV, 1919) and *Abraham Lincoln* (1928). Died April 27, 1927.

The spellbinders who leaped with such enthusiasm and unrestrained eloquence upon the political platforms of 1884[1] caught up the dying echo of the golden age and spoke the prologue to a new era of masterful American oratory.

Vying with them in heated debate were a number of young gentlemen testing their powers in trial flights as they began their ascent to the national forum upon which, within a decade, they were to argue the issues of an imperialistic nationalism. Theodore Roosevelt was one of these, delivering his first speech before a Republican national convention. Jonathan Dolliver was another, speaking with such vigor before the Iowa Republican convention that he achieved national recognition. William Jennings Bryan attended his second Democratic national convention and electioneered in and about Jacksonville, Ill.; and in central Indiana, Albert Jeremiah Beveridge, yet only a college senior, campaigned so brilliantly that the *Indianapolis News* declared him "the finest young orator in the Republican party."[2]

The opportunity to participate in the campaign as a speaker had been eagerly seized, for as a lad, Beveridge had formed a deep desire to emulate

---

[1] "The young Republicans who went forth converted to Democracy in the Blaine Campaign (1884) and with the zeal of new converts held their audiences 'spell bound,' as they wove chaplets of rhetorical flowers about the heads of the Democratic candidates were the first spellbinders, I think, to wear the title."—Curtis Guild, Jr., "The Spellbinders," *Scribner's Magazine* 32 (November, 1902): 561.

[2] Quoted in the *Greencastle Times*, Nov. 6, 1884, p. 5.

the Republican speakers who waved the bloody shirt in the political rallies of the 1870's or the equally impassioned Democratic campaigners who exposed the scandals of General Grant's administration.[1] Many a time, while plowing in the long furrows of an Illinois farm, he had tested his powers upon a stump while his horses rested by the fence row.[2] In school he sought guidance in McGuffey's *Readers*. With enthusiasm he declaimed the oratorical selections. Often he must have reread a passage entitled "The Duty of an American Orator," for he never forgot its closing injunction: "Be it then the noblest office of American eloquence to cultivate in the people of every state a deep and fervent attachment to the Union."[3]

He soon acquired a local reputation as a speaker and participated in political meetings, particularly in the activity of the Francis Murphy temperance movement. In the fall of 1881, Beveridge entered Indiana Asbury University[4] with the oft-reiterated purpose of developing his speaking powers. He found there a congenial atmosphere for his purpose. Annual orations were required of all students, there were a large number of prize contests, and the extracurricular life of the college was centered in the literary societies, where weekly orations, essays, debates, and declamations were an absorbing interest. To excel in public speaking was the common ambition. Beveridge entered these activities with an announced determination to win. He budgeted every hour of time. He had definite hours for reading, for composition, and for oral practice. Rising before sunup, he hurried to a wood at the edge of the town, where he delivered his own orations or declaimed the masterpieces, often competing with the roar of passing freight trains.[5] Returning to his room, he read until the breakfast bell. His college orations reveal the wide range of this self-imposed study.[6]

The formal instruction of the college was also a profound influence. Fundamental political ideas and beliefs were impressed upon him by his teachers and by his textbooks.[7] His theories of oratory developed largely from Whately's *Elements of Rhetoric*, Bacon's *Manual of Gesture*, and Town-

[1] Beveridge, *The Art of Public Speaking* (New York, 1924), pp. 3-9.

[2] Unpublished autobiography, cited by Bowers *Beveridge and the Progressive Era* (Boston, 1932), p. 10.

[3] William H. McGuffey, *New Eclectic Readers*, V, 145. Beveridge's affection for the readers cited by Mark Sullivan, *Our Times*, (New York, 1927), II, p. 13*n*.

[4] The name was changed to DePauw University in 1884.

[5] Agnes Root, "Senator Albert J. Beveridge—The Man," *DePauw Palladium* 4 (Nov. 5, 1900): 1.

[6] H. T. Ross, "Education of an Orator," *Quarterly Journal of Speech*, 18 (February, 1932): 77-78.

[7] *Ibid.* Particularly important were Professors John Clark Ridpath and John P. D. John. Influential texts include Wayland's *Elements of Political Economy* and Woolsey's *Political Science*.

send's *Art of Speech*.[1] The lasting impress of Townsend is unmistakable in Beveridge's *The Art of Public Speaking*, written 40 years after college.[2]

Campaign of 1884. Each year Beveridge won the campus oratorical contests for which he was eligible. As a consequence, he was invited by the Indiana Republicans to be one of their campaign speakers in the fall of 1884. During the summer of 1884, spent in Des Moines, Iowa, as a book salesman, he had been inspired by Ingersoll and fired politically by Jonathan Dolliver. He was, therefore, quick to accept an offer to take the stump for Blaine during the fall canvass. His first speech was made at a country crossroads blacksmith shop; the second was delivered to a crowd of farmers gathered in a barn. Typical of the occasions and of the press notices that came almost daily to Indianapolis was this from Logansport:

> A. J. Beveridge delivered here, last night, one of the best speeches of the campaign. He was escorted from the hotel to the courthouse by the Blaine and Logan Guards and held his audience delighted for an hour and a half, being frequently greeted with loud applause. His speech was scholarly and eloquent. Though a young man, he is a power on the rostrum and is doing good work in this campaign. The local democratic machine had a large number of the voters of the county to a pole raising and had carried off the key to the only public hall in the town. A ladder was got, entrance was effected through a window, the door opened from the inside, lights brought, and an enthusiastic meeting held in spite of these disadvantages.[3]

In October he was summoned to ride the Blaine Special, as the candidate crossed Indiana. In company with William McKinley, Benjamin Harrison, and General Lew Wallace, he listened to Blaine, and since he was quick to note the effectiveness of his clarity and simplicity in public address, he began to debate the relative merits of Blaine and Ingersoll.[4] At Worthington, after Blaine had appeared on the rear platform of the train, Beveridge was almost overwhelmed when he was assigned to step off and address "the vast throng of people who had collected from all parts of the country to see the next president."[5]

College Oratory. Returning to the campus after the election, Beveridge began to prepare for the DePauw oratorical contest, with its prize of $100 in gold. The other students, knowing that Beveridge would win, attempted to force him to withdraw. They refused to compete against him, thinking thereby to invalidate the competition. The faculty decided, however, that Beveridge might speak against a standard of excellence set up by the judges.

[1] Luther Tracy Townsend, *The Art of Speech* (New York, 1880–1881), Vol. II, "Studies in Eloquence and Logic."
[2] Beveridge, *The Art of Public Speaking* (New York, 1924).
[3] *Indianapolis Journal*, Oct. 9, 1884, p. 2.
[4] Bowers, *op. cit.*, p. 23.
[5] *Greencastle Banner*, Oct. 23, 1884, p. 1.

In this way he won the prize. Elated, he wrote the president of the college that he would annually offer a gold medal as the prize in a Beveridge oratorical contest.

A few weeks later, Beveridge climaxed his college career with victories in state and interstate oratorical contests. In the latter competition, he was ranked first on manuscript and third in delivery, defeating the representative from Illinois, who was third on manuscript but tied for first in delivery. His victory had been due to his manuscript, and the manuscript, significantly, he had been revising and perfecting for 3 years.[1] In June, 1885, Beveridge was chosen one of the commencement orators, closing his college experience with a tribute to Robert Burns.

1885–1895. It was an interesting coincidence that, in the year 1885, both Beveridge and Theodore Roosevelt should have been on the frontier; it was no coincidence that both should have found in the expanse of open ranges and in the virility of Western life new visions of national strength and of national possibility. Following his graduation, Beveridge had gone to Dighton, Kan., where he sold real estate. Here it is recorded that he made his first pleading, when, with an extemporaneous but impassioned speech, he prevented a mob from hanging a man accused of horse stealing.[2] Shortly after this incident, Beveridge returned to Indianapolis, where he began to read law in the office of Senator Joseph E. McDonald. A few months later, he was selected as the reading clerk for the Indiana state legislature. Law and politics henceforth became absorbing interests.

In 1888 he was invited to join a party of Hoosiers who attended the Republican convention in Chicago in support of the candidacy of Judge Walter Quinton Gresham. Here, under the leadership of Robert G. Ingersoll he campaigned vigorously for Gresham's nomination, but without success, for the convention named Benjamin Harrison instead. Beveridge's experiences, however, outweighed his disappointment. Here for the first time, he had come into contact with the national leaders of his party, and here he again had had the opportunity of being associated with Ingersoll and of studying his eloquence. Without doubt, he was deeply influenced, and while he later criticized Ingersoll's blank-verse style, he always considered him one of the four greatest public speakers America has produced."[3] Beveridge's support of Gresham did not prevent him from taking the stump for Harrison, and he traveled about the state of Indiana as one of the most vigorous of local speakers. In 1890 he joined in the canvass for the Congressional elections.

---

[1] Four versions of the speech as delivered in 1883, 1884, and 1885, may be found in the manuscript book *Albert J. Beveridge in DePauw,* DePauw University Library.

[2] *Indianapolis Star,* 16 (Jan. 1, 1911), 3; *Indianapolis News,* Jan. 11, 1899, p. 2.

[3] Beveridge, *The Art of Public Speaking* (Boston, 1924), p. 13.

Albert J. Beveridge

The Period of Exuberance

This activity naturally brought him many invitations for occasional addresses. One of his favorites was "Robert Burns," which was apparently a revised version of his commencement oration at DePauw. This address, though polished and graceful and the subject of much thought and preparation, was probably not so important in Beveridge's career as a short but brilliant "Toast to the American Soldier," which, on a moment's notice, he delivered at a reception held for a large gathering of distinguished soldiers of the Civil War, meeting in a convention of the Loyal Legion.[1] Soon after, he was invited to give the toast to George Washington at the annual dinner of the Union Club of Chicago, February 22, 1895. The speech was flamboyant and exaggerated in both words and figures of speech, but it was applauded by an audience that still appreciated the excesses of spellbinding, and the memory of its lofty periods was to make it possible for him to achieve national prominence two years later.

"*The Answer to Altgeld.*" That opportunity came in the frenzied and embittered activity of the Presidential campaign of 1896. In the closing days of that campaign, Federal interference came to the front and vied for a time with the mighty question of free silver. This issue was raised from obscurity to national prominence by Governor John P. Altgeld, of Illinois, speaking at the Cooper Union in New York City, October 16, 1896. It was an issue that had its roots far back in the industrial turmoil and bitter discontent of 1894, when President Cleveland had sent Federal troops into Illinois to stop the disorders growing out of the Pullman strike. This action aroused bitter resentment on the part of Governor Altgeld, who held that President Cleveland had had no right to send troops into his state without his request. Now, in order to align the labor vote behind him in his race for re-election to the governorship, Altgeld brought the issue into the campaign. Bryan supported the governor by speaking in the Chicago area for three days. The Republicans, losing ground, resolved on one last desperate effort. A committee was dispatched to Indianapolis to secure ex-President Benjamin Harrison as speaker for the rally. They found that Harrison's schedule was already crowded with engagements, but as they were about to leave, John Shaffer,[2] the state chairman, suggested that they secure Albert Beveridge. They immediately recalled his Union League speech and agreed. Beveridge accepted their invitation. At last he was to have an opportunity to present his own interpretation of the

---

[1] I. S. Gordon, in *Dinner and Toasts in Honor of Senator Albert J. Beveridge*, Jan. 13, 1899 (Indianapolis, 1899), p. 32.

[2] John C. Shaffer, in *The History of the Republican Party*, (Russell M. Seeds, ed., Indianapolis, 1899), I, 267.

Constitution and the doctrine of State and Federal rights! With all the vigor at his command, he began his preparation for the speech that was to be delivered one week hence. On the day, Beveridge arrived in Chicago in the early morning, rushed to a hotel, and called for a stenographer. He had been so busy gathering material that he had not yet composed his speech. Before night, the speech had been dictated, revised, and released to the press.[1]

The auditorium was packed long before the hour arrived, although most of the audience had never heard Beveridge speak and knew little about him. Of necessity the speaker had to substitute power for prestige. This he accomplished, and the *Chicago Tribune* reported that "he captured his audience in the very first sentence. Indeed every sentence he uttered for several minutes was interrupted by applause, and he continued on the best of terms with his audience to the close of his address."[2] Vigorously he assaulted Altgeld, contending that President Cleveland had been entirely within his rights in sending troops to quell the disorder. "When should he act?" he asked.

When the forces of destruction were gathering or should he have waited until the red glow in the West told him that the flames of arson were already wrapping Chicago in their winding sheet of flame? . . . I say that the head of the Republic is a traitor to his trust if, when he sees the conditions forming under which anarchy acts, he does not draw about the threatened spot the magic circle of his constitutional power.

He concluded with a stirring appeal for nationalism, for a united support of the Federal government by every state and every citizen.

The speech made a strong impression not only upon the audience but upon the whole country. The Republican leaders, impressed by its power, telegraphed it to all parts of the country. Nationalism in the Middle West became more important than free silver.[3] Altgeld was defeated, and Albert J. Beveridge had matched his strength for the first time against William Jennings Bryan, as he mounted at last the national forum.

Here, for more than a decade, he was to stand with Theodore Roosevelt, opposing Bryan, while they strove together to guide the rising tides of nationalism. Each of these men found in the movement the vision of an ideal republic, destined to rise on the crest of a greater American patriotism. To Theodore Roosevelt, this republic was strong and militant, fighting the battles of the weak, contending with the strong, dominant in world affairs. To William Jennings Bryan it was a republic at peace with the

[1] *Ibid.*
[2] *Chicago Tribune*, Oct. 31, 1896, p. 2.
[3] Shafer, *op. cit.*

world, the model of self-government and political equality. To Albert J. Beveridge it was a republic of the common man but a nation so strong that it commanded the commerce of the seas, controlled the economy of colonies, sat with power in the council of the empires of earth. More than this, it was a Republic "charged by an Almighty God to regenerate the earth, and by precept and example, to lead the children of men." Before 1898 these men stressed nationalism; after 1898 they discussed imperialism. During this period, Beveridge delivered many of his most important addresses. The first phase of this period extends from the memorable October 30, 1896, to July 16, 1898.

On December 21, 1896, Beveridge delivered an address entitled "Forefathers' Day" before the New England Society of St. Louis. On February 12 he was again in Chicago to give the toast on "Abraham Lincoln" at the annual dinner of the Marquette Club, composed of the leading Republicans of the Middle West. A year later, he decided to make a speaking trip through the East. On January 4, 1898, he addressed the Allegheny County Bar Association in Pittsburgh on the theme "The Vitality of the American Constitution." Here he clearly expounded his basic conception of the nature and function of the Constitution, a concept to which he consistently adhered throughout his public career. The vitality of the Constitution must reside, he declared, in its "power to grow as the people grow, and furnish scope for the people's power as the Nation's necessities enlarge." The golden rule of constitutional interpretation should be and ought to be: "The Constitution exists for the people, not the people for the Constitution."

On February 12, 1898, he was in New York City as one of the speaker before the New York Republican Club. Chauncey M. Depew was the toasts master, and Elihu Root and Theodore Roosevelt, then Assistant Secretary of the Navy, were fellow speakers. Again Beveridge used the theme "Abraham Lincoln."

"*The Middlesex Speech.*" The climax of these Eastern engagements came on April 27 at a dinner of the Middlesex Club of Boston. War had just been declared on Spain. Boston was seething with activity as preparations for war gathered headway. In such an atmosphere, Beveridge forecast with unusual accuracy the policy of President McKinley both during and after the war, and he also made the pronouncement that has been used to prove him the "original expansionist."[1]

In this speech, Beveridge declared that the nation must look beyond the immediate period of the war and prepare for peace. Labor and capital must unite on a program of unified endeavor; the currency problem must

[1] John A. Coffin, "The Senatorial Career of Albert J. Beveridge," *Indiana Magazine of History*, 24 (September, 1928): 146.

be solved in such a way that the whole country would be benefited; for after the war, the markets of the world must be opened to American commerce. "American factories," he asserted, "are making more than the American people can use; American soil is producing more than they can consume. Fate has written our policy for us; the trade of the world must and shall be ours."

Taking up the policy to be pursued in the war itself, Beveridge foretold with prophetic voice the course that struggle was to take: "We are at war with Spain. Therefore our field of operation is not confined to Cuba . . . In the Pacific is the true field of our earlier operations. There Spain has an empire, the Philippine archipelago."

This address helped to establish Beveridge's reputation in the East. The timeliness of the issues discussed, the saneness of the conclusions, and dramatic effectiveness of his presentation convinced Republican leaders on the seaboard that "a new Lochinvar had come out of the West."[1] This increased popularity in the East also added immeasurably to his growing prestige at home. He was scheduled to open officially the political campaign of 1898, with a speech before a Republican rally in Indianapolis.

Throughout the summer of 1898, the United States engaged in war with Spain. As Beveridge had prophesied, the first important victory was achieved in the Philippines. On May 1, Admiral George Dewey defeated the Spanish-Pacific fleet and gained possession of Manila Bay. In July Admiral Sampson and Commodore Schley annihilated the Spanish fleet defending Cuba, and American troops on land stormed the heights of San Juan before the city of Santiago. This broke the strength of Spanish resistance. The protocol of peace was signed on August 12. October was the date set for the convening of a peace commission to draw up the terms of peace between the two nations.

The interval between August 12 and October 1 was one in which the leaders of the administration and of both political parties were greatly concerned as to the proper terms of peace. The most difficult problem was the future disposition of Cuba, which had been liberated, and of the Philippine Islands, which had been captured. A sharp division of sentiment was soon evident. Many believed that the United States should take control of both Cuba and the Philippines and hold them as colonies. Diametrically opposed to these were others who believed that these islands should be liberated at once. Naturally, among the general citizenry there was indecision.

"*The March of the Flag.*" Both political parties hesitated to take a definite stand before the elections of 1898. The Republicans, although they had won a substantial victory in 1896, naturally faced the normal losses characteristic of off-year elections. They feared that a pronounced state-

[1] *Boston Evening Transcript*, Apr. 28, 1927.

ment might increase Democratic inroads into Congress. To add to the dilemma, the leaders could not agree as to the policy they would like to expound. Senator George Frisbie Hoar was as ardent an anti-imperialist as Theodore Roosevelt was an imperialist. Even President McKinley was uncertain. In the ranks of Democracy, Bryan, although he had served as a colonel of Nebraska Volunteers, was anti-imperialistic, while many of the Eastern Democrats opposed him. But political sidestepping could not postpone the coming elections. On September 16, Beveridge brilliantly committed the Republicans of Indiana to imperialism.

"The March of the Flag" should be ranked as one of Beveridge's greatest speeches. Carefully prepared, lofty in tone and sweeping in its grasp of policies and events, delivered with power and contagious enthusiasm, it presented a solution to a perplexing national problem and exerted a profound influence on the country.

He met the issue squarely. "In this campaign," he said, "the question is larger than a party question. It is an American question. It is a world question. Shall the American people continue their march toward the commercial supremacy of the world?" Urging the nation to accept its opportunities, Beveridge called attention to the possibilities for expansion already within the grasp of the Republic. Reviewing events through which the nation had expanded, Beveridge received tremendous cheers, as he delivered "the march of the flag":

> The march of the flag! . . . Jefferson acquired that imperial territory which swept from the Mississippi to the mountains, from Texas to the British possessions, and the march of the flag began!
>
> The infidels of the gospel of liberty raved, but the flag swept on! . . . Another empire was added to the Republic and the march of the flag went on!
>
> Those who deny the power of free institutions to expand urged every argument, and more, that we hear today; but the people's judgement approved the command of their blood, and the march of the flag went on!
>
> Florida came under the dominion of the Republic, and the march of the flag went on. The Cassandras prophesied every prophecy of despair we hear today, but the march of the flag went on!
>
> And now obeying the same voice that Jefferson heard and obeyed. . . . Our President today plants the flag over the islands of the sea, outposts of commerce, citadels of national security, and the march of the flag goes on![1]

The speech became a campaign document, with thousands of copies printed for distribution throughout the country.[2] It played a part in the elections, but from the standpoint of the speaker it was even more vital, for it was an important factor in his subsequent election to the United

[1] *Indianapolis Journal*, Sept. 17, 1898, p. 4.
[2] *Meaning of the Times*, p. 47.

States Senate. In the midst of that contest Senator Newton W. Gilbert, speaking in the Indiana Senate Chamber, said: "A few months ago I sat in a breathless audience and listened to a distinguished man as he described 'The March of the Flag.'"[1] Senator Gilbert joined with others to send that man to Washington.

Election to the Senate. The political campaign of 1898 was of particular interest to the people of Indiana because the legislature to be elected would select a United States Senator. Each party had a senator at the time, Senator Turpie having entered the Senate with Cleveland's election in 1892 and Senator Fairbanks with McKinley in 1896. Naturally, each party wished to gain control, and each had within its ranks a number of aspirants. Nine Republicans had already announced their candidacy when Beveridge decided that the lack of majority strength on the part of any one candidate might produce a deadlock that would naturally lead to the election of an outsider. With the assistance of several friends, he worked out a clever plan. John C. Shaffer later revealed the strategy: "We mapped out a campaign on this line; that Beveridge should go into every district in the State, help to elect to the legislature the member from that district, whether he was in favor of Judge Taylor, or Lew Wallace or any of the other candidates, but to get the member pledged to one thing: *that his second choice should be Albert J. Beveridge.*"[2]

Accordingly, Beveridge campaigned in every one of the districts in Indiana. At all times he spoke for the party and the favorite son candidates, never for himself, but he quietly secured from the legislators a promise that he should be their second choice. In November, the Republicans won, and when the expected deadlock developed and the second choices were finally voted, Beveridge was elected. Fortunately Beveridge had succeeded, not through the support of a political machine but through his independent efforts and political sagacity. Without restraining obligations, therefore, he could say in his formal speech to the legislature, following his election:

A Senator should never think of himself, but only of the republic and the perpetuity and progress of free institutions among mankind, which the Republic represents. . . .

Your senator is not the senator from Indiana alone. According to the Constitution, and according to the nature of nationhood, he is a Senator of the United States, from Indiana.

"The speech," said the *Indianapolis News*, "was in the Senator-elect's best style."[3]

[1] *Indianapolis Journal*, Jan. 18, 1899, p. 8.
[2] John C. Shafer, *Addresses in Honor of Albert J. Beveridge* (Indianapolis, 1917), p. 24.
[3] *Indianapolis News*, Jan. 18, 1899, p. 2.

Idealism was soon tempered with practicality. As Beveridge looked forward to his years in the Senate, he realized that he must now take a place beside men who were skilled in statecraft and experienced in politics and government. Most of them were older than he; many of them had been national figures for years. What place would he occupy in such company? Earnestly he desired to be a leader; he could never happily follow. But how could he achieve leadership in the Senate? Throughout his life Beveridge had known only one way to succeed in the achievement of his ambitions: hard, thorough, and painstaking preparation for every task and public utterance whenever possible. With characteristic determination he resolved, therefore, to prepare himself once more, with confidence that an opportunity would come to speak to the nation when he was ready.

"On the Philippine Question." To political observers in 1899, it became increasingly evident that the most absorbing topic of Congressional deliberation in the coming session would be the policy to be adopted relative to the future disposition of the Philippine Islands, acquired under the peace treaty with Spain. The treaty had been ratified in the Senate only after Bryan had persuaded certain Democratic members to vote for it, but Bryan's subsequent statements made it clear that he was opposed to the retention of the Islands—that he would make this an issue in the election of 1900. Senator George F. Hoar of Massachusetts, Carl Schurz, and others were organizing a league against "imperialistic" policies, toward which the administration seemed to be tending. The newspapers and the periodicals were filled with arguments reflecting every aspect of the complicated problem. Everyone discussed the issue. In this controversy, Beveridge saw his opportunity. With the forces of the administration and of the opposition in a quandary, he realized that a senator amply prepared and exceptionally well qualified to speak on the Philippine situation could seize leadership and exert real influence upon legislation. He decided to qualify himself for the opportunity. He had already declared himself an expansionist; he had already taken his stand with those who believed that the Philippines should be held by the United States under the American flag; he had already asserted that the islands were the key to the Asiatic trade that must be captured by the United States if the nation was to continue its commercial development. He now decided to visit the Philippines and secure first-hand information. No member of the Senate had ever been there; no one of his colleagues, therefore, could possibly know as much about the archipelago as he.

A drawback to the plan lay in the fact that he would have to be away from the United States for at least six months, an interval of time in which anything might happen politically. He resolved, therefore, to make so impressive a statement of his views that he could not be forgotten or overlooked during the time he was in the Far East. An opportunity for such a pronouncement came to him in the form of an invitation to address the Union League Club of Philadelphia. His address was entitled "The Republic that Never Retreats." In it he incorporated his arguments for colonial expansion. So much publicity and acclaim attached to his words that Bryan felt he must deliver an answer, and he did so in an address that he called "America's Mission."

In the meantime, Beveridge had sailed for the Philippines, where he spent 3 busy months observing every phase of life on the islands. On several occasions he was under fire with the American troops then attempting to subdue native insurgents. Meticulously he noted his observations in notebooks. Then the next 3 months were spent in the Orient, where he investigated potential markets and commercial possibilities. With this wealth of information, he returned to the United States, where he surprised the newspaper men by announcing: "You may say that I absolutely decline to express any opinion at the present time as to General Otis, the future of the Philippines, or anything else."[1] This decision he adhered to through the following months, although he did go to Washington at the request of the President to confer with him.

On December 4, 1899, Beveridge was sworn in as a member of the Senate. The following day, President McKinley sent his message to Congress in which he officially introduced the issue of American policy in the Philippines by saying: "The future government of the Philippines rests with the Congress of the United States. . . . It will be the duty of the Congress to construct a plan of government which shall establish and maintain freedom and order and peace. . . ."[2] The indefiniteness of the message made it evident that at the opportune moment, a party spokesman would be called upon to present the matter in greater detail.

On December 20 Senator Hoar, a militant anti-imperialist, introduced a resolution requiring the government of the United States "to abstain from interfering with the freedom and just rights of other nations or peoples."[3]

Shortly after, Beveridge countered with a resolution worded as follows:

RESOLVED: That the Philippine Islands are territory belonging to the United States; that it is the intention of the United States to retain them as such and to establish and maintain such governmental control throughout the Arch pelago as the situation may demand.[4]

[1] *Indianapolis Journal*, Aug. 10, 1899, p. 5.
[2] *Congressional Record*, Fifty-sixth Congress, First session, p. 34.
[3] *Ibid.*, p. 602, Sec. 8 of the resolution.
[4] *Ibid.*, SR53, p. 644.

"I desire," he said, "that the joint resolution shall lie on the table until next Tuesday, at the expiration of the morning hour, at which time I should like to submit some remarks upon it."[1]

As the noon hour approached on Tuesday, January 10, and the morning business was drawing to a close, the galleries of the Senate chamber began to fill rapidly. Beveridge's announcement that he would speak at this time had been given wide publicity and had occasioned much comment, especially in Washington. The undoubted understanding known to exist between the Senator and President McKinley in the White House gave the proposed utterance the status of an administration pronouncement. The public was also curious as to the information that Beveridge had collected on his visit to the islands and withheld so long. Many also wished to hear his maiden speech in the Senate. His wide reputation as a speaker had grown upon the consistency of his eloquence. In Congressional circles there was not only interest but amazement that a new member of the Senate should break the tradition of the conscript fathers and make an important speech before he had passed through a year of silence. The very audacity of the act, however, drew them to the chamber for the enactment of the scene.

When the hour of 12 had come, the floor of the chamber was crowded with senators and their friends from the House, public galleries were overflowing, and the diplomatic gallery was filled. There were many women, also, equally intent upon the proceedings. Secretary Gage, of the cabinet, came in with other high officials of the administration. Senator Beveridge arose and asked for the reading of his resolution. Instantly the animated undertone of conversation quieted. With a slow, sweeping glance about him at his audience, he began:

Mr. President: I address the Senate at this time because Senators and Members of the House on both sides have asked that I give to Congress and the country my observations in the Philippines and the Far East, and the conclusions which these observations compel; and because of hurtful resolutions introduced and utterances made in the Senate, every word of which will cost and is costing the lives of American soldiers.

Mr. President, the times call for candor. The Philippines are ours, "Territory belonging to the United States," as the Constitution calls them. And just beyond the Philippines are China's illimitable markets. We will not retreat from either. We will not repudiate our duty in the archipelago. We will not abandon our duty in the Orient. We will not renounce our part in the mission of the race. And we will move forward to our work, not howling out regrets, like slaves whipped to their burdens, but with gratitude for a task worthy of our strength, and thanksgiving to Almighty God that He has deemed us worthy of His work.

[1] *Ibid.*

Continuing, Beveridge stressed the commercial advantages awaiting American merchants in the islands and in the Far East. Then he vigorously called upon the government to support the armed forces, which were attempting to subdue the Filipinos and establish order. He urged reinforcements and ample military supplies. Above all, he demanded that members of the Senate cease their opposition to the war, with the words: "I say to those whose voices in America have cheered these misguided natives to shoot our soldiers down, that the blood of those dead and wounded boys of ours is on their hands. In sorrow rather than in anger, I say these words, for I earnestly believe that our brothers knew not what they did."

The future of the Philippines was next considered. Denying to the natives the capacity for self-government, Beveridge declared that the need was for a "strong and simple" government by Americans. This policy of colonial administration, he continued, was legally justified and constitutional. He concluded with a peroration on the mission of America. The following graphic description of him upon this occasion has been preserved:

Slight of form, short of stature, smooth of face, looking ten years younger than his age . . . speaking rapidly in a voice clear and musical as a silver bell, with an enunciation perfectly distinct, and in tones modulated to suit each particular phase of his remarks, the new Senator from Indiana won such a triumph as seldom comes to any public man. His manner was earnest, his delivery graceful, his few gestures, timely and effective. At intervals he drove home telling points with passionate fervor and dramatic force, but for the most part he employed the conversational tone that is now the favorite with the best orators.[1]

As Beveridge resumed his seat a storm of applause swept the galleries, which was prolonged to an unusual extent, although demonstrations of the kind were not ordinarily permitted in the Senate chamber. Senator Hoar was immediately recognized. Deeply moved by this acclaim for imperialism, to which he was unalterably opposed, he opened a bitter assault upon both the speaker and the speech. Later the *Nation* continued the attack with the statement: "There never was a more striking illustration of a man more 'inebriated with the exuberance of his own verbosity' than he now presents. For 'spread-eagleism' the senate chamber has never heard anything to equal that part of the speech in which he turns seer and interprets the meaning of expansion as a policy in national and world development."[2]

[1] *Indianapolis Journal*, Jan. 10, 1900, p. 1. Beveridge's voice was generally described as "metallic" rather than musical.—*Indianapolis Star*, Dec. 13, 1905. Clear, penetrating, and pleasant, it was somewhat sharp and crisp rather than full-volumed and organlike.

[2] *The Nation*, 70, (Jan. 11, 1900): 21.

To these attacks the *Indianapolis Press* replied: "Senator Beveridge could not have had a more effective endorsement of his speech than the criticism of Senator Hoar whose 'comment upon the youth of Indiana's senator, his glittering generalities, and want of common sense' fall flat and unavailing before the array of facts and arguments presented."[1] Edwin Wildman, in *Harper's Weekly*, likewise supported Beveridge, concluding his article thus: "They hurled epithets at him, called him the silver tongued orator, and likened his case to the parable of Satan leading the Savior into a high mount and tempting him, but his speech has not been answered and his leadership is acknowledged."[2]

Equally as intense as the clash on the issues involved was the controversy as to Beveridge's success as a speaker. "Mr. Dooley" set the pace in criticism by saying: "Well, sir, 'twas a gr-reat speech. 'Twas a speech ye cud waltz to. Even younger men thin Sinitor Beveridge had niver made grander orations."[3]

Subsequent judgment, however, confirmed the estimate of the correspondent of the Associated Press: "He justified the reputation which preceded him. He is an orator. That much is acknowledged even by those who hoped in their hearts that he would fail to measure up to the high standard the Senate required its members to reach who aspire to the designation of Orator. The future rests with him. No one else can mar it."[4]

From Beveridge's personal point of view, the address was a success. He was quoted by newspapers all over the country, and he was firmly established not only as governmental spokesman but as an authority on the Philippines and an outstanding advocate of expansion.

His colleagues in the Senate, however, were not willing that he should go unpunished for speaking so soon. When he essayed another important speech on the policy to be followed in Puerto Rico,[5] drawing another crowded gallery, all but six of the Republican Senators left the chamber.[6]

The crux of all this misunderstanding lay in two misconceptions that Beveridge held when he entered the Senate. First, he had, from the outside, considered the Senate as still carrying on the traditions of the Websterian period, wherein the great questions of the day were brought upon the floor for discussion and where those who wished to condemn or defend the policies rose to speak in a lofty and dignified fashion. But the Senate, as he soon came to find, was little more than a legislative business bureau.

---

[1] *Indianapolis Press*, Jan. 10, 1900, p. 6.
[2] Edwin Wildman, "Albert J. Beveridge," *Harper's Weekly*, 44, (Apr. 14, 1900): 349.
[3] F. P. Dunne, "Mr. Dooley," *Harper's Weekly*, 44, (Jan. 27, 1900): 92.
[4] *Indianapolis Journal*, Jan. 10, 1900, p. 2.
[5] *Congressional Record*, Fifty-sixth Congress, first session, Appendix, p. 279–286.
[6] Bowers, *op. cit.*, p. 129.

Policies were agreed upon in committee rooms and brought out for approval, not for argument. The occasional speeches were delivered largely for home consumption.

Again, Beveridge came to the Senate with a definite conception of ·its dignity, gravity, and governmental importance. To be a Senator, as he conceived it, was to dress with a frock coat and a top hat, as befitted a high officer of the Republic. He found the Senate filled with men in sack coats, who conducted the government's business during office hours. As a result, it took time for Beveridge to adjust himself to the Senate as he found it in 1900.

"*The Star of Empire.*" Senatorial differences were temporarily laid aside in the summer of that year, for another Presidential campaign was under way. William Jennings Bryan was again nominated to oppose President McKinley. In his speech of acceptance, he revived the issue of imperialism and declared that the United States should free the Philippines as they proposed doing in the case of Cuba.[1] To meet this challenge, the Republican leaders sent Beveridge to Chicago,[2] where he answered with an address on "The Star of Empire." In considering Bryan's principal argument, he said: "I speak for myself alone, but I believe that in this my voice is the voice of the American millions, as it is the voice of the ultimate future, when I say that Porto Rico is ours, and ours forever; and Cuba ought to have been ours, and ours forever. . . . And so my answer to Mr. Bryan's comparison is that, if we have made a mistake in Cuba we ought not make the same mistake in the Philippines."

Later he predicted that the United States would establish strong bonds with Cuba before granting her freedom. This statement was severely criticized by both Republicans and Democrats, but the Platt Amendment was passed within 3 months, doing this very thing.

Beveridge's Technique. Throughout the decade following, Beveridge spoke with the full maturity of his energy and power. Ever in demand to present his views or to lend his eloquence to the support of issues, he spoke constantly. Formal arguments and informal debate in the Senate, occasional addresses and campaign speeches kept him continually before the public. Beveridge enjoyed his popularity, and he labored assiduously to preserve and enhance his prestige. To every speaking engagement he brought the same meticulous and exhaustive preparation. He followed his own injunction that "the man or woman who presumes to talk to an audience should know more about the subject discussed than anybody and everybody in that audience."[3]

[1] "Imperialism," *Speeches of William Jennings Bryan*, II, 17–49.
[2] Bowers, *op. cit.*, pp. 132–133.
[3] Beveridge, *The Art of Public Speaking* (Boston, 1924), p. 25.

Knowledge alone, however, was not enough. The material gathered was carefully arranged and analyzed. Then for formal speeches, a manuscript was written out and revised. When the speech was to have political significance, he submitted copies to his trusted advisers for their comment and criticism.[1] The final revision was memorized and often practiced aloud. Fortunately for Beveridge, the memorization was not laborious. By reading his manuscript several times, he could absorb it almost verbatim. The fidelity with which the spoken words followed the manuscripts is attested by Fred E. Shortemeier: "I was a reporter on the *Indianapolis Star* for several years that Mr. Beveridge was actively engaged in public affairs. . . . He practically did not deviate at all from the typewritten manuscripts in delivering his addresses, although he did not keep a note before him. After preparing a speech, he seemed to know it by heart, even as to the very language."[2] As a result of this careful, painstaking period of preparation, it was said that Beveridge "never makes a poor speech."[3]

Interestingly enough, while the methods of preparation remained the same, Beveridge changed his speaking style. The change became pronounced in 1902. The period that preceded was one of exuberance, characterized by striking rhetorical passages in the grandiose manner; the period that followed, although equally grounded in strong emotion and equally effective in the direct and logical communication of thought, was eloquent by reason of the lucidity, the dignity, and the noble simplicity of the diction and because of the restrained and perfected delivery of the mature and accomplished orator. In the addresses already discussed in detail, he had perfected the technique of spellbinding, with its obvious faults of excessive and flamboyant rhetoric. Yet beneath these conspicuous passages, Beveridge always set out his arguments clearly, logically and forcefully arranged. His language was simple and easily understood. From his student days, he had studied the strong and natural simplicity of Lincoln's utterances and of favorite Biblical passages.[4] He was not unprepared, therefore, to follow the public taste when it began to demand the blunt, direct, and conversational style of the American businessmen who became dominant at this period.

[1] His speech on the Philippine question was read to John C. Shaffer; most of the important senatorial speeches were criticized by Albert Shaw and George W. Perkins; speeches of the Progressive campaign were submitted to Joseph Dixon; speeches of the 1922 campaign were reviewed by A. M. Glossbrenner.

[2] Letter to the author, Nov. 26, 1930.

[3] W. N. Brigance, "In the Workshop of Great Speakers," *American Speech*, August, 1926: 590.

[4] Of this study, Mr. Fred Shortemeier wrote: "He told me several times that the rhythm and music of his speeches came very largely from his having been a great reader of the Bible." —Letter of Nov. 26, 1930.

Period of Restraint

As early as 1902, Beveridge sensed the change and wrote his friend Leo G. Rothchild, "It appears to me that that period in my life of the spell-binding speech, the 'great cheers' speech, and the 'touch-to-tears' speech is over." He continued, "As to catching the crowd you will observe that my tendency for the last two years has been steadily toward simplicity of style and the elimination of mere phrases. It must keep on at that. The day of the other things has gone by for me."[1] Only once did he deliberately depart from this decision. This was in response to the insistence of some of his close personal friends that he close his campaign for the Senate in 1922 with his old-time eloquence.

Soon after 1902 Beveridge's addresses reflected the change not only in style but in arrangement. Previously each had had six structural divisions: (1) an introduction presenting the thematic idea, often epigrammatically expressed; (2) a brief narrative passage or one giving a swift word picture of the situation; (3) a statement of the issues and the position of the speaker regarding them; (4) then refutation of opposing contentions, (5) followed by his own arguments in support of his position; (6) and finally a peroration picturing America's opportunity under the proposed policy. He now abandoned this essentially classical arrangement for a simpler and less well-defined structure. Generally he opened with an introduction that struck the keynote to his speech; then he followed with a consideration of issues and solutions, in order, and concluded with a short exhortation to duty or the like.

This change in style and disposition did not alter his logic. He continued to build his arguments upon the same three major premises:

1. Whatever will make the United States the greatest nation on earth is desirable as a national policy.

2. Whatever contributes to the inherent welfare of the American people is constitutional.

3. Whatever challenges in any way the fundamental American institutions or the exercise of constitutional government should be condemned. From these points of view Beveridge urged the expansion of America's foreign trade, the tariff, the direct election of senators, woman suffrage, the regulation of the trusts and of big business, the governmental inspection of foods and drugs, the necessity of abolishing child labor, and the conservation of natural resources.

In developing his arguments, Beveridge preferred the method of generalization. It permitted him to support his arguments with the extensive material he gathered, and it fitted nicely into his compositional

[1] Letters to Leo G. Rothchild, Indianapolis, Mar. 26 and Apr. 7, 1902.

predilection for parallel units and repetition. For variety he used an occasional analogy.

Throughout Beveridge's years in the senate he was not only a formal orator but a vigorous and brilliant debater. To the latter activity he brought the same intensive preparation he gave to oratory. Because of this, Beveridge could pick flaws in the minute details of an opponent's arguments and refute them with his own extensive knowledge of the subject. This attention to detail did not prevent him from supporting the major proposal under consideration. Principles he always supported, even though they were subjected to minor modifications that he did not approve.

Beveridge as a Debater. The three most notable of Beveridge's senatorial debates were those with Senators Quay (1902–1903) and Foraker (1904) over the admission of Oklahoma, Indian Territory, Arizona, and New Mexico to statehood and the desperate insurgent Republican attack on the Payne-Aldrich tariff bill in 1909. Beveridge's skill was generally acknowledged. "Senators Dolliver, DePew and Beveridge," wrote Senator Foraker, who had so arduously opposed the latter, "were all great orators, but they were more than that. They were close and logical reasoners and by their entertaining speeches exercised great power of persuasion with respect to all of the debates in which they participated."[1] In the same vein, Albert Shaw declared that "never in recent times has debating in the United States Senate been on a higher plane of ability than in the session now ending."[2]

Beveridge, however, was even much more influential as a political campaigner. From 1884 to 1924 he participated in every national and Congressional canvass but one (1918). He officially opened and closed more Republican campaigns during his lifetime than any other member of his party. In 1908 alone, he delivered more than four hundred fifty political speeches, a record surpassed in extent only by Bryan and Roosevelt.[3]

Beveridge's early exchanges with Bryan have been recounted. Another long-range controversy followed Bryan's Madison Square Garden Speech in 1906, in which he advocated the governmental ownership of railroads. Beveridge answered him in Chicago, asserting that "American institutions are equal to the railroad situation." In late October Beveridge and Bryan both crossed Indiana. Beveridge's attitude toward the Great Commoner is interesting: "I have no patience with the abuse of Mr. Bryan. Mistaken

[1] Joseph Benson Foraker, *Notes of a Busy Life* (Cincinnati, 1916), II, 10.

[2] "Great Debating in the Senate," *Review of Reviews* 43 (March, 1911): 271.

[3] "In 1896 Bryan traversed 29 states, covered 18,000 miles and delivered five hundred speeches to an aggregate of 5,000,000 people."—D. S. Muzzey, United States of America (Boston, 1924), p. 527. Roosevelt in 1900 visited 567 towns, made 673 speeches, and spoke to over three million people.—C. F. Bacon, "Itinerant Speech-making in the Last Campaign," *Arena* 25 (April, 1901) 418.

in policy, he is yet a hero of conscience. At St. Louis he refused to sell his moral birthright for a mass of pottage. . . . And today he is the same undismayed soldier of conviction choosing to utter his thought however it may shatter his fortune."[1]

"*Pass Prosperity Around.*" As early as 1906 Beveridge had begun to oppose the tariff supported by the conservative element of his party. In the campaign of 1908 he had definitely promised revision. He was bitterly disappointed, therefore, when President Taft failed to support him against the Payne-Aldrich tariff bill, which revised many schedules upward rather than downward. His insurgency caused the President practically to read him out of the party. This came for Beveridge at an unfortunate hour, for his second term in the Senate was expiring, and in spite of the tremendous energy with which he entered the campaign for re-election, and even of Theodore Roosevelt's support, he was defeated. His defeat was one of the events that foreshadowed the break-up of the Republican party in 1912.

Beveridge, out of sympathy both with the administration and with its policies, joined with Roosevelt in his fight for the next Presidential nomination. Thwarted by President Taft's firm control of the party machinery, Beveridge became one of the leaders who launched the Progressive party and sent out its call for a national convention. "As the outstanding man to deliver the keynote address . . . Beveridge was selected by common consent," wrote Joseph Dixon, national chairman of the Progressive party.

His speech on that occasion was wholly his own production. He was in full touch and sympathy with the purposes of the movement, and no one questioned his undoubted ability to present our viewpoint in a masterly way. He read his speech over to me twice—for suggestions—first in a Chicago hotel and afterwards in New York City, but I do not recall that I made a single change or suggestion of any possible weight or moment. He had gone into retirement for a week during which he prepared the speech.[2]

The convention was unique in American politics. The delegates were drawn from both parties, but they were mostly Republicans. Many had been denied candidacy by the regular party machines; others were of the reform elements. They assembled for many individual reasons, but they were united in a desire to form a new party, with Theodore Roosevelt as its Presidential candidate. So sincere were they that each delegate paid his own expenses. At the opening session of the convention official delegates and Roosevelt supporters crowded into the auditorium until it was estimated that 10,000 people were present when the gavel sounded. Hundreds

---

[1] *Indianapolis News*, Oct. 5, 1906, p. 14.
[2] Joseph Dixon, in a letter to the author, Dec. 1, 1930.

of woman suffragettes filled the balconies. Although the heat was stifling, the enthusiasm was noisy and intense. To this audience, Beveridge presented the keynote of a new party.

His opening paragraph was so concise and epigrammatical that it became the "vest pocket platform" of the party:

. . . We stand for a nobler America. We stand for an undivided nation. We stand for a broader liberty, a fuller justice. We stand for social brotherhood as against savage individualism. We stand for an intelligent co-operation instead of a reckless competition. We stand for mutual helpfulness instead of mutual hatred. We stand for equal rights as a fact of life instead of a catchword of politics. We stand for the rule of the people as a practical truth instead of a meaningless pretense. We stand for a representative government that represents the people. We battle for the equal rights of man.

Beveridge then denounced the boss systems in the old parties—a denunciation in which they all concurred with equal vigor. He then set up, one by one, the planks of the new party. The reforms appealed at once to the intellectuals as humanitarian and desirable; to the old party men the reforms were campaign material that would influence the masses. The women were pleased with Beveridge's sentiments regarding them and his advocacy of equal suffrage. The delegates from different sections of the country were pleased with the national scope of the party and its possibilities. His closing appeal was for enlistment in a crusade for justice and humanity; and his closing words were from the first stanza of "The Battle Hymn of the Republic":

> He hath sounded forth the trumpet that shall never call retreat;
> He is sifting out the hearts of men before His judgment-seat;
> Oh, be swift, my soul to answer Him! Be jubilant, my feet!
> Our God is marching on.

The audience caught up his words in a swelling chorus of song.[1]

Had Albert J. Beveridge succeeded in one of the most challenging situations he had ever faced? "The answer came at the end," declared the *Outlook:* " . . . not in the applause, not in the cheers, but in the voices of men and women, from North and South, and East and West, singing the Battle Hymn of the Republic."[2] While sections of the press opposed the party and its platform, no reporter who was an eye witness at the convention denied the immediate emotional effect of Beveridge's speech, and

[1] Beveridge, while realizing the full value of this climax to his peroration, did not anticipate that the song would be caught up as it was and that the "Battle Hymn of the Republic" would become the marching song of the party.—Mrs. Albert J. Beveridge, Indianapolis, June 3, 1930.
[2] *The Outlook*, 101 (Aug. 24, 1912): 859.

few who commented upon it denied its inherent fairness, sincerity, and power. "Its effect on the delegates and the crowd of spectators was dramatic and overwhelming," said the *Post*.[1]

The convention nominated Theodore Roosevelt for the Presidency, and Beveridge was the party's candidate for the governorship of Indiana. Both took the platform and engaged in almost continuous speaking. When Roosevelt was shot in Milwaukee, Beveridge was summoned to take over his major appointments. Eloquence alone, however, as American history amply demonstrates, can seldom win an election. The Progressives were defeated in the election and later in the Congressional campaign of 1914. One of the last to abandon the lost cause was Beveridge. In 1916 he was reconciled to the Republican candidacy of Charles Evans Hughes and made a transcontinental speaking tour in his behalf. In 1920 he spoke for Harding, and in 1922 he engaged in a strenuous but losing campaign for his old seat in the senate.

Occasional Addresses. In the meantime he had attracted national attention in the field of historical biography with his *Life of John Marshall*. After his defeat in 1922, he undertook a biography of Abraham Lincoln. Thereafter his speaking was secondary to his literary labors. Occasionally he was prevailed upon to deliver his address on "The Bible as Good Literature" or on "The Art of Public Speaking." The conditions under which he would agree to appear were set forth in one of his letters:

> I make one uniform and iron-clad condition, whether I speak on this subject in Philadelphia or at an Indiana cross-roads church. That condition is:
>
> All churches must unite in a union service; the meeting must be held in the largest auditorium in the place; everybody must be invited and no charge made for admission and no collection taken.[2]

In his correspondence Beveridge always stated definitely that he was not "a professional public speaker or platform entertainer." On one occasion he wrote: "Perhaps I ought to say to you that I have never been on the lecture platform, never in my career have I delivered a lecture as such, and never under any circumstances accepted any compensation for a public address."[3]

On June 2, 1926, Beveridge delivered his last important address, opening the sesquicentennial celebration of the signing of the Declaration of Independence, reiterating his lifetime devotion to Constitutional government.

Beveridge achieved distinction in many fields of endeavor. He was a statesman, a legislator, a journalist, and a historical biographer, but

[1] *Chicago Evening Post*, Aug. 5, 1912, p. 1.
[2] Beveridge to Robert O. Justice, Oct. 2, 1926.
[3] Beveridge MS.

to the citizens of his own generation, he was preeminently an orator. For four decades he was the voice of American nationalism. Through the years his logical eloquence aided in molding public opinion and in establishing principles that are today firmly imbedded in the political philosophy of the Republic.

SELECTED BIBLIOGRAPHY

Beveridge's Life

Beveridge MS, correspondence of Albert J. Beveridge (1900–1927) notebooks, and an unpublished autobiography, in the possession of Mrs. Albert J. Beveridge, Beverly Farms, Mass.

Bowers, Claude G.: *Beveridge and the Progressive Era*, Boston, 1932.

Coffin, John A.: "Senatorial Career of Albert J. Beveridge," *Indiana Magazine of History*, 24 (1928): 159–185; 242–295.

Jones, Edgar DeWitt: *Lords of Speech*, New York, 1937.

Ross, Herold Truslow: The Oratorical Career of Albert J. Beveridge, a Ph.D. dissertation deposited at the State University of Iowa, Iowa City, Iowa, 1932. Appendix I, a complete biography of Beveridge; Appendix II, rare and unpublished speeches. Section treating years 1862–1885 published in "The Education of an Orator," *Quarterly Journal of Speech*, 18 (February, 1932): 70–82.

Tilden, Richard Arnold: *The Senatorial Career of Albert J. Beveridge*, Greencastle, Ind., 1928.

Thompson, Charles Willis: *Party Leaders of the Time*, New York, 1906.

Beveridge's Works

Beveridge, Albert J.: *The Art of Public Speaking*, New York, 1924; *Meaning of the Times*, Indianapolis, 1908, a collection of Beveridge's principal speeches; "Public Speaking," *Modern Eloquence*, 5: xiii–xxiv.

Ross, Herold Truslow: "The Oratorical Principles and Practices of Albert J. Beveridge," *Archives of Speech*, 1 (1936): 99–168.

Beveridge's Principal Addresses

"Answer to Altgeld," 1896, *Chicago Tribune*, Oct. 31, 1896.

"Middlesex Speech," 1898, *Meaning of the Times*, pp. 37–46.

"March of the Flag," 1898, *Meaning of the Times*, pp. 47–57; Reed, *Modern Eloquence*, 1928, XI, 372–377.

"Republic that Never Retreats," 1899, *Indianapolis News*, Feb. 14, 1899; Reed, *Modern Eloquence* (1900), I, 70–72.

"Star of Empire," 1900, *Meaning of the Times*, pp. 118–143.

"On the Philippine Question," *Meaning of the Times*, pp. 58–88; *Congressional Record*, Fifty-sixth Congress, first session, pp. 704–712; Shaw, *History of American Oratory*, pp. 573–578.

"Child Labor," 1907, *Meaning of the Times*, pp. 308–673; *Congressional Record*, Fifty-ninth Congress, second session, 1552–1554, 1792–1826, 1867–1883.

"Pass Prosperity Around," 1912, *Indianapolis Star*, Aug. 5, 1912.

"Speech Opening Republican Campaign of 1916," J. M. O'Neill, *Models of Speech Composition*, 1922, p. 372.

"Sesquicentennial Address," 1926, *Indianapolis Star*, June 3, 1926.

33

Robert M. La Follette

by CARROLL P. LAHMAN

Robert M. La Follette was born in Dane County, Wisconsin, June 14, 1855; his ancestry was chiefly Scotch-Irish and French Huguenot. He was educated in the local schools and the University of Wisconsin (B.S., 1879) and was admitted to the bar in 1880. He served as district attorney of Dane County, 1881–1884; in the United States House of Representatives, 1885–1891; and as governor of Wisconsin, 1901–1905, where he instituted direct primary, ad valorem taxation of public utilities, state regulation of railroads, merit system for state employees. He served in the United States Senate, 1906–1925, where he was active in connection with railroad, tariff, and finance legislation and in support of measures to aid agriculture and labor. He opposed United States entrance into the First World War, 1917, and opposed the Treaty of Versailles and League of Nations in 1919. In 1922 he secured a Senate investigation of naval oil leases; was leader of the insurgent movement within the Republican party, culminating in the national election of 1912, and was Independent Progressive candidate for President, 1924, receiving 4,822,900 popular votes and 13 electoral votes. He died in Washington, D.C., in 1925.

The Growth of a Political Leader

Robert La Follette's place in political history rests upon his leadership of the forces in American life devoted to the rights of the common man as opposed to what he called "special privilege." He had an almost mystical belief in the sound judgment of rank-and-file people when given all the facts. He did not start as a conscious disturber of the economic *status quo* or as an avowed reformer. He was a Republican member of the committee that framed the McKinley tariff, and it was only after his defeat for re-election and the beginning of a personal feud with Senator Philetus Sawyer over an alleged attempt at bribery by the latter that he began to sense the sinister connection between Big Business and politics.[1]

From then on, whether as organizer and leader of the victorious anti-machine faction of the Republican party in Wisconsin; as independent, outspoken member of the Congressional insurgent Republicans and then as recognized leader of the Progressive movement within the Republican party until its mantle fell on Theodore Roosevelt; as stubborn opponent of

[1] *La Follette's Autobiography* (Madison, 1913), pp. 163–164.

942

American entry into the First World War and of our adherence to the Treaty of Versailles; or as independent candidate for President in 1924, for him the basic issue was always the same: "the encroachment of the powerful few upon the rights of the many."[1]

Leader of the Progressive Revolt

The Progressive revolt during the Taft administration, dramatized in the fight against the Payne-Aldrich tariff and in the curbing of the powers of the Speaker of the House of Representatives, found Senator La Follette a seasoned veteran in such a struggle. A number of states had taken the lead in passing various reform measures, particularly in the field of railroad regulation. Popular resentment at the control of government by business and at the reactionary drift of the Taft administration was fanned into an ever hotter fire by the speeches, on Senate floor and public rostrum, of the insurgent leaders. The Populist movement had been swallowed by Bryanism, but Bryan was no longer the major force he once had been, and the country seemed ready for a new reform movement within the Republican party.

In the forefront of the fight none was more active than La Follette, and Wisconsin was pointed to as the best example of what could be accomplished under progressive leadership. The reforms achieved there had been won only in the face of the most determined opposition by corporate interests, old-line political leaders and organization, and to some extent even the national Republican administration. To meet the power, the prestige, and the wealth of his opponents called for skillful leadership on La Follette's part.

One of his greatest assets was his ability to analyze human nature and his capacity to adapt his appeal to the wants and interests of real people, including special groups like the farmers, small businessmen, and such racial groups as the Scandinavians and Germans, both numerous in Wisconsin.

Raised on a farm in a strongly Norwegian community, he knew farmers and their ways of thinking and had some knowledge of the Norwegian language. His belief in agriculture as the cornerstone of a sound democracy was Jeffersonian in its intensity. His attacks on the political machine and his constructive proposals for the democratization of the nominating process were adapted to such an audience. He sensed the increasing popular antagonism to high-handed railroad procedures and the abuses of Big Business and magnetized the antipass struggle already launched into a veritable crusade that eventually encompassed equalized taxation and state regulation. The Populistic ferment of the Middle West found indigenous

---

[1] *Ibid.*, p. 760.

expression in Wisconsin in the movement led by La Follette. For both ideological and practical reasons he operated within, instead of outside, the Republican party.

He showed his appreciation of the essentially conservative temper of the Wisconsin electorate in the avoidance of radical proposals and in the advancing of only one issue or, at most, a very limited number at a time. Partly for this reason he was more successful as governor than as Presidential candidate, when his platform contained a wide assortment of planks.

Background and Training

For leadership in the Wisconsin and national Progressive movements La Follette was fitted by both temperament and training. Descendant in the fourth generation of ancestors in America predominantly Scotch-Irish and French Huguenot, he came of a hardy pioneer stock. His grandfather left Kentucky as an abolitionist. His father was active in the young Republican party until his death, when Robert, his youngest son, was only a baby. Through his widowed mother he had inculcated a pride in family honesty and high principles. She, too, set him an example of industry and good judgment.[1]

He grew up on a near-frontier farm, where he shared the responsibilities of its management with his mother and did the manual labor that later gave him a feeling of kinship and understanding with the mass of voters who work with their hands.[2]

His early education, received in one-room country and village schools and two private schools, was somewhat better than that of the average farm boy of the time, but it was not enough to admit him to the state university without further preparation. He early showed ability in reciting poetry at community gatherings, a special favorite being the dramatic poem "The Polish Boy." He received the training afforded by participation in such community organizations as the semireligious, total-abstinence Order of Good Templars. He was apparently repelled from formal religion by the overzealous piety of a sanctimonious stepfather.[3]

Likewise, he was early influenced by the spirit of the times—not merely by the usual democratic freedom of pioneer agricultural life but by the agitation of such current movements as the Grangers, which left an indelible impression.[4]

[1] *Ibid.*, pp. 147, 312.
[2] *Ibid.*, p. 308.
[3] Personal interviews with Albert O. Barton and Robert M. La Follette, Jr.
[4] *La Follette's Autobiography*, p. 19.

Robert M. La Follette

During his years as an undergraduate at the University of Wisconsin he continued his public recitations; took part in amateur dramatics on campus and off; had his hopes of a career on the stage dashed by John McCullough's dictum that he was too small in stature; owned, managed, and edited the university paper; won the Interstate Oratorical Contest with his character analysis of Iago; won the heart of a less dramatic but more studious class-mate, Belle Case, of Baraboo, who later became his wife and lifelong astute political counselor. So much time had been spent on extracurricular speech work, in attending plays at Milwaukee and Chicago, and in visiting court that the man upon whom his alma mater was to confer the degree of Doctor of Laws 22 years later was allowed to graduate only when a tie vote of the faculty was broken in his favor by President Bascom.[1]

His winning of the Interstate contest stood him in good stead on that vote, as did the reputation he had gained by it when he was elected district attorney 18 months later.

His political methods then and later as Representative in Congress at first grew out of ignorance of the conventional "political game" but soon became based on the conviction of the simple rightness of going directly to the people. In this procedure, whether by personal conference or public address, he showed himself to be highly effective. In first ignoring and then defying the local boss he revealed something of the independence, courage, and stubbornness that marked his subsequent career. As for his political philosophy, it matured slowly. Once formed, however, it remained con-sistent and inflexible.

Methods and Personality

With the possible exception of the direct primary, La Follette, as leader of the Wisconsin Progressive revolt, was not the originator of the issues that he carried through. Even in that field there was already a sizable body of public opinion hostile to the devious, secret methods of party politics. It was La Follette's role to energize, direct, and lead the democratic sympa-thies of pioneers and the sons of pioneers into a practical program of con-crete accomplishment. While he voiced the inarticulate resentment of equilitarian farmers, laborers, and small businessmen against political and economic abuses in the state, he showed strength in offering positive remedies. He was destructive only to clear the way for constructive substitutes.

Lasswell says that if we wish to classify a leader, we should first see "what form of activity means the most to him."[2] On such a basis La

[1] Rasmus Anderson, *Life Story of Rasmus B. Anderson* (Madison, 1915), p. 610.
[2] H. D. Lasswell, *Psychopathology and Politics* (Chicago, 1930), p. 53.

Follette would not be classed as a theorist. Rather, he wanted to see things accomplished, laws passed, abuses ended.

During the 5 years that he was governor of Wisconsin he made the following record of legislative and executive achievements:

First state-wide direct primary law in the United States.

Equitable railroad taxation.

Thoroughgoing railroad regulation by an appointive state commission.

Progressive inheritance tax to take the place of an earlier one held unconstitutional.

Merit system established in the state civil service.

First legislative reference and bill-drafting service in any state.

Corrupt-practices legislation strengthened.

Drastic anti-lobby statute.

Greatly increased financial support of education.

Appointment of women to various significant state positions.

Use of trained experts in both advisory and administrative positions.

Pioneer conservation measures.

Preliminary steps for a state income tax.

Quite as significant as these immediate accomplishments is the fact that they did not end with his leaving the governorship. The program of advanced legislation and administration went steadily forward under his successors until Wisconsin came to be commonly regarded as the social and political laboratory of the nation.

The foundation of such an immediate and continuing record was his basic political method of going directly to the voters—the outgrowth of his profound faith in the soundness of the common people, once they understood the issues. To give them understanding he gave them facts, often unadulterated figures and statistics at great length or in unbelievable quantity. To spread the facts he employed personal and form letters, organized a literary bureau, sowed the state down with pamphlets, engineered the establishment of first a weekly and then a daily newspaper,[1] and, preeminently, took to the hustings for strenuous weeks of personal speechmaking.

With education of the voters went organization. Possessing an almost uncanny memory for names and faces, he developed an enormous personal acquaintance over the state and from it forged a close-knit, well-oiled organization that for political effectiveness rivaled, if it did not exceed, the old machine against which he inveighed. This organization, like the Progressive program, continued to function with little diminution of effectiveness after La Follette went to Washington. By his directions and suggestions and through his influence, sensitively felt and interpreted by able local lieutenants, he remained its actual head until the time of his death. "Bob"

[1] *The State*, 1897; *Milwaukee Free Press*, 1901. *La Follette's Magazine* first appeared in 1909.

became "Old Bob," but his hand was never far from the throttle of the machine.[1]

La Follette was always the practical politician. The resourcefulness that had made him famous as a trial lawyer he carried into his political battles. He learned from bitter experience the methods employed against him, and he bettered the instruction. His sobriquet of "Battling Bob" was well earned. Plans were made with utmost care, and here his ability to foresee and checkmate his opponents' moves were a source of constant wonderment. He was forever on the offensive. Once he was in the governor's chair, he relaxed not a whit in his tireless activity, his attention to practical details, his strategy of going to the people with issues, and he did not hesitate to use the perquisites of office and power to advance his ends. He was not content to be a figurehead executive and frankly used all the influence at his disposal to secure legislation that he believed was for the public good. Long, carefully prepared, and elaborately documented messages to the legislature; personal conferences with individual members; special messages and veto messages that alternately recommended, exhorted, and excoriated; organizing of local sentiment in members' districts to be exerted on behalf of the desired legislation; and, on the public platform, the reading of roll calls to let the people know how their representatives voted—these were the chief devices in his strategic arsenal.

Such methods dramatized La Follette's appeal to the state, but they at times alienated support. He had a well-earned reputation for being uncompromising, and he did not allow considerations of personal feeling to stand in the way of driving an issue through to victory. He seems to have been oversuspicious of the motives of men not in his camp and did little or nothing to heal the ever-widening breach. The Wisconsin warfare was long and bitter, rendered more so by the Progressive leader's unyielding tactics.

He, of course, was not the conventional party head, aiming at harmony at any cost, including the submersion of specific issues beneath vague declarations and glittering generalities. Instead he led the Progressive revolt within the Republican Party until it became the dominant element in the party. Always it was a fighting front on which he served, and the constant struggle tended to unify his followers.

They were unified, too, about their leader's personality. For the rank-and-file "Half-breeds," as the conservatives or "Stalwarts" called the progressives, La Follette and the reforms he espoused were indistinguishable. For them La Follette *was* reform. He who had been personally popular as university student, district attorney, and Congressman carried the same warm, vivid, and magnetic personality into the larger arena of state politics.

[1] Personal interviews with former Congressman John M. Nelson and William T. Evjue, editor of the Madison *Capital Times*.

He possessed the ability of kindling warm affection and deep devotion on the part of very diverse followers—young university students and grizzled veterans like A. R. Hall, railroad workers and rising lawyers, horny-handed farmers, and members of college faculties. It was not without significance that thousands over the state knew him familiarly as "Bob." He met in large measure Young's requirement that "the leader must be able so to appeal to the imagination of his followers that they identify themselves with him and voluntarily follow his lead."[1]

He was forever doing the spectacular and unexpected. He liked to surprise the public and to steal a march on his opponents. His liking for the dramatic and his adeptness in its use is so commonly agreed upon by all commentators that only a few examples need be given. His unheard-of barnstorming of county fairs in the fall of 1897 is one. His delay for 4 years, while rumor grew, in revealing his famous railroad letter in 1900 is another.[2] Then there were such precedent-shattering innovations as reading his message to the legislature in person, his domination of the Republican state central committee and the strong-arm methods at the state convention of 1904, his open bid for Democratic votes and his endorsement of Democratic candidates, his *conditional* acceptance of the United States Senatorship. These are a few. Some of his publicity-getting methods made the judicious grieve, but on the whole they were highly effective in winning public attention and support and in disconcerting the opposition.

Another point should be made in connection with La Follette's dramatizing his appeal. He himself not only stood for action and a positive program in the minds of his followers, but he possessed the ability to make them feel that they too were an essential part in the struggle. They, as free-born American citizens, had a duty and also a personal economic stake in the conflict. They were not mere side-line spectators; they belonged on the team, and the game would be lost without their help. Such an emphasis is inescapable in speech after speech in various campaigns. The note was even stronger in personal conference.[3]

Speech Training and Leadership

La Follette the political leader and La Follette the public speaker are inseparable. Without his power in public speech he never could have dramatized his message effectively and so could scarcely have won such a popular following. Without his desire for a political career and his active championing of political issues, the speaking ability cultivated since the

---

[1] Kimball Young, *Social Psychology* (New York, 1930), p. 383.

[2] *La Follette's Autobiography*, pp. 233–237.

[3] Personal interviews with Emil Baensch, former lieutenant governor, and ex-Congressman John M. Nelson; *Milwaukee Journal* quoted in *Wisconsin State Journal*, May 20, 1903.

days when he "spoke pieces" as a small boy on the farm would have gone into other channels—theatrical or forensic. Two very good reasons gave public speaking the central place among his procedures. One was his proficiency in its use and his realization of its power. The other was necessity. Newspapers of the state fluctuated in their attitude toward him, but in general the press, especially in the larger cities, was hostile after the fight grew hot. To get his message to the people he had to carry it to them by word of mouth.

Despite his reputation at the time as a forceful and effective trial lawyer, his addresses at special occasions while governor and United States Senator, his hundreds of Chautauqua and lyceum addresses over a period of 25 years, La Follette's permanent reputation as a speaker rests almost entirely on his deliberative speaking. As a matter of fact, most of his speaking was essentially that. Aside from his literary lecture on Hamlet, which he gave infrequently through the years, he had just one Chautauqua address—that on "Representative Government," an extemporaneous recital of the fight for good government, first in Wisconsin and then at Washington, and a persuasive portrayal of state and national conditions that were undermining representative government. When he read his long and detailed messages to the legislature, although he delivered them with all the power of oral interpretation that he possessed, their content was directed quite as much to the larger reading audience of the state as to the lawmakers actually before him. Even in his remarks on special occasions there was very often this same serious underlying note. No matter how much he might enjoy the man-to-man relationship of a speaking situation, speaking for him was serious business and a means to an end. His speeches and gubernatorial messages were designed to influence his hearers' thinking and acting.

Such an attitude is not surprising in view of his ambitious nature and his sensitiveness to human needs. The ideas he advanced grew out of first-hand contact on the farm and among farmers with Midwestern agrarian discontent with low prices, high transportation rates, and the growth of Big Business. His democratic, equalitarian leanings were strengthened by the forces he encountered at the University of Wisconsin, where President John Bascom unceasingly preached to the students their civic obligation to the state, and where, as a freshman, La Follette had led a successful anti-fraternity revolt.

"I owe what I am," said La Follette in later years, "and what I have done largely to the inspiration I received while there."[1]

John Bascom was himself an effective speaker, who took an active part in current social and economic affairs and who, both by precept and example, stood staunchly for substance and sincerity in speaking. With the

[1] *La Follette's Autobiography*, p. 26.

admiration that Bob La Follette felt for Dr. Bascom, the older man's indirect influence on his speaking was significant.

The training afforded by the University rhetorical and literary society work was probably similar to that received by hundreds of other college men throughout the country at that period, but a close friend and classmate questions whether his instructors in this field greatly influenced his speaking.[1]

Various people, however, apparently stimulated and helped mold young La Follette's literary tastes: James Smith, the country schoolteacher who lived on the La Follette farm in Primrose Township and was a lover of Burns and Shakespeare; George Anderson, the old man whose horse and cow Bob tended when the La Follettes first moved to Madison and who transmitted some of his love for Burns and enjoyment of Scotch dialect to his young friend; Major Charles G. Mayers, talented Englishman who sponsored amateur theatricals in which La Follette participated; Judge A. B. Braley, Shakespearean student and public reader.[2]

Then there were the speakers that he heard in Madison, of whose influence he himself speaks in his *Autobiography*. Chief Justice Edward G. Ryan's warning of the power of corporate wealth, delivered to the graduating law class of the University in 1873, profoundly impressed him as an eighteen-year-old country boy. Just after he was graduated from the university he heard James A. Garfield and felt that he was more than a mere politician. As a sophomore he had his first chance to hear Robert G. Ingersoll, in the tumultuous Hayes-Tilden campaign of 1876. Years later he wrote:

I would not have missed it for every worldly thing I possessed. And he did not disappoint me. . . . I cannot remember much that he said, but the impression he made upon me was indelible. . . .

Ingersoll had a tremendous influence upon me, as indeed he had upon many young men of that time. It was not that he changed my beliefs but that he liberated my mind. . . . [3]

In his early years he was interested in more than Ingersoll's ideas. He "played the sedulous ape" to capture some of Ingersoll's style, for in preparing his senior-year oration on Iago he read everything of Ingersoll's that he could get his hands on.[4]

Other experiences that apparently exerted an effect in the direction of practical, direct deliberative speaking were his listening to Congressional

---

[1] Personal interview with Judge J. B. Simpson, of Shullsburg, Wis.

[2] Personal interview with Albert O. Barton, former secretary to La Follette.

[3] *La Follette's Autobiography*, pp. 16–17, 22–24, 33–36. Quoted by permission of the Progressive Publishing Co., Madison, Wis.

[4] Personal letter, July 14, 1938, from A. N. Hitchcock, Wisconsin, '80.

debate before taking his seat in the House of Representatives and his careful reading of Elliot's debates on the Constitution and the speeches by Lincoln and Douglas.[1] He made an enviable reputation as a speaker while serving in the lower house of Congress.[2]

It is interesting to note what La Follette himself said about speaking. Unlike Bryan and Beveridge, two progressive contemporaries who placed great reliance on the spoken word, he never delivered a lecture or wrote a treatise expounding his views as to the requisites of good public speaking. All that we can find are brief expressions here and there of views uttered at different times and under various circumstances.[3]

When he was interested in the drama as a young man he wrote:

> The truly great reader like the truly great actor is more than a mere inter-preter of the author. At most—long and short—all of the speeches of the prominent characters of a play furnish but a mere outline of the personality of that character. . . . "Thought is deeper than all speech, feeling deeper than all thought." The great reader with a truly creative mind and wealth of feeling fills out this mere outline into a full-orbed man or woman.[4]

In a commencement address to Howard University law graduates while a first-term Congressman, he insisted that the gift of fluency and moving emotional appeal were not enough; nothing could take the place of thorough preparation and knowledge of the facts and the law. When he helped coach university oratorical contestants in later years, he worked for form and polish through painstaking practice in gesturing and in vocal effects.[5]

As an experienced lawyer he paid tribute to the training received from participating in college debate, and as governor he told a mass meeting of students to study public speaking, because "it is the man on the platform who is able to express his convictions . . . who holds the balance of power."[6] Only a few weeks before his death he wrote: "I have no sympathy with, nor confidence in, the fellow who pretends that he gets the best results on the inspiration of the moment. He may have a flash of mental ecstasy while under the intellectual stress of speaking, but he is more likely to have a brain fluke—with a mediocre result."[7]

[1] *La Follette's Autobiography*, pp. 51–52.

[2] See quotations in campaign literature for 1890 and 1900 in the Wisconsin State Historical Library.

[3] Personal interview with Robert M. La Follette, Jr.

[4] Quoted by Belle Case La Follette, *La Follette's Magazine*, December, 1925, p. 192. Used by permission of the Progressive Publishing Co., Madison, Wis.

[5] Personal conference with H. H. Jacobs, the University of Wisconsin representative for 1893 in the Northern Oratorical League.

[6] University of Wisconsin *Daily Cardinal*, Dec. 20, 1899; *Madison Democrat*, May 10, 1905.

[7] *La Follette's Magazine*, June, 1926, p. 89. Quoted by permission of the Progressive Publishing Co., Madison, Wis.

Genuineness, depth of feeling, thorough preparation in both content and delivery—these are about all the really definite suggestions that we can gain from what La Follette himself said.

Methods of Preparation

What was his own method of preparation for speaking? For important messages and political speeches the first step was to call on authoritative sources for accurate information. Often special research was done by someone, usually a young university-trained man, designated for the task. The next step was for him and Mrs. La Follette—for on such occasions they often worked together—to surround themselves with endless stacks of source material and bury themselves in personal research away from interruptions. For ideas to be included he also welcomed and solicited suggestions from trusted friends and advisers. If they seemed good, they were accepted, but not until they were worked over and incorporated in his own way. He wrote out most of his speeches in longhand, although he also dictated to one or two faithful stenographers who were long with him. He was a slow writer, taking great pains to find the right word to express his thought. The first draft, if time allowed, was submitted to a few close advisers for criticism. Of course, he reserved the right to accept or reject such suggestions, but many were accepted. Mrs. La Follette's role was especially important here, for it was she, to a considerable extent, who put the final stamp of approval on the text of both speeches and other campaign documents.

Not only did La Follette solicit suggestions on the ideas and wording of a speech; at least in the early days he sought criticism of his actual speaking. Until his death Sam Harper, his law partner, thus acted as one such critic and counselor.

When time allowed, he liked to have an hour or so to relax and rest at a hotel before his speech, but in the rush of campaigns this, of course, was usually impossible.[1]

Speech Content and Style

The care with which La Follette prepared his cases as a lawyer influenced his preparation for deliberative speaking. He realized that it was "incumbent upon the reformer who seeks to establish a new order to come equipped with complete mastery of all the information upon which the established order is based."[2]

[1] Data for this discussion of La Follette's preparation come from the following sources: Junius Wood, *Chicago Daily News*, Aug. 18, 1924; Fola La Follette, "Robert M. La Follette—My Father," *Twentieth Century Magazine*, April, 1912, pp. 515–519; Barton, *La Follette's Winning of Wisconsin*, p. 271; personal interviews with Frank H. Bryant, Fred L. Holmes, John J. Hannan, A. T. Rogers, A. O. Barton, Robert La Follette, Jr.

[2] *La Follette's Autobiography*, pp. 444–445

The result was evident in both content and structure, with an organization that led his hearers and readers easily from one idea to the next in language that was crisply businesslike and straightforward. As he grew in experience, it is possible to trace a gradual change in his manner of speech, from the more to the less ornate, from the general to the specific, from appeals to old party shibboleths to pointed discussion of current issues that affected individual hearers. The pictorial and emotional phraseology found in university orations and certain early political and Congressional speeches largely disappeared. Not that emotional appeal was no longer present—for that remained one of his strongest characteristics—but it came through other concepts and through the speaker's own personal force in the use of voice and body.

La Follette's ideas were developed by explication and elaboration and by the copious use of authorities, factual evidence, and statistics. During the height of the battle over railroad rates, they were heavily loaded with detailed figures, but in general, despite the common statement that he regularly deluged his audiences with statistics, concrete evidence of this sort was used only in such amounts and at such points in the speech as could be assimilated by a serious-minded audience.

Probably his single most significant characteristic was the skillful use of adaptation. As a speaker he had the ability to voice popular sentiments for the inarticulate mass in terms that they understood. His ideas were within their comprehension, and the motives to which he appealed were both altruistic and selfish: save and purify representative government in the commonwealth of Wisconsin, and vote for your own economic interests against the secret schemes and greed of political machines and high-handed, wealthy railroad corporations. There was something of class appeal, but this was so interwoven with appeals to disinterested citizenship as largely to avoid giving that impression. The speaker did not hesitate to suggest a specific course of action to his listeners: vote for men who represent *your* interests. And then he often named the candidate who he believed could be trusted or the one who had let the people down in the last legislature.

Thus, at the end of the strenuous campaign of 1902, in his Milwaukee speech of November 1, La Follette admitted that it was not conventional to denounce members of his own party:

But I believe the people have a right to know when their interests are not represented. . . .

Now the question is up to you. You should find out how the men who wish to represent you in the legislature stand upon these important questions. . . . Look out for your own interests. The time to do so is the present hour. But I would not appeal to you on this ground, although it means $1,000,000 a year to the tax-payers of the state, but I would appeal to you on the ground that you should preserve your representative government and that there should be elected men who would not take their orders from any lobby and who would owe allegiance to the people.[1]

This vitalizing of his hearers' deep-laid desires was highly concrete. When La Follette discussed freight rates in a given county he gave exact comparative figures for that county as compared with those for points at similar distances from market in states with regulated rates. He stressed the products produced and consumed in that section. He translated the over-charge in terms of taxes on an acre of farm land, on the income of laboring men. In this way did dry figures come home to his listeners and make them want to do something about the conditions they revealed.

It was during his off-year educational campaigning for state railroad regulation in 1903 that, as governor, he made this application for his hearers at Antigo, in the northern part of the state:

In 1900 Langlade county had 6,357 acres seeded to oats and harvested 198,580 bushels of oats. This is an average of 31 bushels to each acre. As it costs you 1.23 cents per bushel more to produce and market your oats here, on account of exorbitant freight rates, than it does in Iowa, your loss from this source amounts to over 38 cents per acre. Now, what do these 38 cents per acre mean? It means, first, that your net profits from your efforts are reduced by this amount. It means that this extra reduction in your profits reduces in turn the value of your land. . . . For the purpose of raising oats, therefore, your land, under your present freight rates, is worth $6.33 per acre less than if you had as low rates as the Iowa farmers are enjoying. Had you enjoyed the benefit of the same rate for the same service as the Iowa farmers, it would mean that the 6,357 acres seeded to oats in this county last year would be worth $40,239 more than they are at present. Would not that addition to the value of the land of this county mean something to you?[2]

In public address and in messages to the legislature La Follette showed great expertness in identifying himself with the people's cause and in separating the sheep and the goats among public men, newspaper editors, and the general public on this same basis. Since he and his supporters were *for* the people, their opponents *ipso facto* were *against* the people.

In his long and exhaustive message to the legislature in 1903, Governor La Follette employed this technique skillfully. "Efforts may be further continued to obstruct the course of justice," he said as he demanded redemption of platform pledges for tax reform.

These failing, as a last resort efforts will be made to compromise. There has been given into our hands a trust to discharge. Difference of opinion may arise in the performance of public duty upon questions of policy. This is not a question of policy. The railroad companies of this State owe to the State more than a million

[1] *Milwaukee Free Press*, Nov. 2, 1902.
[2] *Milwaukee Free Press*, Sept. 9, 1903.

dollars a year. The people want a million dollars a year, because it is the sum owing. They are not to be wheedled by any soft phrases about "conservatism." There is nothing to compromise. Equal and just taxation is a fundamental principle of republican government. The amount due as taxes from railroads and other public-service corporations should be paid, and paid in full, and I am confident the legislation to secure that payment will be promptly enacted.[1]

His legal training in cross-examination and rebuttal stood him in good stead on the public platform. Almost without exception he ignored all personal attacks and refused to answer them, from the platform or otherwise. When it came to attacks on the principles and program for which he was contending, however, he not only met but anticipated them. Hence in many of his speeches much time was given to the answering of possible and actual objections. His chief reliance in refutation was on general reasoning, but he also used factual evidence to good advantage and at times called in question the consistency and even the good faith of his opponents.

It was in opening his 1902 campaign against Mayor Rose, of Milwaukee, that he thus answered the Democratic party's platform argument that the direct primary would give cities a disproportionate influence in the choice of candidates:

This argument always comes from some city politician who is always much worried about the country voter. It is based upon the claim that the city voter has an advantage in getting to the polls. The farmer must travel a long distance, perhaps over poor roads, and often in bad weather. But how about these disadvantages under the caucus and convention system? In order that his influence shall be felt at all in making nominations the farmer must attend at least half a dozen caucuses and several conventions covering nearly the entire season from spring to fall in his busiest time. This solicitude of the city-bred politician for the country voter lacks the stamp of sincerity. . . .

As to the relative domination of cities in nominations by caucuses and conventions as compared with nominations by direct vote, the fact is of interest that in the recent contests the city of Milwaukee gave 92 out of 144 of her votes to a candidate for governor in one state convention and 93 out of 110 to another candidate for governor in another state convention. Would she have been likely to vote with greater unanimity, would her influence have been more potent as against the country voters under a primary election?[2]

Two years later, when the fight had grown even hotter and more personal, La Follette refuted charges against himself so far as they were connected with the issue of railroad regulation. The verbatim report quoted

[1] Message of Robert M. La Follette, governor of Wisconsin, delivered to the legislature January 15, 1903.
[2] Text of speech given in campaign folder in Wisconsin State Historical Library.

throws interesting light on the speaker's extemporaneous style and how he secured humorous touches without resorting to funny stories.

After making clear the record of court decisions in protecting common carriers from unreasonable restrictions, he said to a great Milwaukee audience:

Now, the only thing that I haven't been called in this long struggle is a fool. (*Laughter and applause.*) And what a miserable, contemptible ninny a man would be to put years into a struggle to get on the statute books a law that would be smashed into smithereens by the supreme court in twenty minutes after they'd heard that the law was of the kind which they say I'm trying to pass, and that wreck of a statute would stand there through all time to come as a monument to the folly of the man who had helped to get it there. (*Great Applause.*)

Now, they say that I'm awfully ambitious, and I am. (*Great applause.*) But I'm not ambitious to earn that kind of a place in history. (*Laughter and applause.*) I'll tell you frankly here tonight I'll be very glad indeed, I am very anxious indeed, to connect my name, with others, in getting upon the statute books some legislation here in Wisconsin that will be just and fair to the railroads and just and fair to the people, that will give a new impetus to manufacturing, to agriculture, and to all the industries of the state and will push the state forward. I'm ambitious to connect my name with legislation that will accomplish that, because I know it will stand there on the statute books long years after I'm dead—will be a better monument, a better legacy to leave to my children than anything else I could leave them. (*Prolonged applause and cheers.*)[1]

Despite the fact that during these strenuous years of La Follette's winning of Wisconsin the combative note was preeminent in his speeches, there were other notes as well. When he campaigned for the national Republican ticket in 1896 and 1900, once as the defeated and once as the successful contender for the gubernatorial nomination, he enunciated conventional party doctrines in conventional, conciliatory, and unifying party terms. He praised his own party and his own candidates, and he attacked the policies and alleged fallacies of Bryan and the Democrats. His speeches were lucid and apparently highly effective, but they were less deadly serious and decidedly less militant than were speeches on state issues when he was speaking as the leader of a fighting faction within the party.

Even then, however, he was too keen a judge of popular psychology and of persuasive techniques always to attack. In his messages to the legislature he knew the value of a tribute to the members' disinterested attachment to the public welfare and of a plea for cooperation between the executive and legislative departments. He was not above complimenting his audiences similarly, but in restrained terms that avoided the appearance of currying favor.

[1] *Milwaukee Free Press*, Nov. 5, 1904.

Robert M. La Follette

He seldom made admissions or concessions, but he was skillful in his use of the "common-ground" technique to win acceptance of propositions by public-spirited voters of all parties. Particularly noticeable, even in some measure in the campaigns of 1896 and 1900, was his nonpartisan appeal for support of principles. Thus he won over to his cause so many thousands of "fair-minded" Democrats that he practically disrupted that party in the state.

The following example of his method is taken from the verbatim report of the first speech La Follette ever gave in Milwaukee, at the close of the campaign of 1896:

Now, my friends, why are you here tonight? I know you have come here tonight to reason together upon what is best for this country of ours. For I say to you that I believe everyone of you in this audience, and I don't care what may be your political faith, I don't care under what banners you have been marching, I believe that everyone of you—Populist, Prohibitionist, Democrat alike—has the same desire for good government and the same desire for the best interests and the advancement of this country as the Republicans have. . . .

Now as to the cause [of the country's business depression], I entreat you, as you have come in here tonight desiring your country's good, to hear me; and if the reasons which I give for the opinions which I hold are not good, then I do not ask you to agree with me. In this country of ours, Mr. Chairman, no man's opinions are worth a whit more than the reasons which are behind them. (*Applause.*)[1]

Some idea of La Follette's rhetorical style can be had from excerpts already quoted. It was distinctly that of a salesman of ideas in the field of economics and government. There was little of embellishment through pictorial or figurative language. Even though his primary purpose was to inform and to persuade rank-and-file voters who had little advanced education, it is surprising, in view of La Follette's own literary interests and background, that there are so few literary allusions. This is true even of his Congressional speeches in both House and Senate, although there one does find a very infrequent brief bit from Shakespeare or other literary source.

More common than literary or Biblical references and quotations were citations of legal and historical precedents, references to modern expert authorities, quotations from great figures in the country's history, whose names carry weight with the average man. He seldom made unfounded assertions. These were the sources upon which he called for support.

Businesslike and communicative, La Follette's written speeches were couched in *oral* style. It is obvious to one reading them that, although they were meant to be used as campaign documents, they were written to be spoken and heard.

[1] *Milwaukee Sentinel,* Nov. 3, 1896.

Manuscript speeches and extemporaneous adaptations abound in rhetorical questions, balanced structure, sentences of varied length, exclamations, cumulative phraseology, restatement and reiteration, and various other earmarks of a style adapted to a dynamic, vigorous speaker and designed for auditory reception.

Repetition is especially noticeable, both of ideas in different words and of certain favorite expressions. Some of this repetition was designed to make clear and to emphasize points that he was making, for he appreciated the impenetrability of the average man's head. Part of it was undesigned and probably unconscious, an accompaniment of extemporaneous delivery.[1]

As La Follette, despite his ultrapragmatic political methods in general, largely avoided intemperate expressions in public documents and addresses on political topics, so he showed a proper restraint and suiting of sentiments and diction to the circumstances in various occasional addresses. These addresses show careful phrasing, a deep seriousness, somewhat less matter-of-factness than in deliberative speeches, a note of sincerity, adaptation to the particular occasion, and often an unmistakable note of civic responsibility. Perhaps the most pictorial bit is found in his Farmers' Institute speech at Oconomowoc, in 1902, where he painted an idyllic picture of farm life.

Put the farm in direct communication with the world by the rural delivery, the telephone, the electric railway, the traveling library, the township school, the improved highway, and you have given it the essential advantages of the city without depriving it of the essential advantages of the country.

There will be left the sweet and vitalizing country air, the isolation of broad acres, the beauty of hill and valley, woodland and meadow, and living, running water. The charm of the ripening grain, coming to its mysterious fullness in the warm embrace of the sunshine, the honest pride in the grazing flocks, and the affectionate interest in their growing young, will always be an inherent and uplifting element of life upon the farm. The rich blessings of unconscious health, the joy of wholesome work, that brings wholesome rest and wholesome appetite, are the natural rewards of this outdoor occupation. Nearness to nature, nearness to God, a truer philosophy, a keener human sympathy, higher ideals, greater individuality, will ever be stamped upon the life and character of the country home.[2]

In summary, it may be said that his mature speech style, that which distinguished his speaking as governor and United States Senator, was lucid but somewhat repetitious, copious but clear; almost completely

[1] Personal interviews with Charles M. Dow and Professor John R. Commons, both close, long-time associates of La Follette.

[2] *Voters' Hand Book* (1902), pp. 114ff.

devoid of rhetorical embellishment and literary allusions, but vigorous and moving; replete with persuasive elements in the way of sentence form and length—a distinctly *oral* style.

Before the Audience: Delivery

One of the features of La Follette's speeches most frequently commented on is their length. Political addresses and campaign speeches of full length regularly lasted 2½ or 3 hours, sometimes even longer. Chautauqua speeches occupied about an hour less, unless extended because of audience response.[1]

One reason they were so long was that he was full of his subject and presented it so interestingly that the audience stayed on. Another was his extemporaneous delivery, which caused considerable repetition and restatement, some of it, at least, caused by the habit, formed in the courtroom with a jury, of watching his listeners' faces and continuing with a point until he saw the light of understanding there.[2]

La Follette did not start a campaign with mere notes and a ready tongue, however. He started with a carefully worded written speech that, in at least some cases, he read at the outset of the campaign from manuscript. Even when he read, however, as in his messages to the legislature, there was a communicativeness that held his auditors and made it a speech and not a "paper."

Since this one careful speech was the basis for the entire campaign, it was given, in whole or in part, many times; it was not long after the first presentation that the manuscript was being used only for occasional reference on statistics, and it soon disappeared entirely. A few notes might take its place, or the speaker might proceed without any aids whatever. Never was the original speech given verbatim, although so retentive was his mind of the ideas and phraseology painstakingly worked out that sections of the manuscript might be given in almost their original form.[3]

During his barnstorming of county fairs in the fall of 1897 the *Milwaukee Journal* ran a feature story, profusely illustrated with snapshots, on this would-be leader who was breaking political precedents of the state. On this matter of notes the reporter wrote:

[1] Personal interviews with Robert Duncan, former Chautauqua man, and John J. Hannan, secretary to La Follette both as governor and Senator.

[2] Personal interview with Fred L. Holmes, former editor of *La Follette's Magazine*. Holmes's statement is borne out by La Follette's own testimony in the course of his speech on the tariff in the Senate, June 3, 1909: " . . . when I am speaking I see the face of every senator and every change of expression, just as in practicing law I saw the face of every juryman and used to think that I knew what was passing in the mind of every juror."

[3] Personal interviews with John R. Commons, C. A. Harper, Fred L. Holmes, John J. Hannan, and Robert La Follette, Jr.

With most public speakers the presence in one hand of a written speech is a considerable drawback. La Follette uses it as an effective weapon. It seems to give added accuracy and precision to his statements. He goes to it for inspiration and does not in any sense occupy the time and patience of his hearers by referring to it. He seems never to lose his place. He uses the written sheet as a man would use a club in a fight. He holds it out before his audience, grasping it tightly in his left hand, and with the fingers of his right hand he taps it impressively, and no one dreams it is not a part of the idea he is advancing.[1]

The communicative, extempore method of speaking explains in part how he could hold audiences, often with many of the people standing, for a discussion of heavy subjects for such long hours. It is only part of the explanation however. Fundamental was La Follette's personality. He captured attention and held it from the moment he rose. With his short muscular body,[2] his high-browed expressive face, his bristling pompadour, his piercing glance from gray-blue eyes—he was instinct with a sort of "general vibrant alertness."

This characteristic, coupled with a warm heartiness of manner, direct eye-to-eye contact as he sat poised on the edge of his chair, and the demonstrative habit of showing his good will by putting his arm about a friend, made him irresistible in private conference.[3]

The throngs who crowded about to shake hands with "Bob" experienced it for a fleeting moment as he recognized old friends and greeted each well-wisher with an appropriate remark.[4]

The entire audience responded as they sat and watched and listened. As a reporter for a Chicago paper wrote: "He takes men right into the narrow circle of his exclusive attention. Every man believes that the orator is talking directly to him."[5]

His manner in campaign speeches, the most typical and by far the most numerous of the whole period under review, was poised yet informal. He was always master of the situation, but he welcomed questions and often solicited reactions from the audience as he paused for effect or threw in a question that evoked a direct response. Seldom was anyone rash enough to heckle him for the sake of disturbance. On the few such occasions the speaker quickly put the heckler in his place. With bona fide, even though hostile, questions he was patient and fair in his answers, although naturally not using them to his own disadvantage.

[1] *Milwaukee Journal*, Oct. 2, 1897.

[2] He was only 5 feet 6 inches tall.

[3] Personal interviews with former Congressman John M. Nelson and Joseph Schafer, superintendent of the Wisconsin State Historical Society.

[4] See account of how La Follette greeted people at the conclusion of his speeches, in the *Milwaukee Free Press*, Feb. 19, 1905.

[5] *Chicago Times-Herald*, Sept. 27, 1897, quoted in Barton, *op. cit.*, p. 86.

His final Milwaukee speech in 1902 illustrated both this practice of responding to audience comments and that of soliciting spoken responses from his audiences. He was speaking of the Democratic state convention when an anti-Rose Democrat on the platform behind him spoke out:

"That was not a Democratic—it was a corporation convention."

"That was what it was," said La Follette. "It was controlled by the public service corporations of the state, and it is the sort of work which the convention did in regard to taxation of these public service corporations which drives honest Democrats out of the party. What can they do? What other course can they take and preserve their honor?"

When the cheers, applause, and nods of approval had ceased, he asked: "Would you trust Democrats who were afraid to mention the subject of railroad taxation in their platform?"

The answer was shouts of "No!"[1]

The way he handled a crowd, as in the soliciting of reactions, was part of his showmanship. Nowhere did he have a chance to indulge his flair better than on the platform. His use of ready-made audiences at county fairs was dramatic in itself. So were the whirlwind campaigns he conducted—by special train in 1900, four strenuous weeks in 1902, twice that long in 1904, when the newly invented and not too dependable automobile was pressed into service. Then there were the invention and devastating use of the "roll call" to let light in on the record of the senator or assemblyman in a given district, the frank attempt to influence the 1904 Republican primaries by stumping the districts of Stalwart legislators, the various incidents of county fairs, including the blocking of the race track at Oshkosh, until he finished his speech—the list is almost inexhaustible.

Such a political leader could scarcely be guilty of making dry speeches. Nor was he. Yet there is little that strikes one as humorous as he reads the prepared manuscript of the speech. La Follette deliberately guarded against humor in advance preparation, fearing to use his native quick wit and keen sense of humor "lest people remember the jest and forget the issue."[2]

In no respect is there greater difference between the manuscript and stenographic versions of one of his speeches than in this matter of humor. The former is severely serious; the latter shows humorous turn of phrase, clever adaptation to something in the speaking situation or to a listener's remark, and frequent indications of laughter by the audience. Seldom

[1] *Milwaukee Free Press*, Nov. 2, 1902.
[2] Fola La Follette, *Twentieth Century Magazine*, April, 1912, p. 516.

did he tell a funny story, and when he did it was likely to be at his own expense.[1]

Aside from these ways, his humorous effects were largely secured through sarcastic jibes at the weaknesses and inconsistencies of his opponents, sometimes including what they said about him. At such times, wording, trained voice, highly expressive face, and physical mimicry combined to produce an effect that "would make his audience roar."[2] This power of mimicry was a part of La Follette's dramatic equipment that never found expression on the stage. He put it to good use on the rostrum. With his open, grasping hands behind his back he could in a moment suggest the crooked politician more vividly and humorously than he could in words.[3]

Physical mimicry was dramatic, but it was only part of the effect produced by bodily action. So completely did he give himself to his speaking that at the end of every speech of any length he was wringing wet with perspiration. As he warmed to his subject he would loosen his collar and finally, if the room was warm, discard his coat. He moved a good deal on the platform, especially walking down to the front. In his county-fair speaking he mounted chairs and tables and even stood on platform railings, the better to see and be seen by his audience. When he stood in one place he was a dynamo of physical energy, tossing his head for emphasis, running his hands through his pompadour, or holding his clenched hands above his head while his head shook with intensity. His hands were eloquent in themselves, always moving, as were the fingers, yet never calling attention away from the speaker's message. With these physical attributes and a poised body in which "every muscle . . . is like a spring of steel" went a speaking countenance capable of the most varied and intense expression. Well might observers say that La Follette had an expressive body, trained to respond to the slightest change in thought and feeling and making the response so quickly and fully as to give the impression of genuineness.[4]

The *Milwaukee Journal* feature writer already quoted thus vividly describes La Follette the actor:

Mr. La Follette is sometimes sarcastic. His words bite like coals of fire; but his face and gestures are unique. Here, as in other phases, they harmonize, and with

[1] Personal interviews with Charles M. Dow and A. O. Barton.

[2] Personal interview with John R. Commons.

[3] Personal interviews with Fred L. Holmes, A. T. Rogers, and William T. Evjue.

[4] This description of physical activity is based on current newspaper accounts; a personal letter from Charles L. Wagner, of New York, formerly secretary of the Slayton Lyceum Bureau; and on interviews with a large number of associates of La Follette who heard him speak many times, including C. A. Harper, A. T. Rogers, Fred L. Holmes, Solomon Levitan, John J. Hannan, O. S. Loomis, Robert Duncan, Charles M. Dow, Joseph Schafer, J. B. Simpson, and Robert M. La Follette, Jr.

his head slightly lowered, his shock of brown hair overtopping the face and the right arm extended, the index finger pointing apparently at the very object of his attack, there is a certain fine frenzy in the man that few public speakers can use to such advantage. Again he will refer to the noble men that have made history in this country in past years as a heritage of which Americans should be proud, and with clenched fists and uplifted arms, he seems to hold that precious heritage aloft and, gazing at it with open mouth and upturned eyes, invite his hearers to see in substance the very thing his fancy has painted. . . .

. . . Near the conclusion of his speech as he folds his arms across his chest with the air of a man who has done all that can be done, and in a quiet and impressive way delivers his peroration, there is a wonderful change. It is a change that does not detract from your opinion of the orator, but rather adds to it. You realize then that he has been speaking a long time. He has tired you out, but you did not know it before. However, he does not seem to have become weary himself. As he bows for the last time and withdraws he seems as fresh as ever.[1]

One other item in La Follette's speaking equipment remains to be mentioned: his voice. It did not have the effortless, bell-like quality of Bryan's, but though it was not especially pleasing, it was a good voice, vigorous and strong, despite overuse. Its owner knew how to use it to save wear and tear on the vocal apparatus. He read much aloud to family and friends in the home. His voice was slightly below a medium key and had a vibrant, moving quality. It was by varied intonation and inflection as well as by changes in quality and the other vocal elements that many of his most telling speech effects were secure. His enunciation was unusually distinct, his general rate of speech neither fast nor slow. He tended to begin rather slowly and then to speak more rapidly as he warmed to his subject.[2]

He was never in such a hurry as to spoil his pauses, for he knew their emphatic and dramatic effect. A Chautauqua man considers him one of the greatest masters of the sustained pause, which he would prolong for five or six seconds until his audience, unable to wait longer, would sometimes call out the answer to the rhetorical question he had posed or furnish the name he had left unsaid in the progress of the "roll call."[3]

If the total effect of La Follette's skill in speech delivery had been to make his listeners go away and remember only its showy, dramatic features, it would have been a liability instead of an asset. They enjoyed the show he put on, but he also made his challenging message stick. In John R. Common's phrase, "He made them *think with him*."

[1] *Milwaukee Journal*, Oct. 2, 1897.
[2] This description of La Follette's voice as a responsive instrument is a composite from current newspaper accounts, a personal letter from Charles L. Wagner, and interviews with Messrs. Dow, Barton, Duncan, Robert La Follette, Jr., Commons, Holmes, and Harper.
[3] Personal interview with Robert Duncan, now of the University of Wisconsin.

Although he was denounced by many as a cheap actor and charlatan, for the thousands upon thousands of common men and women who drove over muddy or dusty country roads to hear him in a campaign speech or at the county fair he was genuine and sincere, speaking with a dead earnestness that carried conviction to farmer, laborer, storekeeper, and university man alike.

Revealing is the comment of the Washington correspondent of a metropolitan paper who came to Wisconsin to interview the governor during the 1902 campaign. After hearing him speak at Boscobel, the reporter wrote:

I have been in every important campaign in this country for a number of years, but I never heard a campaign speech like that. The honesty of this man is apparent. . . . All that is necessary is to hear him to be convinced of his sincerity and of the truth of the propositions he advances. . . . [1]

Outstanding Speeches

Unlike Bryan, Robert M. La Follette did not spring into national prominence with a single great speech. It is difficult to place one's finger even on a select few. His speeches in Wisconsin were always essentially campaign speeches, by a steady succession of which he magnetized the reform forces and broke down the resistance of the opposition. If one were to name two of his gubernatorial and pregubernatorial period, they would probably be his first public presentation of the direct primary idea in the warmly received "Menace of the Machine" speech at the University of Chicago, on Washington's Birthday, 1897, and his constantly developing "Representative Government" address, delivered before hundreds of Chautauqua and lyceum audiences between 1900 and the time of his death.

During his two decades in the United States Senate and his campaigns for the Presidency in 1912 and 1924, he delivered scores of speeches on a great variety of current economic and political questions as the recognized spokesman of the insurgent Republicans or Progressives. Especially noteworthy senatorial speeches were his exhaustive discussions of the Hepburn railroad bill, when he first took his seat in the Senate,[2] and of the Payne-Aldrich tariff of 1909, his "Free Speech and the Right of Congress to Declare the Objects of the War," on October 6, 1917, and his 4-hour speech on April 28, 1922, which resulted in the famous investigation of the Harding-administration oil leases.

[1] Quoted in the *Milwaukee Free Press*, Oct. 13, 1902.
[2] For an account of how La Follette met the studied absence of his Republican colleagues from the Senate floor when he began to speak, see his *Autobiography*, pp. 411–413.

It was in the Wisconsin fight, however, that he perfected his political methods and largely matured in his speaking. His horizon broadened as he became increasingly familiar with his senatorial duties, but as a public speaker and political leader there were few, if any, important changes after he resigned the governorship on January 1, 1906.

In long-range results, perhaps La Follette's Chautauqua speaking was most significant of all. Without his Wisconsin reputation La Follette would not have been a headliner among the "talent," but with that and, later, his senatorial record as background, he was able to reach a large responsive public from one end of the country to the other. It was through the Chautauquas, both permanent assemblies and traveling tent circuits, that millions of Americans derived entertainment, inspiration, and not a little political education toward reform during the decade preceding the election of 1912. Said French Strother, in the *World's Work* for September, 1912: "The progressive movement owes its strength very largely to the Chautauqua, just as the abolition movement gained its momentum chiefly from the free platform of the lyceum."[1]

La Follette played a prominent role in this spreading, deepening Progressive movement. There were other voices: Bryan, Folk, Dolliver, Cummins, to mention four; but none spoke in clearer or more forceful tones. That his words took root is evidenced by the testimony of men all over the country that their lives were profoundly influenced by hearing "Representative Government" at Chautauqua or lyceum.[2]

Measured by the tests of immediate response, practical results, and long-term influence, La Follette was an effective public speaker.

SELECTED BIBLIOGRAPHY

Life and Work

Manuscript Sources

The voluminous La Follette papers in the Wisconsin State Historical Library are not yet available but are to be opened as soon as the biography of Robert M. La Follette being written by his daughter, Fola La Follette Middleton, is completed.

The papers of various men associated with La Follette are to be found in the same library, at Madison. Those of James O. Davidson and Nils P. Haugen are especially helpful.

Contemporary Newspapers

The files of Wisconsin newspapers, particularly those of Madison and Milwaukee, are filled with pertinent material, but because of the widely divergent attitudes toward La Follette, one needs to read papers both favorable and unfavorable to him. The Madison papers are the *Wisconsin State Journal*, the *Madison Democrat*, and, later, the *Capital Times*. The Milwaukee papers are the *Daily News*, the *Journal*, the *Sentinel*, and the *Free Press*. The files of the first

[1] "The Great American Forum," *The World's Work*, 9 (1905): 551–564.
[2] Interview with Robert M. La Follette, Jr.

La Follette journal, the weekly Madison paper *The State*, are also to be found in the Wisconsin State Historical Library, as are those of *La Follette's Magazine*.

Especially valuable are thirty-seven volumes of clippings in the same library from Wisconsin and out-of-state newspapers concerning La Follette and the causes in which he was interested, 1895–1910.

Autobiographical Sources

La Follette's Autobiography—A Personal Narrative of Political Experiences (Madison, 1913) La Follette carried forward in 1924 in a series of ten articles that appeared in various newspapers, including the Madison *Capital Times*, September 19–29. Belle Case La Follette wrote a series of intimate sketches of her husband in *La Follette's Magazine*, December, 1925; May, June, 1926; October, 1927; May, October, November, 1928.

Unpublished Theses

The number of graduate studies of La Follette is limited: Joseph Buren Clayton, La Follette's Campaign for the Presidential Nomination, 1912, Master's thesis, University of Chicago, 1921; John Woodford Crawford, A Study of the Development of Robert M. La Follette as a Speaker, Master's thesis, Northwestern University, 1935; Milton Irvin Goldstein, The La Follette Movement in Wisconsin, Master's thesis, Washington University, 1936; Alfred S. Harvey, The Background of the Progressive Movement in Wisconsin, Master's thesis, University of Wisconsin, 1933; Arzalia S. Johnson, The La Follette-Roosevelt Feud, Master's thesis, University of Wisconsin, 1930; Carroll P. Lahman, Robert Marion La Follette as Public Speaker and Political Leader (1855–1905), Doctoral dissertation, University of Wisconsin, 1939; Wallace S. Sayre, Robert M. La Follette—A Study in Political Methods, Doctoral dissertation, New York University, 1930.

Secondary Sources: Books

Aside from the *Autobiography*, the only book-length biographical treatment is Albert O. Barton's *La Follette's Winning of Wisconsin* (1894–1904) (Madison, 1922).

Of background treatments and of general historical and specialized books that give significant attention to La Follette, there are so many that it would be impossible to include them here.

Secondary Sources: Periodicals

Of the hundreds of magazine articles that have appeared about La Follette and his work, these will be found especially helpful: Richard Barry, "A Radical in Power: A Study of La Follette," *Outlook*, Nov. 29, 1922, pp. 564–567; Bruce Bliven, "Robert M. La Follette's Place in Our History," *Current History*, August, 1925, pp. 716–722; Zona Gale, "The La Follette Family," *Nation*, Feb. 15, 1928, pp. 181–182; William Hard, "Robert M. La Follette" *Review of Reviews*, September, 1924, pp. 275–279; Richard Lloyd Jones, "Among La Follette's People," *Collier's*, Sept. 3, 1910, pp. 17–18; F. A. Ogg, "Robert M. La Follette in Retrospect," *Current History*, February, 1931, pp. 685–691; Lincoln Steffens, "Wisconsin: A State Where the People Have Restored Representative Government," *McClure's Magazine*, October, 1904, pp. 563–579; Mark Sullivan, "Looking Back on La Follette," *World's Work*, January, 1925, pp. 324–331; Louis A. Warren, "The Lincoln and La Follette Families in Pioneer History," *Wisconsin Magazine of History*, 12 (1928–1929): 359–378; Walter Wellman, "The Rise of La Follette," *Review of Reviews*, March, 1905, pp. 299–302.

Miscellaneous Sources

In the Wisconsin Legislative Reference Library, Madison: La Follette's Voting Record in the United States Senate, 1905–1924 (31 pp., typewritten); catalogued chronological clippings

Robert M. La Follette

and other unbound material dealing with La Follette and with the Republican party in Wisconsin. In the Wisconsin State Historical Library: sixteen boxes of miscellaneous papers under heading Wisconsin Politics 1878–; files of material issued by the La Follette-Wheeler National Committee, 1924.

Speeches and Speaking
Texts of Speeches

There is no printed collection of La Follette's speeches. C. P. Lahman's doctoral dissertation includes a 365-page Appendix of representative speeches for the period 1879–1905.

Texts of individual speeches delivered during the years of Wisconsin campaigning are available, in the main, only through the pages of newspapers and in printed campaign literature of that time. The text of the university oration "Iago" is given in Charles Edgar Prather's *Winning Orations of the Inter-state Oratorical Contests* (Topeka, 1891).

The best source for speeches and for floor debate in the House of Representatives and the United States Senate is the *Congressional Record*. Stirn's *An Annotated Bibliography of Robert M. La Follette* (Chicago, 1937) reproduces the *Congressional Record* index and in addition gives La Follette's vote on roll calls in connection with the measures listed.

Governor La Follette's messages to the legislature, many of them delivered in person, may be found in the official journals of the legislature and in separate official printings.

Helpful to an understanding of La Follette's thinking and for a study of his oral and written style is *The Political Philosophy of Robert M. La Follette as Revealed in His Speeches and Writings* (Madison, 1920), compiled by Ellen Torelle.

Two Famous Speeches

The text of La Follette's speech at the banquet of the Periodical Publishers' Association in Philadelphia, Feb. 2, 1912, is given in *La Follette's Autobiography*, pp. 762–797. Comments on conditions surrounding its delivery may be found in many places, including these: *Autobiography*; John R. Commons, *Myself* (New York, 1934); Owen Wister, *Roosevelt—The Story of a Friendship* (New York, 1930).

The text and the circumstances of La Follette's speech before the National Nonpartisan League at St. Paul in 1917, which for a time threatened his expulsion from the United States Senate on grounds of disloyalty, are given in the Senate documents: *Majority Report, Senate Committee on Privileges and Elections, Calendar No. 560*, Sixty-fifth Congress, third session, Report No. 614; *Minority Report, Senate Committee on Privileges and Elections, Calendar No. 560*, Sixty-fifth Congress, third session, Report No. 614, Part 2; also the hearings before the special subcommittee of this committee, Sixty-fifth Congress, first session. With these should also be read the fifth in Senator La Follette's series of autobiographical newspaper articles in 1924, Madison *Capital Times*, Sept. 25.

Discussions of Speaking

Because of the central place held by his speaking, many of the references given under Life and Work contain valuable information on La Follette's speaking, especially Barton's *La Follette's Winning of Wisconsin*; the biographical series on her husband's early career in *La Follette's Magazine*, 1925–1928, by Belle Case La Follette; and contributions in the same magazine by Gilbert E. Roe, August, 1926, and April, May, June, 1929.

The two most thoroughgoing studies of La Follette as a speaker are unpublished theses by Crawford and Lahman, already listed under the first division of this bibliography.

34

Woodrow Wilson

by DAYTON DAVID McKEAN

Thomas Woodrow Wilson—the Thomas was, in later life, dropped for the sake of euphony—was born in Staunton, Va., December 28, 1856. His family moved to Augusta, Ga., in 1858, to Columbia, S. C., in 1870. He never attended a public school but was privately tutored, chiefly by his father. He attended Davidson College in 1873, but illness compelled him to return home, where he remained until he entered Princeton in 1875; he was graduated in 1879. The same year he entered the law school of the University of Virginia, but he withdrew in 1880, when his health failed once more. He studied law at home and was admitted to the Georgia bar in 1882 but gave up the law after a year and enrolled in the graduate school at Johns Hopkins, where he obtained his Ph.D. in 1886. His first and most famous book *Congressional Government* (1885) was accepted as his dissertation. He taught at Bryn Mawr 1885–1888, Wesleyan 1888–1890, Princeton 1890–1902, when he became president of the University. He resigned to run for governor of New Jersey in 1910; elected, he resigned to be inaugurated as President in 1913. He delivered his messages in person before Congress. He obtained the Federal Reserve Act, the Underwood Tariff, and other domestic reforms. He was war President during the First World War; his speeches, especially the address calling for a declaration of war, laid the basis for popular support of the war, and his "Fourteen Points" speech, for the armistice. The League of Nations came into being as a result of his insistence. He died in Washington, D. C., February 3, 1924.

From his earliest youth Woodrow Wilson longed to be a leader; and since the leaders he most admired were orators, he determined to become one. He looked upon oratory as the first tool of leadership: "Its object is persuasion and conviction—the control of other minds. . . . "[1]

The Education of the Orator

The child of the Presbyterian manse was impressed by his adoring and adored father with the appreciation of words. Many years later President Wilson told Ida M. Tarbell:

[1] From the *Princetonian*, June 7, 1877, p. 42, quoted by Ray Stannard Baker, *Woodrow Wilson, Life and Letters* (Garden City, N.Y., 1927) I, 92. Cited hereafter as Baker.

My best training came from him. He was intolerant of vagueness, and from the time I began to write until his death in 1903, when he was eighty-one years old, I carried everything I wrote to him. . . . "What do you mean by that?" [he would ask.] I would tell him, and, of course, in doing so would express myself more simply than I had on paper. "Why didn't you say so?" he would go on. "Don't shoot at your meaning with bird shot and hit the whole countryside; shoot with a rifle at the thing you have to say."[1]

His father influenced his speaking as well as his writing, and in the same direction:

My father would not permit me to blurt things out, or stammer a half-way job of telling whatever I had to tell. If I became excited in explaining some boyish activity he always said, "Steady, now, Thomas; wait a minute. Think! Think what it is you wish to say, and then choose your words to say it." As a young boy, therefore, even at the age of four or five, I was taught to think about what I was going to say, and then I was required to say it correctly. Before I was grown, it became a habit.[2]

This remarkable father and son read aloud to each other passages from favorite authors and orators, took the ideas out of the selections, and then tried to put them together again to improve upon the expression. They even tried to compress Webster's orations without robbing them of either ideas or eloquence. "But," the President said later, "we never got far with Daniel."[3]

At Davidson College Wilson joined the Eumenean Literary Society, delivered orations, and took part in debates. His marks were good in rhetoric, composition, English, and declamation; they were not equally good in Latin or Greek; and were worse in mathematics.[4] Woodrow Wilson never mastered any language but English, though in later years he got up a reading knowledge of French and German.

In every college in which Wilson studied or taught, except Bryn Mawr, he took an active part in the work of the college literary and debating society. He was elected to membership in the American Whig Society at Princeton in September, 1875.[5] Wilson was more prominent in the politics of the society than in its formal exercises in speaking. He was elected first controller for his junior year and speaker for his senior year. Says Beam:

[1] "A Talk with the President of the United States," *Collier's* 58 (Oct. 28, 1916): 5.
[2] Quoted by David Lawrence, *The True Story of Woodrow Wilson* (New York, 1924), p. 18.
[3] Baker, I, 39.
[4] *Ibid.*, p. 75.
[5] Jacob N. Beam, *The American Whig Society of Princeton University* (Princeton, N. J., 1933), p. 187. This history of the Princeton literary and debating society contains the best existing account of Wilson's activities as an undergraduate speaker; Mr. Beam checked through all the minutes of the society and cited in his book all Wilson's appearances.

Wilson's greatest prominence was in the discussions in the business sessions. He was a member of the most important committees, and he spoke often on questions of Hall policy and procedure. In literary exercises and contests he was not as prominent and successful as his later career would lead us to expect. . . . In the Sophomore Oratorical contest he won second prize, but he failed to be included among Whig's four Junior Orators the next year. In debates he won the appointment only once and was not among the three winners of the Competitive Debate in which he participated.[1]

The explanation for this kind and amount of participation by Wilson, in view of his great interest in oratory, lies in part in the fact that during these years he was also editor of the college paper, and he was engaged as well in the preparation of the famous article "Cabinet Government in the United States," which appeared in the *International Review* (edited by Henry Cabot Lodge) shortly after Wilson's graduation.[2] Wilson was, moreover, interested in another debating society, which he organized with some of his classmates, called the Liberal Debating Club. The constitution of this club, drawn up by Wilson, established a society modeled on the House of Commons.[3]

As a law student at the University of Virginia Wilson joined the Jefferson debating society and 4 days after his election became its secretary.[4] He took part in a notable debate with William Cabell Bruce and delivered an oration on John Bright.[5] When he was elected president of the society he headed a committee that revised its constitution.[6]

When he arrived at Johns Hopkins, Wilson joined the Hopkins Literary Society and before long delivered to the members an address on oratory, which he reported to his fianceé Ellen Axson: "I talked . . . about oratory, its aims and the difficulties surrounding its cultivation in a University, where exact knowledge overcrows everything else, and the art of persuasion is neglected on principle . . . "[7] Not only did he reorganize the Hopkins Literary Society but he gave it a new name, the Hopkins House of Commons.[8] Wilson was so well liked by the members of the

---

[1] *Ibid.*, p. 193.

[2] 7 (1879): 146–163; also in *The Public Papers of Woodrow Wilson* (6 vols., Ray Stannard Baker and William E. Dodd, eds., New York, 1925), I, 19–42. This, the authorized edition of Wilson's papers and speeches, will be cited hereafter as *Public Papers*.

[3] Baker, I, 94.

[4] *Ibid.*, p. 118.

[5] *Public Papers*, I, 60–62, has a summary of his speech in the debate, reprinted from the *University of Virginia Magazine*, 19 (1880): 448–450, and the oration on Bright, in full, pp. 43–59, reprinted from the same periodical, 19 (1880): 354–370.

[6] Baker, I, 123.

[7] Quoted by Baker, I, 188.

[8] *Ibid.*, p. 199.

society that on his marriage they presented him with two bronze statuettes.

At Wesleyan University in 1889 Professor Wilson called a meeting of the student body and urged the students to set up a debating society to be called the Wesleyan House of Commons. In this speech he said, "Highest oratory is arrived at through the cultivation of the art of debate. To imitate the House of Representatives would be patriotic, but not interesting. . . . So we shall imitate the British House of Commons, thereby introducing a dramatic element in that a body of ministers resigns when defeated."[1] The Wesleyan House of Commons was, according to Baker, an immediate if not a permanent success.

When he returned to Princeton he resumed his interest in the Whig Society and became a member of the alumni control group, the Whig Senate. He assisted students in the preparation of debates and orations and often acted as one of the faculty judges.[2]

Even before the youthful Wilson went to college he was studying orators, particularly the great British orators. While he was a boy in Columbia he had a picture of Gladstone over his desk.[3] Throughout his life Wilson was an admirer of the great English Liberal; when he was studying law at the University of Virginia he wrote an article for the *University of Virginia Magazine*, entitled "Mr. Gladstone: A Character Sketch."[4] He also studied Bright, Burke, Canning, Cobden, Fox, Macaulay, and Pitt.

Among these orators, Burke was his favorite. A Princeton classmate told Ray Stannard Baker of discovering him in Patter's Woods, near Princeton, practicing one of Burke's orations.[5] His later speeches and writings contain numerous admiring references to Burke and quotations from him, *e.g.*, " . . . those deathless passages of great speech, compact of music and high sense, in which Edmund Burke justified us. . . . "[6] Above all the other orators whom he studied, he absorbed Burke; Bliss Perry, who edited a book of selections from Burke, said, "Wilson was the only colleague I ever had who could be trusted instantly to cap any quotation from Burke."[7] While Wilson was professor of politics at Princeton he published an essay on Burke, an extensive analysis not only of Burke

---

[1] Quoted by Baker, I, 303, from the *Wesleyan Argus*, Jan. 18, 1889.

[2] Beam, *op. cit.*, p. 193; and Dayton David McKean, "Woodrow Wilson as a Debate Coach," *Quarterly Journal of Speech*, 16 (1930): 458–463.

[3] Baker, I, 71.

[4] 29 (1880): 401–426, reprinted in *Public Papers*, I, 63–88.

[5] Baker, I, 92.

[6] "The Ideals of America," an address delivered on the one hundred twenty-fifth anniversary of the battle of Trenton, Dec. 26, 1901, *Public Papers*, I, 420.

[7] *And Gladly Teach* (Boston, 1935), p. 133.

as a statesman but also of Burke as a speaker.[1] Burke greatly influenced Wilson's political thinking: he was, until his entry into politics, like Burke, essentially a conservative; he admired the parliamentary form of government in which he saw opportunity for statesmanship like Burke's, an opportunity he could not see under congressional government; he approved of Burke's views on party—"he gave it principles quite as often as he accepted principles from it"—[2] and above all he appreciated Burke's view of public duty and often quoted as "no bad motto" this sentence from Burke, "Duty demands and requires, that what is right should not only be made known, but be made prevalent; that what is evil should not only be detected, but defeated."[3]

He read also the American orators, particularly Henry and Webster, and he followed the debates in Congress.[4] He read in translation the Greek and Roman orators, and he read some criticism, at least Jebb's *Attic Orators* and Goodrich's *British Eloquence*. Baker tells of an article on "The Orator" in the *Gentleman's Magazine* for April, 1874, that Wilson read as a Princeton undergraduate; this article, according to the biographer, so stirred Wilson "that he remembered all his life the exact place at the head of the south stairs of the Chancellor Green Library where he read it."[5]

Views on Oratory and Orators

Wilson never published any systematic statement of his views on the art of public speaking; he preferred to write about orators rather than oratory. In his essays and addresses on orators, however, he brings out in an incidental fashion his views of the subject. First of all, he was convinced that content is fundamental to eloquence:

No orator ever more signally illustrated [than did Bright] the truth that eloquence is not of the lips alone. Eloquence is never begotten by empty pates. Grovelling minds are never winged with high and noble thoughts. Eloquence consists not in sonorous sound or brilliant phrases. *Thought* is the fibre, thought is the *pith* of eloquence. Eloquence lies in the thought, not in the throat. . . . It is persuasion inspired by conviction.[6]

[1] "The Interpreter of English Liberty," *Mere Literature and Other Essays* (Boston, 1896), pp. 104–160; also in *Selected Literary and Political Papers of Woodrow Wilson* (New York, 1925), III, 104–160; Vols. I and II of this popular edition of Wilson's speeches and papers are based upon the *Public Papers;* Vol. III reprints selected essays not found in *Public Papers*.

[2] *Mere Literature*, p. 140.

[3] *Ibid.*, p. 136.

[4] Baker, I, p. 117, prints a list of the books that Wilson took out of the University of Virginia Library on oratory, history, and law.

[5] *Ibid.*, p. 88.

[6] "John Bright," *Public Papers*, I, 48; italics in the original.

In a youthful article written in the *Princetonian* Wilson recommended for the training of the orator the study of classic models, particularly Demosthenes, "the truest model for all orators. . . . Only as the constant companions of Demosthenes, Cicero, Burke, Fox, Canning, and Webster can we hope to become orators."[1]

Without compromising his convictions, Wilson felt, the orator must, nevertheless, adapt his remarks to his audience. He wrote of Gladstone:

His genius as an orator most conspicuously manifests itself in his power of adapting his style to the audience he is addressing. One day he is speaking to a meeting of the most intelligent and learned members of his constituency, and his style is one of measured calmness, his treatment following the leadings of a strict, though eloquent, logic. The next day, perhaps, he meets the farmers of the country-side upon the hustings, and the style is changed. . . . There is always, however, whatever the audience he is addressing, the same foundation of conviction and the same transparency of truth. Though the treatment be diverse, there is no diversity in the beliefs, no crookedness in the counsels, of the orator.[2]

Wilson felt that his idol, Burke, spoke with insufficient regard for his audience: "He too easily lost sight of his audience in his search for principles, and they resented his neglect of them, his indifference to their tastes. They felt his lofty style of reasoning as a sort of rebuke. . . . He had, before very long, to accustom himself, therefore, to speak to an empty House and subsequent generations."[3]

Wilson appreciated the conversational quality in speaking and in his oration on Bright commented particularly upon it.[4] He felt that the orator should always be self-restrained, for "the orator who maintains complete sovereignty over his emotions is a thousandfold more powerful and impressive than he who 'saws the air' and 'tears a passion to tatters.' Emotional demonstrations should come from his audience and not from the orator himself."[5] Burke did not, Wilson thought, always maintain sufficient self-control: "He was passionate sometimes beyond all bounds: he seriously frightened cautious and practical men by his haste and vehemence. . : . He was capable of falling, upon occasion, into a very frenzy of excitement in the midst of debate, when he would often shock moderate men by the ungoverned license of his language."[6]

It is fair to say that Wilson always tried to follow his own advice on speaking: he always put ideas first; he adapted his appeal to the audience before him; he never lost his self-control while speaking.

[1] The *Princetonian*, June 7, 1877, p. 42, quoted by Baker, I, 93.
[2] "Mr. Gladstone: A Character Sketch," *Public Papers*, I, 82.
[3] "The Interpreter of English Liberty," p. 134.
[4] *Public Papers*, I, 51.
[5] *Ibid.*, p. 50.
[6] "The Interpreter of English Liberty," p. 138.

Wilson thought that a college lecturer should be, in the best sense, an orator. He deplored the dreary lectures he heard at Johns Hopkins, and he wrote to Ellen Axson, "How can a teacher stimulate young men to study, how can he fill them with great ideas and worthy purposes, how can he draw them out of themselves and make them to become forces in the world without oratory? Perfunctory lecturing is of no service in the world. It's a nuisance."[1] Wilson's essay on Adam Smith, "An Old Master," took its title not from Smith's mastery of economics but from his mastery of the art of academic lecturing.[2] Wilson was a great success as a lecturer.[3] He was annually voted the most popular of the college lecturers at Princeton. He always worked on his lectures as carefully as he worked in preparing a speech.[4]

Personality

The personality of Woodrow Wilson is a matter still in dispute. The admirers of Wilson put him only a little lower than the angels; his opponents and his enemies exhausted the vocabulary of abuse upon him, and a few, like Theodore Roosevelt, coined bitter phrases to denounce him.[5] Somewhere between these extremes must lie the real Wilson. The present writer cannot expect to make a definitive appraisal of Wilson; he can only hope that the following sketch is suggestive.

Professor Charles E. Merriam has called attention to the effect of Wilson's physique upon his personality.[6] Wilson did not have the rugged constitution of his contemporaries, Bryan and Roosevelt. He had to leave Davidson College on account of his health and for the same reason to give up finishing the work for his law degree at Virginia. He suffered from a stomach disorder all his life, which he referred to as indigestion. When, in the late nineties, he was trying to support three daughters and build a home on a professor's salary, he worked so hard that he developed a severe attack of writer's cramp, or neuritis, in his right hand. He tried to write with an especially large pen but gave that up and taught himself to write

---

[1] Quoted by Baker, I, 186.

[2] *An Old Master and Other Political Essays* (New York, 1893); also in *Selected Literary and Political Papers of Woodrow Wilson*, III, 3.

[3] Baker, II, 9–12, cites many letters from students of Wilson.

[4] A page of notes for a lecture, "Clay and Webster Contrasted," is reproduced in Baker, I, 311.

[5] The interpretation of Wilson has also a "lunatic fringe." One of the strangest is that of the pseudonymous Wells Wells, whose *Wilson the Unknown* (New York, 1931) asserts that Wilson did not want the Senate to ratify the peace treaty because he wanted to run for a third term in 1920 and wanted an issue. George Sylvester Viereck makes him the dupe of Col. House in *The Strangest Friendship in History* (New York, 1932). William Bayard Hale, in *The Story of a Style* (New York, 1920), stops just short of saying that Wilson was insane.

[6] *Four American Party Leaders* (New York, 1926); see especially pp. 46, 55, 57, 59.

with his left hand.[1] While he was president of Princeton he had several breakdowns of health and had to take long vacations to recuperate. In May, 1906, he lost the vision of his left eye, and he never totally recovered it.[2] At that time the doctors told him that he had arteriosclerosis and that he should give up everything to lead a quiet and retired life. It is needless to say that he disregarded this advice; after another vacation he resumed working as hard as ever. There is a story that, when he was President, someone suggested that he was working too hard, that he would undermine his constitution. "Man," said Wilson, "I have long been living on my by-laws."

Though he pushed his body to the limit, and occasionally and finally beyond it, Wilson knew that he could not, especially as President, do as many things and see as many people as Roosevelt, for instance, had done. He chose to be a statesman rather than a good mixer, "to play," as he said, "for the verdict of history." This necessary decision had two results: it gave him a reputation for coldness and aloofness that he had never had before he became President, and it restricted his acquaintance so that he was often given unfortunate advice.

The general cast of Wilson's thinking was determined in his youth, in his Scotch Presbyterian upbringing. (1) There was intense loyalty and devotion to his family.[3] (2) Wilson got from his family, particularly from his father, strong religious convictions, which he kept all his life. He believed in prayer, in the God of Calvin. He would never enter into religious disputes; for, as he wrote to Dr. Cary T. Grayson, "so far as religion is concerned, argument is adjourned."[4] The Presbyterian doctrine gave Wilson a certain fatalism, an assurance that God directed his ways, and it gave him an intense belief in the validity of moral principles. The refrain of most of Wilson's speeches, the appeal he most often made, was to principle. Edmund Wilson, in an estimate of his illustrious namesake, noted this trait particularly. The Presbyterians, he said:

habitually put moral considerations above material ones. . . . Much of Woodrow Wilson's power was derived from the passionate persistency with which he adhered, in later life, to this ideal of acting on principle. He carried the devotion to principle into fields where people had never thought to see it, and those he encountered were invariably at first demoralized or won. . . . All that vocabulary of idealism—truth, righteousness, service, faith—which the ordinary public speaker

---

[1] Baker, II, 33. A page of notes for a speech delivered Nov. 8, 1896, written with Wilson's left hand, is reproduced by Baker, II, 32.

[2] Baker, II, 201.

[3] See especially Eleanor R. McAdoo and M. Y. Gaffey, *The Woodrow Wilsons* (New York, 1937), *passim*; and Lawrence, *op. cit.*, pp. 124–135.

[4] Quoted by Baker, I, 68. Baker gives (pp. 65–72) a fuller account of Wilson's religious views than space here will permit.

uses without believing in them [*sic*] and almost without the expectation of being believed—all these phrases meant something real to Wilson; and it was the perception of this fact which arrested the attention of the public.[1]

Judge Wescott, one of Woodrow Wilson's most intense admirers, thought that the chief power of Wilson's eloquence was in its high moral quality: "It is his glory to have identified practical statesmanship with the teachings of Christ."[2] The true disciple cannot be tolerant, and Wilson was not. He said, "Tolerance . . . is of little worth in politics. Politics is a war of *causes;* a joust of principles. Government is too serious a matter to admit of meaningless courtesies."[3]

The rigid adherence to moral principles and the strain of intolerance in his nature made Wilson bitter in defeat. He never forgot and never forgave. The wounds made at Princeton never healed. His defeat in the League of Nations fight rankled until his dying day. In his last public address, November 10, 1923, "The High Significance of Armistice Day," delivered less than three months before his death, he said, "We turned our backs upon our associates and refused to bear any responsible part in the administration of peace, or the firm and permanent establishment of the results of the war—won at so terrible a cost of life and treasure—and withdrew into a sullen and selfish isolation, which is deeply ignoble because manifestly cowardly and dishonorable. . . . "[4]

Any man who took himself and his principles so seriously would be ambitious. Woodrow Wilson had a burning ambition that drove his rather frail body all his life. Joseph Jastrow, who knew him in his early years, wrote of him, "He was a youth with a formulated purpose suitable to maturity. From the picture of Gladstone which the boy enshrined above his desk to the cards on which he wrote half in jest and half in prophecy 'Thomas Woodrow Wilson, Senator from Virginia' he knew clearly where he was going."[5]

Had he lived in England he would have stood for Parliament as soon as he left the university, but in America such a career is not open, at least immediately; the aspiring politician in the United States has usually to be a success at something else first. Wilson had no fortune to support a political career, and he turned first to the law and then to teaching and writing. He kept his eye on the main goal, nevertheless; he lost no opportunity to

[1] "Woodrow Wilson: Political Preacher," *The New Republic*, 53 (1927): 36.

[2] John W. Wescott, *Woodrow Wilson's Eloquence* (Camden, N. J., privately printed, 1922), p. 60, *cf.* also p. 76.

[3] "John Bright," *Public Papers*, I, 54; italics in the original.

[4] *Public Papers*, VI, 540. The whole address deserves a careful reading by any student of Wilson's character.

[5] "The Education of Woodrow Wilson," *The Nation*, 126 (1928): 154.

speak on public questions either as professor of politics or as president of Princeton. He even feared that he would be too successful before his major chance might come, that he might be, as he said, "defeated by his own secondary successes."

It might be supposed that this man, with strong moral and religious principles, who was somewhat intolerant and always ambitious, would have no sense of humor. Wilson had, however, a keen sense of humor. He could laugh at himself, tell jokes on himself. He was fond of reciting limericks, especially one that Lawrence asserts Wilson made up about his own appearance:

> For beauty I am not a star,
> There are others more handsome by far,
> But my face—I don't mind it;
> You see I'm behind it;
> It's the fellow in front that I jar.[1]

He was skillful at mimicry and at telling dialect stories. But the humor in important public addresses was no more than an occasional flash of wit or sarcasm.[2] James Kerney, who followed Wilson around New Jersey in his campaign for governor, gives in his *Political Education of Woodrow Wilson* many instances of Wilson's impromptu wit and humor.[3]

Wilson did not make personal friends easily. A group of men in the Princeton class of 1879 were lifelong friends, not separated from him by the disputes in his administration as president of the university or by the political contests that followed. Wilson wanted friends and friendships, but he never quite knew how to make them; for one thing, he demanded a high degree of loyalty from his friends: very rarely would he maintain any sort of friendship with a man who disagreed with him, though he did with Henry van Dyke. He was more likely to see treachery in any opposition to his policies and to break off a friendship abruptly, as he broke with his old friend John Grier Hibben, who was not so much treacherous as weak. From the time of his break with Hibben he was even more reluctant than before to form close friendships. Wilson obtained his sure, swift insight into the movements of public opinion not so much from friendships as from a wide general reading and from a full knowledge of American history and tradition.

[1] Lawrence, *op. cit.*, p. 125.

[2] His speech to the National Press Club, Mar. 20, 1914, "A President's Difficulties," an informal, impromptu address not intended for publication, shows, in the opinion of the writer, more humor than any of his other published speeches. Printed in *Public Papers*, III, 94–98. It is Wilson at his genial best and may well be read alongside "The High Significance of Armistice Day."

[3] *The Political Education of Woodrow Wilson* (New York, 1926), pp. 38–42, 71–72.

He recognized early that he dealt more surely with men in the mass than with men as individuals. When he had established the Hopkins House of Commons he wrote to Ellen Axson:

I have a sense of power in dealing with men collectively which I do not feel always in dealing with them singly. In the former case the pride of reserve does not stand so much in my way as it does in the latter. One feels no sacrifice of pride necessary in courting the favour of an assembly of men such as he would have to make in seeking to please one man.[1]

Not even his enemies denied that Wilson had a powerful mind, alert, clear, keen, especially gifted with the power of analysis and with the ability to state his views in forcible, lucid language. As a writer and political thinker Wilson was at his best in *Congressional Government,* a work that, in American[2] political writing, deserves to be ranked with the *Federalist.*[2] In all his published work, however, he never touched that height again. In his political thinking and writing Wilson was not so much a political scientist, such as Gierke, Dicey, or Burgess, as an essayist on and an interpreter of politics. He had, indeed, a great contempt for scholars and scholarship, the literary man's contempt. He wrote:

There is, indeed, a natural antagonism, let it be frankly said, between the standards of scholarship and the standards of literature. Exact scholarship values things in direct proportion as they are verifiable; but literature knows nothing of such tests. The truths which it seeks are the truths of self-expression. . . . Scholars, therefore, do not reflect; they label, group kind with kind, set forth in schemes, expound with dispassionate method. Their minds are not stages, but museums; nothing is done there, but very curious and valuable collections are kept there.[3]

Career as an Orator

Wilson's career as an orator may, for convenience, be divided into three parts: (1) the academic period, from his college entrance to his resignation as president of Princeton; (2) the period of domestic politics, from his campaign for governor to the outbreak of the First World War; and (3) the period of the war and the League of Nations.

We do not know how many addresses Woodrow Wilson made as professor at Bryn Mawr, Wesleyan, and Princeton and as president of Princeton, but he made a great many. He delivered courses of lectures at Johns Hopkins

---

[1] Quoted by Baker, I, 199. Baker calls this observation of Wilson's an "extraordinary bit of self-revelation . . . [that] illuminates, like a searchlight, his entire career. . . . We find him far more self-revealing, even confidential, in his public addresses than in conversation, save with his most intimate friends."

[2] Published in 1885, *Congressional Government* went through fourteen editions, twenty-nine impressions, 1885–1924; new edition with an introduction by Ray Stannard Baker, 1935.

[3] *Mere Literature,* pp. 19 and 21.

and at Columbia and many public lectures in other places, from New England to Denver.[1] He was in great demand for occasional addresses and for afterdinner speeches. He spoke to Princeton alumni clubs in many places, defending his Princeton policies. He made many addresses to the students of Princeton, including the annual baccalaureate sermon.

The speeches made in this period set forth Wilson's views of higher education. In many ways his thinking on the problems of college and university was a generation ahead of his time, but space here will not permit a discussion of his educational philosophy.[2] In his address at the sesquicentennial celebration of Princeton in 1896 he summarized in a brilliant passage his view of the ideal university:

I have had sight of the perfect place of learning in my thought: a free place, and a various, where no man could be and not know with how great a destiny knowledge had come into the world—itself a little world; but not perplexed, living with a singleness of aim not known without; the home of sagacious men, hard-headed and with a will to know, debaters of the world's questions every day and used to the rough ways of democracy; and yet a place removed—calm Science seated there, recluse, ascetic, like a nun; not knowing that the world passes, not caring, if the truth but come in answer to her prayer; and Literature, walking within her open doors, in quiet chambers, with men of olden time, storied walls about her, and calm voices infinitely sweet; here "magic casements, opening on the foam of perilous seas, in fairy lands forlorn," to which you may withdraw and use your youth for pleasure; there windows open straight upon the street, where many stand and talk, intent upon the world of men and business. A place where ideals are kept in heart in an air they can breathe; but no fool's paradise. A place where to hear the truth about the past and hold debate about the affairs of the present, with knowledge and without passion; like the world in having all men's life at heart, a place for men and all that concerns them; but unlike the world in its self possession, its thorough way of talk; its care to know more than the moment brings to light; slow to take excitement, its air pure and wholesome with a breath of faith; every eye within it bright in the clear day and quick to look toward heaven for the confirmation of its hope. Who shall show us the way to this place?[3]

Wilson rose to national prominence with the Progressive movement. He was a contemporary of Bryan, La Follette, and Theodore Roosevelt.

[1] See M. V. Pennington and J. R. Bolling, *Chronology of Woodrow Wilson* (New York, 1927), pp. 20–25.

[2] The reader particularly interested in this part of Wilson's thinking is referred to these speeches especially: sesquicentennial address, *Public Papers*, I, 259–285; "The Spirit of Learning," *ibid.*, II, 102–119; and "The Training of the Intellect," an admirable speech that strangely is neither in the *Public Papers* nor in the *Selected Literary and Political Papers* but may be found in J. M. O'Neill, *Models of Speech Composition* (New York, 1924), pp. 844–849.

[3] *Public Papers*, I, pp. 284–285. This notable address was reprinted in *The Forum*, 22 (1896): 447–466, and widely commented upon; Grover Cleveland nevertheless said of it, "Magnificent, but what does it mean?"

His early views, as has been pointed out, were, like Burke's, conservative. He was a conservative Southerner but a reconstructed Southerner: "Because I love the South," he said, "I rejoice in the failure of the Confederacy. Suppose that secession had been accomplished? Conceive of this Union as divided into two separate and independent sovereignties!"[1] The conservative Southerner, transplanted to New Jersey, was nominated for governor by conservative interests. Colonel George Harvey, editor of *Harper's Weekly*—which owed J. P. Morgan $400,000—was the spokesman of the group.[2] William C. Whitney and Thomas Fortune Ryan, Democrats who hated Bryan, were the moneyed men behind Harvey. Senator James Smith, Jr., boss of the Democratic party in New Jersey, was the politican who, acting for the others, compelled a reluctant state convention to nominate Wilson.[3]

Even before he was elected, however, Wilson began to change his position from "a conservative Democrat to a very militant two-fisted radical." Among the men who helped to produce the change in his thinking was George L. Record, a progressive Republican who challenged Wilson to a public debate; Wilson countered with an offer to exchange letters, and Record submitted nineteen searching and embarrassing questions. To the surprise of everybody and to the delight of the liberals in both parties Wilson answered all the questions without equivocation; the liberals rallied to him and assured his election.[4] Other progressives who helped in making the change were Martin P. Devlin, John J. Tracy, Joseph P. Tumulty, William W. St. John, and Mark Sullivan. As Wilson's views, as expressed in his speeches, became more and more liberal, he was, of course, charged with inconsistency; he frankly admitted that he had changed his mind.[5] Like Burke, Wilson as often gave his party principles as he accepted principles from it; and as governor and as President he left a long record of progressive legislation. The finest speech of this period is the First Inaugural; it is Wilson the progressive at his best.[6]

Just before Wilson's inauguration Bliss Perry published an essay on Wilson's style in which he said, "I believe that Woodrow Wilson's best

[1] "John Bright," *Public Papers*, I, 56.

[2] Kerney, *op. cit.*, p. 17.

[3] Of the many accounts of the events leading up to Wilson's nomination and election, perhaps the best is Kerney, *op. cit.*, pp. 14–76. Kerney was thoroughly familiar with New Jersey politics; he had Wilson's confidence; yet he was not a blind admirer.

[4] For the Record story, see Kerney, *op. cit.*, pp. 69–76, and Joseph P. Tumulty, *Woodrow Wilson as I Know Him* (New York, 1921), pp. 38–42.

[5] For an example, see Kerney, *op. cit.*, p. 72.

[6] Space will not permit fuller discussion of this speech here. See the writer's "Notes on Woodrow Wilson's Speeches," *The Quarterly Journal of Speech*, 16 (1930): 176–180.

writing has not yet been put on paper."[1] Ten years later he felt that he could say, "I will hazard the opinion that President Wilson's addresses of January 22, 1917, April 2, 1917, and January 8, 1918, are such examples of great writing as can scarcely be matched in the long history of English political prose."[2] The speeches referred to are "Essential Terms of Peace In Europe," delivered to the Senate; "For a Declaration of War against Germany," delivered before both houses of Congress; and "The Fourteen Points Speech," likewise delivered to a joint session.[3] The present writer would add to this list "Presenting the Peace Treaty to the Senate," July 10, 1919.[4] These speeches are the high points of Wilson as war President. The speech on the declaration of war will be analyzed in more detail hereafter; it seems appropriate to examine first his methods of preparation of his speeches, his style, and his delivery.

Methods of Preparation

"I begin," President Wilson told Ida M. Tarbell, "with a list of the topics I want to cover, arranging them in my mind in their natural rela-tions—that is, I fit the bones of the thing together; then I write it out in shorthand. I have always been accustomed to writing in shorthand, finding it a great saver of time. This done, I copy it on my own typewriter, changing phrases, correcting sentences, and adding material as I go along."[5] For important addresses on new material the first stage was a shorthand outline; the second, a shorthand draft; the third, a typewritten draft, usually typed by Wilson on his own machine but amid pressing business, sometimes dictated.[6] When the material was thoroughly familiar to him he made an outline and then dictated the speech to a stenographer. For occasional addresses he did not always write out the speech at all but made an outline and gave the address extemporaneously.[7] And he was called upon for impromptu speeches, which he made by the hundreds.

He submitted, time permitting, the manuscripts of important speeches to others; or he read the speech aloud for the criticism of others. As long

---

[1] "Woodrow Wilson as a Man of Letters," *The Century Magazine*, 85 (1913): 756, reprinted in *In Praise of Folly and Other Papers* (Boston, 1923), p. 160.

[2] *In Praise of Folly and Other Papers*, p. 170.

[3] *Public Papers*, IV, 407–414; V. 6–16 and 155–162, respectively.

[4] *Public Papers*, V, 537–552.

[5] *Collier's, op. cit.*, p. 5.

[6] Miss Tarbell's account of Wilson's statement is confirmed by R. H. Patchin, "Wilson His Own Stenographer," *Harper's Weekly*, 58 (1914): 22–23. Pages of shorthand draft of the message to Congress on Currency and Banking, June 23, 1913, are there reproduced alongside pages from the transcribed draft.

[7] The writer is indebted to Gilbert F. Close, one of Wilson's personal secretaries, for this information.

as his father lived he took his speeches to him. Ellen Axson Wilson went over his speeches with him. As President he depended upon Tumulty, who had, he said, "a very extraordinary appreciation of how a thing will 'get over the footlights.'"[1] When he was preparing an address to Congress he discussed it with party leaders. In his speech to the National Press Club, March 20, 1914, he said:

> I was amused the other day at a remark that Senator Newlands made. I had read him the trust message that I was to deliver to Congress some ten days before I delivered it, and I never stop "doctoring" things of that kind until the day I have to deliver them. When he heard it read to Congress he said: "I think it was better than it was when you read it to me." I said: "Senator, there is one thing I think you do not understand. I not only use all the brains I have, but all I can borrow, and I have borrowed a lot since I read it to you first."[2]

Ray Stannard Baker wrote of the texts of Wilson's speeches:

> Wilson made no systematic attempt to keep copies of his innumerable addresses. . . . He flung them off and let them go. . . . Several times during the crowded days of the Paris Peace Conference, the writer took up to him copies of important speeches he had made, thinking he might like to look them over, possibly make changes before they were published. He cared nothing about seeing them or keeping them: never once made a correction.[3]

The Public Papers of Woodrow Wilson were compiled from "the original manuscripts, proofs, and pamphlets, so far as they exist, of Mr. Wilson's addresses and messages: and others have been gathered from periodicals, from reports of meetings where he was a speaker, or from congressional or other documents preserved in the Library of Congress or in the Library of Princeton University."[4] The editors were careful to cite in every case the source of the text they followed.[5] The relationship between what was reported and what was said naturally differs with the character of individual speeches: the more formal and important ones, such as the inaugurals or messages to Congress, were written out and read from manuscript; for the less important or less formal ones, such as after-dinner and rear-platform speeches given impromptu or from outline notes, we are dependent upon newspaper reports or stenographic notes.

[1] *Collier's, op. cit.,* p. 5.
[2] *Public Papers,* III, 95.
[3] *Baker,* I, xxiv.
[4] *Public Papers,* I, v.
[5] The six volumes of the *Public Papers* are a selection, not the complete works. A bibliography, compiled by H. S. Leach, librarian of Lehigh University, is, however, appended, so that the student may discover what speeches were omitted and where texts may be found.

Style

His friends agreed that Wilson's style was the man; Bliss Perry wrote: "He talks precisely as he writes and he writes as he talks. . . . Mr. Wilson surely has never needed to put himself into the literary state of mind as a preparation for writing, nor into the oratorical state of mind as a preparation for speaking. The mind and the style are the same throughout."[1] Henry Jones Ford, the first time he met Wilson, "noticed that while his talk [in conversation] was manifestly an improvisation, his thoughts came with their clothes on. There was a balance to his periods revealing an instinctive sense of form . . . "[2]

Wilson liked to begin his speeches with a reference to the audience, to his relation to the audience, or to the occasion.[3] His speeches, which are chiefly expository-argumentative in type, usually contain an early statement of points, and these points are then repeated and amplified. The speeches are not, generally, specific: rather, they lay down broad, abstract principles. They often have a somewhat didactic air, like sermons or lectures, for Wilson had long experience as a lecturer, and he gave many religious addresses. They are fully illustrated, often with specific matter but seldom with statistical evidence. There is a clear, climactic order in most of them, and there is a definite conclusion, which, in the more formal addresses, is a peroration.

Wilson was a master of the telling phrase, the slogan. Among his phrases that became famous were: "watchful waiting";[4] "too proud to fight";[5] "a little group of willful men";[6] and "the world must be made safe for democracy."[7] Some of his phrases were, indeed, too good; they were repeated *ad nauseam* by other speakers—Wilson never repeated them—until the slogans lost their edge.

As a device for making phrases memorable Wilson was especially fond of alliteration. His earliest published works contain many examples, such as "cunningly concocted in the closest sessions of partisan committees";[8] or "accusations hurled at him by haughty, hating tories whose hatred was born of fear."[9] His later speeches contained even more alliteration;

[1] "Woodrow Wilson as a Man of Letters," *The Century Magazine*, 85 (1913): 754.

[2] *Woodrow Wilson: The Man and His Work* (New York, 1916), p. 281.

[3] Howard L. Runion, An Objective Study of the Speech Style of Woodrow Wilson, unpublished Ph.D. dissertation, University of Michigan, 1936, p. 150. Runion made a statistical study of fifty of Wilson's speeches.

[4] First annual message to Congress, Dec. 2, 1913, *Public Papers*, III, 72.

[5] "Address to Foreign-born Citizens," Philadelphia, May 10, 1915, *Public Papers*, III, 321.

[6] "Address to the Country," Mar. 4, 1917, *Public Papers*, IV, 435.

[7] "For a Declaration of War against Germany," *Public Papers*, V, 14.

[8] "Cabinet Government in the United States," *Public Papers*, I, 28.

[9] "John Bright," *Public Papers*, I, 52.

the following, for example, will be found in the "Fourteen Points Speech": "confusions of counsel"; "fearless frankness"; "part and parcel"; "principle and purpose"; "processes of peace"; "open covenants of peace, openly arrived at"; and "assured a secure sovereignty."[1]

Wilson never hesitated to drive in a point by the use of repetition. In the same speech occur these instances and many others: "The Central Empires were to keep every foot of territory their armed forces had occupied —every province, every city, every point of vantage. . . . " "An evident principle runs through the whole program. . . . It is the principle of justice . . . unless this principle be made its foundation no part of the structure of international justice can stand. The people of the United States could act on no other principle."

As a student of oratory Wilson knew the use of rhetorical devices. Almost all the usual ones could be illustrated, if space permitted, from his speeches. He liked a neat antithesis: "William Pitt was a noble statesman; the Earl of Chatham was a noble ruin."[2] He could use a rhetorical question or a series of questions with telling effect.[3] He used freely metaphor, simile, and personification.[4]

Wilson had certain favorite words that, beyond doubt, he overused. Among them were *air, business, candid, counsel, essence, eyes, heart, quick, passion, purpose,* and *spirit.* He liked, especially in his earlier days, words of an antique flavor: *ere, fain, 'tis.*[5]

Wilson's style was the despair of his opponents. Owen Wister, biographer and friend of Theodore Roosevelt, said, "The American people had month after month been so drugged by Mr. Wilson's words, those smooth knockout drops of rhetoric . . . that Germany was quite safe from their resentment."[6] William Bayard Hale wrote a whole book on Wilson's rhetoric, *The Story of a Style;* he found in Wilson's style "aristocratic affectations," "learned addictions," "phonetic phenomena," and "a soothing wash of words"; he was sure that Wilson was not great, and he half wondered if he was sane. Such criticism does not deserve further analysis.[7]

[1] *Public Papers,* V, 155–162.

[2] "William Earl Chatham," *Public Papers,* I, 17.

[3] See second paragraph of "Fourteen Points Speech" for example.

[4] Runion, *op. cit.,* p. 112. Runion counted the figures of speech that Wilson used in fifty speeches and concluded that his use of them was almost exactly equal to that of forty-six British and American orators studied by Miss Rousseau.

[5] For analysis of Wilson's vocabulary, see N. B. Miller, A Vocabulary Analysis of Four American Orators, unpublished Master's essay, University of Wisconsin, 1932, *passim.* Miller concluded that Wilson had a larger speaking vocabulary than Bryan, Borah, or Theodore Roosevelt (p. 52).

[6] "If We Elect Mr. Wilson," *Collier's* 58 (Nov. 4, 1916): 22.

[7] Hale wrote a campaign biography, *Woodrow Wilson: The Story of His Life* (Garden City, N.Y., 1911) and expected from Wilson greater favors than he received. He was sent on a

Delivery

Wilson was a vigorous speaker but one who always spoke with power in reserve. Pictures of him in action show him using gestures, notably the index finger or "school-master" gesture but never the sweeping, extremely emphatic gestures of Theodore Roosevelt. He had a pleasant, well-modulated tenor voice; not a powerful, booming voice.[1] He would have made an excellent radio speaker. His platform manner was pleasant, informal, though he could get very angry and denunciatory.[2] His anger never became shrill; it was more likely to break over into some unfortunate expression.

Effect upon the Audience

The effect of Wilson's speeches upon his immediate hearers naturally depended upon the nature of his audience. Sometimes he could win a hostile audience; sometimes he could not. On one occasion he did his best to persuade the Princeton Club of New York of the soundness of his policies at Princeton, "but the assembly listened and dispersed in absolute silence."[3] He faced another hostile audience when he spoke to the Democratic state convention after his nomination for governor, since he had been nominated, not by the rank and file, but by the bosses; even Tumulty and Wescott, who came to be great admirers, had opposed his nomination. Tumulty gives this account of the effect of the speech:

> Men all about me cried in a frenzy: "Thank God, at last, a leader has come!"
> . . . The speech is over. Around me there is a swirling mass of men whose hearts had been touched by the great speech which is just at an end. Men stood about me with tears streaming from their eyes. . . . As I turned to leave the convention hall there stood at my side old John Crandall of Atlantic City, like myself a bitter, implacable foe of Woodrow Wilson in the Convention. I watched him intently to see what effect the speech had had upon him. For a minute he was silent, as if in a dream, and then drawing himself up to his full height, with a cynical smile on his

---

minor mission to Mexico, but disappointed that his talents were not further employed, he went to work at $15,000 a year for the German propagandists in America. Count von Bernstorff tells of Hale's services in *My Three Years in America* (New York, 1920); see especially pp. 48, 115, 338, 346.

[1] Wilson's voice may be heard on two Victor records, numbered 35252 and 35253. The former has two brief addresses entitled "Address to the Farmers" and "Democratic Principles"; the latter two are on "Labor" and "The Tariff."

[2] This information on Wilson's delivery has been collected by the writer from conversations with men who knew and heard Wilson, especially Christian Gauss, George McLean Harper, and Matthew Imbrie.

[3] Robert Edwards Annin, *Woodrow Wilson: A Character Study* (New York, 1925), p. 62. Annin was present.

face, waving his hat and cane in the air, and at the same time shaking his head in a self-accusing way, yelled at the top of his voice, "I am sixty-five years old, and still a damn fool!"[1]

Kerney, Lawrence, Tumulty, and other witnesses testify that Wilson was a very effective campaigner. He was able to catch the mood of a popular audience and to swing the audience his way. If he had not had the breakdown on his trip in behalf of the League of Nations, the story of the Senate and the League of Nations might have been different.

The War Message

Critics will differ as to which was the greatest speech of Wilson's career. The most momentous speech, at least, was the one delivered April 2, 1917, to both houses of Congress, called in special session, urging a declaration of war against Germany. The secondary audience was the American public, if not the whole of mankind. The address was intended not only to bring about a declaration of war with Germany but also to give reasons for the declaration and in doing so to justify the policies of the government of the United States since the war had broken out.

From the neutrality proclamation of August 4, 1914, to the declaration of war speech, April 2, 1917, was a long and painful road for Wilson. He sincerely wished to keep the United States out of the war, although his personal sympathies, because of his admiration for British political institutions and because of his study of English writers, was on the side of the Allies. He had refused for nearly three years to be swayed either by the war hawks in his cabinet or by those outside, like Lodge, Roosevelt, and Wood. He had protested against British interference with our neutral trade, but his protests had been in large part vitiated by Ambassador Page, the full extent of whose pro-Ally work was not revealed until after the war; and the vast market opened up for American goods in the countries of the Allies had so satisfied American business that, in the war prosperity, the British violations of our rights seemed not to matter. In the complex of forces operating upon the public and the President from 1914 to 1917 the British and French propaganda, then largely unrevealed, was of great importance; the German propaganda was so bungling that it did the Allied cause more good than harm. In spite of the sinking of the *Lusitania* and other ships on which Americans lost their lives, in spite of the preparedness campaign and the clamor of the jingoes for war, and in spite of Dumba, von Papen, Boy-Ed, and the Zimmermann note, Wilson kept the United States neutral. He was re-elected on the slogan, "He kept us out of war." He hoped for a "peace without victory" in which the United States would,

[1] Tumulty, *op. cit.*, p. 21. Kerney, *op. cit.*, p. 55, testifies that the speech was a great success.

as the chief neutral, be able to influence a just and lasting peace through the establishment of a League of Nations.[1] Before the United States should join the cause of the Allies—if neutrality could not be maintained until the war ended—Wilson wanted a restatement of their purposes that would bind them to these terms. But his hand was forced by the German declaration of unrestricted submarine warfare for February 1, 1917, which brought an immediate breach of diplomatic relations; even after relations had been severed Wilson hoped that the United States could keep out by an armed neutrality, as had been done in 1798, but the Germans soon sank American vessels, and on March 21 Wilson called for a special session of Congress for April 2.[2]

Wilson consulted House on March 27 and again on March 28 concerning the points he intended to make in his message; he did not consult the cabinet on it because, while they were all for war, he felt that he could not satisfy them all on every point, and the responsibility was his.[3] The actual phraseology of the address was left until the last moment; on April 1 he read the final draft to House, who suggested one change that Wilson accepted.[4]

Congress was not ready to hear the message until 8:30 at night, and the President did not actually begin to speak until 8:40. The delivery took 32 minutes.[5] Before the speaker were the members of both houses, the cabinet, the Supreme Court, and the diplomatic corps. The galleries were packed. Wilson received an ovation as he entered.[6] As soon as the applause subsided he began to read:[7]

Gentlemen of the Congress:

I have called the Congress into extraordinary session because there are serious, very serious, choices of policy to be made, and made immediately, which it was neither right nor constitutionally permissible that I should assume the responsibility of making.

[1] See his speech at Indianapolis, Oct. 12, 1916, *Public Papers*, IV, 356–363; and "Essential Terms of Peace in Europe," address to the Senate, Jan. 22, 1917, *Public Papers*, IV, 407–414.

[2] For general works on the period from the outbreak of the war to American entrance, see C. Hartley Grattan, *Why We Fought* (New York, 1929); Walter Millis, *Road to War* (Boston, 1935); and Charles C. Tansill, *America Goes to War* (Boston, 1938).

[3] Charles Seymour, ed., *The Intimate Papers of Colonel House* (Boston, 1926), II, 468.

[4] According to *The New York Times*, Apr. 3, 1917, he prepared the speech onh is own typewriter and read proof on it himself.

[5] Seymour, *op. cit.*, p. 469.

[6] David F. Houston, *Eight Years with Wilson's Cabinet* (New York, 1926), I, 254. *The New York Times* said of the ovation, "Representatives and Senators not only cheered but yelled. It was two minutes before he could begin his address. When he did begin it . . . he read without looking up, but after a while he would glance occasionally to the right or the left as he made a point, not as if he were trying to see the effect, but more as a sort of gesture—the only one he employed."

[7] For text of the address, see *Public Papers,* V 6–16, *Congressional Record*, Vol. 55, Part 1 pp. 102–104.

He then reviewed briefly the history of the negotiations with Germany over "the cruel and unmanly business" of sending "to the bottom without warning and without thought of help or mercy . . . men, women, and children engaged in pursuits which have always, even in the darkest periods of modern history, been deemed innocent and legitimate." Perhaps he was thinking of British violations of international law when he added, "Property can be paid for; the lives of peaceful and innocent people cannot be."

"The present German submarine warfare," he said, is a war "against mankind. It is a war against all nations. . . . Each nation must decide how it will meet it." This statement not only put the case against Germany on the broadest possible base but also invited all other neutrals to join forces with the United States and the Allies.

Wilson realized that, once the United States entered the war, tolerance would be gone; nevertheless, he made an appeal for calm thinking:

The choice we make for ourselves must be made with a moderation of counsel and a temperateness of judgment befitting our character and our motives as a nation. We must put excited feeling away. Our motive must not be revenge or the victorious assertion of the physical might of the nation, but only the vindication of right, of human right, of which we are only a single champion.

After a short explanation for the failure of armed neutrality, he said: "There is one choice we cannot make, we are incapable of making: we will not choose the path of submission—" At this word he was interrupted by Chief Justice White, who dropped the soft hat he had been holding and, raising his hands high in the air, gave a loud clap, "and House, Senate, and galleries followed with a roar like a storm."[1] As soon as he could, the President concluded his sentence "—and suffer the most sacred rights of our Nation and our people to be ignored or violated." He turned then to his recommendation:

With a profound sense of the solemn and even tragical character of the step I am taking and of the grave responsibilities which it involves, but in unhesitating obedience to what I deem my constitutional duty, I advise that the Congress declare the recent course of the Imperial German Government to be in fact nothing less than war [here Chief Justice White again led the applause] against the government and people of the United States; that it formally accept the status of belligerent which has thus been thrust upon it; and that it take immediate steps not only to put the country in a more thorough state of defense but also to exert all its power and employ all its resources to bring the government of the German Empire to terms and to end the war.

[1] *The New York Times*, Apr. 3, 1917.

To put the onus of beginning the conflict upon the other side is an ancient device of politics, but the device of separating the German government from the German people, to which Wilson twice returned in more detail, was a stroke of propaganda genius.

After asking for the declaration of war, he outlined the steps necessary, in his view, to its effective prosecution: the immediate extension of credits to the Entente, the mobilization of men and materials, the raising of an army by universal concription, and the increase of taxes and the borrowing of money to meet the costs of the war.

He then returned to the reasons for entering the war. "Our object," he said, "is to vindicate the principles of peace and justice in the life of the world as against selfish and autocratic power and to set up amongst the really free and self-governed peoples of the world such a concert of purpose and of action as will henceforth insure the observance of those principles." A war to end war.

We have no quarrel with the German people. We have no feeling towards them but one of sympathy and friendship. It was not upon their impulse that their government acted in entering this war. It was not with their previous knowledge or approval. It was a war determined upon as wars used to be determined upon in the old, unhappy days when peoples were nowhere consulted by their rulers. . . . [1]

A League of Nations was contemplated by Wilson as one of the objects of the war: "A steadfast concert for peace can never be maintained except by a partnership of democratic nations." Fortunately for his argument the Russian Revolution had just removed the great autocracy among the Allies, and Wilson could say, "Here is a fit partner for a League of Honor."

The United States would fight:

For the rights of nations great and small and the privilege of men everywhere to choose their way of life and of obedience. The world must be made safe for democracy. Its peace must be planted upon the tested foundations of political liberty. We have no selfish ends to serve. We desire no conquest, no dominion. We seek no indemnities for ourselves, no material compensation for the sacrifices we shall freely make. We are but one of the champions of the rights of mankind. . . .

Just because we fight without rancor and without selfish object, seeking nothing for ourselves but what we shall wish to share with all free peoples, we shall, I feel confident, conduct our operations as belligerents without passion and ourselves observe with proud punctilio the principles of right and fair play we profess to be fighting for.

After discussing our relations with Austria and after another reference to the German people, he concluded:

[1] According to Baker, it was the Zimmermann note that finally convinced Wilson of Germany's war guilt and of her hostile intentions toward the United States.—Baker, VI, 474.

It is a distressing and oppressive duty, Gentlemen of the Congress, which I have performed in thus addressing you. There are, it may be, many months of firey trial and sacrifice ahead of us. It is a fearful thing to lead this great peaceful people into war, into the most terrible and disastrous of all wars, civilization itself seeming to be in the balance. But the right is more precious than peace, and we shall fight for the things we have always carried nearest our hearts,—for democracy, for the right of those who submit to authority to have a voice in their own Governments, for the rights and liberties of small nations, for a universal dominion of right by such a concert of free peoples as shall bring peace and safety to all nations and make the world itself at last free. To such a task we can dedicate our lives and our fortunes, everything that we are and everything that we have,[1] with the pride of those who know that the day has come when America is privileged to spend her blood and her might for the principles that gave her birth and happiness and the peace which she has treasured. God helping her, she can do no other.[2]

The conclusion of the speech brought the audience once more cheering to its feet.[3] Even Senator Lodge praised the address warmly. The President walked rapidly from the chamber and went immediately to the White House. In the cabinet room later, according to Tumulty, he said, "Think what it was they were applauding. My message today was a message of death for our young men. How strange it seems to applaud that."[4] And after a few minutes he put his head on the cabinet table and wept. It was a message of death for Woodrow Wilson, too, for the strain of the war produced, two years later, a stroke of paralysis from which he never recovered. The crowds of people who knelt in the street on Sunday morning, February 3, 1924, when he died, remembered him as one who played for the verdict of history by stirring the conscience of mankind.

BIBLIOGRAPHY

The following is a selected bibliography, intended to be useful to students of Wilson's career as a speaker, rather than to students of the history of the period. Biographies of prominent men of the time, books about the events leading up to the war, and books about the war and the peace are now to be numbered in the thousands. Only the *Public Papers* is listed for Wilson's speeches because of the admirable bibliography of the speeches that it contains; when such a bibliography is generally available it need not be reproduced here.

Only published books are cited, for the vast periodical material is fully indexed in the well-known guides.

[1] *Cf.* the concluding words of the Declaration of Independence: "We mutually pledge to each other our Lives, our Fortunes, and our sacred Honor."

[2] *Cf.* Martin Luther before Charles V at the Diet of Worms, 1521: "Here I stand. I can do no other. God help me. Amen!"

[3] *The New York Times*, Apr. 3, 1917. The *Times* gave two and a half columns to the reception of the address, printed quotations of praise of it telegraphically gathered from other newspapers, and editorially commented that it was "the most convincing justification of war that any nation has ever put forth in declaring it."

[4] Tumulty, *op. cit.*, p. 256.

Biographies

Annin, R. E.: *Woodrow Wilson: A Character Study*, New York, 1924. A hostile biography, written by a great admirer of Theodore Roosevelt. Annin says of Wilson's eloquence, however, that "he was probably without a peer in his generation."

Baker, Ray Stannard: *Woodrow Wilson: Life and Letters*, 8 vols., Garden City, N.Y., 1927–1939. This, the authorized biography, is the fullest, and in many ways the best, of the biographies. "Mr. Baker's study," said C. Hartley Grattan, "rises far above all competing works." Takes Wilson through the Armistice.

———: *Woodrow Wilson and World Settlement*, 3 vols., Garden City, N.Y., 1922. Continues the story through the Peace Conference and prints many important documents.

Daniels, Josephus: *The Life of Woodrow Wilson*, Philadelphia, 1924. Friendly biography by a member of Wilson's cabinet.

Dodd, William E.: *Woodrow Wilson and His Work*, Garden City, N.Y., 1920. Later editions, 1921, 1928, 1932. Perhaps the best one-volume biography.

Ford, Henry Jones: *Woodrow Wilson: The Man and His Work*, New York, 1916. An early and very friendly biography by a Princeton colleague.

Hale, William Bayard· *Woodrow Wilson: The Story of His Life*, Garden City, N.Y., 1911. A campaign biography.

———: *The Story of a Style*, New York, 1920. A very prejudiced and unfair examination of Wilson's spoken and written style.

Houston, David F.: *Eight Years with Wilson's Cabinet*, 2 vols., Garden City, N.Y., 1926. Contains some good material on Wilson's speeches.

Kerney, James: *The Political Education of Woodrow Wilson*, New York, 1926. The best work on Wilson's political career in New Jersey.

Lawrence, David: *The True Story of Woodrow Wilson*, New York, 1924. Lawrence knew Wilson well before he went into politics and afterward as well as any newspaperman. The book contains a chronology that cites a few speeches.

Low, 'A. M.: *Woodrow Wilson: An Interpretation*, Boston, 1918. An admiring view of an international-minded Englishman, who thought of Wilson, nevertheless, as "an enigma."

McAdoo Eleanor R., and M. Y. Gaffey: *The Woodrow Wilsons*, New York, 1937. A chatty, interesting view of the Wilson household.

Merriam, Charles E.: *Four American Party Leaders*, New York, 1926. Chapter III, on Wilson, is a very penetrating analysis; Merriam makes some interesting comparisons of Wilson and other orators.

Pennington, M. V., and J. R. Bolling, *Chronology of Woodrow Wilson*, New York, 1927. Contains not only 152-page chronological table but also some speeches and writings.

Reid, Edith G.: *Woodrow Wilson: The Caricature, the Myth and the Man*, New York, 1934. Rather highly colored biography by a devoted friend.

Seymour, Charles: *Woodrow Wilson and the World War* in Chronicles of America series, Vol. XLVIII, New Haven, 1921. Historical study by the editor of *The Intimate Papers of Colonel House*.

Tumulty, Joseph P: *Woodrow Wilson as I Know Him*, New York, 1921. This account of Wilson's life by his faithful secretary is most valuable on the New Jersey period and on the intimate details of White House life.

Wells, Wells: *Wilson the Unknown*, New York, 1931. Thin biography, weird interpretation.

White, William Allen: *Woodrow Wilson: The Man, His Times, and His Task*, Boston, 1924. A lively, journalistic biography by a man friendly to Wilson and his policies. White knew Wilson, but not intimately.

Wescott, John W.: *Woodrow Wilson's Eloquence*, Camden, N. J., privately printed, 1922. More on Wescott than on Wilson or on eloquence.

Speeches

Baker, Ray Stannard, and William E. Dodd, ed.: *The Public Papers of Woodrow Wilson*, 6 vols., with a biographical sketch by the editors and a bibliography of Wilson's speeches and writings prepared by H. S. Leach, librarian of Lehigh University, New York, 1925. Includes all the important speeches made by Wilson but not all the speeches he made; reprints many magazine articles, book reviews, and public statements but no published books.

Index

Burgh, James, 203
Burke, Ædanus, 69
Burke, Edmund, 255, 457, 479, 498, 516, 666, 670n., 671, 701, 702, 800, 805, 819, 898n., 971, 972, 973, 980; *quoted*, 17, 515
Burke, Thomas, 37, 38; *quoted*, 36
Burleigh, Charles, 181
Burns, Robert, 363, 374, 375, 383, 914, 922, 950
Emerson's speech on, 518
Burr, Aaron, 40, 616
Burr, Pres. Aaron, 23, 26n.
Burr, Theophilus, 454
Burroughs, John, 277
Bushnell, Horace, 300n.
Butler, Andrew P., 751, 756, 760
Butler, Benjamin F., 445n., 461, 464, 494, 882
Butler, Fanny Kemble, 185
Butler's Book (Butler), 445n.
Byles, Mather, 26; *quoted*, 23
Byrd, William, of Westover, 40
Byron, George Gordon, Lord, 671, 914

C

Cable, George Washington, 123
Cabot, James E., 506
Cadman, S. Parkes, *quoted*, 272, 281
Caesar, 497, 671, 914
Caine, Hall, 123
Caldwell, Josiah, 887, 888
Caleb Cushing (Fuess), 434n.
Calhoun, Florida Bonneau, 639
Calhoun, John C., 70, 90, 105, 107, 109, 136, 364, 373, 398, 610, 612, 613, 625, 626, 639-664, 677, 686, 699, 729, 734, 735, 736, 774, 800, 801, 805, 829, 840, 856n., 891; *quoted*, 106, 107
appearance, 646
attitude of, toward slavery, 657-659
toward tariffs, 651-652
background and early training, 639-642
basic premises of his thinking, 648-659
beliefs on financial policy, 652-654
bibliography, 661-664
biographical data, 639
chief interest in legislative speeches, 659
conception of concurrent majorities, 650-651
conception of nature of government, 648-651
as conversationalist, 644-645
distinction between secession and nullification, 650
idea of international policy, 655-657
ideas on internal improvements, 654-655
manner of speaking, 646-647
personality and character, 642-648
results of speaking, 661
structure of speeches, 659-660
style, 660-661
use of modes of proof, 660
voice, 647-648
Calhoun, Martha, 639
Calhoun, Patrick, 639, 640
Calhoun, William, 434n.

California land cases, 468, 469
Calkins, E. E., 781n.
Callender, Guy Stevens, 783n.
Calvin, John, 214n., 218, 220, 221, 303n., 379
Cambridge Law School, 434, 437, 438
Cambridge Synod, 220
Camm, John, 584
Campaign of 1840 speech (Webster), 718
Campbell, George, 203, 204, 240, 628n.
Campbell, N. H., 108
Canandaigua Academy, 777
"Candle of the Lord" (Brooks), 319
Canning, George, 971, 973
Capen, Charles E., *quoted*, 851n., 858
"Capon Springs Speech" (Webster), 669-670
Carlyle, Thomas, 313n., 495, 774
Carmack, Edward W., 136
Carnegie, Andrew, 275, 416
Carnegie Music Hall Address (B. T. Washington), 426n.
Carpenter, Boyd, 125n.
Carpenter, F. B., *quoted*, 285n., 286
Carpenters' Hall, Philadelphia, 33
Carr, C. E., 805n.
Carroll, Archbishop, 26n.
Carroll, Charles, 51, 684
Carroll, Charles, Sr., 40
Carrollton speech (Lincoln), 864n.
Carson, J. N., *quoted*, 857
Carter, Landon, 584
Carter, Robert, 31n.
Carter, Thomas H., 136
Cartwright, Peter, 84
Carver, George Washington, *quoted*, 420
Cary, Archibald, 31n.
Case and Tryal of Peter Zenger, Printer, 43
Case of Trevett v. Weeden, 43
Case of William Atwood, 43
Cass, Lewis, 96, 625, 800, 873
Castle Garden speech (Evarts), 487-489
Catalogue of Officers and Students in Yale College, 1834-1835, *quoted*, 486
Catholic World, *quoted*, 384
Cato, 554
Catt, Carrie Chapman, 126, 187
Caucus, party, 142-143
Cause between Elizabeth Rutgers and Joshua Waddington, 43
Caverno, C., 458
"Centennial Oration" (Evarts), 496-498
Chaflin, William, 358
Chandler, Peleg, *quoted*, 759, 772
Channing, Edward, 659
Channing, Edward T., 205, 333, 773; *quoted*, 331, 758
Channing, William Ellery, 157, 251, 268, 269, 292, 300n., 303n., 325, 334, 336, 337, 339, 505, 534, 606, 753, 754, 755, 758, 773
address on, (Eliot), 534
Channing, William Henry, *quoted*, 337
Chapman, Ervin S., *quoted*, 852n.
Chapman, Mrs. Maria Weston, *quoted*, 337